SOUTH AMERICA

Map labels:

ARUBA I.
BONAIRE I.
CURAÇAO I.
MARGARITA I.
TOBAGO I.
TRINIDAD I.

Santa Marta Mts.
Gulf of Urabá
R. Catatumbo
R. Magdalena

VENEZUELA
R. Meta
R. Orinoco

COLOMBIA

GUYANA
SURINAM
FRENCH GUIANA

GORGONA I.
R. Vaupés
R. Caquetá
R. Uaupés
R. Negro

ECUADOR
R. Putumayo
Napo
R. Içá
R. Japurá
R. Solimões
R. Amazonas

P E R U

R. Ucayali
R. Juruá
R. Purús
R. Madeira
R. Tapajós
R. Xingú
R. Tocantins

B R A Z I L

R. Huallaga
R. Marañón
R. São Francisco

R. Beni

B O L I V I A

R. Paraguai

PACIFIC
OCEAN

PARAGUAY
R. Paraguay

C H I L E

A R G E N T I N A

URUGUAY

ATLANTIC
OCEAN

FALKLAND
ISLANDS

TIERRA
DEL FUEGO

MTMS

A GUIDE TO
THE BIRDS OF
SOUTH AMERICA

G. M. S.

Illustrated by Earl L. Poole,
John R. Quinn, and George M. Sutton

A GUIDE TO
THE BIRDS OF
SOUTH AMERICA

RODOLPHE MEYER DE SCHAUENSEE

Curator of Birds
The Academy of Natural Sciences of Philadelphia

Published for
The Academy of Natural Sciences of Philadelphia

by
LIVINGSTON PUBLISHING COMPANY
Wynnewood, Pennsylvania

Copyright © 1970
by The Academy of Natural Sciences of Philadelphia
All rights reserved

Library of Congress Catalog Card Number: 76-113640
ISBN: 0-87098-027-0

Seven line drawings in text courtesy of John Wiley & Sons, Inc.

Printed in the United States of America

FOREWORD

The bird fauna of South America is the richest in the world both in numbers and variety of species. This book is the first to describe all the species of birds from this continent, many of which are illustrated for the first time, and it is intended to be equally useful to both the professional and amateur ornithologist.

For more than 200 years, the birds of South America have been described, classified and recorded from many localities in thousands of technical articles and books. Today, the kinds of birds and their relationships are sufficiently well established to make this an opportune time for producing a comprehensive guide of convenient size. The essentials for the identification of nearly 3000 species of birds found in South America have been brought together for the first time in a single volume.

As the author suggests in his introduction, little is still known about the life histories, behavior, nesting and food habits, and migrational movements of the birds. Likewise, there is still much to be learned about which characters are most useful for quick identification in the field. These gaps in knowledge present a challenge and opportunity to the serious bird student.

The Academy of Natural Sciences of Philadelphia earnestly hopes that this substantial and timely work will not only serve as an aid to the scientific study of birds, but also add to the pleasure of those who simply enjoy the aesthetic appeal of observing birds in their natural surroundings.

H. Radclyffe Roberts
Director, Academy of Natural Sciences of Philadelphia

TABLE OF CONTENTS

LIST OF FAMILIES

ix

Fig. 1. HALF-COLLARED GNATWREN
Microbates c. cinerieventris
p. 346

INTRODUCTION

Modern air travel has brought South America within easy reach of the growing band of bird students in the United States and Europe. It seems essential, therefore, for the traveler who is interested in birds to have at his disposal an easily carried, illustrated guide to the birds of South America. The present book was written with this in mind.

No continent supports a bigger and more varied avifauna; no less than 2926 species belonging to 865 genera and 93 families have been recorded. The field student has a splendid opportunity to make valuable observations for little is yet known of the habits and distribution of many South American birds.

In this book all the species of birds regularly found in South America are described, and their approximate size given in inches and tenths of inches. Females are not described if they resemble males. If a species contains one or more subspecies, its scientific name is followed by an asterisk. If the subspecies is distinctive enough to affect field identification, the difference is noted in parentheses followed by a number. This number corresponds to the number given in the range of the species and shows the area occupied by the particular subspecies.

A brief account of each family is given. Many South American bird families contain a bewildering number of species, the flycatchers comprising no less than 315. It is a striking fact that three South American families——the hummingbirds, antbirds, and flycatchers——comprise nearly 100 more species than all those regularly found in North America north of Mexico.

An "Aid to Identification" is provided. It is not a key leading to a specific bird, but rather an elimination key leading to groups with certain common characters such as "all black," or "with red in plumage." Thus one may discard birds not bearing the characters mentioned. These groupings are followed by numbers which correspond to those assigned to each species in the family; as a further aid to elimination, sometimes the letter *a*, *b*, or *c* follows the numbers. The letter *a* indicates the bird is found in only northern South America (the Guianas, Venezuela, northernmost Brazil and Colombia); *b* indicates western South America and the Andes; *c* indicates eastern South America south of the Amazon. Numbers not followed by letters usually apply to widespread Amazonian birds or birds of general distribution.

The range of each species is given, but often not in as much detail as it is in *The Species of Birds of South America* by the present author. Since the publication of that book in 1966, many extensions of range have been discovered, many by the following ornithologists: Olrog, Short (Argentina); Vuilleumier (Bolivia); Pinto, Sick (Brazil); Johnson (Chile); Haffer (Colombia); Lévêque (Ecuador); Schade and Masi-Pallares, Steinbacher (Paraguay); O'Neill, Weske, Plenge (Peru); Mees (Surinam); Phelps (Venezuela); and Gerzenstein

(Uruguay). These extensions have been incorporated in this book. It may be noted here that when a species is said to range widely east of the Andes from Colombia to Bolivia, this denotes that the species is also found in the intervening countries of Ecuador and Peru unless otherwise noted. Discontinuous ranges are implied when periods are used. Thus, "COLOMBIA. PERU; BOLIVIA." indicates the species in question has not been recorded from Ecuador. If the range of a bird is very restricted or little is known, the localities at which it has been taken are noted. Extralimital ranges are given for birds found beyond South America. The avifauna of Trinidad, Tobago, Curaçao, Bonaire and Aruba, islands close to the shores of South America, are included because faunistically they are South American. The avifauna of other islands well off the shore such as the Galápagos, Falkland, Juan Fernández Islands, etc. are not included. In addition to the birds' geographical ranges, the altitudinal zones which they inhabit are given. The zones and their limits are:

> **Tropical Zone:** sea level to 4500-5000 ft.
> **Subtropical Zone:** 4500-5000 to 7500-8500 ft.
> **Temperate Zone:** 7500-8500 to 9500-11,500 ft.
> **Páramo or Puna Zone:** 9500-11,500 ft. to snow line

The forests of the tropical zone are the preferred habitat of a vast number of birds belonging to many families. In these forests, which cover a large part of South America south to Bolivia, northern Paraguay and southern Brazil, tinamous, curassows, guans, trumpeters, eagles and hawks, parrots, toucans and araçaris, many species of hummingbirds, trogons, puffbirds, woodcreepers, honeycreepers, caciques and tanagers are also found in great variety. In dry open woodland, scrubby growth, and semidesert, characteristic birds are chachalacas, thick-knees, many species of doves and parakeets, cuckoos, nightjars, swifts, hummingbirds, jacamars, puffbirds, nunlets, piculets, furnarids, flycatchers, jays, orioles and finches. In wet and swampy areas, rails, ducks, jacanas, herons, ibises and storks are numerous. In the campos, tinamous, screamers, storks, doves, parrots, woodpeckers (the latter two especially in groves of palms), furnarids, flycatchers, jays and finches are common.

In the cooler forests and woods of the subtropical and temperate zones typical birds are tinamous, wood-quails, quail-doves, quetzals, many humming-birds, toucanets, green barbets, woodpeckers, antpittas, tapaculos, flower-piercers, flycatchers, tanagers and finches.

On the open and sometimes rocky slopes of the Andes in the puna and páramo zones, rheas, caracaras, plovers, seedsnipes, hummingbirds, various terrestrial woodpeckers, furnarids and flycatchers, swallows as well as thrushes, and many finches find a congenial habitat. In the lakes and alkaline ponds of these uplands, grebes, ducks, flamingos, coots, avocets and even a gull or two make their home.

In the southern part of the continent, the pampas and bushy plains are the home of the rheas, seriemas, certain tinamous, furnarids, plantcutters, pipits, and various kinds of blackbirds and finches.

The sea coasts are inhabited by boobies, cormorants, gulls, terns, migrant "shorebirds" and, at the southern end of the continent, steamer-ducks and penguins, albatrosses, petrels, shearwaters and storm-petrels inhabit the seas.

An effort has been made to indicate the usual habitat frequented for as many species of birds as possible. In this connection, for species unknown to the author, the writings of the late M. A. Carriker, Jr., and of Jürgen Haffer, A. W. Johnson, Maria Koepcke, Claës C. Olrog, John P. O'Neill, François Vuilleumier and Alexander Wetmore have been most helpful. In addition, Kjell von Sneidern noted on the labels of the birds he collected for the Academy in Colombia the type of habitat in which they were secured. The following terms for habitats have been used:

Forest. Heavy nondeciduous tropical forest.

Dry forest. Rather open, semideciduous forest with a definite dry season.

Capoeria. Second-growth scrub in Brazil where original forest has been cut.

Shrubbery. Open spaces with shrubs and low vegetation.

Savanna. Grassland with scattered trees and shrubs, and sometimes palms and palm groves.

Cerrado. Specialized growth on Brazil's tableland, consisting of a thick, tangled vegetation of semideciduous, gnarled, low trees although sometimes fairly open and carpeted with coarse grass. Cerradão is similar to cerrado but the trees are considerably higher.

Caatinga. A specialized growth found in northeast Brazil from Rio Grande do Norte to southern Bahía, characterized by deciduous, thorny scrubland with many cacti and other succulents, the ground is more or less bare.

Desert. Dry, sandy scrub with thorny growth and cacti.

Puna or Páramo. Bleak often rocky, slopes of the Andes from 10,000 feet to snow line.

Campos. Open grassland with few trees. Isolated campos occur along north sides of the lower Amazon and are also found here and there in the Amazon forest toward headwaters of the southern affluents.

Pampas. Open grassland of Argentina.

Nomenclature here followed is that used by the author and Eugene Eisenmann of the American Museum of Natural History, New York, in an earlier book, *The Species of Birds of South America*, except for a few changes in vernacular names suggested by Eisenmann.

It should be noted that río (not accented in Portuguese) is sometimes capitalized; if so (Río Negro) it refers to a state or city rather than to a river. The names of certain geographic areas have been changed since the publication of *The Species of Birds of South America*, thus British Guiana is now called Guyana; in Brazil, Rio Branco has become Roraima and Guaporé is now called Rondonia.

To conserve space and keep this book to a convenient size, abbreviations have been used in describing geographical ranges; n for north and northern, s for south, etc. In the case of Colombia, E and W Andes denotes specifically the Eastern and Western Andean ranges. If the term "mountains of Colombia" is used, this includes both the Santa Marta Mts. and the Andes. Other abbreviations are: hab., habitat; acc., accidental; ad., adult; imm., immature.

A total of 50 plates—31 of them in color—should aid bird identification, for many families such as seriemas, trumpeters and tapaculos are unfamiliar to students of temperate zone birds. At least one member of each family and birds belonging to 640 genera (almost 80% of the resident genera) and 676 species are illustrated. Thirty plates representing birds found chiefly in southern South America have been painted especially for this work by John R. Quinn of

Plymouth, New Hampshire; the remaining 20 plates are the work of Earl L. Poole of Reading, Pennsylvania, and represent birds found mainly in northern South America. Dr. Poole's paintings appeared in the author's earlier book, *The Birds of Colombia*. Except for one instance, no North American migrants have been illustrated because good colored figures of all the species are easily available in current North American bird guides. Drawings by George M. Sutton represent 22 species not shown on the plates.

It gives me great pleasure to acknowledge the help generously offered by many of my colleagues in allowing me to examine specimens in their charge. Once again I must offer my sincere thanks to Dr. Eugene Eisenmann for his ever-readiness to answer puzzling questions based on his great knowledge of neotropical birds. He has also been kind enough to read carefully the galley proofs and has given me much valuable advice and many suggestions for the improvement of this book. To him I am most grateful. My thanks are also due to Miss Maude T. Meyer de Schauensee for the beautifully drawn maps found on the endsheets of this book.

Fig. 2. BLACK-SPOTTED BARBET
Capito niger punctatus
p. 176

Chart of a Bird

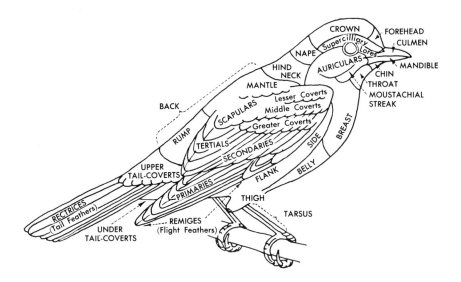

Terms used in this book to describe the plumage and external features of a bird are shown above. Although this drawing is of a thrush-like songbird, the terms used are applicable to all birds regardless of family.

ACCOUNT OF THE BIRDS

Order SPHENISCIFORMES

Family SPHENISCIDAE   PENGUINS

Penguins are found in cold and cool waters of the southern hemisphere. They live in colonies, stand very erect on land, and swim on or below the water surface with paddle-like wings, using feet to steer. Floating low in the water, their large heads and thick necks distinguish them from cormorants. Color: dark above, white below, the head markings usually being the best distinguishing character.

1. KING PENGUIN

Aptenodytes patagonicus *

38". Head and throat black, patch of orange at sides of head narrowing to a point at sides of throat and extending to upper breast. Upperparts blue gray, lowerparts white.

Breeds in small numbers on Horn I., CHILE, and Staten I., ARGENTINA; casually in Strait of Magellan. [Breeds on subantarctic islands, in small numbers on Falkland Is.]

2. EMPEROR PENGUIN

Aptenodytes forsteri

48". Differs from 1 by black of throat being more restricted, and by circular patch at sides of head orange yellow, fading to white on foreneck.

Wanders to se coast of Tierra del Fuego, ARGENTINA, and waters off Cape Horn, CHILE. [Breeds on antarctic ice-shelf.]

3. GENTOO PENGUIN

Pygoscelis papua *

30". Upperparts, head and throat brownish black; eye-to-eye white line across top of head, lowerparts white.

Breeds on Staten I. Winters n to about 43° s on coast of ARGENTINA. [Breeds on subantarctic islands.]

4. ROCKHOPPER PENGUIN

Eudyptes crestatus *

25". Head and throat black, elongated feathers at sides of crown pale yellow. Upperparts slaty black, underparts white.

Breeds on Staten I., ARGENTINA, on Tierra del Fuego and islands about Cape Horn, CHILE. Winters n along coast to Buenos Aires, ARGENTINA, and irregularly to URUGUAY. [Breeds on subantarctic islands.]

5. HUMBOLDT PENGUIN

Spheniscus humboldti

27". Upperparts, sides of head and throat bluish or brownish gray. Underparts white; brown band across chest continued down sides of body, separated from dark upperparts by white line commencing above the eye and extending down entire length of body.

Breeds year-round on islands off coast of Lambayeque (6° 30′ s), PERU, s to Santiago del Norte (34° s), CHILE; winters s as far as Valdivia (40° s).

6. MAGELLANIC PENGUIN

Spheniscus magellanicus *

28". Differs principally from 5 by a broad dark band across lower throat, giving illusion of two underside bands instead of one.

Breeds in coastal CHILE n to Aconcagua, and coast of ARGENTINA n to Santa Cruz. After breeding season migrates n to URUGUAY and s BRAZIL. [Juan Fernández and Falkland Is.]

Plate 20

1

Order RHEIFORMES

Family RHEIDAE

RHEAS

Ostrich-like in appearance, rheas are flightless and live on the pampas or on open Andean highlands where they feed on grass, grain and insects. They are usually seen in small bands, but occasionally as many as 50 are found together. Very wary, they quickly flee from danger. They lay their eggs on bare ground, four or five hens laying in the same "nest" where as many as 20 or 30 large greenish yellow eggs are deposited.

1. GREATER RHEA

Rhea americana *

52″. Upperparts gray, lowerparts white. Crown and patch at base of neck blackish.

Lowlands up to 6000 ft. E and central BRAZIL from Maranhão to Rio Grande do Sul and w to Mato Grosso; PARAGUAY; URUGUAY; BOLIVIAN chaco; n and central ARGENTINA s to Río Negro.

Plate 1

2. LESSER RHEA

Pterocnemia pennata *

38″. Differs from 1 by smaller size, and by feathers of underparts tipped with white.

Puna zone. Extreme s PERU; BOLIVIA in Potosí and Oruro; nw ARGENTINA in Jujuy and Catamarca; also Patagonian lowlands from s Mendoza to Strait of Magellan. N CHILE s to Atacama and from Aysén to Strait of Magellan. Introduced in Tierra del Fuego.

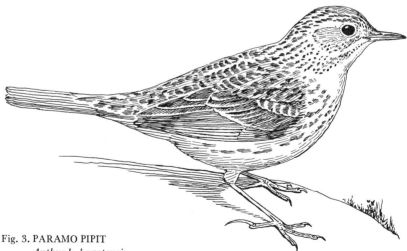

Fig. 3. PARAMO PIPIT
Anthus b. bogotensis
p. 348

2

Order TINAMIFORMES

Family TINAMIDAE   TINAMOUS

Tinamous are shy, forest and brush-inhabiting birds which rarely take wing. They are compact in shape with short, rounded wings, and the tails hidden by tail coverts. They are found only in the Americas from Mexico to Patagonia.

Their coloring is mostly shades of brown and gray with many species conspicuously barred. They feed on fruits, seeds and insects. Their voice is rather flute-like, their frequently repeated notes are often heard at night.

Tinamous nest on the ground and their eggs are notable for a shiny, enamel-like surface showing shades of blue, olive, yellow or purplish. Eggs are incubated by the male.

AID TO IDENTIFICATION

Back uniform brown 10, 11a, 12, 13, 20a, 21b, 24a, 25a, 26b, 27, 28

Back slaty or black 3b, 9

Back with broken or inconspicuous bars 1, 2c, 4, 17, 18c, 19a, 26b, 38c

Back conspicuously banded 13, 14, 15, 16, 17, 18c, 19a, 20a, 21b, 22, 23, 24a, 31b, 32b, 38c, 39; (primaries cinnamon rufous) 29, 46

Wings and upperparts spotted 5, 6b, 7b, 8b, 33b, 35b, 36b, 40, 41, 42c; (streaked) 30b, 34, 37

Crested 43, 44

Neck buff, striped blackish, tarsus short, toes thick 45b, 46b

1. GRAY TINAMOU

Tinamus tao *

18". Above dark gray barred with black; below pale gray vermiculated with black, throat white. Birds in n part of range have olive backs, sparsely barred black.

Tropical, subtropical zones. GUYANA; VENEZUELA n of the Orinoco. N COLOMBIA in Perijá Mts., Cauca Valley and e of Andes in Meta, thence s to Cochabamba and Santa Cruz, BOLIVIA. Central and e Amazonian BRAZIL s of the Amazon from e bank of rios Madeira and Rondonia eastward, thence south to n Mato Grosso. Forest.

2. SOLITARY TINAMOU

Tinamus solitarius *

18". Head and neck ochraceous, throat white. Upper back, breast and center of underparts grayish to olivaceous gray, back barred with black.

E BRAZIL from Pernambuco and Alagoas s to Rio Grande do Sul, and s Mato Grosso; e PARAGUAY; ARGENTINA in Misiones. Forest.

3. BLACK TINAMOU

Tinamus osgoodi *

18". Slaty black, throat gray. Under tail coverts cinnamon.

Subtropical zone. COLOMBIA, known only from s Huila. PERU, known only from Marcapata Valley in Cuzco. Forest.

4. GREAT TINAMOU

Tinamus major *

18". Crown rufous to slaty black, throat white, neck rufous. Back light to dark olivaceous brown (even yellowish olive in some races) with broken bars. Underparts pale grayish buff vermiculated with dusky; center of abdomen white, flanks barred.

Tropical zone. GUIANAS, VENEZUELA and COLOMBIA south to n BOLIVIA. Amazonian BRAZIL south to s Amazonas, s Pará and n Mato Grosso. [Mid. Amer.] Forest.

5. WHITE-THROATED TINAMOU

Tinamus guttatus

13″. Crown slaty, throat white. Back dark chestnut brown, lower back barred black, inner remiges spotted with buff. Underparts light pinkish brown darkest on breast, under tail coverts chestnut.

Tropical zone. From sw VENEZUELA and se COLOMBIA to nw BOLIVIA, e in Amazonian BRAZIL on both sides of the Amazon to e Pará and Amapá. Forest.

Plate 1

6. HIGHLAND TINAMOU

Nothocercus bonapartei *

15″. Crown slaty, throat tawny. Brown above narrowly waved and freckled with black, paler below with wider wavy blackish lines. Inner remiges, upper tail coverts and belly pale-spotted.

Tropical, subtropical zones. .Andes in w VENEZUELA from Aragua westward; Andes of COLOMBIA, e base of Andes in Meta. E ECUADOR; ne PERU in n Cajamarca. [Costa Rica; w Panama.] Forest.

7. TAWNY-BREASTED TINAMOU

Nothocercus julius

15″. Forehead and sides of head bright chestnut, upper throat white, lower gray. Back olivaceous brown waved and barred with black, inner remiges spotted with pale buff. Breast and flanks olivaceous brown, rest of underparts bright cinnamon rufous.

Subtropical, temperate zones of Andes from extreme w VENEZUELA (Táchira) and e and w COLOMBIA southward to about 2° s in e ECUADOR. Forest.

8. HOODED TINAMOU

Nothocercus nigrocapillus *

13″. Rather like 6 in color but crown and

sides of head plumbeous gray and general color lighter.

Subtropical zone of PERU in Amazonas and from Junín s to Cochabamba, BOLIVIA.

9. CINEREOUS TINAMOU

Crypturellus cinereus *

11″. General plumage brownish gray, crown and nape dull reddish brown (or all blackish, 1).

Tropical zone. GUIANAS w through Orinocon region of VENEZUELA to base of E Andes in Meta, COLOMBIA, s in forest to n BOLIVIA; Amazonian BRAZIL to mouth of the Amazon, Marajó I., and e Pará. Nw COLOMBIA in Antioquia, thence south, w of W Andes, to Esmeraldas, ECUADOR, 1. Forest, plantations.

10. LITTLE TINAMOU

Crypturellus soui *

9″. Color varies with race; recognizable by very small size and nearly uniform brown plumage, only flanks lightly barred. Crown and nape slaty to dark brown or rufous brown, throat white. Back dark brown to dark grayish brown, underparts rich rufous chestnut to grayish, palest in center of abdomen. Females usually brighter than males.

Tropical, lower subtropical zones. Virtually throughout south to n BOLIVIA and s BRAZIL. W of Andes to w ECUADOR. [Mid. Amer.] Forest and thickets.

11. TEPUI TINAMOU

Crypturellus ptaritepui

11″. Crown rufous brown, back darker. Underparts dull brownish gray with rufous wash on upper breast. Maxilla yellow, legs olive.

Subtropical zone. Mts. of se Bolívar, VENEZUELA. Forest.

12. BROWN TINAMOU

Crypturellus obsoletus *

11″. Crown and nape grayish black, sides of head and neck gray, throat paler. Upperparts dark chestnut to grayish brown or blackish; below rufous, ochraceous or buffy; flanks barred. Lower mandible flesh color, legs olive gray.

Tropical, subtropical zones. Nw VENE-ZUELA, ne COLOMBIA south to n BO-LIVIA, PARAGUAY and ne ARGENTINA. BRAZIL s of the Amazon.

13. UNDULATED TINAMOU

Crypturellus undulatus *

12". Color varies with race. Two types exist, linked by intermediates. Typical race: entire upperparts including crown evenly barred rufescent and black; throat white, upper breast grayish, remaining underparts buffy white, flanks and under tail coverts barred ochraceous and black. Other extreme: up-perparts dark brown vermiculated with black obscurely barred on head and upper tail coverts; throat white, breast and sides of body light gray, center of abdomen whitish; flanks dark ochraceous, barred buff. Legs yellowish drab to leaden gray.

GUYANA; s VENEZUELA; e COLOMBIA s to BOLIVIA, PARAGUAY and n ARGEN-TINA. W Amazonian BRAZIL and in east from Maranhão and Piauí to Paraná and Mato Grosso. Forest, scrub, cerradão.

14. RUSTY TINAMOU

Crypturellus brevirostris

12". Crown ferruginous chestnut, throat white. Upper back bright rufous, lower back broadly banded ochraceous and black. Breast bright ferruginous, flanks barred.

FRENCH GUIANA. E PERU; w Amazonian BRAZIL to rios Negro and Madeira. Forest.

15. BARTLETT'S TINAMOU

Crypturellus bartletti

Differs from 14 mainly by grayish black crown.

E PERU; w Amazonian BRAZIL s of the Amazon to rio Madeira.

16. VARIEGATED TINAMOU

Crypturellus variegatus *

13". Differs from 15 mainly in larger size and much longer bill.

GUIANAS; VENEZUELA s of the Orinoco; e COLOMBIA s to central PERU. Most of BRAZIL south to n Mato Grosso and Espírito Santo. Forest.

Plate 1

17. RED-LEGGED TINAMOU

Crypturellus atrocapillus *

12". Crown sooty black, throat rufous, mantle dull brown vermiculated with black, lower back and upper tail coverts obscurely barred black. Upper breast dull gray; rest of underparts tawny cinnamon, barred black on flanks. Lower mandible flesh color, legs salmon to scarlet pink. ♀: Differs from ♂ by wing coverts, inner remiges and back—except mantle—evenly barred black and ochraceous, more tawny on back.

GUYANA; SURINAM; VENEZUELA ex-cept in Amazonas; BRAZIL n of the Ama-zon. E PERU; n BOLIVIA. Margarita I. Forest and scrub.

18. YELLOW-LEGGED TINAMOU

Crypturellus noctivagus *

18". In color very like 17 but differs mainly by broad white eyebrow and in the ♀ by light bars on wings much paler. Legs dull yellow instead of red.

E BRAZIL from Piauí and Pernambuco s to Rio Grande do Sul.

19. GRAY-LEGGED TINAMOU

Crypturellus duidae *

Rather similar to 17 but chest clear rufous (in one race tinged gray), more intense rufous head and neck in the male and somewhat narrower and paler bars on back and wings of the ♀. Legs dark brownish gray.

Tropical zone. VENEZUELA in sw Táchira and sw Amazonas; COLOMBIA in s Meta. Forest.

20. THICKET TINAMOU

Crypturellus cinnamomeus *

11". Crown dull brown, sides of head cinnamon, throat white. Back dark brown barred with black on lower back, feathers fringed buffy white, wing coverts marked like lower back. Breast neutral gray be-coming pale buffy on lower breast and abdomen, flanks barred. Legs coral pink. ♀: More richly colored than male; crown chest-nut brown.

Chiefly semiarid tropical zone. Ne COLOM-BIA from Atlántico e to base of Perijá Mts. in w Zulia, VENEZUELA. [Mexico to nw Costa Rica.] Forest, scrub.

21. PALE-BROWED TINAMOU

Crypturellus transfasciatus

11″. Crown dusky brown with prominent, wide, whitish eyebrow. Back grayish olive indistinctly barred with black on lower back. Throat white, lower throat and upper breast light gray, lower throat feathers vermiculated with black. Sides of body gray, center of abdomen buffy white, flanks barred. Legs pink. ♀: Lighter with prominent pale eyebrow but with back (except mantle), wing coverts and inner remiges regularly barred black and ochraceous.

Tropical zone. W ECUADOR from equator to Tumbes and Piura in nw PERU. Deciduous forest.

22. BRAZILIAN TINAMOU

Crypturellus strigulosus *

11″. Above dark reddish brown, lower back and inner remiges barred with buffy. Throat ferruginous, neck and breast ash gray, rest of underparts buffy, flanks barred black. Legs dark brown.

Amazonian BRAZIL and e PERU south of the Amazon; nw BOLIVIA.

23. BARRED TINAMOU

Crypturellus casiquiare

10″. Head and neck bright chestnut, throat white. Entire upperparts boldly barred black and ochraceous. Front and sides of neck and the breast light gray, belly white, flanks barred black.

VENEZUELA, known only from junction of ríos Casiquiare and Guianía; from río Vaupés on COLOMBIA-BRAZIL boundary. Forest.

24. SLATY-BREASTED TINAMOU

Crypturellus boucardi *

11″. Top and sides of head and hindneck chestnut, throat white, lower throat and breast gray, rest of underparts buffy gray with pale bars on flanks. Back dark brown, sometimes with lower back and upper tail coverts barred with fulvous. Lower mandible and legs light pink; legs sometimes brick red. ♀: Like ♂ but with wing coverts and inner remiges barred with pale buff, lower back and rump barred black and brown becoming buffy on tail coverts.

Tropical zone. Nw COLOMBIA in Córdoba, n Antioquia and n Bolívar. [Mexico to n Costa Rica.] Forest.

25. MAGDALENA TINAMOU

Crypturellus saltuarius

11″. Forecrown dark gray; throat white becoming gray on lower neck; breast cinnamon buff, center of abdomen dull white. Above rich brown becoming sepia on lower back. Lower mandible yellowish white.

Tropical zone. Known only from forested middle Magdalena Valley in central COLOMBIA.

26. CHOCO TINAMOU

Crypturellus kerriae

11″. Crown and sides of head blackish, throat dark gray becoming blackish on lower neck. Underparts more or less uniform dark brown, flanks barred. Upperparts dark reddish brown, rump feathers with obscure black bars. Legs light red, toes darker red. ♀: Like ♂ but wing coverts and back barred black. Below dark brown.

Tropical zone. Known only from foothills of Baudó Mts. in Chocó, w COLOMBIA.

27. SMALL-BILLED TINAMOU

Crypturellus parvirostris

8″. Top and sides of head gray to brownish gray, throat pale gray, breast and sides of body darker gray, center of abdomen pinkish buff, flank feathers black, fringed pale buff. Upper mantle grayish, back dark reddish brown. Bill and legs red.

Amazonian and e BRAZIL s of the Amazon from Amazonas and Mato Grosso e to Marajó I., also from Maranhão and Ceará to São Paulo. Se PERU; n BOLIVIA from Beni e to PARAGUAY; ne ARGENTINA in Misiones and possibly Santa Fe and Chaco. Forest, scrub, cerradão.

28. TATAUPA TINAMOU

Crypturellus tataupa *

10″. In color almost exactly like 27 but much larger with much bigger bill and legs dark purplish red to dark purplish drab.

Tropical, subtropical zones. PERU from Cajamarca and Junín s to BOLIVIA; PARAGUAY; n ARGENTINA s to La Rioja, n Córdoba, n Santa Fe and Corrientes. BRAZIL from Maranhão to Rio Grande de Sul. Forest, scrub.

29. RED-WINGED TINAMOU

Rhynchotus rufescens *

16". Top of head and back barred black and sandy brown or buff. Throat white, neck and upper breast cinnamon (or neck streaked, breast barred with black, 1). Underparts pale buff (or grayish, 2) slightly barred on sides of body and flanks. Primaries cinnamon rufous.

Central and e BRAZIL s of the Amazon from rio Madeira e to Maranhão and Piauí, and from Bahía (possibly Pernambuco), Goiás and Minas Gerais s to Rio Grande do Sul; BOLIVIA from Beni s to Chuquisaca and Santa Cruz; PARAGUAY; URUGUAY. N and central ARGENTINA from s Misiones to Río Negro, 2. In s BOLIVIA and nw ARGENTINA, 1. Grassland.

Plate 1

30. TACZANOWSKI'S TINAMOU

Nothoprocta taczanowskii

13". Top and sides of head brown, throat white. Black streak from behind eye and another from gape bordering throat. Lower throat and upper breast gray spotted with white, spots bordered below with black. Sides of body grayish buff barred with blackish, center of abdomen pale buff. Above dusky; feathers margined laterally with buffy giving streaked appearance. Inner webs of primaries conspicuously barred with buff. Legs yellow.

Temperate zone of Andes of central and se PERU in Junín and Cuzco.

31. KALINOWSKI'S TINAMOU

Nothoprocta kalinowski

14". Upperparts grayish brown barred with black, secondaries barred tawny. Lower breast and abdomen gray, dotted and marbled with buffy.

Temperate zone of central and se PERU in Libertad and Cuzco.

32. ORNATE TINAMOU

Nothoprocta ornata *

Rather like 31 but with back barred buffy and black. Throat buffy spotted with black, breast plain gray or spotted dusky. Sides of body tawny buff, sides of abdomen buffy white.

Temperate zone of Andes in central PERU

from Junín s through Puno to Potosí, BOLIVIA. Puna zone of w ARGENTINA from Jujuy to La Rioja. CHILE in cordillera of Tarapacá. Open scrub.

33. CHILEAN TINAMOU

Nothoprocta perdicaria *

12". Upperparts grayish brown spotted with black, finely lined with dark cinnamon and speckled with white. Throat and center of abdomen whitish; lower neck, breast and sides gray; flanks somewhat barred. Primaries gray, secondaries brown.

Mts. of CHILE from s Atacama s to Llanquihue. Grassland, wheatfields.

34. BRUSHLAND TINAMOU

Nothoprocta cinerascens *

12". Entire upperparts sandy brown barred with black, back feathers laterally margined whitish, giving somewhat streaked appearance. Throat whitish, lower throat barred with black. Breast buffy gray spotted with whitish, rest of underparts buffy white. Primaries blackish notched on outer web with buff.

S BOLIVIA in Tarija; w PARAGUAY and w ARGENTINA s to La Pampa. Open scrub, thorn scrub.

35. ANDEAN TINAMOU

Nothoprocta pentlandii *

11". Forehead and sides of crown gray; center of crown and upperparts sandy brown spotted with black, and barred and marbled with rufescent; line behind eye black. Throat and breast gray, pale-spotted; rest of underparts buffy white. Inner secondaries grayish brown, outer webs of secondaries pale brown barred with whitish.

Temperate zone of s ECUADOR s through Andes to BOLIVIA; n CHILE in cordillera of Arica and s to Catamarca in w ARGENTINA between 1500-2500 m. Pasturelands.

36. CURVE-BILLED TINAMOU

Nothoprocta curvirostris *

10". Upperparts dark brown spotted with black and streaked with buffy white. Throat white, breast tawny rufous spotted with black, pale-streaked; rest of underparts tawny buff. Outer webs of secondaries cinnamon rufous barred with black.

Páramo zone of Andes of ECUADOR from Mt. Pichincha s to Huánuco in central PERU.

37. WHITE-BELLIED NOTHURA

Nothura boraquira

10". Upperparts barred black and sandy brown and streaked with buffy white. Throat white, neck buffy streaked with black, breast buff marbled with blackish, rest of underparts buffy white.

Ne BRAZIL from Piauí and Ceará s to Minas Gerais. PARAGUAYAN chaco; e BOLIVIA in Santa Cruz. Grassland, scrub.

38. LESSER NOTHURA

Nothura minor

7". Upperparts rufous chestnut marbled with black. Wing coverts evenly barred blackish and rufous, secondaries and tertials cinnamon barred with dark brown. Throat white, underparts tawny rufous lightly barred on sides with blackish, streaked on breast with rufous chestnut.

E and central BRAZIL from Minas Gerais s to São Paulo and w to Mato Grosso.

39. DARWIN'S NOTHURA

Nothura darwinii *

Rather like 37 but browner above with grayer breast.

PERU from Cuzco s through BOLIVIA to nw ARGENTINA in Salta and Tucumán thence to Mendoza, La Pampa, Buenos Aires, e Río Negro and ne Chubut. Grassland, open savanna.

40. SPOTTED NOTHURA

Nothura maculosa *

10". Crown black, feathers margined and barred with rusty. Back brown, feathers spotted and barred with black and edged with whitish. Throat white, underparts buffy, breast streaked with chestnut and black.

E BRAZIL in Ceará, in Goiás, Minas Gerais and probably s Bahía, and from Rio de Janeiro and São Paulo w to Mato Grosso. PARAGUAY; URUGUAY; e ARGENTINA from Misiones to Corrientes and Formosa s through Santa Fe and Buenos Aires to Chubut. Pastureland, sometimes woodland.

Plate 1

41. CHACO NOTHURA

Nothura chacoensis

Very like 40 but upperparts grayer, underparts somewhat darker and breast streaked with dark brown but no chestnut.

Arid parts of PARAGUAYAN chaco from 100 miles w of río Paraguay, probably at least to Bolivian border, and s to the n bank of río Pilcomayo. N ARGENTINA in Formosa. Pastureland.

42. DWARF TINAMOU

Taoniscus nanus

6". Crown black, feathers edged with gray. Back pale grayish brown spotted with black and waved with grayish buff. Flight feathers uniform grayish brown. Throat and belly white, breast buffy lightly spotted with black, flanks barred with black.

E BRAZIL in São Paulo and Paraná. Doubtfully reported from ne ARGENTINA in Misiones.

43. ELEGANT CRESTED-TINAMOU

Eudromia elegans *

16". Long, thin, black crest curving forward. Top and sides of head brown, streak behind eye and on throat buff, back rather finely spotted black and buff. Breast rather finely barred, rest of underparts more coarsely barred black and buff.

ARGENTINA from Tucumán s through Catamarca, Santiago del Estero and Córdoba to Santa Cruz, e through La Pampa to s Buenos Aires. CHILE in Aysén at Chile Chico. Grassland, arid hills, barren flats.

44. QUEBRACHO CRESTED-TINAMOU

Eudromia formosa

Rather like 43, but much darker; crest feathers shorter, narrower and less tapered.

PARAGUAY in arid w chaco. ARGENTINA in e Salta, e Tucumán, Santiago del Estero, w Chaco and Formosa. Quebracho woodland.

45. PUNA TINAMOU

Tinamotis pentlandii *

18". Crown and hindneck buff, neck streaked with dark gray. Upper back and inner remiges barred olivaceous and cinnamon buff and streaked with violet gray, the gray streaks having powdery blue cast. Lower back and tail yellowish olive barred with pale whitish buff. Breast cinnamon buff barred with violet gray becoming whitish on lower breast where barred with dusky; rest of underparts bright cinnamon rufous. Primaries barred dark brown and buff on outer webs, inner web uniform grayish brown. Tarsus short, toes thick.

Puna zone of Andes of s PERU from Junín s to Antofagasta, CHILE; highlands of BO-LIVIA s through ARGENTINA to Neuquén. Open steppes.

Plate 1

46. PATAGONIAN TINAMOU

Tinamotis ingoufi

15". Head and neck whitish with blackish stripes. Back and breast bluish gray with ochraceous, black-centered marks; abdomen rufous. Primaries rufous.

Western steppes of Río Negro to s Santa Cruz, ARGENTINA. S CHILE in Aysén and Magallanes. Grassland.

Fig. 4. SOOTY SHEARWATER
Puffinus griseus
p. 16

Order PODICIPEDIFORMES

Family PODICIPEDIDAE   GREBES

Grebes are found on freshwater ponds and lakes. They have lobed toes and narrow, pointed bills. Expert divers, they live on fish and other aquatic life. They build floating nests made of reeds; their breeding plumage differs from their winter plumage.

1. LEAST GREBE

Podiceps dominicus *

9". Much the smallest South American grebe. Upperparts and neck ashy gray, throat blackish (white in winter). Below dirty white; flight feathers largely white. Bill black, tipped white.

Tropical to temperate zone. From COLOMBIA and VENEZUELA south, e of Andes, to Tierra del Fuego, ARGENTINA; w of Andes s to Lambayeque in w PERU. Curaçao, Bonaire. Trinidad and Tobago. [Tex.; Mid. Amer; W Indies.]

2. WHITE-TUFTED GREBE

Podiceps rolland *

12". Above black, feathers broadly edged brown; lengthened feathers at sides of head mixed black and white. Neck blackish, underparts rufescent. Inner remiges white. Winter: white below, brownish only on neck; no plumes.

Tropical to temperate zone. S PERU s through BOLIVIA, PARAGUAY, se BRAZIL in Rio Grande do Sul, URUGUAY, ARGENTINA and CHILE to Tierra del Fuego. [Falkland Is.]

3. PUNA GREBE

Podiceps taczanowskii

14". Upperparts gray, blackish on nape and hindneck; below white. Plumes at sides of head gray. In winter lacks black on nape and hindneck; no plumes.

Puna zone of Andes of central PERU in Junín.

4. SILVERY GREBE

Podiceps occipitalis *

11". Like 3 but smaller (or with cinnamon patch on breast, 1).

Temperate, lower páramo zones from Central Andes in s COLOMBIA s to Catamarca, ARGENTINA; from Rio Negro to Tierra del Fuego, CHILE, 1. [Falkland Is.]

5. EARED GREBE

Podiceps nigricollis *

(Called *P. caspicus* in *Sp. Bds. S. Amer.*)

12". Above blackish with a greenish gloss. Plumes at sides of head golden buff shading to chestnut. Throat black, foreneck and sides of body chestnut, underparts and inner remiges white. In winter white below with no chestnut on neck and sides; no plumes. Bill slightly upturned.

Breeds on a few lakes in temperate zone of E Andes of COLOMBIA from Bogotá northward. [N Amer., s to Guatemala in winter. Eurasia; n Africa.]

Plate 44

6. GREAT GREBE

Podiceps major

24". At once distinguishable by large size and long bill (4"). Above brownish black glossed green. Sides of head and throat gray becoming blackish on lower throat, foreneck chestnut; underparts white. In winter throat white and chestnut on foreneck duller.

Se BRAZIL in Rio Grande do Sul; PARAGUAY; URUGUAY; ARGENTINA except

10

Andean region. Coast of PERU in Piura, and in Ancash and Lambayeque. CHILE from Coquimbo to Tierra del Fuego.

7. SHORT-WINGED GREBE

Centropelma micropterum

11″. Crown blackish, feathers basally chestnut, nape chestnut, plumes at sides of head black. Throat and foreneck white, rest of plumage dark brownish, paler below. In winter white below, no plumes.

PERU from Lake Titicaca s to Lake Poopó, BOLIVIA.

Plate 22

8. PIED-BILLED GREBE

Podilymbus podiceps *

13″. Distinguishable in breeding plumage from other grebes by thick yellowish bill with black band. Upperparts and neck grayish brown, throat black; underparts dirty white. No white visible in wing in flight. In winter throat white, bill plain greenish.

Tropical to temperate zone. From COLOMBIA, n VENEZUELA and GUYANA s to CHILE and ARGENTINA to Santa Cruz. Aruba, Curaçao, Bonaire. Trinidad, Tobago. [N and Mid. Amer.; W Indies.]

Fig. 5. BROWN PELICAN
Pelecanus occidentalis
p. 20

Order PROCELLARIIFORMES

Family DIOMEDEIDAE   ALBATROSSES

Albatrosses are the largest seabirds. They have long, very narrow wings on which they glide effortlessly. They alight on water to feed and can only take off again by running on water's surface against the wind. They often follow ships, feeding on sea life and refuse churned up in the water. Almost all live in southern oceans.

AID TO IDENTIFICATION

Whole body, including center of back, white 1, 2

Mainly white, center of back dark 4, 5b, 6, 7c, 8

All or mostly sooty 3b, 9b, 10

1. WANDERING ALBATROSS

Diomedea exulans *

42-48". Wingspread 11'. Mainly white, wing tips blackish. Bill pink. Imm.: Sooty brown with white face and throat.

Occurs off coast of CHILE n to Tropic of Capricorn and still farther in Humboldt current. Coasts of ARGENTINA and URUGUAY n to Cabo Frio, BRAZIL. [Breeds on subantarctic islands.]

2. ROYAL ALBATROSS

Diomedea epomophora *

42-48". Wingspread 10'. Virtually indistinguishable from 1 except by more slender bill, horn color with black cutting edge.

Possibly breeds in Tierra del Fuego. Occurs off coast of CHILE n to PERU and coasts of ARGENTINA, URUGUAY and São Paulo, BRAZIL. [Breeds in New Zealand region.]

3. GALAPAGOS ALBATROSS

Diomedea irrorata

35". Wingspread 8'. Head white; rest of plumage sooty, waved on back with white. Bill yellow.

Occurs from Pacific coast of COLOMBIA s to Independencia Bay, PERU. [Breeds on Hood I., Galápagos Is.]

4. BLACK-BROWED ALBATROSS

Diomedea melanophris *

34". Wingspread 8'. White; wings, tail and middle of back black; narrow black line above eye; underwing white with broad black border. Bill straw yellow, tip pink.

Breeds on Staten I., ARGENTINA, and San Ildefonso and Diégo Ramírez islets off Cape Horn, CHILE. Ranges n to coast of PERU, and BRAZIL as far as Bahía. [Breeds on subantarctic islands.]

Plate 20

5. BULLER'S ALBATROSS

Diomedea bulleri

32". Wingspread 8'. Cheeks and hindneck pale gray, darker in front of eye; forehead white. Back and wings sooty brown; rump, upper tail coverts and underparts white; underwing white with narrow black border. Bill gray, yellow band on top of upper mandible.

Wanders to coast of PERU (June) and CHILE (March and May). [Breeds on islands off New Zealand.]

6. WHITE-CAPPED ALBATROSS

Diomedea cauta *

36". Wingspread 8'. White; nape and cheeks gray, gray line above eye. Wings dark grayish brown, middle of back light grayish brown. Underwing virtually all white, black border very narrow. Bill dark greenish gray, yellow tip.

Occurs off coast of PERU from Lima s to Llanquihue, CHILE, and off coast of Buenos Aires, ARGENTINA. [Breeds in islands off Tasmania and New Zealand.]

7. YELLOW-NOSED ALBATROSS

Diomedea chlororhynchos

32". Wingspread 6.5'. Head, neck, rump and undersurface white; wings dark sooty gray; back lighter, brownish; underwing white with narrow black border. Bill black, ridge yellow becoming pink to scarlet at tip.

Casual off coast of BRAZIL and ARGENTINA. [Breeds on Tristan and Gough Is.]

8. GRAY-HEADED ALBATROSS

Diomedea chrysostoma

32". Head and neck slaty gray (white in old birds); back and tail dark gray, wings blackish; rump and underparts white; underwing white with black border. Bill has dark central stripe, edged above and below by rich yellow, becoming bright pink at tip.

Breeds on San Ildefonso and Diégo Ramírez islets off Cape Horn, CHILE; ranges n along coast of CHILE and ARGENTINA. Sight records from PERU. [Breeds on subantarctic islands.]

9. SOOTY ALBATROSS

Phoebetria fusca

33". Much like 10 but somewhat larger, darker and browner. Bill black, groove in lower mandible yellow or orange.

Casual in Magellanic waters of CHILE. [Breeds on Tristan and Gough Is.]

10. LIGHT-MANTLED ALBATROSS

Phoebetria palpebrata *

28". Pale sooty gray; darker on head, wings and tail. An interrupted white eye ring. Tail rather long, wedge-shaped. Bill black, groove in lower mandible pale blue; feet fleshy white.

Occurs off CHILE from Tarapacá to Cape Horn, and has been taken at Bahía de Yendegaia and Beagle Channel, ARGENTINA. Accidental off coast of s São Paulo, BRAZIL. [Breeds on subantarctic islands.]

Family PROCELLARIIDAE

SHEARWATERS, FULMARS, PETRELS

Birds of this family are strictly pelagic, coming ashore only to nest. They are usually seen far out at sea, gliding on stiff wings near the surface of the water. They feed on plankton and other marine life and nest in burrows and rock crevices. Fulmars are distinguishable by heavier bodies, larger bills and more gull-like appearance.

AID TO IDENTIFICATION

Dark above (and below) 1, 5c, 17, 22b, 24; (white or partially white below) underwing white 3, 8a, 11c, 12b, 19c, 20b, 21c, 26c, underwing dark 6c, 7c, 9b, 10c, 16, 18b, 22b, 23b, 25c, 27a

Spotted or checkered above 1, 4

Pale gray above, white below 2, 13, 14, 15

1. GIANT FULMAR (or Petrel)

Macronectes giganteus

35". Wingspread 7'. Differs from rest of family by very large size; differs from albatrosses by broad wings. Sooty brown, sooty gray or white spotted with brown; underwing dark. Bill massive, pale yellow.

Occurs off entire CHILEAN coast year-round; n to Talara, PERU, July, Aug. Atlantic coast off ARGENTINA; URUGUAY, particularly off Isla de Lobos; BRAZIL n to Cabo Frio. [Breeds on Tristan da Cunha and subantarctic islands.]

2. SOUTHERN (or Silver-gray) FULMAR

Fulmarus glacialoides *

20". Wingspread 4'. Upperparts light gray, head and underparts white. Wing tip dark, white flash in wing. Tail short, rounded. Bill pink with black tip, heavy and hooked.

Occurs off s coasts n to 6°s in PERU, and Cabo São Roque, BRAZIL. [Breeds in Antarctica and subantarctic islands.]

3. ANTARCTIC PETREL

Thalassoica antarctica `

17". Above brown, below white. Inner secondaries and greater wing coverts white; underwing white. Tail white, tipped brown.

Casual about Cape Horn and in channels among islands of southernmost CHILE and Tierra del Fuego, ARGENTINA. [Breeds in Antarctica.]

4. CAPE (or Pintado) PETREL

Daption capense

16". Wingspread 3'. Checkered black and white above; white below, throat sooty. Two large white areas on wings; underwing white.

Occurs off coast of CHILE year-round north to Guayaquil Bay, ECUADOR, at times even crossing Equator. Atlantic coast from Tierra del Fuego, ARGENTINA, n to São Paulo, BRAZIL. [Breeds in Antarctica and subantarctic islands.]

Plate 20

5. GRAY-FACED (or Great-winged) PETREL

Pterodroma macroptera *

(Called *P. brevirostris* in *Sp. Bds. S. Amer.*)

10.5". Tail long, wedge-shaped. Blackish brown; face and throat pale gray; underwing dark. Bill stout, legs black.

Recorded off coasts of se BRAZIL and ARGENTINA. [Breeds on Kerguelen, Marion, Tristan and Crozet Is. Islands off New Zealand and w Australia.]

6. WHITE-HEADED PETREL

Pterodroma lessonii *

18". Rather like 2. Front of head white, around eye black. Back pale gray, underparts white; upper and underwing dark. Bill black.

Casual off coast of ARGENTINA, URUGUAY and BRAZIL, and off Pacific entrance of Strait of Magellan, CHILE. [Breeds in subantarctic islands.]

7. HOODED (or Schlegel's) PETREL

Pterodroma incerta

18". Uppersurface, throat, foreneck and underwing dark brown; lower breast and belly white. Bill black, feet yellow.

Casual off coast of ARGENTINA, URUGUAY and BRAZIL n to 29° s. [Breeds on Tristan da Cunha.]

8. BLACK-CAPPED PETREL

Pterodroma hasitata

15". Sooty brown above, cap darker, collar whitish. Forehead, rump and underparts white. Underwing white with black border. Dark phase: sooty brown, rump white. Bill short, black.

Sw Caribbean between Guajira Pen., COLOMBIA and Aruba. Off coast of BRAZIL. [Breeds in W Indies.]

9. DARK-RUMPED PETREL

Pterodroma phaeopygia *

17". Tail dark, wedge-shaped. Forehead white; ocular region, trailing edge of wing and tail black. Back dusky; underparts white. Undersurface of flight feathers dark, under wing coverts mostly white.

Occurs off COLOMBIA (Malpelo I.), ECUADOR and n and central PERU. [Breeds in Hawaiian and Galápagos Is.]

10. SOFT-PLUMAGED PETREL

Pterodroma mollis *

15". Above ashy gray, tail paler. Below white, gray band across upper breast, occasionally all pale gray below. Underwing all dark gray.

Casual off coast of ARGENTINA and URUGUAY. [Breeds from Madeira and Cape Verde Is. s to Gough and the Kerguelen Is.]

11. WHITE-NECKED PETREL

Pterodroma externa *

16". Dark ashy gray above, tail paler. Face, underparts, underwing and base of tail white.

Casually on coast of ARGENTINA. Probably Pacific coast of S America. [Breeds on Juan Fernández and Kermadec Is.]

12. BLUE-FOOTED (or Cook's) PETREL

Pterodroma cookii *

10.5". Much like 10 but no gray band across breast. Undersurface of wings all white, inner webs of primaries white.

Occurs off Ancón, Lima, PERU, and Corral, Valdivia, CHILE; possibly breeds on islands between Guaitecas Is., and Strait of Magellan. [Breeds in New Zealand waters and Juan Fernández Is.]

13. BLUE PETREL

Halobaena caerulea

11". Pale blue gray above, white below. Tail square; outer tail feathers mostly white, rest pale gray, tipped white. Dark *W* across wings.

Occurs from Cape Horn n off coast of CHILE to latitude of Valparaíso; off coast of ARGENTINA. [Breeds on subantarctic islands.]

14. DOVE PRION

Pachyptila desolata *

12". Rather like 11 but tail wedge-shaped with blackish terminal band; blackish ear coverts. Dark *W* across wings. Bill bluish.

Casual on coast of CHILE off Concepción and Llanquihue (50 km. n of Taltal). Atlantic n to São Paulo, BRAZIL. [Breeds in Antarctica and antarctic islands.]

15. SLENDER-BILLED PRION

Pachyptila belcheri *

12". Similar to 14 but bill narrower at base.

Winters off coast of ARGENTINA (possibly breeding on Staten I. and Tierra del Fuego) n to São Paulo, BRAZIL. Occurs off s PERU and n CHILE. [Breeds on Kerguelen and Falkland Is.]

16. GRAY PETREL (or Pediunker)

Adamastor cinereus

18". Wingspread 4'. Uniform dark bluish gray above, white below; underwing dark. Bill long, pale.

Occurs from Cape Horn, CHILE, n along Pacific coast to about 12°s off coast of PERU; on Atlantic coast n to Rio Grande do Sul, BRAZIL. [Breeds on Tristan and Gough Is.]

17. WHITE-CHINNED PETREL (or Shoemaker)

Procellaria aequinoctialis *

22". Wingspread 5'. Brownish black. Chin white; sometimes white extends to eyes and forehead. Bill greenish white and black; legs black.

Occurs off Pacific coast n in PERU to about 6°s and Atlantic coast to s BRAZIL, casually as far n as Bahía and even the lower Amazon. [Breeds on subantarctic islands.]

18. PARKINSON'S PETREL

Procellaria parkinsoni *

18". Sooty black; underside of primary shafts white. Bill bluish horn with black tip and ridge of culmen.

Off coast of ECUADOR. [Breeds in New Zealand; recorded off Galápagos.]

19. CORY'S (or Mediterranean) SHEARWATER

Puffinus diomedea *

17". Wingspread 4'. Above uniform brownish gray; underparts and underwing white. Bill yellow.

Recorded only from GUYANA and Bahía, BRAZIL. Accidental in Trinidad. [Breeds from Azores to Canary and Cape Verde Is.]

20. PINK-FOOTED SHEARWATER

Puffinus creatopus

20". Differs from 19 by dusky flanks and dark tip to yellow bill. Underparts sometimes mottled with gray.

Breeds on Mocha I. in Arauco Bay, most probably on Huafo and other islands about Chiloé, CHILE. In nonbreeding season found n as far as PERU and ECUADOR. [Breeds in Juan Fernández Is.]

21. GREATER SHEARWATER

Puffinus gravis

19". Wingspread 4'. Cap dark, back light gray brown, incomplete pale collar on hindneck, and pale patch at base of tail. Underparts and front of underwing white. Bill dark.

At sea from Tierra del Fuego n to Buenos Aires, ARGENTINA, more or less yearround; URUGUAY, off coast of Rocha Prov., and Maldonado. Trinidad. [Breeds on Tristan da Cunha; winters in N Atlantic.]

22. WEDGE-TAILED SHEARWATER

Puffinus pacificus *

15". Above dark chocolate brown, wings and tail blackish; below paler grayish brown, throat dark. Tail long, very wedge-shaped. Bill reddish flesh, tip dark. A phase occurs with light underparts.

Recorded from Gulf of Guayaquil, ECUADOR, to Pacific coast of COLOMBIA. [Breeds on Revilla Gigedo Is. and islands of central and western Pacific, also Seychelles Is., Indian Ocean. Recorded off Costa Rica, Panama, and Galápagos Is.]

23. GRAY-BACKED SHEARWATER

Puffinus bulleri

16". Much like 11 in color, but with less or no white on forehead or tail. Bill longer, more slender.

Found occasionally in CHILE off Concón and Valparaíso (Feb.-Mar.), and coast of PERU off Talara. [Breeds on islands in New Zealand waters.]

24. SOOTY SHEARWATER

Puffinus griseus

20". Wingspread 3.5'. Dark grey. Distinguishable from other large dark petrels by white underwing. Tail short, rounded. Bill long, dark.

Breeds in CHILE in Strait of Magellan. Breeds on Staten I., ARGENTINA. In winter n along coast to URUGUAY; n along Pacific coast to COLOMBIA. [Breeds in Falkland Is. and islands off New Zealand.]

Fig. 4, p. 9

25. COMMON (or Manx) SHEARWATER

Puffinus puffinus *

14". Wingspread 2.5'. Above blackish brown extending on sides of head to below eye. Underparts and underwing white.

Migrant from Europe to coast of BRAZIL and URUGUAY s to Buenos Aires, ARGENTINA. Acc. in Trinidad. [Breeds on islands in Atlantic and Pacific oceans, and Mediterranean and Black seas.]

26. LITTLE SHEARWATER

Puffinus assimilis

10". Above slaty blackish; sides of head, underparts and underwing white. Bill and legs blue.

Recorded from coast of ARGENTINA. [Breeds in Azores, tropical African islands, Tristan group and New Zealand seas.]

27. DUSKY-BACKED (or Audubon's) SHEARWATER

Puffinus lherminieri *

11". Like 25 but smaller and with black under tail coverts. Very like 26 but legs flesh colored.

Breeds on Los Roques, recorded from La Orchila and Los Hermanos off coast of VENEZUELA. Recorded off Pacific coast of ECUADOR. Tobago. [Breeds in Bermuda, islands in Caribbean, and Ascension I. Recorded off coasts of Panama, Galápagos Is.]

Family HYDROBATIDAE   STORM-PETRELS

Small pelagic birds, storm-petrels flit over the waves with rapidly beating wings, occasionally "dancing" on the surface, their feet touching the water. They eat plankton and small fish and sometimes follow ships.

AID TO IDENTIFICATION

With white below 2b, 3, 4, 5b, 6, 13

All dusky 7b, 11b, 12b, with white rump 1, 8b, 9, 10

Tail forked 8b, 9, 10, 11b, 12b, 13b

1. WILSON'S STORM-PETREL

Oceanites oceanicus*

7". Tail square. Brownish black, rump white; pale band on wings, underwing all black. Webs between toes yellow, legs long, feet extending beyond tail.

Breeds on islets near Cape Horn n in winter along coast of CHILE to latitude of Ancón, PERU, and acc. to ECUADOR. Occurs off Tierra del Fuego, ARGENTINA, and coast of URUGUAY, n to Bahía, BRAZIL. Recorded from n coast of VENEZUELA, off GUYANA and SURINAM. [Migrates to N Atlantic, casually to n Pacific.]

2. WHITE-VENTED STORM-PETREL

Oceanites gracilis*

6". Tail square. Sooty black; center of abdomen and rump white.

Found off Pacific coast from COLOMBIA to CHILE between 3°n and 33°s. [Nesting grounds unknown.]

Plate 20

3. WHITE-FACED STORM-PETREL

Pelagodroma marina*

8". Tail short, square. Forehead, face, eyebrow, underparts and underwing white. Back light gray, paler and grayer on rump; darker on crown, wings and tail.

Recorded off Point Piñas, ECUADOR; also off Patagonia and Mar del Plata, ARGENTINA, and s coast of URUGUAY. [Breeds on African Atlantic islands, Tristan and in Australian-New Zealand region; recorded off Galápagos Is.]

4. WHITE-BELLIED STORM-PETREL

Fregetta grallaria*

8". Tail square. Sooty gray above; rump, lower breast and belly white. Inner under wing coverts and base of outer tail feathers white.

Strays to coast of CHILE off Valparaíso. Accidental off coast of ARGENTINA.

[Breeds in Juan Fernández Is., islands of central Pacific and Tristan da Cunha.]

5. BLACK-BELLIED STORM-PETREL

Fregetta tropica

7.5". Like 4 but with dark band down center of white belly.

Occurs in waters about Cape Horn, CHILE; off Cañete, PERU. [Breeds in subantarctic islands.]

6. GRAY-BACKED STORM-PETREL

Garrodia nereis

7". Tail square. Slaty black above shading to bluish gray on rump. Breast, abdomen and inner under wing coverts and underwing white. Tail pale gray broadly edged black.

Occurs in waters about Cape Horn, CHILE, and off coast of Patagonia, ARGENTINA. [Breeds on subantarctic islands.]

7. LEAST STORM-PETREL

Halocyptena microsoma

5.7". Sooty blackish brown. The smallest petrel and the only storm-petrel with wedge-shaped tail.

Occurs off coast of COLOMBIA and ECUADOR to 2°s. [Breeds on islands off Baja California and in the gulf.]

Fig. 7, p. 37

8. WEDGE-RUMPED STORM-PETREL

Oceanodroma tethys*

6.5". Tail forked. Sooty blackish brown. Triangular white rump patch.

Breeds on San Gallán and Pescadores Is. off coast of PERU, ranging s to 20°s off coast of CHILE. Galápagos breeders wander to waters off COLOMBIA and ECUADOR. [Occurs in Gulf of Panama.]

9. BAND-RUMPED STORM-PETREL

Oceanodroma castro*

8". Tail forked. Sooty blackish brown, wings with pronounced pale wing bar.

Upper tail coverts white, broadly tipped black, outer tail feathers basally white.

Occurs off coast of BRAZIL and probably off Pacific coast. [Breeds on islands of tropical Atlantic and Pacific.]

10. LEACH'S STORM-PETREL

Oceanodroma leucorhoa *

8.5". Sooty blackish gray. Difficult to distinguish from 9 but white rump patch divided in middle, shafts of feathers black instead of white, and tail more deeply forked.

Recorded from Gulf of Paria, VENEZUELA, s to BRAZIL (Bahía). Trinidad. [Breeds on islands of N Atlantic and Pacific.]

11. SOOTY STORM-PETREL

Oceanodroma markhami *

9.5". Sooty brown. Pale wing band prominent. Tail long, deeply forked.

Occurs off coast of CHILE from latitude of Valparaíso north to n PERU. Probably breeds inland in n CHILE. [Recorded off Galápagos, Clipperton and Cocos Is.]

12. BLACK STORM-PETREL

Oceanodroma melania

9". Differs from 11 by being blacker and lacking prominent wing band.

Migrant to Pacific coast s at least to 8°s. [Breeds on islands off Baja California and w Mexico.]

13. RINGED STORM-PETREL

Oceanodroma hornbyi

8.7". Above mainly dusky brown, below mainly white. The only South American petrel with dark band across white underparts and pale band across hindneck. Tail deeply forked.

Probably breeds in Andes of PERU ? and n CHILE. Recorded off Pacific coast n to ECUADOR.

Family PELECANOIDIDAE   DIVING-PETRELS

In appearance and flight diving-petrels resemble dovekies, with little resemblance to conventional petrels. They dive with ease, using wings to propel themselves under water. They have a rapid, whirring flight close to the surface. They are usually found in coastal waters and channels.

1. PERUVIAN DIVING-PETREL

Pelecanoides garnotii

9". Above shiny black, scapulars gray, edged white; underparts white.

Breeds on islands off coasts of PERU and CHILE from Lobos de Tierra to Corral, occasionally found off coast at Ancud, Chiloé I.

2. MAGELLANIC DIVING-PETREL

Pelecanoides magellani

8.5". Differs from 1 by back feathers tipped white, and by conspicuous white patch at sides of neck.

Breeds in coastal and inland waterways from Chiloé I., CHILE, s to Cape Horn and on Staten I., n in winter along coast of ARGENTINA to vicinity of Puerto Deseado, Santa Cruz.

Plate 20

3. SUBANTARCTIC (or Common) DIVING-PETREL

Pelecanoides urinatrix *

7". Differs from 1 by smaller size, by grayish band across upper breast, and by much smaller bill.

Magellanic channels of CHILE between 47° and 54°s where it probably breeds. Occurs in winter off coast of Buenos Aires, ARGENTINA. [Breeds also on Tristan da Cunha, the Falkland and subantarctic islands, New Zealand and Australia.]

Order PELECANIFORMES

Family PHAETHONTIDAE   TROPICBIRDS

Adult tropicbirds are distinguishable from other seabirds by quill-like, much lengthened central tail feathers (18-23"). Their flight is pigeon-like, rapid and direct. They feed on squid and fish which they catch by diving from a considerable height, and sometimes they join terns which are fishing. On the water their long tails are held high.

1. RED-BILLED TROPICBIRD

Phaethon aethereus *

24", with quills 40". White; line through eye and encircling crown black; back barred with black, outer webs of primaries black. Lengthened tail feathers white. Bill red. Imm.: No lengthened tail feathers. Bill yellow.

Breeds on Los Hermanos and Los Roques off coast of VENEZUELA. Breeds also on La Plata I., ECUADOR, and San Lorenzo I., off Lima, PERU. Acc. off Maranhão, BRAZIL, and Taltal, CHILE (?). Curaçao. Little Tobago, St. Giles islets, nesting. [Tropical oceans and seas.]

Plate 21

2. RED-TAILED TROPICBIRD

Phaethon rubricauda *

18", with quills 36". White, sometimes tinged rosy. Mark in front of eye and eyebrow black; tertials in center and shafts of flight feathers black. Lengthened tail feathers red. Bill yellow, orange or vermilion. Imm.: Much like adult of 1 but primaries white with black shafts. Bill black.

Occurs off coast of CHILE. [Breeds in tropical Indian and Pacific oceans.]

3. WHITE-TAILED TROPICBIRD

Phaethon lepturus *

16", with quills 32". Body plumage rather like 2 but lesser wing coverts edged black, tertials almost all black, outer webs of primaries black. Lengthened tail feathers white. Bill orange. Imm.: Much like 2 but smaller, and outer web of outermost primaries black.

Occurs off Caribbean coast of COLOMBIA, off coast of BRAZIL, off coast of CHILE. [Tropical oceans and seas.]

Family PELECANIDAE   PELICANS

Very large size, long bill and hunchback appearance in flight distinguish pelicans from other seabirds. They live on fish and are often seen plunging after them, head first, hitting the water with a splash. They nest on low bushes or on the ground and do not venture far from land.

19

BROWN PELICAN

Pelecanus occidentalis *

40-54" (or 60-65", 1). Head and stripe down neck white, rest of neck chestnut; silvery gray above, browner below. In non-breeding season adult has white head and neck. Young birds have brownish gray head and neck, and white underparts.

Coasts of COLOMBIA and VENEZUELA including adjacent islands. Migrant to n BRAZIL (rio Uraricuera), s of the Amazon on rio Tapajós; coast of ECUADOR. Humboldt current waters along coast of PERU to Corral and occasionally Chiloé I., CHILE; acc. in Tierra del Fuego, ARGENTINA, 1. Aruba to Trinidad and Tobago. [N and Mid. Amer.; W Indies. Galápagos Is.]

Fig. 5, p. 11

Family SULIDAE   BOOBIES

Boobies are distinguished from other seabirds by narrow wedge-shaped tails. Often seen in long straggling lines flying near sea's surface, they frequently glide over the waves like an albatross. Like pelicans they dive head first after fish. Immature birds are brown, usually lighter below.

1. BLUE-FOOTED BOOBY

Sula nebouxii

34". Top of head and neck white streaked brown. Upper back and rump white, middle of back brown mottled with white. Underparts white. Wings and tail brown. Bill dull blue; feet bright blue.

Breeds on islands along Pacific coast s to PERU, wanders s as far as Chincha Is., Ica, PERU. [Gulf of Panama and Galápagos Is.]

2. PERUVIAN BOOBY

Sula variegata

29". Head, neck and underparts white; back and rump dark brown checkered with white. Wings and tail silvery brown. Bill purplish blue; feet dull blue.

A bird of the Humboldt current. Breeds from Point Pariñas, PERU, s to Concepción, CHILE. Ranges casually north to sw COLOMBIA and s to Chiloé I., CHILE.

3. MASKED (or White, or Blue-faced) BOOBY

Sula dactylatra *

31". White; wings and tail dark brown. Bill orange yellow with dark tip; or pink or light red (♀).

Pacific coast of COLOMBIA, ECUADOR (breeding on La Plata I.) and off Talara, PERU. Occurs in estuary of the Amazon and Cabo Frio and Rio de Janeiro; breeds on Fernando de Noronha off coast of ne BRAZIL. Islands off the coast of VENEZUELA. [Caribbean Sea, Gulf of Mexico, Pacific Panama, w and central Pacific, islands off n Australia.]

Plate 21

4. RED-FOOTED BOOBY

Sula sula *

28". Much like 3 but tail white or all grayish brown although usually with white rump, tail and belly. The only South American booby with a white tail.

Caribbean coast and islands off VENEZUELA from Paraguaná Peninsula to Cape Codera. Acc. off ne coast of BRAZIL. Trinidad and Tobago. [Caribbean Sea, S Atlantic Ocean, islands off Pacific coast of Mexico, Galápagos Is., W and central Pacific and Indian Oceans.]

5. BROWN BOOBY

Sula leucogaster *

28". Chocolate brown; wing lining, lower breast and belly white.

Breeds in Gulf of Urabá and on Gorgona I.

off Pacific coast of COLOMBIA; VENE-ZUELA from Falcón to Sucre, breeding on many islands off coast. Breeds also on coast of BRAZIL from Bahía to Paraná, casual in Santa Catarina. Recorded casually s to ECUADOR and ARGENTINA. Aruba to Trinidad and Tobago. [Gulf of Mexico, Caribbean Sea, tropical Atlantic, Gulf of Panama, tropical Pacific and Indian Oceans.]

Family PHALACROCORACIDAE   CORMORANTS

Cormorants are found along larger rivers, on seacoasts and off shore islands. Some species are important producers of guano. Immature cormorants look more or less alike, brownish or grayish above and paler below. In flight the neck is extended and the tail appears short. They fly in loose lines or V-shaped ones. Cormorants live in colonies and feed on fish.

1. NEOTROPIC CORMORANT

Phalacrocorax olivaceus*

28". Entirely glossy purplish black with tuft of white feathers at each side of head, and white outline to throat pouch in breeding season.

Breeds generally throughout South America near water—both coastal salt-water and inland fresh-water—s to Cape Horn. Found from sea level to temperate zone of Andes. Aruba to Trinidad. [Gulf States; Mid. Amer.; Cuba, Bahamas.]

2. ROCK CORMORANT

Phalacrocorax magellanicus

26". Head, neck and upperparts glossy greenish black, breast and belly white. Rather like 3 but readily distinguishable by all black neck. Bare facial skin red.

Breeds on coast of CHILE from Valdivia to Cape Horn and coast of ARGENTINA n to Santa Cruz; in winter n to URUGUAY. [Falkland Is.]

3. GUANAY CORMORANT

Phalacrocorax bougainvillii

30". Much like 2 but chin and base of neck white, feathers on back of head elongated. Bare facial skin red.

Breeds on islands off coast of PERU to Mocha I., CHILE. Casual n to Buenaventura Bay, COLOMBIA. [Casual e Panama.]

4. RED-LEGGED CORMORANT

Phalacrocorax gaimardi

28". Mostly pale gray, patch of white on each side of neck; wings and back checkered with silvery.

Coast of PERU from Punta Aguja s regularly to Chiloé I., more rarely to Strait of Magellan, CHILE. In ARGENTINA only at Puerto Deseado, Santa Cruz.

Plate 21

5. BLUE-EYED CORMORANT

Phalacrocorax atriceps*

28". Upperparts black glossed with green, blue and violet; below white; white band on wing formed by lesser wing coverts and white patch on center of back. Black on sides of head *arched up* toward eye.

Coasts, sometimes inland lakes, of s CHILE from Mocha I. to Strait of Magellan in ARGENTINA. Breeds along coast of AR-GENTINA from Puerto Deseado s to río Gallegos; in winter n to URUGUAY. [Antarctica and subantarctic islands.]

6. KING CORMORANT

Phalacrocorax albiventer

28". Differs from 5 mainly by no white patch in center back and by more extensive black at side of head, reaching across lower head in a *straight line*.

Breeds from Strait of Magellan to Cape Horn in CHILE, from Staten I. and Tierra del Fuego to Puerto San Julián, and on larger lakes in Neuquén and Río Negro, ARGENTINA. Migrates casually n as far as URUGUAY. [Falkland Is.]

Family ANHINGIDAE   DARTERS

Anhingas differ from cormorants by long dagger-like bills, small heads, thin necks and long tails which are carried spread when flying. They are often seen swimming with only heads and necks above water, and when perching their dangling wings are characteristic. They feed on fish which they spear under water. Anhingas are also found in Africa and Asia to New Zealand.

ANHINGA

Anhinga anhinga *

34". Mainly glossy greenish black, wing coverts mostly silvery white; tail long, feathers pale-tipped. ♀: Differs from ♂ by grayish buff head, neck and breast.

Tropical zone generally s to BOLIVIA and n ARGENTINA. W of Andes only to w ECUADOR. Trinidad and Tobago. [Southern US; Mid. Amer.; Cuba; Grenada.] Rivers, freshwater marshes.

Plate 21

Family FREGATIDAE   FRIGATEBIRDS

These large marine birds are easily recognized by long, narrow, angled wings and deeply forked tails which open and shut in flight. They never land upon water but feed on fish caught on the surface, or stolen from boobies or other birds. They do not wander far from land, and nest and roost in trees or bushes.

MAGNIFICENT FRIGATEBIRD

Fregata magnificens

42". Entirely black, naked gular pouch red. ♀: Black, breast white. Imm.: Head and underparts white.

Breeds on islands along Pacific coast s to Gulf of Guayaquil, ECUADOR; wanders s to about 5°s, n PERU, and Iquique, CHILE (once). On Atlantic coast breeds on islands s to São Paulo, BRAZIL; URUGUAY, summer resident; wanders to coast of Buenos Aires, ARGENTINA. Acc. inland (Cauca Valley, COLOMBIA). Aruba, Curaçao. Trinidad, Tobago, [Islands off Mid. Amer.; Caribbean. Galápagos Is. Cape Verde Is.; off Gambia.]

Plate 21

Order CICONIIFORMES

Family ARDEIDAE   HERONS, EGRETS

Herons are long legged, long billed birds found along coastal and inland waters. They subsist on fish and vertebrates and nest in colonies. They fly with necks retracted and legs extended. The sexes are similar in most species.

AID TO IDENTIFICATION

White (bill yellow) legs black 3, legs greenish to yellowish 11; (bill black) feet yellow 4; (bill dark gray) tip black 5, with livid blue streak, cap black 13; (bill flesh, tip black) 6a

Back gray (size very large) 1a, 2; (size small) 5, 6a, 7

Back green or black 8a, 9, 10, 14, 19, 21

Back brown, vermiculated 16, 17, 18a

Back other than above (back streaked) 12, 15, 20; (back banded) 16, 17, 18a, 19, 22

1. GREAT BLUE HERON

Ardea herodias *

46". Crown white broadly bordered with black (ad.) or all black (imm.); neck buffy; back blue gray; underparts black streaked white; tibial feathers rufous.

Migrant from N America and resident. N COLOMBIA (Oct.-Apr.). N VENEZUELA. Resident on islands from Aruba to Trinidad and Tobago. [N Amer. s to Mexico; W Indies; Galápagos Is.]

2. WHITE-NECKED HERON

Ardea cocoi

50". Differs from 1 by entirely black crown, much whiter neck (ad.), blacker underparts and white tibial feathers.

Generally distributed s to Chubut, ARGENTINA, and Aysén, CHILE. Trinidad. [E Panama; acc. Falkland Is.]

3. GREAT (or Common) EGRET

Casmerodius albus *

38". All white. Bill yellow, feet and legs black.

Generally distributed s to Strait of Magel-
lan, CHILE and to Santa Cruz and accidentally Tierra del Fuego, ARGENTINA. Aruba to Trinidad and Tobago. [US southward.]

4. SNOWY EGRET

Egretta thula *

23". All white. Bill and legs black, feet yellow.

Generally distributed s to Valdivia, CHILE, and Córdoba and Buenos Aires, and acc. to Río Negro, ARGENTINA. Aruba to Trinidad and Tobago. [US southward.]

5. LITTLE BLUE HERON

Florida caerulea *

23". Dark blue gray, head and neck mostly maroon. Imm.: All white. Bill dark blue gray with black tip; feet and legs black.

COLOMBIA south w of Andes to central PERU (Lima). East of Andes generally distributed south to n Mato Grosso and Paraná, BRAZIL, and URUGUAY. Birds banded in N America casually reach COLOMBIA and VENEZUELA in winter. Aruba, Curaçao, Bonaire. Trinidad and Tobago. [Southern US southward.]

23

6. REDDISH EGRET

Dichromanassa rufescens*

30''. Dark gray, head and neck rufous brown. Imm.: All white. Bill flesh color, tip black; feet and legs black.

Migrant. Coastal VENEZUELA from Falcón e and islands off coast. Curaçao, Aruba, Bonaire. [Gulf States southward.]

7. TRICOLORED (or Louisiana) HERON

Hydranassa tricolor*

24''. Mostly dark slaty gray; throat and line down center of neck rufous, lower breast and belly white. Imm.: Much like adult but neck rufous.

N VENEZUELA and GUIANAS s to Piauí, BRAZIL; n COLOMBIA to Pacific and south to nw PERU. Aruba to Trinidad and Tobago. [Southern US southward.] Mangroves, coastal mudflats, marshes.

8. GREEN HERON

Butorides virescens*

18''. Crown and wings glossy greenish black, wing coverts edged buff. Feathers of mantle bronzy green, edged gray, elongated in breeding season. Sides of head and neck rich rufous, throat white, front of neck and upper breast white streaked with black, belly grayish brown.

Breeds from Aruba to Tobago. Winter resident in n COLOMBIA and n VENEZUELA from sea level to temperate zone; straggler to GUYANA and SURINAM. [S Canada southward.]

9. STRIATED HERON

Butorides striatus*

16''. Much like 8 but sides of head and neck gray, and general plumage lighter and grayer.

Tropical to lower temperate zone. Generally distributed s in ARGENTINA to Buenos Aires and La Pampa. CHILE (once). Margarita I. Trinidad, Tobago. [Costa Rica southward. Africa, Asia, Australia, islands of w Pacific.] Swamps, mangroves.

10. CHESTNUT-BELLIED HERON

Agamia agami

28''. Upperparts and wings shiny dark green, shoulders and underparts rich chestnut.

Long occipital feathers blue gray. Throat white, line down center of throat and neck chestnut.

GUIANAS, VENEZUELA and COLOMBIA south, w of Andes to nw ECUADOR; e of them to n Beni and Santa Cruz, BOLIVIA. Amazonian BRAZIL south to n Mato Grosso and rio Paraguai drainage. Trinidad. [Mexico southward.]

Plate 3

11. CATTLE EGRET

Bubulcus ibis*

17''. White; in breeding plumage the crown, dorsal plumes, neck and breast intense pinkish buff. Bill yellow, feet and legs dull yellow to dull greenish or blackish. Accompanies cattle.

GUYANA, SURINAM, VENEZUELA, COLOMBIA, ECUADOR, PERU (up to 11,000 ft.), BOLIVIA, BRAZIL (Marajó I., Pará), n CHILE. Trinidad, Tobago. [S and e N Amer.; Mid. Amer.; W Indies. Warmer parts of Eurasia and Africa.]

12. WHISTLING HERON

Syrigma sibilatrix*

21''. Crown black, bare orbital skin bright blue. Neck buffy; back, tail ad underparts white; wing coverts buffy, streaked black. Bill pink with black tip.

N VENEZUELA s to the Orinoco; ne COLOMBIA s to Meta. S BRAZIL from São Paulo to Mato Grosso. Lowlands of BOLIVIA; PARAGUAY; URUGUAY; n ARGENTINA s to Tucumán, Santa Fe and Buenos Aires.

Plate 2

13. CAPPED HERON

Pilherodius pileatus

22''. White; crown black. Bare orbital skin cobalt. Bill bluish gray, lower mandible with livid blue streak; legs gray.

Generally distributed s through BRAZIL to e PERU, w BOLIVIA, n PARAGUAY. W of Andes in n COLOMBIA. Los Roques. [Panama.] Forested rivers, swampy woods.

14. BLACK-CROWNED NIGHT-HERON

Nycticorax nycticorax*

25''. Crown, mantle and scapulars black; forehead and underparts white; wings, lower back and tail gray. Imm.: Above grayish brown spotted and streaked with buffy white; neck brown, streaked white; underparts white, streaked brown.

Generally distributed throughout s to Tierra del Fuego. Aruba to Trinidad and Tobago. [Virtually world-wide.] Swampy woods.

15. YELLOW-CROWNED NIGHT-HERON

Nyctanassa violacea *

28". Head black, center of crown buffy yellow, broad streak below eye white; rest of plumage gray, streaked paler on wings and back. Imm.: Like 14 but darker.

W and n COLOMBIA, s along Pacific coast to n PERU. N VENEZUELA, GUIANAS; n and e BRAZIL from Amazonas, Pará and Maranhão, s to Rio Grande do Sul. Aruba to Trinidad and Tobago. [US southward; W Indies; Galápagos Is.] Swampy woods, mangroves.

16. RUFESCENT TIGER-HERON

Tigrisoma lineatum *

28". Top and sides of head and neck chestnut; back and closed wing brown finely vermiculated and streaked with black. Breast brown broadly streaked with white, lower breast and belly grayish brown; axillaries black barred with white. Imm.: Neck and upperparts black broadly banded with orange buff; underparts white with broken blackish bars.

Lowlands. COLOMBIA and VENEZUELA s to about 2°s in w ECUADOR and e of Andes to BOLIVIA, PARAGUAY and ARGENTINA s to Mendoza and Buenos Aires; BRAZIL south to w Amazonas, Mato Grosso and Paraná; n URUGUAY. Trinidad. [Honduras southward.] Swampy woods.

17. FASCIATED TIGER-HERON

Tigrisoma fasciatum *

26". Crown black, sides of neck and upperparts grayish black narrowly barred with buff; breast brownish streaked with white, belly grayish brown. Imm.: Much like 16 but bill stouter and shorter.

Chiefly forested hill country and highlands. N VENEZUELA; COLOMBIA s to BOLIVIA and nw ARGENTINA. Se BRAZIL from Rio de Janeiro to Rio Grande do Sul and sw Mato Grosso. [Costa Rica, Panama.] Forest, streams.

18. BARE-THROATED TIGER-HERON

Tigrisoma mexicanum *

30". In color much like 17 but larger and immediately distinguishable in all plumages from other tiger-herons by wholly bare throat.

Lower Atrato Valley in nw COLOMBIA. [Mid. Amer.] Wooded streams, marshes.

19. ZIGZAG HERON

Zebrilus undulatus

12.5". Crown and ample crest black, sides of head and neck chestnut. Above black, back and wing coverts crossed by narrow, wavy, buffy bars. Underparts buffy. Rufous phase: Back more coarsely banded and forecrown rufous.

E COLOMBIA. Ne and s VENEZUELA; GUIANAS; n and e BRAZIL to Belém region and to Mato Grosso (rios Guaporé and upper Paraguai); e PERU. Forest ponds and streams.

20. STRIPE-BACKED BITTERN

Ixobrychus involucris

13". Above sandy buff, line down center of crown and broad streaks on back black. Below buffy white, streaked fawn.

Ne COLOMBIA. N VENEZUELA. GUYANA; SURINAM. Se BRAZIL from Rio de Janeiro and São Paulo to Rio Grande do Sul; URUGUAY; PARAGUAY; se BOLIVIA in Tarija. ARGENTINA s to Río Negro. CHILE from Aconcagua to Llanquihue. Trinidad (May), reported breeding but this has been doubted. Birds found in n South America may be migrants from south.
                                                    Plate 2

21. LEAST BITTERN

Ixobrychus exilis *

10.5" (or 13.5", 1) Crown, nape, back and tail glossy greenish black; upper mantle chestnut. Underparts buffy, deepest on breast.

GUIANAS; VENEZUELA in Guárico and Miranda. COLOMBIA in Santa Marta and Cauca Valley. Bogotá savanna, 1. BRAZIL n of the Amazon from rio Negro to Monte Alegre, s of the Amazon from rio Tapajós to Marajó I., and from Alagoas to São Paulo and possibly Mato Grosso; PARAGUAY; ne ARGENTINA. BOLIVIA in Beni. Coast of

PERU from Libertad to Lima. Trinidad. [S Canada southward. Northern migrants reach Colombia.]

22. PINNATED BITTERN

Botaurus pinnatus

25". Crown black; throat white completely feathered; neck banded black and buff, streaked with rufous in front. Back streaked and banded with buff. Underparts white, striped with buff.

Tropical to temperate zone. GUIANAS, VENEZUELA, COLOMBIA s to about 2°s in w ECUADOR. E and central BRAZIL from Pernambuco, s to Rio Grande do Sul and w to Goiás and Mato Grosso; PARAGUAY; URUGUAY; ARGENTINA in Tucumán, Córdoba, Santa Fe and n Buenos Aires. Trinidad. [Mexico, Br. Honduras, Nicaragua, Costa Rica.] Swamps.

Family COCHLEARIIDAE   BOAT-BILLED HERONS

Boat-bills perhaps should not be separated from herons and are, in fact, not distantly related to night-herons. They are gregarious, live in swampy woods and mangroves and are mainly nocturnal.

BOAT-BILLED HERON

Cochlearius cochlearius*

24". Distinguishable from other herons by very broad, flat bill. Forehead white, crown and ample crest black. Above mostly pale gray. Breast pinkish buff; sides black; center of abdomen chestnut. Imm.: Mostly dull brown.

GUIANAS; VENEZUELA; n COLOMBIA. E and w ECUADOR; e PERU. E BOLIVIA. BRAZIL in Amazonia, and in e from Goiás and Bahía s to São Paulo and Mato Grosso (rio Paraguai). Casual in n ARGENTINA. Trinidad. [Mid. Amer.]

Plate 22

Family CICONIIDAE   STORKS

Storks somewhat resemble herons but are not as dependent on water, being found often in dry fields as well as marshes. They fly with necks extended and feet protruding beyond the tail. Usually gregarious, they live on insects, small reptiles and fish.

1. AMERICAN WOOD-IBIS
   ## (or Wood-Stork)

Mycteria americana

40". Head and neck bare, slaty gray. Plumage white, flight feathers and tail black. Bill black, heavy, slightly curved; legs black, feet pinkish yellow.

GUIANAS; VENEZUELA; COLOMBIA s to middle Magdalena Valley and e of Andes to Meta. ECUADOR south to nw and e PERU, acc. in high Andes. BRAZIL; BOLIVIA; PARAGUAY; URUGUAY; ARGENTINA, acc. as far s as Chubut. Trinidad, doubtfully Tobago. [Southern US; Mid. Amer.; Greater Antilles.]

2. MAGUARI STORK

Euxenura maguari

38". White; wings and tail black. Bill orange red, straight.

GUYANA; SURINAM; n and se VENE-ZUELA; e COLOMBIA; BRAZIL s to BO-LIVIA and ARGENTINA to Chubut. Occasional visitor to CHILE s to Magallanes.

Plate 21

3. JABIRU

Jabiru mycteria

52". White. Bare head and neck black, red at base of neck. Bill straight, black, very heavy.

GUIANAS; VENEZUELA; COLOMBIA from lower Magdalena to e llanos. E PERU, rarely on coast. BRAZIL in Roraima, Marajó and Mexiana Is., and lower rio Madeira, in e from Pernambuco to São Paulo and Mato Grosso; PARAGUAY; URUGUAY; n ARGENTINA, acc. to Buenos Aires. [Mid. Amer.]

Fig. 12, p. 96

Family THRESKIORNITHIDAE   IBISES

Ibises are distinguishable from herons and storks by very much thinner curved bills. Like storks they fly with neck extended. They live in swampy woods and marshes and are gregarious. Most species of young ibises resemble each other in their grayish brown coloration.

AID TO IDENTIFICATION

Mostly gray 1c, (with white or buffy neck) 2

Mostly blackish green 3, 4, 5

Pink, white or red 10, (with black wing tips) 6a, 7

Neck and underparts maroon 8, 9b

1. PLUMBEOUS IBIS

Harpiprion caerulescens

32". The only ibis almost entirely gray. Bill black, feet and legs salmon.

S BRAZIL in Mato Grosso and Rio Grande do Sul south to n ARGENTINA, casually to Córdoba and Buenos Aires.

2. BUFF-NECKED IBIS

*Theristicus caudatus**

29". Head, neck and upper breast buffy white, shaded orange rufous; upperparts gray; greater wing coverts white. Breast and belly black (or breast and belly white, 1; or neck and breast light chestnut, breast crossed by gray band, 2).

Tropical zone. GUIANAS, n VENEZUELA; COLOMBIA to Valle and Meta. BRAZIL virtually throughout s to PARAGUAY, URUGUAY and n ARGENTINA. Puna zone of ECUADOR, PERU and n BOLIVIA, 1. CHILE and s ARGENTINA to Tierra del Fuego, 2. Savanna, marshes.

Plate 3

3. SHARP-TAILED IBIS

Cercibis oxycerca

29". Glossy greenish black. Bill, bare patch around eye, and legs red.

GUYANA; VENEZUELA locally in llanos; llanos e of Andes in COLOMBIA. W Amazonian BRAZIL n and s of the Amazon. Ponds, riverbanks.

4. GREEN IBIS

Mesembrinibis cayennensis

23". Head gray, back and sides of neck shining dark emerald green, upperparts and wings dark bronze green. Bill green; feet and legs jade green.

GUIANAS; VENEZUELA; n COLOMBIA; e ECUADOR; PERU; BRAZIL; PARAGUAY; ne ARGENTINA. [Costa Rica, Panama.] Swampy forest, wooded streams.

Plate 2

5. BARE-FACED (or Whispering) IBIS

Phimosus infuscatus

19". Greenish black. Bill, face and legs reddish flesh color. Much lighter, less chunky in build than 3.

GUYANA; SURINAM; VENEZUELA south to nw Amazonas and sw Bolívar; n COLOMBIA from río Sinú e; extreme n BRAZIL in Roraima, and s of the Amazon from Maranhão to Rio Grande do Sul, and w to Mato Grosso; BOLIVIA from Beni to Santa Cruz; PARAGUAY; URUGUAY; ARGENTINA s to Tucumán, Córdoba and Buenos Aires. Swampy forest, wooded streams.

6. WHITE IBIS

Eudocimus albus

24". All white, tips of primaries blue black. Bill and legs red.

FRENCH GUIANA, VENEZUELA in Falcón, Aragua, Carabobo and Apure. COLOMBIA in lower Magdalena Valley and on coast in Atlántico and Bolívar. Curaçao. Trinidad. [Southern US; Mid. Amer.; Greater Antilles.] Marshes, mangroves.

7. SCARLET IBIS

Eudocimus ruber

22". All scarlet, tips of primaries blue black.

GUIANAS; VENEZUELA locally in swampy lowlands except Amazonas and s Bolívar; COLOMBIA from lower Magdalena Valley e to Arauco and Meta. E BRAZIL, locally chiefly near coast, s to Paraná. Trinidad. Chiefly coastal lagoons.

8. WHITE-FACED IBIS

Plegadis chihi

20". Head, neck and underparts rich chestnut; face outlined in white in breeding season, bare loral skin red. Crown, wing coverts and inner remiges glossy metallic purple; primaries and lower back metallic bronzy green.

BOLIVIA. CHILE from Antofagasta to Valdivia. Se BRAZIL in São Paulo, Rio Grande do Sul and Mato Grosso; URUGUAY; PARAGUAY; ARGENTINA s to Río Negro and acc. to Tierra del Fuego. Birds recorded from VENEZUELA and COLOMBIA probably belong to *P. falcinellus* (see appendix). [Breeds in western US; in winter s to El Salvador. Acc. Falkland Is.] Marshes, estuaries.

9. PUNA IBIS

Plegadis ridgwayi

22". Rather like 8 but larger, much darker, and without white markings on face.

Puna zone of Andes of PERU from Junín, (acc. on coast of Lima), s to BOLIVIA. Casual in nw ARGENTINA and Cordillera de Arica in n CHILE. Swamps, ponds.

10. ROSEATE SPOONBILL

Ajaia ajaja

32". Rosy pink; neck white, shoulders and rump rosy crimson; whole head bare black and greenish yellow. Bill flat, very wide, expanded and rounded at tip.

GUIANAS; VENEZUELA; n COLOMBIA; BRAZIL virtually throughout; ECUADOR; PERU, (w of Andes only in Tumbes and Piura.) Casual in CHILE s to Colchagua. BOLIVIA; PARAGUAY; URUGUAY; n ARGENTINA, s accidentally to s Patagonia. Aruba, Bonaire. Trinidad and Tobago. [Gulf States; Mid. Amer.; Greater Antilles.] Marshes, swampy woods.

Family PHOENICOPTERIDAE   FLAMINGOS

Flamingos are distinguishable from other wading birds by very long necks and legs and by bent, thick, black-tipped bills. In flight they carry necks and legs extended. They live in colonies and feed on minute mollusca, algae and diatoms which they sift with their bills. They frequent shallow lagoons and lakes and build columnar mud nests.

1. AMERICAN FLAMINGO

Phoenicopterus ruber

45″. General plumage rosy pink, neck darker; primaries black. Legs pink. Bill pink with black tip.

Coasts of GUIANAS, and VENEZUELA in Falcón (Chichiriviche; Adícora) and Miranda (Laguna de Tacarigua). Irregularly in ne BRAZIL to mouth of the Amazon. Curaçao, Bonaire (breeding), Aruba; La Orchila, Margarita I., formerly Los Roques, Las Aves. [Bahamas; Cuba; Hispaniola. Yucatán. Galápagos Is.] Coastal lagoons.

2. CHILEAN FLAMINGO

Phoenicopterus chilensis

Like 1 but somewhat larger; head, neck and back white, tinged pink. Basal half of bill yellow, distal half black. Legs horn color, joints red.

Highlands of central and s PERU and along entire coast from Tumbés southward. Flamingos seen in w ECUADOR probably belong to this species. Highlands of CHILE from Tarapacá to Magallanes, winters or wanders to Tierra del Fuego. BOLIVIA in La Paz and Tarija. PARAGUAY, URUGUAY; BRAZIL in Rio Grande do Sul; ARGENTINA throughout, breeding chiefly in mts. and in s part of the country. [Acc.

Falkland Is.] Highland salt lakes, brackish estuaries, coastal marshes.

3. ANDEAN FLAMINGO

Phoenicoparrus andinus

Somewhat larger than 2, differing by basal portion of neck and upper breast rosy carmine, and by black tertials as well as primaries and secondaries. Bill black, base yellow.

Puna zone of southwest PERU. Highlands of Tarapacá, Antofagasta and Atacama, CHILE, BOLIVIA in Oruro, and Potosí. W ARGENTINA in Jujuy, Salta, Catamarca and Tucumán; in winter descends to lower elevations. Highland salt lakes, lowland marshes in winter.

Plate 3

4. PUNA (or James') FLAMINGO

Phoenicoparrus jamesi

Distinguishable from 1 or 2 by smaller size. Bill mostly yellow with black tip; legs dark brick red.

Puna zone. S PERU at Lake Titicaca; CHILE in Tarapacá; BOLIVIA in w Oruro and Potosí; nw ARGENTINA in Jujuy, Salta, Catamarca and Tucumán. Highland salt lakes.

Fig. 6. BOGOTA RAIL
   Rallus semiplumbeus
   p. 66

Order ANSERIFORMES

Family ANHIMIDAE   SCREAMERS

These large, ungainly birds are found on open lowlands, grasslands and marshy areas. They often fly to great heights, sailing in wide circles almost out of sight. Their trumpet-like voices carry for a great distance. Screamers feed on vegetable matter.

1. HORNED SCREAMER

Anhima cornuta

35". General plumage glossy greenish black; shoulders, belly and mottling on head and neck white. Horn-like quill on top of head. Legs thick, feet very large.

GUIANAS; VENEZUELA n of the Orinoco; n COLOMBIA to Cauca Valley and e of Andes to the Amazon. ECUADOR w of Andes at Balzar, Guayas, and e of them on upper río Pastaza; e PERU; BRAZIL s to São Paulo and Mato Grosso; BOLIVIA from Beni to Tarija. Probably extreme nw ARGENTINA.

Fig. 11, p. 89

2. NORTHERN SCREAMER

Chauna chavaria

34". Crown and crest gray, rest of head white; neck black, rest of plumage dark gray glossed green above; under wing coverts white.

Nw VENEZUELA from Trujillo west through n COLOMBIA to lower río Atrato.

Plate 44

3. SOUTHERN SCREAMER

Chauna torquata

Differs from 2 by only base of neck being black, underparts much paler, feathers gray broadly edged white.

S BRAZIL from Rio Grande do Sul to w São Paulo and Mato Grosso, e to BOLIVIA, s to Buenos Aires and La Pampa, ARGENTINA. Cultivated fields, marshes.

Family ANATIDAE   DUCKS, GEESE, SWANS

The most distinctive ducks of South America are the Torrent Ducks. They inhabit fast-flowing mountain streams and fend themselves off rocks with their stiff tails. Other distinctive ducks are the long-necked Tree-Ducks and the forest-inhabiting Muscovy Ducks from which the domestic species is descended.

AID TO IDENTIFICATION

With conspicuous head pattern
    Front of head white 2, 8b, 12b, (or black) 39
    Crown dusky, sides of head white or buffy 3, 19, 22, 23b, 28, 33, 37b

Crescent or spot before eye 15b, 24, 33

Crown buffy white 17a

Stripe through or below eye 28, 29b, 37b, 38, 39

Head chocolate with white stripe down sides of neck 21

Without conspicuous head pattern

Goose or swan (mostly white) 4c, 5c, 6b, 10; (not white, barred below) 7b, 8b, 9b, 10; (neck buff, sides and belly chestnut) 11

Mostly pale gray, bill yellow 13b, 14b

Above black or greenish black 31, 32a, 34, 35, (bill pink) 30, (long thin crest) 12b, 36c, (breast white, sides rufous) 26a

Back striped or banded 1, 29b, 39

Nondescript, mostly brown (back mottled, bill gray) 16, 17a, 21a, 24, 25, 26a; (bill yellow) 16, 20; (back uniform) 30, 31, 32a, 40; (head black) 38, 40

1. FULVOUS TREE- (or Whistling-) DUCK

Dendrocygna bicolor

19". Above mostly blackish, mantle barred with rufous. Underparts rufescent, lengthened plumes at sides of body cream color, upper and under tail coverts white.

GUIANAS; n VENEZUELA from Zulia and Táchira to Aragua; COLOMBIA in Cauca Valley and E Andes to temperate zone; e and w ECUADOR; e and nw PERU, acc. in central highlands. E BRAZIL from Pará s to PARAGUAY, URUGUAY and n and central ARGENTINA. Acc. in CHILE. Trinidad. [Breeds also in US s to Honduras; casual Panama. Also Africa to India and Burma.] Marshes, lagoons.

2. WHITE-FACED TREE- (or Whistling-) DUCK

Dendrocygna viduata

17". Face and foreneck white; back of head and neck, and band across throat black; back brown, feathers pale-edged; rump, tail and center of underparts black; chest rufous chestnut, sides of body barred black and white.

Tropical zone. GUYANA; SURINAM; VENEZUELA n of the Orinoco; ne CO-LOMBIA occasionally to temperate zone; PERU, occasionally in highlands; virtually all BRAZIL; PARAGUAY; URUGUAY; BOLIVIA in Beni and Santa Cruz; n AR-GENTINA to Córdoba, and Buenos Aires. Curaçao. Trinidad. [Breeds also in Costa Rica and Africa.] Marshes, lagoons.

Plate 2

3. BLACK-BELLIED TREE- (or Whistling-) DUCK

Dendrocygna autumnalis *

19". Sides of head, neck and lower breast gray; back and upper breast rufous brown, wing with considerable white; rump and belly black. Bill bright pinkish red.

Tropical zone. GUYANA; SURINAM; n VENEZUELA w in COLOMBIA to Cauca Valley and Meta and s along Pacific coast to w ECUADOR. E BRAZIL from Pará to Rio Grande do Sul, thence w to Mato Grosso; PARAGUAY; e and occasionally coastal PERU; n and e BOLIVIA; nw ARGENTINA to Santiago del Estero. Margarita I. Trinidad. [Breeds in Tex. and Mid. Amer.] Coastal marshes, lagoons.

4. COSCOROBA SWAN

Coscoroba coscoroba

29". White, primaries tipped black. Bill, feet and legs bright rosy pink.

Breeds from BRAZIL in Rio Grande do Sul and PARAGUAY s to Cape Horn and Magellanic CHILE. [Falkland Is.] Lakes with dense vegetation.

5. BLACK-NECKED SWAN

Cygnus melancoryphus

40". White; neck black. Base of bill and caruncle scarlet; legs and feet pale flesh.

Se BRAZIL from s São Paulo to URU-GUAY, PARAGUAY, and ARGENTINA to Tierra del Fuego. CHILE from Coquimbo s. [Falkland Is.] Lakes, coastal areas.

6. ANDEAN GOOSE

Chloephaga melanoptera

30″. White; wings and tail black, glossed green. Bill and legs red.

Breeds from 10,000 ft. upward, winters at lower altitudes. Andes of central PERU s to Ñuble, CHILE and nw ARGENTINA to Catamarca; acc. to Río Negro. Andean lakes and marshes.

7. ASHY-HEADED GOOSE

Chloephaga poliocephala

24″. Head and neck gray, breast and upper back chestnut, sides of body barred black and white; center of abdomen, shoulder and secondaries white; lower back, rump and tail black glossed green. ♀: Similar but breast barred black.

Breeds in ARGENTINA from Río Negro to Tierra del Fuego, winters n to Buenos Aires. Breeds in CHILE from Malleco to Llanquihue in Andes, and from Chiloé s in coastal islands to Cape Horn. Lake shores, boggy forest clearings.

Plate 2

8. RUDDY-HEADED GOOSE

Chloephaga rubidiceps

24″. Head and neck grayish cinnamon, mantle grayish finely barred black. Breast cinnamon finely barred black, sides of body buffy white barred black, center of abdomen reddish cinnamon. Shoulder and secondaries white.

Semiarid open plains. S Magallanes and Tierra del Fuego in CHILE, and ARGENTINA, n in winter to Buenos Aires. [Falkland Is.]

9. UPLAND GOOSE

Chloephaga picta *

28″. Head, rump, secondaries and shoulder white; rest of plumage coarsely barred black and white; or (white phase) head, neck and underparts white, flanks barred black. ♀: Rather like 8 but larger, darker and more coarsely barred particularly on flanks. Center of underparts barred instead of plain.

S CHILE from Colchagua s to Cape Horn. ARGENTINA from Río Negro s to Tierra del Fuego and Staten I., in winter n to Buenos Aires. Acc. in URUGUAY [Falkland Is.] Semiarid, open plains.

10. KELP GOOSE

Chloephaga hybrida *

30″. Entirely white. Bill black, legs yellow. ♀: Top of head graying brown, rest of head and neck black vermiculated with buffy white, mantle black. Breast and sides of body coarsely barred black and white; shoulders, secondaries, back and tail white. Bill pink; legs yellow.

Nests on coast of s Tierra del Fuego, ARGENTINA, and in CHILE from Cape Horn to Chiloé I. Winters n to coast of Río Negro, ARGENTINA, and Cautín, CHILE. [Falkland Is.]

11. ORINOCO GOOSE

Neochen jubata

23″. Head, neck, breast and upper mantle pale ashy buff; belly chestnut; lower back, wings and tail black strongly glossed green; wing speculum white.

GUIANAS; llanos of VENEZUELA and e COLOMBIA; e PERU; Amazonian BRAZIL south to s Amazonas and n Mato Grosso and in São Paulo; PARAGUAY; BOLIVIA in Beni, Santa Cruz and Tarija; adjacent ARGENTINA in Salta. Rivers, marshes. Perches in trees.

12. CRESTED DUCK

Lophonetta specularioides *

24″. Tail rather long, pointed; crest greenish black. Front and sides of head and neck whitish finely speckled darker, ocular region blackish; top of head and back grayish brown mottled on upper back and paler on rump. Underparts buffy more or less spotted on breast; wings and tail dark brown, wing speculum purple shot with green, inner remiges white.

Andean lakes from Huánuco, PERU, s through CHILE to Cape Horn. Highlands of BOLIVIA and ARGENTINA to Tierra del Fuego and along Atlantic coast from Chubut s; in winter n to Buenos Aires. [Falkland Is.] In winter found also in coastal areas.

Plate 2

13. FLIGHTLESS STEAMER-DUCK

Tachyeres pteneres

27″. Pale gray mottled on back, breast and sides with blue gray; throat tinged rusty;

lower breast, belly and inner remiges white. Wing very short. Bill yellow.

Coast of CHILE from Corral to Cape Horn. S ARGENTINA from Chubut to Tierra del Fuego and Staten I.

14. FLYING STEAMER-DUCK

Tachyeres patachonicus

22". Much like 13 but considerably smaller, darker, throat and sides of head strongly rufescent, wings longer.

CHILE from Concepción s to Tierra del Fuego. ARGENTINA in the interior from Neuquén, and from coast of Chubut s to Tierra del Fuego. [Falkland Is.] Coasts, rivers, lakes.

15. SPECTACLED DUCK

Anas specularis

18". Head, back of neck and broad patch in front of eye blackish brown; throat, front and sides of neck white. Back dark brown, feathers pale-edged; breast grayish brown, sides of body paler with prominent black spots. Wings and tail purplish black, speculum metallic purple shot with green.

Andes of CHILE and ARGENTINA from Talca on the w and Neuquén on the e to Tierra del Fuego. N in winter to Aconcagua, CHILE and Buenos Aires, ARGENTINA. Fast-flowing rivers, woodlands or open country.

16. SPECKLED TEAL

Anas flavirostris *

16-18". Head somewhat crested, bill dark (northern birds) or mostly yellow (southern birds). Head and neck freckled black and brown; upperparts dark to pale brown, mottled paler (northern birds) or darker (southern birds); underparts soiled white mottled on breast with blackish. Wing speculum black, posteriorly metallic green, edged above and below with buffy.

Andes of VENEZUELA from Trujillo s through COLOMBIA in E and Central Andes to ECUADOR. Puna zone of PERU from central Cajamarca s through BOLIVIA, CHILE and ARGENTINA to Tierra del Fuego. BRAZIL in Rio Grande do Sul; URUGUAY; PARAGUAY. [Falkland Is.] Lakes, swamps, reedbeds.

17. AMERICAN WIGEON

Anas americana

20". Top of head, shoulders and most of underparts white; line extending from behind eye green, sides of head and neck freckled black and buff, rest of plumage generally pinkish brown vermiculated on back with black. ♀: Much like ♂ but lacks white crown patch.

Winter resident (Oct.-Apr.). COLOMBIA in Cauca Valley and E Andes. Casual in VENEZUELA. Aruba to Trinidad and Tobago. [Breeds in N Amer.; winters in Mid. Amer.; W Indies.] Ponds, shallow coastal waters. Sometimes grazes like goose.

18. SOUTHERN (or Chiloé) WIGEON

Anas sibilatrix

19". Forecrown and front of face white, broad streak behind eye bottle green. Upper back and breast barred black and white, rest of underparts white, sides of body sometimes rufous. ♀: Much like ♂ but duller.

Breeds in CHILE from mouth of río Huanco in Atacama and in ARGENTINA from Córdoba and Buenos Aires, s to Tierra del Fuego. In winter n to Rio Grande do Sul, BRAZIL; URUGUAY (where some breed), and PARAGUAY. [Falkland Is.] Lakes, marshes with abundant vegetation.

19. WHITE-CHEEKED (or Bahama) PINTAIL

Anas bahamensis *

17". Top of head to below eye, and body plumage generally, brown spotted with black; sides of head white sharply defined from brown cap, throat and foreneck white. Tail pointed, pale buff. ♀: Like ♂ but smaller.

GUIANAS; n VENEZUELA; n COLOMBIA in lower Magdalena Valleys. Sw ECUADOR. E BRAIL w to the Tapajós and s to Rio Grande do Sul. URUGUAY; PARAGUAY; e ARGENTINA s to La Pampa and Buenos Aires. E BOLIVIA. Coast of PERU from Tumbes southward. Occasionally in n CHILE. Aruba to Trinidad. [Bahamas; W Indies; Galápagos Is.] Estuaries.

20. YELLOW-BILLED (or Brown) PINTAIL

Anas georgica *

22", 1; or 26", 2. Top of head rufescent

brown (or blackish, 1), sides of head and neck finely (or coarsely, 1) speckled dusky. Upperparts brown, feathers edged fulvous, underparts dirty white (or brown, 1) more or less spotted with dusky. Speculum black tinged green, bordered buff above and below; tail pointed.

COLOMBIA in E Andes, Cauca Valley, 1; from Nariño s through ECUADOR to CHILE and BOLIVIA, thence east to s BRAZIL and s to Tierra del Fuego. [Falkland Is.; S Georgia I.] Lakes, marshes, rivers.

21. COMMON (or Northern) PINTAIL

Anas acuta

26". Head and neck chocolate brown, line at side of neck white; back mostly gray vermiculated with black; underparts white. Speculum bronze green. ♀: Rather like 20 but readily distinguishable by white margins to feathers of upperparts.

Winter resident in COLOMBIA (Oct.-Apr.). Straggler to GUYANA, SURINAM and n VENEZUELA. [Breeds in N Hemisphere. Winters to Mid. Amer., Africa, India, Philippines, Hawaii.] Lakes, rivers.

22. SILVER TEAL

Anas versicolor *

16". Cap to below eye blackish brown; upper back blackish, feathers edged buff, lower back and tail barred black and white. Throat and sides of head fulvous, breast fulvous spotted with black, sides of body broadly barred black and white. Shoulders gray; speculum green, margined above and below with white. Bill blue, upper mandible yellow basally.

CHILE from Santiago s to Tierra del Fuego; BOLIVIAN chaco; PARAGUAY; URUGUAY; s BRAZIL in Rio Grande do Sul; all of ARGENTINA. [Falkland Is.] Lakes, reedbeds.

23. PUNA TEAL

Anas puna

19". Rather like 22 but cap blacker, lower back uniform grayish brown, sides of body finely barred black and white. Bill much larger, all blue. ♀: Differs from ♂ by being much browner below and having tail and upper tail coverts unbarred or slightly barred.

Puna zone. PERU from Lima (where found occasionally on coast) and Junín s in Andes of CHILE to Antofagasta; BOLIVIA in La Paz, Cochabamba and Oruro. ARGENTINA in Jujuy. Mountain lakes.

24. BLUE-WINGED TEAL

Anas discors

15". Top of head black, broad white crescent in front of eye, rest of head gray. Shoulder blue, speculum green. ♀: Above dark brown, feathers edged fulvous; lowerparts buffy white spotted with brown. Shoulder blue, speculum green.

Winter resident (Sept.-Apr.). GUIANAS; VENEZUELA n of the Orinoco; COLOMBIA, ECUADOR and PERU s to Junín and rarely n CHILE, BRAZIL in Pará and Maranhão. URUGUAY; ARGENTINA to Buenos Aires. Aruba to Trinidad and Tobago. [Breeds in N Amer., winters to Panama and W Indies.] Marshes, lagoons.

25. CINNAMON TEAL

Anas cyanoptera *

16". Head, neck and underparts reddish chestnut, lightly spotted black (migrants unspotted). Shoulder blue, speculum green. ♀: Almost indistinguishable from 24 but differs by having the green of speculum only suggested.

Resident in COLOMBIA in E Andes from 1000 to 3600 m., and in the Cauca and middle Magdalena Valleys. Resident in PERU from Lake Titicaca s to Strait of Magellan; PARAGUAY; URUGUAY; Rio Grande do Sul, BRAZIL. Migrants occasionally winter s to COLOMBIA, VENEZUELA and probably ECUADOR. [Breeds also in N Amer. s to Mexico, winters to Panama, occasionally Cuba.] Rivers, marshes, reedbeds.

26. NORTHERN SHOVELER

Anas clypeata

18". Bill broad at tip. Boldly patterned with much white. Head and neck bottle green, breast and base of hindneck white, rest of lowerparts dark chestnut. Shoulder blue, speculum green. ♀: Above dark brown, feathers slightly edged fulvous; below buffy brown inconspicuously spotted darker on breast.

Winter resident (Oct.-Mar.). COLOMBIA in Cauca Valley and temperate zone of n portion of E Andes. Casual in Trinidad. [Breeds in N Amer. and Eurasia. Winters through Mid. Amer., W Indies, N Africa, s Asia.] Marshes, ponds.

27. RED SHOVELER

Anas platalea

18". Head fulvous white spotted with black, unspotted at base of bill and throat. Upperparts, breast and sides of body cinnamon spotted with black; rump and upper tail coverts black glossed with green. Tertials dark glossy green with broad white shaft streaks, shoulder blue, speculum green. ♀: Differs from ♀ of 26 by uppersurface feathers blackish brown conspicuously edged with fulvous, breast feathers conspicuously mottled with blackish.

S PERU in Cuzco. BOLIVIA; PARAGUAY; URUGUAY; se BRAZIL in Rio de Janeiro and Rio Grande do Sul; CHILE and ARGENTINA, except Andean region, s to Strait of Magellan. [Falkland Is.] Lakes with dense reedbeds.

28. RINGED TEAL

Anas leucophrys

14". Top of head and hindneck black; sides of breast, throat and neck dull white streaked dusky; mantle grayish brown, lower back velvety black glossed with green. Breast pinkish with round black spots. Wing coverts black with white patch on secondary coverts; inner remiges elongated, bronze green on outer web, scapulars chestnut. ♀: Top of head dark brown, sides of head whitish with dark line below eye. Back and wings like ♂ but scapulars brown. Throat whitish, underparts dull white, breast spotted with pale brown.

S BRAZIL in Rio Grande do Sul and Mato Grosso; URUGUAY; PARAGUAY; e BOLIVIA from Santa Cruz to Tarija; ARGENTINA s to Buenos Aires. Open marshes.

Plate 3

29. TORRENT DUCK

Merganetta armata *

15". Bill red, very narrow; tail long, stiff. Crown and back of neck black, sides of head and rest of neck white with black stripe extending downward from eye. Back grayish to reddish striped with black; below white to dark reddish brown or almost black,

striped with black. ♀: Gray above, narrowly barred with black; cinnamon rufous below.

Andean torrents from nw VENEZUELA and COLOMBIA to Tierra del Fuego.

Plate 2

30. ROSY-BILLED POCHARD

Netta peposaca

20". Bill and knob at forehead rosy pink. Head, neck and breast purplish black; belly white vermiculated black. Back black vermiculated with white. Greater wing coverts and secondaries white, tipped black; underside of wing and under tail coverts white. ♀: Brown; chin and throat white. Secondaries and under tail coverts white.

Se BRAZIL in Rio Grande do Sul; URUGUAY; PARAGUAY; ARGENTINA s to Río Negro; CHILE from Atacama s to Valdivia. Lakes with dense vegetation.

31. SOUTHERN POCHARD

Netta erythrophthalma *

17". Top of head black, sides of head and throat dark maroon. Back black vermiculated with brown. Breast blackish, belly dark brown, sides of body tinged rufescent. Secondaries partly white. Bill blue gray. ♀: Brown; white marks on sides of head and base of bill.

Spottily distributed. VENEZUELA in Zulia and Aragua. COLOMBIA on Caribbean coast, temperate zone of E Andes, Cauca Valley and in the se. ECUADOR. PERU w of Andes from Lambayeque to Arequipa. CHILE in Arica. Sporadic in e BRAZIL. Nw ARGENTINA. Trinidad (?). [Breeds also in Africa.] Rivers, mountain lakes, coasts in winter.

Plate 21

32. LESSER SCAUP

Aythya affinis

16". Head and neck black glossed with purple. Breast, upper back and rump black; center of back white with wavy black lines. Belly and patch on wing white. ♀: Head, neck, upper breast and back dark brown; white patch at base of bill. Lower breast, belly and patch on wing white.

Winter resident (Jan.-Feb.). N VENEZUELA; COLOMBIA in E Andes and Cauca Valley; acc. in w ECUADOR; Aruba to

Trinidad and Tobago. [Breeds in N Amer., winters through Mid. Amer.] Marshy lakes.

33. BRAZILIAN DUCK (or Teal)

Amazonetta brasiliensis *

15". General plumage brown, rufescent on breast. Crown, back of neck, lower back, rump, tail and inner wing coverts black. Greater wing coverts and outer secondaries brilliant, metallic green turning to purplish on secondaries which are broadly tipped white. Bill orange; legs red. ♀: Much like ♂ but with white spot before eye and larger one at base of bill. Bill olive; legs red.

GUYANA; e VENEZUELA; COLOMBIA e of Andes; BRAZIL; n and e BOLIVIA; PARAGUAY; URUGUAY; n ARGENTINA s to Córdoba and n Buenos Aires. SURINAM (?). Open lagoons, bogs. Perches in trees.

Plate 2

34. COMB DUCK

Sarkidiornis melanotos *

♂ 30", ♀ 22". Bill black with high, fleshy wattle at base. Head, neck and underparts white; head and neck spotted with black. Upperparts black glossed with green and purple. ♀: Generally similar to ♂ but much smaller; bill normal.

A forest duck of local distribution. GUYANA; VENEZUELA in Orinoco basin; COLOMBIA in upper tropical, temperate zones of Andes. W ECUADOR. Nw and e PERU, acc. in highlands (Lake Junín). BRAZIL from mouth of the Amazon w to rio Negro and s to Mato Grosso and Rio de Janeiro URUGUAY; PARAGUAY; ARGENTINA s to Santa Fe and acc. to Buenos Aires. Trinidad. [E Panama, Africa, s Asia.] Perches in trees.

35. MUSCOVY DUCK

Cairina moschata

♂ 33", ♀ 26". Mostly blackish, back and wings glossed bronzy green, shoulders extensively white. Face bare, black. ♀: Much like ♂ but much smaller.

Tropical zone. GUIANAS; most of VENEZUELA and COLOMBIA; ECUADOR; casual in e PERU and on Pacific coast. BRAZIL. N URUGUAY; PARAGUAY; e BOLIVIA. N ARGENTINA s to Santa Fe,

accidentally in Buenos Aires. Trinidad. [Mid. Amer.] Forested rivers and lakes. Perches in trees.

36. BRAZILIAN MERGANSER

Mergus octosetaceus

22". Long, thin crest; head and neck black with green reflections. Upperparts dark greenish brown. Breast and sides gray finely vermiculated with white, rest of underparts irregularly barred brown and white; wing patch white. Bill long, thin, red.

Drainage of upper and middle Paraguai and Paraná rivers in BRAZIL, PARAGUAY and ARGENTINA. Rivers, or small streams. Feeds on fish.

37. RUDDY DUCK

Oxyura jamaicensis *

17". Head black (cheeks spotted with white, 1), chin white; back, foreneck, breast and belly mottled grayish brown and black; tail stiffened, black. Bill blue. ♀: Brown above spotted and vermiculated with black; underparts ferruginous brown; pale stripe below eye.

COLOMBIA in temperate and páramo zones of E and Central Andes, 1; Andes of Nariño s to PERU (also found on coast) and BOLIVIA; Andes of CHILE to Aysén and in lowlands in Aconcagua; w ARGENTINA s to Tierra del Fuego. [N Amer. to Guatemala. Bahamas. W Indies.] Lakes with dense vegetation.

38. LAKE DUCK

Oxyura vittata

14.5". Much like 37 but smaller, no white on cheeks and black of head extending farther down neck especially at back. Bill blue.

BRAZIL in Rio Grande do Sul; URUGUAY; PARAGUAY; ARGENTINA to Tierra del Fuego; CHILE from s Tarapacá to Llanquihue. Southern breeding birds migrate north to ne ARGENTINA, URUGUAY and s BRAZIL. Lakes with dense vegetation.

39. MASKED DUCK

Oxyura dominica

14.5". Front of head black, rest of head and.

neck chestnut; back and sides of body chestnut, feathers with broad black centers. Large wing patch white; tail black, stiff, carried erect, fan-shaped. Bill blue. ♀: Rather like females of 37 and 38 but with pale stripe above eye and broader stripe below it.

Tropical to temperate zone. COLOMBIA, south, in the west through w ECUADOR to s Lambayeque, PERU. VENEZUELA and GUIANAS s through BRAZIL and e BOLIVIA to Santiago del Estero and Buenos Aires, ARGENTINA. Trinidad and Tobago. [Texas; Mid. Amer.; W Indies.] Lakes with dense vegetation.

Plate 2

40. BLACK-HEADED DUCK
Heteronetta atricapilla

14.5″. Head and neck blackish brown; upperparts and breast dark brown, freckled and vermiculated paler; secondaries edged white, wing coverts tipped white. Underparts dull white mottled dusky. Bill yellow. ♀: Like ♂ but top and sides of head brown, mottled paler and throat whitish.

BRAZIL in Rio Grande do Sul; URUGUAY; PARAGUAY; e BOLIVIA in Santa Cruz; ARGENTINA from Entre Ríos, Santa Fe and Córdoba to Buenos Aires, La Pampa and Mendoza; central CHILE from Santiago to Valdivia. Southern birds migrate north. Parasitic. Reedbeeds.

Fig. 7. LEAST STORM-PETREL
Halocyptena microsoma
p. 17

Order FALCONIFORMES

Family CATHARTIDAE   AMERICAN VULTURES

Except for the King Vulture, American vultures are chiefly black. In South America some are a familiar sight in towns and villages; others are found in forests and open country away from towns. They feed on carrion and are useful in ridding towns of refuse.

1. ANDEAN CONDOR

Vultur gryphus

42″. Wingspan about 10′. Head and neck bare, purplish flesh with comb on top of head, white ruff at base of neck; rest of plumage black except for large patch of silvery gray on wings. ♀: Similar to ♂, but with no comb. Imm.: Dull brownish; ruff brown, no silvery in wings.

Andes of Me/rida, VENEZUELA, but not since 1912. Santa Marta Mts. and Andes of COLOMBIA, rare and local. Andes of ECUADOR; Andes and seacoast of PERU, s through mts. and lowlands to Cape Horn. ARGENTINE lowlands from Río Negro southward. Open country.

2. KING VULTURE

Sarcoramphus papa

30″. Head and neck bare, orange, red and blue. Body plumage and under wing coverts creamy white; rump, wings and tail black. Imm.: Sooty black with varying amounts of white below, depending on age.

Generally distributed, chiefly lowlands, e of Andes s to La Rioja, n Santa Fe and Corrientes, ARGENTINA. W of Andes to n PERU. Trinidad (occasionally). [Mid. Amer.] Forest.

Fig. 14, p. 114

3. BLACK VULTURE

*Coragyps atratus**

25″. Head and neck bare, grayish black. Black; patch on underside of primaries whitish. Tail short, rounded, shorter than outstretched legs.

Generally distributed s in the e to Río Negro, ARGENTINA, and in the w to Aysén, CHILE. Margarita I. Trinidad. [Southern US; Mid. Amer.] Towns, villages, open country.

4. TURKEY VULTURE

*Cathartes aura**

29″. Head bare, purplish red, some races have whitish or yellow bands on hindneck. Brownish black. Tail long, narrow, much longer than outstretched legs. Underside of primaries silvery gray.

Generally distributed s to Tierra del Fuego. Margarita I. Trinidad. [S Canada s through Mid. Amer., Greater Antilles. Falkland Is.] Open country.

5. LESSER YELLOW-HEADED VULTURE

*Cathartes burrovianus**

28-32″ (or 22-25″, l). Above dull black, feathers edged with dull grayish brown; below brownish black. Head bare, crown bluish green, rest of head orange to orange yellow sometimes with greenish; tarsi grayish white.

Nw VENEZUELA; n and w COLOMBIA, l. Coastal GUYANA and SURINAM, and from Meta, COLOMBIA s generally to n ARGENTINA. [Coastal se Mexico to Panama.] Marshes and open grassland away from habitation.

Plate 22

38

6. GREATER YELLOW-HEADED VULTURE

Cathartes melambrotos

33″. Very like 5 but slightly larger with longer tail, the plumage entirely deep black with greenish or bluish sheen, no admixture of brown tones. Head and neck largely yellow, some bluish gray on forehead and about eyes, sometimes dull purplish pink on nape.

GUYANA; SURINAM; s and e VENEZUELA along the Orinoco; e COLOMBIA from s Meta to n BRAZIL s to Belém, rios Xingú and Tapajós. E PERU in Loreto and Huánuco. Ne BOLIVIA. Forest, forest edge.

Family ACCIPITRIDAE   EAGLES AND HAWKS

This family differs from falcons (Falconidae) by more rounded and broader wings and more frequent sailings in flight. In habits they do not differ from eagles and hawks found elsewhere. They exhibit a variety of color phases and immature birds are usually quite different from adults. Females are usually considerably larger than males.

Many species, particularly larger eagles, are often rare and very local although widely distributed.

This aid to identification is based on adult plumage only.

AID TO IDENTIFICATION

Plain white below (above gray) 1, 2, 16, 18, 33c, 34c, 36, 37b, 54a; (above black) 3, 4, 22, 28, 35, 51; (above brown) 19b, 20b, 50b

Barred below 5, 7, 13, 14b, 15, 16, 17, 20b, 24, 25, 29, 40b, 42, 43c, 54a, 55, 57

Moderately to heavily streaked below 7, 21, 23, 27b, 50b, 54a, 56

Body plumage all or mostly blackish 5, 10, 17, 18, 19b, 20b, 21b, 23, 26, 28, 30, 44a, 45, 56; (or gray) 6, 8c, 9, 11, 12, 15, 18, 19b, 38, 39b, 46b, 57; (or white) 31, 32b, 34c, 35

With band across chest 15, 19b, 23, 41, 49, 56; (crested) 15, 47c, 48, 49, 50b, 52, 53

1. WHITE-TAILED KITE

Elanus leucurus *

15″. Above (including central tail feathers) pale gray becoming white on forecrown. Extensive shoulder patch and small one on underside of bend of wing, black. Sides of head, underparts and all but central tail feathers white. Imm.: Brownish above, mottled white; below white, streaked cinnamon brown. Tail white with narrow subterminal blackish bar.

Tropical, rarely to temperate zone. GUIANAS; n VENEZUELA; n COLOMBIA. BRAZIL in Roraima and from Marajó I. s to Rio Grande do Sul. PARAGUAY; URUGUAY; ARGENTINA s to Buenos Aires and Córdoba. CHILE s to Valdivia. Trinidad. [Sw US; Mid. Amer.] Open country, semiarid regions.

Plate 22

2. PEARL KITE

Gampsonyx swainsonii *

8″ (or 10″, 1). Forehead and sides of head buff; throat and underparts white; patch at sides of breast black or rufous; thighs pale rufous. Back slaty gray, collar on hindneck white edged with chestnut. Inner remiges broadly tipped white, wing lining pure white. Tail like back. Imm.: Much like ad., but feathers of upperparts edged rufous, below suffused with yellowish buff.

Tropical zone. GUYANA; SURINAM; VENEZUELA; n COLOMBIA; Amazonian

PERU and BRAZIL south to n ARGEN-TINA and south in e BRAZIL to São Paulo. W ECUADOR, nw PERU, 1. Margarita I. Trinidad. [Nicaragua.] Savanna, often near palm trees, open woodland, arid scrub, cerrado.

Plate 43

3. SWALLOW-TAILED KITE

Elanoides forficatus *

24''. Tail very long, deeply forked. Head, neck, underparts and inner remiges white. Upperparts and tail black, interscapular region glossed green (or purplish, 1). Imm.: Like ad. but head, neck and underparts finely streaked dusky.

Tropical zone. Resident, generally distributed south to w ECUADOR and BOLIVIA, PARAGUAY and ne ARGENTINA. Migrant to COLOMBIA and n ECUADOR and probably to s BRAZIL (Paraná, Mato Grosso), 1. [Breeds from central US southward. Greater Antilles.] Swamps, open country, humid forest.

4. GRAY-HEADED KITE

Leptodon cayanensis

18-20''. Head and breast light gray, back blackish, lower breast and belly white. Tail black, tipped white with three (two visible) gray bands. Underside of wings white broadly barred black on primaries, bars narrowing toward tertials. From below: Wing coverts blackish. Remiges barred. Tail with three white bars. Imm.: Crown patch black; head, hindneck and entire underparts white; back dark brown; tail ashy tipped buff with three black bands. Dark phase: Upperparts and sides of head dark brown, sometimes with indistinct rufous nuchal collar. Below white or buffy, heavily streaked blackish; sometimes almost solid black on throat and upper breast; rarely lightly striped and with dark median throat stripe.

Tropical zone. Generally distributed; on the west to w ECUADOR, e of Andes to BO-LIVIA, n ARGENTINA and s BRAZIL to Rio Grande do Sul. Forest, near streams.

5. HOOK-BILLED KITE

Chondrohierax uncinatus *

15-18''. Variable in size (particularly bill) and color. Above slaty blue, below paler; breast and belly sometimes barred white, buff or cinnamon. Tail black with two broad white or slaty bars. Underside of wing barred black and white. Cere and orbital skin usually green or greenish; iris white or yellow. Black phase: Black; tail with one or two white or ashy bars. ♀: Above dark brown or sooty black with cinnamon nuchal collar; below broadly barred white and reddish brown. Tail black with two wide gray bars. Imm.: Brownish black above, nuchal collar and underparts white. Tail with three gray bars and light tip.

Tropical zone rarely to lower temperate zone. Generally distributed e of Andes to São Paulo, BRAZIL, n ARGENTINA and BOLIVIA; w of Andes to Lima, PERU. Trinidad. [Mid. Amer.; Cuba; Grenada; Acc. s Texas.] Wet woodland, forest creeks, coffee plantations.

Plate 22

6. RUFOUS-THIGHED KITE

Harpagus diodon

12-14''. Above slaty gray, darker on head; below pale gray, throat paler with black median stripe; thighs and under wing coverts bright ferruginous. Quills dark brown banded with white on inner web. Tail blackish with three or four gray bars. Much like 12 but latter lacks black throat stripe and has white under wing coverts. Legs orange yellow. Imm.: Above brown, mottled white; below white with black line down center of throat and dark brown drop-shaped marks on breast and upper belly. Thighs ferruginous. Much like 12 but at once distinguishable by black median line on throat.

Tropical zone. GUIANAS; central and Amazonian BRAZIL and from Bahía to Rio Grande do Sul; PARAGUAY; n ARGEN-TINA. Forest.

7. DOUBLE-TOOTHED KITE

Harpagus bidentatus *

Dusky throat stripe. Differs mainly from 6 by color of underparts which vary from almost solid rufous chestnut to rufous barred black and white; or grayish on chest with rufous confined to sides, the belly pale gray barred rufescent. ♀: Like male but more conspicuously barred. Imm.: Differs from 6 mainly by white thighs.

Tropical zone. GUIANAS; VENEZUELA; COLOMBIA, e and w ECUADOR; central and e PERU; e BOLIVIA; Amazonian BRAZIL and from Maranhão to Rio de Janeiro. Trinidad. [Mid. Amer.] Forest, savanna.

8. MISSISSIPPI KITE

Ictinia misisippiensis

14". Head, underparts and inner remiges pale gray, back dark gray; primaries black sometimes with some dark maroon on inner webs. Lower back and tail slaty black. From below tail appears all black, somewhat forked. Legs dusky. Juv.: Upperparts dark brown, streaked white on head and mottled white on back. Throat white, rest of underparts white broadly streaked rufous brown.

Migrant. Recorded in winter from PARAGUAY and ARGENTINA, migration route unknown. [Breeds in central and s US. Recorded from Mexico, Guatemala and Costa Rica.] Pastureland, open scrub.

9. PLUMBEOUS KITE

Ictinia plumbea

14". Darker than 8 and at once distinguishable by bright rufous inner webs of primaries; inner webs of lateral tail feathers with two distinct spots on inner webs, visible as band from below. Tail square-ended. Legs orange to yellow. Juv.: Above brownish black, head and nape streaked white. Throat white finely streaked gray, rest of underparts white coarsely streaked gray. Primaries blackish, sometimes with some rufous on inner web. Tail as in ad.

Tropical, subtropical zones. Generally distributed e of Andes to BOLIVIA, n ARGENTINA and BRAZIL s to Rio Grande do Sul. W of Andes to ECUADOR. [Mid. Amer., where summer res.] Groves of trees, forested rivers.

Plate 43

10. EVERGLADE (OR SNAIL) KITE

Rostrhamus sociabilis *

16". Bill very slender; iris, bare lores, cere and legs bright orange red. Slaty gray; upper and under tail coverts white. Tail rather long, slightly forked, black, extensively white at base, ashy at tip. ♀: Dark brown, blotched white or buff below, eyebrow white. Tail as in ♂. Imm.: Much like ♀ above; below tawny, broadly streaked dusky. Tail as in ad.

Marshes of tropical to rarely temperate zone. Generally distributed w of Andes to ECUADOR and e of them to URUGUAY and n ARGENTINA. Trinidad. [Mid. Amer.; Cuba.]

11. SLENDER-BILLED KITE

Helicolestes hamatus

14.5". Bill, as in 10, soft parts more yellow; tail much shorter and solid black. General color much paler and grayer; no white tail coverts. Imm.: Differs by two to four white tail bars, rusty edges on wing coverts.

Spottily distributed. SURINAM; se and n VENEZUELA; n and se COLOMBIA. Amazonian BRAZIL; e PERU. [E Panama.] Wooded swamps, plantations, forest pools.

Fig. 10, p. 71

12. BICOLORED HAWK

Accipiter bicolor *

14-17". In *Accipiter* the tail is rather long and narrow. Adults of this variable species are recognizable by bright ferruginous thighs. Slaty gray above, top and sides of head sometimes blackish, light gray below (or underparts with black shaft streaks, 1; or throat whitish spotted ashy, gray underparts shaded with rufous and barred and spotted whitish, 2; or underparts strongly cinnamon, imm. with drop-shaped spots on throat and upper breast and white bars on belly, 3). Underside of wings narrowly barred. Tail blackish with two or three pale gray or whitish bars, cf. 6. Imm.: Above sooty brown, feathers pale-edged, with conspicuous white or buff nuchal collar. Below white to tawny, thighs amber brown (or streaked below, thighs amber, barred black, 2). Tail blackish with four white bars and white tip, cf. 6.

W ECUADOR, 1. GUIANAS to COLOMBIA south to e PERU; Amazonian BRAZIL, in the e from Maranhão to Rio Grande do Sul; PARAGUAY; n ARGENTINA. BOLIVIA and nw ARGENTINA to Santa Fe, 3. CHILE from O'Higgins and ARGENTINA from Neuquén to Tierra del Fuego, 2. [Mid. Amer.] Forest edge, clearings.

13. TINY HAWK

Accipiter superciliosus *

8-11". Above slaty gray; below white very narrowly barred except on throat, with grayish brown. Tail ashy with four dark bars. Imm.: Grayish brown above; below pale buff barred brown except on throat and thighs. Tail with six or seven black bars. Rufous phase: Crown blackish, sides of head and neck and rest of underparts bright rufous, barred lightly on back and wings with dusky. Below cinnamon buff barred rufous brown. Tail with four broken black bars.

Generally distributed south to w ECUADOR, e PERU, BRAZIL to Santa Catarina, PARAGUAY and ne ARGENTINA [Nicaragua to Panama.] Forest borders, second growth, clearings.

14. SEMICOLLARED HAWK

Accipiter collaris

12-14". Crown blackish, cheeks and ill-defined collar on hindneck white. Back sooty brown, tail ashy brown with five dark bars. Below white broadly barred blackish brown except on throat. Imm.: Above rufous brown, spotted black; crown black, nuchal collar rufous. Tail rufous with six dark bars. Below buffy obsoletely barred amber brown.

Tropical, subtropical zones. W VENEZUELA; COLOMBIA west of E Andes including Santa Marta to w ECUADOR. Forest.

15. GRAY-BELLIED HAWK

Accipiter poliogaster

17-20'" Superficially like *Micrastur mirandollei* (see 4, p. 51). Crown black, sides of head black or gray. Above blackish feathers edged slate gray; below pale gray with dark hair streaks. Tail black with three dark gray bars. Underside of wings virtually unbarred. Imm.: Remarkably like 52 in color but much smaller. Crown black, back dark brown, nuchal collar rufous. Throat white, edged laterally with black. Sides of head and breast rufous, center of breast white, rest of underparts white barred and spotted with black. Tail evenly barred black and ashy. Once considered a distinct species, *A. pectoralis*.

Widely but very locally distributed. GUYANA; VENEZUELA; ne COLOMBIA; e ECUADOR; ne PERU; BRAZIL; n and e BOLIVIA; PARAGUAY; ARGENTINA in Misiones. Forest.

16. SHARP-SHINNED HAWK

Accipiter striatus *

11-13". Slaty gray above; below white with obsolete black shaft lines and bars, thighs bright chestnut. Tail brown with five (or four, 1) ashy bars (or above deep slaty gray, below bright chestnut, usually barred with grayish white and dark rufous, throat and upper chest often tinged ashy, thighs bright chestnut; tail blackish with four ashy bars, 2). Imm.: More or less like ad., but streaked below.

Upper tropical to temperate zone. Andes of w VENEZUELA and in Santa Marta, COLOMBIA, 1. From w COLOMBIA s through Andes to nw BOLIVIA, 2. From e BOLIVIA e to Bahía, BRAZIL, and URUGUAY and s to Córdoba and Buenos Aires, ARGENTINA. [N Amer.; Guatemala to Nicaragua; W Indies; N Amer. birds winter south to w Panama.] Woodlands.

17. BLACK-CHESTED BUZZARD-EAGLE

Geranoaetus melanoleucus *

24-27". Above slaty black, wing coverts ashy gray, barred black. Breast slaty black, belly white, finely (or coarsely, imm.) barred with black. Tail short, wedge-shaped, dark slaty tipped light gray. Feathers of head and neck lanceolate. From below not unlike 49 but much smaller and at once distinguishable by uniformly dark, unbarred tail. Imm.: Above somewhat like ad. Below tawny buff streaked on breast and barred on belly and thighs with blackish. Tail longer than in ad., gray with numerous blackish bars.

Subtropical, temperate zones of Andes from Mérida, VENEZUELA, s in the Andes to Tierra del Fuego and crossing to the Atlantic coast through PARAGUAY and n ARGENTINA to São Paulo and Rio Grande do Sul, BRAZIL, URUGUAY and Buenos Aires, ARGENTINA. Open woods and pasturelands, desert and dunes.

18. WHITE-TAILED HAWK

Buteo albicaudatus *

24". Occurs in three color phases: (1) Most of head, neck, back and wings gray; shoulders and scapulars rufescent, underparts white, sometimes with blackish throat. (2) Similar above but underparts gray. (3) Dark brown above and below, often with some rufous on shoulder. In all phases tail is white with many very narrow inconspicuous dusky bars and broad, black subterminal band conspicuous also from below. Imm.: Usually blackish with pale tail, and wing lining darker than flight feathers, sometimes with suggestion of rufous on shoulders.

Tropical, subtropical zones. GUYANA w to COLOMBIA, s to Río Negro, ARGENTINA. Not recorded from Ecuador, Peru or Chile. Aruba to Trinidad. [Sw US; Mid. Amer.] Plains, eroded hills, open woods, plantations.

Plate 43

19. RED-BACKED HAWK

Buteo polyosoma *[1]

18-21". Much like 18 but tail relatively longer, usually distinguishable by no rufous on shoulders. Occurs in five color phases: (1) Chestnut; whole head, thighs sooty brown to slate. (2) Similar above, entire undersurface white variably barred with very narrow grayish bars on belly. (3) Gray to slaty black above and below, sometimes with some chestnut on mantle. (4) Very pale to pale slate gray above, white below. (5) Similar to (1) above, throat and breast dark slate with band of chestnut across lower breast, belly and thighs boldly banded gray and white. In all phases tail is white with very narrow blackish bars and broad black subterminal band and ashy tip, conspicuous also from below. Imm.: Usually dark brown above more or less mottled with white on nape and rufous on mantle. Below dark buff to pale ochraceous; upper throat, sides of neck heavily streaked dark brown; lower breast and belly irregularly barred reddish brown. Very rarely sooty black above and below. Tail pale grayish closely barred brown.

Tropical to páramo zone. Central COLOMBIAN Andes s to Cape Horn. [Falkland and Juan Fernández Is.] Open steppes, arid country.

20. VARIABLE (or Puna) HAWK

Buteo poecilochrous

20-24". Indistinguishable in the field from 19 but lacks color phase (1), and usually occurs at higher elevations. Imm.: Similar to 19 but dark phase present in about half the individuals. Differs structurally by larger size and by third primary shorter than the fifth instead of longer as in 19.

Mainly puna zone. Andes from sw COLOMBIA south to n CHILE, n BOLIVIA and nw ARGENTINA. Open steppes, usually above 10,000 ft.

21. RUFOUS-TAILED HAWK

Buteo ventralis

21-24". Above blackish, feathers of hindneck edged light ferruginous, sides of head strongly tinged cinnamon. Throat white, bordered black at sides; rest of underparts ochraceous white streaked and blotched blackish, thickest at flanks and abdomen, breast strongly ferruginous. Thighs cinnamon rufous narrowly barred reddish brown. Tail light rufous with nine black bands, tip white. Deep black phase not uncommon, in which underside of wings and tail is whitish. Imm.: Black above with a few white streaks or spots; below white with sides of head and body streaked black. Tail ashy gray narrowly barred dusky, tipped dirty white.

CHILE from Ñuble to Magallanes. ARGENTINA in Santa Cruz. Forest edge.

22. ZONE-TAILED HAWK

Buteo albonotatus *

20". Black, tinged slaty. Tail black with three bands (distal one widest), gray above, white below, and pale tip. Imm.: Like ad. but spotted white on breast and thighs. Tail barred with brown above, below whitish with numerous narrow blackish bars and broader subterminal band.

Generally but locally distrubuted south to w PERU, e BOLIVIA, PARAGUAY, and e BRAZIL in Marajó I., Ceará and Paraná. Trinidad. [Sw US; Mid. Amer.] Open woodland, river banks.

23. SWAINSON'S HAWK

Buteo swainsoni

20". Upperparts, sides of head and neck dark brown. Throat white, breast dark reddish brown; rest of underparts buffy white, sparsely barred on sides with rufous. Tail ashy brown, narrowly barred dusky with whitish patch near base; tail from below pale gray faintly barred dusky. Rufous phase: Below mostly reddish brown. Dark phase: Blackish above and below, tail as above. From below: In light phase throat and belly white, breast dark, wing and tail tips black; in dark phase below all dark, wings and tail as in light phase. Imm.: Above dark chocolate brown varied with white on head and neck, rufous on back. Below buffy white, variably spotted dark brown. Tail as in ad. In dark phase lower surface dark with rufous or buffy spots.

Winter resident, mainly in ARGENTINA s to Río Negro. Recorded spottily from central and se COLOMBIA; nw VENEZUELA; w PERU; e BRAZIL; PARAGUAY; e BOLIVIA. Trinidad. [Breeds in w and central US, and n Mexico. Migrates through Mid. Amer. Winter range not well understood. Some found wintering in Florida.] Open country.

24. BROAD-WINGED HAWK

Buteo platypterus *

14-18". Above dark brown. Throat white, rest of underparts regularly and closely banded cinnamon rufous. Tail black with two broad white bands and white tip. Not unlike 25 but distinguishable by white instead of ashy or rufous tail bars. Rare black phase resembles 28 but distinguishable by smaller feet. From below: Tail broad, rather short with three black bars; underside of wing light, tipped black. Imm.: Dark brown above, here and there spotted and streaked white. Below white lightly to heavily streaked dusky, tail ashy boldly barred with five or six narrow dusky bars. Not unlike 27 but always distinguishable by few dark streaks in center of throat.

Tropical, subtropical zones. Winter resident (Oct.-Apr.). FRENCH GUIANA, VENEZUELA, COLOMBIA, in the w south to w PERU, e of Andes to BOLIVIA. Nw BRAZIL and sw Mato Grosso. Tobago, resident. Trinidad, migrant. [Breeds in N Amer. s to Texas, winters in Mid. Amer.; resident, W Indies.] Open woodland.

25. ROADSIDE HAWK

Buteo magnirostris *

13-15". Head, breast and upperparts brown to brownish gray to pale gray; lower breast and belly regularly banded white and cinnamon. Inner webs of remiges barred rufous. Tail brown or ashy brown with four or five gray to cinnamon brown to tawny buff bars. Imm.: Above brown; below tawny,

streaked brown on throat and breast, barred reddish brown on belly.

Tropical, subtropical zones. Widely distributed s to central ARGENTINA in La Rioja, Córdoba and Santa Fe. W of Andes to nw PERU. [Mid. Amer.; Pearl Is.] Open woodland, savanna.

Plate 22

26. WHITE-RUMPED HAWK

Buteo leucorrhous

13-15". Black; tibial feathers rufous. Upper and under tail coverts white. Tail black, white at base, crossed by single ashy white bar. From below under wing coverts are white and tail shows two white bars. Imm.: Mottled with rufous on head, neck and wings; below much mottled with rufous, thighs barred.

Subtropical zone. W VENEZUELA; COLOMBIA; e and w ECUADOR; nw PERU; PARAGUAY; BRAZIL from Minas Gerais to Rio Grande do Sul. N ARGENTINA from Salta and Tucumán eastward. Open forest clearings.

27. WHITE-THROATED HAWK

Buteo albigula

16-19". Above blackish brown. Below white; sides of neck and breast chestnut brown; sides of body and belly streaked and splotched brown; solid dark patch at sides of belly; thighs buffy, barred ferruginous. Tail dark brown with numerous inconspicuous black bars. Dark phase is very rare. Imm.: Much like ad. but wing coverts pale-edged and sides of neck and breast duller and darker. Thighs buff, barred black. In all stages differs from 28 by longer tail.

Subtropical to temperate zone, in the n usually above 7500 ft. Andes from COLOMBIA s to PERU, n ARGENTINA in Salta, and CHILE to Valdivia. Open mountain slopes.

28. SHORT-TAILED HAWK

Buteo brachyurus *

15-17". Upperparts and sides of head slaty black, forehead white. Underparts and wing lining white. Underside of tail whitish with two narrow, and one broader, subterminal black bars; tail rather short. Dark phase: Slaty black, or dusky brown above and below. Wing lining whitish barred dusky.

Tail black with five ashy bars and tip. Tail banding often indistinct in both phases. Imm.: Above dusky brown more or less streaked whitish, below white, sometimes with a few fine shaft streaks. Tail with more bars than ad. Much like 27 but distinguishable by plain white instead of barred thighs, lack of conspicuous streaking below, and no brown at sides of breast. Dark phase: Like ad. but below streaked white.

Usually tropical to lower subtropical zone below 7000 ft. GUIANAS; n and w VENEZUELA; COLOMBIA w of E Andes; w ECUADOR. Central and se PERU; BOLIVIA; BRAZIL; PARAGUAY; n ARGENTINA. Chacachacare I.; Tobago. [Florida; Mid. Amer.] Open woodland, swamps.

29. GRAY HAWK

Buteo nitidus *

15-17″. Above pale gray narrowly barred darker gray; below white narrowly barred gray. Tail black with broad white bar and white tip. Imm.: Above dark brown mixed with cinnamon buff; below whitish to buff, spotted sooty brown; throat with dark median streak, thighs barred. Tail ashy with many dark bars, underside whitish barred dusky.

Tropical zone. GUIANAS w to Caribbean coast of COLOMBIA and e of Andes to n ARGENTINA and BRAZIL to Rio de Janeiro and Mato Grosso. Trinidad, Tobago. [Sw US; Mid. Amer.] Open woodland, cerrado.

30. BAY-WINGED (or Harris') HAWK

Parabuteo unicinctus *

19″. Dark ashy brown. Shoulders, under wing coverts and thighs chestnut. Upper tail coverts white. Tail black, extensively white at base, with white terminal band. Imm.: Above blackish brown feathers rusty-edged, wing coverts rufescent; head and neck streaked ochraceous, underparts ochraceous with drop-shaped blackish streaks. Thighs rusty, barred black. Tail grayish brown, white at base with numerous dusky bars, tipped white.

Tropical zone, generally distributed s to about 42°s. Margarita I. [Sw US; Mid. Amer.] Open or dry woodland, sometimes swampy areas.

31. WHITE HAWK

Leucopternis albicollis *

18-22″. White, interscapular region spotted black. Wings black, inner remiges and wing coverts edged white. Tail black with white base and broad white tip (or whiter on back, crown spangled with black, tail white with broad subterminal black band, 1; or white, remiges broadly edged white, tail white with narrower black subterminal band, 2). Imm.: Like ad. but buff instead of white and streaked blackish on head.

Tropical zone. GUIANAS, VENEZUELA except nw; se COLOMBIA south to n and e BOLIVIA; Amazonian BRAZIL to Maranhão and central Mato Grosso. Nw VENEZUELA to COLOMBIA in Boyacá, middle Magdalena Valley and Caribbean lowlands, 1. COLOMBIA on Pacific slope south to s Chocó, 2. Trinidad. [Mid. Amer.] Forest edge, deciduous forest.

Plate 43

32. GRAY-BACKED HAWK

Leucopternis occidentalis

17-20″. Rather like 31 but differs by plumbeous, white-streaked crown and blackish gray interscapular region. Tail white with wide black subterminal band. Imm.: Like ad. but paler, chest blotched gray, sides lightly barred.

Tropical, subtropical zones. W ECUADOR to Peruvian border. Forest.

33. MANTLED HAWK

Leucopternis polionota

20-24″. Head, neck and underparts white; back slaty gray, upper tail coverts tipped white. Upper wing coverts edged white, remiges slaty, secondaries tipped white. Basal half of tail black, distal half white. Imm.: Differs from ad. by head streaked black, back darker, feathers edged white.

E BRAZIL from Alagoas and Bahía to Santa Catarina; n PARAGUAY; ARGENTINA in Misiones. Forest.

34. WHITE-NECKED HAWK

Leucopternis lacernulata

18-21″. Crown to upper back white, shaded gray; rest of back dark slaty gray here and there spotted and barred white, particularly on lower back and rump. Below white.

Primaries blackish. Tail basally blackish, distally white with blackish subterminal band. Imm.: Differs by blacker, less slaty upperparts and head and upper back streaked black.

E BRAZIL from Alagoas to Santa Catarina. Forest.

35. BLACK-FACED HAWK

Leucopternis melanops

15". Head, neck and underparts white; crown and nape streaked black, ocular region black. Upperparts black, spotted white. Primaries and tail black, the latter with narrow central white band. Imm.: Head, neck and underparts tinged buff, black feathers of uppersurface edged buff. Tail with two white bands and pale tip.

GUIANAS; s VENEZUELA; se COLOMBIA; e ECUADOR; BRAZIL n of the Amazon. Savanna, forest near water, mangroves.

36. WHITE-BROWED HAWK

Leucopternis kuhli

13-14". Above black, feathers of upper mantle mottled white; eyebrow white; sides of head streaked white, ocular region deep black. Below, white slightly streaked on sides of breast. Tail black with narrow white median bar and ashy tip. Imm.: Tail with three narrow irregular white bars.

E PERU; BRAZIL s of the Amazon from rios Madeira and Jiparaná east to e Pará. Forest.

37. SEMIPLUMBEOUS HAWK

Leucopternis semiplumbea

13-14". Leaden gray above, upper tail coverts black; below white. Tail black, usually with one, sometimes two white bars. Cere and legs orange to reddish orange. Imm.: Like ad. but with dusky shaft streak above and below; tail with two or three white bars.

COLOMBIA from middle Magdalena Valley to Pacific, south to w ECUADOR. [Honduras to Panama.] Forest.

38. SLATE-COLORED HAWK

Leucopternis schistacea

15-17". Uniform bluish slate. Tail black with median white band and tip. Imm.: Lower breast and belly banded slaty and

white. Underside of wing barred black and white. Tail as in ad.

Sw VENEZUELA; se COLOMBIA south to n BOLIVIA and Amazonian BRAZIL. Forest, especially near water's edge.

39. PLUMBEOUS HAWK

Leucopternis plumbea

Much like 38 but smaller; wings blackish, under wing coverts white, and no white tip to tail. Cere and legs orange. Imm.: Much like ad. but thighs barred.

Pacific slope of COLOMBIA south to nw PERU. [Panama.] Forest.

40. BARRED HAWK

Leucopternis princeps

18-20". Head, neck, upperparts and upper breast black, feathers edged slaty; lower breast, belly and under wing coverts white narrowly barred black. Tail black with narrow median white bar. From below underside of body, wing coverts and remiges appear all narrowly barred black and white. Tail black with two median white bars. Imm.: Like ad. but wing coverts edged white.

Upper tropical zone. N and w COLOMBIA to w ECUADOR. [Costa Rica, Panama.] Forest.

41. BLACK-COLLARED HAWK

Busarellus nigricollis *

18-20". Head buffy white, nape streaked dusky. Extensive black patch on foreneck; rest of plumage bright chestnut rufous. Primaries and distal part of tail black, base of tail black barred rufous. Imm.: Head whiter than ad.; tibia, upper tail coverts and secondaries barred black, back darker, breast buff, streaked black. Black patch on foreneck.

Tropical zone. Generally distributed e of Andes to URUGUAY, BOLIVIA and n ARGENTINA; w of Andes in COLOMBIA. [Mid. Amer.] Forested rivers, swamps, mangroves, flooded rice fields. Eats fish.

42. SAVANNA HAWK

Heterospizias meridionalis

20-25". Whole head, neck, shoulders, and entire underparts rufous brown, latter palest and barred black. Remiges bright rufous tipped black. Back slaty gray, feathers edged rufous; rump, upper tail coverts and tail black, tail with broad white median band and narrow white tip. From below tail seems to have broad black subterminal bar margined white on both sides. Legs long, yellow. Imm.: Dark brown above, shoulders mixed with rufous; below buffy, sides of breast and scattered streakes dusky. Wings as in ad. but rufous parts somewhat barred black. Tail black with ill-defined central ashy bar.

Generally distributed to nw PERU and BOLIVIA, n ARGENTINA and URUGUAY. Trinidad. [Panama.] Grassland, swampy savanna.

43. RUFOUS CRAB-HAWK

Buteogallus aequinoctialis

18". Head and upperparts black, feathers of back and wing coverts edged rufous, inner remiges partly rufous. Underparts and under wing coverts bright rufous with narrow black bars. Tail blackish with poorly marked white median band and well-marked white tip. Imm.: Pale superciliary. Brown above, buff below mottled dusky on sides. Wing patch tawny. Tail grayish brown with about twelve dark bars.

Atlantic coastal swamps and mangroves from VENEZUELA and GUIANAS s to Paraná, BRAZIL.

44. COMMON BLACK HAWK

Buteogallus anthracinus*

18-21". Head inconspicuously crested. Black, base of primaries white (more extensive in 1). Tail black with wide median white band and white tip. Lores, cere and legs orange. From below: Black; small whitish patch at wing angle, two white tail bars. Imm.: Brownish black spotted and streaked above with buff. Below buff broadly streaked black, thighs barred. Tail pale buff with many irregular, narrow black bars. (Occasionally pale washed-out specimens occur due to lack of melanin, 1).

Coastal and interior forests and mangroves. Restricted to coastal mangroves and mud flats, 1. Pacific coast of COLOMBIA and ECUADOR, 1. Caribbean and e COLOMBIA to Meta; n VENEZUELA; GUYANA. Trinidad. [Mid. Amer.; Cozumel I.; Bay Is.; Cuba, Lesser Antilles. Confined to man-groves of Pacific coast and islands off Mid. Amer., 1.]

45. GREAT BLACK HAWK

Buteogallus urubitinga*

24-26". Black; upper tail coverts tipped white. Tail white, distal third of it black, tip white. From below: Black; white patch at wing angle. Tail white with broad black terminal band. Imm.: Above brownish black; below tawny to white, streaked and spotted black, tibia barred black. Tail buff to grayish with many irregular black bars. Much like 44 but larger, rump white and more white in tail.

Generally distributed from nw PERU to BOLIVIA, n ARGENTINA and URUGUAY. Trinidad, Tobago. [Mid. Amer.] Near water in arid, open or humid forested country.

46. SOLITARY EAGLE

Harpyhaliaetus solitarius*

26-28". Head slightly crested, tail short. Dark bluish gray; tail black with broad white median band and narrow white tip. Not unlike 45 but larger with shorter tail. From below: Black, no white wing patch. Tail with broad white median band. Imm.: Dark brownish gray above, back feathers edged cinnamon. Sides of head and underparts ochraceous tawny, streaked black. Tail black, marbled gray with blackish terminal band.

Tropical, subtropical zones. N VENEZUELA; n and w COLOMBIA; e ECUADOR; e and central PERU. [Mid. Amer.] Forest.

47. CROWNED EAGLE

Harpyhaliaetus coronatus

25-27". Head with long blackish crest, tail short. Above dark grayish brown, below somewhat lighter. Tail black with white median bar and white tip distinctly visible from below. Underside of wings unbarred or lightly so. Imm.: Not as dark as 46, sides of head and underparts buffy white, spots on underparts dark brown instead of black. Crest long as in ad.

BRAZIL from Goiás to Rio Grande do Sul and Mato Grosso; PARAGUAY; e BOLIVIA, ARGENTINA to Río Negro. URUGUAY (?). Forest.

48. CRESTED EAGLE

Morphnus guianensis

33". Flat crest, longest feathers black, tipped white. Head, neck and breast pale gray, back black. Throat, lower breast and belly white. Tail with three broad grayish bands. Primaries conspicuously barred black. Dark phase: Sides of head and upper breast blackish, throat paler, rest of underparts boldly to lightly barred black and white. Rare blackish phase also exists. From below, wing coverts pure white, flight feathers heavily barred. Tail with four black bars, tail longer and narrower than in 49. Imm.: Head, neck and breast white, back dark brown mottled white; crest white, black near tip. Primaries conspicuously barred. Tail gray with numerous narrow dusky bars.

Tropical zone. GUIANAS; n VENEZUELA; COLOMBIA; e and w ECUADOR s to BOLIVIA, PARAGUAY; BRAZIL to Mato Grosso and ARGENTINA in Misiones. [Honduras to Panama.] Forest.

49. HARPY EAGLE

Harpia harpyja

34-37". Head gray adorned with blackish, ashy tipped, divided crest and wide ruff. Uppersurface and chest blackish; rest of underparts white, thighs barred black. Tail black crossed by four ashy bars. Primaries noticeably banded black and white. From below: Underside of wings including wing coverts barred. Black breast band. Tail broad with three white bars and tip. Imm.: Head white, crest feathers with dark tips. Upperparts and breast paler than ad.

Tropical zone. GUIANAS; VENEZUELA; COLOMBIA s to BOLIVIA, nw ARGENTINA and BRAZIL s to São Paulo. [Mid. Amer.] Forest.

50. BLACK-AND-CHESTNUT EAGLE

Oroaetus isidori

25-29". Head with long, black crest. Head, throat and upperparts black, below chestnut rufous with black streaks. Thighs black, tarsus chestnut, feathered. From below: Wing coverts mottled with dusky, primaries unbarred, tips black, inner remiges lightly barred. Tail grayish with broad terminal black bar. Imm.: Upperparts brown, feathers pale-edged, crest tipped black. Lowerparts white. Tail marbled gray and brown

with three black bands. Not unlike 51 and 52 but rarely occurs in tropical zone.

Subtropical to temperate zone, occasionally near sea level. N VENEZUELA and COLOMBIA s through Andes to nw ARGENTINA. Forested mountain country.

51. BLACK-AND-WHITE HAWK-EAGLE

Spizastur melanoleucus

22-24". Head, neck and underparts white; lores, orbital region, short crest and crown patch black. Back black, wings brownish black. Tarsus feathered. Tail evenly barred black and grayish brown. From below: Wing coverts pure white, remiges lightly barred. Tail with four narrow black bars and wider subterminal bar. Imm.: Like ad. but above browner, wing coverts tipped white.

Tropical zone. GUIANAS; n and sw VENEZUELA; COLOMBIA in E Andes and in Meta; n and e BRAZIL s to Mato Grosso and Rio Grande do Sul; PARAGUAY; n ARGENTINA from Misiones to Tucumán. [Mid. Amer.] Forest, savanna, river courses.

52. ORNATE HAWK-EAGLE

Spizaetus ornatus *

23-25". Crown and long crest black. Above blackish. Throat white, bordered laterally by broad black band; nape, hindneck and sides of breast tawny rufous; center of breast white, rest of underparts and feathered tarsi boldly barred black and white. Tail ashy gray with four black bands (see also 15 imm.). From below: Wings narrowly barred dusky. Tail with five black bars. Imm.: Head and neck white, tinged cinnamon; underparts white, barred on sides and tarsi. Above grayish brown, tail broadly barred grayish and black.

Tropical, lower subtropical zones. GUIANAS; VENEZUELA and COLOMBIA south to e and w ECUADOR, e PERU, n BOLIVIA, PARAGUAY, BRAZIL to Rio Grande do Sul and ne ARGENTINA in Misiones. [Mid. Amer.] Forest.

Plate 43

53. BLACK HAWK-EAGLE

Spizaetus tyrannus *

25-28". Black. Base of long bushy crest feathers, spots on belly (sometimes) and bars on thighs and tibial feathers white. Tail long, black with three grayish brown bars.

Under wing coverts and undersurface of remiges prominently barred white. From below: Flight feathers sharply banded black and white. Underside of body black. Tail boldly banded black and white. Imm.: Brownish black above, crown mixed with white to buff, lower back to upper tail coverts barred white. Throat white; breast buffy streaked blackish, rest of underparts blackish mottled and barred with white. Thighs and tibia white barred black. Tail with five or six grayish bars.

Tropical zone. GUIANAS; n VENEZUELA; COLOMBIA; e ECUADOR s to BOLIVIA, PARAGUAY; BRAZIL to Rio Grande do Sul; ne ARGENTINA in Misiones. [Mid. Amer.] Forest and savanna.

54. NORTHERN HARRIER

Circus cyaneus*

18-21". Harriers differ from other hawks by possessing a facial ruff. Their tails are long and narrow. Head, neck, chest, upperparts and central tail feathers pale gray, outer remiges tipped dusky. Rump and underparts white, latter lightly spotted and barred rufous. Remiges basally white, distally black, tail feathers barred black. ♀: Above dark brown, crown and wing coverts streaked ferruginous, rump white. Below tawny buff with dark streaks on throat and breast. Tail grayish brown becoming buff toward outermost with four or five dark bars. Imm.: Like ♀ but paler below and more streaked.

Winter resident in COLOMBIA w of E Andes, casually in nw VENEZUELA. [Breeds in Northern Hemisphere. Winters from southern US through Mid. Amer. and W Indies; also Africa, s Asia.] Open country, marshes. Sails low over ground.

55. CINEREOUS HARRIER

Circus cinereus

17-20". Head, throat, upper breast and back light ashy gray; upper tail coverts white; central tail feathers like back with dark subterminal band, rest buffy with four dark bars. Lower breast and belly narrowly but conspicuously barred orange rufous and white. Underwing white, remiges tipped black. ♀: Head and upperparts blackish brown; rump white. Below closely barred orange rufous and white. Imm.: Sepia brown above with cinnamon margins to

feathers; breast rusty white with long reddish brown streaks; belly fulvous white spotted ferruginous, spots coalescing into bands on lower belly.

Open country to temperate zone. Generally distributed in w and s South America from COLOMBIA s through CHILE and ARGENTINA to Tierra del Fuego and e through PARAGUAY to se BRAZIL and URUGUAY. [Falkland Is.] Marshes, grassland.

56. LONG-WINGED HARRIER

Circus buffoni

18-24". Upperparts and breast band blackish brown. Forehead, eyebrow, throat, breast and belly white with a few dark shaft streaks. Remiges gray, barred black. Upper tail coverts white, tail light gray with five black bars, outer feathers with rufous borders to black bars. Dark phase: Sooty black, forehead and eyebrow white. Upper tail coverts barred black and white. Thighs and under tail coverts dark chestnut. Wings and tail as in normal phase. ♀: In light phase browner above and more heavily spotted below than ♂; thighs tawny. In dark phase like ♂. Imm.: Light phase resembles ♀ ad. but more heavily streaked below. Dark phase: Dusky with rufous thighs and under tail coverts.

GUIANAS; VENEZUELA; COLOMBIA. E BRAZIL s of the Amazon to Rio Grande do Sul and Mato Grosso; URUGUAY, PARAGUAY; e BOLIVIA; ARGENTINA to Tierra del Fuego. Central CHILE (very rare). Trinidad (nesting). [Juan Fernández Is.] Open country, marshy ranch lands.

57. CRANE HAWK

Geranospiza caerulescens*

17-21". Legs very long, salmon; tail long. Distinctive white bar parallel to body on underside of wing. Plain blue gray (or regularly and narrowly banded below and on under wing coverts with white, upper wing coverts irregularly barred, 1). Tail black with two broad white bars. Imm.: Like ad. above. Throat whitish, underparts mixed gray and fawn, under tail coverts ochraceous, bars on tail all or partly ochraceous (or like ad., 1, but more heavily banded). From below white bar on wing is distinctive.

Tropical zone. VENEZUELA and COLOMBIA south to nw PERU and n BRAZIL. E and s BRAZIL, PARAGUAY, e BOLIVIA and ARGENTINA s to La Rioja and Buenos Aires, 1. [Mid. Amer.] Mangroves, swamps, plantations, near water. Forages on tree trunks.

Plate 43

Family PANDIONIDAE   OSPREYS

Ospreys live near the seacoast or inland on large bodies of water. They feed on fish which they catch by plunging after them feet first. They are recognizable in flight by their strongly angled wings when sailing.

Ospreys are found in South America year-round but do not breed there.

OSPREY

Pandion haliaetus *

20-24". Somewhat crested. Above dark brown. Head, neck and underparts white, crown and hindneck and stripe through eye dark brown. Under wing coverts white, remiges barred, dusky patch at bend of wing. Underside of tail pale with five to seven dark bars. ♀: Similar but chest somewhat spotted. Imm.: Similar but feathers of back pale-edged and chest more heavily spotted.

Tropical to temperate zone. Mainly winter resident south to n CHILE, n ARGENTINA and URUGUAY. Aruba to Tobago. [Worldwide except arctic regions. In Western Hemisphere breeds from Alaska and Canada to Florida and Br. Honduras.] Coastal and inland waters.

Plate 21

Family FALCONIDAE   FALCONS, CARACARAS

Falcons differ from accipiters by pointed, rather than rounded, and narrower wings. In flight they soar much less and often hover with rapidly beating wings while looking down for prey. They feed on small mammals, birds, snakes and insects. Caracaras differ from Falcons by their bare, often brightly colored throat and facial region. Some are partly terrestrial.

AID TO IDENTIFICATION (adults)

Dark above, below white to buff 1, 2, 3b, 4, 9

Barred rufous and black above, wings gray 23

Barred below 2, 3b, 5, 6b, 10, 15, 17, 18

Streaked below 11b, 14, 16, 17, 18, 22, 23

Black and white 2, 11b, 12b, 13b

Black above, below largely chestnut 19, 20, (or tawny) 21

Skin of face and throat red or yellow 11b, 12b, 13b, 14b

1. LAUGHING FALCON

Herpetotheres cachinnans *

18-22". Crown, hindneck, upper mantle and underparts buffy white, crown streaked black; sides of head and nuchal collar blackish. Back chocolate brown, upper tail coverts white to buff. Tail rounded, narrowly barred black and buff. Imm.: Like ad. but feathers of upperparts broadly pale-edged and tail with fewer bars. Light portions of plumage white rather than buff.

Tropical, subtropical zones. Generally distributed to nw PERU and BOLIVIA, PARAGUAY, BRAZIL to São Paulo, and n ARGENTINA. [Mid. Amer.] Feeds on snakes. Forest edge, open woodland, riverbanks, cerrado.

Plate 43

2. COLLARED FOREST-FALCON

Micrastur semitorquatus *

18-24". Face with facial ruff, not as distinct as in harriers. Tail long, somewhat wedge-shaped. Upperparts sooty brown, nuchal collar, sides of head and underparts white (or tawny in tawny phase; or all brown in dark phase). Underside of wing barred; tail long, blackish with three or four narrow white bars and white tip, outer feathers with six bars. Legs long, yellow or greenish yellow. Imm.: Upperparts dark brown or barred dark brown and amber brown in dark phase. Tail blackish with five narrow white bars and white tip.

Tropical, subtropical zones. Generally distributed to nw PERU and BOLIVIA, PARAGUAY, BRAZIL to São Paulo, and n ARGENTINA from Tucumán to Corrientes. [Mid. Amer.] Forest, occasionally mangroves.

3. BUCKLEY'S FOREST-FALCON

Micrastur buckleyi

Almost exactly like 2, but smaller with much shorter tarsus, 55-65 mm. vs. 78-87 mm., and tail with four instead of six white bands on outer feathers.

Tropical, subtropical zones. E ECUADOR; ne PERU. Forest.

4. SLATY-BACKED FOREST-FALCON

Micrastur mirandollei *

14-16". Above slaty gray, darker on head;

below creamy white. Tail black, tipped white, with three narrow white (or ashy, 1) bars. Imm.: Like ad. but underparts buffier, feathers edged dusky.

Tropical zone. GUIANAS; VENEZUELA s of the Orinoco; e COLOMBIA. E PERU; nw BOLIVIA; Amazonian BRAZIL and in Bahía and Espírito Santo. W COLOMBIA to Buenaventura, 1. [Costa Rica, Panama, 1.] Forest.

5. BARRED FOREST-FALCON

Micrastur ruficollis *

(Includes *M. gilvicollis,* treated as distinct species in *Sp. Bds. S. Amer.*)

13-15". Rufous phase: Rufous brown above, darker on crown. Throat and breast rufous, rest of underparts evenly banded black and white. Wings like back; tail black with three or four narrow white bands. Gray phase: Above gray, wings with brownish cast; below banded black and white, generally with suffusion of brown on sides of breast. Intermediates between the two phases occur. Imm.: In rufous phase much like ad. but throat white; in gray phase dark brown above, below buff barred black, bars widely spaced or plain buff unbarred.

Tropical, subtropical zones. N VENEZUELA; COLOMBIA; ECUADOR; PERU; BOLIVIA; PARAGUAY; e and s BRAZIL from Piauí to Mato Grosso and Rio Grande do Sul; n ARGENTINA. Rufous phase occurs only in s part of range. Forest.

Plate 43

6. PLUMBEOUS FOREST-FALCON

Micrastur plumbeus

(Treated as a race of *M. gilvicollis* in *Sp. Bds. S. Amer.*)

Above pale slate gray. Tail black with one conspicuous white median bar. Throat and breast pale gray finely barred black, center of abdomen white. Much like gray phase of 5, but tail much shorter with single bar. Imm.: Much like 5, but tail shorter.

Tropical zone. Sw COLOMBIA and nw ECUADOR. Forest.

7. BLACK CARACARA

Daptrius ater

17-19". Black with greenish gloss. Tail

rather long, white basally. Bare skin of face and throat orange red, sometimes yellow on throat; legs orange to red. Imm.: Less glossy than ad., feathers of breast tipped buff. Basal two-thirds of tail white with three or four black bars. Skin of face and throat lemon yellow.

Tropical zone. E of Andes south to e PERU, n BOLIVIA and BRAZIL south to n Mato Grosso and n Maranhão. Feeds mostly on carrion, fruit and insects. Savanna, forest near rivers.

8. RED-THROATED CARACARA

Daptrius americanus *

19-22". Glossy black, sides of head streaked white. Belly, thighs and under tail coverts white. Skin of face, throat and legs vermilion. Tail all black, longer than in 7. Imm.: Like ad. but face more feathered.

Tropical forest. Generally distributed south to w ECUADOR, e PERU and BRAZIL to Mato Grosso and São Paulo. [Mid. Amer.] Feeds mostly on fruit and larvae of wasps.

9. YELLOW-HEADED CARACARA

Milvago chimachima *

16-18". Head, neck and underparts buff, black stripe behind eye. Above brown, feathers pale-edged. Tail buffy with many wavy dark bars and black tip. From below: Wing coverts pale; outer remiges pale with dark tips, inner remiges lightly barred. Imm.: Like ad. but mottled and barred below with chocolate; crown streaked.

Tropical and subtropical grasslands, often with cattle. Mainly e of Andes s to BOLIVIA, n ARGENTINA and URUGUAY. W of Andes in COLOMBIA. Curaçao. Chacachacare I. [Panama.]

10. CHIMANGO CARACARA

Milvago chimango *

15-17". Cinnamon brown (or rufous brown, 1), narrowly streaked dark brown on crown and nape, feathers of upperparts pale-edged. Upper tail coverts white; tail buffy white finely freckled and barred dusky with wide subterminal dusky band and pale tip. From below differs from 9 by darker wing coverts, thus pale area at end of wing more prominent. Imm.: Much like ad. but tinged rufous, subterminal tail band indistinct.

PARAGUAY; BRAZIL in Rio Grande do Sul; URUGUAY; ARGENTINA throughout. CHILE from Tarapacá to Cape Horn, 1. Accompanies cattle, often near water.

11. CARUNCULATED CARACARA

Phalcoboenus carunculatus

20-22". Head with short curled crest, neck and back bluish black. Below striped black and white. Remiges tipped white. Belly, thighs, upper and under tail coverts and under wing coverts white. Upper tail coverts long, white. Tail black, tipped white. Skin of face, throat and legs orange red. Imm.: Pale brown, rump buff. Outer tail feathers deep buff. Face duller than ad., legs dusky.

Temperate, páramo zones. COLOMBIA from s part of Central Andes to Andes of ECUADOR. Open mtn. slopes, sometimes with cattle.

Plate 22

12. MOUNTAIN CARACARA

Phalcoboenus megalopterus

19-21". Head without curled crest. Blue black with white shoulders, belly, flanks, tips of remiges and upper tail coverts. Tail black, tipped white. Face reddish orange, bill bluish tipped yellow. Legs orange yellow. Imm.: Very like 11 but considerably darker. Face paler than ad. Bill black, legs dusky.

Temperate, páramo zones from nw PERU s to Talca in CHILE, w BOLIVIA and nw ARGENTINA to Catamarca. Remote mountain slopes.

13. WHITE-THROATED CARACARA

Phalcoboenus albogularis

19-21". Crown feathers curled. Above black; upper tail coverts white. Tail black, white tipped. Below white, flanks with dusky spots. Face and legs yellow. Imm.: Much like 11 but darker, crown feathers less curly.

CHILE from Aysén, and ARGENTINA from Neuquén, to Tierra del Fuego. Open mountain slopes, low woodland.

14. STRIATED CARACARA

Phalcoboenus australis

21-23". Above and below blackish brown with pale-streaked nuchal collar, throat, breast and belly. Neck feathers long, narrow and pointed. Thighs amber brown. Tail black, tipped white. Face and legs bright orange yellow. Imm.: Dark smoky brown with pale nuchal collar and plain ochre tail. Face and legs light gray.

S ARGENTINA in Tierra del Fuego and Staten I.; CHILE on islands s of Beagle Channel. [Falkland Is.] Rocky coasts, scavenges around sea bird colonies.

15. CRESTED CARACARA

Polyborus plancus *

20-24". Crown, flat crest black. Sides of head, neck and throat buffy white. Back blackish, barred buffy white (or barred on mantle only, 1). Breast barred like back. Belly and thighs blackish. Tail buffy white with numerous dusky bars and broad black terminal band. Primaries mostly buffy, narrowly barred. Face orange red, legs long, yellow. Imm.: Mostly pale brown, feathers splotched and edged buffy white. Wings and tail as in ad. Face and legs like ad. but duller.

Tropical to temperate zone. From GUIANAS, VENEZUELA and COLOMBIA to nw PERU and Amazonia n of the Amazon, 1; thence s to Tierra del Fuego. Aruba to Trinidad. [Southern US, s to Panama; Cuba.] Open country, sparsely wooded savanna.

16. SPOT-WINGED FALCONET

Spiziapteryx circumcinctus

11". Above ashy brown, back with dark streaks; eyebrow, nuchal collar, rump and upper tail coverts white. Wing coverts spotted white. Below dull white with blackish streaks. Remiges and tail with white spots, central tail feathers uniform dark brown. Imm.: Like ad.

PARAGUAY (100 km. w of Orloff); w ARGENTINA from Salta to La Pampa, acc. eastward. Dry open country with scattered trees and cacti.

Plate 22

17. PEREGRINE FALCON

Falco peregrinus *

15-20". Above dark blue gray, darkest on crown, inconspicuously barred; broad moustachial streak blackish, hindcheek white (or blackish, 1). Throat and breast white to buff, sides of belly barred gray. Tail like

back with five or six dark bars and white tip. Imm.: Above brown, below buffy white broadly streaked dusky.

Breeds from Santa Cruz, ARGENTINA, and Atacama, CHILE, to Tierra del Fuego; winters n to URUGUAY, and through Andes occasionally as far n as COLOMBIA (June-July), 1. [Falkland Is., 1.] Winter resident (Oct.-Mar.), s as far as Buenos Aires, ARGENTINA and Valdivia, CHILE. Aruba to Trinidad and Tobago. [Breeds in N Amer. from Alaska to Mexico. Also in Old World.] Coastal lagoons, rocky seacoast, open savanna.

18. PALLID FALCON

Falco kreyenborgi

Much like 17 but much paler. Head pale ochraceous, streaked and washed with gray and black on crown. Back clear gray sharply barred with black. Below white sparingly flecked and barred and shaft-streaked with black on sides of belly. Tail with about ten sharp, buffy gray and black bars, conspicuous white tip. ♀: Similar but upper back washed ochraceous. Imm.: Crown cinnamon buff, streaked blackish. Back brownish black, barred deep buff to tawny, upper tail coverts broadly edged white. Cheeks, throat and underparts creamy white, moustachial streak black, lower breast with blackish brown streaks. Tail brownish black with buffy paired spots forming about ten uneven, pale bars. (Description after Stresemann and Amadon.)

From Río Negro, ARGENTINA, to islands s of Tierra del Fuego, CHILE. Plains country, cliffs.

19. ORANGE-BREASTED FALCON

Falco deiroleucus

13-15". Above black, feathers bordered slate gray. Sides of head black, throat buffy white; chest, belly, thighs and under tail coverts chestnut; lower breast black, barred and spotted rufous buff. Tail black with three narrow white bars. Imm.: Dark brown above, chest streaked black, rest of underparts and flanks black, spotted white. Tail as in ad.

Tropical, subtropical zones. GUIANAS west to w COLOMBIA in Cauca, and e of Andes to n ARGENTINA. Trinidad. [Mid. Amer.] Coasts and forest edge, mountain forest.

20. BAT FALCON

Falco rufigularis *

9-12". Like 19 but without rufous chest; lower breast black, narrowly barred white; tail black with four or five narrow, slaty bars. Size smaller. Imm.: Similar to ad. but duller with abdomen sooty brown.

Tropical zone. GUIANAS w to COLOMBIA and w ECUADOR and south to s BRAZIL, BOLIVIA and n ARGENTINA. Trinidad. [Mid. Amer.] Forest edge, dead trees in clearings.

Plate 43

21. APLOMADO FALCON

Falco femoralis *

15-18". Crown blackish, eyebrow tawny buff continued around back of head to form nuchal collar. Moustachial streak and space behind eye black. Upperparts gray, tail with six or seven conspicuous white bars. Sides of neck, throat and underparts tawny buff with broad, often broken black band across belly, feathers narrowly edged white. Imm.: Like ad. but brown above, breast heavily streaked brown, and band across belly more solid and black.

Tropical to temperate zone. GUYANA; n and se VENEZUELA; COLOMBIA; e and w ECUADOR s through ARGENTINA and CHILE to Tierra del Fuego. Margarita I., Trinidad. [Sw US to Panama. Acc. Falkland Is.] Dry savanna, arid country, plains.

22. MERLIN (or Pigeon Hawk)

Falco columbarius *

10-13". Above dark slaty blue, narrowly streaked black. Below white to buffy, streaked brown to rufous brown. Tail blue gray with three or four black bars and broad black subterminal band and white tip. ♀: Similar, but dark brown above, upper tail coverts and rump gray. Imm.: Similar to ♀ but without gray rump or upper tail coverts.

Winter resident (Oct.-May). Tropical to temperate zone. N VENEZUELA; COLOMBIA w of Andes; ECUADOR; n PERU s to Libertad. Acc. in Bahía, BRAZIL. Aruba to Trinidad and Tobago. [Breeds in N Amer. from Alaska and Labrador to Michigan and the Dakotas. Also in Eurasia, wintering to n Africa, n India, s China.] Open woods, marshes, seacoast.

23. AMERICAN KESTREL (or American Sparrow Hawk)

Falco sparverius *

9-11". Center of crown chestnut surrounded by gray. Throat and sides of head white, sides of head with two vertical black stripes and black spot on ear coverts. Hindneck and back chestnut, barred black. Tail rufous with broad subterminal black bar and white tip. Wings blue gray. Undersurface buffy white to pinkish to cinnamon, lightly to heavily spotted black. ♀: Differs from ♂ by wings like back, crown rufous, streaked black. Below broadly streaked rusty brown, tail with numerous black bars. Imm.: Like ♀.

Tropical to temperate zone. Throughout to Tierra del Fuego except in heavily forested regions. Aruba to Trinidad. [Breeds in N Amer. to Nicaragua and W Indies. N Amer. migrants reach Panama. Juan Fernández Is., resident. Acc. Falkland Is.] Open country, savanna woodland.

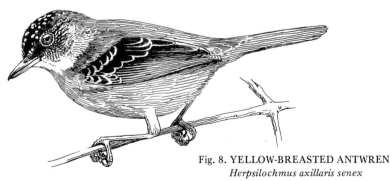

Fig. 8. YELLOW-BREASTED ANTWREN
Herpsilochmus axillaris senex
p. 240

Order GALLIFORMES

Family CRACIDAE

CHACHALACAS, GUANS AND CURASSOWS

These large, gregarious, turkey-like game birds, 17" to 38" long, differ from other members of the order by each possessing a well-developed hind toe. Chiefly arboreal, they are very good to eat and are assiduously hunted.

They feed on fruit and vegetable matter, and roost and nest in trees; indeed, guans spend most of their time in the forest canopy. They, like the chachalacas, which inhabit thickets, are clothed in shades of bronzy brown to grayish olive or green, but differ in possessing flat crests and dewlaps or wattles. The sexes in both are similar.

The curassows live on the forest floor but quickly fly into trees if disturbed. Males are usually almost all black, and the heads of some species are adorned with casques or bony wattles, and in *Crax* are handsomely crested. Females are often barred, their color sometimes brown.

AID TO IDENTIFICATION

Upperparts olive to grayish olive, belly rufous or brown:
Primaries and tail without chestnut (legs dusky) 1, 11, 14; (legs red) 8, 9a, 10, 12b, 15b, 16b, 17c, 18c, 19, 25b

Outer tail feathers partly chestnut 2b, 3, 4a; (or white) 4, 20b

Primaries chestnut 5a, 6b, 7, (or white) 13b

All or mainly dark glossy green or purplish:
With white crest 21, 22, 23c, (no crest) 24b

Black and white:
Head with conspicuous recurved crest, plumage black and white (tail all black) 26, 27, 31, 32a, 33, 34b; (tail tipped white) 28, 29a, 30a; (head with bony casque) 36a, 37b

Chestnut and black or buff and black 27c, 28, 29a, 31, 32a, 35a, 36a
38; (head with bony casque) 36a

1. LITTLE CHACHALACA

*Ortalis motmot**

19" (or 17", 1). Head reddish chestnut, back and wings brown; underparts gray. Four central tail feathers brown strongly glossed greenish, rest chestnut.

Tropical zone. GUIANAS; VENEZUELA n of the Orinoco. E Amazonian BRAZIL n of the Amazon from rio Negro, s of the Amazon from rio Tapajós, 1. Thick scrub.

2. BUFF-BROWED CHACHALACA

Ortalis superciliaris

21". Eyebrow buffy or whitish. Head, upper back, throat and breast brown, feathers pale-edged; lower back and rump rufous. Belly pale gray to whitish. Primaries edged light gray. Tail bronzy olive, the three outer feathers mostly chestnut.

Ne BRAZIL from Pará to Maranhão, n Piauí and extreme n Goiás. Thick scrub.

3. SPECKLED CHACHALACA

*Ortalis guttata**

21". Top and sides of head gray; back olive brown (or olive gray, 1) becoming rufescent on rump. Throat and breast dark brown, feathers with conspicuous white tips (or narrowly edged all around with white, 1). Lower breast and belly pale ashy gray (or white, 2). Tail as in 2.

Tropical zone. COLOMBIA in Cauca and Magdalena Valleys, 1. COLOMBIA east of E Andes south to n and central BOLIVIA, nw Amazonian BRAZIL. E BRAZIL from Pernambuco to Espírito Santo, 2; in Santa Catarina and Rio Grande do Sul. Thick scrub.

Plate 44

4. RUFOUS-VENTED CHACHALACA

*Ortalis ruficauda**

21". Top and sides of head plumbeous gray. Back olive brown, grayer on upper mantle. Throat and upper breast gray becoming paler on abdomen; flanks and under tail coverts rufous. Tail dark bronzy green, all but central feathers broadly tipped chestnut (or white, 1).

Tropical, occasionally subtropical zone. VENEZUELA n of the Orinoco w to Falcón, Lara, Táchira, Apure and nw Arauca; ne COLOMBIA. Guajira Peninsula, COLOMBIA, and w Zulia, VENEZUELA, 1. Margarita I.; Tobago. Forest edge, scrub.

5. CHESTNUT-WINGED CHACHALACA

*Ortalis garrula**

21" (or 18", 1) Primaries chestnut. Top and sides of head and hindneck rufous (or gray, 1). Back olive brown (or brown, 1). Throat and breast pale olive brown, lower breast and belly white (or throat and breast chestnut brown, abdomen buffy brown, 1). Tail dark bronzy green, all but central feathers broadly tipped white (or dark buff, 1).

Tropical zone. N COLOMBIA from w base of Santa Marta Mts. w to lower Cauca and upper Sinú Valleys; extreme nw Chocó, 1 (*cinereiceps*, Gray-headed Chachalaca, sometimes treated as a species). [Nicaragua southward.] Dense undergrowth, open woodland.

6. RUFOUS-HEADED CHACHALACA

Ortalis erythroptera

22". Differs from 5 by head, neck and upper breast dark chestnut, under tail cov-

erts light chestnut, and chestnut tip to outer tail feathers much wider and deeper in color.

Tropical zone. W ECUADOR from Esmeraldas s to Tumbes and Piura, PERU. Arid scrub.

7. CHACO CHACHALACA

*Ortalis canicollis**

22". Forehead black; crown and hindneck gray; throat silvery gray. Back grayish olive, feathers pale-edged, lower back and rump tinged rufescent. Breast gray, belly paler, under tail coverts chestnut. Central tail feathers gray, the outer two or three with broad chestnut tips (or darker and browner throughout, without pale margins to dorsal feathers, 1).

Tropical zone. Se BOLIVIA s to Córdoba and Santa Fe, ARGENTINA. Basin of rio Paraguai in sw Mato Grosso, BRAZIL, 1. Trees with thick scrub below.

8. MARAIL GUAN

*Penelope marail**

33". Mainly dark bluish green. Forehead, sides of crown and cheeks dark gray, feathers of hindneck and mantle indistinctly edged gray, feathers of breast margined white, belly brown. Outer tail feathers black, glossed purple. Legs red.

Tropical zone. GUIANAS; VENEZUELA s of the Orinoco; BRAZIL n of the Amazon e of rio Negro. Thick to somewhat open forest.

9. CRESTED GUAN

*Penelope purpurascens**

36". Crest bushy, the feathers broad without pale margins. General color dark olive brown, feathers of upper mantle indistinctly margined with gray, breast feathers broadly edged laterally with white. Belly and lower back chestnut. Central tail feathers like back, outer ones blackish. Legs dark red.

Tropical zone. VENEZUELA n of the Orinoco; most of COLOMBIA but not s of Boyacá in the e or in Nariño in the w. West ECUADOR. [Mid. Amer.] Forest.

Plate 44

10. SPIX'S GUAN

*Penelope jacquacu**

35". Crest feathers much narrower and

longer than in 9 and margined pale gray. Back and breast olive brown (or bluish green, 1), feathers edged laterally with white (or all around narrowly with gray, 2). Lower back brown (or rufescent, 2); belly extensively rufous (or dark brown, 1). Legs red.

Tropical zone. GUYANA and ne Bolívar, VENEZUELA, 1; remainder of the country s of the Orinoco w to e COLOMBIA, ECUADOR and PERU to n and central BOLIVIA. W Amazonian BRAZIL e to rios Negro and Madeira. Subtropical zone, slopes above Cauca Valley, COLOMBIA, 2 (*perspicax,* Cauca Guan, sometimes treated as a species). Forest.

11. DUSKY-LEGGED GUAN

*Penelope obscura ***

35". Differs from 10 by having only the feathers of forepart of crest pale-edged, lower breast and belly dark brown instead of rufous, and legs blackish horn instead of red.

Se BRAZIL from Minas Gerais, to URUGUAY, PARAGUAY, e BOLIVIA, nw ARGENTINA up to 6000 ft. Forest.

12. BAUDO GUAN

Penelope ortoni

26". Crest short, not well developed. Chiefly dark bronzy brown, feathers of breast and belly broadly margined with white. Feet and legs light red.

Tropical, occasionally lower subtropical zone. W COLOMBIA from upper río Atrato s to Chimbo, w ECUADOR. Forest.

13. WHITE-WINGED GUAN

Penelope albipennis

24". Differed from all other guans in having white outer primaries.

Formerly nw PERU in Piura (extinct).

14. RUSTY-MARGINED GUAN

*Penelope superciliaris ***

27". Differs from all other species by having scapulars, upper wing coverts and secondaries margined with rufous. General plumage dark olive bronze, breast feathers edged all around with grayish white. Buff or white eyebrow present in some races. Legs dusky.

BRAZIL s of the Amazon from rio Madeira eastward. PARAGUAY e of río Paraguay; ne ARGENTINA in Misiones. Forest.

15. ANDEAN GUAN

*Penelope montagnii ***

24". Throat more feathered than in preceding species. Feathers of crest long, narrow, somewhat pointed, edged pale gray. General plumage bronzy brown (or bronzy olive, 1), lower breast and belly rufescent. Feathers at sides of head, neck, upper mantle, breast and belly edged all around with grayish white giving scaled appearance (or only margined laterally giving streaked appearance; below eye more or less solid white, 1). Legs pinkish red.

Subtropical to temperate zone. VENEZUELA from Trujillo w to Central Andes of COLOMBIA, s to ECUADOR. PERU to BOLIVIA and ARGENTINA in Salta, 1. Forest.

16. RED-FACED GUAN

Penelope dabbenei

31". Rather like 11 but instantly distinguishable by pale pinkish flesh instead of blackish horn legs, and red instead of dark blue facial skin. Somewhat paler and browner in color, considerably smaller in size.

Subtropical zone. Se BOLIVIA and nw ARGENTINA in Jujuy. Forest.

17. WHITE-BROWED GUAN

Penelope jacucaca

28". Crest black, feathers long and narrow. Forehead and broad eyebrow white. General plumage warm brown, slightly glossed olive above. Wing coverts, scapulars and breast feathers edged whitish. Legs red.

Drier portions of ne BRAZIL in Ceará, w Paraiba, s Piauí and Bahía interior. Caatinga.

18. CHESTNUT-BELLIED GUAN

Penelope ochrogaster

28". Crest dull reddish brown, feathers faintly edged paler; very narrow eyebrow present but not prominent. Upperparts olive brown, wing coverts and upper back feathers inconspicuously pale-edged. Breast dark brown gradually becoming ferruginous on belly and chestnut on thighs and under tail coverts. Wings and tail with strong coppery bronze luster. Legs red.

Central BRAZIL in w Minas Gerais, Goiás and Mato Grosso. Forest.

19. WHITE-CRESTED GUAN

Penelope pileata

28″. Crest white, tinged buffy; feathers long and hairy in texture. Hindneck and upper mantle chestnut; rest of back, wings and uppersurface of tail dark, glossy olive green; wing coverts and mantle feathers edged white. Underparts bright chestnut, feathers of neck and breast edged laterally with white. Legs red.

BRAZIL s of the Amazon from lower rio Madeira e to lower rio Tapajós. Forest.

20. BAND-TAILED GUAN

Penelope argyrotis *

24″. The only guan with pale-tipped tail. General plumage bronzy olive, tinged rufescent on belly. Crest feathers very long and narrow, edged whitish. Feathers of mantle and breast edged laterally with white; lower back and rump plain rufescent brown. Tail bronzy brown, all feathers with diffused dull rufous or buffy white tips, (or similar but conspicuous eyebrow, sides of head whitish, general color browner, 1).

Upper tropical and subtropical zones. VENEZUELA n of the Orinoco w to Santa Marta Mts. and n portion of e slope of E Andes of COLOMBIA. W. slope of Andes of ECUADOR south to 7°s in nw PERU, 1 (*barbata*, Bearded Guan, sometimes treated as a species). Forest.

21. BLUE-THROATED PIPING-GUAN

Pipile pipile *

(Includes *Pipile cumanensis* of *Sp. Bds. S. Amer.*)

24″. Crest white, feathers dark-shafted. General plumage glossy purplish brown (or bluish green, 1; or olive green, 2). Wing coverts extensively white, upper breast streaked white. Skin of face, throat and dewlap bright cobalt blue (or dewlap replaced by slim, pendulous caruncle about 1¼″ long, 2). Legs red.

Tropical zone. Trinidad. GUIANAS, s VENEZUELA, se COLOMBIA, e ECUADOR, e PERU and nw BRAZIL, 1. BOLIVIA, PARAGUAY, central and probably s Mato Grosso, BRAZIL, 2. Forest.

Plate 1

22. RED-THROATED PIPING-GUAN

Pipile cujubi *

(Includes *nattereri*, listed under *P. cumanensis* of *Sp. Bds. S. Amer.*)

Much like 21 but dewlap bright red; less white on wing coverts.

Amazonian BRAZIL s of the Amazon from rio Purús e to Belém region and south to n Goiás and Mato Grosso. Probably n BOLIVIA. Forest.

23. BLACK-FRONTED PIPING-GUAN

Pipile jacutinga

Differs from 21 and 22 by forehead, upper throat and sides of head covered by dense, velvety, black feathers. Dewlap red. Upperparts strongly glossed rich violet blue, lower parts less glossy and violaceous, and conspicuously streaked white. Legs red.

E BRAZIL from s Bahía s to Rio Grande do Sul, e PARAGUAY and Misiones and Corrientes, ARGENTINA. Forest.

24. WATTLED GUAN

Aburria aburri

28″. Uniform black, glossed bronze green. Skin of lower throat and pendant caruncle yellowish white. Cere light blue; legs pale yellow.

Upper tropical and subtropical zones. Nw VENEZUELA from Mérida e to mtns. of COLOMBIA southward, w of Andes, to about 7°s in ECUADOR and e of them to Junín, PERU. Forest.

25. SICKLE-WINGED GUAN

Chamaepetes goudotii *

25″. Whole head, neck, uppersurface, wings and tail bronze green (or front of neck rufescent 1; or feathers of head, throat and chest margined with ashy gray, 2). Underparts mostly rufous chestnut. Outer primaries narrow, curved.

Upper tropical to temperate zone. COLOMBIA in Santa Marta Mts., 1. COLOMBIAN Andes to w ECUADOR. E ECUADOR and ne PERU, 1; Huánuco and Junín, 2. Forest.

Plate 1

26. BLACK CURASSOW

Crax alector

35″. Crest prominent, feathers curled at tip. Black with bluish violet sheen, belly and under tail coverts white. Tail black. Base of bill yellow to orange with no knobs or swelling. Legs bluish gray. ♀: Similar to ♂ but crest feathers with a few white spots and bars.

Tropical zone. GUIANAS; VENEZUELA s of the Orinoco and in the delta; e COLOMBIA in Meta and Vichada; n BRAZIL from rio Negro east. Forest.

27. RED-BILLED CURASSOW

Crax blumenbachii

Very like 26 but smaller; plumage glossed green. Bill smaller, bright red at base and on swellings on sides of mandible; legs pink. ♀: Mainly black, crest barred white. Wing coverts vermiculated chestnut; belly cinnamon. Tail black, median feathers vermiculated chestnut at base.

Coastal BRAZIL from s Bahía and e Minas Gerais to Rio de Janeiro and Espírito Santo. Now extinct except in Espírito Santo and Bahía. Forest.

28. BARE-FACED CURASSOW

Crax fasciolata *

33". Differs at a glance from 27 by white, terminal tail band. Base of bill sulphur yellow; legs dull vermilion. ♀: Crest feathers white, tipped black (or black narrowly banded with white, 1). Head, neck and upper breast black, latter barred with white; rest of underparts ochraceous buff. Upper back black, barred ochraceous; lower back mixed buff and black. Wing coverts ochraceous, barred black; wings and tail black barred white, tail with broad white tip (or upper back black; rest of back, wing coverts and remiges black with narrow, wavy black lines; sides of body barred with black; tail black, sometimes with few wavy white lines at sides, broadly tipped white, 1).

Tropical zone. BRAZIL in Pará from rio Tocantins eastward to n Maranhão, 1; s through Goiás, w Minas Gerais and w Paraná to Mato Grosso, PARAGUAY, e BOLIVIA and ne ARGENTINA to Formosa and Chaco. Forest.

Plate 1

29. BLUE-BILLED CURASSOW

Crax alberti

36". Black with little sheen. Belly, under tail coverts and terminal tail band white.

Base of bill and large bony swellings on sides of mandible light cobalt blue. Legs light pinkish violet. ♀: No swellings on mandible. Mainly black; crest, back, wings and tail narrowly (or broadly, 1) barred and tail broadly tipped with white, outer primaries chestnut. Breast chestnut shading to cinnamon on belly (or underparts barred black and white or black and buff, belly pale buff, primaries black, 1.) (1 = imm. plumage, "*Crax annulata.*")

Tropical zone. N COLOMBIA from w and n foothills of Santa Marta region, middle Magdalena to lower Cauca Valley and Gulf of Urabá. Forest.

30. YELLOW-KNOBBED CURASSOW

Crax daubentoni *

36". Differs from 29 by base of bill being bright yellow with large, yellow, bony knob at base of culmen and swellings at each side of mandible; crest feathers much longer. Legs gray. ♀: Like ♂ but crest feathers basally white; breast, sides and wing coverts narrowly barred with white. Bill dusky, without knobs or swellings.

Tropical zone. VENEZUELA n of the Orinoco west to e foothills of Santa Marta Mts. and in Arauca, COLOMBIA.

31. WATTLED CURASSOW

Crax globulosa

35". Black with strong green sheen; belly and under tail coverts white. Large, red, bony knob at base of culmen, cere yellow; mandible with two round, yellow swellings, the yellow mixed with red. ♀: Like ♂ but lower breast with fine, wavy rusty colored bars, belly and under tail coverts dark ochraceous. No knobs or swellings.

Tropical zone. Se COLOMBIA to ne PERU; n BOLIVIA; w Amazonian BRAZIL e to rios Negro and Madeira and in n Mato Grosso. Forest.

32. GREAT CURASSOW

Crax rubra *

38". Black; belly and under tail coverts white. Bill black, knob at base of culmen yellow, base of lower mandible yellow without swellings. ♀: Head and neck black thickly spotted white, crest barred black and white. Upperparts cinnamon rufous with variable amount of greenish black on upper mantle. Breast chestnut shading to cinnamon on belly. Wings and tail mottled, sometimes barred, with black. No knobs.

Tropical zone. Pacific slope of COLOMBIA e to Gulf of Urabá and upper Sinú Valley. [Mid. Amer.] Forest.

33. RAZOR-BILLED CURASSOW

Mitu mitu *

35". Bill red, narrow, compressed; culmen elevated, arched, and swollen above nostrils. Shiny blue black; crest flat but erectile; belly and under tail coverts light chestnut. Central tail feathers black, rest tipped white (or all feathers tipped white, 1). Legs red.

Littoral forests of BRAZIL in Alagoas and ne Bahía, where probably extinct. Se CO-LOMBIA on the Amazon (Puerto Nariño) and Amazonia s of the Amazon w to BOLIVIA and e PERU, 1. Forest, sometimes near streams.

34. SALVIN'S CURASSOW

Mitu salvini

35". Much like 33, but belly and under tail coverts white. Tail tipped white. Bill less arched and elevated and less swollen.

Tropical zone. Se COLOMBIA south to ne PERU. Forest.

Plate 44

35. LESSER RAZOR-BILLED CURASSOW

Mitu tomentosa

33". Differs from 33 mainly by scarcely developed crest and tail feathers tipped chestnut instead of white. Bill less elevated than in 34.

Tropical zone. GUYANA; VENEZUELA s of the Orinoco; se COLOMBIA and adjacent n BRAZIL. Forest.

36. HELMETED CURASSOW

Pauxi pauxi *

36". Large, bony, fig-shaped casque springing from forehead. Plumage mainly black with strong bottle green sheen, dorsal feathers broadly edged dull black, neck feathers black, plush like. Belly, under tail coverts and tip of tail white. Bill and legs red. Rufous phase (♀ only): Head and neck black, remainder of plumage mainly buffy brown, back feathers with subterminal black bars, wing coverts margined whitish. Wings and tail vermiculated black. Casque as in ♂.

Upper tropical and subtropical zones. Nw VENEZUELA from Miranda west to ne COLOMBIA in Perijá Mts. and n Norte de Santander. Forest.

Plate 44

37. HORNED CURASSOW

Pauxi unicornis

36". Casque cylindrical, horn-like 2.5" high. Feathers of hindneck tightly curled and shiny. Plumage mainly black with dull olive green gloss, black edges to dorsal feathers indistinct. Belly, under tail coverts and tip of tail white. Bill red, horn dark blue; legs rose colored.

Known from two specimens from the Yungas of Cochabamba, 2500 ft., BO-LIVIA, 1936. Recently collected on río Catacapes, upper río Beni, BOLIVIA (Cordier), and in Huánuco, e PERU, 1969 (Weske).

38. NOCTURNAL (or Rufous) CURASSOW

Nothocrax urumutum

26". Crown and long, flat crest black. Neck and underparts orange rufous. Back and tail vermiculated brown and black. Bill and legs red, skin above eye vivid lemon yellow.

Tropical zone. S VENEZUELA, se COLOMBIA south to e PERU; w BRAZIL e to rios Negro and Purús. Forest.

Family PHASIANIDAE   PARTRIDGES AND QUAILS

Quails and partridges belong to the pheasant family. Phasianidae reach their highest development in Asia and are poorly represented in the Americas. The most numerous group in South America are the wood-quails, found chiefly in forested country and scrub.

AID TO IDENTIFICATION

Throat differently colored from breast 1a, 4b, 6b, 7a, 8b, 9a, 10a, 13b

Breast and/or belly spotted or streaked 1a, 5a, 9a, 11b

Lower parts barred or scalloped 2. 13b

Underparts plain 3c, 6b, 7a, 12, with narrow band across breast 8

1. CRESTED BOBWHITE
Colinus cristatus*

9". Conspicuous sandy colored crest. Chin, forehead and ear coverts white to chestnut; hindneck and extreme upper back blackish spotted with white, rest of upperparts brown spotted and vermiculated with black. Breast chestnut, spotted with white (or unspotted, 1); rest of underparts cinnamon buff barred with black (or chestnut with white spots, 1). ♀: Above mixed brown and black, hindneck spotted with white, underparts somewhat like male but duller.

Tropical to temperate zone. GUIANAS; VENEZUELA; n COLOMBIA from Sinú Valley eastward; on e slope of E Andes, 1; n BRAZIL in upper rio Branco region and Amapá. Aruba, Curaçao. Margarita I. [Central and w Panama.] Campos, fields, open mountain slopes, semiarid scrub.

Plate 44

2. MARBLED WOOD-QUAIL
Odontophorus gujanensis*

11". Above chiefly dark brown vermiculated with black, sometimes grayish on upper mantle; inner remiges spotted with black and edged fulvous. Below dark brown inconspicuously spotted and barred with black and buff or ochraceous brown.

Tropical zone. GUIANAS; VENEZUELA; n and e COLOMBIA; e ECUADOR south to e BOLIVIA. Amazonian BRAZIL s of the Amazon in Amazonas to n Mato Grosso. [Costa Rica, Panama.] Forest undergrowth; scrub.

3. SPOT-WINGED WOOD-QUAIL
Odontophorus capueira*

11". Top of head rufescent brown spotted fulvous; upper back grayish brown streaked with white and spotted with black, lower back paler and almost uniform. Sides of head and entire underparts gray.

E BRAZIL in Ceará and Alagoas, and from Bahía s to Rio Grande do Sul and se Mato Grosso; PARAGUAY; ARGENTINA in Misiones. Caatinga; forest.

4. RUFOUS-FRONTED WOOD-QUAIL
Odontophorus erythrops*

11". Forehead, sides of head and underparts chestnut; throat and foreneck black with white gorget. Upperparts blackish brown finely vermiculated with sandy.

Tropical zone. W COLOMBIA e to lower Cauca Valley and south in w ECUADOR to Loja. Forest.

5. BLACK-FRONTED WOOD-QUAIL
Odontophorus atrifrons*

12". Forehead, cheeks and throat black; hindcrown and nape rufous brown. Mantle brown finely vermiculated with sandy, lower back pale sandy brown; wing coverts edged rufous. Breast brown variegated with white, center of lower breast and belly cinnamon buff, streaked black. ♀: Similar but underparts much more rufescent.

Upper tropical and subtropical zones. VENEZUELA in Perijá Mts.; COLOMBIA in Santa Marta Mts. and n end of E Andes. Forest.

6. DARK-BACKED WOOD-QUAIL
Odontophorus melanonotus

11". Above dark brown very finely vermiculated with rufous; throat and breast chestnut, rest of underparts brown vermiculated with black.

Lower subtropical zone. Nw ECUADOR.

7. CHESTNUT WOOD-QUAIL
Odontophorus hyperythrus

11". Differs mainly from 6 by being much paler above, feathers of back and inner remiges with conspicuous black spots, and by white facial area. ♀: Differs from male by having only throat and extreme upper breast chestnut, rest of underparts dark gray.

Subtropical zone. Andes of COLOMBIA. Forest.

8. RUFOUS-BREASTED WOOD-QUAIL

Odontophorus speciosus *

11". Above like 7 but darker. Eyebrow mixed black and white; throat and sides of neck black; breast and underparts mostly chestnut. ♀: Differs from male by dark gray underparts with narrow chestnut band across breast.

Tropical zone. E ECUADOR s through PERU to n and e BOLIVIA. Forest.

9. GORGETED WOOD-QUAIL

Odontophorus strophium

10". Crown and ear coverts blackish brown, sides of head white speckled with black, chin white, throat black crossed by broad white crescent. Underparts reddish chestnut more or less spotted or streaked with white. Above brown variegated black and buff. ♀: Chin and throat white, band of black spots across center of throat.

Temperate zone. COLOMBIA, known only from E Andes at Subía near Bogotá.

10. VENEZUELAN WOOD-QUAIL

Odontophorus columbianus

10". Much like 9 but throat barred black and white, and white spots of underside much more prominent and edged with black.

Subtropical zone. N VENEZUELA in sw Táchira and coast from Carabobo to Miranda. Forest.

11. STRIPE-FACED WOOD-QUAIL

Odontophorus balliviani

11". Crown rufous chestnut, back reddish brown vermiculated with blackish, inner remiges variegated with black and buffy white. Throat and sides of head black, conspicuous eyebrow and line from base of bill extending back to encircle ear coverts cinnamon. Underparts dark chestnut, each feather with subterminal white mark surrounded by black. ♀: Like ♂ but much lighter above, underparts much more rufescent.

Subtropical zone. Andes of se PERU (Cuzco) and n BOLIVIA (Cochabamba). Forest.

Plate 1

12. STARRED WOOD-QUAIL

Odontophorus stellatus

10". Head conspicuously crested, crown bright rufous chestnut, forecrown dark brown. Throat, sides of head and upper mantle gray, lower back olive brown. Wing coverts and inner remiges dark brown, former dotted with fulvous, latter variegated with black. Underparts rufous chestnut, under tail coverts barred black. ♀: Differs from ♂ by brownish black crest.

Tropical zone. W Amazonia in e ECUADOR, e PERU, and w BRAZIL s of the Amazon e to rio Madeira, and in immediately adjacent BOLIVIA.

13. TAWNY-FACED QUAIL

Rhynchortyx cinctus *

7.5". Lores, eyebrows and cheeks bright orange rufous, crown dark reddish brown, streak behind eye black. Throat and upper breast gray, rest of underparts mostly tawny buff. Mantle gray, feathers edged reddish brown, rest of back grayish dotted with black and buff. Inner remiges dark brown spotted with black and mottled with buff. ♀: Above rather like ♂; sides of head like crown, streak behind eye and throat buffy white; upper breast dark reddish brown, rest of underparts white broadly banded with black.

Tropical zone. Extreme nw COLOMBIA from the Panama border e to Magdalena Valley and along Pacific coast south to nw ECUADOR. [Honduras through Panama.] Forest.

Plate 44

Family OPISTHOCOMIDAE   HOATZINS

These peculiar birds vaguely resemble pheasants. They frequent the banks of forested streams, moving about awkwardly near the water's edge in the low trees and bushes which they inhabit. Their voice consists of a low croak, often heard at night. They feed entirely on leaves. Nestlings swim and dive with ease and clamber from the water into overhanging branches with the aid of claws on their wings. These powers are lost in adult birds.

HOATZIN

Opisthocomus hoazin

25". Face bare, bright blue; iris red. Head adorned with untidy, conspicuous crest. Above mostly bronzy olive, hindneck and mantle streaked buff; shoulders pale buff, wing coverts and tips of tail feathers pale-edged, outer remiges chestnut. Throat and breast buff, rest of underparts chestnut.

GUIANAS, and basins of the Orinoco and Amazon systems s to Maranhão, Piauí, nw Mato Grosso and sw Goiás, BRAZIL and n BOLIVIA.

Plate 3

Fig. 9. WHITE-HEADED MARSH-TYRANT
Arundinicola leucocephala
p. 291

Order GRUIFORMES

Family ARAMIDAE

LIMPKINS

Limpkins rather resemble ibises and, like them, fly with legs and neck outstretched. However they differ radically in habits and are related to rails and cranes. They live on fresh water mussels and snails found in marshy woods and swamps. To a certain extent they are nocturnal.

LIMPKIN

Aramus guarauna *

26''. Generally brown, streaked heavily on back and sides of neck with white; feathers of underparts with concealed white centers. Bill long, thin, curved.

Tropical zone. Generally distributed e of Andes to central ARGENTINA and w of Andes to w ECUADOR. Trinidad. [Southern US; Mid. Amer.; Greater Antilles.] Wooded swamps, edge of mangroves.

Plate 23

Family PSOPHIIDAE

TRUMPETERS

Trumpeters resemble miniature rheas in shape, are mainly terrestrial, inhabit tropical forest and nest in trees and tops of palms. They have a variety of notes, the most characteristic one being a loud booming sound. They are often kept as pets due to their reputed prowess in killing snakes. Actually they feed mainly on vegetable matter and insects.

1. GRAY-WINGED TRUMPETER

Psophia crepitans *

22''. Head and neck clothed in short, velvety black feathers, feathers at base of neck metallic purple; rest of body mainly black; feathers of lower mantle broadly tipped ochraceous. Inner remiges gray, the feathers rather decomposed and hair-like.

GUIANAS; VENEZUELA s of the Orinoco, n of it in Sucre and Monagas; COLOMBIA e of Andes from Meta south to ne PERU and Amazonian BRAZIL n of the Amazon. Forest.

2. PALE-WINGED TRUMPETER

Psophia leucoptera *

22''. Differs from 1 mainly by some of the wing coverts edged bronzy green, inner remiges white or cinnamon buff.

Amazonian BRAZIL, n of the Amazon on n bank of rio Solimões, and s of the Amazon from w bank of rio Madeira west to e PERU and south to n and e BOLIVIA. Forest.

Plate 1

3. DARK-WINGED TRUMPETER

Psophia viridis *

22''. Differs from 2 mainly by having inner remiges mostly green and upper surface dark brown, glossed green.

BRAZIL s of the Amazon from e bank of rio Madeira east to e Pará. Forest.

64

Family RALLIDAE   RAILS, GALLINULES, COOTS

Rails inhabit coastal and inland swamps, marshy woods and moist meadows; a few are found high in the Andes. Secretive, they are rarely seen, preferring to run rather than fly from danger. Females are usually considerably smaller than males.

Coots are more like ducks than rails; they are dark gray in color, have lobed toes, and dive expertly.

AID TO IDENTIFICATION

Spotted or barred above 8, 21, 30, 31

Streaked above (below buff to cinnamon) 5b, 20; (below gray) 6, 7a, 19

Not streaked or spotted above (below gray or partially white) 1, 2, 15c, 16, 18a, 22b, 23, 24, 25, 27c, 32, 33; (below buffy to chestnut) 3, 4a, 9, 10c, 11a, 12, 13b, 14c, 17, 26a, 28, 29; (below blue to purplish blue) 35, 36; (all slaty gray) 34, 37, 38b, 39a, 40, 41, 42, 43b, 44b

1. PLUMBEOUS RAIL

Rallus sanguinolentus *

11". Front of head and most of underparts plumbeous gray; upperparts olive brown. Bill rather long, grass green, red at base.

Pacific and central PERU from Lambayeque and Cajamarca s in temperate zone to Lake Titicaca, BOLIVIA, PARAGUAY, URUGUAY and se BRAZIL to Tierra del Fuego. [Acc. Falkland Is.] Swamps.

2. BLACKISH RAIL

Rallus nigricans *

11". Much like 1 but throat paler than rest of underparts. Bill rather long, yellowish green, greener at tip.

W COLOMBIA. E ECUADOR; e PERU. E BRAZIL from Pernambuco s to Rio Grande do Sul; PARAGUAY; ne ARGENTINA. Swamps.

3. CLAPPER RAIL

Rallus longirostris *

13". Olive brown above, feathers with dark brown centers and gray edges; eyebrow white. Underparts pale fulvous to cinnamomeus, flanks barred dark brown and white.

A coastal species. COLOMBIA in Guajira Peninsula; VENEZUELA in Falcón and Carabobo; GUIANAS, s coastally in BRAZIL to Santa Catarina. ECUADOR from Esmeraldas south to nw PERU. Margarita I.

Trinidad. [US s to Br. Honduras.] Salt marshes, mangroves.

Plate 21

4. PLAIN-FLANKED RAIL

Rallus wetmorei

Much like 3 but with flanks unbarred.

Coastal VENEZUELA in Aragua. Mangroves.

5. LESSER (or Virginia) RAIL

Rallus limicola *

9". Entire upperparts broadly streaked brown and black. Sides of head gray, throat white; underparts pinkish cinnamon, flanks and under tail coverts barred black and white.

Subtropical zone of s COLOMBIA in e and w Nariño and in ECUADOR; coastal PERU. [S Canada s to Mexico; in winter to Guatemala.] Swampy grassland.

6. AUSTRAL RAIL

Rallus antarcticus

9". Upperparts buffy brown streaked with black, wing coverts rufous. Throat and sides of head pale gray, eyebrow pale buff becoming deep buff and turning to gray posteriorly, rest of underparts plumbeous gray; flanks broadly barred black and white. Upper mandible dark red, lower mandible bright red; legs dark purplish.

CHILE in Santiago, Llanquihue and Magallanes; ARGENTINA in Buenos Aires, Chubut and Santa Cruz. Marshy fields, lake shores.

7. BOGOTA RAIL

Rallus semiplumbeus

10". Rather like 6 but much lighter in color. Bill red, culmen and tip black.

Temperate zone. E Andes of COLOMBIA in Boyacá and Cundinamarca. Lake shores and marshes.

Fig. 6, p. 29

8. SPOTTED RAIL

Rallus maculatus *

10". Above blackish brown streaked with white; below white, neck streaked, breast and belly mostly barred with black. Bill yellowish with red base.

Tropical zone. SURINAM; FRENCH GUIANA; w through VENEZUELA to Cauca Valley in COLOMBIA. Nw PERU. E BRAZIL from Pará s to Rio Grande do Sul; URUGUAY; PARAGUAY; ARGENTINA s to Córdoba and Buenos Aires. Trinidad and Tobago. [E Mexico; Br. Honduras; Costa Rica; Cuba.] Marshes with rushes.

9. UNIFORM CRAKE

Amaurolimnas concolor *

9". Upperparts olivaceous brown; underparts rufous chestnut, throat paler. Bill yellowish green, legs vermilion.

Tropical zone. GUIANAS; COLOMBIA; e and w ECUADOR; e PERU; BRAZIL, very locally in Amazonia and from Bahía to São Paulo. E BOLIVIA. [Mid. Amer.] Swampy woods.

10. LITTLE WOOD-RAIL

Aramides mangle

13". In this genus the bill is proportionately short. Head, upper neck and mantle gray, back olive. Primaries and underparts light chestnut; under wing coverts barred black and white. Bill greenish with red base. Legs red.

E BRAZIL from Maranhão to Rio de Janeiro. Usually coastal mangroves but sometimes inland.

11. RUFOUS-NECKED WOOD-RAIL

Aramides axillaris

12". Differs principally from 10 by head and neck rufous chestnut instead of gray.

Tropical zone. Pacific COLOMBIA to w ECUADOR. Caribbean coast of COLOMBIA from Atlántico east to n VENEZUELA (where occasionally in subtropical zone) and to GUYANA and SURINAM. Los Roques. Trinidad. [Mexico to w Panama. Bay Is., Honduras.] Mangroves, forest.

12. GRAY-NECKED WOOD-RAIL

Aramides cajanea *

15". Head, neck and thighs gray, throat white; back olive, rump black. Underparts cinnamon rufous to chestnut, center of abdomen black. Bill yellowish green; legs pink.

Generally distributed e of Andes s to Santa Fe and Buenos Aires, ARGENTINA. Pacific slope s only to s Chocó, COLOMBIA. Trinidad. [Mid. Amer.] Swamps, mangroves, rice fields, humid forest.

Plate 3

13. BROWN WOOD-RAIL

Aramides wolfi

13". Top and sides of head and back of neck gray, throat white. Back chestnut brown to olivaceous brown; closed wing olive. Underparts like back but paler, center of abdomen black.

Tropical zone. Pacific COLOMBIA from Baudó Mts. to sw ECUADOR. Mangroves, tall forest.

Plate 44

14. GIANT WOOD-RAIL

Aramides ypecaha

19". Top and sides of head gray becoming cinnamon on hindneck, throat white; lower neck and upper breast blue gray. Back olive, rump and tail black; sides of body cinnamon pink, center of abdomen white. Bill yellowish; legs pink.

E BRAZIL in s Piauí to Rio Grande do Sul and e Mato Grosso; PARAGUAY; URUGUAY; e ARGENTINA s to Buenos Aires. Saw grass swamps, lagoons; sometimes found far from water.

15. SLATY-BREASTED WOOD-RAIL

Aramides saracura

16". Top of head dark gray, throat white. Hindneck and mantle reddish brown becoming olive on center of back and inner remiges; rump and tail black. Underparts slaty gray.

Se BRAZIL from Minas Gerais to Rio Grande do Sul; PARAGUAY; ne ARGENTINA in Misiones. Forest, more or less independent of water.

16. RED-WINGED WOOD-RAIL

Aramides calopterus

14". Top of head brown, back olive, rump and tail black, sides of neck and greater wing coverts chestnut red. Underparts plumbeous gray. Bill greenish; legs pink.

E ECUADOR; e PERU. BRAZIL in sw Amazonas. Forest streams.

17. CHESTNUT-HEADED CRAKE

Anurolimnas castaneiceps

9". Front and sides of head, neck and breast rufous chestnut, rest of plumage dark olive brown. Legs orange red.

Tropical zone. Se COLOMBIA to e PERU. Forest.

18. SORA

Porzana carolina

9". Face and throat black, sides of head and neck and the breast gray, rest of underparts white broadly banded with black on sides. Back olive brown mottled with black and streaked with white. Bill and legs yellowish olive.

Winter resident (Oct.-May). Tropical to temperate zone. GUYANA, VENEZUELA and COLOMBIA s to ECUADOR and central PERU. Curaçao, Bonaire. Trinidad. [S Canada to w Mexico. Winters to Panama.] Marshes, rice fields.

19. ASH-THROATED CRAKE

Porzana albicollis *

10". Above olive broadly streaked with black; center of throat white, sides of head, neck and entire underparts pale gray; flanks barred black and white.

GUIANAS; n and se VENEZUELA; COLOMBIA from Magdalena Valley e to Arauca and Meta. E BRAZIL, PARAGUAY,

n BOLIVIA and n ARGENTINA. Trinidad. Grassland, drier parts of marshes.

20. YELLOW-BREASTED CRAKE

Porzana flaviventer *

5.5". Eyebrow yellowish white, crown and stripe through eye black. Back black streaked with white; closed wing brownish yellow mottled and barred with black and white. Breast buffy, center of abdomen white, sides of body barred black and white.

GUIANAS; n VENEZUELA from Mérida to Miranda, and in ne Bolívar; central n COLOMBIA. BRAZIL in rio Negro region, and from e Pará s to Minas Gerais. PARAGUAY; ARGENTINA in Tucumán, Santa Fe and Buenos Aires. [S Mexico; El Salvador; Nicaragua; Panama.] Grassy marshes.

21. DOT-WINGED CRAKE

Laterallus spilopterus

6". Top of head, back and rump rufescent olive brown coarsely spotted with black, wings sparsely spotted with white; underparts plumbeous gray, flanks barred with white.

URUGUAY in Canelones. ARGENTINA from Buenos Aires w to San Juan and La Rioja. Swamps; wet, marshy meadows; sometimes dry grassland.

22. BLACK CRAKE (or Rail)

Laterallus jamaicensis *

6". Head and underparts plumbeous gray, flanks barred white. Upper back dull chestnut, rest of back olive brown dotted white; rump black, barred white. Imm.: Mantle dotted white.

Coast of PERU (Lima). CHILE from Atacama to Malleco. W ARGENTINA in Mendoza and San Juan. [US to Br. Honduras; Greater Antilles. Winters to Guatemala.] Hab. as in 21.

23. GRAY-BREASTED CRAKE

Laterallus exilis

6". Front and sides of head, neck and breast gray, nape to upper mantle rufous chestnut, back light olive brown; throat and center of underparts white, sides of body barred black and white. Imm.: Like 22 but mantle unspotted.

GUIANAS; n VENEZUELA; COLOMBIA. N Amazonian BRAZIL on both sides of the

Amazon from rio Negro to at least Óbidos, and from rio Solimões to e Pará; e PERU. W ECUADOR once. Trinidad. [Br. Honduras to Panama.] Hab. as in 21.

24. RUFOUS-FACED CRAKE

Laterallus xenopterus

7". Top and sides of head, hindneck and mantle dark rufous, back and rump brown, upper wing coverts broadly barred with white; foreneck and breast buffy ochraceous, rest of underparts white, sides of body broadly barred black.

PARAGUAY (Horqueta). Known from one specimen.

25. RUFOUS-SIDED CRAKE

Laterallus melanophaius *

7". Forehead, sides of head, neck and breast orange rufous; throat, foreneck and central underparts white, sides of body barred black and white; under tail coverts chestnut. Upperparts dull brown. Imm.: Much like 23.

Tropical zone. Generally distributed e of Andes s to La Rioja and Buenos Aires, ARGENTINA. W of Andes in COLOMBIA and ECUADOR. [Nicaragua to Panama.] Hab. as in 21.

Plate 44

26. RUSTY-FLANKED CRAKE

Laterallus levraudi

7". Rather like 25 differing mainly in sides of body being vinous chestnut instead of barred black and white.

Subtropical zone. VENEZUELA n of the Orinoco. Hab. as in 21.

27. RED-AND-WHITE CRAKE

Laterallus leucopyrrhus

7". Top and sides of head, upper mantle, sides of neck and breast dark rufous chestnut, rest of back reddish brown; underparts white, barred with black on sides.

Se BRAZIL from Rio de Janeiro s to URUGUAY, PARAGUAY, and ARGENTINA to Buenos Aires. Hab. as in 21.

28. BLACK-BANDED CRAKE

Laterallus fasciatus

7". Whole head, neck and breast rufous chestnut, rest of underparts orange ochraceous banded with black. Back olive.

Se COLOMBIA south to e PERU; w Amazonian BRAZIL. Hab. as in 21.

29. RUSSET-CROWNED CRAKE

Laterallus viridis

6.5". Crown rufous chestnut, sides of head gray. Upperparts olive; underparts orange ochraceous. Legs salmon.

GUIANAS; VENEZUELA s of the Orinoco; COLOMBIA w to middle Magdalena Valley; e ECUADOR; e PERU; almost all of BRAZIL s to Rio de Janeiro and Mato Grosso and s Amazonas. Hab. as in 21.

30. OCELLATED CRAKE

Micropygia schomburgkii *

5.5". Mostly ochraceous; crown black dotted with white. Wing coverts and sides of breast with round, black-encircled white spots. Center of abdomen white.

GUYANA and FRENCH GUIANA; locally through VENEZUELA; e COLOMBIA. Se and central BRAZIL from Bahía and São Paulo w through Goiás to Mato Grosso. [Costa Rica.] Marshy grassland.

Plate 2

31. SPECKLED CRAKE

Coturnicops notata

5.5". Upperparts dark olive brown dotted with black and white; throat whitish, lower neck and breast finely streaked, rest of underparts barred black and white.

Very spottily distributed, northern birds possibly being migrants from south. GUYANA; n VENEZUELA; ne COLOMBIA. Se BRAZIL; URUGUAY; PARAGUAY; ARGENTINA. [Acc. Falkland Is. (?)] Rice and alfalfa fields, marshes.

32. PAINT-BILLED CRAKE

Neocrex erythrops *

8". Forecrown, sides of head, neck and underparts blue gray, throat white; upperparts olive brown, flanks and under tail coverts barred black and white (or plain drab, unbarred, 1). Bill yellow, bright orange basally.

Tropical to temperate zone. VENEZUELA n of the Orinoco (once in Bolívar); e

COLOMBIA. E BRAZIL n of the Amazon in Pará s to Espírito Santo and n Mato Grosso; PARAGUAY. Nw ARGENTINA. W PERU from Lambayeque to Lima. Ne COLOMBIA w to Pacific and south to w ECUADOR, 1. [E Panama, 1] Reedbeds.

Plate 2

33. SPOT-FLANKED GALLINULE

Porphyriops melanops*

11″ (13″, 1). Center of crown black; rest of head, neck, breast and upper mantle gray; wing coverts chestnut; back and sides of body olive brown with round white spots on flanks. Center of belly and under tail coverts white. Bill and legs greenish.

Temperate zone of E Andes of COLOMBIA, 1. E PERU (?). E BOLIVIA. E BRAZIL from Ceará s through URUGUAY and PARAGUAY to Santa Cruz, ARGENTINA. CHILE from Atacama to Aysén. Ponds, wet grassland.

Plate 44

34. COMMON GALLINULE

Gallinula chloropus*

15″. Tip of bill yellow, rest of bill and frontal shield scarlet. Mainly dark gray, head and neck blackish, back tinged brownish. White stripe at sides of body. Under tail coverts black, bordered white laterally.

Generally distributed s to Mendoza and Buenos Aires, ARGENTINA, and n CHILE in Andes of Tarapacá. Trinidad. [S Canada; US; Mid. Amer.; W Indies. Galápagos. Africa. Eurasia.] Ponds and marshes.

35. PURPLE GALLINULE

Porphyrula martinica

13″. Tip of bill yellowish green, rest vermilion; frontal shield bright, pale blue. Head, neck and underparts bluish purple, back dull bronzy green, under tail coverts white.

Usually tropical, but occasionally to the temperate zone. Generally distributed south to n Buenos Aires, n Santa Fe and Tucumán ARGENTINA and to n CHILE. Curaçao, Aruba. Trinidad, Tobago. [Southern US; Mid. Amer.; W Indies.] Marshes, rice fields.

36. AZURE (or Little) GALLINULE

Porphyrula flavirostris

10″. Bill and frontal shield greenish, legs

yellow. Crown, hindneck and upper back brownish olive, lower back and rump blackish. Sides of head, neck, breast and wing coverts light blue, throat, center of breast and rest of underparts white.

Tropical zone. GUIANAS; rarely in VENEZUELA and in se COLOMBIA; e ECUADOR; Amazonian BRAZIL and in Goiás, Minas Gerais and Mato Grosso; n BOLIVIA; PARAGUAY; ARGENTINA (Formosa). Marshes, rice fields.

Plate 3

37. AMERICAN COOT

Fulica americana*

18″. Bill white, frontal shield maroon to chocolate brown. General plumage slate gray, inner remiges edged white.

Temperate zone. COLOMBIA s through Andes to BOLIVIA, CHILE to Antofagasta and w ARGENTINA in Andean zone of Jujuy, Salta and n Catamarca. [N Amer., in winter to Panama and W Indies.] Ponds, marshes.

38. SLATE-COLORED COOT

Fulica ardesiaca

16″. Bill and frontal shield white. General plumage slate gray, no white tip to inner remiges.

Temperate zone. Sw COLOMBIA s through Andes to s PERU, (once at sea level near Pisco). Ponds, marshes.

Plate 44

39. CARIBBEAN COOT

Fulica caribaea

15″. Bill white, frontal shield white to sulfur. General plumage slate gray; inner remiges edged white.

VENEZUELA in Zulia and Aragua. Curaçao. Probably Trinidad and possibly Tobago. [W Indies.] Ponds, marshes.

40. RED-GARTERED COOT

Fulica armillata

17″. Bill yellow, spot in front of nostril and base of upper mandible red, frontal shield red bordered with yellow. General plumage slaty, no white on inner remiges.

Se BRAZIL from Rio de Janeiro to URUGUAY, PARAGUAY s through ARGENTINA (except the altiplano) and CHILE (from Coquimbo) s to Tierra del Fuego. [Acc. Falkland Is.] Ponds, marshes.

41. WHITE-WINGED COOT

Fulica leucoptera

13". Bill and frontal shield lemon yellow. General plumage slaty, inner secondaries edged white.

Extreme se BRAZIL w to BOLIVIA and CHILE, s to Tierra del Fuego. Ponds and marshes.

42. RED-FRONTED COOT

Fulica rufifrons

19". Bill lemon yellow, basally red, frontal shield dark red. General plumage slaty, blacker on head and neck; inner remiges without white.

Se BRAZIL; URUGUAY; ARGENTINA (not altiplano) south to n Tierra del Fuego. CHILE from Atacama to Cautin. Rarely PARAGUAY. [Falkland Is.] Ponds, marshes.

43. GIANT COOT

Fulica gigantea

26". Bill dark crimson, tipped white; basal half of maxilla and median line of shield white, sides of shield saffron. The only coot with red legs and feet. General plumage slaty black.

Puna zone. S PERU from Junín south to w BOLIVIA and n CHILE in Tarapacá (only to 18°s), and Andes in Jujuy, ARGENTINA. Highland lakes, often alkaline.

44. HORNED COOT

Fulica cornuta

24". Bill yellowish green, ridge black; frontal shield replaced by fringed, black, horn-shaped wattle. General plumage slaty black.

Puna zone. Andes of sw BOLIVIA; w ARGENTINA from Jujuy to n Catamarca and Tucumán; CHILE from Tarapacá to Atacama, (19°s to 28° 46's). Highland lakes, often alkaline.

Family HELIORNITHIDAE   SUNGREBES

Sungrebes live on quiet forest streams. They are related to rails, have webbed toes, can dive, and often swim half-submerged. Their note is said to resemble a dog's bark. They nest in bushes, up to 12 feet above the water, and feed on aquatic life and seeds.

SUNGREBE

Heliornis fulica

11". Top of head, hindneck and stripe on sides of neck black; eyebrow, throat, rest of neck and most of underparts white, tinged clay color on breast. Upperparts olive brown, tail tipped white.

Tropical zone. Generally distributed in streams over tropical parts of continent s to Mato Grosso and São Paulo BRAZIL, n BOLIVIA, PARAGUAY, and ARGENTINA in Misiones. Acc. in Trinidad. [Mid. Amer.]
Plate 22

Family EURYPYGIDAE   SUNBITTERNS

Sunbitterns superficially resemble herons but are at once distinguishable by their long tails and short legs. They live along shallow forest streams, and feed on insects and other small animal life, capturing their prey with a swift, darting thrust of the bill.

SUNBITTERN

Eurypyga helias*

20″. Wings and tail strikingly patterned. Primaries broadly banded gray, black, white and chestnut; tail narrowly barred black and white, and crossed by two broad black bars margined above with chestnut. Back barred rufescent and black (♀ gray and black). Top and sides of head black with white bar above and another below eye.

Tropical zone. Greater part of continent south to s PERU, BRAZIL to s Goiás, Mato Grosso and Amazonas and n BOLIVIA. West of Andes south to w ECUADOR. [Mid. Amer.]

Plate 3

Family CARIAMIDAE   SERIEMAS

These large birds are at once distinguishable from all other South American birds by their hawklike heads, long necks, tails and legs. They live on the pampas, feeding on small reptiles and mammals. They are mainly terrestrial and fly little. They nest in trees.

1. RED-LEGGED SERIEMA

Cariama cristata

30″. Mainly ochraceous gray, conspicuous crest at base of bill; primaries banded black and white, outer tail feathers tipped white. Legs salmon.

E and central BRAZIL from s Piauí and Ceará to URUGUAY, PARAGUAY and n ARGENTINA s to Entre Ríos, and San Luis. E BOLIVIA in Santa Cruz. Shrubby plains.

Plate 1

2. BLACK-LEGGED SERIEMA

Chunga burmeisteri

30″. No frontal crest. Head, neck and breast gray, belly white. Back, closed wing and tail grayish ochraceous vermiculated with black, remiges barred black and white. Tail with subterminal black bands. Legs black.

PARAGUAY; w ARGENTINA from Jujuy, Salta and w Formosa to San Luis. Shrubby plains.

Fig. 10. SLENDER-BILLED KITE
Heliocolestes hamatus
p. 41

Order CHARADRIIFORMES

Family JACANIDAE   JACANAS

Jacanas are distinguishable from other birds by very long toes and nails which enable them to run over lily pads and floating vegetation. They are good swimmers and dive easily. They feed on vegetable matter, small snails, insects and other animal life.

WATTLED JACANA

Jacana jacana *

10". Head, neck, upper mantle, breast, central belly and under tail coverts black. Back chestnut maroon (or greenish black, 1); outer remiges pale yellow with black tips. Bill yellow, bare forehead and wattles red; legs dusky green. Imm.: Bronzy brown above, white below; broad, buffy eyebrow.

Tropical zone. Widespread e of Andes from GUIANAS, VENEZUELA and COLOMBIA to BOLIVIA and Mendoza and n Buenos Aires, ARGENTINA. W of Andes in w COLOMBIA, in upper Cauca Valley; in Magdalena Valley, 1. W ECUADOR. Nw PERU. Accidental in CHILE. Trinidad. [Panama n to Veraguas.] Marshes, swampy riverbanks and lakes.

Plate 3

Family ROSTRATULIDAE   PAINTED-SNIPES

Somewhat snipe-like but with a curved bill which is green basally and yellow distally. An inhabitant of bogs and wet meadows.

SOUTH AMERICAN PAINTED-SNIPE

Nycticryphes semicollaris

8.5". Crown blackish with pale median stripe; back grayish brown mottled with chestnut and black; at each side of back an ochraceous line formed by edges of scapulars, remiges with round white spots. Throat and breast brown with white crescentic mark at sides of breast, rest of underparts white.

Lowlands. CHILE from Coquimbo s to Arauco. PARAGUAYAN chaco; URUGUAY; ARGENTINA s to Río Negro. Accidental in São Paulo and Rio de Janeiro, breeding in Rio Grande do Sul, BRAZIL. Grassy marshland.

Plate 23

Family HAEMATOPODIDAE   OYSTERCATCHERS

Oystercatchers are distinguishable from other shorebirds by their peculiarly shaped bills which are narrow, compressed, blade-like, and red in color. They usually frequent the seashore where they feed on shellfish opened with the bill, as well as crabs, marine worms and other animal life.

1. AMERICAN OYSTERCATCHER

Haematopus palliatus*

17". Head, neck and upper breast black, rest of underparts white. Back brown; inner remiges mainly white; upper tail coverts white; tail blackish.

Coasts of South America s to Chiloé I., CHILE, and to Chubut and occasionally Santa Cruz, ARGENTINA. Aruba, Trinidad and Tobago. [Southern US; Mid. Amer.; W Indies. Galápagos Is.] Stony beaches, small rocky islands.

Plate 20

2. MAGELLANIC OYSTERCATCHER

Haematopus leucopodus

17". Differs from 1 by being much blacker and by base of tail broadly white.

CHILE, casually from Valdivia and regularly from Chiloé I. to Cape Horn; ARGENTINA in Tierra del Fuego and Staten I., n in winter to Chubut. [Falkland Is.] Hab. as in 1.

3. BLACKISH OYSTERCATCHER

Haematopus ater

19". Head, neck and underparts sooty black; back, wings and tail bronzy brown.

From Lambayeque, PERU, and from Chubut, ARGENTINA, to Tierra del Fuego and Staten I. and Cape Horn; in winter n to Buenos Aires and possibly URUGUAY. [Falkland Is.] Hab. as in 1.

Family CHARADRIIDAE   LAPWINGS, PLOVERS

Although plovers are often seen on the seashore, many species inhabit open plains country, mountain grasslands, and sometimes desert regions. In some species the winter plumage is very different from the breeding plumage. This key is based on breeding plumage. Some North American species wintering in South América summer there without breeding.

AID TO IDENTIFICATION

Back streaked or mottled 4, 5, 14, 18b

Back neither streaked nor mottled (breast black) 1, 3, 7b, 19; (breast gray) 2b, 17b; (breast cinnamon rufous) 13; (breast white) 15; (one black band across breast) 6, 8b, 10, 12; (two bands across breast) 9, 11; (breast finely barred) 16b

1. SOUTHERN LAPWING

Vanellus chilensis*

13". Forehead, long thin occipital crest, foreneck, breast and outer remiges black. Upperparts light bronzy grayish green, lesser wing coverts metallic purplish green; scapu-lars rosy bronze, basally white, distally black. Belly white. Base and tip of tail white, rest black.

Fig. 20, p. 434

GUIANAS w across VENEZUELA to s Cauca, COLOMBIA. E and central BRAZIL; n and e BOLIVIA; ARGENTINA, PARAGUAY; URUGUAY and CHILE (from Atacama) to Tierra del Fuego. Trinidad (sight). [E Panama. Acc. in Falkland Is., Juan Fernández Is.] Savanna, wet grassland.

Fig. 4, p. 29

2. ANDEAN LAPWING

Vanellus resplendens

13". Head, upper mantle and breast pale gray, rest of underparts white. Back bronze green, lesser wing coverts shiny metallic purple, greater wing coverts and inner remiges mostly white. Tail white with black subterminal band.

Temperate zone. Sw COLOMBIA, acc. to Bogotá; Andes from ECUADOR s to Antofagasta, CHILE. Highlands of BOLIVIA and nw ARGENTINA to Catamarca. Nests between 9000 and 13,000 ft., in winter descends to 6000 ft. Marshy fields, lakeshores.

3. PIED LAPWING (or Plover)

Hoploxypterus cayanus

9". Forecrown, sides of head and neck, upper mantle and breast black. Hindcrown sandy brown encircled by white. Throat, underparts and lower back white. Upper back, wing coverts and inner remiges sandy brown, black line at sides of back. Outer remiges black. Tail white with broad subterminal black bar.

Tropical zone. Generally distributed e of Andes to se PERU, n and e BOLIVIA, PARAGUAY and acc. in ARGENTINA (Misiones). Possibly w ECUADOR (sight rec. Guayaquil). Pools in savanna, river banks.

Plate 44 (♂), 23 (♀)

4. BLACK-BELLIED PLOVER

Pluvialis squatarola

12". Forehead and eyebrow white, upperparts black spotted with white, tail barred black and white; underparts mostly black; axillaries black, white flash in wing. Winter: Upperparts light grayish; forecrown, rump and underparts white slightly streaked on breast. Tail white lightly barred dusky.

Winters (Sept.-Apr.) chiefly along Pacific coast to Concepción, CHILE. Rarer on Atlantic coast where recorded s to URUGUAY and occasionally Buenos Aires, AR-

GENTINA. Caribbean coast and islands from Aruba to Trinidad and Tobago. [Breeds in circumpolar regions. Winters to s Asia, s Africa, Australia etc.] Mud flats, sandy beaches.

5. AMERICAN (or Lesser) GOLDEN PLOVER

Pluvialis dominica *

9-11". Differs from 4 mainly by upperparts black spotted with pale yellow, axillaries pale sandy, and no white rump or flash in wing. Winter: Differs from 4 by having upperparts spotted with yellow, rump like back, axillaries pale sandy, and tail dark.

Migrates chiefly e of Andes. Winters (Sept.-Mar.) mostly in s South America to ARGENTINA. Very rare in spring in CHILE. Aruba, Curaçao; Trinidad and Tobago. [Breeds in N Amer. and n Asia. Winters to s Asia, Australia, etc.] Sandy beaches, mud flats, pampas.

6. SEMIPALMATED PLOVER

Charadrius semipalmatus

7-8". Forecrown, sides of head, band across chest continued around upper mantle black. Forehead, throat, collar on hindneck, and underparts white; crown and back sandy brown. Bill yellow with black tip. Winter: Differs by black parts of plumage replaced with brown, and an all-black bill.

Winter resident (July-Mar.). Recorded from all South American countries with seacoasts to Llanquihue, CHILE, and Santa Cruz, ARGENTINA. Recorded also from Tarija, BOLIVIA. Aruba to Trinidad and Tobago. [Breeds in arctic America. Winters from California and S Carolina southward. Galápagos Is.] Beaches, mud flats, inland pools.

7. SNOWY PLOVER

Charadrius alexandrinus *

6". Forecrown, ear coverts and sides of breast black; forehead, sides of head, collar on hindneck and entire underparts white. Back and crown pale sandy gray. Bill black. Winter: Differs by lacking black.

Resident on Pacific coast from sw ECUADOR s to Chiloé I., CHILE. Recorded from BOLIVIA. Aruba to Margarita I. [Breeds in s and w US, Mexico, W Indies; also in Eurasia, n Africa. American migrants winter casually s to the w Caribbean and Panama,

Old World migrants to Africa, Asia and Australia.] Sandy beaches, occasionally inland.

8. PUNA PLOVER

Charadrius alticola

7". Forehead and underparts white, bar across crown black, hindcrown and nape cinnamon, ill-defined dark band across lower breast. Winter: Similar but lacking black bar and cinnamon coloration.

Puna zone. Andes of s PERU from Junín to Antofagasta, CHILE; w BOLIVIA. Andean zone of ARGENTINA to Catamarca. Marshy shores of mountain lakes.

Plate 2

9. TWO-BANDED PLOVER

Charadrius falklandicus *

7". Forehead white, bar across forecrown black, hindcrown and sides of head tinged cinnamon. Breast with two black bars, lower one very broad. Back sandy grayish. Bill, legs black. Winter: Similar but no black band on head, bands on lower parts ill-defined.

CHILE from Antofagasta and ARGENTINA on coast and Patagonian lakes and rivers s to Tierra del Fuego. In winter north to n CHILE, URUGUAY and Rio Grande do Sul, BRAZIL. [Falkland Is.]

10. COLLARED PLOVER

Charadrius collaris

6.5". Forehead white, lores and crown black, bordered behind with cinnamon. Upperparts sandy brown; underparts white with black band across breast. Outer tail feathers white. Bill longer than in 6, all black; legs orange yellow.

Generally distributed in lowlands e of Andes s to Mendoza and Buenos Aires, ARGENTINA; w of Andes south to w ECUADOR. In winter recorded in CHILE from Valparaíso to Malleco (Apr.-Sept.). Aruba to Trinidad and Tobago. [S Mexico southward.] Sandy beaches, also inland.

11. KILLDEER

Charadrius vociferus *

10". Forehead, eyebrow, throat and collar on hindneck white; upper back brown, lower back and upper tail coverts cinnamon. Underparts white with two black breast bands. Tail variegated cinnamon, black and white. Bill black, legs flesh.

Resident in PERU from Piura south to w CHILE. Winter resident (Dec.-Mar.) in COLOMBIA, w ECUADOR, rarely VENEZUELA. Aruba, Curaçao, Bonaire. Tobago. [Breeds in N Amer. and W Indies.] Pastures, cultivated lands.

12. THICK-BILLED (or Wilson's) PLOVER

Charadrius wilsonia *

8". Bill black, long and heavy; legs blue gray. Forehead, eyebrow, throat and collar on hindneck white; lores and bar on forecrown black. Upperparts sandy brown; underparts white with broad black band across breast. Winter: Black markings replaced by brownish gray; some specimens show considerable cinnamon about head and breast.

Resident and breeding on coasts of COLOMBIA, VENEZUELA, and probably to extreme ne BRAZIL; also on Pacific coast s to nw PERU. Winter resident. E VENEZUELA s to Bahía, BRAZIL, accidental in e ECUADOR. Aruba to Trinidad and Tobago. [Breeds from Virginia to Texas. Migrant and resident in Mid. Amer.] Mud flats, sandy beaches.

13. RUFOUS-CHESTED DOTTEREL

Zonibyx modestus

8". Forehead and eyebrow white. Upperparts uniform brown. Throat gray, breast cinnamon rufous bordered below by black band, rest of underparts and outer tail feathers white. Winter: Mostly dull brown, throat and belly white.

Breeds in CHILE from Llanquihue to Cape Horn, wintering from Valdivia to Atacama. In ARGENTINA breeds in Tierra del Fuego, wintering n to URUGUAY and rarely to São Paulo, BRAZIL. Coasts and pasturelands.

Plate 21

14. TAWNY-THROATED DOTTEREL

Oreopholus ruficollis *

11". Crown and mantle sandy grayish, eyebrow buff. Back, wing coverts and inner remiges streaked black and tawny, lower back and upper tail coverts unstreaked. Throat cinnamon, breast tinged grayish, rest of underparts buff with black patch on center of abdomen. Tail variegated tawny, gray and black. Legs salmon.

Resident (?) on coast of n PERU in Lambayeque. Breeds in highlands of s PERU from Puno s in Andes to Tierra del Fuego. Winters north to s ECUADOR and to Buenos Aires and Entre Ríos, ARGENTINA, and in URUGUAY. Andean bogs, winters on open grasslands.

Plate 23

15. MAGELLANIC PLOVER

Pluvianellus socialis

8″. Above pale dove gray; upper tail coverts white with black streak down center; underparts mostly white. Tail white, the central feathers black. Legs short, red.

Breeds in Magallanes, CHILE, and in n Tierra del Fuego, ARGENTINA n in winter to Chubut. Sea and lakeshores.

Plate 20

16. DIADEMED SANDPIPER-PLOVER

Phegornis mitchellii

7″. Sandpiper-like. Bill slightly decurved. Head and neck dark gray, bar across center of crown encircling hindcrown and spot below eye white. Upper mantle orange rufous, rest of back brown. Underparts finely barred gray and white, patch on breast white.

Puna zone of central and s PERU from Lima and Junín s through Andes to ARGENTINA

in Chubut and CHILE in Curicó. Mountain bogs and lakeshores.

Plate 23

17. SURFBIRD

Aphriza virgata

10″. Upperparts, throat and breast variegated black and pale sandy, upper tail coverts and most of underparts white. Middle wing coverts broadly edged white. Winter: Plain dove gray, somewhat speckled below. Legs yellow.

Winters along Pacific coast s to Strait of Magellan and w Tierra del Fuego, CHILE. [Breeds in mts. of Alaska. Winters also in s California and Panama.]

18. RUDDY TURNSTONE

Arenaria interpres *

9″. Strikingly patterned in black, white and chestnut above. Breast and stripes at sides of head black, rest of underparts and sides of head white. Broad white wing stripe. Legs red, short. Winter: More or less similar but all much duller, and chestnut replaced by brown.

Winters (Sept.-May) along coasts s to Buenos Aires, ARGENTINA, and to Llanquihue, CHILE. Aruba to Trinidad and Tobago. [Breeds in circumpolar regions. Winters to s Africa and s Asia.] Sandy beaches, pebbly shores.

Family SCOLOPACIDAE   SNIPES AND SANDPIPERS

Except for snipes all the species of this family are migrants from the Northern Hemisphere to South America. Most of the migrants are usually found in flocks along the seacoast and arrive in late August and leave again in April.

AID TO IDENTIFICATION

Primaries barred 16, 17c, 18, 27, or with very large white area 6

Primaries unbarred (rump or upper tail coverts white or white barred black) 2, 3, 7, 10c, 14, 15, 20c, 22b, 23; (rump not white, bill very long, straight or curved) 19, 21b, 24, 25b, 26b, 28b, 29a, bill not conspicuously long 1, 4, 5b, 8, 9, 11, 12, 13

1. SOLITARY SANDPIPER

Tringa solitaria *

7″. Above dark olive brown streaked on

head and neck and speckled on back with white. Below white narrowly streaked on head and breast; no wing stripe. Outer tail feathers barred black and white. Legs olive greenish. Winter: Grayer, less streaked.

Winters along coastal and inland waters south to w PERU, BOLIVIA, and Río Negro, ARGENTINA. Curaçao. Los Roques. Trinidad. [Breeds in Alaska and Canada.] Mud flats, rivers.

2. LESSER YELLOWLEGS

Tringa flavipes

10". Above dark brown spotted and barred with white; rump and tail white, latter lightly barred. Below white streaked on sides of neck and breast. Legs yellow. Winter: Streaking and spotting reduced.

Winters both inland and coastally, occasionally as far s as the Strait of Magellan. Aruba to Trinidad and Tobago. [Breeds in Alaska and Canada.]

3. GREATER YELLOWLEGS

Tringa melanoleuca

14". Like 2 in color, but larger. Legs very long.

Winters both inland and coastally, occasionally as far s as Strait of Magellan. Aruba to Trinidad and Tobago. [Breeds from Alaska to Labrador.]

4. SPOTTED SANDPIPER

Actitis macularia

7.5". Above olive brown obscurely barred; eyebrow and underparts white, latter with conspicuous round dark spots. Outer tail feathers barred. White stripe on wing. Bill flesh, tip black. Legs pinkish. Winter: Plain grayish brown above, plain white below.

Winters chiefly inland, regularly s to BOLIVIA and s BRAZIL occasionally to CHILE, URUGUAY and ARGENTINA. Aruba to Trinidad and Tobago. [Breeds in N Amer. to tree limit.]

5. WANDERING TATTLER

Heteroscelus incanus

10". Above plain gray, below white heavily barred with dark gray; no wing stripe. Legs dull ocher yellow. Winter: Above plain gray, white stripe above dusky lores; below white, breast pale gray.

Casual winter visitor. Coastal ECUADOR and PERU. [Breeds in mts. of Alaska.]

6. WILLET

Catoptrophorus semipalmatus *

16". Above pale grayish brown streaked dusky on head and neck and barred on back, rump white; below white spotted and barred dusky. Greater wing coverts and tips of remiges black, wing with broad white band. Tail mostly white, Legs blue gray. Winter: Pale gray above, plain white below.

Winters from coasts of COLOMBIA and VENEZUELA to ne BRAZIL and to PERU and occasionally n CHILE. Aruba to Trinidad and Tobago. [Breeds in interior and on coasts of N Amer.]

7. RED KNOT

Calidris canutus *

10.5". Above gray, variegated with black and rufous; underparts cinnamon rufous. Wing with narrow white stripe. Bill rather short; legs greenish olive. Winter: Above gray, feathers with subterminal black band and pale fringe; underparts white, lightly spotted on breast with dusky.

Winters coastally in s South America to Strait of Magellan. [Breeds in arctic America and Eurasia.]

8. LEAST SANDPIPER

Calidris minutilla

6". Upperparts dark brown, feathers rufous-edged; rump black; wing stripe white. Below white, breast streaked dark brown. Outer tail feathers gray. Legs yellowish green. Winter: Upperparts dark grayish brown, feathers without rufous edges.

Winters on all coasts and occasionally inland, south to n CHILE and BRAZIL. Aruba to Trinidad and Tobago. [Breeds in arctic America.]

9. BAIRD'S SANDPIPER

Calidris bairdii

7". Above dark brown, feathers edged clay color giving streaked appearance; central tail coverts black, outer tail coverts white. Sides of neck and breast pinkish buff lightly streaked dusky, underparts white; pale wing stripe indistinct. Legs rather short, dusky green. Tip of bill not broadened. Winter: Appears darker above due to wear of pale feather edges.

Winters chiefly in s South America, locally in Andes of ECUADOR and central PERU. Transient in COLOMBIA and VENE-ZUELA. Apparently not recorded from Brazil. [Breeds in arctic America and e Siberia. Acc. Falkland Is.]

10. WHITE-RUMPED SANDPIPER

Calidris fuscicollis

7". Above rather like 9 but feather edges more rufous and rump white. Legs dark lead color; tip of bill somewhat broadened. Winter: Above sandy grayish with occasional black or rusty feathers.

Winters chiefly e of Andes from s BRAZIL and PARAGUAY to Tierra del Fuego. Aruba to Trinidad and Tobago. [Breeds in w arctic America. Acc. Falkland Is.]

11. PECTORAL SANDPIPER

Calidris melanotos

9". Upperparts blackish, feathers broadly edged with buff and rufous, rump black; upper throat and belly white in sharp contrast to buffy, closely streaked lower neck and breast. Legs olive yellow. Winter: Rufous edges to feathers of upperparts reduced or absent. Foreneck and upper breast grayish white.

Winters in wet meadows and grassy mud flats from PERU and s BRAZIL to Santa Cruz, ARGENTINA, and in CHILE from Arica to Osorno. Aruba to Trinidad and Tobago. [Breeds in arctic America and ne Siberia.]

12. SEMIPALMATED SANDPIPER

Calidris pusilla

6". Much like 8, but with black legs; less rusty brown; bill longer.

Winters on Caribbean and Atlantic coasts (occasionally inland) to ARGENTINA. Uncommon on Pacific coast to n CHILE. Aruba to Trinidad and Tobago. [Breeds in arctic America.]

13. WESTERN SANDPIPER

Calidris mauri

6.5". Much like 12, bill longer, particularly in ♀. Legs black. Winter: Males are almost indistinguishable from 12, but often show a little rufous in scapulars. ♀: Differs by longer bill.

Winter resident on Caribbean and Atlantic coasts from COLOMBIA to SURINAM; on Pacific coast to Trujillo, PERU. Aruba to Trinidad. [Breeds in w Alaska, ne Siberia.]

14. SANDERLING

Calidris alba

8". Above variegated cinnamon, black and white. Breast cinnamon spotted with black, rest of underparts white. Inner webs of primaries mostly white. Legs black. Winter: Pale gray above; forehead, sides of head, wing stripe and underparts white. Bill rather thick, black; legs black.

Winters on all coasts s to Aysén, CHILE, and Tierra del Fuego, ARGENTINA; rare inland. Aruba to Trinidad and Tobago. [Breeds on arctic islands from Greenland to e Siberia. Winters from Gulf Coast s. Also to S Africa, Australia and tropical Pacific islands.]

15. STILT SANDPIPER

Micropalama himantopus

8.5". Crown mixed rufous, black and buff; eyebrow whitish, stripe behind eye rusty buff. Upperparts blackish, feathers edged buffy, upper tail coverts white barred with black. Underparts whitish, throat spotted, rest of underparts heavily barred with dusky. No wing stripe. Legs olive. Winter: Much resembling 11 in color but with much longer bill and legs.

Winters from n BOLIVIA to s BRAZIL and n ARGENTINA. Casual in CHILE. Aruba to Trinidad. [Breeds in arctic America.]

16. BUFF-BREASTED SANDPIPER

Tryngites subruficollis

8". Upperparts black, feathers sharply edged buff giving scaled appearance; underparts uniform buff. Bill rather short; legs greenish yellow.

Winters mostly inland from BOLIVIA to s and w BRAZIL, central ARGENTINA and w PERU. Trinidad. [Breeds in Alaska and nw Canada.]

17. UPLAND SANDPIPER (or Upland Plover)

Bartramia longicauda

12". Above black, the feathers broadly edged cinnamon; rump black. Throat and belly white, foreneck buffy streaked dusky, sides of body barred with black. Tail long, the outer feathers barred buff and black. Bill short and straight, legs pale yellowish.

Winters inland chiefly in s BRAZIL from São Paulo s to URUGUAY and on pampas of PARAGUAY and ARGENTINA s to Río Negro; a few winter in n S America. Acc. in CHILE. [Breeds in N Amer. s to Colorado and Virginia. Acc. Falkland Is.]

18. WHIMBREL

Numenius phaeopus*

17". Bill long, decurved. Sides of crown and stripe through eye blackish, eyebrow and median coronal stripe buff; back dark grayish brown variegated with buff. Neck and breast streaked fulvous and brown, sides barred; center of underparts plain buffy. Tail barred brown and fulvous.

Winters along all coasts s to Bahía, BRAZIL, and to Tierra del Fuego, CHILE. Casual in Tierra del Fuego, ARGENTINA (presumably via Pacific). Aruba to Trinidad. [Breeds in arctic America and Eurasia.]

19. ESKIMO CURLEW

Numenius borealis

13". Much like 18 but differs principally by unbarred inner webs of primaries. Difficult to separate from 18 in the field, but smaller, undersurface of wings cinnamon buff.

Virtually extinct. Last recorded in ARGENTINA, Mar del Plata, Sept. 29, 1914, and near General Lavalle, Prov. Buenos Aires, Jan. 17, 1939 (sight). Formerly wintered in s BRAZIL; URUGUAY; ARGENTINA s to Chubut and CHILE from Arica to Chiloé I. [Breeds in arctic Amer. Spec. shot in Barbados 1964.]

20. HUDSONIAN GODWIT

Limosa haemastica

15". Bill long, upcurved, basally pink, distally black. Head whitish streaked with dusky; upperparts blackish, variegated with pale cinnamon and buff; shoulder plain grayish; rump white. Neck and underparts cinnamon rufous streaked on neck and barred on rest of underparts with blackish. Tail black. Winter: Rather like 6 but easily distinguished by white rump and black tail, much less white in wing, and by bill.

Winters coastally and inland from s BRAZIL, PARAGUAY and URUGUAY to Tierra del Fuego. Casual on Pacific coast. Trinidad. [Breeds in arctic America. Acc. Falkland Is.]

21. MARBLED GODWIT

Limosa fedoa

18". Rather like 20 with similar bill but below pale pinkish buff, finely barred with black; no white rump; tail barred rufous and black. Winter: Quite different from 20. Upperparts much as in summer, below uniform pinkish buff.

Winters casually on Pacific coast to n CHILE. Trinidad and Tobago. [Breeds in w Canada to Montana and Wisconsin.]

22. LONG-BILLED DOWITCHER

Limnodromus scolopaceus

12". Snipe-like; bill long. Top of head, stripe through eye and mantle black, mantle variegated with rufous and buff; lower back and rump white. Hindneck and underparts pinkish buff, spotted on hindneck and breast and barred on sides with black. Tail finely barred black and white. Winter: Above grayer and much less spotted, breast gray, rest of underparts white barred on sides with dusky.

Probably casual winter visitor. Old records only from COLOMBIA, w ECUADOR, nw PERU and ARGENTINA. [Breeds in nw N Amer. and ne Siberia.]

23. COMMON (or Short-billed) DOWITCHER

Limnodromus griseus*

12". Very difficult to distinguish from 22, but bill averages shorter; paler below, sides of breast spotted rather than barred with black, and black bars in tail narrower. Winter: Top of head usually unspotted, breast paler gray with markings on breast and sides of body more prominent.

Winters coastally and inland s to Bahía, BRAZIL, and to nw PERU. Aruba to Trinidad and Tobago. [Breeds in Alaska and Canada.]

24. COMMON SNIPE

Gallinago gallinago*

11". Top of head and stripe through eye black, median crown stripe and eyebrow buffy. Back black variegated with pale buff, upper tail coverts barred black and buff.

Throat and abdomen white, breast variegated with buffy. North American migrants are much buffier than residents and much more barred on sides of body.

Resident, tropical zone, in marshy areas e of Andes from GUIANAS, VENEZUELA and COLOMBIA s to Buenos Aires and Mendoza, ARGENTINA; birds from extreme s breeding at least from Neuquén and Río Negro to Tierra del Fuego winter n to Salta and Buenos Aires and URUGUAY; breed also in CHILE from Atacama to Cape Horn. Migrant (July-Mar.). COLOMBIA, VENEZUELA, (mostly n of the Orinoco) GUIANAS and e ECUADOR. Aruba to Trinidad, Tobago. [Breeds in N Amer. to California and Pennsylvania. Europe and Asia. Falkland I.]

25. PUNA SNIPE

Gallinago andina *

9". Much like 24 (migrant), but smaller with much narrower black bars on axillaries.

Puna zone. High Andes of s PERU; w BOLIVIA; CHILE in Tarapacá and Antofagasta; nw ARGENTINA. Bogs.

26. NOBLE SNIPE

Gallinago nobilis

12". Much like 25 in color but very much larger with much longer bill.

Temperate and páramo zones. Extreme w VENEZUELA in Andes of Táchira. E and Central Andes of COLOMBIA to ECUADOR. Bogs.

27. GIANT SNIPE

Gallinago undulata *

17". In addition to much larger size, instantly separable from all other snipes by barred primaries, otherwise of usual snipe coloration.

GUIANAS, VENEZUELA and e COLOMBIA s to BOLIVIA, PARAGUAY, se BRAZIL; probably URUGUAY. Dry or marshy savanna.

28. CORDILLERAN SNIPE

Gallinago stricklandii *

14". In color much like other snipes, but underparts more extensively barred and tail without rufous chestnut; bill heavier.

Andes of nw VENEZUELA; COLOMBIA in Santa Marta Mts. and E and Central Andes, s in Andes to w BOLIVIA, possibly to n CHILE and in the south from Tierra del Fuego to Cape Horn. [Falkland Is.] Swampy woods, bogs, long grass.

Plate 23

29. BANDED SNIPE

Gallinago imperialis

12". Differs from all other snipes by mantle being banded rufous and black. Sides of head, neck and chest rufous chestnut streaked on neck and banded on breast with black; rest of underparts broadly banded black and white.

Known only from two old specimens from "Bogotá," COLOMBIA. Recently collected in Cuzco, se PERU, 1969 (Weske).

Family RECURVIROSTRIDAE   AVOCETS AND STILTS

Stilts inhabit fresh- and salt-water lagoons, are gregarious and nest in colonies. Avocets in South America are birds of the high Andes where they are found on the shores of mountain lakes.

1. COMMON STILT

Himantopus himantopus *

18-20". Unmistakable. Mostly black above, entirely white below with very long red legs.

Generally distributed both resident and migrant s to BOLIVIA and ARGENTINA. [Virtually worldwide in warmer temperate or tropical zones.]

Plate 23

2. ANDEAN AVOCET

Recurvirostra andina

17-18". Bill sharply upturned. White; band across middle of back, upper tail coverts, wings and tail chocolate brown.

Puna zone of Andes of s PERU and n CHILE s to Salar de Maricunga in Atacama and nw ARGENTINA in Jujuy, Salta and Catamarca.

Plate 23

Family PHALAROPODIDAE   PHALAROPES

Phalaropes resemble short-legged sandpipers but differ in having lobed toes. Wilson's Phalarope winters in the Andes as well as along the coast; the Red Phalarope and the Northern Phalarope winter mainly at sea. At sea they occur in large flocks. They sit high in the water and fly in compact flocks showing alternately their white undersurface and darker uppersurface. Females are larger and more brightly colored than males. In winter the sexes are alike, and the three species are separable from other similar waders by a blackish stripe behind the eye.

1. RED PHALAROPE

Phalaropus fulicarius

8". ♀: Crown, lores and throat grayish black, cheeks and ear coverts white. Underparts and hindneck pinkish brick red. Upperparts mainly streaked black and cinnamon, shoulders gray, wing stripe white. ♂: Like ♀ but differs by crown streaked black and cinnamon. Winter: Upperparts plain gray, entire underparts white. Wing stripe white. Blackish stripe behind eye. Feet pale; bill basally yellow, relatively stout.

Winters chiefly at sea but recorded spottily both on seacoast and inland. Pacific coast from COLOMBIA to PERU. Regularly in CHILE offshore from Arica to Chiloé I. Acc. in PARAGUAY and ARGENTINA. [Breeds in arctic America and Eurasia.]

2. NORTHERN PHALAROPE

Lobipes lobatus

7". ♀: Crown dark gray, lower cheeks white, sides of neck chestnut, front of neck gray. Back gray sparsely streaked with cinnamon. Underparts white. ♂: Differs from ♀ mainly by being much paler. Crown streaked dark brown. Winter: Much like 1; differs mainly by back somewhat streaked with white and

bill much thinner and all black.

Casual migrant. Off PERU, occasionally in coastal salt lagoons; CHILE from Arica to Santiago; ARGENTINA (Chaco; Patagonia). [Breeds in arctic America and Eurasia.]

3. WILSON'S PHALAROPE

Steganopus tricolor

9". ♀: Crown grayish white, broad stripe through eye continued down sides of neck black, gradually changing to rich chestnut and continued down sides of back; center of back gray. Throat white, lower throat tinged cinnamon, rest of underparts white. Upper tail coverts white. Legs, longer than in other two species, dull yellowish. ♂: Like ♀ but much duller. Winter: Much like 1 and 2 but distinguishable by white rump and no wing stripe.

Migrant. COLOMBIA, transient on Pacific coast and Cauca Valley and in w ECUADOR. Winters in highlands of PERU; inland and coastal waters of CHILE; BOLIVIA; PARAGUAY; URUGUAY; ARGENTINA s to Chubut. Accidental in interior of BRAZIL (Mato Grosso). [Breeds in interior of N Amer. Accidental in Falkland Is.]

Plate 23

Family BURHINIDAE   THICK-KNEES

Thick-knees resemble enormous plovers. They are somewhat nocturnal and are usually found in arid regions.

1. DOUBLE-STRIPED THICK-KNEE

Burhinus bistriatus *

18". Mostly dark brown, streaked on back with fulvous. Throat and belly white. Broad superciliary white, surmounted by a black band. Broad patch on wing and bars on tail white. Eye large. Bill black; legs olive.

Ne COLOMBIA; VENEZUELA s to the Orinoco; GUYANA and Roraima, n BRA-ZIL. Curaçao. Margarita I. [Mexico to Costa Rica. Hispaniola.]

Plate 23

2. PERUVIAN THICK-KNEE

Burhinus superciliaris *

16". Generally like 1 but back sandy brown vermiculated with buff and dusky.

Arid littoral of the Pacific from Punta Santa Elena, ECUADOR, south to n CHILE.

Family THINOCORIDAE   SEEDSNIPES

Although "snipe" forms part of the name of these birds, they bear no resemblance whatsoever to snipes; they look like partridges and only recall snipes in their rapid, erratic flight and alarm note. They have short legs and short finch-like bills. They are found in coveys, and in the northern part of their range occur on mountain moors. They feed on seeds, shoots and leaves.

1. RUFOUS-BELLIED SEEDSNIPE

Attagis gayi *

12". Upperparts blackish coarsely vermiculated with grayish buff to cinnamon; breast feathers cinnamon buff, scalloped with black; rest of underparts cinnamon buff.

High Andes from ECUADOR s to Magallanes, CHILE. W and central BOLIVIA and w ARGENTINA. Semiarid mountain slopes.

2. WHITE-BELLIED SEEDSNIPE

Attagis malouinus

11". Upperparts sandy rufous, feathers spotted and bordered with black; outer wing coverts black, bordered with white. Sides of head and throat whitish, front of neck and breast dull white spotted with black, rest of underparts white. ♀: Upperparts blackish, feathers edged and mottled with cinnamon buff. Breast cinnamon buff, feathers scalloped with black; throat and rest of underparts white.

Mts. from Río Negro, ARGENTINA, and Magallanes, CHILE, s to Staten I. and Tierra del Fuego. [Acc. Falkland Is.] Bushy pastureland.

3. GRAY-BREASTED SEEDSNIPE

Thinocorus orbignyianus *

9". Forehead gray; hindcrown and back variegated black, brown and pale buff. Sides of head and neck and the breast gray, throat white enclosed by black gorget. Belly white, separated from gray of breast by black bar. ♀: Above like male but without gray on head. Sides of neck and breast pinkish buff streaked with dark brown.

Andes of PERU from Libertad s through Andes of CHILE to Tierra del Fuego; w and central BOLIVIA; w ARGENTINA. Dry puna, in the south on lowland plains.

Plate 20

4. LEAST SEEDSNIPE

Thinocorus rumicivorus*

7.5". Much like 3 but smaller and with black stripe down center of breast. ♀: Much like 3 but smaller and paler.

Arid coast of sw ECUADOR s coastally to Tierra del Fuego. W BOLIVIA; w ARGENTINA, in winter in the east to Entre Ríos. [Acc. Falkland Is.] Arid foothills with low vegetation.

Family CHIONIDIDAE   SHEATHBILLS

These strange seabirds resemble pigeons in flight and have the voice of a crow. Although the feet are not webbed, they swim with ease and feed on fish and carrion. One species forms the family.

1. SNOWY SHEATHBILL

Chionis alba

16". Entirely white. Bill, with sheath over nostrils, flesh color with coffee color tip and yellow base. Bare patch below eye flesh color with white caruncles.

Visitor from Antarctic to Tierra del Fuego (where found all year) and coast of ARGENTINA; regularly off coast of URUGUAY from May to Sept. [Breeds in antarctic islands and Grahamland.]

Plate 20

Family STERCORARIIDAE   SKUAS AND JAEGERS

These marine birds differ strikingly from gulls, have hooked bills and sharp claws. In a sense they are birds of prey; they chase gulls and terns robbing them of their prey, and feed on young birds and eggs as well as fish. They breed in polar regions and in the non-breeding season are found far out at sea.

1. GREAT SKUA

Catharacta skua*

24". Back brown with some light streaking. Underparts brown to cinnamon brown to almost white; large white patch on wing. Wings rather broad, angled. Tail wedge-shaped.

Breeds in CHILE from Arauco to Cape Horn and in s ARGENTINA from Chubut to Tierra del Fuego. In nonbreeding season in Pacific n at least to n PERU. Birds breeding in antarctic islands migrate n to Buenos Aires, ARGENTINA, and Cabo Frio, BRAZIL, and occasionally Marajó I. Birds breeding on Antarctic continent may reach south-ernmost South America. Arctic breeders acc. in GUYANA. [Arctic and antarctic regions.]

Plate 20

2. POMARINE JAEGER

Stercorarius pomarinus

22". Crown, wings and upperparts dark chocolate brown; sides of neck yellowish; collar on hindneck and underparts white; band across breast chocolate brown. Central tail feathers protruding about 2-4", twisted and blunt. Prominent patch on wing white. Dark phase: Similar but dark above and below. Imm.: Similar but barred below and central tail feathers barely protruding.

Winters off Pacific coast s to PERU and off coasts of VENEZUELA and GUYANA. [Breeds in arctic regions.]

3. PARASITIC JAEGER

Stercorarius parasiticus

18". Much like 2 but paler above, band across breast much less conspicuous, and lengthened tail feathers sharply pointed.

Winters off Pacific coast s to Magallanes, CHILE, and off Atlantic coast s to Tierra del Fuego, ARGENTINA. Acc. in interior BRAZIL (Roraima). Curaçao. [Breeds in Arctic.]

4. LONG-TAILED JAEGER

Stercorarius longicaudus

Much like 3 but smaller; paler and grayer above with black cap and no band across breast. Central tail feathers much longer, protruding 5-8" beyond others, and very narrow. Dark phase is very rare. Imm.: Difficult to separate from that of 3, usually less white on wing, bill more slender.

Winters usually far at sea off Pacific coast s to Valparaíso, CHILE, and Atlantic coast to Buenos Aires, ARGENTINA. [Breeds in Arctic.]

Family LARIDAE   GULLS AND TERNS

Gulls are essentially birds of bays and seacoasts, few species straying far from land. Some inhabit inland lakes and rivers, one even living high in the Andes. They swim well and live on animal food. Gulls have rather broad wings, rather thick, hooked bills and usually square tails.

Terns differ from gulls in their slender pointed bills, narrower wings and forked tails. They are more pelagic than gulls, but some inhabit inland waters. They live on small fish caught by diving from the air. The winter plumage of both gulls and terns differs somewhat from the breeding plumage. This key is based on breeding plumage.

AID TO IDENTIFICATION

Tail not forked
    Head dusky 6, 7, 8b, 9b, 10, general plumage dusky 33a, 34a
    Head light 1b, 2b, 3, 4a, 5
Tail forked
    Head and/or upperparts dark gray to chocolate 11b, 12b, 13, 23a, 24, 32b
    With or without black cap, general plumage light (bill greenish yellow) 14, 21, 25, 26b, 27, 30; (bill black) 15, 22a, 31; (bill orange or red) 16a, 17, 18, 19, 20c, 28, 29b

1. DOLPHIN GULL

Leucophaeus scoresbii

16.5". Pearl gray, wings dark gray, inner remiges broadly tipped with white. Tail pure white. Bill short, very thick, red; feet red. Winter: Head becomes dusky.

Nests in CHILE from Chiloé I. to Cape Horn, casually n to Talcahuano; ARGENTINA in Tierra del Fuego, n in winter to Río Negro. [Falkland Is.]

2. GRAY GULL

Larus modestus

17.5". Mostly pale gray, front of head white; primaries black, secondaries with white tip. Tail with black subterminal bar. Bill and feet black. Head pale coffee color in winter.

Pacific coast from Gorgona I., COLOMBIA (accidental), and Manta Bay, ECUADOR, s to Corral, CHILE. Nests in w PERU and the interior of n CHILE. [Gulf of Panama; Falkland Is.]

3. BAND-TAILED GULL
Larus belcheri*

20". White; center of back, wings and broad tail band brownish black (or slaty black, 1), secondaries tipped white. Wing lining gray (or white, 1). Bill and feet yellow, tip of bill red with black subterminal spot. Winter: Head dusky brown (or white, 1).

From Lobos de Tierra, PERU, s to Coquimbo, CHILE. ARGENTINA in s Buenos Aires, n to URUGUAY in winter, 1. [Casual e Panama.] Seacoast. River mouths, brackish lagoons, 1.

4. RING-BILLED GULL
Larus delawarensis

18". White, mantle pale gray. Bill and feet greenish yellow, bill with black ring near tip. Winter: Head streaked dusky.

Winters to Trinidad. [Breeds inland in N Amer.; in winter both coasts s to W Indies and Panama.]

5. KELP GULL
Larus dominicanus*

21". Much like 3 but larger with thicker bill and completely white tail. Scattered dark feathers on head in winter. Bill yellow, red at tip of mandible; legs greenish yellow. The only South American black-backed gull with a wholly white tail.

Breeds from Lobos de Tierra, PERU, and Rio de Janeiro, BRAZIL, to Tierra del Fuego; also on lakes in s Andes. Occasionally in winter n to ECUADOR and to 10°s on Atlantic coast. [Breeds in antarctic regions, New Zealand, S Africa.]

Plate 20

6. LAUGHING GULL
Larus atricilla

16". Head blackish gray, upper and lower eyelid white. Back and wings dark gray; upper back, underparts and tail white. Primaries black, inner remiges broadly tipped white. Bill and feet red. Winter: Similar, but head and nape white mottled with dusky; bill dusky red.

Winters off both coasts s to Lima, PERU, and mouth of Amazon, BRAZIL. Aruba to Trinidad and Tobago. [Breeds in N Amer. to Mexico and Gulf states.]

7. GRAY-HOODED GULL
Larus cirrocephalus*

16". Head lavender gray; back and inner remiges pale gray; underparts, rump and tail white; outer primaries black with subterminal white patches. Bill and feet scarlet. Winter: Head white, hindcrown and nape pale gray.

Coastal BRAZIL, breeding from Rio de Janeiro to Bahía Blanca, ARGENTINA. Larger lakes and rivers of interior, breeding on Paraguai and Paraná rivers in Mato Grosso, BRAZIL, and in URUGUAY, PARAGUAY, BOLIVIA and n ARGENTINA s to Córdoba and Santa Fe. From río Guayas, w ECUADOR s to 17°s on the coast of PERU. [Coast and lakes of Africa.]

8. ANDEAN GULL
Larus serranus

18". Head black, hindpart of eye encircled with white. Upper back, tail and underparts white; center of back and wings pale gray, outer primaries white with black tips and inner webs. Bill and feet dark crimson. Winter: Head white with grayish markings. Distinguishable from other gulls by wing markings.

Breeds on high Andean lakes, descending in winter to coast and lowland rivers from ECUADOR to Aysén, CHILE, and nw ARGENTINA.

9. FRANKLIN'S GULL
Larus pipixcan

14". Rather like 6 but smaller with blacker head, and outer primaries mostly pale gray with white flash separating conspicuous subterminal black patches. Bill and legs red. Winter: Head white with hindcrown and nape dusky.

Winters along Pacific coast from COLOMBIA to Valdivia, CHILE. [Breeds in interior western N Amer.]

10. BROWN-HOODED GULL
Larus maculipennis

14". Rather like 6 but smaller, back paler, head browner. Wings different, outer wing coverts white, outer primaries mostly white, partially black on inner web. Bill dusky red;

feet reddish. Winter: Head white, hindcrown and nape dusky.

Ranges from Arica, CHILE, and Alagoas, BRAZIL, to Tierra del Fuego, breeding from URUGUAY, ARGENTINA and central CHILE (Valdivia). Found inland as well as on coast. [Falkland Is.]

11. SABINE'S GULL

Xema sabini *

13". Head slate gray with narrow black collar around neck. Upper mantle and underparts white, center of back and wing coverts pearl gray. Primaries black, a white triangle on spread wing. Tail forked, white. Bill blackish with yellow tip. Winter: Nape and upper mantle dusky.

Winters off Pacific coast s to PERU (Lima). [Breeds in circumpolar regions.]

12. SWALLOW-TAILED GULL

Creagrus furcatus

20". Head dark gray with white patch at base of bill. Upperparts pale gray, a white triangle on spread wings; underparts and deeply forked tail white. Bill greenish gray with pale tip, feet pinkish. Winter: Head whitish with grayish ring around eyes and neck.

Casual off coast of ECUADOR to s PERU. [Breeds in Galápagos Is. and Malpelo I. Casual (?) in e Panama (?)]

13. BLACK TERN

Chlidonias niger *

10". Head black; back, wings and tail slate gray. Underparts blackish gray, under tail coverts white. Tail forked. Bill black; feet purplish brown. Winter: Forehead, collar on hindneck and entire underparts white (except dark patch on sides of breast).

Winters coastally s to SURINAM and PERU; accidentally to CHILE. Trinidad. [Breeds on fresh water lakes in N Amer. Also in Europe and w Asia, wintering in Africa.]

14. LARGE-BILLED TERN

Phaetusa simplex *

15". Forehead and space before eye white, cap black; underparts and wing coverts white; upperparts and tail gray, primaries black. Tail slightly forked. Bill thick, greenish yellow; feet olive.

Larger rivers flowing into Caribbean and Atlantic and adjacent coasts south to e BOLIVIA and Buenos Aires, ARGENTINA. W of Andes only in ECUADOR. Aruba; Margarita I. Trinidad. [Acc. Cuba.]

Plate 21

15. GULL-BILLED TERN

Gelochelidon nilotica *

14". Crown and nape black; back, wings and tail pale pearl gray; underparts white. Tail short, forked. Bill all black, short, thick; feet black. Winter: Similar but hindcrown streaked with gray, patch behind eye black.

Resident on Atlantic coast south to s Buenos Aires, ARGENTINA, and inland to Corrientes and along Paraná and Uruguay rivers; also in sw ECUADOR. Migrant from N Amer. to Caribbean coast of VENEZUELA (Oct.-May), ECUADOR, nw PERU. Curaçao. Margarita I. Trinidad. [Breeds in salt marshes and lagoons in southern N Amer. Also in Europe and n Africa; Asia to Australia.]

16. CASPIAN TERN

Hydroprogne caspia

21". Crown and nape black; back and primaries silvery gray; underparts and tail white, tail somewhat forked. Bill coral red, very heavy. Winter: Similar but crown and nape streaked black and white, solid black below and behind eye. (See also 28)

Winter resident on Caribbean coast and lower Magdalena River in COLOMBIA. [Breeds in N Amer., Europe, Africa. Winters to Mexico, occasionally to Panama.]

Plate 21

17. SOUTH AMERICAN TERN

Sterna hirundinacea

17". Crown and nape black, upperparts pale gray; underparts white. Tail deeply forked, outer feathers projecting beyond closed wing. Bill and feet coral red. Winter: Similar but forecrown white.

Breeds from Cabo Frio, BRAZIL, and Ica, PERU, s to Cape Horn. Winters n to Bahía, BRAZIL, and Ancash, PERU.

18. COMMON TERN

Sterna hirundo *

16". Very similar to 17 but somewhat

smaller. Bill coral red with black tip, feet coral red. Outer tail feathers not longer than closed wing. Winter: Similar but forecrown white and bill blackish, base often reddish, feet orange.

Winters on all coasts, s to Lima, PERU, and Santa Cruz, ARGENTINA. Recorded from interior of BRAZIL on rio Araguaia. Aruba to Trinidad nesting on Los Roques and Las Aves. [Breeds in N Amer. and Eurasia.]

19. ARCTIC TERN

Sterna paradisaea

15". Crown and nape black, cheeks and chin white. Upper and underparts pale gray, rump white. Tail very deeply forked, outer feathers projecting only slightly beyond closed wing. Bill blood red, feet coral red. Winter: Similar but crown white, ocular region and nape black. Bill black.

Migrates offshore from COLOMBIA to CHILE and from Bahía, BRAZIL, to n ARGENTINA. [Breeds in circumpolar regions. Winters in the Antarctic.]

20. ANTARCTIC TERN

Sterna vittata *

15". Crown black; back and wings pale silvery gray, rump white. Tail rather deeply forked, almost white. Bill vermilion, feet orange red. Winter: Forecrown white. In breeding plumage when 19 is in winter plumage.

Winters off coast of s BRAZIL (breeds on islands one mile off Macaé, Rio de Janeiro), URUGUAY and ARGENTINA, probably CHILE. [Breeds in subantarctic islands.]

21. SNOWY-CROWNED (or Trudeau's) TERN

Sterna trudeaui

14". Head white, line through eye black. General plumage light gray, rump white. Bill yellow with black tip; feet orange. Winter: Mantle mottled with brown.

Breeds usually in interior marshes of URUGUAY and ARGENTINA to Buenos Aires, casually south to s Santa Cruz. Also in CHILE to Strait of Magellan. Winters n to Rio de Janeiro, BRAZIL.

22. ROSEATE TERN

Sterna dougallii *

15". Crown and nape black; mantle pale

silvery gray; outer portion of primaries dusky. Tail very deeply forked, outer feathers protruding well beyond closed wing. Bill black with vermilion red base; feet vermilion red. Winter: Forecrown white spotted with black. Bill black; feet orange.

Winters along Caribbean coast of VENEZUELA. (?) Accidental in BRAZIL (Piauí, Bahía). Aruba, Trinidad and Tobago. [Breeds in e N Amer., also in Europe and n Africa, s Asia and Australia.]

23. BRIDLED TERN

Sterna anaethetus *

14". White forehead and eyebrow, extending well *beyond* eye. Lores, crown, nape and ear coverts black; hindneck whitish, rest of upperparts smoky, grayish brown. Underparts white. Tail very deeply forked, outer feathers mostly white, rest like back. Bill and feet black. Winter: Similar but forecrown white.

Ranges to Caribbean coast of VENEZUELA; coast of GUYANA and Pacific coast of COLOMBIA. Breeds in Aruba, Curaçao. Occasional off Tobago and Soldado Rock. [Breeds in Bahamas, W Indies, Mid. Amer., nw Africa.]

24. SOOTY TERN

Sterna fuscata *

16". Rather like 23 but darker brown above with no white on hindneck. Forehead white, eyebrow extending back only *to* eye; tail not as deeply forked. Bill and feet black. Imm.: Mostly dark brown. Forked tail and white-tipped feathers of upperparts distinguish it from Brown Noddy (33).

Mainly pelagic. Wanders to Caribbean coast of VENEZUELA and down Atlantic coast to mouth of Amazon, BRAZIL; also to coasts of PERU and CHILE. Aruba to Trinidad and Tobago, breeding on Venezuelan islands. [Breeds in Bahamas, W Indies and nw Africa.]

25. YELLOW-BILLED TERN

Sterna superciliaris

10". Forehead white; lores, crown and nape black. Upperparts pale gray; underparts white. Five outer primaries mostly black. Tail somewhat forked. Bill yellow, rather heavy; feet dull yellow. Winter: Crown streaked black and white.

Rivers and lakes e of Andes from VENE-
ZUELA and COLOMBIA south to n
ARGENTINA, URUGUAY, PARAGUAY
and n BOLIVIA. Trinidad and Tobago.

26. PERUVIAN TERN

Sterna lorata

9". Much like 25 and 27 but underparts
tinged gray and tail somewhat more forked.
Bill basally dusky yellow with apical half
black, smaller and much more slender; feet
brownish yellow. Winter: Forecrown spotted with white.

Pacific coast from Gulf of Guayaquil,
ECUADOR to n CHILE.

27. LEAST TERN

Sterna albifrons *

9". Rather like 25 but bill more slender, tail
more deeply forked and only outer two
primaries black on outer portion. Bill yellow
with black tip. feet orange yellow. Bill
shorter than 26, underparts less gray. Winter: Forecrown white; bill black.

Winter visitor to n VENEZUELA, and Atlantic coast s to Piauí, BRAZIL, and rarely
Buenos Aires, ARGENTINA. Aruba to Trinidad. [N Amer., Europe, w Africa.]

28. ROYAL TERN

Sterna maxima *

19". Rather like 16 but somewhat smaller
with less heavy orange to yellow bill, more
crested head and much more deeply forked
tail. Winter: Differs from 16 by pure white
forehead, rest of crown white streaked with
black.

Not found along rivers. Winters, and may
breed, on all coasts from COLOMBIA and
VENEZUELA s to Pisco, PERU, and Chu-
but, ARGENTINA. Aruba to Trinidad and
Tobago. [Breeds in southern US, Mexico; W
Indies. Africa.]

29. ELEGANT TERN

Sterna elegans

16". Very similar to 28 but considerably
smaller with much more slender orange red
bill. Winter: Similar to 28, but bill more
slender, crown blacker.

Winters along Pacific coast from sw ECUA-
DOR to Corral, CHILE. [Breeds in s California and Baja California.]

30. CAYENNE TERN

Sterna eurygnatha

16". Much like 29 and 31 but immediately
distinguishable by pale yellow bill. Winter:
Similar to 29.

Caribbean coast of COLOMBIA and VENE-
ZUELA. Atlantic coast to Chubut, ARGEN-
TINA. Aruba to Trinidad and Tobago.

31. SANDWICH TERN

Sterna sandvicensis *

16". Much like 28 but smaller and immediately distinguishable by black, yellow-tipped
bill, feet black.

Migrant. Winters along Caribbean coast and
Atlantic coast south to n Santa Cruz,
ARGENTINA. Casual off coast of ECUA-
DOR (Nov.-Dec.). Aruba. Occasionally Trin-
idad. [Breeds in N Amer., islands off Mid.
Amer. Europe. In winter W Africa.]

32. INCA TERN

Larosterna inca

16". Uniform dark gray, white stripe below
eye extending backward in long plumes.
Secondaries tipped white. Tail forked. Bill
and feet red.

From Gulf of Guayaquil, ECUADOR, s to
Valdivia, CHILE, breeding chiefly on islands
off PERUVIAN coast and rarely in CHILE
(Bay of Iquique).

Plate 21

33. BROWN NODDY

Anous stolidus *

16". Dark sooty brown; crown gray to
white. Tail wedge-shaped. Feet and bill
black (see also 24).

Casual in GUYANA and Caribbean coast of
VENEZUELA. Breeds on Octavia Rocks off
coast of Chocó, COLOMBIA. Breeds on
islands from Curaçao to Trinidad and Tobago. [Bahamas, W Indies and central tropical Atlantic; irregular off coasts of Panama.]

34. LESSER NODDY

Anous tenuirostris *

12". Much like 33 but considerably smaller
with more slender and relatively longer bill, .
pale color of crown extending to mantle.

More pelagic than 33. Bonaire, Los Roques (breeding), Las Aves (probably breeding). Trinidad. [Breeds off Br. Honduras. Trop. central and w Atlantic waters to s Africa.]

Family RYNCHOPIDAE   SKIMMERS

Skimmers are notable for their peculiar bill which is blade-like with the mandible longer. They are often seen flying with the mandible skimming the surface of the water. They inhabit coastal waters, bays, and large rivers, and assemble on sand bars.

BLACK SKIMMER

Rynchops nigra *

18″. Upperparts and wings brownish black, secondaries broadly edged white. Forehead, sides of head and underparts white. Tail slightly forked, feathers pale gray, edged white. Bill red with black tip. Winter: Mottled with white above.

Generally distributed s to Buenos Aires, ARGENTINA, and from e and w ECUADOR s to Magallanes, CHILE, possibly not breeding s of Gulf of Guayaquil. Rarely in Andean lakes (Lake Titicaca). Trinidad. [Breeds on Atlantic and Gulf coasts of US to Mexico; on Pacific coast from Mexico to Guatemala; casual to both coasts of Panama.]

Plate 23

Fig. 11. HORNED SCREAMER
Anhima cornuta
p. 30

Order COLUMBIFORMES

Family COLUMBIDAE

PIGEONS AND DOVES

There are a great many varieties of pigeons and doves in South America and some exhibit rather bright colors. They are found from sea level to the temperate zone and in desert regions as well as tropical rain forests. The sexes are usually alike but the female is duller.

AID TO IDENTIFICATION

Size medium to large, 9" or over
> Tail banded or contrastingly tipped (underparts buff to chestnut) 1b, 2b, 7, 14, 15b, 24b, 32b, 33b, 34, 35b, 36b, 37b, 38; (underparts gray or white) 30, 31a, 39b

> Tail not banded or contrastingly tipped (below buff to chestnut) 4, 5, 6a, 8, 9b, 10, 11, 12b, 28b, 40, 42b, 44a, 45b, 46b; (below gray or white) 3a, 13b, 22, 23c, 41, 43b

Size very small, under 8"
> Tail banded or contrastingly tipped (underparts ochraceous pinkish) 16c, 17, 18, 19, 21b, 25b, 26b; (underparts gray or white) 20, 29

> Tail not banded or contrastingly tipped (below brown or vinaceous) 22, 23c, 27b

1. BAND-TAILED PIGEON

Columba fasciata *

14". Head and underparts vinaceous, band across hindneck white. Feathers of upper back edged metallic bronze green; lower back gray. Wings bronzy brown. Tail gray with broad, dark terminal band.

Subtropical to temperate zone. N VENEZUELA, s of the Orinoco in Bolívar; COLOMBIA through e and w PERU to nw ARGENTINA in Catamarca and Tucumán. Trinidad. [Western N Amer., south through Mid. Amer.] Alder woods, forest.

2. CHILEAN PIGEON

Columba araucana

15". Head and underparts vinous chestnut shot with violet, band across nape buff. Feathers of hindneck metallic bronze purple, upper back vinous chestnut, lower back and sides dark gray. Wings and tail grayish brown, tail with black subterminal band and light tip.

CHILE from s Atacama s to Taitao Peninsula in Aysén; s ARGENTINA in Neuquén, Río Negro and Chubut. Woodland, particularly araucarias.

3. SCALY-NAPED PIGEON

Columba squamosa

15". Head and breast dark vinaceous, feathers of hindneck and upper mantle metallic purple edged maroon red; rest of plumage dark gray. Bill red with pale tip.

Aruba (formerly), Curaçao, Bonaire. Los Testigos, Los Frailes, VENEZUELA. [W Indies.] Humid or dry woodland.

4. SCALED PIGEON

Columba speciosa

12". Top of head, lower back, wing coverts, inner remiges vinous chestnut; feathers of upper mantle with white subterminal spot and metallic purple fringe; feathers of lowerparts whitish edged on upper breast with metallic purple, on lower breast and abdomen with dull purple giving a scaled appearance. Bill bright crimson red. ♀: Duller; back brown, metallic edges of feathers dull purplish black.

Virtually throughout lowland s to BOLIVIA, PARAGUAY and BRAZIL to Santa Catarina. ARGENTINA in Misiones and Santa Fe. Pacific slope south to w ECUADOR. Trinidad. [Mid. Amer.] Savanna, open forest.

5. PICAZURO PIGEON

Columba picazuro *

14". Head and underparts vinous brown, belly paler. Feathers of hindneck silvery white, edged black; of upper mantle metallic purple, edged dusky. Back mostly dark gray. Wings dull brown, wing coverts grayer, pale-edged. Tail black. Orbital skin red.

E BRAZIL from Piauí and Pernambuco s to Bahía, and from Rio Grande do Sul w to Mato Grosso and e BOLIVIA; ARGENTINA to La Pampa and n Buenos Aires, occasionally to Río Negro. Woodland, caatinga, often near habitations.

Plate 4

6. BARE-EYED PIGEON

Columba corensis

13". Head, neck and underparts vinous pink, upper back and wing coverts pale brown, greater wing coverts broadly edged white. Lower back and tail gray. Orbital skin blue. Bill flesh color.

Arid n coast of COLOMBIA from Barranquilla (?) and Santa Marta east in n VENEZUELA to Monagas; Margarita I. Aruba, Curaçao, Bonaire.

7. SPOT-WINGED PIGEON

Columba maculosa *

13". Head, neck and underparts vinous gray, back mostly gray; wings brown, wing coverts spotted white, greater coverts narrowly (or broadly, 1) edged white.

Temperate zone of s PERU from Lima south to w BOLIVIA and nw ARGENTINA. PARAGUAY, URUGUAY, s BRAZIL and e ARGENTINA to Chubut, 1. Woods, feeds on ground.

8. PALE-VENTED PIGEON

Columba cayennensis *

12". Forehead gray, crown metallic bronzy green, sides of head pale gray, throat white. Upper back and wing coverts vinous brown, lower back dark gray. Breast vinous, belly gray, under tail coverts white. Wings and tail dull brown. Bill black.

Tropical zone. Generally distributed w of Andes to sw ECUADOR, e of Andes to n ARGENTINA acc. to La Rioja. Trinidad and Tobago. [Mid. Amer.]

9. PERUVIAN PIGEON

Columba oenops

12". Rather like 8, but throat vinous like breast, and lower back and belly much darker gray; under tail coverts dark gray and tail blackish instead of dull brown. Bill leaden blue with crimson base.

Subtropical zone of n PERU in upper Marañón Valley s to Libertad. Woodland.

10. RUDDY PIGEON

Columba subvinacea *

13". Mainly purplish brown, upper mantle shot with metallic violet; wings and tail bronzy brown, wing lining dull chestnut. ♀: Duller, much less violet.

Tropical and subtropical zones. COLOMBIA, VENEZUELA and GUIANAS south to n BOLIVIA, Amazonian BRAZIL and Maranhão. W of Andes south to w ECUADOR. [Costa Rica, Panama.] Forest treetops.

11. PLUMBEOUS PIGEON

Columba plumbea *

12". Much like 10 but underparts paler with a less violet tinge, wing lining dull brown with no trace of chestnut.

Tropical and subtropical zones. Generally distributed e of Andes to BOLIVIA, Amazonian BRAZIL, and from s Bahía and s Goiás to Rio Grande do Sul; n PARAGUAY. W of Andes to ECUADOR.

12. SHORT-BILLED PIGEON

Columba nigrirostris

12". Much like some forms of 10 but readily distinguishable from them by being much paler and grayer below, and by back and wings being bronzy brown instead of vinaceous brown. Under wing coverts and wing lining dull cinnamon.

Tropical zone. Nw COLOMBIA in n Chocó. [Mid. Amer.] Forest treetops, clearings.

13. DUSKY PIGEON

Columba goodsoni

10.5". Top of head pinkish gray, hindneck and upper mantle shot with purple; back, wings and tail bronzy brown shot with purple. Throat pale gray, rest of underparts vinous gray. Wing lining cinnamon, under wing coverts, axillaries and under tail coverts pale chestnut. Bill black; legs red.

Tropical zone. Headwaters of río Atrato in w COLOMBIA to Pichincha, w ECUADOR. Forest.

14. EARED DOVE

Zenaida auriculata. *

10". Top of head gray; forehead, sides of head and uderparts vinous pink; line behind eye and on ear coverts purple black. Upperparts olive brown glossed iridescent purple and gold on upper mantle. Inner remiges spotted with black. Outer tail feathers broadly tipped white or cinnamon rufous. ♀: Similar but little if any gray on top of head.

Tropical to temperate zone. Generally distributed to n Tierra del Fuego. Aruba to Bonaire. Trinidad and Tobago. [S Lesser Antilles. Acc. Falkland Is.] Fields, open woodland, semiarid country.

15. WHITE-WINGED DOVE

Zenaida asiatica *

11". Upperparts pale olive brown, wing coverts broadly edged white. Black spot below ear coverts; sides of neck shot with violet. Breast pale sandy, tinged pink; rest of underparts grayer. Outer tail feathers gray with dusky subterminal bar and pale tip.

Sw ECUADOR s along coast to n CHILE in Tarapacá. [From sw US to w Panama. Bahamas. W Indies.] Cultivated lands, wooded river courses; in dry country, oases.

16. BLUE-EYED GROUND-DOVE

Columbina cyanopis

6". Head vinaceous chestnut. Back olive brown, upper tail coverts cinnamon rufous. Throat white, upper breast and sides dull ochraceous, abdomen pale buff, under tail coverts white. Lesser wing coverts cinnamon, median coverts with steel blue spots. Tail much rounded, outer feathers blackish,

three outermost with white tips on outer web. ♀: Similar but paler.

Central BRAZIL in Mato Grosso (Cuyabá), s Goiás (rio Verde); extreme w São Paulo (Itapura). Cerrado.

17. COMMON GROUND-DOVE

Columbina passerina

6.5". Upperparts grayish or olive brown. Forehead and underparts pinkish, breast feathers with dark centers. Wing coverts pinkish with steel blue spots, remiges mostly cinnamon. Outer tail feathers gray at base, black terminally. ♀: Paler.

Tropical zone. GUIANAS; VENEZUELA; COLOMBIA s to río Dagua and middle Magdalena Valley, extreme e in Vaupés; ECUADOR in temperate zone. N and ne Amazonian BRAZIL and from Pernambuco to Bahía. Aruba to Trinidad. [Southern US s to Costa Rica. Bahamas. W Indies.] Open, arid country, populated areas. Largely terrestrial.

18. PLAIN-BREASTED GROUND-DOVE

Columbina minuta *

6". Head and nape blue gray. Back pale grayish brown, underparts pinkish. Primaries chestnut, wing coverts spotted with steel blue. Outer tail feathers gray basally, black distally. ♀: Duller.

GUIANAS; VENEZUELA usually s of the Orinoco only; n COLOMBIA. E and central BRAZIL from e Pará, to São Paulo and Mato Grosso; n PARAGUAY. W PERU from Trujillo to Lima, and e of Andes in Cuzco and Huánuco. Trinidad. [Mid. Amer.] Open scrub, pastures, towns, cerrado, dry grassland.

Plate 31

19. RUDDY GROUND-DOVE

Columbina talpacoti *

7" Top and sides of head gray. Uppersurface cinnamon rufous; primaries black, wing coverts spotted with black, under wing coverts black. Throat white, rest of undersurface cinnamon pink. Outer tail feathers black, tipped cinnamon. ♀: Olive brown above, wing coverts mottled with black, underparts pale buffy brown (or rather like 18 but larger and instantly separable by black instead of chestnut under wing coverts and primaries, 1).

Drier parts of GUIANAS, VENEZUELA and COLOMBIA south to n ARGENTINA, accidentally as far s as Tucumán and Buenos Aires. Accidental in CHILE. URUGUAY (sight records). Arid coastal ECUADOR and nw PERU, l. Margarita I. Trinidad and Tobago. [Mid. Amer.] Shrubby savanna, pastures, gardens, towns.

20. PICUI GROUND-DOVE

Columbina picui *

7″. Upperparts sandy olive brown; underparts whitish, tinged vinous on breast. Primaries black; wing coverts broadly edged with white, inner ones with a few purple spots. Outer tail feathers mostly white.

COLOMBIA in Amazonas. PERU (once, Puno); n BOLIVIA; ne and s BRAZIL; PARAGUAY; URUGUAY; ARGENTINA s to Río Negro. N CHILE. Forest edge, open country, towns.

21. CROAKING GROUND-DOVE

Columbina cruziana

7″. Much like 18 but larger, primaries black instead of chestnut. Bill much longer, yellow basally with black tip instead of all horn color.

Coastal ECUADOR to n CHILE, extending e in PERU to valley of Marañón. Arid scrub, oases, gardens.

22. BLUE GROUND-DOVE

Claravis pretiosa

8.5″. Uppersurface blue gray, wing coverts and tertials spotted with purple black. Underparts pale gray, lightest on throat, darkest on under tail coverts. Outer tail feathers black. ♀: Uppersurface tawny brown, upper tail coverts rufous; spots on wing coverts and inner remiges rufous purple. Throat and abdomen whitish, breast tinged brown. Central tail feathers rufous, outer ones black.

Generally distributed e of Andes to n ARGENTINA, w of Andes to nw PERU. Trinidad. [Mid. Amer.] Forest edge, borders of mangroves, shrubbery; terrestrial.

23. PURPLE-WINGED GROUND-DOVE

Claravis godefrida

9″. Rather like 22 but wing coverts with three broad purple bars, and outer tail feathers white instead of black. ♀: Rufes-

cent brown, paler on throat and abdomen. Wing coverts with three purple bars. Outer tail feathers blackish, broadly tipped cinnamon.

Se BRAZIL from s Bahía to Santa Catarina. Ne PARAGUAY Wooded country; terrestrial.

24. MAROON-CHESTED GROUND-DOVE

Claravis mondetoura *

9″. Much like 23 but instantly separable by maroon foreneck and chest. ♀: Much like 23 but tail feathers narrowly tipped white.

Subtropical zone. Andes of nw VENEZUELA; n COLOMBIA s to Cauca; e ECUADOR through e PERU to La Paz, BOLIVIA. [Se Mexico to w Panama.] Forest undergrowth, bamboo; terrestrial.

Plate 4

25. BARE-FACED GROUND-DOVE

Metriopelia ceciliae *

7.5″. Upperparts sandy grayish or pinkish grayish, spotted on lower back and wing coverts with buffy white; bare skin around eye orange red outlined in black. Throat white, breast pinkish, rest of underparts pale buff, outer tail feathers blackish, tipped white.

Temperate and puna zones of PERU south to n CHILE; BOLIVIA. Rarely in nw ARGENTINA in Salta and Jujuy. Cultivated land, pastures, villages.

26. BARE-EYED GROUND-DOVE

Metriopelia morenoi

7″. Above grayish brown, tinged gray on head and mantle; upper tail coverts rufous. Undersurface pale brownish gray, reddish brown on under tail coverts. Remiges and underwing black. Outer tail feathers black tipped with white. Orbital skin bright orange, leg flesh color.

Andean zone of w ARGENTINA s to La Rioja. Pastureland.

27. GOLDEN-SPOTTED GROUND-DOVE

Metriopelia aymara

7.5″. Uniform light grayish brown, tinged vinaceous below. Wing coverts spotted with golden bronze; primaries black, rufous at base. Outer tail feathers black.

Puna zone of s PERU; w BOLIVIA. Andean zone of w ARGENTINA to Mendoza; CHILE s to Coquimbo. Pastures, villages.

28. BLACK-WINGED GROUND-DOVE

Metriopelia melanoptera *

9". Much like 27 but considerably larger with longer tail; bend of wing white, wing coverts unspotted.

Temperate and páramo zones, sometimes coastally in winter. Sw COLOMBIA s through Andes to Aysén, CHILE. W BOLIVIA and w ARGENTINA from Jujuy to Santa Cruz. Wooded hillsides, farmland, arid scrub.

29. LONG-TAILED GROUND-DOVE

Uropelia campestris *

7". Tail much graduated. Forecrown gray, rest of upperparts sandy brown, wing coverts with purple spots bordered by white. Throat and breast pinkish gray, rest of underparts soiled white. All but central tail feathers broadly tipped white. Base of bill orange.

Campos of e and central BRAZIL from Amapá and Marajó I., s to Goiás, w Minas Gerais, and n and central Mato Grosso; e BOLIVIA in Santa Cruz.

Plate 30

30. SCALED DOVE

Scardafella squammata *

8.5". Sandy gray above, white below, all feathers edged dusky giving scaled appearance. Primaries mostly rufous. Tail graduated, outer feathers mostly white.

FRENCH GUIANA; VENEZUELA n of the Orinoco and on the Meta, w to arid portions of n COLOMBIA and along the Orinoco. E and central BRAZIL from se Pará south through central plateau in Goiás to Paraná and Mato Grosso; PARAGUAY; ne ARGENTINA. Margarita I. Trinidad. Villages, gardens, dry country scrub.

Plate 30

31. GRAY-CHESTED DOVE

Leptotila cassinii *

10". Forehead grayish; top of head, back, wings and tail bronzy brown. Throat and crissum white, breast gray. Tail pale grayish, outermost feathers wih small white tip.

Tropical zone of COLOMBIA from nw coast east to lower Magdalena Valley. [Mid. Amer.] Humid forest. Terrestrial.

32. TOLIMA DOVE

Leptotila conoveri

10". Crown blue gray, forehead whitish, sides of head grayish. Back bronzy brown, upper mantle shot with purple. Throat white, breast dark tawny pink, rest of underparts pale brown. Outermost tail feathers with small white tip.

Subtropical zone of e slope of the Central Andes of COLOMBIA in Tolima and Huila.

33. OCHRE-BELLIED DOVE

Leptotila ochraceiventris

9.5". Crown tawny brown, paler on forehead, sides of head tawny, throat white. Underparts tawny, tinged violet on breast. Back bronzy brown; two outermost tail feathers with broad white tips.

Tropical and subtropical zones of sw ECUADOR and nw PERU in Piura. Forest.

34. WHITE-TIPPED DOVE

Leptotila verreauxi *

11". Forecrown pinkish white deepening to violet on hindcrown and becoming iridescent purple green on hindneck and upper mantle, rest of upperparts pale brown. Throat, crissum and under tail coverts white, rest of underparts pale pinkish. Central tail feathers like back, outer feathers black, all but central pair broadly margined with white.

Tropical to lower temperate zone. GUIANAS, VENEZUELA and COLOMBIA south to w PERU and ARGENTINA to Mendoza, La Pampa and n Buenos Aires. Aruba to Trinidad and Tobago. [Mid. Amer.] Semiarid scrub, brushy pastures, forest borders. Terrestrial.

Plate 1

35. LARGE-TAILED DOVE

Leptotila megalura *

12". Much like 34 but hindneck and upper back without metallic green gloss; crown, hindneck and upper mantle vinous pink in contrast to sandy brown back.

Subtropical BOLIVIA; nw ARGENTINA to Catamarca and Tucumán. Alder groves, forest.

36. GRAY-HEADED DOVE

Leptotila plumbeiceps *

9.5". Forecrown pale gray, hindcrown darker. Above olive brown, below mostly pinkish vinaceous. Lateral tail feathers black, tipped white.

Upper tropical and subtropical zones. W COLOMBIA in Cauca Valley and w slope of W Andes s to Valle. [S Mexico to w Panama.] Forest, clearings, thickets. Terrestrial.

37. PALLID DOVE

Leptotila pallida

10". Somewhat like 35 but back much darker and redder brown. Tail much redder.

Tropical zone. W COLOMBIA from río San Juan south to sw ECUADOR. Forest.

38. GRAY-FRONTED DOVE

Leptotila rufaxilla *

11". Rather like 37 but distinguishable by upperparts, especially central tail feathers, much less reddish.

Tropical zone. Generally distributed e of Andes. The GUIANAS, from COLOMBIA and e ECUADOR through BRAZIL to BOLIVIA, n ARGENTINA and URUGUAY. Forest.

39. SAPPHIRE QUAIL-DOVE

Geotrygon saphirina *

10.5". Forehead white, center of crown gray, hindcrown and nape bronze green, stripe below eye white bordered below by broad violet stripe. Upper mantle bronze, center of back rich purple, lower back and rump deep violet blue. Underparts white, gray at sides of breast. Tail black, lateral feathers with gray terminal band, outer feathers with small white tip.

Tropical zone. COLOMBIA west of W Andes from upper río Atrato south to nw ECUADOR and from e ECUADOR south in e PERU to Cuzco. Forest. Quail-doves are largely terrestrial.

Plate 31

40. RUDDY QUAIL-DOVE

Geotrygon montana *

9". Upperparts, wings and tail rich rufous, forehead paler, mantle shot with violet, stripe below eye violet brown. Underparts tawny, whitish on throat, darkest on breast. ♀: Olive brown above shot with green; forehead, sides of head and underparts tawny to dull brownish, throat white.

Tropical, occasionally temperate zones. GUIANAS, VENEZUELA and COLOMBIA s through BRAZIL to BOLIVIA, n PARAGUAY, and ne ARGENTINA in Misiones. Trinidad. [Mid. Amer.; W Indies.] Forest undergrowth, second growth, woodland.

41. VIOLACEOUS QUAIL-DOVE

Geotrygon violacea *

9.5". Upperparts bronzy brown, crown, hindneck and upper mantle strongly shot with purple, remiges rufous. Breast gray shot with purple, throat and rest of underparts white. Tail rich purplish brown.

Tropical zone. SURINAM; n VENEZUELA to n COLOMBIA in Santa Marta region and base of Macarena Mts. E BRAZIL s of the Amazon from e Pará (Belém region) s to Paraná; PARAGUAY; ne ARGENTINA in Misiones; BOLIVIA in La Paz and Santa Cruz. [Nicaragua to Panama.] Thick forest.

42. OLIVE-BACKED QUAIL-DOVE

Geotrygon veraguensis

9.5". Upperparts and breast dark bronzy or olive brown, shot on hindcrown and mantle with violet. Forecrown white to buffy, broad streak below eye white. Abdomen mostly tawny brown. Tail bronzy brown.

Tropical zone. W COLOMBIA in lower Cauca Valley and along Pacific slope south to nw ECUADOR. [Caribbean slope of Costa Rica; Panama.] Dense, humid forest.

Plate 31

43. RUSSET-CROWNED QUAIL-DOVE

Geotrygon goldmani *

11". Crown and sides of head rufous, moustachial streak black. Upperparts dark brown, mantle strongly shot with purple; throat white, underparts mainly blue gray.

Tropical zone. Extreme nw COLOMBIA. [E Panama.] Humid forest.

44. LINED QUAIL-DOVE

Geotrygon linearis *

12.5". Above somewhat like 43 but browner, below tawny rufous instead of gray.

Tropical and subtropical zones. N COLOM-
BIA from lower Cauca Valley e to Santa
Marta region and in Macarena Mts.; VENE-
ZUELA n of the Orinoco. Trinidad and
Tobago. [Mexico to w Panama.] Humid
forest.

45. WHITE-THROATED QUAIL-DOVE

Geotrygon frenata *

13″. Like 43 but crown gray instead of
rufous; below less pure gray, more brownish.

Upper tropical and subtropical zones. Pacific
COLOMBIA e to Central Andes, and e of
Andes in Nariño; e and w ECUADOR;
PERU; n BOLIVIA. Nw ARGENTINA. For-
est.

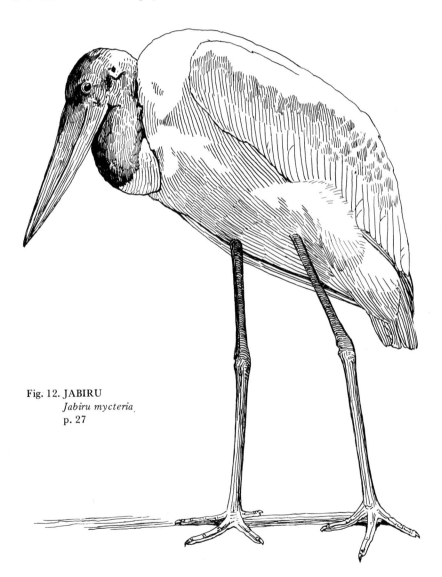

Fig. 12. JABIRU
Jabiru mycteria
p. 27

Order PSITTACIFORMES

Family PSITTACIDAE   MACAWS, PARROTS, PARAKEETS

Parrots are found throughout tropical portions of the world extending to south temperate regions. They are abundant and widespread in South America from lowland tropics to above the tree line of the Andes.

Noisy and conspicuous, they fly swiftly on rapidly but shallow-beating wings. They live on fruit, nuts and seeds, sometimes doing considerable damage to crops. They nest in holes in trees and lay round, white eggs.

In size and shape parrots are very variable, some being chunky with stubby tails, others, usually referred to as parakeets, more slender with long, pointed tails. The largest species are found among the gaudily colored, long-tailed macaws which attain a length of over three feet, while in contrast the tiny parrotlets are hardly as big as a sparrow. Virtually all species, however, show a certain amount of green in their plumage, and irrespective of color or shape, all are recognizable as parrots.

AID TO IDENTIFICATION

Size very large, over 20"
   Tail long, pointed (underparts blue) 1c, 2c, 3c, 4c; (underparts yellow) 5; (underparts red) 8, 9; (underparts all or mostly green) 6b, 7b, 10b, 12, 13, 14c
Size smaller, 8" to 17"
   Tail long, pointed, under wing coverts green (tail mostly green) 17, 19, 20b, 25, 26c, 27, 29b, 30b, 31, 32c, 34c, 45b, 47b, 52, 53b, 54b, 64c, 65; (tail mostly red) 37, 38, 39a, 40, 41, 44, 48a, 49a, 50b, 51b; (tail red and blue) 15b; (tail blue) 11, 24, 28

   Under wing coverts red 16, 21b, 23, 33, 35c, 36, 42a, 47b, 85a

   Under wing coverts all or partly yellow 18c, 22, 23, 24, 43a

   Tail square or rounded (head in contrast to rest of plumage) 79, 80, 82b, 83a, 84, 86b, 88, 90, 93b, 94b, 95b, 96, 102c, 103a, 110; (head not in contrast, sometimes forecrown red) 81c, 87b, 89, 91, 92, 97c, 98, 99, 100, 101, 104, 105, 106, 107b, 108, 109c, 111c
Size smaller, 5.5" to 8"
   Tail short (under wing coverts green) 55, 56b, 57b, 68, 70, 71a, 73a, 74c, 75c, 77c, 78a; (under wing coverts yellow or orange) 66b, 67a, 68, 76b; (under wing coverts blue) 58, 59, 60a, 61, 62b, 63b, 72a; (under wing coverts red) 75, 77b

1. HYACINTHINE MACAW

*Anodorhynchus hyacinthinus**

37". Uniform deep purplish blue. Bare skin around eye and at base of lower mandible yellow.

E BRAZIL s of the Amazon from rio Tapajós e to Maranhão, s through w Bahía and Goiás to Minas Gerais and Mato Grosso. Swamps, forest, palm groves.

2. INDIGO MACAW

Anodorhynchus leari

30". Purplish blue, shaded with grayish

green on sides of head and breast. Bare skin on head as in 1 but paler.

E BRAZIL; known with certainty only from Joazeiro, on rio São Francisco, Bahía.

3. GLAUCOUS MACAW

Anodorhynchus glaucus

27". Pale blue above, greenish blue below; cheeks and throat shaded brownish. Bare skin on head as in 2.

PARAGUAY and URUGUAY (Artigas) n to BRAZIL borders. Forest, palm groves.

4. LITTLE BLUE MACAW

Cyanopsitta spixii

21". Blue, shaded greenish below; head paler, grayish on cheeks; differs from other blue macaws by bare, whitish cheeks.

E BRAZIL in s Piauí and nw Bahía. Palm groves.

5. BLUE-AND-YELLOW MACAW

Ara ararauna

33". Blue above, yellow below.

GUIANAS; VENEZUELA s of the Orinoco, n of it in Monagas; COLOMBIA (not Cauca Valley nor w Nariño) s to BOLIVIA, PARAGUAY, and through e and w ECUADOR to se BRAZIL. Trinidad. [E Panama.] Forest.

6. MILITARY MACAW

Ara militaris *

28". Mainly green; forehead scarlet; remiges blue; tail feathers blue, central pair with red basal half.

Nw VENEZUELA. COLOMBIA w of Andes from Dagua Valley to middle Magdalena Valley and Santa Marta region, e of Andes in Putumayo; e ECUADOR; n PERU s to Lambayeque and Cajamarca. BOLIVIA from Santa Cruz to nw ARGENTINA. [Mexico.] Open, sometimes dry woodland.

7. GREAT GREEN MACAW

Ara ambigua *

33". Very similar to 6 but considerably larger and more yellow green; tail paler blue, basal part of central feathers more orange.

COLOMBIA west of W Andes s only to headwaters of río Atrato. W ECUADOR in Guayas. [Nicaragua to Panama.] Forest.

8. SCARLET MACAW

Ara macao

35". Mainly scarlet. Tertials and median wing coverts mainly yellow; flight feathers, rump and upper tail coverts blue; central tail feathers scarlet, rest increasingly blue.

Generally distributed e of Andes to e Pará and south to n Mato Grosso, BRAZIL; PERU and BOLIVIA in Santa Cruz. W of Andes in Magdalena Valley, COLOMBIA. Trinidad. [Mid. Amer.] Deciduous forest, open woodland.

9. RED-AND-GREEN MACAW

Ara chloroptera

38". Rather similar to 8 but larger; red plumage darker. Median wing coverts green instead of yellow; central tail feathers tipped blue.

Generally distributed e of Andes; s in BRAZIL to Paraná and Mato Grosso, n and e BOLIVIA, PARAGUAY and n ARGENTINA in Formosa. W of Andes in COLOMBIA from upper Atrato eastward. [E Panama.] Humid forest.

10. RED-FRONTED MACAW

Ara rubrogenys

24". Mainly pale green; crown, ear coverts, shoulders, under wing coverts and thighs orange red; tail red and blue.

BOLIVIA in Cochabamba and probably Santa Cruz. Forest.

Plate 4

11. GOLDEN-COLLARED MACAW

Ara auricollis

15". Green; crown and cheeks black, collar on hindneck golden yellow. (See also 28)

BOLIVIA in Beni, Santa Cruz and Tarija; PARAGUAY; BRAZIL in Mato Grosso; nw ARGENTINA in s Jujuy and n Salta. Forest, palm groves.

12. CHESTNUT-FRONTED MACAW

Ara severa *

20". Mainly green. Forehead chestnut, crown bluish green. Under wing coverts scarlet; underside of primaries dull red (only species of the group with this feature).

GUIANAS; w VENEZUELA; COLOMBIA, (on the west s only to headwater of the

Atrato); e PERU; BRAZIL in Amazonia, also s Bahía. N BOLIVIA. [E Panama.] Forest, swampy forest.

13. RED-BELLIED MACAW

Ara manilata

21". Mainly green; forecrown and cheeks blue; center of abdomen dull red.

GUIANAS; n and se VENEZUELA; COLOMBIA e of Andes from Meta south to ne PERU; BRAZIL in Amazonia and from w Bahía and Goiás to Mato Grosso. Trinidad. Savanna.

14. BLUE-WINGED MACAW

Ara maracana

Not unlike 13; differs by larger size, forehead and patch on lower back orange red and central tail feathers basally red instead of green.

E BRAZIL from Pará and Maranhão s to Mato Grosso and Rio Grande do Sul; PARAGUAY; ne ARGENTINA in Misiones. Forest.

15. BLUE-HEADED MACAW

Ara couloni

16". Much like 14, differs mainly by no red on forehead, back and abdomen.

E PERU in Huallaga Valley from Loreto, Huánuco; in the upper Purús drainage and probably adjoining sw BRAZIL.

16. RED-SHOULDERED MACAW

*Ara nobilis**

14". Mainly green; forecrown blue; bend of wing and under wing coverts red. Only macaw with green primaries.

GUYANA; SURINAM; VENEZUELA in e Monagas and Bolívar; BRAZIL n of the Amazon in Roraima and Pará, s of the Amazon from se Pará and Maranhão to São Paulo and se Mato Grosso. Savanna, palm groves, campos.

17. BLUE-CROWNED PARAKEET

*Aratinga acuticauda**

15". Forecrown blue, rest of plumage green; outer tail feathers with red on inner web. All *Aratingas* have long, pointed tails.

E COLOMBIA east across n VENEZUELA to Monagas, s of the Orinoco only in n

Bolívar. E BRAZIL in Piauí and n Bahía, and in w Mato Grosso; e BOLIVIA from Cochabamba to Tarija; PARAGUAY; URUGUAY; ARGENTINA from Jujuy and Salta s to La Pampa and n Buenos Aires. Margarita I. Open forest.

18. GOLDEN PARAKEET

Aratinga guarouba

15". Golden yellow; remiges green.

BRAZIL s of the Amazon in Pará from rio Xingú e to rio Capím and in adjacent Maranhão. Forest.

19. SCARLET-FRONTED PARAKEET

*Aratinga wagleri**

15". Green; forecrown and tibia red, a few red spots on sides of neck, (bend of wing red, 1); under wing coverts green.

VENEZUELA n of the Orinoco; COLOMBIA west of E Andes (except Nariño), e of them in Caquetá. W ECUADOR to w PERU s to Arequipa and e to upper río Marañón and s to Cuzco, 1. Bushy country, cultivated lands, sometimes town parks.

20. MITRED PARAKEET

*Aratinga mitrata**

15". Green; forehead, ocular region, throat and sides of neck scarlet; under wing coverts green.

Central and s PERU south through e BOLIVIA to La Rioja and w Córdoba in w ARGENTINA. Forest.

Plate 4

21. RED-MASKED PARAKEET

Aratinga erythrogenys

13". Rather like 20 but red extending over cheeks; under wing coverts red and green.

Arid zone of w ECUADOR south in w PERU to Lambayeque.

22. WHITE-EYED PARAKEET

*Aratinga leucophthalmus**

14". Green; spots on cheeks red (forecrown also red, 1); lesser under wing coverts red, greater ones yellow.

GUIANAS; VENEZUELA n of the Orinoco in Anzoátegui and Monagas, s of it in Delta Amacuro and Bolívar; COLOMBIA east of E Andes (in Meta, 1) s through ECUADOR and

BRAZIL to Catamarca, n Santa Fe and Entre Ríos, ARGENTINA. Trinidad. [Nicaragua to Panama.] Savanna, palm groves.

23. SUN PARAKEET

Aratinga solstitialis *

13". Sides of head orange red, crown and back golden yellow sometimes mixed with green, underparts yellow shading to red on lower breast and belly; remiges deep blue, edged green; tail olive tipped blue (or head yellow, ocular region and most of lower-parts red, back green, 1; or forehead and ocular region red, crown yellow, abdomen red, rest of plumage green, 2).

GUIANAS; se VENEZUELA (Cerro Rorai-ma only); n BRAZIL n of the Amazon in Roraima, s bank of the Amazon at Santarém. In the e from Maranhão to Ceará and Alagoas, 1; and from Goiás s to Rio Grande do Sul, 2. Savanna, campos, palm groves, cerrado.

24. DUSKY-HEADED PARAKEET

Aratinga weddellii

11". Green, head grayish blue. Wings par-tially blue; under wing coverts green; tail blue.

Se COLOMBIA s to PERU; Amazonian BRAZIL in s Amazonas from rio Juruá e to rio Madeira and w Mato Grosso; BOLIVIA in Beni and Cochabamba. Forest.

25. BROWN-THROATED PARAKEET

Aratinga pertinax *

11". Green; crown blue to greenish blue; sides of head, throat and upper breast brown to grayish brown, belly yellowish green. Yellow ocular ring in some races (with yellow forehead, sides of head and throat, 1).

GUIANAS; VENEZUELA; n COLOMBIA from Córdoba eastward and e of Andes s to Meta; n BRAZIL in Roraima and on upper rio Negro, s of the Amazon on upper rio Tapajós. Aruba to Margarita I., 1. [W Panama; W Indies.] Savanna, mangroves, cultivated lands, campos, cerrado.

26. CACTUS PARAKEET

Aratinga cactorum *

11". Rather like 25 but with dull orange lower breast and abdomen.

BRAZIL in e Pará (Belém region) and from Piauí, Ceará, and Pernambuco to Minas Gerais. Caatinga, cerrado.

27. PEACH-FRONTED PARAKEET

Aratinga aurea *

11.5". Rather like 25 but forecrown peach color, hindcrown blue.

Virtually all of BRAZIL s of the Amazon; n PARAGUAY; BOLIVIA in Beni (and Santa Cruz?); ARGENTINA in extreme n Salta. Forest, cerrado.

28. BLACK-HOODED PARAKEET

Nandayus nenday

14". Tail long, pointed. Mostly green; crown and cheeks black, breast washed with blue. Wings and tail mostly blue. (See also 11)

Se BOLIVIA; s BRAZIL in Mato Grosso; PARAGUAY; ARGENTINA in Formosa and Chaco, occasionally in n Santa Fe. Open woodland, palm groves.

29. GOLDEN-PLUMED PARROT

Leptosittaca branickii

14". Tail long and pointed. Mostly green; frontlet burnt orange; dull yellow streak below eye prolonged in narrow line across ear coverts, the feathers lengthened; center of abdomen dull orange.

Temperate zone. Central Andes of COLOM-BIA. Sw ECUADOR in El Oro and Loja. Central PERU in Junín. Forest.

Plate 31

30. YELLOW-EARED PARAKEET

Ognorhynchus icterotis

17". Tail long and pointed. Above green, below greenish yellow; forehead, cheeks, and ear coverts golden yellow, ear covert feathers lengthened.

Subtropical to temperate zone of Andes in COLOMBIA and n ECUADOR in Imbabura and n Pichincha. Frequents wax palms.

Plate 31

31. BURROWING PARROT

Cyanoliseus patagonus *

18". Tail long, pointed. Above mostly olive, mantle shaded brown; lower back and upper tail coverts olive yellow. Forehead, throat and breast ashy brown; flanks yellow, center of abdomen red. Flight feathers blue. Tail olive.

CHILE from s Atacama to Valdivia. W ARGENTINA from Salta and Tucumán to Chubut, and from s Buenos Aires to Río Negro; southern birds migrate n as far as Entre Ríos and possibly URUGUAY in winter. Plains; nest in sandstone cliffs and ravines.

32. OCHRE-MARKED PARAKEET

Pyrrhura cruentata

11". Mainly green. Crown and nape dusky brown; below eye and ear coverts maroon, buffy behind ear coverts. Breast, collar on hindneck and primaries blue; shoulder scarlet; center of abdomen red. Tail pointed, olive, underside red. Only one of the genus with blue breast.

E BRAZIL from s Bahía and Minas Gerais to ne São Paulo.

33. BLAZE-WINGED PARAKEET

Pyrrhura devillei

10". Mostly green. Crown ashy brown; breast ashy olive feathers pale-edged; upper tail coverts olive green; tail pointed, olive green, underside red. Only species with red under wing coverts and green tail.

E BOLIVIA, n PARAGUAY and sw Mato Grosso, BRAZIL.

34. REDDISH-BELLIED PARAKEET

*Pyrrhura frontalis**

11". Mostly green. Ear coverts grayish; breast olive brown, feathers pale-edged; center of abdomen dull red; narrow frontlet maroon. Tail pointed, olive, underside red.

Se BRAZIL from Bahía to Rio Grande do Sul; URUGUAY; PARAGUAY; n ARGENTINA in Misiones, Corrientes, Chaco, Formosa. Woodland, orchards.

35. PEARLY PARAKEET

*Pyrrhura perlata**

10". Mostly green. Crown dark brown; nape feathers pale-edged; ear coverts pale brownish, cheeks bluish; upper breast dark brown, feathers with pinkish brown edges; under wing coverts mostly scarlet. Tail pointed, maroon red.

BRAZIL in e Pará from rio Xingú to Belém region, and in n Maranhão. Forest.

36. CRIMSON-BELLIED PARAKEET

Pyrrhura rhodogaster

9". Crown, nape and breast dark brown, feathers pale-edged; forehead and upper mantle blue; rest of upperparts green. Lower breast and belly crimson; tail pointed, black, tinged red above. Only species with crimson breast and belly.

Amazonian BRAZIL s of the Amazon between rio Madeira and rio Tapajós, e of the Tapajós along rio Jamauchim; n Mato Grosso. Forest.

37. GREEN-CHEEKED PARAKEET

*Pyrrhura molinae**

11". Mostly green. Crown and nape dull brown; breast brownish, scaled; center of abdomen red. Tail pointed, red.

S Mato Grosso, BRAZIL; n and e BOLIVIA from La Paz to Tarija; nw ARGENTINA in Salta and Jujuy, and acc. to Tucumán. Forest.

38. YELLOW-SIDED PARAKEET

Pyrrhura hypoxantha

11". Crown dusky brown; back green, feathers of rump and upper tail coverts margined with red and yellow. Throat and upper breast whitish, streaked with dusky; sides of body and thighs yellow, feathers edged green; center of abdomen shading to red. Tail pointed, red.

Known only from three specimens from Urucúm and Corumbá in Mato Grosso, BRAZIL.

39. BLOOD-EARED PARAKEET

*Pyrrhura hoematotis**

10". Mainly green; forecrown dull brown, hindcrown and nape dull green, feathers pale-tipped; ear coverts dull red. Breast olive, feathers pale-edged. Tail pointed, red.

Subtropical zone. Coastal range of VENEZUELA from Aragua to Miranda, and in Lara. Forest.

40. MAROON-FACED PARAKEET

*Pyrrhura leucotis**

8". Narrow frontlet and sides of head maroon, ear coverts whitish, forecrown and nape blue, hindcrown dark brown. Breast green, feathers edged with pale, straight bar;

center of abdomen. lower back and tail maroon red; shoulder scarlet. Tail pointed, dull red.

Tropical to lower subtropical zone. N VENEZUELA from Yaracuy e to Sucre and Monagas. E BRAZIL in Ceará and Goiás and from s Bahía to São Paulo. Forest.

41. PAINTED PARAKEET

Pyrrhura picta *

9". Variable species, rather like 40 but at once distinguishable by shape of the pale edges of breast feathers, either V- or U-shaped. In some subspecies the preocular region or entire front of head is dark red with no blue on forecrown; some have red shoulder, others do not.

GUIANAS; VENEZUELA s of the Orinoco; n COLOMBIA w to río Sinú. E PERU; BRAZIL to sw Amazonas, n Mato Grosso and Goiás. BOLIVIA in La Paz. Forest.

Plate 31

42. SANTA MARTA PARAKEET

Pyrrhura viridicata

10". Green; ear coverts dull maroon, narrow frontlet red; scattered feathers on lower breast scarlet and orange; edge of wing and lesser under wing coverts mottled scarlet and orange. Tail pointed, green, red below.

Subtropical zone. COLOMBIA in Santa Marta Mts. Forest, grassy mountain scrub.

43. FIERY-SHOULDERED PARAKEET

Pyrrhura egregia *

10". Green; crown mottled with brown; breast feathers edged pinkish buff; center of abdomen maroon; under wing coverts orange, green and yellow; bend of wing orange red. Tail pointed, maroon.

Tropical and subtropical zones. GUYANA. Se VENEZUELA. Woodland.

44. MAROON-TAILED PARAKEET

Pyrrhura melanura *

Very like 43 but differing in scarlet greater wing coverts and green under wing coverts; crown much browner, breast feathers narrowly (or very broadly, 1) edged with pale ashy. Tail maroon.

Tropical and subtropical zones. S VENEZUELA. COLOMBIA generally, except

Santa Marta, (subtropical zone, Central Andes, 1). E ECUADOR and ne PERU; w BRAZIL to río Negro. Forest.

45. BERLEPSCH'S PARAKEET

Pyrrhura berlepschi

10". Very similar to 44 (1) but tail green with some maroon on inner webs instead of all maroon.

Tropical zone. E PERU in valley of río Huallaga.

46. ROCK PARAKEET

Pyrrhura rupicola *

11". Much like 45 but tail entirely green.

Subtropical zone. PERU from Junín s to Beni, BOLIVIA. Sw BRAZIL in Acre.

47. WHITE-BREASTED PARAKEET

Pyrrhura albipectus

10". Crown brown, feathers streaked with green and pale-edged; ear coverts orange. Broad collar on hindneck whitish; throat and extreme upper breast pinkish white shading to yellow on lower breast, rest of underparts and back green. Primary coverts scarlet; tail pointed, maroon, central feathers edged green.

Tropical zone. Se ECUADOR. Forest.

48. FLAME-WINGED PARAKEET

Pyrrhura calliptera

10". Mostly green; ear coverts maroon; breast brown, feathers with paler pinkish edges; wing coverts yellow. Tail pointed, maroon.

Subtropical zone of both slopes of E Andes of COLOMBIA. Forest.

49. ROSE-HEADED PARAKEET

Pyrrhura rhodocephala

10". Mostly green; crown rosy red; ear coverts maroon red; primary coverts white. Tail pointed, red.

Subtropical zone. Mts. of w VENEZUELA in Táchira, Mérida and Trujillo. Forest.

50. AUSTRAL PARAKEET

Enicognathus ferrugineus *

13". Green, body feathers edged black.

Forehead, lores, center of abdomen red. Tail long, pointed, red.

CHILE from Colchagua, and ARGENTINA from Neuquén, s to Tierra del Fuego. Oak forest, open woods.

51. SLENDER-BILLED PARAKEET

Enicognathus leptorhynchus

16". Very like 50 but much larger, with red of lores extending backward to encircle eyes, and no red on abdomen. Bill remarkably straight and slender for a parrot.

CHILE from Aconcagua to Chiloé I. and occasionally to Aysén. Araucaria forest, farm lands.

52. MONK PARAKEET

Myiopsitta monachus *

11". Forecrown and breast gray, breast feathers edged paler (or uniform pale gray, 1), lower breast yellowish, rest of underparts green. Remiges blue on outer web. Tail long and pointed, green, outermost feathers with yellow inner webs (or tail all bluish green,1).

BOLIVIA in e Cochabamba, 1; and from Tarija e through PARAGUAY, URUGUAY, ARGENTINA to Río Negro. Open woods, cultivated lands, palm groves.

53. GRAY-HOODED PARAKEET

Bolborhynchus aymara

8.5". Top and sides of head ashy brown; back, wings, and tail green. Throat and breast gray shading to green on flanks. Tail rather long, pointed.

Mts. of BOLIVIA south in w ARGENTINA from Jujuy to Mendoza and w Córdoba. Shrubby hillsides.

54. MOUNTAIN PARAKEET

Bolborhynchus aurifrons *

8". Green; forehead and throat golden yellow (or green, 1); underparts yellowish green; wings blue. Female lacks yellow about head as does male of southernmost race.

Coast and Andes of PERU to temperate zone. BOLIVIA from Cochabamba to Oruro s in CHILE to Santiago, and w ARGENTINA to Catamarca; thence to Córdoba, 1. Scrub, cultivated lands, occasionally city parks.

Plate 4

55. BARRED PARAKEET

Bolborhynchus lineola *

7". Green; back and sides barred with black; shoulders black. Tail pointed, green and black.

Subtropical zone. Nw VENEZUELA in Táchira and Mérida; Andes of COLOMBIA. Central PERU in Cuzco. [Mexico to w Panama.] Forest.

Fig. 16, p. 163

56. RUFOUS-FRONTED PARAKEET

Bolborhynchus ferrugineifrons

8". Green, shaded olive below; forehead and chin dull orange. Bill heavy and swollen.

Temperate zone of Central Andes of CO-LOMBIA in Tolima. Scrubby mountain slopes.

57. ANDEAN PARAKEET

Bolborhynchus orbygnesius

7". Rather like 56 but smaller with no orange on forehead and chin.

Subtropical and temperate zones. PERU from Cajamarca s to Cochabamba, BO-LIVIA. Bushy slopes.

58. GREEN-RUMPED PARROTLET

Forpus passerinus *

5". Green with sky blue lesser wing coverts, cobalt blue greater coverts and blue-tinged rump. ♀: All green, rump slightly brighter and forecrown sometimes tinged with yellow.

Tropical zone. GUIANAS, w through VEN-EZUELA (except Amazonas) to ne CO-LOMBIA e of Santa Marta Mts., and in Zulia Valley; BRAZIL on upper rio Branco s to n bank of the Amazon, and in Macapá; s of the Amazon from the Tapajós e to rio Anapú. Trinidad. Curaçao (introduced?) [Panama?] Savanna, thorny scrub and cactus.

59. BLUE-WINGED PARROTLET

Forpus xanthopterygius *

5". Green; wing coverts and rump blue. ♀: Hardly distinguishable from 58 but lower parts more yellowish green.

Tropical zone. Semiarid n COLOMBIA w of Santa Marta Mts., and in extreme lower Magdalena Valley. Ne PERU, e in BRAZIL, on both sides of the Amazon to e Amazonas, also in e BRAZIL from Maranhão and Ceará s to Rio Grande do Sul; PARAGUAY; ne ARGENTINA in Misiones and Corrientes. BOLIVIA in Beni and Santa Cruz. Open woodland, shrubbery.

60. SPECTACLED PARROTLET

Forpus conspicillatus *

5". Much like 59 but at once distinguishable by bright blue ocular region. ♀: Like 59 but ocular area bluish green.

Tropical zone. COLOMBIA from Cauca and Patía valleys e to Meta and Boyacá; VENEZUELA on the Meta. [E Panama.] Open woods, pasture borders.

Plate 31

61. DUSKY-BILLED PARROTLET

Forpus sclateri *

5". Much like 59 but darker with bill dusky instead of pale. ♀: Crown and underparts yellowish green; back dark green, rump blue green.

Tropical zone. GUYANA and FRENCH GUIANA; VENEZUELA in Carabobo and Bolívar; e COLOMBIA in Caquetá south to e PERU; Amazonian BRAZIL from rios Juruá and Negro e to the Belém region, Pará. N BOLIVIA. Open woodland.

62. PACIFIC PARROTLET

Forpus coelestis

5". Crown and cheeks bright green, spot behind eye deep blue; nape pale violet blue, upper back dull grayish green, lower back deep cobalt, tail coverts greenish blue. Greater wing coverts and inner remiges dark purplish blue. Underparts light green, sides of body grayish green. ♀: Like 59 but larger and spot behind eye tinged blue.

Tropical zone. W ECUADOR from río Chone s to Trujillo, PERU.

63. YELLOW-FACED PARROTLET

Forpus xanthops

6.5". Forecrown, cheeks and throat bright yellow, hindcrown and nape greenish gray. Upper back pale sage green, lower back and rump cobalt blue; greater wing coverts and inner remiges purplish blue. Underparts greenish yellow. ♀: Similar but lower back and rump pale blue, greater wing coverts

and inner remiges only tinged blue.

Upper tropical and subtropical zones. N PERU in Marañón Valley in Libertad. Dry, open scrub.

64. PLAIN PARAKEET

Brotogeris tirica

10". Green, yellower below. Central tail feathers bluish, considerably longer than the rest.

E BRAZIL from e Bahía and Goiás to Rio Grande do Sul. Low woods, parks.

65. CANARY-WINGED PARAKEET

Brotogeris versicolurus *

9". Green; inner wing coverts yellow, lesser wing coverts and tertials white (or inner wing coverts yellow, tertials green, 1).

Tropical zone. FRENCH GUIANA. Se COLOMBIA; e ECUADOR; e PERU; BRAZIL in Amazon Valley on both sides of river to Amapá and Belém. From s Pará, Maranhão, Piauí and Ceará, south to w São Paulo and Mato Grosso, PARAGUAY, BOLIVIA and n ARGENTINA, 1. Forest, cerrado.

66. GRAY-CHEEKED PARAKEET

Brotogeris pyrrhopterus

8.5". Green; crown pale blue, cheeks and throat soiled white. Primary coverts deep blue; under wing coverts and axillaries bright orange.

Tropical zone. W ECUADOR from río Chone s to Piura, PERU. Arid scrub.

67. ORANGE-CHINNED PARAKEET

Brotogeris jugularis *

7". Green; top of head and rump bluer, chin spot orange. Inner wing coverts bronzy brown, under wing coverts bright yellow.

Tropical zone. VENEZUELA n of the Orinoco from Guárico w; n COLOMBIA from Norte de Santander w to Chocó. [Mid. Amer.] Savanna, woodland, gardens.

Plate 31

68. COBALT-WINGED PARAKEET

Brotogeris cyanoptera *

8". Green; forehead yellowish, chin spot orange. Upper wing coverts variable, green or yellow depending on race; under wing coverts bluish green (or partially yellow, 1).

Tropical zone. Upper Orinoco Valley in VENEZUELA and COLOMBIA to nw BO-LIVIA and w Amazonian BRAZIL e to rios Negro and Purús. Upper río Huallaga, PERU, 1. Open country with scattered trees.

69. GOLDEN-WINGED PARAKEET

Brotogeris chrysopterus *

7". Green; head bluer. Primary coverts bright orange.

Tropical zone. GUIANAS; e VENEZUELA from Sucre and Monagas s to Bolívar; e and central Amazonian BRAZIL from rios Negro and Madeira, east to e Pará and n Maranhão. Forest, savanna.

70. TUI PARAKEET

Brotogeris sanctithomae

6.5". Forecrown and spot behind eye yellow; wings, mantle and central tail feathers green; lower back, undersurface and outer tail feathers yellowish green.

Tropical zone. Ne PERU from lower río Napo e to both banks of the lower Amazon, BRAZIL. Forest.

71. TEPUI PARROTLET

Nannopsittaca panychlora

5.5". Tail short and square. Green, darker above; forehead, ocular area and under tail coverts yellowish. Rather like *Bolborhynchus* or *Forpus* but bill much more slender and maxilla less sharply curved.

Subtropical zone. W GUYANA; VENE-ZUELA on higher mountain peaks in Bolívar and Amazonas, known n of the Orinoco only from Cerro Papelón, Sucre.

72. LILAC-TAILED PARROTLET

Touit batavica

6". Head greenish yellow; back and wings black; undersurface greenish blue; bend of wing red; wing coverts and inner remiges yellow. Tail short, square, violet with black subterminal bar.

Tropical zone. GUYANA; SURINAM; VENEZUELA n of the Orinoco locally from Mérida to Sucre, s of the Orinoco in e Bolívar. Trinidad and Tobago. Forest tree-tops.

73. SAPPHIRE-RUMPED PARROTLET

Touit purpurata *

7". Green; crown and scapulars brown (or crown green, 1), patch on lower back cobalt blue. Tail short, square, central feathers green, the rest crimson, edged purplish black (or edged green, ♀).

Tropical zone. GUIANAS; e VENEZUELA s of the Orinoco; ne BRAZIL s to Belém region. Se COLOMBIA, sw VENEZUELA and nw BRAZIL along Uaupés and Içaná rivers e to río Negro, 1. Forest, savanna.

74. BLACK-EARED PARROTLET

Touit melanonota

6". Green; sides of body pale bluish; mantle, scapulars and primary coverts brownish black, patch on lower back deep black. Tail short, square, central feathers green with subterminal black patch, rest red with broad black terminal band.

Se BRAZIL from s Bahía to s São Paulo.

75. SCARLET-SHOULDERED PARROTLET

Touit huetii

6". Green, yellower on abdomen; under tail coverts mostly yellow. Forehead, front of face and greater wing coverts dark blue; bend of wing, under wing coverts and axillaries flame scarlet. Tail short, square, central feathers green, rest red (or yellow, ♀) with narrow, terminal black bar.

Tropical zone. GUYANA; VENEZUELA in Monagas, w Bolívar and Amazonas. CO-LOMBIA at base of Macarena Mts. E ECUA-DOR; e PERU; BRAZIL s of the Amazon from lower río Tocantins to Belém, Pará and s to Serra do Cachimbo. Trinidad and Tobago. Forest treetops.

Plate 4

76. RED-WINGED PARROTLET

Touit dilectissima *

8". Green; crown blue, lores and below eye red, chin and throat yellow. Upper wing coverts scarlet, yellow and black; lesser under wing coverts scarlet, rest and axillaries golden yellow. Tail short, square, central feathers yellow at base then green with broad black tip; rest all yellow, tipped black. ♀: Like male but crown and upper wing coverts green.

Tropical zone. Nw VENEZUELA; w and n COLOMBIA; nw ECUADOR. [E Panama.] Forest.

77. GOLDEN-TAILED PARROTLET

Touit surda *

6″. Green; front of face tawny buff; scapulars bronzy brown. Tail short, square, central feathers green, rest golden narrowly edged and tipped with black (or green, ♀).

E BRAZIL in Pernambuco and Alagoas, and from Goiás and Bahía to São Paulo. Forest.

78. SPOT-WINGED PARROTLET

Touit stictoptera *

7″. Green, ocular region , yellowish. Wing coverts and scapulars brown, tipped whitish; median wing coverts dull orange. Tail short, square, green, outer feathers tinged red on inner web. ♀: Like ♂ but wing coverts green, feathers with black bases.

Upper tropical and subtropical zones. COLOMBIA on w slope of Central Andes in Cauca, w slope of E Andes in Cundinamarca, and Macarena Mts. in Meta. E slope of Andes in ECUADOR. Forest.

79. BLACK-HEADED PARROT

Pionites melanocephala *

9″. Crown and nape black; spot before eye blue green; cheeks, throat, collar on hindneck, thighs and under tail coverts orange to lemon yellow. Upperparts and tail green; primaries black, edged blue. Tail short, square.

Tropical zone. GUIANAS; VENEZUELA s of the Orinoco, n of it only in Sucre; COLOMBIA e of Andes from Meta south to ne PERU and n BRAZIL in rio Branco-rio Negro regions and n bank of lower Amazon in Pará. Forest, savanna.

Plate 4

80. WHITE-BELLIED PARROT

Pionites leucogaster *

9″. Crown apricot, sides of head and throat yellow, upperparts green, primaries black. Underparts white, flanks green (or yellow, 1, 2); tail green (or yellow, 2).

Tropical zone. E Amazonian BRAZIL in ne Mato Grosso and Pará; rio Madeira to rio Purús, 2; from rio Juruá to e ECUADOR, e PERU and n BOLIVIA in Beni, 1. Forest.

81. RED-CAPPED PARROT

Pionopsitta pileata

9″. Green; forecrown to below eye rosy red. Outer tail feathers mostly blue. ♀: Lacks red on head.

Se BRAZIL from s Bahía s to Rio Grande do Sul; PARAGUAY; ne ARGENTINA. Forest.

82. BROWN-HOODED PARROT

Pionopsitta haematotis *

9.5″. Green; head brown; throat, collar on foreneck, and ear coverts rose (or face rose, whitish on chin and lower cheeks, 1). Chest and nape tinged brownish olive. Under wing coverts and wing lining cobalt blue, axillaries red. Central tail feathers green, outer tail feathers basally red, all tinged blue. Females have less rose on chest, sometimes lack red axillaries.

Tropical, occasionally subtropical zone. Extreme nw COLOMBIA e to Sinú Valley; from upper río Atrato south to w ECUADOR, 1. [Mid. Amer.] Forest.

83. CAICA PARROT

Pionopsitta caica

9″. Green; head blackish; upper breast olive; collar on hindneck rusty. Primary coverts cobalt blue. Tail green, inner webs yellow tipped with blue.

Tropical zone. GUIANAS; e VENEZUELA in Bolívar; ne BRAZIL n of the Amazon from Roraima eastward. Forest treetops.

84. ORANGE-CHEEKED PARROT

Pionopsitta barrabandi *

10″. Green; head black; cheeks and shoulder orange; chest olive yellow; bend of wing and under wing coverts scarlet; inner webs of outer tail feathers yellow.

Tropical zone. S VENEZUELA; se COLOMBIA; e ECUADOR; e PERU; w Amazonian BRAZIL on both sides of the Amazon e to rios Negro and Madeira, s to Mato Grosso. Forest.

Plate 4

85. SAFFRON-HEADED PARROT

Pionopsitta pyrilia

9.5″. Head and shoulders orange yellow; back and belly green; chest olive; bend of wing, under wing coverts and axillaries scarlet. Inner webs of outer tail feathers yellow, tail pointed.

Tropical to upper subtropical zone. W VENEZUELA w through n COLOMBIA to middle río San Juan. [E Panama.] Forest.

86. BLACK-EARED PARROT

Hapalopsittaca melanotis *

10". Green; forehead, lores and sides of neck pale blue; crown and nape pale blue mixed with green, ocular area bright pale green. Wing coverts black; wing lining verditer blue. Tail green, broadly tipped blue.

Temperate zone. Central PERU in Junín. BOLIVIA in Cochabamba and La Paz.

Plate 4

87. RUSTY-FACED PARROT

Hapalopsittaca amazonina *

9". Front of head red (or dull yellow, 1); occiput bluish; feathers of ear coverts somewhat lengthened, olive with yellow shaft streaks (or without shaft streaks, 1, 2). Back green; breast olive green, rest of underparts yellowish green; shoulder red (or mainly blue with no red, 2). Central tail feathers green, rest dull red, broadly tipped blue.

Upper subtropical and temperate zones. Andes of nw VENEZUELA and w slope of E Andes of COLOMBIA to Cundinamarca; Central Andes in Caldas, 1. Andes of ECUADOR, 2. Forest.

88. VULTURINE PARROT

Gypopsitta vulturina

9". Head bare, skin of forehead, ocular region and chin orange, rest black. Collar around neck golden yellow broadly margined posteriorly by black; back green; shoulders orange. Underparts greenish blue; under wing coverts and axillaries crimson. Tail blue, inner webs of outer feathers yellow. (In color very like 84.)

Tropical zone. E Amazonian BRAZIL s of the Amazon from e bank of lower río Madeira east to e Pará. Erroneously recorded from Guyana and Venezuela. Forest.

89. SHORT-TAILED PARROT

Graydidascalus brachyurus

10". Green; wing coverts and tertials narrowly but sharply edged greenish yellow. Tail very short, pale yellowish green.

Tropical zone. Se COLOMBIA from Caquetá south to e PERU; BRAZIL in Amazon Valley to its mouth, n to coast of Amapá. Forest.

90. BLUE-HEADED PARROT

Pionus menstruus *

11". Base of maxilla red. Whole head, neck and breast bright blue somewhat mixed with red on lower throat (or without red, 1). Back, lower breast and belly green (or belly feathers edged cobalt blue, 1). Under tail coverts and inner webs of outer tail feathers red. Young birds have red forehead and very little blue on head and breast.

Tropical zone. GUIANAS; VENEZUELA; COLOMBIA; ECUADOR; e PERU and n BOLIVIA; Amazonian and e BRAZIL s to Mato Grosso. Coastal BRAZIL from Bahía to Espírito Santo, 1. Trinidad. [Costa Rica, Panama.] Forest treetops, cornfields.

Plate 31

91. RED-BILLED PARROT

Pionus sordidus *

11". Bill red. Crown dusky greenish; back dull green, feathers edged sandy in some races. Throat and extreme upper breast blue, rest of underparts pale green to brownish olive. Under tail coverts and tail much as in 90.

Tropical, subtropical zones. Mts. of n VENEZUELA; COLOMBIA in Santa Marta and Perijá Mts. and E Andes; e and w ECUADOR; e PERU; n BOLIVIA. Forest.

92. SCALY-HEADED PARROT

Pionus maximiliani *

12". Differs from 91 by bill black and yellow, throat and breast violet, and underparts not tinged with brown.

E and s BRAZIL from Piauí and Goiás to Rio Grande do Sul and Mato Grosso; e and s BOLIVIA; PARAGUAY; n ARGENTINA. Forest, woodland.

93. PLUM-CROWNED PARROT

Pionus tumultuosus

11". Bill olive yellow. Head and neck plum color darkening to purple on breast, rest of plumage green; under tail coverts red. Base of outer tail feathers red on inner web, purple on outer web.

Upper tropical and subtropical zones.

PERU, e of Andes (on w slope at Taulis) s to La Paz and Cochabamba, BOLIVIA. Forest.

94. WHITE-CAPPED PARROT

Pionus seniloides

11". Bill pale olive yellow. Head feathers white, edged with blackish and tinged rose on forehead and throat; breast dull purplish brown, center of belly dull brownish red, under tail coverts red. Upperparts and sides of body green. ♀: Duller, without red patch on abdomen.

Subtropical, temperate zones. Nw VENEZUELA w to Central Andes of COLOMBIA and s through ECUADOR almost to borders of Peru. Forest.

95. BRONZE-WINGED PARROT

Pionus chalcopterus *

11". Head dull blue, feathers basally white; mantle dusky bronzy green, lower back and outer remiges dark purple blue; wing coverts and tertials bronzy brown, pale-tipped. Throat white, patch on upper breast pinkish, rest of underparts dark blue, under tail coverts pinkish red; wing lining verditer blue.

Upper tropical and subtropical zones. N VENEZUELA in Sierra de Perijá; Andes of COLOMBIA, ECUADOR and nw PERU. Forest.

96. DUSKY PARROT

Pionus fuscus

10". Spot at nostril red. Top and sides of head dull slaty blue, patch at sides of neck dull white. Upperparts dark brown, feathers pale-edged; underparts brown, paler than back, feathers broadly edged with plum color or blue; wing lining blue. Under tail coverts pinkish red.

Tropical zone. Ne COLOMBIA in Sierra de Perijá. VENEZUELA s of the Orinoco; GUIANAS; n BRAZIL, n of the Amazon from rio Negro to at least rio Branco, s of the Amazon from rio Madeira to Maranhão. Forest.

97. RED-SPECTACLED PARROT

Amazona pretrei

13". Mainly green, body feathers edged black. Forecrown, lores and ocular region, thighs, bend of wing, shoulders and primary coverts crimson.

Se BRAZIL from São Paulo to Rio Grande do Sul. Ne ARGENTINA in Misiones. Forest.

98. ALDER PARROT

Amazona tucumana

13". Differs from 97 by having only the forehead and primary coverts red, thighs orange.

Tropical, subtropical zones. Se BOLIVIA in Chuquisaca and Tarija. N ARGENTINA from Jujuy to Misiones. Alder forest.

99. RED-LORED PARROT

Amazona autumnalis *

13". Mainly green. Lores and forehead red; feathers of crown and nape edged lilac. Wing speculum red.

Tropical zone. Extreme nw VENEZUELA in Zulia; n half of COLOMBIA west of E Andes. W ECUADOR s to Gulf of Guayaquil. Nw BRAZIL n of the Amazon to rio Negro. [Mid. Amer.] Tall trees and mangroves, river courses.

100. BLUE-CHEEKED PARROT

Amazona brasiliensis *

14". Mainly green. Forecrown red, hindcrown yellow, feathers edged green; cheeks purplish blue; base of tail crimson (or with yellow lores and blue cheeks, wing speculum orange and tail green with patch of red on inner web of outer feathers, 2; or with forehead and lores orange yellow, crown yellowish, feathers edged green, cheeks cornflower blue, patch of orange on inner webs of outer tail feathers, 1).

GUIANAS, 1. VENEZUELA in se Bolívar. BRAZIL from e Alagoas s through e Minas Gerais, Bahía and Espírito Santo, 2; from São Paulo to Rio Grande do Sul. Forest.

101. FESTIVE PARROT

Amazona festiva *

15". Mainly green. Only species of *Amazona* with red lower back. Forehead and lores dark crimson; broad streak above and behind eye and center of throat blue. Primaries dark blue; no color patch on wing.

Nw GUYANA; VENEZUELA on the Meta and along middle Orinoco to Delta Amacuro. Amazonian COLOMBIA, ECUADOR, PERU and w BRAZIL from lower rio Madeira to rio Branco. Forest.

102. YELLOW-FACED PARROT

Amazona xanthops

11″. Mainly green. Only species of *Amazona* with yellow band across abdomen, terminating on each side in orange patch. Head yellow, ear coverts tinged orange.

E and central BRAZIL from s Piauí and Goiás to São Paulo and Mato Grosso. Cerrado.

103. YELLOW-SHOULDERED PARROT

Amazona barbadensis *

13″. Mostly green, body feathers edged black especially above. Head mostly yellow, shoulders and thighs yellow. Wing speculum red.

Arid coastal range of VENEZUELA from Falcón to Anzoátegui. Aruba (formerly), Bonaire. La Blanquilla, Margarita I.

104. TURQUOISE-FRONTED PARROT

Amazona aestiva *

15″. Mainly green, body feathers edged black. Forecrown and lores light blue; throat yellow; shoulders red, (or with yellow hindcrown, ocular region and shoulders, 1). Large wing speculum red.

E BRAZIL from Piauí to Rio Grande do Sul; in Goiás, Mato Grosso, PARAGUAY, n and e BOLIVIA, and n ARGENTINA south to n Santa Fe, 1.

Plate 4

105. YELLOW-HEADED PARROT

Amazona ochrocephala *

14″. Mainly green. Center of crown yellow; shoulders red.

Tropical zone. GUIANAS; VENEZUELA except extreme s; COLOMBIA west of E Andes from Atrato Valley to Santander, e of Andes from Meta south to e PERU; Amazonian BRAZIL to nw Mato Grosso and e Pará (Marajó I.). Trinidad. [Mid. Amer.] Forest, woodland, cornfields.

106. ORANGE-WINGED PARROT

Amazona amazonica *

13″. Mainly green. Center of crown pale

yellow edged posteriorly by pale blue, or sometimes crown pale blue with a little yellow in center; cheeks orange yellow; wing speculum orange red.

Tropical zone. Generally distributed e of Andes to e PERU and Amazonian and e BRAZIL s to Paraná and Mato Grosso (upper rio Paraguai). W of Andes in n COLOMBIA. Trinidad and Tobago. Forest, swampy woods.

107. SCALY-NAPED PARROT

Amazona mercenaria *

13″. Mainly green. Feathers of hindcrown, nape and breast with dusky edges. Bend of wing orange, wing speculum red, (usually absent, 1). Body plumage variable, parrot green to olive green especially below; rump usually pale yellowish green. Tail distinctive: Central feathers green, pale-tipped, the rest tipped yellowish with green bases and with variable amount of red between; outermost feather with purple blue outer web, this color in variable amounts on outer web of other feathers.

Upper tropical to temperate zone. Nw VENEZUELA in Zulia and Mérida, and mts. of COLOMBIA and ECUADOR, 1. PERU to n BOLIVIA. Forest.

108. MEALY PARROT

Amazona farinosa *

16″. Mainly green with powdery bloom. Center of crown yellow sometimes mixed with red or all green; feathers of hindcrown and nape with dusky edges; bend of wing and extensive speculum red; basal half of tail dark green, distal half greenish yellow.

Tropical zone. GUIANAS, VENEZUELA and COLOMBIA s to Mato Grosso and São Paulo, BRAZIL, and BOLIVIA from La Paz to Santa Cruz. [Mid. Amer.] Forest, cornfields.

109. VINACEOUS-BREASTED PARROT

Amazona vinacea

14″. Partially green. Bill, lores and forehead red; feathers of extreme upper mantle pale blue broadly edged black; breast plum color shaded bluish, feathers with dusky edges. Bend of wing, wing speculum and base of inner tail feathers crimson; primaries edged bright blue.

Se BRAZIL from Bahía to Rio Grande do

Sul; PARAGUAY; ARGENTINA in Misiones. Forest.

110. RED-FAN PARROT

Deroptyus accipitrinus *

14″. Head rather hawk-like, brown, feathers with pale shaft streaks; nape feathers long, broad, erectile, crimson broadly edged blue. Back, belly, wings and tail green; breast and center of abdomen dark crimson, feathers broadly edged blue. Tail black on underside.

GUIANAS; VENEZUELA in Bolívar. CO- LOMBIA e of Andes from Meta south to ne PERU; Amazonian BRAZIL e to Amapá and e Pará south to n Mato Grosso, and possibly Maranhão. Forest, savanna.

111. BLUE-BELLIED PARROT

Triclaria malachitacea

9″. Mossy green, belly violet blue. Tail square. ♀: All green.

Se BRAZIL from s Bahía to Rio Grande do Sul. Forest.

Plate 4

Fig. 13. RUSTY-BELTED TAPACULO
Liosceles thoracicus dugandi
p. 260

Order CUCULIFORMES

Family CUCULIDAE   CUCKOOS

Cuckoos in South America are mainly birds of brush and forest of the tropical zone where they are widespread, but only one species is found in Chile. Usually dull in color, they have rather long, graduated tails. The ground-cuckoos, *Nemorphus* are large, long-tailed, terrestrial birds of the forest.

Only the genera *Tapera* and *Dromococcyx* are parasitic. The rest build flimsy nests of twigs, except for the Anis which construct bulky communal nests, and cover their eggs with green leaves when left unattended.

AID TO IDENTIFICATION

Above uniform (ashy or bronzy brown) 1a, 2, 3, 4, 5, 6a; (or chestnut) 9, 10, 11

Crown gray, back brown 7, 8a

Black above and below 12, 13, 14

Upperparts streaked 15c, 16

Dark brown above, tail feathers very wide, long 17, 18

Very large, terrestrial, pheasant-like 19, 20, 21b, 22a, 23

1. DWARF CUCKOO

Coccyzus pumilus

8.5″. Crown gray, back ashy gray; throat and upper breast orange rufous, rest of underparts white. Tail with subterminal dark area and narrow white tip. Bill black.

Tropical, occasionally subtropical zone. N COLOMBIA in lower Magdalena Valley, occasionally to temperate zone of E Andes. N VENEZUELA south to n Bolívar and n Amazonas. Margarita I. Open woods.

2. ASH-COLORED CUCKOO

Coccyzus cinereus

9.5″. Pale ashy brown, breast paler, rest of underparts white. Tail with small black subterminal area and narrow white tip, tail not graduated. Bill black.

URUGUAY; PARAGUAY; e BOLIVIA; n ARGENTINA s to La Pampa and Buenos Aires. Acc. in BRAZIL in Bahía. Open woods, scrub.

3. BLACK-BILLED CUCKOO

Coccyzus erythropthalmus

11.5″. Rather like 2 but much larger with strongly graduated tail. Uppersurface browner, throat and breast little different from rest of undersurface. Bill black.

Winter resident. Nw VENEZUELA; CO-LOMBIA; ECUADOR; n PERU; acc. in n ARGENTINA. Trinidad. [Breeds in N Amer. Migrates through Mid. Amer. Acc. Europe.] Forest, scrub.

4. YELLOW-BILLED CUCKOO

*Coccyzus americanus**

12″. Rather like 3 but inner webs of flight feathers mainly rufous, outer tail feathers with much larger white tips, outer web of outermost tail feather mostly white. Mandible yellow.

Winter resident. Generally distributed e of Andes s to La Rioja, Córdoba and Buenos Aires, ARGENTINA. W of Andes in CO-LOMBIA. Aruba to Trinidad and Tobago.

[Breeds in Canada, US, Mexico and W Indies. Migrates through Mid. Amer. Acc. Europe.] Open woodland.

5. PEARLY-BREASTED CUCKOO

Coccyzus euleri

10". Very like 4 but at once distinguishable by no rufous on flight feathers. Separable from 3 by yellow mandible and blackish outer tail feathers, broadly tipped white.

Tropical zone. GUYANA; SURINAM; VENEZUELA in Mérida, n Bolívar and Amazonas. E COLOMBIA and at Cartagena. E BRAZIL from Pará to Rio de Janeiro and Mato Grosso. ARGENTINA in Misiones. Thickets, forest edge.

Plate 24

6. MANGROVE CUCKOO

Coccyzus minor*

12.5". Rather like 4 but with undersurface rusty buff, no rufous in wing and well-marked black ear coverts. Mandible yellow.

GUIANAS; ne BRAZIL on Cajutuba I., off coast of Pará. Aruba, Curaçao, Bonaire. Trinidad. Possibly Colombia and Venezuela. [S Florida; Mid. Amer.; islands of Caribbean.] Coastal mangroves, thickets.

7. DARK-BILLED CUCKOO

Coccyzus melacoryphus

10.5". Top of head dark gray, ear coverts black; sides of neck and breast light gray, rest of undersurface buff. Uppersurface grayish brown; central tail feathers like back; rest black, tipped white. Bill black.

Tropical, occasionally subtropical zone. Generally distributed e of Andes s to La Rioja, La Pampa and Buenos Aires, ARGENTINA. W of Andes to PERU. Margarita I. Trinidad. [Galápagos Is. Acc. Falkland Is.] Mangroves, plantations, capoeira, bushy stream banks.

8. GRAY-CAPPED CUCKOO

Coccyzus lansbergi

10". Top and sides of head dark gray in sharp contrast to rufous brown back and wings; tawny rufous below. Tail black, outer feathers broadly tipped white.

Tropical zone. N VENEZUELA; w COLOMBIA from Bolívar to Santa Marta. W ECUA-DOR. Migrant to w PERU. [Panama (?)] Thickets.

9. SQUIRREL CUCKOO

Piaya cayana*

16". Chestnut brown above. Throat and upper breast pinkish buff; rest of underparts gray, darkening to blackish on belly and under tail coverts. Tail chestnut maroon, black on undersurface, very long, strongly graduated, broadly tipped white. Bill yellow green, orbital region red or yellow.

Tropical, subtropical zones. Generally distributed e of Andes to n ARGENTINA, occasionally to Buenos Aires. W of Andes from w COLOMBIA south to nw PERU in Piura. Trinidad. [Mid. Amer.] Forest, savanna, cerrado.

Plate 24

10. BLACK-BELLIED CUCKOO

Piaya melanogaster*

14.5". Top and sides of head pale gray; upperparts rufous brown tinged maroon on tail. Throat and breast orange buff; lower breast and belly blackish. Bill crimson. Tail considerably shorter than 9, otherwise similar.

Tropical zone. GUIANAS; VENEZUELA s of the Orinoco; se COLOMBIA; e ECUADOR; e PERU. BRAZIL from rio Branco and rio Negro s to rio Madeira and n Mato Grosso. Forest.

11. LITTLE CUCKOO

Piaya minuta*

11". Miniature of 9, but upperparts, throat and breast deeper rufous brown; belly grayish olive. Tail as in 9 but much shorter, orbital ring red.

Tropical zone. GUIANAS; VENEZUELA; COLOMBIA; e ECUADOR; e PERU; Amazonian and central BRAZIL to Mato Grosso and Goiás; n BOLIVIA. Trinidad. [E Panama.] Mangroves, stream banks, marshy thickets.

12. GREATER ANI

Crotophaga major

19". Metallic blue black, feathers of mantle and breast broadly fringed with metallic green; tail metallic purple. Bill compressed, strongly arched. Iris pale.

Tropical, casually to temperate zone. Generally distributed e of Andes s in ARGENTINA to La Rioja, Córdoba and Buenos Aires. W of Andes only in COLOMBIA s to río San Juan in Chocó. Trinidad. [Central and e Panama.] Swampy places, mangroves.

Plate 44

13. SMOOTH-BILLED ANI

Crotophaga ani

13". Black, feathers of crown, mantle and breast with metallic edges; wings and tail purplish. Bill strongly arched with high narrow ridge. Iris dark.

Tropical, occasionally to lower temperate zone. Generally distributed e of Andes in open habitats s in ARGENTINA to La Rioja, Córdoba and Santa Fe, casually to n Buenos Aires. W of Andes to w ECUADOR. Margarita I. Trinidad. [S Florida; islands of Caribbean; sw Costa Rica; Panama.] Ranches, open country, wet cerrado.

14. GROOVE-BILLED ANI

Crotophaga sulcirostris*

Much like 13 but slightly smaller; bill grooved, without ridge.

Tropical zone. GUYANA; VENEZUELA generally n of the Orinoco, s of it in n Bolívar, n Amazonas; COLOMBIA e of Andes in Vichada. W of Andes from COLOMBIA to PERU, casually to n CHILE in Tarapacá. N ARGENTINA in extreme n Jujuy and Salta. Aruba, Curaçao, Bonaire. Trinidad. [S Texas; Mid. America.] Dry pastures, dry savanna.

15. GUIRA CUCKOO

Guira guira

15.5". Crown rufous with dark shaft stripes; upper back and wing coverts dark brown streaked with white, rest of back buffy white. Underparts buffy white with narrow black shaft streaks on upper breast. Central tail feathers like back, rest pale buffy basally, central part blackish, and broadly tipped white.

Islands in mouth of the Amazon south through e BRAZIL to Río Negro, ARGENTINA, and w to BOLIVIA. Campos, parks.

Plate 24

16. STRIPED CUCKOO

Tapera naevia *

11.5". Crown somewhat crested, rufous streaked with black; back sandy brown to buffy brown streaked with black, upper tail coverts long. Throat and upper breast pale sandy or grayish, belly white. Tail somewhat graduated, mostly brown.

Tropical, lower subtropical zones. Generally distributed e of Andes s to La Rioja, La Pampa and Buenos Aires, ARGENTINA. W of Andes to sw ECUADOR. Margarita I. Trinidad. [Mid. Amer.] Thickets, open woodland, edge of mangroves, cerrado.

17. PHEASANT CUCKOO

Dromococcyx phasianellus *

15". Crown dark rufous, strongly crested; upperparts blackish brown, wing coverts and scapulars edged white. Throat and breast buffy with small dusky spots, rest of underparts white. Tail unusual: Upper tail coverts very long and plume-like tipped with white spot, tail feathers very broad, graduated, dark brown, pale-edged.

Tropical zone. VENEZUELA; COLOMBIA e of Andes from Arauca to Meta. Most of BRAZIL s to Paraná and Mato Grosso; n BOLIVIA; PARAGUAY; ne ARGENTINA in Misiones. [Mid. Amer.] Forest, thickets.

18. PAVONINE CUCKOO

Dromococcyx pavoninus*

10". Very much like 17 but back darker, throat and upper breast uniform rufous brown, size much smaller.

Tropical zone. GUYANA and FRENCH GUIANA; VENEZUELA; e ECUADOR; e PERU. BRAZIL in Roraima and in the e from Goiás s to Paraná and Mato Grosso and Rondonia; PARAGUAY; ne ARGENTINA in Misiones. Forest.

19. RUFOUS-VENTED GROUND-CUCKOO

Neomorphus geoffroyi*

18". Head with dark blue, flat crest; back metallic bronzy green to bronzy purple; underparts grayish to buffy, feathers of throat and upper breast pale-tipped; narrow pectoral band black; crissum chestnut.

Tropical zone. W COLOMBIA in Córdoba s to río Baudó and e of Andes from Caquetá south to e ECUADOR. Central PERU in

Puno and Huánuco. Nw BOLIVIA. BRAZIL s of the Amazon to Rio de Janeiro and n Mato Grosso. [Nicaragua southward.] Forest with fairly open undergrowth.

20. SCALED GROUND-CUCKOO

Neomorphus squamiger

Much like 19, differing chiefly by indistinct pectoral band.

Known only from central Amazonian BRAZIL on both sides of lower rio Tapajós in Pará. Forest.

21. BANDED GROUND-CUCKOO

Neomorphus radiolosus

18". Long, flat crest; hindneck and extreme upper mantle blue black; rest of mantle blackish, barred buffy white; rest of back and inner remiges maroon. Below broadly banded black and buffy white; upper tail coverts metallic purple green. Central tail feathers metallic green, rest deep purple green.

Tropical zone. Sw COLOMBIA from lower río San Juan south to nw ECUADOR. Forest.

Plate 44

22. RUFOUS-WINGED GROUND-CUCKOO

Neomorphus rufipennis

18". Head crested; head, neck, upper back and upper breast deep purplish blue, ashy on throat; lower breast and belly pale ashy brown, becoming dusky on under tail coverts. Back metallic olive, shaded purple; inner remiges purplish maroon. Central tail feathers metallic purple, rest greenish black. Face bare, red.

Tropical zone. GUYANA; VENEZUELA s of the Orinoco; BRAZIL in n Roraima. Forest.

23. RED-BILLED GROUND-CUCKOO

*Neomorphus pucheranii **

18". Crest dark blue; mantle metallic olive becoming bronzy and darker on lower back and upper tail coverts, inner remiges maroon. Throat and upper breast ashy, some feathers narrowly edged black; narrow black pectoral band; lower breast ashy white, sides of body and flanks brown darkening to dusky on under tail coverts. Central tail feathers metallic greenish purple, rest greenish black. Face bare, red.

Tropical zone. Ne PERU east in w BRAZIL along rio Solimões to rios Purús and Negro. Forest.

Fig. 14. KING VULTURE
Sarcoramphus papa
p. 38

Order STRIGIFORMES

Family TYTONIDAE   BARN OWLS

Barn Owls are mostly nocturnal but are sometimes seen at dusk flying over meadows and clearnings. They often nest in buildings but if there are none they use holes in trees or burrows. Their voice is varied comprising hissing sounds, shrill cries and clicks made with the bill.

BARN OWL

Tyto alba *

15". Facial disk white, surrounded by dark border, ocular region dusky. Back buffy brown to blackish brown, dotted with white; underparts white to dark buff, dotted with dusky. Primaries and tail barred buffy and black.

Tropical to temperate zone. Recorded from all countries virtually throughout, although often local, s to Tierra del Fuego. Curaçao, Bonaire. Trinidad and Tobago. [Virtually cosmopolitan, except in polar regions.] Open country, meadows, towns.

Plate 22

Family STRIGIDAE   OWLS

Except for pygmy, burrowing and short-eared owls, the species found in South America are strictly nocturnal and rarely seen. In habits and appearance they differ little from owls in other parts of the world.

They are distinguishable from other nocturnal birds by large, prominent eyes, set in front of the head. Their feet have sharp claws to catch mice, rabbits and other small animals on which they feed. Most owls have a rufous phase.

AID TO IDENTIFICATION

With ear tufts (size small) 1, 2b, 3, 4c, 5b, 6, 7a, 8b; (size large) 9, 10, 25, 26, 27

Without ear tufts (size small) 14, 15b, 16, 17, 18, 28; (size large) 11, 12c, 13b, 19b, 20, 21, 22b, 23c, 24

1. VERMICULATED SCREECH-OWL

Otus guatemalae *

8". Above dark brown vermiculated dusky. Scapulars white, barred brown; wing coverts spotted white. Below rather dark, vermiculated. Differs from 3 by lacking heavy

vertical streaks in underparts, feathers without golden buff bases. Ear tufts present.

Tropical, lower subtropical zones. N VENEZUELA, s of the Orinoco on Cerros Roraima, Duida and La Neblina. W COLOMBIA s to Baudó Mts. E and w ECUADOR.

115

BOLIVIA in Cochabamba. [Mid. Amer.] Forest.

2. WEST PERUVIAN SCREECH-OWL

Otus roboratus

9.5". Rather like 3 but differs by white of underparts not basally cinnamon (or basally cinnamon like 3, 1), center of belly clear white and outer webs of primaries notched with buffy, inner webs almost uniform. Ear tufts present.

Tropical to temperate zone. W PERU in the Marañón Valley (in upper Marañón, 1), coastal Cajamarca and nw Andes s to Lima, up to 9500 ft. Woodland.

3. TROPICAL SCREECH-OWL

Otus choliba *

9.5". Above brown, feathers with narrow black streaks and buffy spots. Face mask bordered posteriorly by black. Underparts white with black streaks and narrower wavy crossbars, feathers cinnamon basally; cinnamon showing through everywhere. Outer webs of scapulars and of inner wing coverts buffy white; inner webs of primaries with distinct broad bands of cinnamon brown to pale gray. Ear tufts present.

Tropical, subtropical zones. Generally distributed e of Andes to San Luis and n Buenos Aires, ARGENTINA. W of Andes to upper Cauca Valley, COLOMBIA. [Costa Rica southward.] Forest, savanna, arid regions, towns.

Plate 24

4. LONG-TUFTED SCREECH-OWL

Otus atricapillus *

10". Much like 3 but somewhat larger with black streaks on crown wider, ear tufts longer.

Se BRAZIL from Bahía to Rio Grande do Sul, w to Goiás; PARAGUAY; ne ARGENTINA in Misiones. Forest.

5. RUFESCENT SCREECH-OWL

Otus ingens *

10.5". Ear tufts and collar on hindneck whitish. Above sandy brown, unstreaked but heavily vermiculated with blackish; below whitish, heavily vermiculated and narrowly and sparsely streaked with brown, the feathers golden buff basally. Primaries cin-

namon with dusky bars. Tail narrowly barred cinnamon and dusky.

Subtropical to temperate zone. Andes of nw VENEZUELA. COLOMBIA in upper Cauca Valley. E slope of Andes of ECUADOR to nw BOLIVIA. Forest.

6. TAWNY-BELLIED SCREECH-OWL

Otus watsonii *

9". Very dark screech-owl with long ear tufts. Dark brown above and tawny, collar on hindneck buffy. Underparts ochraceous tawny streaked with black, vermiculated dusky on chest and obscurely barred with whitish on belly. Ear tufts.

Tropical zone. SURINAM; VENEZUELA in extreme nw, nw Bolívar and in Amazonas; COLOMBIA e of E Andes south to nw BOLIVIA and BRAZIL on both sides of the Amazon, e to rio Tapajós and south to n Mato Grosso. Forest.

7. BARE-SHANKED SCREECH-OWL

Otus clarkii

10". Rather large screech-owl, dark reddish brown above, feathers of crown tipped white, of back spotted with black and buff. Underparts mostly white streaked with black and barred with tawny, often giving a spotted effect. Ear tufts present. Tarsus bare.

Subtropical zone. Nw COLOMBIA in mts. on Panama border. [Costa Rica, Panama.] Forest.

8. WHITE-THROATED SCREECH-OWL

Otus albogularis *

11.5". Throat conspicuously white. Upperparts and breast dark brown, spotted and vermiculated with tawny; belly tawny buff, sparsely barred and streaked with dusky. Ear tufts present.

Subtropical, temperate zones. Andes of nw VENEZUELA; Andes of COLOMBIA; e ECUADOR, and ne PERU in Amazonas and in nw at Taulis. BOLIVIA in Cochabamba. Forest.

9. CRESTED OWL

Lophostrix cristata *

16". Long, plume-like white ear tufts; forehead and eyebrow white, cheeks chestnut. Back dark brown, chest and underparts much paler, chest mixed with white, rest of underparts vermiculated with whitish. Wing coverts with round white spots.

Tropical zone. GUIANAS, VENEZUELA, COLOMBIA, south, e of Andes, to Cochabamba, BOLIVIA, and Amazonian BRAZIL e to middle Amazon. [Mid. Amer.] Forest.

10. GREAT HORNED OWL

Bubo virginianus *

21''. Largest South American owl; conspicuous ear tufts. Above brown mixed with white, below closely barred dusky and whitish. Face pale, large patch on lower throat white. Toes feathered.

Tropical to páramo zone. Very local in tropical lowlands, more widespread in cooler elevations and temperate lowlands s to Tierra del Fuego and Cape Horn Archipelago. [N and Mid. Amer.; w Panama.] Forest, second growth, coastal mangroves.

11. SPECTACLED OWL

Pulsatrix perspicillata *

18''. Back uniform dark chocolate brown; underparts buff with broad chocolate breast band. Forehead, eyebrow, line encircling face and patch on lower throat white. No ear tufts.

Tropical zone. Generally distributed e of Andes to Rio Grande do Sul, BRAZIL, PARAGUAY, BOLIVIA and nw ARGENTINA. W of Andes south to w ECUADOR. Trinidad. [Mid. Amer.] Forest, savanna, plantations, mangroves.

12. TAWNY-BROWED OWL

Pulsatrix koeniswaldiana

Much like 11 but smaller and differing mainly by face being encircled by ochraceous instead of white.

Se BRAZIL from Espírito Santo and e Minas Gerais to Paraná; e PARAGUAY; ne ARGENTINA in Misiones. Forest.

13. BAND-BELLIED OWL

Pulsatrix melanota *

16.5''. Above chocolate brown with a few buffy white spots; forehead, lores and upper breast white; rest of underparts white barred with brown. No ear tufts.

Tropical zone. Se COLOMBIA south to n BOLIVIA in Cochabamba. Forest.

14. LEAST PYGMY-OWL

Glaucidium minutissimum *

6''. Two black spots surrounded by ochraceous, rather like "eyes," on back of head. Top of head brown, minutely dotted with white. Back russet brown, nuchal collar white. Underparts white with lower throat, sides of breast and streaks on abdomen rufous brown. Tail black notched with white, or coarsely barred. Imm.: Crown usually duller, unmarked.

GUYANA. Nw COLOMBIA. Se PERU; BRAZIL in Roraima, Amapá, Pará, Bahía and Mato Grosso; PARAGUAY. [Mid. Amer.] Open, bushy country, forest.

15. ANDEAN PYGMY-OWL

Glaucidium jardinii *

6.5''. Somewhat larger than 14 and crown either uniform or with fulvous dots. Tail more finely barred.

Andes in upper subtropical and temperate zones from Mérida, VENEZUELA, and COLOMBIA s through Andes to BOLIVIA in Cochabamba. [Mts. of Costa Rica, w Panama.] Forest, scrub.

16. FERRUGINOUS PYGMY-OWL

Glaucidium brasilianum *

6.5''. Much like 15 but usually inhabiting lowlands instead of mountains. Crown streaked rather than spotted.

Tropical and subtropical zones. Generally distributed s to central ARGENTINA and n CHILE. Trinidad. [S Arizona; Mid. Amer.] Forest, scrub, arid woodland; sometimes in towns, cerrado.

Plate 24

17. AUSTRAL PYGMY-OWL

Glaucidium nanum

7.5''. Distinguished from other pygmy-owls by numerous white spots on wing coverts and scapulars, and by narrowly barred tail.

S CHILE from Atacama, and ARGENTINA from Neuquén and Río Negro to s Tierra del Fuego; in winter migrates n to Buenos Aires, Entre Ríos, Santa Fe and Tucumán. Woods, thickets.

18. BURROWING OWL

Speotyto cunicularia *

9''. Distinguishable from any other South

American owl by diurnal and terrestrial habits and long legs. Above brown spotted with white; below white sparsely barred with brown. No ear tufts.

Tropical to temperate zone. Generally but locally distributed in open, arid and semiarid regions south to n Tierra del Fuego. Aruba. Margarita I. [W North Amer., Florida; Mexico to Honduras; acc. Panama. W Indies.]

19. BLACK-AND-WHITE OWL

Ciccaba nigrolineata

15". Upperparts uniform brownish black except for white bars on hindneck. Underparts white regularly barred with black. Tail black with four or five narrow white bars. No ear tufts.

Tropical to subtropical zone. Nw VENEZUELA e to Caracas and Guárico; central and ne COLOMBIA. W ECUADOR; ne PERU. [Mid. Amer.] Forest, clearings.

20. BLACK-BANDED OWL

Ciccaba huhula *

15". Black; uppersurface with very narrow wavy white bars, undersurface regularly barred with white. Tail with four white bars. No ear tufts.

Tropical zone. GUYANA and FRENCH GUIANA; VENEZUELA s of the Orinoco; COLOMBIA e of Andes in Meta; e ECUADOR; e PERU; BRAZIL in Amazonia from rio Juruá to e Pará, and Maranhão, s to Santa Catarina and Mato Grosso; PARAGUAY; n ARGENTINA. Forest.

Plate 24

21. MOTTLED OWL

Ciccaba virgata *

13". Very variable species. Upperparts either blackish brown everywhere finely dotted and barred with fulvous, or reddish brown finely waved with blackish. Scapulars with white spots. Eyebrows white to fulvous. Chest brown, everywhere dotted and lined with whitish; rest of underparts white to fulvous broadly streaked. Remiges and rectrices barred. No ear tufts.

Tropical to subtropical zone. Generally distributed e of Andes to se PERU, BOLIVIA in La Paz and Cochabamba, PARAGUAY, and ne ARGENTINA. W of Andes s to río Chone, w ECUADOR. Trinidad. [Mid. Amer.] Forest.

22. RUFOUS-BANDED OWL

Ciccaba albitarsus *

15.5". Uppersurface banded black and rufous; eyebrow and lores white. Below bright tawny orange with large silvery white spots, divided in center by chestnut line. Primaries notched with rufous on outer web. No ear tufts.

Subtropical to temperate zone of Andes. N VENEZUELA in Mérida and Trujillo; COLOMBIA; ECUADOR; n PERU, on w slope of Andes at Taulis (6° 50′ s), on e slope above Marañón Valley, south to n BOLIVIA. Forest.

23. RUSTY-BARRED OWL

Strix hylophila

Rather like 22; differs mainly by inner webs of outer remiges being conspicuously barred and by face buff, barred with blackish. No ear tufts.

Se BRAZIL from Minas Gerais and São Paulo to Rio Grande do Sul; PARAGUAY; n ARGENTINA in Misiones and e Formosa. Forest.

24. RUFOUS-LEGGED OWL

Strix rufipes *

15". Upperparts dark brown barred with white; below white barred with blackish, everywhere orange bases of feathers showing through. Primaries rufescent barred with dusky. Tail blackish with six or seven buffy to white bars. Tarsi plain buff. Face margined posteriorly by black. No ear tufts.

PARAGUAYAN chaco; ARGENTINA and CHILE to Tierra del Fuego. [Acc. Falkland Is.] Forest.

25. STRIPED OWL

Rhinoptynx clamator *

15". Buffy ochraceous boldly streaked with black, lower back and inner remiges freckled with black. Facial disk buffy white, bordered black. Ear tufts prominent, black on outer web; deep black band surrounding face. Tail and flight feathers barred. Tarsi and toes feathered, buff.

Tropical zone. GUIANAS; VENEZUELA n of the Orinoco, s of it in Bolívar; COLOMBIA e of Andes. E PERU; central and e BRAZIL from Bahía and Goiás s to Rio Grande do Sul and Mato Grosso; BOLIVIA;

PARAGUAY; URUGUAY; n ARGENTINA to Santa Fe and Buenos Aires. Tobago. [Mid. Amer.] Bushy grassland, marshes, savanna.

26. STYGIAN OWL

Asio stygius *

17". Above dark brown with a few buff spots on crown and hindneck; small ear tufts. Upper tail coverts barred with fulvous; inner remiges sparsely spotted with fulvous. Underparts mottled buff and dark brown. Tail dark brown barred with buff. Tarsi feathered.

Tropical to temperate zone. W VENE-ZUELA; Andes of COLOMBIA; ECUADOR; BRAZIL, spotty records in Amazonia, s to Mato Grosso, also from Minas Gerais and São Paulo to Rio Grande do Sul; PARAGUAY; n ARGENTINA. [Mts. of Mexico, Br. Honduras, Guatemala, Nicaragua; Greater Antilles.] Forest, woodland.

27. SHORT-EARED OWL

Asio flammeus *

17". Somewhat like 26 but lower parts ochraceous buff, streaked with dark brown rather than mottled. Primaries banded with orange buff instead of more or less plain and toes feathered as well as tarsi. Ear tufts short and inconspicuous.

Tropical to páramo zone in open, usually semiarid areas. GUYANA; SURINAM; n VENEZUELA; E Andes of COLOMBIA; ECUADOR; nw and s PERU, also along coast; BOLIVIA. S BRAZIL from São Paulo to Rio Grande do Sul; PARAGUAY; URU-GUAY; ARGENTINA and CHILE s to Tierra del Fuego. [Galápagos and Juan Fernández Is.; Falkland Is. N America wintering to Costa Rica. Greater Antilles. Europe and Asia, wintering to N Africa and E Indies. Caroline Is. Hawaii.]

28. BUFF-FRONTED OWL

Aegolius harrisii *

8.5". Above chocolate brown, darkest on head. Forecrown, collar on hindneck and entire underparts yellowish buff. Primaries notched with white, wing coverts with white spots. Tail blackish tipped white, with two broken white bars. No ear tufts.

Subtropical to temperate zone. VENE-ZUELA (Mérida); COLOMBIA ("Bogotá"; upper Cauca Valley); ECUADOR. Se BRA-ZIL from São Paulo to Rio Grande do Sul; PARAGUAY; URUGUAY; n ARGENTINA in Misiones, Tucumán and Jujuy. Forest.

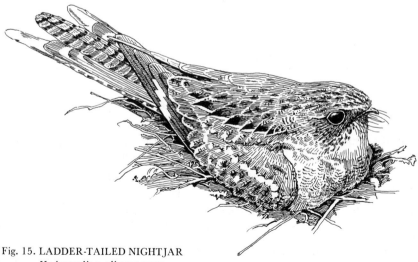

Fig. 15. LADDER-TAILED NIGHTJAR
Hydropsalis c. climacocerca
p. 124

Order CAPRIMULGIFORMES

Family STEATORNITHIDAE   OILBIRDS

These large, nocturnal birds related to nightjars have rather hawk-like bills and claws. They live in colonies, roost and nest in caves, and eat fruits of trees and palms. When disturbed they are very noisy.

The nestlings become exceedingly fat, and were used as a source of oil by indigenous tribes. This, of course, is the reason for their common name.

OILBIRD

Steatornis caripensis

18". Above brown; head rufescent, spotted with white; wing coverts with white spots encircled with black. Outer primaries notched buff. Underparts pinkish brown, spotted with white. Tail long, graduated, brown, barred and freckled with black, very stiff.

Local in tropical to temperate zone. GUYANA; VENEZUELA; mts. of COLOMBIA to nw BOLIVIA. Trinidad. [E Panama.] Forest, near caves, stands of palms.

Plate 24

Family NYCTIBIIDAE   POTOOS

Potoos are strictly nocturnal and related to nightjars. Most of the species, except for the Common Potoo, are rare. They nest on tree stumps, lay but a single egg, and when incubating as well as perching they assume an erect position, blending with the stumps to avoid detection. They dwell in the forest and open woods feeding on insects caught on the wing.

1. GREAT POTOO

Nyctibius grandis

20". White or grayish white marbled with thin wavy lines of black and rufous, appearing gray from afar. Remiges black on inner web. Tail with about eight or nine dusky bars.

Tropical zone. GUIANAS; VENEZUELA; COLOMBIA; e ECUADOR; e PERU; BRAZIL in Amazonia from rio Juruá to e Pará and in the e from Bahía to São Paulo and Mato Grosso. [Guatemala; Panama.] Forest borders, savanna, plantations.

2. LONG-TAILED POTOO

Nyctibius aethereus *

18". Rufous brown, feathers marbled with black and with black spots on inner wing coverts and lower breast. Tail strongly graduated, central feathers pointed.

Tropical zone. GUYANA; s VENEZUELA; w COLOMBIA in Chocó, and extreme e in

Vaupés. E ECUADOR; e PERU; BRAZIL in w Amazonia n of the Solimões, and in the e from e Pará and Bahía s to Paraná; PARAGUAY. Forest.

3. COMMON POTOO

Nyctibius griseus *

15". Two color phases. Brown phase rather like 2 but much smaller and tail only slightly graduated. Gray phase rather like 1 but much smaller and much darker.

Tropical zone. GUIANAS; VENEZUELA; COLOMBIA; e and w ECUADOR; e PERU; virtually throughout BRAZIL s in ARGENTINA to La Rioja and n Santa Fe. Trinidad. [Mid. Amer.; Jamaica; Hispaniola.] Forest, plantations, cerrado.

Plate 24

4. WHITE-WINGED POTOO

Nyctibius leucopterus *

10". Rather like gray phase of 3 but much smaller with much shorter tail, and at once distinguishable from any other potoo by white inner wing coverts and axillaries.

Tropical zone. VENEZUELA in Táchira. COLOMBIA e of E Andes; e ECUADOR. Coastal BRAZIL in Bahía.

5. RUFOUS POTOO

Nyctibius bracteatus

9". Mostly rufous with white spots on axillary tips, breast and belly; breast feathers with narrow, wavy black lines. Tail feathers barred black, tipped white.

Tropical zone. GUYANA. COLOMBIA e of Andes; e ECUADOR; e PERU. Forest.

Family CAPRIMULGIDAE   NIGHTJARS AND NIGHTHAWKS

Except for nighthawks which are crepuscular, birds of this family are strictly nocturnal. All look more or less alike, except for the long-tailed species (nos. 22-26), and owing to their nocturnal habits are best distinguished by voice. They feed mainly on insects caught on the wing. They lay their eggs on the ground, making no nest.

Nighthawks can be distinguished in flight from nightjars by their narrow pointed wings. They usually fly higher than nightjars.

No key is given for this family, as most of the species resemble each other to a great degree and a superficial one would be of little use.

1. SEMICOLLARED NIGHTHAWK

Lurocalis semitorquatus *

9-10.5". Distinguishable from other nighthawks by short tail and very long wings. Upperparts and chest black, sprinkled everywhere with rufous or gray dots and rings; belly rufous, plain or barred with black. Throat and innermost remiges white, latter marbled and spotted with black. Primaries black without white. Two species may be involved.

Tropical, subtropical, temperate zones. GUIANAS; VENEZUELA; COLOMBIA except the west; e ECUADOR; e PERU; BRAZIL; n ARGENTINA in Misiones and e Formosa.

Trinidad. [Nicaragua; Panama.] Campos, forest.

Plate 24

2. LEAST NIGHTHAWK

Chordeiles pusillus *

6". Smallest nighthawk. Above dark brown finely mottled with rufous and buff. Four outer primaries with white band toward middle, inner remiges broadly tipped with pale buff. Underparts regularly barred white and dark brown. Tail feathers, except for outermost and central feathers, tipped white on inner web (mottled with brown in ♀).

Tropical zone. COLOMBIA along the Orinoco; VENEZUELA s of the Orinoco, acc. n of it. GUYANA; BRAZIL in Roraima and s of the Amazon in se Pará and from Piauí to Minas Gerais and Mato Grosso. Campos, savanna.

3. SAND-COLORED NIGHTHAWK

Chordeiles rupestris*

8.5″. Tail more forked than other night-hawks'. Above sandy mixed with black; underparts white mottled with sandy on chest. Outer four primaries blackish, rest of remiges white, tipped black. All but central tail feathers white, tipped black.

Tropical zone. E COLOMBIA; VENE-ZUELA in Amazonas; e ECUADOR; e PERU; w BRAZIL e to rio Negro and rio Tapajós and s to Mato Grosso. N BOLIVIA. Sandbars, riverbanks.

4. LESSER NIGHTHAWK

Chordeiles acutipennis*

8″. Upperparts and chest grayish, speckled and marbled with black. Spots on wing coverts and inner remiges buff. Throat white. Band across four outer primaries white; in ♀ buff, nearer tip than in 5; all but central tail feathers barred black and fulvous on basal two-thirds, distal third black bi-sected by broad white band. (See also 21)

Resident and migrant, tropical zone. N and w COLOMBIA and in upper Magdalena Valley (N American migrants winter in n and w Colombia); VENEZUELA and the GUIANAS s through BRAZIL to PARA-GUAY and n BOLIVIA. On the west s to Arequipa, PERU; once in CHILE. Margarita I. Trinidad and Tobago. [Western US; Mid. Amer.] Savanna, open country.

5. COMMON NIGHTHAWK

Chordeiles minor*

9″. Rather like 4 but more coarsely marked above and below, and white band on the four outer primaries nearer base of feathers.

Tropical zone. Possibly breeding in extreme nw COLOMBIA, otherwise migrant (and in part winter resident) over most of continent s to Córdoba and Buenos Aires, ARGEN-TINA. Curaçao. Tobago. [N Amer.; Mid. Amer.; Bahamas; Greater Antilles.] Open woodland, savanna.

6. BAND-TAILED NIGHTHAWK

Nyctiprogne leucopyga*

7″. Differs from other nighthawks (except 2) by small size. No white in wing, band across tail feathers more toward center than tip of feather.

Tropical zone. GUIANAS; VENEZUELA; extreme e COLOMBIA; BRAZIL from rios Negro and Madeira e to Pará and Piauí, and south to sw Mato Grosso. Savanna.

7. NACUNDA NIGHTHAWK

Podager nacunda*

11″. Upperparts sandy brown vermiculated and spotted with black; breast brown, barred and vermiculated with black. Band across throat, lower breast, belly and under tail coverts pure white. Base of primaries white. Central tail feathers like back with five black bars, three outermost feathers with distal third white (no white in tail, ♀).

Tropical zone. N COLOMBIA from lower río Magdalena to Guajira Peninsula, and e of Andes generally from VENEZUELA and GUIANAS s to Río Negro, ARGENTINA. Trinidad and Tobago. Open country, sa-vanna, campos.

8. PAURAQUE

Nyctidromus albicollis*

11″. Above grayish brown to reddish brown, handsomely marked on scapulars with velvety black spots margined with buff, and on wing coverts with round, rich buff spots. First five primaries crossed by broad white band. Outermost tail feather black, part of inner web fringed white, next two white, rest like back but with black bars. ♀: Differs from ♂ by outer primaries and outer tail feathers being black, barred rufous; next pair similar but with white tip to inner web.

Tropical, subtropical zones. GUIANAS, VENEZUELA and COLOMBIA s to BO-LIVIA and ne ARGENTINA. W of Andes to nw PERU. Trinidad. [S Texas; Mid. Amer.] Forest clearings, brush, capoeira.

Plate 24

9. OCELLATED POORWILL

Nyctiphrynus ocellatus*

8.5″. Mainly reddish brown very finely vermiculated with black, breast grayer (or all very dark, almost blackish, 1). Scapulars with round black spots. Bar across throat white, round spots on belly (and on wing coverts, 1) white. Remiges without white. Three outermost tail feathers laterally tipped white (or all tipped white, 1).

Tropical zone. Pacific slope south to nw ECUADOR, 1. E ECUADOR to n BOLIVIA; BRAZIL in w Amazonia and east, s of the Amazon, to Goiás and Pernambuco s to Rio Grande do Sul; PARAGUAY. Ne ARGENTINA in Misiones. [Nicaragua.] Forest.

Caprimulgus

Birds belonging to this genus look much alike in body plumage. All are mostly brown or grayish brown vermiculated and spotted with black and rufous, crown and scapulars heavily spotted or streaked with black. White or buff band usually crosses lower throat. Lower breast and belly buffy, usually with fine dusky bars. Central tail feathers much like back but barred with black. Best differentiating characters between the species are markings of wings and tail, and these are relied upon in describing the following 12 species. Females usually resemble males except for markings of wings and tail.

10. CHUCK-WILLS-WIDOW
Caprimulgus carolinensis

11.5". A large nightjar with buff band across throat. Primaries black barred with rufous. Three outer tail feathers mostly white on inner web and tipped buff. ♀: Three outer tail feathers barred black and rufous, narrowly tipped pale rufous.

Tropical, subtropical zones. Winter resident in COLOMBIA west of E Andes. VENEZUELA in Mérida, once. [Breeds in N Amer. Winters through Mid. Amer.; Greater Antilles.] Forest and woodland.

11. RUFOUS NIGHTJAR
Caprimulgus rufus *

10.5". Much like 10, but smaller. Outermost tail feather with large subterminal white patch on inner web, next two with large subterminal patch covering both webs. ♀:

Only distinguishable from 10 by smaller size.

Tropical zone. N COLOMBIA; n VENEZUELA to n Bolívar and n Amazonas. GUIANAS s through BRAZIL to BOLIVIA, PARAGUAY and n ARGENTINA. Trinidad. [Costa Rica; Panama. St. Lucia] Open woodland, second growth.

12. SILKY-TAILED NIGHTJAR
Caprimulgus sericocaudatus

11.5". Band across throat buff. Primaries blackish brown notched on outer web only with rufous. Tail much rounded, three outer feathers with wide, diagonal, silky white band across tip. ♀: Tail much rounded, three outer feathers brownish black with rufous bars interrupted in middle and narrow, diagonal, rufous band at tip.

E PERU (Yarinacocha). BRAZIL (Santarém; near Curitiba, Paraná). PARAGUAY (Capitán Meza, alto Paraná). ARGENTINA (Misiones).

13. BAND-WINGED NIGHTJAR
Caprimulgus longirostris *

9". Four outermost primaries with white band across middle of feather. Three outer tail feathers with large white terminal patch and white spot or bar near base of inner web. Belly buffy, barred dusky. ♀: Like ♂ but white marks in tail smaller.

Subtropical to temperate zone. Mts. of n VENEZUELA and isolated peaks in s Bolívar and Amazonas; COLOMBIA from Santa Marta Mts. s through Andes and arid littoral of PERU to CHILE to Magallanes. Se BRAZIL from Minas Gerais to Rio de Janeiro. URUGUAY; ARGENTINA s to Santa Cruz. Campos, open woodland, towns in e Brazil.

14. WHITE-TAILED NIGHTJAR
Caprimulgus cayennensis *

8.5". Four outer primaries with white band toward distal half of feathers; rest of remiges with white spot on inner web, innermost tipped white. Outermost tail feather mostly white with diagonal black bar on inner web, next three white on inner web except for dusky tip and bar near base. Belly white. ♀: Wing as in ♂ but marking ochraceous instead of white; outer four tail feathers barred pale ochraceous and black with marbled tips. Belly buff.

Tropical, subtropical zones. GUIANAS; VENEZUELA; COLOMBIA in Cauca and Magdalena Valleys and on Caribbean coast; BRAZIL in Roraima. Aruba to Trinidad and Tobago. [Costa Rica; Panama. Martinique; Antigua, Barbados.] Campos, savanna.

15. WHITE-WINGED NIGHTJAR
Caprimulgus candicans

9″. Rather pale nightjar. Primaries black with white bases. Abdomen, under wing coverts and outer rectrices white. ♀: Differs from ♂ by barred primaries and tail.

S BRAZIL in Mato Grosso and São Paulo. PARAGUAY.

16. SPOT-TAILED NIGHTJAR
Caprimulgus maculicaudus

8″. Primaries dark brown barred with rufous. Four outer tail feathers terminating in white bar, outer webs notched with rufous, inner webs with three or four round white spots. ♀: Similar but no white in tail.

Tropical zone. GUIANAS; VENEZUELA in Miranda, Barinas and s Amazonas; COLOMBIA in n Chocó, Boyacá, Meta and Vaupés. BRAZIL on rio Madeira, Amazon delta, Rio de Janeiro and in n São Paulo (?). Se PERU. N BOLIVIA in Beni. [Breeding, s Mexico, Honduras.] Savanna, marshy places.

17. LITTLE NIGHTJAR
Caprimulgus parvulus *

8″. Outermost primary with white spot on inner web, next three with broad white band across middle of feather. Scapulars conspicuously black and white (or black and buff). Four outer tail feathers with small white patch at tip of inner web, sometimes on both webs of outermost pair (or with inner web of outermost two tail feathers mostly white, 1). ♀: Primaries blackish notched with rufous near base of outer web and with two or three spots of rufous on inner web. Outer tail feathers dusky with interrupted bars of buff. Rather like 21 but much darker.

Tropical zone. N VENEZUELA; ne COLOMBIA. E PERU; BRAZIL s of the Amazon e to Pará; BOLIVIA; ARGENTINA s to Córdoba and n Buenos Aires. Sw ECUADOR, nw PERU, 1 (*anthonyi*, probably a distinct species). Woodland.

18. CAYENNE NIGHTJAR
Caprimulgus maculosus

8.5″. A dark nightjar. Primaries black with white spot on inner web of four outermost. Outermost tail feather virtually uniform, next two tipped white. ♀: Unknown.

FRENCH GUIANA (Tamanoir). Dry open country.

19. BLACKISH NIGHTJAR
Caprimulgus nigrescens *

8.5″. Outer two primaries uniform blackish, next two with white spot on inner web. Outermost tail feather virtually uniform next two tipped white. ♀: Primaries uniform blackish brown; outer tail feathers dusky, obscurely barred.

Tropical zone. GUIANAS; VENEZUELA s of the Orinoco; e COLOMBIA south, e of Andes, to n BOLIVIA and BRAZIL to n Maranhão and n Mato Grosso. Rocky outcrops in forest, sandy savanna.

20. RORAIMAN NIGHTJAR
Caprimulgus whiteleyi

Like 19 but slightly larger, white terminal patch on tail feathers confined to inner web, and outermost primary with white bar.

VENEZUELA in Bolívar on Cerros Roraima and Ptari-tepui. Forest.

21. PYGMY NIGHTJAR
Caprimulgus hirundinaceus *

7″. Wing pattern rather like *Chordeiles*. Outer three primaries with white patch on inner web, fourth with white on both webs, sometimes even on second and third; shafts dark (or with white bar across first five primaries, shafts white, 1); white patch at tip of two outer tail feathers. ♀: Rather like 17 but paler and no white on scapulars.

E BRAZIL in Ceará and n Bahía, 1; s Piauí and central Bahía.

22. LADDER-TAILED NIGHTJAR
Hydropsalis climacocerca *

11″. Four outer primaries with white bar, fourth with additional spot near base. Tail rather long, W-shaped; central and outer pair of feathers longest, outermost pair with wide diagonal white patch, next three mostly white with vermiculated tips. ♀: 9″. Very different. Much browner with pale cinnamon belly barred with black. Outermost primary mostly uniform dusky but with cinnamon spot on inner web, next two with cinnamon bar and barred rufous basally. Tail normal, outer feathers barred brown and dusky.

Tropical zone. GUIANAS; VENEZUELA s of the Orinoco; e COLOMBIA n to Meta; e ECUADOR; e PERU; w Amazonian BRAZIL e at least to Óbidos and rio Tapajós; BOLIVIA in La Paz. Sandbars, adjacent forest.

Fig. 15, p. 119

23. SCISSOR-TAILED NIGHTJAR

*Hydropsalis brasiliana ***

20″ (or 15″, 1). Outer tail feather very long, dusky, tapering to white tip; rest of feathers notched with white on outer web and fringed with white on inner web, barred with white near base; next three feathers with broad pale tips, central tail feathers longer than any except outer ones. ♀: 11.5″. Outer primary with pale fringe near base of outer web, rest notched and barred with cinnamon. Tail forked, central pair of feathers longer than any except outermost, rather coarsely notched and barred with sandy.

Tropical, subtropical zones. E PERU in Junín and BRAZIL s of the Amazon, 1. BOLIVIA; PARAGUAY; URUGUAY; n and central ARGENTINA s to Mendoza and Buenos Aires. Woodland, cerrado.

24. SWALLOW-TAILED NIGHTJAR

*Uropsalis segmentata ***

26″ (or 20″, 1). Outer tail feathers very long, uniform blackish; outer web very narrow, pale notched (or white, 1), shaft white. Primaries uniform dusky. No rufous nuchal collar. ♀: 9″ Crown black, spotted rufous. Primaries mostly uniform dusky. Tail of normal length, slightly forked, blackish, feathers coarsely barred with rufous.

Temperate, páramo zones. E and Central

Andes of COLOMBIA s through Andes to Cochabamba, BOLIVIA. Central PERU, 1. Open mountain slopes.

25. LYRE-TAILED NIGHTJAR

*Uropsalis lyra ***

31″. Tail very long, lyriform, black, tapering to white tip; shaft black, outer web narrow. Nuchal collar rufous. ♀: Much like 24 but primaries notched on outer web with deep rufous, and crown vermiculated grayish with median black spots rather than black spotted with rufous.

Upper tropical and subtropical zone. From Andes in Mérida, VENEZUELA, s through e and central COLOMBIA and ECUADOR to Cuzco, PERU. Savanna, open woodland.

26. LONG-TRAINED NIGHTJAR

Macropsalis creagra

28″. Outer tail feathers very long (central pair very short, 2″), mostly white on inner web; outer feathers dusky, fringed with white on inner web. Pale rufous nuchal collar. ♀: 8″. Tail normal, outer feathers dark brown, barred rufous. General color like ♂.

Se BRAZIL from Espírito Santo and Rio de Janeiro to Rio Grande do Sul.

27. SICKLE-WINGED NIGHTJAR

Eleothreptus anomalus

7.5″. First six primaries curved inward and equal in length, inner primaries somewhat longer than outer ones; primaries blackish with large white tips on first five, basally rusty fawn. Tail very short, outer rectrices fawn color tipped whitish, irregularly barred with blackish. ♀: Like ♂ but wings banded with rufous and normal in shape.

Se BRAZIL from Minas Gerais to Rio Grande do Sul; URUGUAY; PARAGUAY and ne ARGENTINA in e Chaco, n Santa Fe and Buenos Aires. Swamps.

Order APODIFORMES

Family APODIDAE   SWIFTS

Swifts differ from swallows by their long narrow wings, very swift, often gliding flight, usually blackish plumage, and twittering and screaming notes. They never perch on wires but cling to rocks and hollows in trees. They fly in small groups, feeding on insects caught on the wing. *Cypseloides* swifts have rumps of the same color as the back; *Chaetura* swifts have the rump paler than the back, and the throat more or less paler than the back. Many swifts cannot be reliably identified in the field.

AID TO IDENTIFICATION

Tail slightly to deeply forked 1, 3, 7a, 8a, 9a, 18, 19b, 20, 21a, 22

Tail square 2c, 3, 4c, 5, 13, 14, 15

Tail very short, not conspicuous, bird cigar-shaped 3, 6a, 7, 10, 11b, 12a, 13, 16, 17

1. WHITE-COLLARED SWIFT

Streptoprocne zonaris *

8.5". Very large blackish swift with white collar on hindneck joined to large white breast patch. Tail slightly forked.

Tropical to temperate zone. GUYANA; VENEZUELA and COLOMBIA and s in Andes to e BOLIVIA; BRAZIL in nw Amazonia, Roraima and Mato Grosso, and in e from Minas Gerais to Rio Grande do Sul; n ARGENTINA from Jujuy to Mendoza; on migration to Entre Ríos and Córdoba. Trinidad. [Mid. Amer.] Clearings in hill and mountain country, cliffs, sometimes over cities.

Plate 24

2. BISCUTATE SWIFT

Streptoprocne biscutata

Differs from 1 by being slightly smaller, and by white collar on hindneck not joined to pectoral patch. Tail square.

E BRAZIL from Piauí and Minas Gerais to Rio Grande do Sul.

3. CHESTNUT-COLLARED SWIFT

Cypseloides rutilus *

5.7". Sooty; collar on hindneck, auriculars, lower throat and breast rufous. ♀: Usually lacks rufous collar (with rufous collar, 1).

Tropical, subtropical zones. GUYANA; VENEZUELA (mountains of Venezuela, 1); COLOMBIA, south to n BOLIVIA. Trinidad. [Mexico to w Panama.] Hill country.

4. GREAT DUSKY SWIFT

Cypseloides senex

7.5". Uniform sooty brown, slightly grayer on head and throat, latter with black shaft streaks. Tail square short.

Central and s BRAZIL in s Pará, Mato Grosso and São Paulo; PARAGUAY; ne ARGENTINA in Misiones.

5. SOOTY SWIFT

Cypseloides fumigatus *

6.5-7.5". Much like 4 in color but smaller, more uniformly colored. Tail longer. Probably two species involved.

126

Se BRAZIL from Espírito Santo to Rio Grande do Sul (possibly Pará). Nw ARGEN-TINA in Salta, Tucumán and Santiago del Estero. Open hill country.

6. SPOT-FRONTED SWIFT

Cypseloides cherriei

5.5". Sooty black, sides of forehead and small postocular streak white. Tail very short.

Subtropical zone. COLOMBIA in Santander (Jan.). VENEZUELA in Aragua. [Costa Rica.]

7. WHITE-CHINNED SWIFT

Cypseloides cryptus

6". Sooty brown, small white patch on chin usually present. Tail very short.

GUYANA; VENEZUELA in Táchira, Bolívar and Aragua. COLOMBIA in Cauca and Córdoba. ECUADOR. E PERU. [Br. Honduras southward.]

8. WHITE-CHESTED SWIFT

Cypseloides lemosi

6". Sooty black with irregular white patch on chest. Tail somewhat forked.

COLOMBIA in upper Cauca Valley. Open country.

9. BLACK SWIFT

Cypseloides niger *

6". Sooty black, forecrown and belly whitish. Tail forked. ♀: Belly barred whitish.

Recorded in GUYANA (Merumé Mts.). Casual in Trinidad (sight record). [Breeds from se Alaska to mts. of Honduras and possibly Costa Rica. Migrant W Indies.]

10. CHAPMAN'S SWIFT

Chaetura chapmani *

5.5". Glossy blue black above, rump only slightly contrasting with back. Remiges and underparts sooty gray. Tail short.

GUIANAS; VENEZUELA in Sucre, Aragua, Zulia and w Amazonas. COLOMBIA in Antioquia (Apr.; possibly migrant from s.). Se PERU in s Loreto. Ne BRAZIL in Amapá and e Pará and in central Mato Grosso and Acre. Trinidad. [Central Panama.] Lowland forest, savanna.

11. CHIMNEY SWIFT

Chaetura pelagica

5.5". Much like 10 but differing by throat paler than rest of underparts. Tail very short.

Migrates through COLOMBIA and w VENEZUELA. Winters in PERU in Amazonia and on w coast from Libertad to Lima. Nw BRAZIL (sight record). [Breeds from s Canada to Texas and Florida. Migrates through Mid. Amer. Recorded Hispaniola.]

12. VAUX'S SWIFT

Chaetura vauxi *

4". Very similar to 11 but much smaller.

Resident in mts. of n VENEZUELA from Lara to Monagas. [Breeds from se Alaska s through western N Amer. and Mid. Amer.] Pastures, savanna, woodland.

13. GRAY-RUMPED SWIFT

Chaetura cinereiventris *

4.3". Crown, mantle and wings blue black; rump, upper tail coverts and underparts gray, whitish on throat. Tail much longer than in 12.

Tropical, subtropical zones. GUYANA; VENEZUELA; COLOMBIA; e and w ECUADOR; e PERU; BRAZIL in w Amazonia and in se from Bahía to Rio de Janeiro and Santa Catarina. E PARAGUAY; ARGENTINA in Misiones. Trinidad. [Caribbean slope, Nicaragua to w Panama.] Forest.

14. PALE-RUMPED SWIFT

Chaetura egregia

Rather similar to 13 but somewhat larger; differing by darker belly, bronzy instead of bluish back, and whiter, less grayish, rump.

Se PERU in s Loreto; BOLIVIA in Santa Cruz n to Acre, and to ne Mato Grosso (Serra Roncador), BRAZIL.

15. BAND-RUMPED SWIFT

Chaetura spinicauda *

Much like 13 but breast and belly much darker, whitish throat in strong contrast, and rump band much paler, contrasting with upper tail coverts.

Tropical zone. GUIANAS; VENEZUELA from Orinoco delta to w Amazonas. COLOMBIA w of Andes to Chocó and Valle, e of

Andes in Putumayo and Caquetá; n Amazonian BRAZIL. Trinidad. [Costa Rica; Panama.] Wooded hills.

16. ASHY-TAILED SWIFT

Chaetura andrei *

6". Above deep smoky brown; below smoky brown, distinctly paler on throat, rump and upper tail coverts. Tail very short.

SURINAM; VENEZUELA in Carabobo, Sucre, Guárico and Bolívar. N COLOMBIA in Magdalena (Aug.; migrant from s ?). BRAZIL in Roraima and from Piauí to Rio Grande do Sul, and w to Mato Grosso; n PARAGUAY; n ARGENTINA probably breeding in Tucumán and Salta, after breeding season in Santiago del Estero, Formosa and Santa Fe. [Panama, migrant.] Campos, woodland.

17. SHORT-TAILED SWIFT

Chaetura brachyura *

4.5". Glossy blue black; lower back, rump, tail and tail coverts ashy gray. Tail very short.

Tropical zone. GUIANAS; VENEZUELA; s COLOMBIA e and w of Andes; e ECUADOR; nw and e PERU, w through BRAZIL to Pará, Mato Grosso and Acre. Trinidad. [Panama, migrant (?)] Open country.

Plate 24

18. WHITE-TIPPED SWIFT

Aeronautes montivagus

5.2". Brownish black, scapulars tipped white; throat, breast, center of abdomen dingy white; sides of body and under tail coverts ashy brown. Tail slightly forked, feathers narrowly edged and tipped white.

Mts. of VENEZUELA n of the Orinoco and on isolated peaks s of it; n BRAZIL in Serra Imerí. Sw COLOMBIA. Andes of ECUADOR and PERU s to Lima and Junín, thence to Santa Cruz, BOLIVIA. Often nests in buildings.

19. ANDEAN SWIFT

Aeronautes andecolus *

5.7". Upperparts brown; collar on hindneck, band across rump, and underparts white. Tail rather long, forked.

Andes of se PERU and in W Andes from Cajamarca (occasionally on coast) south in n CHILE to Tarapacá; Andes of BOLIVIA s to Tarija and Potosí; w ARGENTINA from Jujuy and Salta s to Río Negro. Open country.

20. LESSER SWALLOW-TAILED SWIFT

Panyptila cayennensis *

5.3". Deep blue black; white spot before eye, white of throat and breast connected to white collar on hindneck. Tail forked, feathers sharply pointed.

Tropical zone. N COLOMBIA e through VENEZUELA to GUIANAS. E ECUADOR south to e PERU. BRAZIL locally in Amazonia, in Pará and Mato Grosso, also in Maranhão, Bahía, Espírito Santo and São Paulo. Trinidad and Tobago. [Mid. Amer.] Open country, plantations, sometimes forest.

21. PYGMY SWIFT

Micropanyptila furcata *

4". Above ashy brown, below paler, whitish on center of throat and abdomen. Tail deeply forked, feathers rather pointed and white at base.

Tropical zone. VENEZUELA in Mérida, Zulia and COLOMBIA in Norte de Santander.

22. FORK-TAILED PALM-SWIFT

Reinarda squamata *

5.5". Above brown, glossed with bluish. Throat and lores white, rest of underparts mixed brown and white. Tail very long, very deeply forked, feathers pointed.

Tropical zone. GUIANAS; locally throughout VENEZUELA; COLOMBIA e of E Andes. Ne PERU in Loreto; BRAZIL in Amazonia, in the e and interior from Ceará, Paraiba and Pernambuco to Espírito Santo, w Minas Gerais and Goiás. Trinidad. Savanna near Mauritia palms, usually near water.

Family TROCHILIDAE   HUMMINGBIRDS

Although hummingbirds form one of the largest bird families, among them are found the smallest of birds. They are notable for extreme brilliance of plumage, and are often decorated with elaborate crests, ruffs and unusual tails. In many species the plumage is highly iridescent. In spite of their brilliant coloring many species appear almost black in poor light.

Hummingbirds are found only in the Americas and occur from Alaska to Tierra del Fuego but are most abundant in the tropics. They occupy all kinds of terrain, deserts, forests, and open country from sea level to snow line in the Andes. Two hundred and thirty-five species are known from South America.

Their powers of flight are remarkable, the wings beating so rapidly that they are practically invisible when hovering motionless in front of a flower, the birds darting backward or in any direction with the greatest abruptness.

Hummingbirds feed on nectar and minute insects. Their tiny feet are usually unsuitable for anything but perching. They are extremely belligerent, attacking and driving off other birds which invade their territory.

Their nests are prettily constructed of lichens, spider webs, vegetable down and are attached to branches or rocks, or fastened to leaves or in crotches of branches. They lay one or two white eggs.

In the following descriptions two measurements are given; the first is the length of the bird, the second the length of the bill, the two combined giving the total length.

AID TO IDENTIFICATION

Body plumage shining or glittering green without contrasting colors
> With contrasting cap (bill black) 78c, 108b, 128b, 176b, 179b; (mandible basally pink) 85, 86b, 87, 88b, 104a, 110a
>
> Without contrasting cap (large) 11b, 38a, 46b, 47b, 48, 150b, 162b; (small) lower mandible basally pink 52, 68, 70, 71a, 82a, 93, 103, 111a, 112, 114a, bill all black 69, 72a, 73a, 74a, 75a, 92a, 113a, 117a, 118b, 157b, 174a, 175b, 177a, 178b, 182b, 183b, 194b, 197b, 198b

Underparts all or mostly white, gray or black, usually with no glittering colors on throat
> Underparts white 90c, 99b, 100, 101a, 108b, 109c, 214b, 215a, 216b, 227b, 228b, 232b
>
> Underparts gray (size large with stripe down throat, bill curved) 10b, 12b, 15a, 16c, 17, 18a, 19, 22a; (with glittering throat) 30, 45, 218; (throat not glittering) 1, 2b, 35, 40a, 41b, 95b, 117a, 118b, 119c, 139b, 140b, 141b, 163, 220; (size small) 53, 54, 55c, 69, 70c, 71a, 72a, 73a, 74a, 75a, 76, 77c, 78c, 79b, 80a, 84
>
> Underparts black or blackish 1, 8a, 44c, 63b, 66b, 141b, 148b, 149b, 184b, throat glittering 173b, 192b, 199b

Underparts all or mostly uniform buff to chestnut
> Bill distinctly curved (basal portion of mandible pale) 5c, 6b, 7, 13b, 14, 21, 23, 24, 25c, 26c, 28c, 29, 30, 31c; (base of mandible dark) 36a
>
> Bill straight or nearly so (rufous in tail) 20, 37a, 56a, 57c, 58c, 59b, 60b, 89a, 125c, 145b, 165b, dusky band across chest 27, 223b, 224b, 225, 229b, 230b, 231b, 233a; (no rufous in tail) size very large 144, 150, size medium to small 94a, 120b, 121b, 124b, 151b, 155a, 156a, 209b, 221a, 222b, 226b, 227b

Throat or underparts spotted, or white or buff with green disks

Size large 34a, 88a, 89a, 92a, 98, 122b, 128b, 129b, 134b, 135a, 136a, 142b, 149b, 158a, 162b, 188b, 189b, 207b

Size medium to small 83, 86b, 87, 88a, 91, 97, 101a, 102, 106b, 107b, 120b, 122b, 182b, 185b, 191a

Underparts streaked or with conspicuous streak down center

Streaked 3b, 4c, 32b, 33

Streak down center 49, 50, 51, 52, 139b, 217b, 219c

Breast color different from belly

Belly green or grayish (breast violet blue or purple) 39a, 41, 42, 80b, 83, 84, 105, 106b, 107b, 136a, 172b, 195b

Belly not green or grayish (breast blue or purple) 40a, 55c, 79b, 81a, 120b, 122b; (breast green) 76, 115a, 117a, 135a, 156a, 158a, 176b, 180b; (breast black) 166b

Narrow pointed throat patch, usually of more than one color, narrowing to point on breast 200b, 201b, 202b, 203a, 204b, 205a, 206b, 216c

Small, isolated, glittering patch of color on center throat 127b, 129b, 130a, 131, 132b, 133b, 134b, 153a, 156a, 157a, 158a, 159b, 160b, 161b, 171b, 173b, 174a, 193b, 196b

White or pale buff patch or band on breast 9, 9bis, 10b, 90c, 116b, 123b, 136a, 146b, 147b, 148b, 152b, 154b, 167a, 168a, 169b, 170b, 181b, 210b, 211c, 212c, 213b, 223b, 225, 229b, 230b, 231b, 232b, 233a

Above, all or mostly purple or black 44c, 77c, 153a, 154b, 159b, 190b, 191a, 192b, 199a, 202b

Upper back dull brown or black, lower back and rump glittering green, purple, etc., 145b, 146b, 147b, 148b

Rump crossed by white or buff band, size very small 56a, 57c, 58c, 59, 60b, 61, 62a, 64, 66b, 67

Outer tail feathers differently colored from rest

All or mostly white 38a, 43, 44c, 91, 100, 139b, 140b, 143b, 149b, 154b, 155a, 166b, 205a, 206b, 214b, 215, 216c

Buff or chestnut 7, 9, 33b, 36a, 37a, 39a, 53, 89a, 114b, 115a, 116b, 125c, 126, 137, 142b, 145b, 146b, 148b, 149b, 160b, 161b, 164b, 165b

Tail long, forked or terminating in a racquet. Bright colors present

Forked (size very small) 63b, 64, 65, 66b, 76, 77c, 187b, 216c, 222b; (size large) 42, 134b, 135a, 137, 138b, 186b, 189b, 208b

Tail glittering 188b, 209, 210b

Racquet 67, 185b, 217b

Tail long, central tail feathers pointed, terminal portion white or buff. No bright colors present; olive above, buffy or light gray below 11b, 12b, 13b, 14, 15a, 16c, 17, 18a, 19, 20, 21, 22a, 23, 24, 25c, 25bis, 26c, 27, 28, 29, 30, 31c

Shaft of outer primary much thickened 34a, 35, 36a, 37a, 38a, 39a, 40a, 41b, 42

Bill remarkable (enormously long) 162b; (turned up at tip) 52, 207b; (sickle-shaped) 32b, 33b; (flesh color with black tip) 56a, 57c, 58c, 59, 60b, 68, 70c, 83, 84, 85, 86b, 87, 91, 94a, 114a, 116b

1. BLUE-FRONTED LANCEBILL

Doryfera johannae *

3.5" (1.1"). Very dark bird. Frontlet glittering violet; back dark bronzy green, upper tail coverts bluish. Underparts black. Tail slightly rounded, blue black. ♀: Forehead shining blue green, occiput coppery. Bronzy green above, upper tail coverts bluish. Underparts grayish green. Tail blue black, outer feathers tipped gray.

Tropical, subtropical zones. GUYANA; isolated peaks in s VENEZUELA. E slope of E Andes of COLOMBIA south to se PERU. N BRAZIL in Roraima. Scrub, savanna.

2. GREEN-FRONTED LANCEBILL

Doryfera ludoviciae*

4" (1.4"). Both sexes much like ♀ of 1 but considerably larger and with glittering green frontlet.

Upper tropical and subtropical zones. Andes of Mérida, VENEZUELA, COLOMBIA, ECUADOR and PERU to BOLIVIA in La Paz. [Costa Rica; w Panama.] Forest.

Plate 5

3. TOOTH-BILLED HUMMINGBIRD

Androdon aequatorialis

4.1" (1.5"). Bill slightly upcurved. Bronze green above, hindcrown blue. Throat and upper breast streaked gray and black, rest of underparts white. Lateral upper tail coverts white. Central tail feathers gray with broad bluish green tip, remainder bluish black with gray bases and broad white tips. ♀: Like ♂ but without blue on occiput.

Tropical zone. COLOMBIA from middle Magdalena Valley w to Pacific coast, thence south to w ECUADOR. [E Panama.] Forest.

Plate 8

4. SAW-BILLED HERMIT

Ramphodon naevius

5.7" (1.4"). Bill heavy, straight, hooked at tip, lower mandible yellow. Above dark coppery olive, feathers with dusky subterminal band and pale fringe. Postocular streak buff. Throat and sides of neck tawny ochraceous with dark streak down center, rest of underparts buff heavily streaked with blackish. Central four tail feathers dark bronzy purple, rest with purple black bases and broad tawny tips. ♀: Like ♂ but smaller.

Se BRAZIL from Minas Gerais and Espírito Santo to Rio Grande do Sul, possibly Goiás. Forest.

Plate 5

5. HOOK-BILLED HERMIT

Ramphodon dohrnii

4" (1"). Bill much as in 4. Upperparts bronze green, rump feathers fringed buff. Conspicuous white postocular streak, ear coverts dusky. Underparts cinnamon, speckled dusky on sides of abdomen. Tail reddish bronze, each feather tipped white. ♀: Tail without white tip.

Se BRAZIL, in Espírito Santo and possibly adjacent Bahía. Forest.

6. BRONZY HERMIT

Glaucis aenea*

3.2" (1.3"). Bill curved. Above coppery bronzy green, below uniform cinnamon. Central tail feathers bronze with narrow white tip, rest with basal half cinnamon rufous, distal half black, tip white.

Tropical zone. Pacific COLOMBIA from upper río Baudó s to nw ECUADOR. [Nicaragua southward.] Forest.

7. RUFOUS-BREASTED HERMIT

Glaucis hirsuta*

4.2" (1.3"). Differs from 6 by larger size, heavier bill, much greener upperparts and usually duller underparts.

Tropical zone. GUIANAS, VENEZUELA and COLOMBIA (s only to río San Juan in the w) to n BOLIVIA in La Paz, Beni and Cochabamba and BRAZIL s to Rio Grande do Sul. Trinidad and Tobago. [Panama, Grenada.] Forest.

Plate 6

8. SOOTY BARBTHROAT

Threnetes niger

3.9" (1.1"). Bill slightly curved. Entire body plumage dark olive bronze, duskier below; throat black, bordered below by a fulvous band. Tail dark bronze green above, black slightly glossed violet below.

FRENCH GUIANA. Forest.

9. PALE-TAILED BARBTHROAT

Threnetes leucurus*

4" (1.3"). Bill slightly curved. Upperparts bronze green; feathers, especially of crown, edged buff. Throat black, bordered on each side by white line and below by broad orange buff band; breast dusky bronze green, rest of underparts buffy white. Central tail feathers bronze green, next two buffy white, outermost two with subterminal black band and white tip.

Tropical zone. GUIANAS; VENEZUELA s of the Orinoco; COLOMBIA e of Andes; e ECUADOR; w Amazonian BRAZIL to Amapá and e Pará, and Maranhão; e PERU; BOLIVIA to Beni and Cochabamba. Forest.

Plate 8

9bis. BRONZE-TAILED BARBTHROAT

Threnetes loehkeni[1]

Differs from 9 principally by uniformly dark bronzy tail, the feathers narrowly tipped white, the inner webs of the feathers narrowly edged ochraceous.

Tropical zone. Known from six specimens from Amapá, BRAZIL.

10. BAND-TAILED BARBTHROAT

*Threnetes ruckeri**

Similar to 9 except all but central tail feathers white with broad band of black across distal end.

Tropical zone. W VENEZUELA from Zulia to Apure; n COLOMBIA from Santa Marta and Norte de Santander to Pacific coast, thence south to nw ECUADOR. [Guatemala southward.] Forest.

Phaethornis

Phaethornis (22 species). Characteristics: Bill long, curved (straight in 19 and 20), mandible yellow or red basally. No bright colors; above bronzy olive, brown or green, below gray, buff or cinnamon; line down center of throat pale, line through eye dusky. Tail long, much graduated, feathers distally white or buff. In the following descriptions, only the salient characters of each species are given. Most species inhabit undergrowth in or at edge of forest.

11. WHITE-WHISKERED HERMIT

*Phaethornis yaruqui**

4.5" (1.8"). Dark and very distinct species with top of head bronze, small moustachial streak and eyebrow white. Back and breast dark green with pale line down center of throat and rest of underparts blackish; under tail coverts white. Tail much graduated, purple blue, central feathers tipped white. ♀: Differs from ♂ in having longer white or buff moustachial streak, and line down throat and center of breast white, belly grayish.

Tropical zone. W COLOMBIA from lower Atrato s along Pacific coast to nw ECUADOR.

12. GREEN HERMIT

*Phaethornis guy**

4.5" (1.6"). Above rather like 11; below gray with buff line down center of throat, moustachial streak and eyebrow. Tail feathers black, blue at base, tipped white; central pair noticeably longer than others, narrow with distal third white.

Tropical, subtropical zones. N VENEZUELA; COLOMBIA s on Pacific coast to vicinity of Buenaventura east to e slope of E Andes in Boyacá and Meta. E ECUADOR to se PERU. Trinidad. [Costa Rica; Panama.]

13. TAWNY-BELLIED HERMIT

*Phaethornis syrmatophorus**

5" (1.6"). Below cinnamon buff; rump and upper tail coverts ochraceous orange. Central tail feathers very much longer than rest, white for distal half, others broadly tipped cinnamon.

Tropical to subtropical zone. COLOMBIA west to w slope of E Andes; e ECUADOR south to ne PERU in San Martín.

Plate 32

14. LONG-TAILED HERMIT

*Phaethornis superciliosus**

4.5-5" (1.6"). Differs principally from 13 by underparts gray tinged with buff, outer rectrices with paler buff or whitish tips, and under tail coverts white to pale buff instead of ochraceous.

[1] Grantsau, Pap. Avuls., Zool., Aug. 1969, *22*, art. 23, p. 246 (Serra do Navio, Amapá, Brazil).

Tropical, lower subtropical zones. GUIANAS; VENEZUELA s of the Orinoco; n and e COLOMBIA; w and E ECUADOR; e PERU; n BOLIVIA. BRAZIL throughout Amazonian drainage. [Mid. Amer.]

15. GREAT-BILLED HERMIT

Phaethornis malaris

5" (1.8"). Very similar to 14 but at once distinguishable by very much wider rectrices, longer and heavier bill and in area of overlap by larger size.

Tropical zone. FRENCH GUIANA and adjacent extreme ne BRAZIL in Amapá.

16. SCALE-THROATED HERMIT

Phaethornis eurynome *

5" (1.5"). Only large species with broad black throat feathers edged with buff, giving scaled appearance. Crown black, feathers edged rufescent.

Se BRAZIL from Minas Gerais to Rio Grande do Sul; e PARAGUAY; ne ARGENTINA in Misiones.

17. WHITE-BEARDED HERMIT

Phaethornis hispidus

4.5" (1.3"). Only species in which feathers of rump and upper tail coverts are fringed with gray. Throat and breast dark gray with very prominent white streak down center.

Tropical zone. Central VENEZUELA west to e slope of E Andes of COLOMBIA, thence south to n BOLIVIA and w BRAZIL.

18. PALE-BELLIED HERMIT

Phaethornis anthophilus *

4.2" (1.3"). Conspicuous black patch behind eye. Below grayish, center of belly paler and center of throat streaked with black. Tail feathers bronzy green, subterminal band black, tip white.

Tropical zone. VENEZUELA n of the Orinoco; n COLOMBIA. [E Panama.] Clearings, open forest.

19. STRAIGHT-BILLED HERMIT

Phaethornis bourcieri *

4.2" (1.3"). Plumage much like rest with grayish underparts and white gular streak, but instantly distinguishable from others (except for 20) by straight bill. Tail feathers

bronze green with broad subterminal black band, all but central pair tipped buff.

Tropical zone. GUIANAS; s VENEZUELA; se COLOMBIA; e ECUADOR; ne PERU; Amazonian BRAZIL, n of the Amazon from rio Negro e to Amapá, s of it in rio Tapajós region.

20. NEEDLE-BILLED HERMIT

Phaethornis philippi

4.7" (1.3"). Color almost indistinguishable from 13 but bill straight instead of curved. Color differs from 19 by tawny underparts and tips to all but central tail feathers.

E PERU; w BRAZIL s of the Amazon e to rio Madeira; Bolivia (?).

21. DUSKY-THROATED HERMIT

Phaethornis squalidus *

3.5" (1"). Upperparts dull olive; crown dusky, feathers edged dull ochraceous. Throat dusky, rest of underparts dull ochraceous to grayish white. Central tail feathers much longer than rest, apical third white, rest tipped white or buffy.

GUYANA; VENEZUELA s of the Orinoco; extreme e COLOMBIA in Vichada. BRAZIL from Roraima s to both banks of the lower Amazon, and in se from Minas Gerais and Espírito Santo to Santa Catarina.

22. SOOTY-CAPPED HERMIT

Phaethornis augusti *

4.8" (1.3"). Rather like 17 but differing mainly by paler, grayer underparts, distinct white superciliary and malar stripe. Upper tail coverts fringed rufous and central tail feathers longer, basal two-thirds shining coppery green instead of blackish.

Upper tropical zone. GUYANA; VENEZUELA; e COLOMBIA from Santa Marta Mts. s to Macarena Mts.

23. PLANALTO HERMIT

Phaethornis pretrei

4.8" (1.3"). Rather like 13 but underparts pinkish buff instead of tawny. Central tail feathers basally coppery green, rest tipped white instead of tawny, and central rectrices not as markedly longer than next pair.

Planalto region of central and e BRAZIL in Maranhão, Piauí and Ceará s to São Paulo and Mato Grosso. E BOLIVIA; extreme n Salta, ARGENTINA. Forest, savanna, parks.

24. BUFF-BELLIED HERMIT

Phaethornis subochraceus

4.1" (1"). Much like 21 but considerably larger and with feathers of crown dark coppery edged with buffy.

BOLIVIA in Santa Cruz; BRAZIL in w Mato Grosso.

25. CINNAMON-THROATED HERMIT

Phaethornis nattereri

3.3" (1.2"). Rather like 23 but smaller. All but four central tail feathers tipped with pale fulvous instead of white.

BRAZIL, spotty records in Maranhão, Piauí and Mato Grosso; ne Santa Cruz, BOLIVIA.

25bis. MARANHÃO HERMIT

Phaethornis maranhaoensis[1]

Differs from 25 by darker and more rufescent coloration; green, rufous-tipped rump feathers, and shorter tail, blackish basally instead of orange rufous.

Known only from Imperatriz, Maranhão, BRAZIL.

26. BROAD-TIPPED HERMIT

Phaethornis gounellei

3.5" (1"). Above grayish green, upper tail coverts fringed rufous, underparts cinnamon rufous. Tail with more white than in other species; central pair bronze green, tipped white; next pair with green and black basal two-thirds and white distal third, rest with broad white tips.

E BRAZIL in Piauí, Ceará, and Bahía.

27. REDDISH HERMIT

Phaethornis ruber *

3" (.8"). Rump and underparts rufous, narrow black band across lower breast. Tail rather evenly graduated, coppery, feathers tipped cinnamon, central pair sometimes with white. ♀: Paler below than ♂.

Tropical zone. GUIANAS; VENEZUELA s of the Orinoco; e Amazonian COLOMBIA

from Caquetá south to n BOLIVIA in Beni. Most of BRAZIL. Forest, scrub, savanna, gardens.

28. WHITE-BROWED HERMIT

Phaethornis stuarti *

3.3" (.9"). Much like ♀ of 27 but larger and tail feathers greener, less coppery basally; central pair tipped white, rest tipped white or buff, paler than in 27.

Tropical zone of south-central and se PERU, and n BOLIVIA.

29. GRAY-CHINNED HERMIT

Phaethornis griseogularis *

3.1" (.9"). Distinguishable from 28 mainly by having the central part of the tail feathers black.

Tropical, subtropical zones. Locally in VENEZUELA in Zulia, Táchira, Bolívar (Cerro Roraima) and extreme s Amazonas; e base of E Andes of COLOMBIA south to ne PERU, w slope of Andes in Tumbes. Nw BRAZIL.

30. LITTLE HERMIT

Phaethornis longuemareus *

3.6" (.9"). Much like 29 but distinguishable by dusky throat, in some races, and greener central tail feathers. Distinguishable from 28 mainly by more coppery tail and from 27 by larger size, no black band across breast.

Tropical zone. GUIANAS, VENEZUELA and COLOMBIA s through e and w ECUADOR to e PERU and w and central Amazonian BRAZIL to rio Tapajós. Trinidad. [Mid. Amer.]

31. MINUTE HERMIT

Phaethornis idaliae

3.1" (.6"). Differs from all other species by green upper tail coverts. Chin black, throat and breast reddish buff, rest of underparts dark gray. Tail bronze green, tipped buff. ♀: Differs from ♂ by uniform buff throat and underparts.

Se BRAZIL in Espírito Santo and Rio de Janeiro. Forest, scrub, savanna.

---

[1] Grantsau, Pap. Avuls., Zool., Sept. 1968, *22*, art 7, p. 57 (Imperatriz, Maranhão, Brazil).

32. WHITE-TIPPED SICKLEBILL

Eutoxeres aquila *

5" (1", chord). Bill sickle-shaped. Crown dark brown; back bronze green, feathers fringed fulvous. Underparts striped buffy and black. Tail graduated, bronze green, feathers pointed, white tips increasing in size toward outermost.

Tropical zone. COLOMBIA along Pacific slope, head of Magdalena Valley and e of Andes from Meta s to ECUADOR; ne PERU. [Costa Rica southward.]

33. BUFF-TAILED SICKLEBILL

Eutoxeres condamini *

Differs from 32 by blue patch on sides of neck; stripes on underparts buffier; mainly by outer three tail feathers being buff with whitish tips.

Tropical zone. Se COLOMBIA south to se PERU. Forest.

Plate 32

34. SCALY-BREASTED HUMMINGBIRD

Phaeochroa cuvierii *

4.1" (.9"). Above, including four central tail feathers, shining green; below rusty gray with partly concealed shining green disks producing a scaled effect. Four outer tail feathers with broad black subterminal patch and broad white tip. This species and those through 42 have outer primary shaft much thickened in males, less so in females.

Caribbean coast of COLOMBIA from Cartagena to Barranquilla, and lower Magdalena Valley to Gamarra. [Guatemala southward.] Open woodland.

35. GRAY-BREASTED SABREWING

Campylopterus largipennis *

4.6" (1.2"). Above shining green to bronzy green; below uniform gray. Small white spot behind eye. Central tail feathers bluish green, outer ones blue black with white or gray tips.

Tropical zone. GUIANAS; VENEZUELA s of the Orinoco; COLOMBIA e of E Andes from Meta south to n and e BOLIVIA; BRAZIL in Amazonia s to Mato Grosso and n Maranhão, and in Minas Gerais (Serra do Espinhaço). Forest, scrub.

Plate 5

36. RUFOUS-BREASTED SABREWING

Campylopterus hyperythrus

4" (.8"). Above shining bronze green, greener on head; below uniform cinnamon. Four central tail feathers golden bronze, outer ones cinnamon rufous.

Subtropical zone. Se VENEZUELA on isolated mt. summits in Bolívar including Cerro Roraima, but not Cerro Guaiquinima; n BRAZIL in ne Roraima (Cerro Uei-Tepui). Forest, scrub.

37. BUFF-BREASTED SABREWING

Campylopterus duidae *

Differs from 36 by drab underparts, tinted with tawny on sides. Outer tail feathers have dull bronze basal portion.

Subtropical zone. S VENEZUELA in central Bolívar (Cerro Guaiquinima) and isolated mts. in central and s Amazonas; mts. of adjacent n BRAZIL. Forest, scrub.

38. WHITE-TAILED SABREWING

Campylopterus ensipennis

5.1" (1.1"). Glittering green above. Throat glittering violet, rest of underparts shining green. Three outermost tail feathers with basal third blue black, distal two-thirds white. ♀: Differs from ♂, by pale gray underparts with green disks, and throat mixed with green.

Tropical, subtropical zones of n VENEZUELA in Sucre, Monagas and Anzoátegui. Trinidad and Tobago. Forest.

39. LAZULINE SABREWING

Campylopterus falcatus

4.3" (.9"). Uppersurface glittering green, blue on crown. Throat and breast glittering dark violet blue shading to glittering blue green on belly. Tail feathers chestnut, central pair broadly tipped bronze green. ♀: Upperparts and tail like ♂, throat glittering blue, rest of undersurface gray.

Subtropical to temperate zone. N VENEZUELA from Caracas w in COLOMBIA to Cauca Valley; e ECUADOR. Forest, scrub.

40. SANTA MARTA SABREWING

Campylopterus phainopeplus

5" (.9"). Crown, throat and upper breast glittering dark blue, rest of plumage glittering green. Tail dark steel blue, central rectrices tinged green. ♀: Upperparts shining green; underparts gray. Tail green, tips to outer rectrices gray.

COLOMBIA in Santa Marta Mts. from 3800 to 5500 ft. (Feb.-May.) and up to 14,000 ft. (June-Oct.). Forest, open slopes.

41. NAPO SABREWING

Campylopterus villaviscensio

4.5″ (1.1″). Top of head glittering golden green, back and central tail feathers shining bronze green. Throat and breast glittering violet blue, rest of underparts dark gray with green disks. All but central tail feathers dark blue. ♀: Above like male, below dull gray. Outermost pair of tail feathers with small gray tips.

Tropical, subtropical zones of e ECUADOR near headwaters of río Napo. Forest.

42. SWALLOW-TAILED HUMMINGBIRD

Eupetomena macroura *

5.6″ (.8″). Tail long, deeply forked, dull, dark blue. Whole head, throat and breast violet to violet blue, rest of plumage shining blue green or bronzy green. ♀: Similar but head and breast somewhat bluer.

GUIANAS; BRAZIL in Amazonia and from Maranhão, Piauí, Ceará, s to São Paulo and Mato Grosso. Se PERU in Cuzco south to n BOLIVIA and e through Santa Cruz to PARAGUAY. Savanna, scrub.

Plate 6

43. WHITE-NECKED JACOBIN

Florisuga mellivora *

4″ (.8″). Head, throat and breast shining blue, belly white. Back shining bronze green, broad white crescent across upper mantle. Lengthened upper tail coverts, covering central tail feathers, shining bronze green; tail pure white, feathers edged and tipped black. ♀: Shining bronze green above. Throat feathers basally black with broad white fringes, breast and sides gray with green disks producing a scaled effect, center of belly white. Central tail feathers green; rest dull blue green, tipped bluer; outermost tipped white.

Tropical zone. GUIANAS, VENEZUELA, COLOMBIA, s to BOLIVIA and Amazonian BRAZIL to Mato Grosso, and e to Pará and Maranhão. In the west s to ECUADOR.

Trinidad and Tobago. Acc. in Aruba and Curaçao. [Mid. Amer.] Forest clearings, often near streams.

Plate 5

44. BLACK JACOBIN

Melanotrochilus fuscus

4″ (.9″). Black; lower back, upper tail coverts and upper wing coverts bronzy olive. Central tail feathers black; rest white, tipped black. ♀: Differs from ♂ principally by broad chestnut band on each side of throat, and uppersurface feathers fringed chestnut. Tail feathers purple except outermost which are white, the next with white outer web.

E BRAZIL from Alagoas and Pernambuco to Rio Grande do Sul. Forest, capoeira, gardens.

Plate 5

45. BROWN VIOLETEAR

Colibri delphinae *

4.5″ (.6″). Upperparts olive brown, feathers of rump, upper and under tail coverts broadly fringed rufescent. Long auriculars glittering purple. Center of throat glittering green becoming glittering blue on lower throat, bordered on each side by white to fulvous band. Tail olive with broad subterminal coppery purple band.

Tropical, subtropical zones. GUIANAS; VENEZUELA; COLOMBIA; south to n and e BOLIVIA. BRAZIL in n in Roraima and in the e in Bahía (Serra do Sincorá). Trinidad. [Guatemala southward.] Forest border, savanna, cerrado.

46. GREEN VIOLETEAR

Colibri thalassinus *

3.9″ (.9″). Upperparts, breast and belly shining green. Lengthened auriculars purple. Throat glittering green to glittering blue depending on the light. Tail shining blue or green with broad subterminal dusky bar.

Subtropical, temperate zones. VENEZUELA n of the Orinoco; COLOMBIA; ECUADOR; e PERU; BOLIVIA; nw ARGENTINA. [Mexico to w Panama.] Open mountain slopes.

47. SPARKLING VIOLETEAR

Colibri coruscans *

5.5″ (1″). Above shining green. Chin, upper

throat, lengthened auriculars and center of abdomen glittering purple blue, lower throat and breast glittering emerald green, sides of belly and under tail coverts shining green. Tail as in 46.

Upper tropical to temperate zone. VENE-ZUELA n of the Orinoco, and on isolated peaks in Bolívar and Amazonas; COLOM-BIA; ECUADOR; e PERU and on w slope in Lima; BOLIVIA; nw ARGENTINA to Cata-marca. Open mountain slopes.

Plate 32

48. WHITE-VENTED VIOLETEAR

Colibri serrirostris

Much like 46 but somewhat larger. Differing mainly by glittering blue subocular region, violet purple lengthened auriculars, and pure white instead of green and buff under tail coverts.

Tropical to temperate zone. BOLIVIA from La Paz to Chuquisaca and Santa Cruz; nw ARGENTINA in Tucumán and Santa Fe. S BRAZIL from Mato Grosso e to Paraná, thence n to Espírito Santo, Bahía and Goiás. Scrub, savanna, grassland.

49. GREEN-THROATED MANGO

Anthracothorax viridigula

4.1" (1"). Upperparts shining bronzy green. Throat glittering emerald green, center of breast and abdomen black, sides of body shining green. Tail shining purple, outer feathers tipped dark blue. ♀: Like ♂ above. Underparts mostly white with black band, more or less mixed with shining green, extending from chin to belly. Tail much as in ♂ but tipped white.

Tropical zone. E VENEZUELA in Delta Amacuro; GUIANAS; BRAZIL in Amapá, at Santarém, and in Maranhão. Trinidad. Scrub, savanna.

50. GREEN-BREASTED MANGO

Anthracothorax prevostii *

3.9" (1.1"). Throat, center of breast and abdomen blue black, bordered on each side with glittering green, slightly bluish where it meets the black. Central tail feathers bronze green, rest purple, tipped and edged blue. ♀: Much like 49, possibly distinguishable by bluer green feathers mixed with black ones on throat and belly.

Tropical zone. VENEZUELA, very locally n of the Orinoco. COLOMBIA in Guajira Peninsula and middle Cauca Valley. W EC-UADOR from Gulf of Guayaquil s to extreme n PERU. [Mexico to n Costa Rica. Islands of sw Caribbean.] Second growth, clearings.

51. BLACK-THROATED MANGO

Anthracothorax nigricollis

Distinguishable from 50 only by shining dark blue, instead of glittering greenish blue, border to black throat and breast. ♀: Possibly distinguishable by smaller white tips to tail feathers.

Tropical zone. Generally distributed e of Andes s to PERU; BRAZIL; e BOLIVIA; PARAGUAY; ne ARGENTINA. W of Andes in n COLOMBIA. [Panama.] Forest borders, clearings, grassland.

Plate 5

52. FIERY-TAILED AWLBILL

Avocettula recurvirostris

3" (.7"). Distinguishable from any other hummingbird (except 207) by strongly upturned tip of bill. Upperparts shining green. Throat and breast glittering emerald green, center of belly black. Tail dull violet, central feathers dull green, underside of tail glistening coppery purple. ♀: Above like ♂, below white with median black band, sides coppery green. Tail much as in ♂ but outer feathers tipped white.

Tropical zone. GUIANAS; se VENEZUELA (Cerro Roraima); ne Amazonian BRAZIL from Monte Alegre and Santarém east to e Pará and Maranhão. E ECUADOR.

Plate 7

53. RUBY-TOPAZ HUMMINGBIRD

Chrysolampis mosquitus

3.1" (.5"). Crown and nape glittering ruby, bordered behind by black; back dull olive. Chin, throat and upper breast glittering topaz (glittering green against the light); lower breast and belly pale smoky brown, under tail coverts rufous. Tail rufous chestnut tipped dusky. ♀: Above coppery pale green, below pale smoky gray. Central tail feathers greenish olive, rest grayish with black subterminal band, tipped white.

Tropical zone. GUIANAS; VENEZUELA e to Meta, COLOMBIA; e and central[1] BRA-

ZIL from Pará and Maranhão s to Espírito Santo, Minas Gerais and Mato Grosso; ne BOLIVIA in Santa Cruz. Aruba to Trinidad and Tobago. Forest, scrub, savanna.

Plate 5

54. VIOLET-HEADED HUMMINGBIRD

Klais guimeti *

3.5″ (.4″). Head shining purple, small spot behind eye white. Above shining green; below gray. Tail feathers pale green, outer feathers with dusky subterminal patch and pale tip. ♀: Like ♂ but without purple, crown bluish green and throat like rest of underparts.

Tropical and subtropical zones from Mérida, VENEZUELA to w slope of E COLOMBIAN Andes, south through e ECUADOR and PERU, and w BRAZIL to Cochabamba, BOLIVIA. [Nicaragua southward.] Forest, scrub, savanna.

Plate 5

55. BLACK-BREASTED PLOVERCREST

Stephanoxis lalandi *

3.5″ (.4″). Crown glittering green (or glittering violet, 1), with very long crest of thin, pointed, glittering green feathers, the longest ones black. Back shining green. Spot behind eye white; subocular region, sides of neck and breast gray; central underparts mostly glittering purple blue. Central tail feathers like back; rest basally bronze green, black distally, tipped white. ♀: Upperparts and central tail feathers shining green, outer feathers mostly black with pale tips. Undersurface gray.

Se BRAZIL in Espírito Santo and Minas Gerais; from São Paulo to PARAGUAY and ne ARGENTINA, 1. Upland scrub, savanna.

Plate 7

56. TUFTED COQUETTE

Lophornis ornata

2.7″ (.4″). Forehead, face and throat glittering emerald green. Crown and crest rufous; long plumes springing from cheeks ochraceous rufous, tipped with glittering green disks. Mantle and underparts shining pale green. Rump dark shiny violet, bordered above by white band. Tail feathers mostly rufous. ♀: No decorations. Above light coppery green, rump dull purple crossed by buff band. Underparts rufescent. Tail bas-

ally coppery green, distally coppery brown. Both sexes have dark-tipped flesh color bills in this and the next four species.

Tropical zone. GUIANAS; ne VENEZUELA in Sucre, and s of the Orinoco in Bolívar and to mouth of the Meta in Apure; n BRAZIL (Roraima). Trinidad.

57. DOT-EARED COQUETTE

Lophornis gouldii

Differs from 56 chiefly by elongated cheek feathers being pure white, tipped with round green disks. ♀: Much like 56.

Ne and central BRAZIL s of the Amazon from Pará and Maranhão s to Goiás and n Mato Grosso. BOLIVIA in ne Santa Cruz. Forest, scrub, savanna.

58. FRILLED COQUETTE

Lophornis magnifica

Much like 57 but elongated plumes of cheeks much shorter, spatulate, white, edged terminally with green bar. ♀: Differs from 56 mainly by rufous throat, rest of underparts bronzy green.

E and central BRAZIL from Bahía to Rio Grande do Sul and w through Goiás to Mato Grosso. Forest, scrub, parks.

59. RUFOUS-CRESTED COQUETTE

Lophornis delattrei *

Rather like 58 but crest longer, feathers narrowed to sharp point, longest tipped with small green dot. Cheek feathers only slightly lengthened, rufous with green tips. Tail mostly rufous, edged and tipped with dusky green. ♀: Forecrown, throat and breast rufous; belly grayish buff. Outer tail feathers rufous with broad black subterminal band. Upperparts like 56.

Tropical, subtropical zones. Magdalena Valley, COLOMBIA. E PERU. N BOLIVIA from Beni to Santa Cruz. [Sw Mexico. Sw Costa Rica; Panama.] Forest, scrub, weedy fields.

60. SPANGLED COQUETTE

Lophornis stictolopha

Much like 59 but crest feathers not narrowed to point, tipped with blackish disk from hindcrown. ♀: Much like 59.

Tropical, lower subtropical zones. Andes of w VENEZUELA from Caracas to both

slopes of E Andes of COLOMBIA; e EC-
UADOR; ne PERU (Marañón Valley).
Scrub.

Plate 33

61. FESTIVE COQUETTE

Lophornis chalybea *

3.3" (.6"). Forehead, throat and line below
eye glittering green, latter edged below by
velvety black line. Cheek feathers much
elongated, narrow, shining green, tipped
with small white dot. Back shining coppery
green, band across rump white; breast grayish white. Tail shining purple. ♀: Crown and
back bronze green, band across rump white,
upper tail coverts shining purple. Chin and
moustachial streak buff. Underparts dull
brownish, feathers tipped buff, patch on
center of abdomen white. Tail mostly dark
purple, outer feathers pale-tipped. Bill in
both sexes black.

Tropical zone. VENEZUELA in e Bolívar. E
slope of E Andes of COLOMBIA s to
BOLIVIA in Cochabamba; w BRAZIL n of
the Amazon e to Roraima and s of it in
upper rio Juruá to Mato Grosso, also in s
Pará, the se from Minas Gerais to Santa
Catarina. Forest, scrub.

62. PEACOCK COQUETTE

Lophornis pavonina *

3.8" (.5"). Sides of crown glittering golden
green, center black, cheek tufts shining
green, feathers wide with large subterminal
blue black spot; throat black, rest of plumage mostly shining dark green. White band
across rump. Tail purple bronze. ♀: Green
above, stripe through eye black, subocular
region buff; underparts mixed black and
white and buff. Tail gray with broad subterminal bronze purple band, outer feathers
pale-tipped.

GUYANA; VENEZUELA on isolated peaks
in Bolívar and Amazonas. Forest.

63. WIRE-CRESTED THORNTAIL

Popelairia popelairii

♂ 4.5" (.5"), ♀ 3". Head crested, longest
feathers very long, thin and wire-like. Crown
and throat glittering emerald green. Sides of
head, back and upper tail coverts bronzy
green; rump blue black. Underparts black
with white tuft on flanks. Tail long, steel
blue; feathers with white shafts, outer ones

longest, curving outward, pointed. ♀: Above
bronze green, white band across rump.
Throat, breast and center of belly black.
Moustachial streak, flanks, leg puffs white.
Tail normal, steel blue crossed by gray band
at base and tipped white.

Tropical, subtropical zones. COLOMBIA, è
slope of E Andes in Cundinamarca and
Meta. E ECUADOR and ne PERU. Thickets.

64. BLACK-BELLIED THORNTAIL

Popelairia langsdorffi *

♂ 5.7" (.5"), ♀ 3". Above much like 63 but
without crest. Throat and breast glittering
emerald green, bordered below by glittering
golden copper. Underparts mainly black.
Outer tail feathers very narrow, grayish,
narrowing to shaft near tip; rest dark blue
with shafts white on underside. Tail much
longer than 63. ♀: Differs from 63 by throat
and breast white with green disks, bordered
below by golden copper. Tail forked, feathers tipped white, central ones much shorter
than rest.

Tropical zone. VENEZUELA in s Amazonas. Amazonian COLOMBIA to e PERU
and in w Amazonian BRAZIL e to rios Negro and Madeira and w Mato Grosso; and in
se in Bahía, Espírito Santo and Rio de Janeiro. Forest.

65. COPPERY THORNTAIL

Popelairia letitiae

♂ 4" (.5"), ♀ 3". Head, throat and breast
glittering golden green. Upperparts shining
reddish, coppery brown; band across rump
white, shorter tail coverts purple red, longer
golden green. Underparts green with white
patch on breast. Tail rather like that of 64,
but much shorter, less graduated, feathers
wider. ♀: Unknown.

BOLIVIA (known from two males without
precise locality).

66. GREEN THORNTAIL

Popelairia conversii

♂ 4" (.4"), ♀ 2.5". Upperparts and tail much
like 63 but without crest, and outer tail
feathers narrowing suddenly rather than
gradually to shafts near tip. Throat and
upper breast glittering green, rest of underparts coppery green with steel blue spot in
center of breast. ♀: Much like 63, differing
mainly in short central tail feathers, outer

feathers gray with broad black subterminal band and white tip.

Tropical zone. Pacific COLOMBIA to sw ECUADOR. [Costa Rica to Panama.] Forest.

Plate 33

67. RACKET-TAILED COQUETTE

Discosura longicauda

♂ 3.7″ (.4″), ♀ 2.7″. Upperparts shining green with buff band across rump. Throat and breast glittering emerald green, rest of underparts blackish with shining coppery golden disks. Tail forked, purple, outer feathers with bare shaft terminating in a racket. ♀: Above like ♂. Throat black bordered on each side by white; underparts mostly greenish. Tail gray with broad purple subterminal band and pale tip to outer feathers; central feathers much shorter than rest.

Tropical zone. GUIANAS; VENEZUELA in Amazonas; n and e BRAZIL in Pará and Amapá, and from Pernambuco to Bahía. Forest, scrub, savanna.

Plate 5

68. BLUE-CHINNED SAPPHIRE

Chlorestes notatus*

3.5″ (.7″). Above shining bronze green, below glittering golden green to glittering blue green, glittering blue on chin. Tail steel blue. ♀: Upperparts and tail like ♂. Underparts white with glittering green disks on throat and breast and shining disks on rest of underparts, under tail coverts green. Mandible in both sexes flesh color, tipped dusky. (See also 70)

Tropical zone. GUIANAS, VENEZUELA and extreme e COLOMBIA south to ne PERU (Loreto), and BRAZIL e along Amazon Valley to Pará, s to Bahía and Espírito Santo. Trinidad and Tobago. Forest, scrub.

Chlorostilbon

Chlorostilbon (9 species). Characteristics: Very small, green; males with glittering crown (sometimes) and underparts. Most species resemble each other closely and are difficult to tell apart. Females are usually green above and gray below, sometimes with dusky face patch. Only salient features of each species are given in the following descriptions.

69. BLUE-TAILED EMERALD

Chlorostilbon mellisugus*

2.7″ (.55″). Crown and underparts glittering green, bluer on throat. Tail dark blue to black, square to forked. Bill black. ♀: Tail dark blue, outermost feathers with grayish tip. Some races with dusky face patch.

Tropical to temperate zone. GUIANAS to COLOMBIA. E and w ECUADOR; e PERU to n and e BOLIVIA. BRAZIL in lower Amazon Valley. Aruba to Trinidad. [Costa Rica; Panama.] Scrub, savanna.

70. GLITTERING-BELLIED EMERALD

Chlorostilbon aureoventris*

3.5″ (.7″). Crown and belly glittering bronze to glittering bronze green. Throat and upper breast glittering blue green. Tail steel blue, forked to only slightly forked. Bill pink with dusky tip. ♀: Bill as in ♂. Tail feathers with basal portion green and distal portion steel blue, outer four all blue with pale gray tips.

E BRAZIL from Maranhão s to Rio Grande do Sul w to Mato Grosso; URUGUAY; PARAGUAY; BOLIVIA except the w; ARGENTINA s to Mendoza and n Buenos Aires. Scrub, savanna, grassland, cerrado.

71. RED-BILLED EMERALD

Chlorostilbon gibsoni*

Rather like 69 but basal part of mandible pink. Tail longer and more deeply forked. ♀: Much like 69 but with whitish eyebrow and green central tail feathers; rest with broad white tips.

Tropical and subtropical zones. Nw VENEZUELA; n COLOMBIA w to Sinú delta s to Magdalena Valley and possibly upper Cauca Valley; e of E Andes in Norte de Santander. Scrub.

Plate 32

72. COPPERY EMERALD

Chlorostilbon russatus

2.7″ (.3″). Crown and underparts glittering golden green. Back shining green, tail golden copper in sharp contrast. Bill black. ♀: Coppery green above, tail greenish copper, all but central pair of feathers with coppery purple subterminal band and pale tip.

Upper tropical and subtropical zones. COLOMBIA in Santa Marta Mts. and e slope of Andes to Cundinamarca; Perijá Mts. and e slope of latter in VENEZUELA. Forest edge, scrub.

73. NARROW-TAILED EMERALD

Chlorostilbon stenura

2.7" (.6"). Crown and underparts glittering golden green. Tail shining emerald green, somewhat forked, feathers narrow, outer ones acuminate. ♀: Tail shaped as in ♂, outermost feathers grayish white at base, becoming coppery green with shining blue subterminal patch and broad white tip.

Tropical to temperate zone. VENEZUELA from Falcón, Lara and Trujillo to e slope of E Andes of COLOMBIA. Scrub.

74. GREEN-TAILED EMERALD

Chlorostilbon alice

Like 73 in color but tail feathers normal. ♀: Differs from 73 by basal part of outer rectrices coppery green and white tip much smaller.

Subtropical zone of mts. of VENEZUELA n of the Orinoco from Sucre and Monagas w to Trujillo. Scrub.

75. SHORT-TAILED EMERALD

Chlorostilbon poortmanni *

3.1" (.7"). Differs from 74 by larger size, longer bill, and proportionally shorter tail. ♀: Much like 74 but larger.

Tropical, lower subtropical zones. Nw VENEZUELA in Táchira and Mérida; COLOMBIA on both slopes of the n Eastern Andes. Scrub.

76. FORK-TAILED WOODNYMPH

Thalurania furcata *

4.2" (.9"). Crown glittering green or glittering purple or plain, like back. Upperparts blackish green to bronzy green sometimes mixed with a little purple. Throat and breast glittering green, rest of underparts glittering purple (or all glittering green below, 1). ♀: Tail forked, blue black. Above shining green, more coppery on crown. Underparts plain gray or with green disks on lower breast and belly. Tail slightly forked, mostly dark steel blue, outermost feathers with white tips.

Mostly tropical, occasionally subtropical zone. Generally distributed e of Andes s through Amazonian BRAZIL to PERU, BOLIVIA and n ARGENTINA. W of Andes in COLOMBIA. W ECUADOR, 1. [Mid. Amer.] Forest, stream banks, clearings.

Plate 32

77. LONG-TAILED WOODNYMPH

Thalurania watertonii

4.5" (.9"). Crown and hindneck dusky green, back glittering green. Underparts glittering golden green. Tail dark steel blue, longer and more deeply forked than 76. ♀: Much like 76 with longer and more deeply forked tail, outer rectrices narrowed and shaft mostly white.

Coastal BRAZIL from e Pará to Pernambuco and Bahía. Guyana? Forest, scrub.

78. VIOLET-CAPPED WOODNYMPH

Thalurania glaucopis

4.3" (.8"). Crown glittering violet blue, back bronzy green. Underparts glittering golden green. Tail forked, steel blue. ♀: Usual type but with tail more deeply forked than 76 and less than 77.

E BRAZIL from Bahía to Rio Grande do Sul and s Mato Grosso; URUGUAY; PARAGUAY; ne ARGENTINA (Misiones). Forest, scrub.

79. VIOLET-BELLIED HUMMINGBIRD

Damophila julie *

3" (.6"). Above shining green to coppery green with (or without, 1) glittering golden green cap. Throat and extreme upper breast glittering golden green to blue green, rest of underparts glittering violet blue. Tail steel blue, outermost feather shorter than the rest which are equal. Lower mandible flesh color. ♀: Shining green above, grayish white below. Tail as in ♂ but outermost feather pale-tipped.

Tropical zone. COLOMBIA in Magdalena and lower Cauca Valleys w to río Sinú; upper río Sinú w to Pacific coast thence south to w ECUADOR, 1. [Panama.] Forest, mangrove borders.

80. SAPPHIRE-THROATED HUMMINGBIRD

Lepidopyga coeruleogularis *

3" (.7"). Upperparts shining green becoming

more coppery on lower back. Throat and upper breast glittering violet blue, rest of underparts shining green. Tail forked, central feathers copper, rest blue black. Mandible flesh color. ♀: Coppery golden green above, grayish white below. Tail forked, central feathers coppery green, rest blue black, outer feathers with pale tips.

Tropical zone. Extreme nw COLOMBIA near mouth of Atrato, and from mouth of Magdalena at Ciénaga Grande e to Santa Marta. [Pacific Panama.] Mangroves, gardens, scrub.

81. SAPPHIRE-BELLIED HUMMINGBIRD

Lepidopyga lilliae

3" (.7"). Upperparts shining blue green. Throat glittering purple, sides of neck and breast shining blue green, rest of underparts glittering sapphire blue. Tail forked, blue black, feathers narrower than 80. Mandible flesh color. ♀: Unknown but probably much like 80.

Tropical zone. COLOMBIA near mouth of Magdalena at Ciénaga Grande. Mangroves.

82. SHINING-GREEN HUMMINGBIRD

Lepidopyga goudoti *

3.2" (.7"). Above shining green; below glittering green (or glittering golden green, 1). Tail more deeply forked than in 81, short central feathers like back, rest steel blue. Mandible flesh color. ♀: Much like ♂ but duller and tail less deeply forked.

Tropical zone. Nw VENEZUELA from Trujillo westward, COLOMBIA in Norte de Santander, 1; from Santa Marta and Magdalena Valley w to lower Atrato Valley. Open woodland.

83. RUFOUS-THROATED SAPPHIRE

Hylocharis sapphirina

3.4" (.7"). Above dark green. Chin and upper throat rufous, lower throat and upper breast glittering violet, belly grayish. Upper tail coverts and central tail feathers coppery violet, rest chestnut, edged dusky. Bill flesh color, tipped dusky. ♀: Coppery green above. Upper throat rufous, lower throat with glittering blue disks, rest of underparts grayish with green disks. Tail as in ♂ but outer feathers pale-tipped.

Tropical zone. Generally distributed to e PERU; BRAZIL in Amazonia and from

Bahía to São Paulo. PARAGUAY; BOLIVIA in ne Santa Cruz; ne ARGENTINA to Formosa and Chaco. Forest, scrub.

Plate 8

84. WHITE-CHINNED SAPPHIRE

Hylocharis cyanus *

Differs mainly from 83 by crown glittering purple, chin white, and tail blue black. ♀: Differs by being greener above, chin white and tail blue black (without blue disks on lower throat, 1).

Tropical zone. Generally distributed to e PERU, nw BOLIVIA and BRAZIL in Amazonia; from Bahía to São Paulo, 1. Forest, scrub, often near streams.

85. GILDED HUMMINGBIRD

Hylocharis chrysura *

4" (.8"). Shining golden green, chin pale rufous. Tail above and below glittering gold. Bill flesh color, tipped dusky.

South-central BRAZIL from Minas Gerais to Rio Grande do Sul and Mato Grosso; URUGUAY; PARAGUAY; e and n BOLIVIA; n ARGENTINA s to Tucumán, Santiago del Estero, and Buenos Aires. Scrub, savanna, grassland.

86. BLUE-HEADED SAPPHIRE

Hylocharis grayi *

3.5" (.9"). Entire head glittering sapphire blue to violet blue, back shining bronze green. Underparts glittering emerald green. Tail steel blue or blue green. Bill flesh color, tipped dusky. ♀: Shining green above, white below with a few glittering green disks. Tail steel blue or bronze green, pale-tipped.

Tropical zone. Cauca Valley and Pacific slope of COLOMBIA to nw ECUADOR. [E Panama.] Forest, scrub, mangroves.

87. GOLDEN-TAILED SAPPHIRE

Chrysuronia oenone *

Much like 86, but head more purple, color extending to upper breast (or purple confined to crown; throat and upper breast glittering blue green, 1), and tail shining golden copper. ♀: Best distinguished from 86 by golden bronze instead of steel blue tail.

Tropical, subtropical zones. VENEZUELA n of the Ornioco; COLOMBIA east of E Andes south to e ECUADOR. E PERU to n BOLIVIA and w BRAZIL, l. Trinidad. Forest, scrub.

88. VIOLET-CAPPED HUMMINGBIRD

Goldmania violiceps

3.5" (.6"). Superficially like 87 (1) but back bluer green, underparts glittering grass green instead of blue green; and maroon, bronze-bordered tail feathers. Under tail coverts short, shining grass green; three central ones long, silky white, curled and stiff. ♀: Immediately distinguishable from 87 by under tail coverts similar to ♂.

Upper tropical to subtropical zone. Extreme nw COLOMBIA in Chocó. [E Panama.] Forest.

89. PIRRE HUMMINGBIRD

Goethalsia bella

3.5" (.6"). Chin and lores rufous chestnut. Upperparts shining golden green, patch of rufous on secondaries. Underparts whitish with green disks. Tail feathers buff, tipped dusky bronze, central feathers mostly bronze. Under tail coverts buff, central ones like 88 but longer. ♀: Differs from ♂ by buff throat, rest of underparts buffy white.

Upper tropical zone. Extreme n Chocó, COLOMBIA. [E Panama.] Forest.

90. WHITE-THROATED HUMMINGBIRD

Leucochloris albicollis

4" (.8"). Upperparts, chin and broad band across breast shining green; throat, sides of neck, the belly and long under tail coverts white. Central tail feathers like back, rest steel blue with large white tips. ♀: Differs from ♂ by considerably smaller size.

Se BRAZIL from Minas Gerais to Rio Grande do Sul; PARAGUAY; ARGENTINA in Misiones and Buenos Aires. Forest, scrub.

91. WHITE-TAILED GOLDENTHROAT

Polytmus guainumbi *

4.1" (.9"). Bill distinctly curved, pinkish. Above golden bronze, below glittering golden green. Stripe above and below eye white. Tail much rounded, mostly bronze green with increasing white toward outermost feathers. ♀: Above like ♂ but smaller and duller with white chin and pale gray rufous-tinged underparts.

Tropical zone. GUIANAS; VENEZUELA; COLOMBIA e of Andes in Meta. BRAZIL in Amapá and from Maranhão s to São Paulo and Mato Grosso; PARAGUAY; e BOLIVIA; ARGENTINA in Corrientes and Buenos Aires. Trinidad. Savanna, grassland.

Plate 8

92. TEPUI GOLDENTHROAT

Polytmus milleri

4.4" (1"). In body color much like 91 but bill black, no white at eye. Tail feathers bronze green above, shining green below, all but central pair with broad white band at base and white tips. ♀: Similar but smaller, underparts dull white with bronze green disks, thickest on breast.

Subtropical zone. Mts. of s VENEZUELA. Scrub, savanna, grassland.

93. GREEN-TAILED GOLDENTHROAT

Polytmus theresiae *

3.4" (.8"). Much smaller than 92 and differing by greener general color and tail with only extreme base and narrow tip white. ♀: Differs from ♂ in the same manner as 92.

GUIANAS; VENEZUELA; se COLOMBIA. E PERU in Loreto s of the Marañón. Amazonian BRAZIL from rio Negro and rio Purús eastward. Scrub, savanna, grassland.

94. BUFFY HUMMINGBIRD

Leucippus fallax *

3.5" (.8"). Forecrown, sides of head and neck grayish brown, upperparts bronzy to olive green. Underparts uniform buff, under tail coverts whiter. Tail feathers dull olive green, all but central feathers with dusky subterminal patch and broad white tip.

Arid Caribbean littoral of COLOMBIA in Santa Marta e along coast to Sucre, VENEZUELA. La Tortuga, Chimana Grande, Coche and Margarita Is. Mangroves, xerophytic desert.

95. TUMBES HUMMINGBIRD

Leucippus baeri

3.7" (.8"). Crown dull brownish. Back dusty, dull green; underparts pale gray. Central tail feathers dull green with dusky bronze tips, outer feathers gray with broad subterminal black band.

Arid littoral of PERU in Tumbes and Piura.

96. SPOT-THROATED HUMMINGBIRD

Leucippus taczanowskii

4" (1"). Above dull, dusty green; below pale gray, throat spotted with glittering green. Tail mostly dull olive green, outer feathers with subterminal bronzy area. Bill rather heavy.

Arid coastal PERU from Piura s to Ancash.

Plate 7

97. OLIVE-SPOTTED HUMMINGBIRD

Leucippus chlorocercus

3.5" (.7"). Above dull, dusty green; underparts grayish white rather mottled with dusky, throat inconspicuously spotted with olive. Tail feathers green, outer feathers with subterminal dusky patch and grayish tip.

Se ECUADOR; PERU in valleys of Ucayali, Marañón and lower Napo rivers. W BRAZIL. Dry scrub.

98. MANY-SPOTTED HUMMINGBIRD

Taphrospilus hypostictus *

4.5" (1"). Upperparts shining grass green; underparts white, thickly spotted everywhere except on central belly with shining green disks. Tail blue green becoming dusky blue on tip.

Tropical zone. E ECUADOR; PERU from Amazonas to Junín. E BOLIVIA s to Tarija; sw BRAZIL; nw ARGENTINA from Jujuy and Salta to La Rioja. Dry scrub.

99. GREEN-AND-WHITE HUMMINGBIRD

Amazilia viridicauda

3.7" (.9"). Upperparts shining green; center of throat, breast and belly white, sides of body green. Central tail feathers green, rest with white tips increasing in size to outermost which is also white on outer web.

Upper tropical and subtropical zones. PERU from s Huánuco to s Puno.

100. WHITE-BELLIED HUMMINGBIRD

Amazilia chionogaster *

Differs from 99 mainly by more white below and by bronzy green tail, outer feathers with inner web mostly white.

Subtropical to temperate zone. N PERU from Amazonas s to BOLIVIA and w

ARGENTINA to Tucumán and Formosa. BRAZIL in Mato Grosso. Scrub, savanna.

101. WHITE-CHESTED EMERALD

Amazilia chionopectus *

3.2" (.6"). Crown, cheeks and sides of neck glittering green, throat white, breast white mixed with green, belly grayish white. Upperparts shining golden bronzy green. Tail golden bronze with indefinite dusky subterminal area.

Tropical zone. GUIANAS; ne VENEZUELA to Miranda, and in Bolívar and n Amazonas. Trinidad. Forest, scrub.

102. VERSICOLORED EMERALD

Amazilia versicolor *

3" (.6"). Upperparts shining bronzy green with or without glittering blue cap. Sides of neck glittering green or blue, center of throat and breast white with glittering green disks, center of abdomen white, flanks shining bronze green (or throat and underparts mostly white, with glittering disks confined to sides of throat and breast, 1). Tail dull olive with dusky subterminal mark.

Tropical zone. VENEZUELA, n of the Orinoco only in Apure and generally s of it, COLOMBIA e of E Andes and BRAZIL n of the Amazon from rio Negro region to rio Jamundá, 1; in east and south from e Pará (rio Tocantins) to Maranhão and Ceará s to Rio Grande do Sul and w to Mato Grosso; PARAGUAY; BOLIVIA in Santa Cruz. Ne ARGENTINA in Misiones. Forest, scrub, savanna, cerrado.

103. GLITTERING-THROATED EMERALD

Amazilia fimbriata *

3.2" (.7") [or 4" (.9"), 1]. Upperparts shining grass green or bronzy green. Throat, breast and upper abdomen glittering green, center of abdomen white. Central tail feathers bronzy green, rest black.

Tropical zone. GUIANAS; VENEZUELA; COLOMBIA e of Andes to e PERU; BRAZIL s to Santa Catarina and Mato Grosso (coastally from Rio de Janeiro to Santa Catarina, 1); PARAGUAY; n BOLIVIA in Cochabamba. Forest, scrub, grassland, cerrado.

104. TACHIRA EMERALD

Amazilia distans

Differs principally from 103 by crown glittering bluish green, foreneck and upper breast glittering blue, center of abdomen olive gray.

Tropical zone. Known only from Táchira, VENEZUELA. Forest.

105. SAPPHIRE-SPANGLED EMERALD

Amazilia lactea *

3.5" (.8"). Upperparts shining green, bronzy on crown. Throat, breast and sides of neck glittering purple; narrow line down center of breast and belly pure white, sides gray with green disks; under tail coverts white (or center of belly gray; under tail coverts gray, edged white, 1).

Tropical zone. VENEZUELA in Bolívar. E and se PERU to Junín, and BOLIVIA in La Paz and Beni, 1. E BRAZIL from Bahía to São Paulo. Forest, scrub, savanna.

106. BLUE-CHESTED HUMMINGBIRD

Amazilia amabilis

3" (.8"). Above shining green, upper tail coverts dull bronze. Crown and sides of neck glittering emerald green, center of throat blackish, lower throat and upper breast glittering purple blue, rest of underparts gray with a few bronze green disks. Tail blackish bronze. ♀: Like ♂ but much duller, throat with black disks.

Tropical zone. Pacific COLOMBIA and e across Caribbean lowlands to middle Magdalena Valley; w ECUADOR. [Nicaragua southward.] Forest, flowering treetops, plantations.

107. PURPLE-CHESTED HUMMINGBIRD

Amazilia rosenbergi

Differs mainly from 106 by no glittering crown and by entire throat glittering green, purple confined to patch on chest. Central tail feathers bronze, rest black. ♀: Above like ♂. Throat and breast white with glittering green disks, belly gray, under tail coverts white. Outer tail feathers with small white tips.

Pacific coast of COLOMBIA and nw ECUADOR. Scrub.

108. ANDEAN EMERALD

Amazilia franciae *

3.5" (.8"). Crown glittering green or blue; sides of head, neck and breast glittering golden green, belly white. Upperparts and tail shining bronze green, tail with dusky subterminal area.

Subtropical zone. COLOMBIA from w slope of E Andes westward; w ECUADOR. E slope of Andes in n PERU s to Cajamarca.

Plate 33

109. PLAIN-BELLIED EMERALD

Amazilia leucogaster *

Differs mainly from green-capped 108 by tail color. Central feathers bronzy purple, rest black; otherwise sides of throat and breast more extensively glittering golden green, only center of underparts white.

Tropical zone. Ne VENEZUELA; GUIANAS. E BRAZIL in Pará (Belém region), e to Ceará and s to Bahía. Mangroves, plantations, gardens.

110. INDIGO-CAPPED HUMMINGBIRD

Amazilia cyanifrons *

3.5" (.7"). Crown glittering dark indigo blue. Upperparts shining bronzy green, bronzier on lower back; underparts glittering emerald green. Tail steel blue. ♀: Similar but duller.

Tropical, subtropical zones. COLOMBIA in sw Atlántico, slopes of Andes above Magdalena Valley, and e of E Andes in Norte de Santander. [Costa Rica.] Forest.

111. STEELY-VENTED HUMMINGBIRD

Amazilia saucerottei *

Differs from 110 by crown shining green like back. Tail bright steel blue (or blue black, 1).

Tropical, subtropical zones. Drier parts of ne VENEZUELA; COLOMBIA in Norte de Santander, Caribbean lowlands s to Patía Valley; in interior valleys of Nariño, 1. [Nicaragua; Costa Rica.] Forest, semiarid scrub.

112. COPPER-RUMPED HUMMINGBIRD

Amazilia tobaci *

3.2" (.8"). Crown and upper back bronze green; lower back, wing coverts and upper tail coverts purple bronze. Underparts glittering emerald green, under tail coverts cinnamon. Tail steel blue.

Tropical, subtropical zones of VENE-ZUELA, except s Amazonas. Margarita and Patos Is. Trinidad, Tobago. Forest, scrub, savanna.

113. GREEN-BELLIED HUMMINGBIRD

Amazilia viridigaster *

Differs from 112 mainly by tail shining rosy purple instead of blue.

Tropical, subtropical zones. GUYANA (Merumé Mts.). VENEZUELA in Mérida, mts. w of lower río Caura, Cerros Roraima and Duida; COLOMBIA e of Andes to Meta; n BRAZIL on Cerro Uei-tepui. Forest, scrub, plantations.

114. RUFOUS-TAILED HUMMINGBIRD

Amazilia tzacatl *

3.5″ (.9″). Bill pink with dark tip. Upperparts bronze green. Throat and breast glittering emerald green, belly gray; upper and under tail coverts and tail dark rufous, tail edged bronze.

Tropical, occasionally subtropical zone. Nw VENEZUELA; n half of COLOMBIA w of E Andes, e of them s to Cúcuta; w ECUADOR. [Mid. Amer.] Forest edge, scrub, plantations.

115. CHESTNUT-BELLIED HUMMINGBIRD

Amazilia castaneiventris

3.3″ (.8″). Differs mainly from 114 by belly rich chestnut, upperparts much less green, more reddish bronze.

Subtropical zone. West slope of E Andes of COLOMBIA in Boyacá.

116. AMAZILIA HUMMINGBIRD

Amazilia amazilia *

3.5″ (.8″). Upperparts bronzy green to bronzy golden green. Throat and breast glittering green to glittering blue, belly rufous, under tail coverts white or mostly so. Tail rufous, edged bronze (or with white center of breast, and bronze or bronze and rufous tail, 1).

Arid sw ECUADOR s along littoral of PERU to Ica, 1. Interior of se ECUADOR and adjacent interior of n PERU. East and s PERU, 1. Arid scrub, open woods, gardens.

117. WHITE-VENTED PLUMELETEER

Chalybura buffonii *

4″ (1″). Upperparts shining bronzy green. Throat, breast and upper belly glittering golden green to emerald green (or violet blue to bluish green, 1). Central tail feathers dark bronze green, rest blue black (or all dark blue, 1). Under tail coverts white, long, wide, plume-like. ♀: Like ♂ above, grayish below; all but central tail feathers with large white tips. Under tail coverts like ♂.

Tropical zone. N VENEZUELA in Miranda and Zulia; COLOMBIA in Santa Marta, Magdalena Valley and n Chocó. COLOMBIA e of Andes from Arauca to Meta and in sw ECUADOR chiefly in subtropical zone, 1. [Panama.] Forest, savanna, often near streams.

Plate 5

118. BRONZE-TAILED PLUMELETEER

Chalybura urochrysia *

Differs from green-throated varieties of 117 mainly by shining greenish bronze tail in both sexes, and more restricted glittering underparts.

Tropical zone. COLOMBIA on Pacific coast, w shore of Gulf of Urabá and in middle Magdalena Valley; nw ECUADOR. [Nicaragua southward.] Humid forest.

119. SOMBRE HUMMINGBIRD

Aphantochroa cirrhochloris

4″ (.7″). Upperparts shining light green, gray bases of feathers showing through. Underparts dull gray, feathers of throat and breast inconspicuously centered pale green. Central tail feathers like back, rest black glossed with bronze.

E and central BRAZIL from Pernambuco and Bahía to Santa Catarina, w through Minas Gerais and Goiás to Mato Grosso. Forest and scrub.

120. SPECKLED HUMMINGBIRD

Adelomyia melanogenys *

3.4″ (.5″). Above shining bronzy green. Streak behind eye white to buff, cheeks dusky. Underparts dull white to dark buff, speckled on throat and breast with dull green (or spotted with purple blue, 1). Tail bronzy purple, all but central feathers with white or buff tips.

Subtropical zone. N VENEZUELA from Anzoátegui w to COLOMBIA (e of Andes s only to Meta). E and w ECUADOR; PERU (on w slope only to Libertad). BOLIVIA and nw ARGENTINA in Salta and Jujuy, 1. Thickets.

121. BLOSSOMCROWN

Anthocephala floriceps*

3" (.6"). Forecrown buffy white, hindcrown chestnut, spot behind eye white. Back shining green becoming bronzy on rump. Underparts dull gray to buffy. Central tail feathers bronze; rest bronze basally, black medially, and white (or buff, 1) distally.

Upper tropical and subtropical zones. COLOMBIA in Santa Marta Mts.; on e slope of Central Andes in their center section, 1. Forest or patches of woods.

Plate 7

122. WHITETIP

Urosticte benjamini*

3.7" (.9"). Above shining grass green, spot behind eye white. Upper throat glittering green, lower throat shining purple (or entire throat glittering green, 1). Upper breast whitish, becoming grayish on belly, thickly spotted with green disks. Tail somewhat forked, dusky bronze, central pair of feathers shorter, tipped white. ♀: Like ♂ above, underparts white with green disks, glittering on throat. Tail shining bronze, outermost feather tipped white.

Subtropical zone. Pacific slope of COLOMBIA form headwaters of the San Juan south to w ECUADOR. Head of Magdalena Valley, COLOMBIA, e ECUADOR and ne PERU in Amazonas, 1. Forest and scrub.

Plate 32

123. ECUADOREAN PIEDTAIL

Phlogophilus hemileucurus

3" (.7"). Upperparts shining grass green. Throat and breast white with green spots and immaculate white band across center of breast; abdomen white. Tail rounded, central feathers blue green, rest dark blue with white bases and broad white tips.

Tropical zone around headwaters of río Napo, e ECUADOR. Forest.

124. PERUVIAN PIEDTAIL

Phlogophilus harterti

3" (.6"). Above shining green. Underparts pale buff, whitish on throat and central abdomen. Tail rounded, central feathers like back but with large blackish terminal area; other feathers buff with broad, black diagonal median band.

Tropical zone. PERU in s Huánuco, Cuzco and Puno. Forest.

125. BRAZILIAN RUBY

Clytolaema rubricauda

4" (.7"). Center of crown glittering emerald green. Upper surface bronze green shading to bronze purple on lower back. Chin blackish, throat glittering ruby red, breast and sides of neck glittering emerald green, rest of underparts dark gray, feathers centered green. Central tail feathers like back, rest chestnut rufous, margined bronze. ♀: Shining grass green above, white spot behind eye. Underparts uniform cinnamon. Tail as in ♂.

E BRAZIL from Goiás and Minas Gerais to Rio Grande do Sul. Forest, scrub.

Plate 6

126. GOULD'S JEWELFRONT

Polyplancta aurescens

4.5" (.8"). Narrow line from bill to center of crown glittering purple, sides of crown and upperparts shining grass green. Upper throat velvety black; lower throat, sides of neck, and upper breast glittering golden green; broad band across chest rufous, rest of underparts green. Central tail feathers bronze green, rest rufous chestnut edged bronze green. ♀: Differs from ♂ by lacking glittering purple line on crown and being generally duller.

S VENEZUELA; Amazonian COLOMBIA; e ECUADOR s through e PERU to Puno; Amazonian BRAZIL on rios Solimões, Javarí and Juruá, possibly to rio Madeira, and n Mato Grosso. Forest, scrub.

Plate 6

127. FAWN-BREASTED BRILLIANT

Heliodoxa rubinoides*

4" (.9"). Above green to coppery green; below fawn, spot on lower throat glittering violet.

Subtropical zone. Andes of COLOMBIA; e and w ECUADOR; ne PERU s to Junín. Forest, occasionally pastures and gardens.

128. VIOLET-FRONTED BRILLIANT

Heliodoxa leadbeateri *

4.5" (.9"). Crown glittering violet, back bronze green. Throat and breast glittering emerald green, belly dark green. Under tail coverts gray, tipped white. Tail rather deeply forked, central feathers bronze, rest black. ♀: Above coppery green, below white, throat and breast densely sprinkled with glittering green disks, abdomen tinged buff. Tail as in ♂ but tipped white.

Tropical, lower subtropical zones. VENE-ZUELA n of the Orinoco from Miranda westward; COLOMBIA in Magdalena and Cauca Valleys and from e slope of E Andes south to BOLIVIA in La Paz and Cocha-bamba. Forest, scrub.

129. GREEN-CROWNED BRILLIANT

Heliodoxa jacula *

4.5" (1"). Differs from 128 by crown glittering green, purple spot on center of throat, and tail as deeply forked but uniform steel blue. ♀: Very similar to 128 but center of abdomen not tinged buff.

Subtropical zone. COLOMBIA in n Chocó and n part of W, Central and E Andes, both slopes; w ECUADOR. [Costa Rica; Panama.] Forest.

130. VELVET-BROWED BRILLIANT

Heliodoxa xanthogonys

4" (.8"). Center of crown glittering golden green, rest of crown velvety black. Upperparts bronze green. Throat and breast glittering golden green with blue spot on center throat, rest of underparts dark green. Central tail feathers dusky green, rest black. Base of lower mandible orange. ♀: Differs from 129 mainly by abdomen coppery green and lower mandible mostly orange.

Subtropical zone. GUYANA (Merumé Mts.); VENEZUELA on isolated peaks in Bolívar and Amazonas; extreme n BRAZIL on Venezuelan border (Serra Imerí). Forest, scrub, savanna.

131. BLACK-THROATED BRILLIANT

Heliodoxa schreibersii *

4.7" (.9"). Forehead glittering green, crown and upperparts shining green. Underparts black; patch on lower throat glittering purple, bordered below by narrow band of glittering green (or without green band, 1). Tail rather deeply forked, steel blue. ♀: Rather like ♂ but at once distinguishable by long white subocular line, bronze green belly and green central tail feathers.

Tropical zone. E ECUADOR, adjacent PERU; nw Amazonian BRAZIL on upper rio Negro. PERU in Cuzco, 1. Forest, scrub.

132. PINK-THROATED BRILLIANT

Heliodoxa gularis

4" (1"). Shining grass green. Spot behind eye white. Glittering rosy red patch on center of throat, center of abdomen gray, under tail coverts white. Central tail feathers green, outer feathers purplish green. ♀: Generally like ♂ but gape white, patch on throat smaller.

Tropical zone. Ne ECUADOR, south to ne PERU and adjacent Amazonian COLOM-BIA. Forest.

133. RUFOUS-WEBBED BRILLIANT

Heliodoxa branickii

4" (.9"). Line from base of bill through center of crown glittering green changing to blue posteriorly, sides of crown blackish. Body plumage dark shining green. Plaque at center of throat glittering, iridescent rosy red changing to green in certain lights. Outer web of outer remiges and basal part of inner ones cinnamon rufous. Central tail feathers green, rest dark blue. ♀: Unkown.

Se PERU. N BOLIVIA (supposedly from Beni). Forest edge, plantations.

134. EMPRESS BRILLIANT

Heliodoxa imperatrix

5.5" (1"). Tail long, deeply forked, dark bronze. Upperparts dark bronzy green. Area around base of bill and the breast glittering dark green, spot on center of throat glittering violet, abdomen glittering greenish gold. ♀: Much like others of genus but distinguishable by glittering greenish gold disks on abdomen.

Subtropical zone. W slope of W Andes of COLOMBIA from upper río San Juan south to nw ECUADOR. Forest.

Plate 32

135. SCISSOR-TAILED HUMMINGBIRD

Hylonympha macrocerca

7.5″ (1″). Tail long, deeply forked; outer feathers much longer than rest, blackish purple. Forehead and center of crown glittering purple, rest of crown black. Upperparts shining dark green. Throat and upper breast glittering emerald green; belly black, sides with green disks. ♀: 4.5″. Tail forked but not abnormally long. Above dark shining green, below white with shining green disks, center of breast plain white, abdomen and under tail coverts rufous chestnut. Central tail feathers basally green, distally steel blue, outer feathers mostly cinnamon with subterminal dusky area and buffy white tip.

Lower subtropical zone. Mts. of Paria Peninsula in ne VENEZUELA. Forest.

136. VIOLET-CHESTED HUMMINGBIRD

Sternoclyta cyanopectus

4.5″ (1.2″). Uppersurface shining grass green. Throat glittering emerald green, breast glittering violet, abdomen gray with green disks. Tail bronze, outer feathers tipped white on inner web. ♀: Upperparts and tail like ♂. Throat, breast and sides of body grayish white with bronze green disks, center of abdomen rufescent.

Lower subtropical zone. Andes of VENEZUELA from Táchira and Mérida to Miranda. Forest.

Plate 8

137. CRIMSON TOPAZ

Topaza pella *

7″ (1″). Top and sides of head and neck black; nape and upper back glittering purple, shading to glittering gold on upper tail coverts. Throat iridescent glittering topaz, breast and belly glittering crimson, under tail coverts glittering gold. Inner remiges chestnut. Central tail feathers shining gold; next two black, narrow, curved, crossing each other, protruding 2.5″ beyond rest; remainder chestnut. ♀: Above shining green. Throat with glittering crimson disks, underparts with glittering golden green disks, under tail coverts shining green. Central tail feathers bronzy, next pair violet, outermost pair rufous.

Tropical zone. GUIANAS; s VENEZUELA, e Bolívar; ne BRAZIL in Amapá and in vicinity of Belém. E ECUADOR (headwaters of río Napo). Forest.

138. FIERY TOPAZ

Topaza pyra

Differs from 137 by throat glittering golden green, underparts glittering orange red, inner remiges black instead of chestnut. Upper and under tail coverts shining green, not gold. Central tail feathers bronze green; rest, including lengthened crossed feathers, blackish violet. ♀: Differs from 137 mainly in tail color. Central feathers bronze, rest steel blue, outermost with cinnamon outer web.

Tropical zone. VENEZUELA in w and central Amazonas. Extreme e COLOMBIA in Vaupés; nw BRAZIL in rio Negro region. E ECUADOR and adjacent ne PERU.

Plate 32

139. ANDEAN HILLSTAR

Oreotrochilus estella *

4.6″ (.8″). Above olive green; below white with dark stripe down center. Whole head and throat glittering violet (or violet with patch of glittering green in center of throat, 1; or only a few green feathers in center of throat, 2; or top of head shining green, entire throat and sides of neck glittering emerald green, 3). Central tail feathers shining blue green, rest except outermost mostly white. ♀: Upperparts dull olive green. Throat white spotted with green, rest of underparts pale grayish. Tail dark shining green, outer feathers white with median shining green band. (Includes *O. chimborazo* of Ecuador.)

Temperate, páramo zones. Andes of ECUADOR on Mts. Pichincha, Antisana, Cotopaxi, and Iliniza; on Quillotoa, 2; on Chimborazo, 1. PERU, w BOLIVIA, CHILE in Arica and Tarapacá and w ARGENTINA to Catamarca, 3. Hillstars inhabit rocky slopes.

140. WHITE-SIDED HILLSTAR

Oreotrochilus leucopleurus

Very like 139 (3); outermost tail feathers narrower than rest and curving inward.

Temperate zone. Andes of se BOLIVIA in Tarija. Central CHILE from Antofagasta s to Bío-Bío. W ARGENTINA from Jujuy and Salta to Chubut.

141. BLACK-BREASTED HILLSTAR

Oreotrochilus melanogaster

4″ (.6″). Upperparts dark shining green. Throat and sides of neck glittering emerald green, breast and upper abdomen velvety black, sides of body sandy brown. Tail dark blue green. ♀: Much like 139 but tail dark blue green, three outermost feathers with broad white tips.

Temperate zone. Andes of PERU in Junín and Lima.

Plate 6

142. WEDGE-TAILED HILLSTAR

Oreotrochilus adela

4.5" (1.1"). Crown dull brown; back dull olive, feathers pale-edged. Throat and sides of neck glittering emerald green, center of breast and abdomen black, sides of body chestnut. Tail feathers dull dark brown, all but central pair with pale buff inner webs. ♀: Above like ♂. Throat white, heavily spotted; breast and abdomen cinnamon. Tail rather like ♂ but with dusky subterminal area and white tip to outer feathers.

Temperate zone. Andes in Cochabamba, Potosí and Chuquisaca, BOLIVIA.

143. WHITE-TAILED HILLSTAR

Urochroa bougueri *

4.7" (1.2"). Upperparts shining purplish, bronzy green (or bronzy green, 1), gape dark rufous (or without rufous, 1). Throat and breast glittering blue, rest of underparts dark gray with shining green disks. Central and outermost tail feathers black; rest white, edged black (or central tail feathers bronze; rest white, edged black on outer web, 1).

Upper tropical, lower subtropical zones. Pacific slope of COLOMBIA from headwaters of río San Juan south to nw ECUADOR. E slope of E Andes of COLOMBIA in Nariño south to e ECUADOR, 1. Forest.

144. GIANT HUMMINGBIRD

Patagona gigas *

7.5" (1.7"). Unmistakable; the largest hummingbird. Above olive brown, rump white. Underparts and sides of neck dull cinnamon, under tail coverts white. Tail forked, bronzy olive, outermost feathers with central portion pale grayish. Young birds are grayish below with speckled throats.

Arid temperate zone. From n ECUADOR s through Andes to Mendoza, ARGENTINA, and Aysén, CHILE. Some southern breeders

of typical race migrate n from s CHILE or ARGENTINA to Tucumán and Catamarca.

Plate 8

145. SHINING SUNBEAM

Aglaeactis cupripennis *

4" (1"). Crown and mantle dusky brown, lower back and rump glittering purple shading to glittering green on upper tail coverts. Below rufous (or with brown belly, 1) sometimes with dusky marks on throat; patch on breast slightly paler. Tail feathers with cinnamon inner webs and bases (or all bronze, 1). ♀: Differs only by less glittering rump.

Upper temperate zone. Andes of COLOMBIA and ECUADOR. PERU in Cuzco and Puno, 1. Open slopes.

146. WHITE-TUFTED SUNBEAM

Aglaeactis castelnaudii *

Differs from 145 by being dark brown below with spot on throat and center of abdomen dark rufous, pectoral tuft white, Glittering feathers of lower back amethyst purple without green.

Temperate zone. Andes of PERU in Huánuco, Junín and Cuzco. Open glades in woodlands.

147. PURPLE-BACKED SUNBEAM

Aglaeactis aliciae

4.6" (.7"). Mostly dark, earth brown. Lores, chin, patch on lower throat, pectoral tuft, under wing- and under tail coverts white. Lower back and rump amethyst, shading to golden green on upper tail coverts. Tail bronze with white base.

Temperate zone of Andes of n PERU in Libertad and Ancash.

148. BLACK-HOODED SUNBEAM

Aglaeactis pamela

4.2" (.7"). Black. Pectoral tuft white. Lower back, rump and upper tail coverts glittering green. Tail and under tail coverts rufous, latter tipped and edged dusky.

Temperate zone. BOLIVIA in La Paz and Cochabamba.

Plate 7

149. MOUNTAIN VELVETBREAST

Lafresnaya lafresnayi*

3.5″ (1.1″). Bill thin, curved. Upperparts shining grass green. Throat and breast glittering emerald green, belly velvety black, under tail coverts white, tipped bronze. Central tail feathers bronze green, rest white (or buff, 1) edged terminally with black. ♀: Upperparts and tail like ♂, underparts white (or buff, 1) with shining green disks.

Subtropical, temperate zones. Andes of nw VENEZUELA in Mérida and Táchira; COLOMBIA in Santa Marta Mts., s through E and n Central Andes; from W and s Central Andes to Junín, PERU, 1. Forest, scrub.

150. GREAT SAPPHIREWING

Pterophanes cyanopterus*

6.5″ (1.1″). A large dark green hummingbird, somewhat glittering below, with dark blue wings and somewhat forked greenish black tail. ♀: Top and sides of head ashy brown. Back shining green. Wing coverts dark blue. Underparts cinnamon with green disks on sides. Tail as in ♂ with white outer web on outermost feather.

Temperate zone. The Andes of COLOMBIA s to BOLIVIA in La Paz and Cochabamba. Open slopes.

151. BRONZY INCA

Coeligena coeligena*

4.9″ (1.1″). Upperparts shining reddish bronzy, feathers obscurely edged green. Feathers of throat and breast edged white giving scaled appearance, rest of underparts dark brown to rufous brown. Tail bronze.

Upper tropical and subtropical zones. Nw VENEZUELA from Miranda to Zulia and Barinas, w to COLOMBIA, thence s through Andes to n BOLIVIA. Forest.

152. BROWN INCA

Coeligena wilsoni

4.5″ (1.3″). Upperparts and tail like 151. Underparts, including chin, dark grayish brown; throat amethyst. Conspicuous white patch at each side of breast.

Upper tropical and subtropical zones. W slope of W Andes of COLOMBIA from sources of río San Juan south in w ECUADOR to Zaruma. Forest.

153. BLACK INCA

Coeligena prunellei

4.5″ (1.2″). Black. Lesser wing coverts glittering blue. Throat patch glittering greenish blue. Patch at each side of breast white. Tail purple black.

COLOMBIA, probably subtropical or temperate zone of E Andes.

154. COLLARED INCA

Coeligena torquata*

4.5″ (1″). Mantle blackish green, becoming dark shining green on lower back (or entire upperparts shining green, 1, 2, 3). Large white (or cinnamon, 3) breast patch, rest of underparts black (or shining green, 1, 2, 3). Crown patch purple (or no patch, 1; or glittering green surrounded by black, 2; or crown black with glittering green frontal spot, 3). Central tail feathers golden green; rest white, tipped golden green. ♀: Above shining green. Throat and breast white, throat with shining green disks, belly gray with a few shining disks. Tail as in ♂.

Subtropical to temperate zone. Andes of nw VENEZUELA and adjacent COLOMBIA, 1. Rest of COLOMBIA and ECUADOR. N and central PERU, 2; s PERU and n BOLIVIA, 3. Forest, scrub.

155. WHITE-TAILED STARFRONTLET

Coeligena phalerata

4.5″ (1″). Crown glittering turquoise blue. Back shining dark green. Throat glittering violet, rest of underparts glittering blue green. Tail and under tail coverts white. ♀: Above shining green, below uniform cinnamon rufous. Tail bronzy, outer feathers with small buff tips.

COLOMBIA. Forest and open slopes of the Santa Marta Mts. between 4000-10,000 ft.

Plate 32

156. GOLDEN-BELLIED STARFRONTLET

Coeligena bonapartei*

4.5″ (1″). Cap black with glittering green frontlet. Upper back shining grass green, turning to glittering golden orange on lower back and upper tail coverts. Upper throat and breast glittering emerald green, patch on center of throat glittering violet blue, belly glittering golden orange. Tail golden bronze (or rufous, tipped golden bronze, 1). ♀: Differs from ♂ mainly by green crown and rufous throat.

Subtropical, temperate zones. Andes of nw VENEZUELA in Táchira, Mérida and Barinas, 1; Perijá Mts. in VENEZUELA and COLOMBIA and on w slope of E Andes s to latitude of Bogotá. Forest.

157. DUSKY STARFRONTLET

Coeligena orina

4.5" (1.2"). Uniform dark shining green above and below, crown feathers edged black, spot on throat glittering blue. Tail dark green. ♀: Unknown.

COLOMBIA in temperate zone of the n Western Andes. Forest.

158. BLUE-THROATED STARFRONTLET

Coeligena helianthea *

4.5" (1.1"). Frontlet glittering green. Back blackish green, rump and upper tail coverts glittering steely blue shot with purple. Throat and breast blackish green, patch in center of throat glittering purplish blue (or violet, 1), belly and under tail coverts glittering rosy purple. Tail dull black. ♀: Like ♂ but crown green, back lighter. Throat cinnamon, breast buff with green disks. Tail bronzy purple.

Subtropical, temperate zones. Andes of extreme w VENEZUELA in Táchira, 1; COLOMBIA on both slopes of E Andes from Bogotá n to Norte de Santander. Forest, scrub.

159. BUFF-WINGED STARFRONTLET

Coeligena lutetiae

4.6" (1.3"). Frontlet glittering green, crown and back velvety black glossed with purple on rump, tertials pale buff. Underparts glittering green, spot in center of throat violet blue. Tail bronzy black. ♀: Shining green above, glittering golden green below. Throat and tertials buff. Tail bronzy green.

Temperate zone. From w slope of Central COLOMBIAN Andes through Nariño to both slopes of Andes of ECUADOR. Forest.

160. VIOLET-THROATED STARFRONTLET

Coeligena violifer *

4.8" (1.3"). Top of head greenish black

(with glittering green frontlet, 1). Back bronzy green. Throat and breast green, violet patch in center of throat and with (or without, 1) white band across breast, rest of underparts cinnamon (with green disks, 1). Tail and upper tail coverts rufous, latter with bronze tips (or central tail feathers bronze, rest rufous basally and bronze distally, 1). ♀: Much like ♂, but crown green and no violet patch on throat.

Subtropical zone of Andes of PERU from Amazonas to Cuzco. N BOLIVIA to La Paz and Cochabamba, 1.

161. RAINBOW STARFRONTLET

Coeligena iris *

4.3" (1.3"). Upper back dark bronzy green; lower back, belly, wings and tail rufous chestnut. Crown glittering iridescent green to fiery orange, violet blue posteriorly. Throat and breast glittering green, purple blue spot on center of throat (or back all bronzy, crown with purple stripe down center of iridescent crown patch, 1; or nape black, rest of upperparts light rufous chestnut, crown iridescent green to blue, 2). ♀: Much like ♂ but duller.

Subtropical, temperate zones. Andes of s ECUADOR and n PERU to Libertad. E slope of w Andes in s Cajamarca, 1. E slope of w Andes in central Cajamarca, 2.

Plate 6

162. SWORD-BILLED HUMMINGBIRD

Ensifera ensifera

5.2" (4"). Unmistakable due to enormous bill. Crown and tail coppery, back shining green. Throat black, sides of neck and upper breast glittering green, rest of underparts grayish with green disks. Tail forked. ♀: Above like ♂; underparts dull white, throat spotted with bronze, rest with shining green disks.

Upper subtropical and temperate zones. Andes of Mérida, VENEZUELA w to COLOMBIAN Andes and s through Andes to n BOLIVIA. Shrubby slopes.

Plate 33

163. GREEN-BACKED FIRECROWN

Sephanoides sephaniodes

4" (.6"). Top of head glittering iridescent, opalescent red. Above, including tail, bronzy green; below dirty white, speckled on throat and breast with bronze. ♀: Differs from ♂ by no glittering crown; feathers of underparts with broad subterminal dusky patches.

W ARGENTINA from Mendoza to n Tierra del Fuego, in winter in e lowlands to Buenos Aires. CHILE from Atacama to Magallanes and Tierra del Fuego. [Juan Fernández Is.] Scrub, gardens.

164. BUFF-TAILED CORONET
Boissonneaua flavescens*

4.2" (.6"). Crown, throat and breast glittering green, upperparts shining green, belly buff with green disks. Inner webs of innermost remiges and inner under wing coverts cinnamon. Central tail feathers bronze, rest pale buff edged with bronze.

Upper subtropical, lower temperate zones. Andes of nw VENEZUELA w to Andes of COLOMBIA and south to w ECUADOR. Shrubby slopes.

165. CHESTNUT-BREASTED CORONET
Boissonneaua matthewsii

4.2" (.6"). Above shining green, below chestnut, throat thickly speckled with glittering green disks. Central tail feathers bronze, outermost rufous; rest rufous, tipped bronze.

Subtropical zone. Andes of se COLOMBIA s to Cuzco, PERU, on w slope of Andes to Cajamarca.

166. VELVET-PURPLE CORONET
Boissonneaua jardini

4.2" (.7"). Crown dark glittering violet. Nape, sides of head and throat, and upper breast velvety black; rest of underparts glittering purple mixed with blue green. Upperparts glittering blue green. Upper wing coverts glittering golden green, under wing coverts chestnut. Central tail feathers blackish bronze; rest white, edged with blackish bronze. ♀: Like ♂ but slightly duller.

Tropical, subtropical zones of Pacific CO-LOMBIA from headwaters of río San Juan south to nw ECUADOR. Forest.

Plate 32

167. ORANGE-THROATED SUNANGEL
Heliangelus mavors

3.7" (.6"). Upperparts shining green. Fore-

head, throat and upper breast glittering orange; pectoral band buff, rest of underparts buff with green disks. Tail bronzy.

Subtropical, temperate zones. Andes of nw VENEZUELA; COLOMBIA on e slope at n end of E Andes. Forest, shrubbery.

168. MERIDA SUNANGEL
Heliangelus spencei

3.7" (.5"). Upperparts bronzy green, crown dusky, forehead glittering steely green. Throat and upper breast glittering violet, pectoral band white, rest of underparts buff with green disks. Central tail feathers bronze, rest blackish.

Subtropical, temperate zones in Andes of Mérida, VENEZUELA. Forest, shrubbery.

169. AMETHYST-THROATED SUNANGEL
Heliangelus amethysticollis*

Differs mainly from 168 by forehead glittering blue green (breast band buff, 1), under tail coverts white instead of bronze green edged white, and outer tail feathers blue black.

Subtropical, temperate zones. Andes of nw VENEZUELA in sw Táchira and Perijá Mts., w in COLOMBIA to both slopes of E Andes from Norte de Santander to Cundinamarca; s ECUADOR to central PERU. Se PERU to n BOLIVIA in La Paz and Cochabamba, 1. Forest.

Plate 33

170. GORGETED SUNANGEL
Heliangelus strophianus

Differs from 169 mainly by dark gray belly with green disks and dark steel blue tail, longer and somewhat forked.

Subtropical zone. Sw COLOMBIA to nw ECUADOR. Forest.

171. TOURMALINE SUNANGEL
Heliangelus exortis

4" (.5"). Upperparts dark shining green. Forehead dark glittering green, chin and upper throat dark shining purple blue, rest of throat glittering violet (or glittering coppery gold, 1). Breast glittering green, rest of underparts dusky with green disks. Tail rather long, forked, central feathers dark bronze, rest blackish.

Subtropical, temperate zones. COLOMBIA on the three Andean ranges, e slope of s Eastern Andes; e ECUADOR to n PERU to Cajamarca, 1. Forest.

172. PURPLE-THROATED SUNANGEL

Heliangelus viola

4.7″ (.5″). Back shining grass green. Forehead and forecrown glittering blue green; throat glittering violet purple, bordered by glittering blue; changing to glittering green on rest of underparts. Tail rather long, deeply forked, central feathers like back, outer ones blackish.

Subtropical, temperate zones of w ECUADOR s in PERU to n Cajamarca on the west, and valley of the Marañón on the east. Forest.

173. BLACK-BREASTED PUFFLEG

Eriocnemis nigrivestis

3.2″ (.7″). Blackish. Throat and under tail coverts glittering violet blue. Upper tail coverts shining dark blue, tail steel blue. Downy leg puffs white. ♀: Shining bronzy green, becoming glittering blue green on rump and upper tail coverts. Throat patch glittering light blue. Under tail coverts glittering purple blue. Female pufflegs have leg puffs similar to those of males.

Temperate zone. N ECUADOR in mountains around Quito.

174. GLOWING PUFFLEG

Eriocnemis vestitus *

3.5″ (.7″). Crown, back and breast shining dark bronze green; belly and rump glittering golden green. Under tail coverts glittering purple. Tail dark steel blue. Downy leg puffs white. ♀: Upperparts shining golden green, glittering on rump. Patch on throat and under tail coverts glittering blue. Sides of neck and the breast buff with green disks, rest of underparts white with glittering golden green disks.

Temperate, páramo zones. Nw VENEZUELA in Mérida and Táchira; E Andes of COLOMBIA, Central Andes at s end, W Andes at n extremity; e ECUADOR. Forest, shrubbery.

175. TURQUOISE-THROATED PUFFLEG

Eriocnemis godini

3.8″ (.8″). Above shining bronze green, glittering on rump. Underparts glittering emerald green, more golden on abdomen, diffused gular patch glittering blue. Tail forked, blue black. Downy leg puffs white.

Temperate zone. COLOMBIA, known only from "Bogotá." Nw ECUADOR.

176. SAPPHIRE-VENTED PUFFLEG

Eriocnemis luciani *

4.5″ (.8″). Forecrown shining dark blue. Back shining bronze green. Underparts glittering golden green, bluish on throat (or belly mostly glittering dark blue, 1); under tail coverts glittering purple. Tail deeply forked, blue black. Downy leg puffs white.

Subtropical zone. W slope of Andes of Nariño, COLOMBIA, south to e and w ECUADOR. PERU to Cuzco, 1.

Plate 33

177. COPPERY-BELLIED PUFFLEG

Eriocnemis cupreoventris

3.2″ (.7″). Above shining green, bluer on upper tail coverts. Underparts glittering green becoming golden copper on center of abdomen, under tail coverts glittering purple. Tail blue black. Downy leg puffs white.

Subtropical, temperate zones. Nw VENEZUELA in Táchira and Mérida and both slopes of E Andes of COLOMBIA s to Cundinamarca. Shrubbery.

178. GOLDEN-BREASTED PUFFLEG

Eriocnemis mosquera

4.7″ (.8″). Above shining coppery green, below mostly glittering golden coppery green, more coppery on upper breast. Under tail coverts dark grayish; only species in group with dull-colored under tail coverts. Tail rather long, deeply forked, central feathers blue green, rest blackish bronze. Downy leg puffs white.

Temperate, occasionally upper tropical zone. The three Andean ranges of COLOMBIA south to n ECUADOR. Forest.

179. BLUE-CAPPED PUFFLEG

Eriocnemis glaucopoides

3.2″ (.7″). Forecrown and under tail coverts glittering blue. Uppersurface shining bronze green. Throat and breast glittering golden green, bluish on lower breast. Tail blue black. Downy leg puffs white. ♀: Above shining green. Underparts cinnamon; under tail coverts glittering blue, fringed buff.

Temperate zone of Andes of BOLIVIA in Cochabamba, Chuquisaca and Santa Cruz and nw ARGENTINA from Jujuy to Tucumán. Shrubbery.

180. COLORFUL PUFFLEG

Eriocnemis mirabilis[1]

3.2" (.6"). Forehead and forecrown glittering emerald green, postocular patch white. Back dark shining green. Throat and sides of neck glittering blue green merging into shining dark green at breast. Belly deep glittering indigo blue speckled with glittering red. Under tail coverts mixed glittering ruby and glittering brassy gold. Tail dusky, bronzy olive above, glistening bright brassy olive below. Downy leg puffs white, tipped cinnamon in front, all cinnamon behind. ♀: Upperparts and sides of breast shining dark green. Center of throat and breast white with shining green disks. Belly white with shining reddish bronze disks, longest under tail coverts subterminally shining reddish bronze. Tail mostly bronzy green, tipped and edged blue black.

Subtropical zone of w slope of s Western Andes in Cauca, COLOMBIA. Forest.

Plate 6

181. EMERALD-BELLIED PUFFLEG

Eriocnemis alinae *

3" (.6"). Above bronzy green. Forehead, throat, abdomen and under tail coverts glittering bluish green; center of breast white, feathers edged glittering green. Tail green, shining on undersurface, short and slightly forked. Downy leg puffs white.

Tropical, subtropical zones. COLOMBIA on e slope of E Andes from Boyacá to Nariño. Se ECUADOR; e PERU in Amazonas, San Martín and Libertad.

182. BLACK-THIGHED PUFFLEG

Eriocnemis derbyi *

3.5" (.8"). Shining golden, coppery green above and below; upper and under tail coverts glittering green. In certain lights underparts look black. Tail short, slightly forked, black, outer feathers pointed.

Downy leg puffs black. ♀: Differs from ♂ by white, green-spangled, underparts.

Temperate, páramo zones of Central Andes of COLOMBIA south to n ECUADOR. Shrubbery.

183. GREENISH PUFFLEG

Haplophaedia aureliae *

3.5" (.8"). Crown coppery, back shining coppery green. Underparts coppery green, feathers edged pale gray, under tail coverts dull green. Tail blue black. Leg puffs white externally, pinkish buff internally (or all pinkish buff, 1). ♀: Differs from ♂ in underparts grayish with green disks.

Subtropical zone of COLOMBIAN Andes south to e ECUADOR. PERU and BOLIVIA in La Paz, 1. [E Panama.] Forest undergrowth.

184. HOARY PUFFLEG

Haplophaedia lugens

Above like 183. Underparts dark sooty gray, feathers of throat and upper breast edged whitish. Leg puffs white.

Upper tropical and subtropical zones of Andes of w Nariño, COLOMBIA, and nw ECUADOR. Forest.

185. BOOTED RACKET-TAIL

Ocreatus underwoodii *

♂ 4.8", ♀ 3.1" (.5"). Tail forked, outer feathers very much longer than rest, terminating in bare shaft and purple black racket, (these feathers crossed, 1). Upperparts shining green. Throat and breast glittering green. Leg puffs white or buff. ♀: Upperparts and leg puffs as in ♂. Underparts white spotted with green. Tail forked but without lengthened feathers, central feathers shining green, outer ones blue black, tipped white.

Upper tropical to temperate zone. Andes of n VENEZUELA from Miranda w to Andes of COLOMBIA and south through e and w ECUADOR to ne PERU. Central PERU to n BOLIVIA, 1. Forest clearing and scrub.

Plate 6

[1]Meyer de Schauensee, Not. Naturae, 1967, no. 402, p. 1 (Charguayaco, 7200 ft., w slope of W Andes, Cauca, Colombia).

186. BLACK-TAILED TRAINBEARER

Lesbia victoriae *

♂ 10″, ♀ 5.5″ (.5″). Tail very long, deeply forked, black, all but outermost feathers tipped bronze green. Above shining green. Center of throat glittering golden green, breast and belly buff with green disks. ♀: Above like ♂, below white, throat with glittering green disks, breast and belly with shining disks. Tail as in male but much shorter, basal three-quarters of outer web of outer feather whitish.

Upper subtropical and temperate zones. COLOMBIA in E Andes, and w Nariño s through ECUADOR to central and s PERU. Grassy slopes, shrubbery.

Plate 33

187. GREEN-TAILED TRAINBEARER

Lesbia nuna *

6.3″ (.3″). Rather like 186 but very much smaller and greener. All but outer tail feathers shining green; outer feathers blackish becoming bronzy on distal part, tips shining green. ♀: Rather like 186 but smaller and with much greener tail.

Subtropical, temperate zones. Nw VENE-ZUELA (Mérida, once). COLOMBIA in E Andes from Norte de Santander to Cundina-marca and at headwaters of río Putumayo, also in upper Cauca Valley; Andes of e ECUADOR, PERU and nw BOLIVIA.

188. RED-TAILED COMET

Sappho sparganura *

♂ 6.8″, ♀ 4.8″ (.8″). Tail long, deeply forked, glittering rosy red or reddish gold, each feather tipped dusky purple. Top and sides of head shining green, back shining rosy purple. Throat glittering golden green, rest of underparts shining green. ♀: Shining green above, rump purple. Underparts white, throat buffy sprinkled with green disks. Tail much shorter, much less deeply forked than in ♂, with buffy white outer web to outermost feather.

Temperate zone. Andes of BOLIVIA in La Paz, and from Cochabamba south in w ARGENTINA to Neuquén; CHILE (Portillo Pass). Shrubbery.

Plate 7

189. BRONZE-TAILED COMET

Polyonymus caroli

♂ 4.7″, ♀ 4.2″ (.7″). Above and below bronzy green. Throat glittering rosy violet. Tail forked, central feathers bronzy green; rest dusky purple, tipped bronze; outer feather with pale outer web. ♀: Above like ♂. Throat with glittering orange disks, underparts grayish with green disks. Tail like ♂ in color, much shorter and less forked.

Subtropical, temperate zones. Pacific slope of Andes of PERU s to Arequipa, and central parts of country from Cajamarca to Cuzco. Mountain woodland, shrubbery.

Plate 7

190. PURPLE-BACKED THORNBILL

Ramphomicron microrhynchum *

3.2″ (.3″). Above shining purple. Throat glittering golden green, rest of underparts bronze green. Tail rather long, forked, blackish purple. ♀: Bronzy green above, underparts white with green disks. Tail as in ♂ but shorter and less forked, outer feathers tipped white.

Subtropical, temperate zones. Nw VENE-ZUELA in Mérida, s through Andes of COLOMBIA to ECUADOR and w slope of PERUVIAN Andes in Cajamarca (Taulis), and in Junín and Cuzco. Forest, bushy hillsides.

Plate 33

191. BLACK-BACKED THORNBILL

Ramphomicron dorsale

4″ (.3″). Upperparts black, upper tail coverts tipped purple bronze. Center of throat glittering golden olive, underparts dark gray with green disks. Tail rather long, forked, purple black, outer feathers exceptionally wide. ♀: Above shining grass green; upper tail coverts purple bronze. Below buffy white, throat and flanks with shining green disks.

Temperate, páramo zones. Santa Marta Mts. of COLOMBIA. Woods, grassy slopes.

192. BLACK METALTAIL

Metallura phoebe

4.7″ (.6″). Brownish black, wings bronzy. Gular patch glittering greenish blue. Tail, above coppery purple or coppery gold;

underside glittering golden copper. In this genus the color of tail's upperside depends on the incidence of the light. The color given first is that as seen with the light, then against it.

Subtropical, temperate zones. Andes of PERU from San Martín s to Tacna. N BOLIVIA (?). Barren slopes, woodland.

193. COPPERY METALTAIL

Metallura theresiae

3.7'' (.5''). Mostly reddish coppery green, reddest on head. Throat glittering green. Tail above shining blue or iridescent olive; below glittering green.

Temperate zone. N PERU in Amazonas, Cajamarca, Libertad and Huánuco.

194. SCALED METALTAIL

*Metallura aeneocauda**

4'' (.7''). Mostly bronzy green. Throat glittering green, feathers of underparts with buff subterminal bar giving scaled appearance. Tail above shining blue or coppery purple; below glittering bronzy green (or glittering purple red, 1).

Upper subtropical and temperate zones. Andes of PERU from Urubamba Valley in Cuzco s through Puno to La Paz, BOLIVIA; in Cochabamba, 1.

195. VIOLET-THROATED METALTAIL

Metallura baroni

4.5'' (.5''). Mostly bronzy green. Throat to upper breast glittering violet purple. Tail above shining olive or violet purple; below glittering green.

Temperate zone. Andes of sw ECUADOR in Prov. of Cuenca, 11,500 ft. Arid country.

196. FIRE-THROATED METALTAIL

Metallura eupogon

3.7'' (.5''). Bronzy green, throat patch fiery red. Tail above shining blue or coppery olive; below glittering coppery green.

Temperate zone. Andes of central PERU in Huánuco and Junín.

197. VIRIDIAN METALTAIL

*Metallura williami**

3.2'' (.7''). Coppery green, throat glittering green (or black, 1). Tail above shining

purplish blue, or green shot with blue; below glittering coppery green.

Temperate, páramo zones. Both slopes of Central Andes of COLOMBIA south to n ECUADOR; in s ECUADOR, 1. Open slopes.

198. TYRIAN METALTAIL

*Metallura tyrianthina**

3.5'' (.4''). Coppery green, throat glittering emerald green. Tail above shining coppery purple or purple; below shining purple.

Subtropical to páramo zone. N VENEZUELA from mts. of Aragua and Miranda w to COLOMBIA, including Santa Marta, s through Andes to Cochabamba, BOLIVIA. Forest and shrubbery.

199. PERIJA METALTAIL

Metallura iracunda

4.1'' (.4''). Black glossed with coppery greenish gold. Forecrown shining dark green, throat glittering emerald green. Tail above and below glittering purplish red.

Subtropical to temperate zone. Perijá Mts. in COLOMBIA and VENEZUELA.

Plate 33

200. RUFOUS-CAPPED THORNBILL

Chalcostigma ruficeps

3.5'' (.5''). Crown rufous. Back bronzy green. Throat patch narrow, pointed, glittering blue green turning to golden green on upper breast. Underparts buffy with green disks. Tail olive bronze, rather short for the group.

Temperate zone. Se ECUADOR s through Andes to La Paz and Cochabamba, BOLIVIA.

201. OLIVACEOUS THORNBILL

Chalcostigma olivaceum

5.5'' (.6''). Uniform dark grayish olive. Throat patch narrow, pointed, glittering green, becoming golden violet, then turning to purple. Tail shining olive.

Temperate, páramo zones. Central PERU from Junín s to La Paz, BOLIVIA. Grassland, sometimes walks on matted grass in search of insects.

202. BLUE-MANTLED THORNBILL

Chalcostigma stanleyi *

4.7" (.4"). Crown dusky greenish blue, back purplish blue. Throat patch narrow, pointed, glittering green, turning to violet (or steel blue, 1) on breast. Tail steel blue. ♀: Differs from ♂ by almost no throat patch.

Temperate, páramo zones. Andes of ECUADOR; PERU from Amazonas and Libertad s to Huánuco; from Puno to La Paz, BOLIVIA, 1. Habits as in 201.

203. BRONZE-TAILED THORNBILL

Chalcostigma heteropogon

4.7" (.5"). Bronzy green, upper tail coverts reddish bronze. Throat patch narrow, pointed, glittering green, turning to rosy violet on upper breast. Tail coppery bronze.

Temperate, páramo zones. W VENEZUELA in Táchira; E Andes of COLOMBIA s to Cundinamarca.

204. RAINBOW-BEARDED THORNBILL

Chalcostigma herrani *

4" (.5"). Slightly crested, center of crown rufous bordered laterally with black. Back bronzy green, bronzier on rump. Throat patch narrow, pointed, glittering green, turning to glittering orange and becoming fiery red on breast. Tail rather short, rounded, violet purple, outer feathers with broad white tips.

Temperate zone. COLOMBIA in Central Andes in Tolima; s end of W Andes south to n ECUADOR. Shrubbery, grassy slopes.

Plate 33

205. BEARDED HELMETCREST

Oxypogon guerinii *

4.5 (.3"). Crown and sides of head black with crest of long, narrow white feathers; sides of neck white. Back shining olive. Narrow throat patch bluish turning to green on lower throat (or all white, 1; or all violet, 2; or bluish turning to orange on lower throat, 3); longest feathers of lower throat narrow, white, forming a beard. Underparts grayish with olive disks. Tail somewhat forked, bronzy olive, outer feathers mostly white (or central feathers bronzy olive, rest reddish bronze, outermost with buff outer web, 3; or central feathers bronzy olive, outer ones dark violet bronze with white shafts, 1). ♀: Shining bronzy green above,

white below with bronze discs. No crest or beard. Tail as in respective male.

Páramo zone. Nw VENEZUELA on high peaks in Mérida and Trujillo, 1; COLOMBIA in Santa Marta Mts. above 9000 ft., 2; in the E Andes; in the central part of Central Andes, 3. Bushy or grassy slopes. Sometimes walks on matted grass in search of insects.

Plate 32

206. BEARDED MOUNTAINEER

Oreonympha nobilis *

5.5" (1"). Band down center of crown maroon, bordered laterally by glittering violet blue; sides of head black. Throat patch narrow, tapering to point, glittering green becoming glittering violet and then glittering purple on breast. Back olive, underparts white. Upper and under tail coverts shining reddish bronze. Tail forked, central feathers shining bronzy olive, rest with increasing amounts of white, outermost almost entirely white. ♀: Like ♂ but duller, green throat patch not lengthened.

Temperate zone. Andes of PERU in Huancavelica and Cuzco. Arid slopes.

Plate 7

207. MOUNTAIN AVOCETBILL

Opisthoprora euryptera

4" (.5"). Bill upturned at tip. Above shining green, coppery on crown. Below white becoming buff on crissum, everywhere thickly spangled with green disks. Central tail feathers like back; rest blue black, narrowly tipped white.

Temperate zone. Central Andes of COLOMBIA. Ne ECUADOR. Bushy slopes.

Plate 8

208. GRAY-BELLIED COMET

Tephrolesbia griseiventris

6" (.7"). Above shining bronze green, below pale gray, throat glittering blue. Tail rather long, deeply forked, evenly graduated, central feathers golden greenish bronze, rest with increasing amounts of blue, outermost bronzy only at tip. ♀: Differs chiefly from ♂ by no blue throat patch and by shorter tail.

Temperate zone. Middle nw PERU on both slopes of w Andes and w slope of central Andes from s Cajamarca to w Huánuco.

Plate 5

209. LONG-TAILED SYLPH

Aglaiocercus kingi *

♂ 7", ♀ 3.75" (.6"). Tail graduated, central feathers very short, outermost much the longest, 4.75"; feathers basally blue black, exposed portions glittering purple, blue or green; undersurface blackish. Crown patch glittering green. Throat patch glittering violet blue. Above shining dark green, below duller shaded with olive. ♀: Above much like ♂. Throat buffy white with green disks, rest of underparts cinnamon. Tail forked, of normal length; central feathers short, shining green; outer ones with green outer web and tip and dark blue inner web, outermost dark blue with white tip.

Upper tropical and subtropical zones. Mts. of VENEZUELA n of the Orinoco from Sucre w to COLOMBIA in E and Central Andes, and e slope of W Andes in upper Cauca Valley, s through Nariño to w and e ECUADOR, e PERU and BOLIVIA to La Paz and Cochabamba. Forest, scrub.

210. VIOLET-TAILED SYLPH

Aglaiocercus coelestis *

♂ 7", ♀ 3.5" (.6"). Much like 209 but throat patch larger, lower back bluer and all but central tail feathers with glittering peacock blue tips. ♀: At once distinguishable from 209 by glittering blue crown and white breast.

Upper tropical and subtropical zones. CO-LOMBIA on e slope of W Andes at head of Cauca Valley and w slope from headwaters of río San Juan s through Nariño to sw ECUADOR. Forest, scrub.

Plate 32

211. HOODED VISORBEARER

Augastes lumachellus

3.5" (.7"). Crown and sides of throat velvety black, forehead and throat glittering golden green, spot of glittering fiery red at base of throat. Body plumage bronze green. Tail glittering golden bronze above, golden orange below. ♀: Differs mainly from ♂ by no black on head.

Ne part of BRAZILIAN plateau in Bahía on Serra do Sincorá and Serra Geral from Barra de Estiva to Morro do Chapéu, 3000-5000 ft. Cerrado.

Plate 6

212. HYACINTH VISORBEARER

Augastes scutatus *

3" (.6"). Crown and back bronze green. Forehead and throat glittering golden green edged with black, ruff at sides of neck deep purplish blue, pectoral band creamy white, abdomen dark blue. Tail glittering bronzy green above and below. ♀: Rather like ♂ but no black border to green of crown; abdomen paler blue, becoming bronze green on sides; tail considerably bluer.

Se part of BRAZILIAN plateau in Minas Gerais and s Bahía in Serra Cipó, Serra Caraça, Serra da Mantiqueira, Chapada Diamantina, and Serra do Espinhaço from Ouro Preto to Grão Mogól, 3000-5000 ft. Cerrado, open rocky slopes.

213. WEDGE-BILLED HUMMINGBIRD

Schistes geoffroyi *

3.2" (.6"). Upperparts bronzy green becoming bronze on lower back. Throat glittering golden green (with forecrown glittering green, 1), pectoral band white. Patch on each side of breast glittering violet, rest of underparts light gray with green disks. Under tail coverts white (or shining bronze green, 1). Tail bronze green with broad subterminal blue band on all but central feathers. Sexes similar (or differing from ♂ by bronze green crown, pure white throat with shining blue patch at each side of breast, 1).

Upper tropical and subtropical zones. N VENEZUELA s through COLOMBIA to BOLIVIA. W Andes and w slope of Central Andes of COLOMBIA, 1. Forest.

Plate 5

214. PURPLE-CROWNED FAIRY

Heliothryx barroti *

♂ 4", ♀ 4.75", (.6"). Upperparts shining green, underparts pure white. Crown glittering purple; subocular band black, terminating in glittering purple on ear coverts; sides of neck glittering emerald green. Tail rounded, outer feathers white, central ones dark blue. ♀: No purple cap, otherwise like ♂ but subocular band black, central tail feathers considerably longer than rest.

Tropical zone. N COLOMBIA from Gulf of Urabá e to middle Magdalena and along

Pacific slope south to sw ECUADOR. [Mid. Amer.] Forest.

Plate 33

215. BLACK-EARED FAIRY

Heliothryx aurita *

Like 214 but crown glittering green (or with crown and upper throat glittering green, 1). ♀: Like 214.

Tropical zone. GUIANAS, VENEZUELA s of the Orinoco, (n of it only in Sucre); COLOMBIA east of E Andes south to n BOLIVIA, BRAZIL n of the Amazon. S of the Amazon from Pará and Maranhão to Paraná and Mato Grosso, 1. Forest, orange groves, parks.

216. HORNED SUNGEM

Heliactin cornuta

3.7" (.5"). Center of crown glittering dark blue; iridescent tufts at sides of crown glittering ruby red at base, turning to gold and greenish gold. Upperparts coppery greenish gold. Sides of head and throat velvety black which joins and ends in point on upper breast; sides of neck, breast and belly white. Tail feathers narrow and pointed, much graduated, central four longest, central pair greenish, rest white. ♀: Like ♂ but without glittering feathers on head or black throat. Outer tail feathers with black oblique band near base.

SURINAM (Sipaliwini). Central BRAZIL from Maranhão and Piauí to São Paulo and w through Goiás to w Mato Grosso and adjacent ne Santa Cruz, BOLIVIA. Caatinga, cerrado, open forest.

Plate 6

217. MARVELOUS SPATULETAIL

Loddigesia mirabilis

5" (.5"), not including tail feathers with racket. Unmistakable due to extraordinary tail. Outermost feathers much lengthened, each with long, bare shaft curved in semicircle, crossing each other and terminating in enormous blackish purple racket; next pair long, straight narrow and acuminate; remainder rudimentary. Crown and crest glittering purple. Back bronze green. Throat glittering blue, edged glittering green; underparts whitish with black stripe down center. ♀: 3.75". Outer tail feathers somewhat lengthened, pale grayish terminating in

blunt spatule; rest of tail feathers very short, rather wide, dark blue apically. Above bronze green, below mostly white.

Andes of PERU known only from Chachapoyas region on e side of valley of río Utcubamba, an affluent of río Marañón, between 7500-8500 ft., in s Amazonas.

Plate 6

218. LONG-BILLED STARTHROAT

Heliomaster longirostris *

3.5" (1.4"). Crown glittering bluish green. Back coppery green with concealed white patch on lower back. Chin black; throat glittering rosy to violet, bordered laterally by white; breast grayish, center of belly white, sides of body bronzy. Tail feathers bronze, all but central pair with broad black subterminal band, outer feathers tipped white. ♀: Lacks glittering crown patch.

Tropical, subtropical zones. GUIANAS, VENEZUELA, and COLOMBIA south to nw PERU on west, and e of Andes to La Paz and Santa Cruz, BOLIVIA, and to s BRAZIL; in e only to São Paulo. Trinidad. [Mid. Amer.] Scrub, savanna, grassland.

219. STRIPE-BREASTED STARTHROAT

Heliomaster squamosus

4" (1.2"). Crown glittering green. Throat glittering violet, lateral feathers lengthened. Upperparts bronze green; underparts greenish black with white band down center. Tail somewhat forked, central feathers like back, rest dull bluish green. ♀: Above coppery green. Throat feathers blackish, edged white; rest of underparts bronzy green with white line down center. Outer tail feathers black, tipped white.

E BRAZIL from Pernambuco, Bahía and Goiás to São Paulo. Forest, scrub, savanna, grassland.

220. BLUE-TUFTED STARTHROAT

Heliomaster furcifer

4.2" (1"). Crown, nape and upper mantle glittering brassy green, rest of back shining coppery green. Throat glittering violet, tufts at sides of neck and underparts glittering ultramarine. Tail forked, feathers pointed, shining dark green above, glistening blue green below. ♀: Coppery green above, gray below, line down center of abdomen white, sides of body with green disks. Tail less forked than in ♂, feathers pointed, bronze green, all but central pair distally black, undersurface shining blue green, outer feathers tipped white.

Tropical zone. COLOMBIA in Amazonas. BRAZIL in Mato Grosso, Goiás and Rio Grande do Sul; BOLIVIA from Cochabamba to Tarija; PARAGUAY; URUGUAY; w and central ARGENTINA s to Buenos Aires, Córdoba and Catamarca. Forest, scrub, savanna, grassland.

Plate 7

221. OASIS HUMMINGBIRD

Rhodopis vesper*

4.2" (1.3", curved). Above shining olive green, rump and upper tail coverts rufous. Throat glittering rosy violet, underparts buffy white. Tail forked, central feathers very short, inner feathers grayish olive; outer four much narrower than rest, dark purplish brown. ♀: Differs from ♂ by no violet throat patch. Tail slightly forked, feathers shining olive; outer ones black on terminal quarter, tipped white.

Arid, tropical coastal to temperate zone. W PERU from Piura south to n CHILE from Arica to Atacama. Oases, near wells, up mountain slopes in valleys to 10,000 ft.

Plate 7

222. PERUVIAN SHEARTAIL

Thaumastura cora

♂ 5", ♀ 3.7" (.4"). Above shining green. Throat rosy violet, breast white, rest of underparts grayish with green disks. Tail 3.2"; central feathers very short (.3"), mostly white; next pair much the longest, white for most of inner web, outer web and tip dark brown, remaining outer rectrices gradually shorter toward outermost. ♀: Above like ♂, below white. Central tail feathers like back, rest mostly black with white tips, outer feathers shortest.

Arid coastal zone up to lower temperate zone. W PERU from Libertad s to Arequipa. Hab. as in 221.

Plate 7

223. PURPLE-THROATED WOODSTAR

Philodice mitchellii

3" (.6"). Above dusky bronze green. Throat and sides of neck glittering violet, breast white, belly dusky bronze, flanks chestnut.

Tail brownish purple, central feathers very short, outer two pairs equal and longest, outermost narrow. ♀: Like ♂ but throat white, line behind eye white, band across breast blackish, belly rufous. Central tail feathers like back, rest dark cinnamon with broad, black subterminal band.

Tropical, lower subtropical zones. COLOMBIA on both slopes of W Andes south to w ECUADOR. Forest, pastures.

Plate 33

224. SLENDER-TAILED WOODSTAR

Microstilbon burmeisteri

♂ 2.7", ♀ 2.5" (.5"). Above dark shining green, sides of head black. Throat and long moustachial tufts glittering rosy violet. Underparts gray with green disks bordering throat patch and on flanks. Outer tail feathers lengthened (.7"), black, part of inner web of next to outermost pale cinnamon; rest of tail feathers very short, central ones green, ♀: Above dark shining green, underparts buffy cinnamon. Tail square, central feathers green, rest cinnamon with broad black medial band.

Upper tropical to temperate zone. E BOLIVIA in Santa Cruz, Chuquisaca and Tarija; nw ARGENTINA to Catamarca. Forest.

Plate 7

225. AMETHYST WOODSTAR

Calliphlox amethystina

3" (.6"). Above dark bronze green. Throat and sides of neck amethyst bordered with dull white, rest of underparts gray with green disks. Tail rather long, deeply forked, outer six feathers dark purplish brown, tipped bronze. ♀: Like ♂ but throat whitish with a few glittering amethyst disks, underparts mostly rufous. Tail short, square, central feathers green, rest black with cinnamon tips.

Tropical zone. Generally distributed e of Andes south to n BOLIVIA, BRAZIL s to Rio Grande do Sul and Mato Grosso, PARAGUAY and ne ARGENTINA (Misiones). Forest, scrub, savanna, grassland.

Plate 5

226. PURPLE-COLLARED WOODSTAR

Myrtis fanny*

3" (.7"). Upperparts bronze green, throat and sides of neck glittering aquamarine bordered below by glittering violet band; underparts dirty white. Tail long (1"), central feathers shorter, dull brown with greenish gloss. ♀: Bronzy green above, buffy below, whitest on throat and center of belly. Tail normal, central feathers bluish green, next pair with black tips, rest black with white tips.

Tropical to temperate zone. S ECUADOR; PERU from Amazonas s through nw Huánuco and along w slope of Andes s to Arequipa. Semiarid lands, woodland.

227. CHILEAN WOODSTAR

Eulidia yarrellii

3.1" (.5"). Above shining olive green. Throat glittering violet red, underparts white. Central rectrices very short, green; outer rectrices one inch, blackish brown. ♀: Above shining green, below white tinged buff. Central tail feathers like back; lateral feathers black, buff at base with broad white tips.

N CHILE at Arica and neighboring valleys, occasionally s to Antofagasta. Arid country, gardens.

228. SHORT-TAILED WOODSTAR

Myrmia micrura

2.5" (.5"). Above shining pale green. Chin and line from gape to below eye white, throat and sides of neck violet, rest of underparts white. Tail black, very short concealed by upper and under tail coverts, feathers narrow and stiff. ♀: Above like ♂. Throat and breast cinnamon buff, belly buffy white. Tail black, tipped white.

Tropical zone in arid parts of w ECUADOR from La Plata I. s in PERU to Libertad.

Plate 5

229. WHITE-BELLIED WOODSTAR

Acestrura mulsant

3" (.7"). Upperparts and sides of body shining dark green. Throat and sides of neck amethyst; white line from behind eye to pectoral band. Tail black, forked, feathers pointed, two outermost reduced to shafts only. ♀: Above bronze green, sides of head blackish, line from behind eye connected to buffy underparts, which become cinnamon on sides of body. Tail normal, outer feathers cinnamon with broad black subterminal band.

Subtropical, lower temperate zones. COLOMBIA in Central and E Andes from Cundinamarca south to n BOLIVIA. Forest, scrub.

Plate 7

230. LITTLE WOODSTAR

Acestrura bombus

2.5" (.4"). Above bronze green. Throat rosy violet, buff line behind eye curving down to join buffy pectoral band; rest of underparts mostly bronzy green. Central tail feathers very short, next pair narrow and longest, rest becoming narrower and shorter toward outside. ♀: Above bronze green, cinnamon buff below. Outer tail feathers cinnamon with broad subterminal black band.

Tropical zone of e and w ECUADOR s, up to subtropical zone in PERU to Libertad and to Huallaga Valley in Huánuco. Forest, scrub.

231. GORGETED WOODSTAR

Acestrura heliodor *

2.5" (.5"). Upperparts and belly dark bluish green; throat glittering rosy violet, feathers at sides much lengthened; breast grayish (or back dark shining blue, throat glittering reddish violet, breast whitish, 1). Tail black, central feathers very short, next two pairs much longer, outermost much shorter and very narrow. ♀: Rather like 229 but smaller, greener above.

Subtropical zone. Nw VENEZUELA in Andes of Mérida and COLOMBIA in E and Central Andes; Santa Marta Mts., 1. ECUADOR. [E Panama.] Forest, scrub.

232. ESMERALDAS WOODSTAR

Acestrura berlepschi

2.5" (.5"). Above coppery green. Throat glittering violet rose, breast grayish white. Outer tail feathers slightly narrower but equal in length to next pair. ♀: Much like 230 but underparts white, throat tinged buff.

Tropical zone of w ECUADOR.

233. RUFOUS-SHAFTED WOODSTAR

Chaetocercus jourdanii *

Much like 229 in color but tail different. Tail forked, central feathers like back; three lateral feathers not particularly narrowed, equal in length, blackish with rufous near base. Bill shorter (.5"). ♀: Much like 229 but upper tail coverts green instead of rufous.

Tropical, subtropical zones. Ne VENE-ZUELA in Sucre and Monagas, and in nw from Aragua and Carabobo west to E Andes of COLOMBIA in Santander. Trinidad. Forest, scrub.

Fig. 16. BARRED PARAKEET
Bolborhynchus l. lineola
p. 103

Order TROGONIFORMES

Family TROGONIDAE   TROGONS

Trogons are among the most beautiful of birds. Males are metallic green above with crimson or yellow stomachs. Their tails are rather long, graduated, broad and square-ended.

They are solitary, sluggish and confiding; usually inhabit the middle stages of heavy forest and feed on small fruits and insects. Insects are often caught on the wing, the birds darting off their perch after them, then returning, flycatcher-like, to their starting point. Fruit is also picked off on the wing.

Nests are dug in soft, rotting wood or in wasp or termite nests. The "song" is a soft, low, oft-repeated note.

Trogons are also found in tropical Asia and Africa, but are best represented in the New World.

AID TO IDENTIFICATION

With lengthened upper wing coverts and upper tail coverts 1b, 2a, 3b, 4

Normal tail and wing coverts (belly red) 5b, 6, 7b, 9, 10b, 12c, 13; (belly yellow) 8, 11, 14

1. CRESTED QUETZAL

Pharomachrus antisianus

13.5". Upperparts and breast coppery grass green, belly crimson. Three outer tail feathers white except at base, rest of tail feathers and remiges black. Bill orange yellow. ♀: Head mouse brown. Upperparts bronzy green; breast and underparts mostly brown, mottled with green on breast; belly and under tail coverts crimson. Outer tail feathers black notched with white on outer web. Bill black.

Subtropical zone. W VENEZUELA from Mérida and Trujillo, west to e slope of W Andes of COLOMBIA and s through Andes to n BOLIVIA. Forest.

2. WHITE-TIPPED QUETZAL

Pharomachrus fulgidus *

Differs from 1 mainly by only distal portion of outer tail feathers being white. ♀: Differs mainly from 1 by outer tail feathers tipped white, and barred on both webs.

Subtropical zone. GUYANA (?); mts. of VENEZUELA n of the Orinoco from Sucre and Monagas w to Yaracuy. Ne COLOMBIA in Santa Marta Mts. E ECUADOR (?). Forest, coffee plantations.

3. GOLDEN-HEADED QUETZAL

Pharomachrus auriceps *

♂ and ♀ differ from 1 mainly by outer tail feathers entirely black. ♂: Bill orange yellow. ♀: Bill horn brown, ridge black.

Upper tropical and subtropical zones. Nw VENEZUELA; Andes of COLOMBIA south to n BOLIVIA. [E Panama.] Forest.

Plate 34

4. PAVONINE QUETZAL

Pharomachrus pavoninus *

Very similar to 3 but head less crested. Bill red instead of yellow. ♀: Very like 1 but bill smaller, black with red base.

Tropical zone. S VENEZUELA and se COLOMBIA south to nw BOLIVIA and w Amazonian BRAZIL. Forest.

5. SLATY-TAILED TROGON

Trogon massena

12.5". Facial area and throat black. Upperparts and breast glossy greenish blue, bluer on rump; lower breast and under tail coverts red. Wing coverts finely vermiculated black and white. Undersurface of tail black, outer feathers tipped and somewhat mottled with white on outer web. Bill salmon red, eye ring orange red. ♀: Upperparts, wings and tail, throat and breast gray; belly and under tail coverts rosy red. Lower mandible mainly reddish.

Tropical zone of Pacific COLOMBIA from Atrato Valley to nw ECUADOR. [Mid. Amer.] Forest, sometimes mangroves.

6. BLACK-TAILED TROGON

Trogon melanurus *

11". ♂: Differ from 5 mainly by white band across breast. Iris rarely white or gray, usually brown. Bill wholly or largely orange yellow in both sexes. Eye ring orange red.

Tropical, subtropical zones. GUIANAS, s VENEZUELA and in Perijá Mts.; COLOMBIA south to nw PERU and n BOLIVIA. Amazonian BRAZIL. [Central and e Panama.] Forest.

7. BLUE-TAILED TROGON

Trogon comptus

Distinguishable from 6 by much bluer uppersurface and breast; rump and tail peacock blue. No white band across chest. Iris white to bluish gray, no eye ring; bill yellow. ♀: Very similar to 6 but darker throughout. Upper mandible black, yellow at base; lower mandible yellow.

COLOMBIA in lower Cauca Valley and from upper Atrato Valley to w Nariño. Forest.

8. WHITE-TAILED TROGON

Trogon viridis *

11.5". Crown and breast purplish blue, throat black, belly orange yellow. Back bronzy green, rump purplish blue. Central tail feathers greenish blue, broadly tipped black; outer feathers black, tipped white (or mostly white, 1). Bill pale greenish (or bluish gray, 1); eye ring pale bluish. ♀: Upperparts, breast and sides of body dark gray; belly orange yellow. Wing coverts black finely barred white, outer tail feathers tipped and barred with white.

Tropical, subtropical zones. GUIANAS; VENEZUELA, except the nw; e COLOMBIA south to nw BOLIVIA. BRAZIL through Amazonia and from Maranhão s to São Paulo and Mato Grosso. W of Andes in COLOMBIA and ECUADOR, 1. Trinidad. [Central and e Panama.] Forest, scrub, savanna.

Plate 34

9. COLLARED TROGON

Trogon collaris *

10.5". Upperparts and breast golden green, white bar across breast; belly crimson. Wing coverts vermiculated black and white. Outer tail feathers barred black and white and tipped white. Bill greenish yellow; no noticeable eye ring. ♀: Upperparts and breast sandy brown, white about eye, breast band white; belly light crimson. Central tail feathers rufous, outer feathers tipped white with black subterminal bar, outer webs partially white vermiculated with blackish.

Tropical, subtropical zones. GUIANAS, VENEZUELA and COLOMBIA, south to n BOLIVIA; BRAZIL locally in Amazonia e to rio Tapajós and Mato Grosso, and in s Bahía and Rio de Janeiro. W of Andes in COLOMBIA and nw ECUADOR. Trinidad and Tobago. [Mid. Amer.]

10. MASKED TROGON

Trogon personatus *

Very like 9, but bill smaller and tail bars much finer. ♀: Very like 9, but facial area black and outer webs of tail feathers finely barred with black.

Upper tropical to temperate zone. GUYANA, VENEZUELA and COLOMBIA s through Andes to n BOLIVIA. On w slope of Andes from nw COLOMBIA to Piura, PERU. Forest.

11. BLACK-THROATED TROGON

Trogon rufus *

10.5". Upperparts coppery green, throat black, breast bluish green, belly yellow. Central tail feathers coppery green (or coppery gold, 1), outer feathers barred black and white. Bill greenish; eye ring blue. ♀: Similar to 9 but belly yellow and outer tail feathers barred black and white.

Tropical zone. Generally distributed e of Andes from GUIANAS, VENEZUELA and COLOMBIA south to e PERU and Amazonian BRAZIL, in e from Bahía to Paraná; PARAGUAY; ne ARGENTINA. W of Andes in COLOMBIA and ECUADOR, 1. [S Honduras southward.] Forest.

12. SURUCUA TROGON

Trogon surrucura *

11". Back coppery green; crown and breast peacock blue, belly crimson (or orange, 1). Wing coverts freckled black and white. Central tail feathers peacock blue, tipped black; outer feathers mostly white. Bill greenish. ♀: Differs from ♂ mainly by slaty gray throat and breast, wing coverts black finely barred white, and outer tail feathers white on outer web.

E and south-central BRAZIL from s Bahía to Rio Grande do Sul, 1; west to s Goiás and s Mato Grosso, PARAGUAY and n ARGENTINA. Forest.

13. BLUE-CROWNED TROGON

Trogon curucui *

9.5". Differs from red bellied race of 12 mainly by size, indistinct white bar across breast, and outer tail feathers broadly barred white. ♀: Largely gray; differs from ♀ of 12 in same manner as ♂.

Tropical zone. COLOMBIA e of Andes from Meta s to BOLIVIA, PARAGUAY and n ARGENTINA. BRAZIL in w Amazonia e to rios Negro and Tapajós and Mato Grosso; in the e from e Pará to Rio Grande do Sul. Forest.

14. VIOLACEOUS TROGON

Trogon violaceus *

9". Top of head blue (or black, 1). Back bluish green to bluish violet; breast blue; belly orange yellow. Tail blue to purplish blue tipped black. Bill bluish gray; eye ring orange yellow. ♀: Upperparts, flanks and breast gray; belly yellow. Outer tail feathers white, barred black on outer web.

Tropical zone. GUIANAS; nw VENEZUELA and in s Bolívar and Amazonas; COLOMBIA south to n BOLIVIA and Amazonian BRAZIL. W of Andes in COLOMBIA and w ECUADOR, 1. Trinidad. [Mid. Amer.] Forest edge, clearings, open woodland.

Fig. 17. BLACK-FACED ANTTHRUSH
Formicarius a. analis
p. 253

Order CORACIIFORMES

Family ALCEDINIDAE   KINGFISHERS

Kingfishers are found everywhere except in polar regions, but are very poorly represented in the Americas. They live chiefly on small fish caught by diving. The Pygmy Kingfisher, however, lives mostly on insects caught on the wing. Kingfishers nest in holes in banks dug with their bills, scraping out the loose earth with their feet. Their voices, loud and unmusical, consist of a rattling sound.

1. RINGED KINGFISHER

*Ceryle torquata**

15". Crest and upperparts blue gray; breast and belly chestnut with broad white band across throat. Remiges black with large white patch on inner webs. Tail mostly black, banded with white. ♀: Similar but with gray band, margined white below, across breast.

Found in every country s to Tierra del Fuego, usually in lowlands, but in tropics occasionally to temperate zone. Margarita I. Trinidad. [Mid. Amer., Lesser Antilles.] Forested rivers, creeks, ricefields.

2. BELTED KINGFISHER

*Ceryle alcyon**

12". Above blue gray, below white with gray band across breast. Wings and tail as in 1. ♀: Like ♂ but with breast band and sides chestnut.

Occasional in winter. GUYANA; coastal VENEZUELA. COLOMBIA (once). Curaçao to Trinidad and Tobago. [Breeds in N Amer., migrates through Mid. Amer., W Indies.] Rivers, lakes.

3. AMAZON KINGFISHER

*Chloroceryle amazona**

11". Upperparts dark oily green with white band across hindneck. Underparts white with broad chestnut band across lower throat and breast. ♀: Similar but chestnut band replaced by green spots.

Tropical zone. Virtually throughout e of Andes to middle ARGENTINA. W of Andes only in COLOMBIA. Trinidad, Tobago. [Mid. Amer.] Forested rivers, creeks, lakes.

4. GREEN KINGFISHER

*Chloroceryle americana**

8". Virtually a miniature replica of 3, but more white on outer tail feathers. ♀: Much like 3 but with two oily green bands across throat and breast.

Generally distributed south to n ARGENTINA and n CHILE. Trinidad, Tobago. [Mid. Amer.] Rivers, mangroves, lakes.

Plate 9

5. GREEN-AND-RUFOUS KINGFISHER

Chloroceryle inda

9". Above dark oily green, wings and tail spotted with buffy white. Throat buff, deeping to ferruginous on belly. ♀: Similar but with green and white breast band.

E of Andes from GUIANAS, VENEZUELA and COLOMBIA, south to s BRAZIL, e PERU and n BOLIVIA. W of Andes to w ECUADOR. [Nicaragua to Panama.] Forested rivers, mangroves.

6. PYGMY KINGFISHER

Chloroceryle aenea *

5.5". Miniature replica of 5 but center of belly white.

E of Andes from GUIANAS, VENEZUELA and COLOMBIA, south to s BRAZIL, e PERU and n BOLIVIA. W of Andes to w ECUADOR. Trinidad. [Mid. Amer.] Mangroves, ditches, creeks, small forest pools.

Family MOMOTIDAE   MOTMOTS

Motmots are confined to the American tropics. They have rather long, curved bills, and except for the Tody Motmot, long, graduated tails often ending in rackets. They are sluggish and solitary in habits, and frequent the forest substage. They excavate holes in the ground for nesting, feed on fruit, insects and sometimes small mammals. They often flick their tails from side to side like pendulums. Their notes consist of low, carrying, hooting sounds.

1. TODY MOTMOT

Hylomanes momotula *

7". Top of head dull chestnut; eyebrow blue; ear coverts black, bordered below by white. Back, wings and tail dull green. Throat and center of abdomen dull white, rest of underparts pale olive brown. Bill heavy, 1". Tail short.

Tropical zone. COLOMBIA west of W Andes s to Baudó Mts. [S Mexico to nw Costa Rica. E Panama.] Light undergrowth in humid forest.

2. BROAD-BILLED MOTMOT

Electron platyrhynchum *

14". Bill flat, broad, 1.7" long. Head, throat and breast cinnamon rufous, mask and spot on breast black. Back green; belly blue green; remiges and rectrices blue. Tail long with (or without, 1) spatulate tip.

Tropical zone. W COLOMBIA s to lower Cauca Valley and down Pacific coast to w ECUADOR. E of Andes in Amazonia from Caquetá, COLOMBIA, s in BOLIVIA to Cochabamba and Santa Cruz and BRAZIL locally in w and middle Amazonia; in e Pará, Goiás and n Mato Grosso, 1. [Honduras through Panama.] Forest edge.

3. RUFOUS MOTMOT

Baryphthengus ruficapillus *

18". Bill serrated, not flat, 1.5". Mask and small spot on breast black, head and underparts rufous (or underparts olive with broad cinnamon rufous band across belly, 1). Back green. Tail long, green to bluish green, with or without spatulate tip.

Tropical zone. COLOMBIA w of Andes, and e of Andes from se COLOMBIA s to BOLIVIA and w BRAZIL, n of the Amazon to rio Negro and s of it to e bank of rio Tapajós. From Bahía to Rio Grande do Sul, PARAGUAY, and ARGENTINA in Misiones, 1. [Nicaragua through Panama.] Forest.

4. BLUE-CROWNED MOTMOT

Momotus momota *

15" (19", 1). Bill serrated, 1.6". Crown and sides of head black, crown surrounded by broad blue to purplish blue band. Upperparts green to olive brown; below olive green to dull cinnamon. Tail green or blue, with blue spatula.

Tropical zone. Virtually throughout to s BOLIVIA, PARAGUAY, nw ARGENTINA and BRAZIL to w São Paulo and Mato Grosso. Subtropical zone of COLOMBIA and parts of ECUADOR and PERU, 1. Trinidad, Tobago. [Mid. Amer.] Forest, thickets, cerradão.

Plate 34

Order PICIFORMES

Family GALBULIDAE JACAMARS

Jacamars are exclusively tropical American. There are two types, the better known varieties with shining, metallic green upperparts and mostly rufous underparts; the other, smaller, with short tails, dull brown or blackish with white throat and belly. All (except 15) have long, very straight, sharply pointed bills. The sexes are much alike.

Jacamars inhabit forest and savanna country. They perch fairly low on exposed branches from which they dart out after insects, returning to their starting point. They excavate holes in banks in which they nest.

In the following descriptions two measurements are given, the first that of the bird, the second that of the bill.

AID TO IDENTIFICATION

Above not brilliant metallic green 1, 2, 3a, 4a, 5, 6c, 14

Above brilliant metallic green 7, 8, 9, 10, 11, 12, 13, 15

1. CHESTNUT JACAMAR

Galbalcyrhynchus leucotis *

8" (2"). Bill kingfisher-like, pink with dark tip. Plumage mostly dark chestnut. Ear coverts white (or chestnut, 1); wings and tail black, glossed green.

From se COLOMBIA south, e of Andes, to e ECUADOR and e PERU. N BOLIVIA and w Amazonian BRAZIL, between rios Juruá and Purus, 1. Forest clearings. All species of this family belong to the tropical zone unless otherwise stated.

Plate 9

2. BROWN JACAMAR

Brachygalba lugubris *

6.7" (1.5"). Above dull brown; rump glossed greenish black; chest brown, reddish brown or blackish; throat whitish, belly white or buff. Wings and tail black, glossed green. Bill black.

GUIANAS; VENEZUELA s of the Orinoco; COLOMBIA e of E Andes south to n BOLIVIA and BRAZIL to Amazonas, Mato

Grosso and w São Paulo. Open, bushy country; forest.

3. PALE-HEADED JACAMAR

Brachygalba goeringi

6.5" (1.5"). Crown, nape and chest ashy brown; throat and center of belly white, band across belly pale rufous. Back, wings and tail blackish glossed with blue. Bill black.

Nw VENEZUELA from Lara to Guárico; ne COLOMBIA in Boyacá and Arauca. Open woods, thickets.

Plate 45

4. DUSKY-BACKED JACAMAR

Brachygalba salmoni *

6.7" (.7"). Upperparts, wings and tail blackish brown glossed with green. Throat white, breast black glossed with green, belly rusty rufous. Bill black.

Nw COLOMBIA in Bolívar, Córdoba and Antioquia. [E Panama.] Forest, forest edge often near streams.

169

5. WHITE-THROATED JACAMAR

Brachygalba albogularis

6.2" (2"). Mainly blackish glossed with greenish blue. Top of head brownish, sides of head and throat white, center of abdomen ferruginous. Bill pale.

Borders of PERU and BRAZIL along río Javarí, and on upper rio Purús, BRAZIL. Forest.

6. THREE-TOED JACAMAR

Jacamaralcyon tridactyla

6.2" (1.5"). Whole head chestnut brown streaked with buffy. Upperparts blackish glossed with green, sides of body dusky grayish, center of breast and abdomen white. Bill black.

Se BRAZIL from Minas Gerais to Paraná.

7. YELLOW-BILLED JACAMAR

Galbula albirostris *

7.5" (1.5"). Crown metallic blue to purplish blue, back metallic golden green. Underparts chestnut (throat white ♂). Central rectrices like back, outer ones rufous. Bill mostly yellow.

GUIANAS; VENEZUELA s of the Orinoco; COLOMBIA east of E Andes; e ECUADOR; e PERU; Amazonian BRAZIL and in Maranhão and Goías. Forest edge, open woodland.

8. GREEN-TAILED JACAMAR

Galbula galbula

7.7" (1.7"). Upperparts and breast metallic golden green, throat white (or buffy, ♀), rest of underparts rufous chestnut. Tail metallic bluish green. Bill black.

GUIANAS; VENEZUELA s of the Orinoco; extreme e COLOMBIA; n BRAZIL south to s bank of the Amazon between rios Tapajós and Madeira. Forest, near streams.

9. WHITE-CHINNED JACAMAR

Galbula tombacea *

8.7" (2"). Top of head dusky brownish, glossed with blue posteriorly. Upperparts, throat and chest metallic golden green, chin white; underparts ferruginous chestnut (or cinnamon, ♀). Central tail feathers golden green, outer ones chestnut, tipped bronzy green. Bill black.

COLOMBIA e of Andes from Meta south to

e PERU and w Amazonian BRAZIL. Forest near streams and ponds.

10. BLUISH-FRONTED JACAMAR

Galbula cyanescens

Like preceding but slightly larger, crown metallic blue.

E PERU s of the Amazon; w BRAZIL e to rio Purús (east bank). Forest and forest borders.

11. COPPERY-CHESTED JACAMAR

Galbula pastazae

Like the preceding but larger, tail more coppery and bill heavier.

Upper tropical and subtropical zones in e ECUADOR s of equator. Recorded from BRAZIL in s Amazonas (rio Purús).

12. RUFOUS-TAILED JACAMAR

Galbula ruficauda *

9" (2"). Upperparts and chest metallic golden green, throat white to buff (or with upper throat black, 1), rest of underparts rufous chestnut to buff. Two (or four, 1) central tail feathers metallic green, outer ones cinnamon. Bill black.

GUIANAS; VENEZUELA n of the Orinoco and in nw Bolívar and Apure; n COLOMBIA from Norte de Santander and Arauca westward. West of the W Andes s to nw ECUADOR, 1. BRAZIL s to Mato Grosso and Paraná; n BOLIVIA. PARAGUAY Ne ARGENTINA. Trinidad and Tobago. [Mid. Amer.] Forest clearings, second growth, scrubby woodland.

Plate 34

13. BRONZY JACAMAR

Galbula leucogastra *

8.5" (1.5"). Top and sides of head metallic bluish bronze, back and chest metallic purplish shot with green. Throat and belly white (or buff, ♀). Tail bronze green, outermost feathers edged and tipped with white. Bill black.

GUIANAS; VENEZUELA in Delta Amacuro and central Amazonas. Se COLOMBIA. E PERU; w Amazonia e to ne Mato Grosso (Serra Roncador), BRAZIL. Forest.

14. PARADISE JACAMAR

Galbula dea *

12.2" (2"). Crown ashy brown, throat and upper breast white, rest of plumage metallic bronzy black. Tail metallic bronzy black, central feathers narrowed, much lengthened, up to 7" long. Bill black.

GUIANAS; s VENEZUELA; se COLOMBIA; e ECUADOR; e PERU; Amazonian BRAZIL; nw BOLIVIA. Forest edge, savanna.

15. GREAT JACAMAR

Jacamerops aurea *

12" (1.7"). Upperparts metallic golden green to fiery purple, upper throat like back (bordered below by white ♂), rest of underparts tawny rufous. Central tail feathers shining coppery green, rest bluer. Bill heavy, curved, black.

GUIANAS, VENEZUELA s of the Orinoco and COLOMBIA south to ne BOLIVIA and BRAZIL in Amazonia, s in east to Goiás. West of the Andes to w ECUADOR. [Costa Rica, Panama.] Forest.

Plate 34

Family BUCCONIDAE   PUFFBIRDS

Puffbirds are confined to the neotropics. They form a characteristic family of stocky birds with large heads, thick necks and either thick, hooked, black bills or slender curved bills which can be orange or yellow. They are silent and sluggish inhabitants of the substage of thick forest or clearings, often sitting quietly on exposed branches from which they fly out after insects, or pounce upon them on the ground. They nest in holes in banks or in the ground. They are most abundant in Amazonia. As most species inhabit the tropical zone, the habitat of only those which range to higher elevations will be mentioned here.

AID TO IDENTIFICATION

Black and white 1, 2b, 3, 4

With brown, buff or rufous in plumage (bill thick, hooked) 1, 3, 5, 6, 7b, 8, 9b, 10, 11, 12, 27b; (bill more slender, curved) 14c, 15, 16, 17, 18, 19b, 20a; (size very small) 21, 22, 23, 24b, 25, 26

Body plumage all or mostly gray or black, bill yellow or red 28, 29, 30, 31

1. WHITE-NECKED PUFFBIRD

Notharchus macrorhynchus *

10". Crown, back and broad band across lower breast black. Forehead, cheeks, throat, collar on hindneck, throat and belly white, (or similar but belly buff, 1). Bill thick, hooked.

GUIANAS; VENEZUELA; n COLOMBIA and in upper Cauca Valley; ECUADOR; e PERU; BRAZIL in Amazonia. BRAZIL from Espírito Santo to Santa Catarina, PARAGUAY, n BOLIVIA and ne ARGENTINA, 1. [Mid. Amer.] Treetops in open forest, savanna, cerradão.

Plate 45

2. BLACK-BREASTED PUFFBIRD

Notharchus pectoralis

8". Upperparts, sides of neck, wings and tail glossy blue black; white ear coverts joined to white collar across hindneck. Throat and belly white, broad blue black band across breast. Bill thick, hooked.

COLOMBIA from middle Magdalena Valley w across Antioquia to Atrato Valley and down Pacific coast to nw ECUADOR. [E Panama.] Forest treetops.

3. BROWN-BANDED PUFFBIRD

Notharchus ordii

8". Rather like 1 but much smaller. Narrow

frontal band white, black breast band narrow, lower breast ochre brown, belly white; all but central rectrices with white spot on inner web.

VENEZUELA in Amazonas; adjacent BRAZIL and s of the Amazon between rios Xingú and Tapajós. Forest.

4. PIED PUFFBIRD

Notharchus tectus *

6". Almost a miniature of 1 differing by white-speckled crown and eyebrow, white scapulars, and outer tail feathers tipped and marked on inner web with white.

GUIANAS; s VENEZUELA; COLOMBIA west of E Andes; ECUADOR; e PERU. N and ne BRAZIL from rios Negro and Tapajós to Maranhão. [Costa Rica, Panama.] Forest, mangroves, savanna.

5. CHESTNUT-CAPPED PUFFBIRD

Bucco macrodactylus *

5.5". Crown chestnut, sides of head black, stripe below ear coverts white; nuchal collar orange rufous; back brown, speckled with white and fulvous. Throat and upper breast white with broad black band across lower throat; rest of underparts buffy, lightly barred with dusky. Tail brown. Bill thick, hooked.

S VENEZUELA w to base of COLOMBIAN Andes and south to e PERU, w Amazonian BRAZIL and n BOLIVIA. Forest.

6. SPOTTED PUFFBIRD

Bucco tamatia *

7". Back and head markings rather like 5 but without black collar across throat. Throat orange buff, rest of lower parts white heavily spotted with black.

GUIANAS; VENEZUELA s of the Orinoco; e COLOMBIA to e PERU and Amazonian BRAZIL. Forest edge, shrubbery, savanna.

7. SOOTY-CAPPED PUFFBIRD

Bucco noanamae

7.5". Above dark brown, feathers conspicuously fringed buff. Forehead and sides of head grayish; throat white, broad brownish black band across breast, rest of lower parts buffy white spotted with blackish.

COLOMBIA from w shore of Gulf of Urabá to río San Juan on Pacific slope. Forest, scrub.

8. COLLARED PUFFBIRD

Bucco capensis *

7.5". Bill mostly orange. Upperparts rufous brown banded with narrow black bars. Broad buff band across upper back bordered by black band. Throat white, breast band black, rest of underparts buff.

GUIANAS, s VENEZUELA and e COLOMBIA to ne PERU and Amazonian BRAZIL. Forest.

9. BARRED PUFFBIRD

Nystalus radiatus

8.5". Bill greenish gray. Above rather like 8 but much more coarsely banded. Lower parts cinnamon buff narrowly barred on breast and sides with black.

COLOMBIA from middle and lower Magdalena w to Pacific and s to Gulf of Guayaquil, ECUADOR. [Panama.] Open forest bordering streams.

Plate 34

10. WHITE-EARED PUFFBIRD

Nystalus chacuru *

8.5". Bill salmon red. Upperparts brown indistinctly spotted and barred with blackish, nuchal collar white. Ear coverts white surrounded by black. Underparts white.

E PERU from Amazonas south to n BOLIVIA. Campo region of BRAZIL in Mato Grosso, s Amazonas (rio Madeira), Maranhão and Piauí, s to Rio Grande do Sul; PARAGUAY; ARGENTINA in Misiones. Open woodland, campos, cerrado.

11. STRIOLATED PUFFBIRD

Nystalus striolatus *

8.5". Upperparts dark brown, feathers edged with cinnamon; collar on hindneck buff. Throat and center of belly white, rest of underparts buff streaked with black. Tail black, barred cinnamon.

E ECUADOR south to n BOLIVIA. BRAZIL in sw Amazonia and n Mato Grosso, and in e Pará. Forest.

12. SPOT-BACKED PUFFBIRD

Nystalus maculatus *

8″. Above rather like 11 but much more conspicuously spotted with buff. Upper throat white, lower throat buffy orange; rest of underparts white, streaked or spotted with black.

BRAZIL s of the Amazon from rio Tapajós east to e Pará, Maranhão and Ceará, thence s to Minas Gerais, and Mato Grosso. E BOLIVIA; PARAGUAY; ARGENTINA from Jujuy to La Rioja and Córdoba. Forest, shrubbery, campos.

13. RUSSET-THROATED PUFFBIRD

Hypnelus ruficollis *

9″. Bill black. Above earthy brown somewhat spotted with whitish. Below buff, darker on throat; breast crossed by single bar (or by two bars and traces of a third, 1).

Nw VENEZUELA w through COLOMBIA to Guajira Peninsula, Catatumbo lowlands and middle Magdalena Valley. VENEZUELA, except the nw, south to n Bolívar and Amazonas and w to Boyacá and Meta, COLOMBIA, 1. Margarita I. Open dry scrub, arid coastal regions, open woodland.

14. CRESCENT-CHESTED PUFFBIRD

Malacoptila striata *

8.5″. Back rufous brown streaked with buff. Lores and eyebrow buff, crown black, moustachial streak whitish. Broad crescent-shaped white band across breast, bordered below by narrow black band, rest of underparts pale, dull brown inconspicuously barred and streaked. Bill black.

E BRAZIL in Maranhão, and from s Bahía south to Santa Catarina. Forest.

15. WHITE-CHESTED PUFFBIRD

Malacoptila fusca *

7.5″. Bill orange, ridge black. Differs mainly from 14 by no black band below white crescent on chest.

GUIANAS; VENEZUELA in sw Amazonas; COLOMBIA e of Andes south to e PERU; w Amazonian BRAZIL n of the Amazon e to Óbidos. Forest.

16. SEMICOLLARED PUFFBIRD

Malacoptila semicincta

Differs mainly from 15 by darker brown coloration and whiter shaft stripes, and by rusty collar on hindneck.

Se PERU in Puno; sw BRAZIL on upper rio Purús; n BOLIVIA on lower río Beni.

17. BLACK-STREAKED PUFFBIRD

Malacoptila fulvogularis *

9″. Bill black. Differs from 16 mainly by throat and chest buff with no white crescent.

COLOMBIA in subtropical zone at head of Magdalena Valley and in tropical zone e of E Andes in Meta. E ECUADOR to n BOLIVIA in La Paz. Savanna, open woodland.

Plate 9

18. RUFOUS-NECKED PUFFBIRD

Malacoptila rufa *

8″. Crown gray streaked with white, rufous cheeks joined to narrow rufous collar on hindneck. Underparts fulvous brown with narrow white crescent across lower throat, crescent bordered narrowly below with black.

Ne PERU from mouth of río Curaray s to the Ucayali; Amazonian BRAZIL s of the Amazon.

19. WHITE-WHISKERED PUFFBIRD

Malacoptila panamensis *

8″. Upperparts earthy brown to reddish brown spotted with buffy white or cinnamon rufous. Throat and upper breast buff to cinnamon; rest of underparts whitish, streaked with dusky on lower breast. Mandible greenish yellow.

N COLOMBIA e to middle Magdalena Valley and s along Pacific coast to w ECUADOR. [Mid. Amer.] Forest undergrowth, shrubbery.

20. MOUSTACHED PUFFBIRD

Malacoptila mystacalis *

9″. Much like 19 but considerably larger and streaks on underparts obsolete.

Upper tropical and subtropical zones. N VENEZUELA; COLOMBIA in Santa Marta Mts., e slope of E Andes s to Macarena Mts., and generally w of E Andes. Forest.

21. LANCEOLATED MONKLET

Micromonacha lanceolata

5.5". Forehead and lores white. Above rufous brown, mantle feathers somewhat fringed with buff. Below white boldly streaked black. Tail short, with subterminal black bar. Bill short, rather thick.

Tropical, subtropical zones. Pacific COLOMBIA from headwaters of río San Juan to Nariño and e of Andes from Meta south to e PERU and w Amazonian BRAZIL. [Costa Rica, Panama.] Forest.

Plate 9

22. RUSTY-BREASTED NUNLET

Nonnula rubecula*

6.5". Above dull brown, forehead and spot below eye whitish. Throat and breast cinnamon, belly white. Bill, as in all nunlets, is rather long, slender and curved, mostly leaden blue; orbital skin pink.

Sw SURINAM. Sw VENEZUELA. Ne PERU; BRAZIL in w Amazonia e at least to rios Jamundá and Tapajós, in e from Bahía s to Paraná; PARAGUAY; ne ARGENTINA. Forest.

23. FULVOUS-CHINNED NUNLET

Nonnula sclateri

6". Differs from 22 by no white spot below eye, by frontal band, lores and chin tinged ochraceous buff.

Sw BRAZIL at headwaters of rio Juruá, rio Purús and upper rio Madeira (w bank). Se PERU in se Loreto.

24. BROWN NUNLET

Nonnula brunnea

6". Above dull brown, forehead and underparts dull cinnamon.

East base of E Andes of COLOMBIA from Meta south to e PERU.

25. GRAY-CHEEKED NUNLET

Nonnula ruficapilla*

6". Crown rufous chestnut or reddish brown. Cheeks and sides of neck and breast gray. Back brown, underparts cinnamon rufous to cinnamon buff, whitish on belly.

N COLOMBIA e to Santa Marta region and middle Magdalena Valley. E PERU; w BRAZIL in Amazonas and w Mato Grosso. [E

Panama.] Open forest, second growth, thickets.

Plate 34

26. CHESTNUT-HEADED NUNLET

Nonnula amaurocephala

Differs from 25 mainly by sides of head and neck as well as the crown deep rufous chestnut.

W Amazonian BRAZIL along n bank of lower rio Solimões.

27. WHITE-FACED NUNBIRD

Hapaloptila castanea

10". Above olive grayish, below chestnut, upper throat white. Forehead and lores white outlined in black. Bill black.

Subtropical zone. COLOMBIA on w slope of W Andes south to nw ECUADOR. Ne PERU in Huallaga drainage. Forest.

Plate 9

28. BLACK NUNBIRD

Monasa atra

10.5". Blackish gray above, grayer below. Inner wing coverts white, outer gray, edged white. Bill red, slender, curved.

GUIANAS; VENEZUELA generally s of the Orinoco; n BRAZIL to n bank of the Amazon e of rio Negro. Forest.

29. BLACK-FRONTED NUNBIRD

Monasa nigrifrons*

11.5". Blackish gray, forehead black. Bill red, slender, curved.

COLOMBIA e of E Andes to n BOLIVIA; BRAZIL n of the Amazon from rio Negro region e to Óbidos and s of the Amazon generally to e Piauí and w São Paulo. Forest.

30. WHITE-FRONTED NUNBIRD

Monasa morphoeus*

11.5". Bill red, slender, curved. Forehead and chin white (or only forehead white, 1). General plumage dark gray, somewhat paler below. Wings and tail black (or head and breast black, belly and wing coverts pale gray, 1). Tail black.

VENEZUELA in extreme w Amazonas; e COLOMBIA; e ECUADOR; e PERU; BRAZIL in Amazonia, in the e from Piauí s to

Rio de Janeiro; n BOLIVIA. Northern and western COLOMBIA, 1. [Panama, 1.] Forest.

Plate 45

31. YELLOW-BILLED NUNBIRD

Monasa flavirostris

10.5". Black; upper and under wing coverts largely white. Bill yellowish white, slender, curved.

COLOMBIA along e base of E Andes south to e PERU; w Amazonian BRAZIL. Forest.

32. SWALLOW-WING

Chelidoptera tenebrosa*

6.5". Blackish; rump and upper tail coverts white; belly cinnamon, separated from surrounding black by indefinite pale gray area; under tail coverts grayish. Wings long, swallow-like, under wing coverts white. Bill black, slender, curved.

Generally distributed e of Andes to n BOLIVIA and BRAZIL, but in se not south of São Paulo. Forest edge, savanna; dead trees, clearings.

Family CAPITONIDAE   BARBETS

Barbets are usually guadily colored inhabitants of tropical forests and woodlands. They are rather thick set, heavy-billed birds, solitary and sedentary. They feed on fruit and insects, and nest in holes in trees. They are found abundantly in Africa and Asia, less so in American tropics. In South America most species inhabit the tropical zone in the northwestern part of the continent.

AID TO IDENTIFICATION

Back green or olive 1, 8, 9b, 10b, 11b, 12b

Back black or partly black 2b, 3b, 4b, 5b, 6, 7

1. SCARLET-CROWNED BARBET

Capito aurovirens

7.2". Crown scarlet (or hoary white, ♀): upper surface olive. Throat and breast orange, abdomen olive.

COLOMBIA from Caquetá south to e PERU and w Amazonian BRAZIL. Forest.

2. SPOT-CROWNED BARBET

Capito maculicoronatus*

7.2". Crown brown with whitish spots; forehead and uppersurface black. Underparts mostly white with yellow breast band (or with black throat and breast, ♀), flanks spotted with black, feathers tipped scarlet.

N COLOMBIA south to Buenaventura and e to middle Magdalena Valley. [Central and e Panama.] Forest treetops, vine-covered trees.

3. ORANGE-FRONTED BARBET

Capito squamatus

7.2". Forecrown orange to scarlet, hindcrown and nape white. Back blue black (feathers fringed white, ♀), inner remiges partly white. Underparts mostly white (or throat and breast black, ♀).

Sw COLOMBIA in sw Nariño and w ECUADOR. Second growth.

Plate 45

4. WHITE-MANTLED BARBET

Capito hypoleucus

7.2". Forecrown crimson, hindcrown to center of mantle white, rest of upperparts blue black. Throat and breast white, pale dull violet suffusion across breast; belly yellowish white, flanks pale yellow.

Central COLOMBIA in lower Cauca and middle Magdalena Valleys. Forest.

5. FIVE-COLORED BARBET

Capito quinticolor

7.2". Crown and nape blood red (or black finely streaked yellow, ♀). Upperparts black, back feathers tipped greenish yellow. Throat white, tinged yellow; breast and abdomen orange; flanks olive, mottled black.

Pacific COLOMBIA from upper río San Juan south to w Nariño. Forest.

6. BLACK-GIRDLED BARBET

Capito dayi

7.2". Top of head scarlet (or black, ♀). Back black, white patch on mantle, upper tail coverts olive. Throat and cheeks tawny olive, finely barred black; underparts buffy white shading to yellowish green on belly, flanks black, under tail coverts mostly scarlet.

BRAZIL s of the Amazon in Rondonia and from upper rio Madeira to n Mato Grosso and Pará. Forest.

7. BLACK-SPOTTED BARBET

Capito niger *

7.5". Forecrown scarlet, or crown old gold or old gold streaked red. Upperparts black spotted and streaked greenish yellow. Throat orange to scarlet (spotted with black, ♀), rest of underparts creamy yellow to yellow lightly (or heavily, ♀) spotted with black.

GUIANAS; VENEZUELA s of the Orinoco; COLOMBIA east of E Andes s to PERU and BOLIVIA in Beni; w Amazonian BRAZIL e to Roraima, Óbidos and rio Tapajós. Forest, swampy woods, second growth.

Fig. 2, p. xiv

Eubucco

The species of *Eubucco* differ from each other in pattern of head, throat and breast. All have bright grass green back, wings and tail; belly greenish yellow streaked with green. Only the pattern of head, throat and breast is described here.

8. LEMON-THROATED BARBET

Eubucco richardsoni *

6". Top and sides of head, chin spot crimson (or black, 1), nape blue (or yellowish green, 2). Throat yellow, breast orange. ♀: Sides of head black, throat gray, upper breast orange yellow.

E base of COLOMBIAN Andes from Meta s to PERU n of the Marañón; near Pebas, 1; e PERU s of the Marañón and w Amazonian BRAZIL to rio Madeira, 2. Forest and scrub.

9. RED-HEADED BARBET

Eubucco bourcierii *

6.5". Whole head scarlet, narrow collar on hindneck blue. Throat scarlet shading to orange on breast. ♀: Much like 8 but sides of head blue.

Upper tropical and subtropical zones of Andes. COLOMBIA; ECUADOR; ne PERU in n Cajamarca. [Costa Rica, Panama.] Forest undergrowth, clearings.

Plate 34

10. SCARLET-HOODED BARBET

Eubucco tucinkae

6.5". Like 8 but back golden olive and nuchal collar yellow. ♀: Much like ♂, differs from other *Eubucco* females by having red on head.

Se PERU in Puno and se Loreto. Second growth.

11. VERSICOLORED BARBET

Eubucco versicolor *

6.5". Head scarlet; broad moustachial streak and band surrounding red of head and throat blue (or similar but with yellow moustachial streak, 1; or similar to latter, but blue band confined to nape, 2). ♀: Sides of head and the throat blue, throat bordered below by red crescent.

Tropical, subtropical zones. Northern 2, central 1, and se PERU and n BOLIVIA. Forest.

12. TOUCAN BARBET

Semnornis ramphastinus *

8". Back olive brown, rump yellow. Top of head shining enamel-like black, eyebrow white; throat, wings, tail and sides of head blue gray; breast scarlet shading to yellow, crissum olive.

Upper tropical and subtropical zones. COLOMBIA on w slope of W Andes in Valle and s Cauca, south to w ECUADOR. Forest.

Plate 34

Family RAMPHASTIDAE   TOUCANS, ARAÇARIS

Toucans are one of the most characteristic avian families of the American tropics. They are at once distinguishable from other neotropical birds by immense, often brightly colored, bills.

The sexes are usually similar, but bills in males are generally about a third longer than in females. In the following descriptions, the length of the bill (♂) is given separately in parentheses, the two given measurements showing total length.

Toucans are noisy and gregarious, active and inquisitive. They feed on fruits swallowed whole, and nest and roost in holes in trees. Inhabitants of forests, they are found from southern Mexico to northern Argentina and Bolivia.

AID TO IDENTIFICATION

Mostly bright green above and below
   chestnut) 3, 4b, 5b, 6b, 7b

Back all or mostly dark slaty green, belly yellow (one or more narrow black or red bands across lower breast or belly) 8a, 9b, 10b, 11, 12, 13; (with breast and belly plain yellow) 14, 15; (with breast all or mostly red) 16, 17, 18

Back mostly crimson, crest of curled and scale-like feathers 19

Back olive to olive brown

   With yellow ear tufts (throat and breast black) 20b, 21a, 22, 23a, 24; (throat and breast chestnut) 22, 23, 24; (throat and breast gray) 21a

   Without ear tufts (underparts saffron yellow) 25c; (underparts blue) 26b, 28b, 29b; (with gray nuchal collar) 27b, 28b

Chiefly black with white or yellow throat and breast

   Throat and breast yellow or orange 30, 33c, 34a, 35b, 36b, 37b

   Throat and breast white or pale sulphur 31a, 32, 38, 39a, 40, 41

1. GROOVE-BILLED TOUCANET

Aulacorhynchus sulcatus*

11″ (3″). Mainly grass green; ocular region blue, throat gray. Bill mainly dark red with white patch at base of lower mandible (or with base of bill bright red, 1).

Subtropical zone. Coastal mountains of VENEZUELA in Sucre and Monagas, 1; from Miranda to Falcón. Forest.

2. YELLOW-BILLED TOUCANET

Aulacorhynchus calorhynchus

11″ (3.7″). Much like 1 in color. Upper mandible mostly olive yellow, lower mandible mostly black with olive yellow tip and base.

Upper tropical, subtropical zones of nw VENEZUELA, w to Santa Marta Mts., COLOMBIA. Forest.

3. CHESTNUT-TIPPED TOUCANET

Aulacorhynchus derbianus*

13″ (3.5″). Green; nuchal spot and eye region blue, throat bluish white. Tips of central tail feathers chestnut. Bill black, basal portion and tip dark crimson.

Upper tropical and subtropical zones. Mts. of GUYANA; mts. of s VENEZUELA and adjacent n BRAZIL; COLOMBIA probably in se Nariño; e ECUADOR to nw BOLIVIA. Forest.

4. EMERALD TOUCANET

Aulacorhynchus prasinus *

12" (3"). Green; throat white, gray, blue or black. Under tail coverts and tips of all tail feathers chestnut. Bill black, ridge of culmen olive yellow, base of lower mandible red (or black, 1) sharply outlined in white.

Subtropical, lower temperate zones of the Andes. N VENEZUELA; COLOMBIA (in Santa Marta Mts., 1); e ECUADOR; e PERU s to Puno. [Mid. Amer.] Forest.

Plate 31

5. CRIMSON-RUMPED TOUCANET

Aulacorhynchus haematopygus *

15" (4"). Green; diffused blue band across breast; crimson rump. Tips of four central tail feathers chestnut. Bill dark red with some black on ridge, culmen and lower mandible; base sharply outlined in white.

Tropical, subtropical zones. Perijá Mts. in VENEZUELA; Andes of COLOMBIA south to w ECUADOR. Forest.

6. BLUE-BANDED TOUCANET

Aulacorhynchus coeruleicinctis

14" (3.2"). Green; rump dark crimson. Short line behind eye bluish white. Throat white; band across lower breast blue, brightest at sides. Two central tail feathers tipped with chestnut. Bill leaden blue with pale tip.

Subtropical zone. Andes of e PERU from Junín to n BOLIVIA. Forest.

7. YELLOW-BROWED TOUCANET

Aulacorhynchus huallagae

14" (4"). Green; blue band across belly. Throat greenish white; short line behind eye and under tail coverts bright yellow. Four central tail feathers with chestnut tips. Bill leaden blue, paler toward tip, base sharply outlined in white.

Subtropical zone. Ne PERU in Libertad. Forest.

8. COLLARED ARAÇARI

Pteroglossus torquatus *

12.5" (4.5"). Head black. Nuchal collar and flanks chestnut. Mantle dark slaty, rest of back crimson. Breast and belly yellow stained with red, small black patch on center of breast; band across belly red at sides, black in middle. Tail dark slaty. Upper mandible ivory white, ridge and tip black; lower mandible black, bill outlined with white at base.

Tropical zone. VENEZUELA from Aragua w in COLOMBIA to Norte de Santander, Santa Marta and Gulf of Urabá. [Mid. Amer.] Forest.

9. STRIPE-BILLED ARAÇARI

Pteroglossus sanguineus

16" (4.5"). Differs from 8 in no chestnut nuchal collar, and in longitudinal black stripe on upper mandible. Hybridizes with 8 in nw Colombia.

Tropical zone. COLOMBIA on the Gulf of Urabá south to nw ECUADOR. Forest.

10. PALE-MANDIBLED ARAÇARI

Pteroglossus erythropygius

Differs from 9 in ivory white lower mandible blackish only toward tip, instead of all black.

Tropical zone. W ECUADOR from Esmeraldas to Chanchan Valley. Forest.

11. CHESTNUT-EARED ARAÇARI

Pteroglossus castanotis *

14" (5.5"). Crown, nape and upper breast black. Throat, cheeks and nuchal collar dark chestnut. Mantle, wings and tail slaty green, rump crimson. Lower breast and belly yellow, band across belly crimson. Bill black, tawny brown stripe on upper mandible, basal band and "teeth" ochraceous yellow.

Tropical zone. E slope of COLOMBIAN Andes s to BOLIVIA, PARAGUAY and ne ARGENTINA. W and s BRAZIL n of the Amazon e to rio Negro, and s of it to Goiás, Minas Gerais and Paraná. Forest.

12. BLACK-NECKED ARAÇARI

Pteroglossus aracari *

13.5" (4.7"). Head, nape and upper breast black; ear patch deep chestnut. Back, wings and tail slaty green; rump crimson. Lower breast and belly light yellow crossed by broad crimson band. Upper mandible white, culmen and lower mandible black, base of bill outlined in white.

Tropical zone. E VENEZUELA from Sucre south to e Bolívar; GUIANAS; e BRAZIL w to Óbidos and rio Madeira, and from Maranhão, Piauí and Bahía to Santa Catarina. Forest, savanna, plantations.

13. MANY-BANDED ARAÇARI

Pteroglossus pluricinctus

Differs mainly from 12 by black band across breast and another across belly which is crimson mixed with black.

Tropical zone. VENEZUELA n of the Orinoco in Barinas and Táchira, s of it in Amazonas and s Bolívar; adjacent BRAZIL; COLOMBIA e of Andes south to ne PERU. Forest.

14. GREEN ARAÇARI

Pteroglossus viridis

11″ (3.2″). Head and throat black (or chestnut, ♀). Back, wings and tail slaty green; rump crimson. Underparts yellow. Ridge of bill yellow, red, wedge-shaped stripe at side of upper mandible, lower mandible black with red base.

Tropical zone, GUIANAS; VENEZUELA in n and e Bolívar; ne BRAZIL n of the Amazon from e bank of lower rio Negro e to Amapá. Forest, savanna.

15. LETTERED ARAÇARI

Pteroglossus inscriptus *

11″ (3.2″). Color much like 14. Bill dirty yellow; black ridge, tip and small, vertical, wavy lines along cutting edge of upper mandible (with lower mandible all black, 1). ♀: Differs from 14 by black crown.

Tropical zone. Se COLOMBIA, e ECUADOR, ne PERU, nw BRAZIL e to lower rio Solimões and rio Madeira and n BOLIVIA, 1. BRAZIL in n Mato Grosso, e Pará and Pernambuco. Forest, palm groves.

16. RED-NECKED ARAÇARI

Pteroglossus bitorquatus *

11″ (3.2″). Top of head black, throat and sides of head dark chestnut; chestnut of throat edged with black below, and bor-dered by narrow yellow pectoral band. Breast, nape, upper mantle, and rump crimson. Lower back, wings and tail slaty green (or similar with whole head and throat blackish maroon and no yellow pectoral band, 2). Upper mandible green, basal portion of lower mandible white, distal portion black (or lower mandible all black, 1).

Tropical zone. BRAZIL s of the Amazon from e bank of rio Madeira to nw Mato Grosso, 1; between rios Tapajós and Tocantins, 2; east to e Pará and n Maranhão.

17. IVORY-BILLED ARAÇARI

Pteroglossus flavirostris *

12″ (3.5″). Top of head black (or dark chestnut, ♀). Throat and sides of head dark chestnut, rest of underparts yellow; band on upper breast scarlet; broader band on lower breast black, bordered with scarlet. Back dull green, mantle spotted with maroon red, rump scarlet. Wings, tail and thighs dull green. Bill ivory white, bright yellow at nostril; upper mandible with row of black spots on cutting edge and brownish longitudinal mark along upper edge of lower mandible.

Tropical zone. VENEZUELA s of the Orinoco; Amazonian COLOMBIA; e ECUADOR; nw Amazonian BRAZIL n of the Amazon to rio Negro, s of it on upper rio Solimões. Forest.

Plate 31

18. BROWN-MANDIBLED ARAÇARI

Pteroglossus mariae

Differs from 17 only in color of lower mandible, pale brown to chocolate brown, with yellowish olive tip and base.

E PERU; n BOLIVIA in Beni; w Amazonian BRAZIL s of the Amazon e to rio Purús. Forest.

19. CURL-CRESTED ARAÇARI

Pteroglossus beauharnaesii

15″ (4″). Crown black, feathers shiny, curled, broad and enamel-like. Cheeks and throat yellowish white; feathers stiff, shiny and black-tipped. Mantle and rump crimson; wings, tail, and center of back dull green. Breast yellow, stained scarlet; belly yellow crossed by crimson band. Upper mandible black, ridge and tip brownish orange; lower mandible white.

E PERU; w Amazonian BRAZIL s of the Amazon e to rio Madeira and n Mato Grosso; n BOLIVIA in Beni. Forest.

20. YELLOW-EARED TOUCANET
Selenidera spectabilis

12" (3.7"). Crown, nape, throat, breast and center of belly glossy black. Plume-like ear coverts golden yellow. Back and wings olive green, patch on sides of body orange yellow, flanks chestnut, under tail coverts crimson. Tail blue gray. Upper part of bill greenish gray, rest black. ♀: Similar but crown and nape dark chestnut, ear coverts black.

Tropical zone. COLOMBIA along w coast s to the Baudó Mts. and e to lower Cauca. Esmeraldas, nw ECUADOR. [Honduras southward.] Forest.

21. GUIANAN TOUCANET
Selenidera culik

10.5" (3"). Crown, nape and most of underparts glossy black. Ear coverts and band across upper mantle yellow. Back olive green, wings and tail blue gray, flanks greenish gray with chestnut patch, under tail coverts crimson. Tip of tail chestnut. Bill mostly black with red at base. ♀: Differs from ♂ by chestnut nuchal collar and mostly gray underparts.

Tropical zone. GUIANAS; VENEZUELA in extreme se Bolívar; adjoining n BRAZIL. Forest, savanna.

22. GOLDEN-COLLARED TOUCANET
Selenidera reinwardtii *

Differs from 21 by shorter bill, brighter green back, green instead of gray wings and tail, orange flanks and chestnut thighs. Basal two-thirds of bill reddish brown, distal third and ridge black. ♀: Like ♂ but crown chestnut, nape and underparts mainly light chestnut.

Tropical zone. E base of COLOMBIAN Andes from Caquetá s to PERU and w BRAZIL, e to middle Purús. Forest.

Plate 9

23. TAWNY-TUFTED TOUCANET
Selenidera nattereri

Very similar to 22, differing mainly in reddish brown bill with black base and many transverse black stripes.

Tropical zone. GUYANA and FRENCH GUIANA; VENEZUELA in s Bolívar and sw Amazonas; se COLOMBIA east in n BRAZIL to rio Negro. Forest.

24. SPOT-BILLED TOUCANET
Selenidera maculirostris *

Both sexes similar to 22 but bill different color: Upper mandible has black basal two-thirds, olive distal third; lower mandible is olive with black patch in center (or bill milky white with ridge and three transverse black blotches on upper mandible, 1).

Tropical zone. BRAZIL s of the Amazon from lower rio Madeira east to e Pará and n Ceará, 1; from Bahía s to Rio Grande do Sul and ne ARGENTINA.

25. SAFFRON TOUCANET
Baillonius bailloni

13.7" (2"). Above dark olive green, brighter and strongly yellowish on forecrown; rump crimson. Underparts saffron yellow. Wings and tail dark olive green. Bill olive with red near base.

Se BRAZIL from Espírito Santo to Santa Catarina. Forest.

26. PLATE-BILLED MOUNTAIN-TOUCAN
Andigena laminirostris

16" (3.5"). Crown and nape black, back and wings olive brown, rump pale yellow. Underparts light blue, patch on sides of breast yellow, thighs chestnut maroon, under tail coverts crimson. Tail slaty gray, central feathers tipped chestnut. Bill black, reddish at base; raised ivory white plate near base of upper mandible.

Upper tropical to lower temperate zone. COLOMBIA in w Nariño and w ECUADOR south to 2° 30' s. Forest.

27. GRAY-BREASTED MOUNTAIN-TOUCAN
Andigena hypoglauca *

16" (4"). Crown, nape and sides of head black. Broad band across upper mantle and the underparts blue gray, back reddish olive, rump yellow, flanks chestnut, under tail coverts crimson. Tail black, central feathers chestnut. Ridge and distal part of upper mandible red bordered below with black, basal half of bill yellow, distal portion of lower mandible and band at base of both mandibles black.

Temperate zone. W slope of Central CO-LOMBIAN Andes in Caldas and Cauca. E ECUADOR s to Junín, PERU.

Plate 31

28. HOODED MOUNTAIN-TOUCAN

Andigena cucullata

17" (3.7"). Upperparts much as in 27 but rump yellowish green. Throat and upper breast blackish, belly blue gray. Thighs and under tail coverts as in 27. Tail slaty gray. Bill olive green with tip and spot at base of lower mandible black.

Subtropical, temperate zones. E PERU from Amazonas south to n BOLIVIA.

29. BLACK-BILLED MOUNTAIN-TOUCAN

Andigena nigrirostris*

18" (4.5"). Crown to upper mantle glossy black, back olive brown, rump pale yellow. Throat and upper breast white, rest of underparts light blue, thighs chestnut, under tail coverts crimson. Inner remiges and tail slaty gray, central tail feathers tipped chestnut. Bill black, base and basal portion of ridge dark red.

Subtropical, temperate zones. Nw VENE-ZUELA in Trujillo and Táchira; COLOM-BIA in Andes to ne ECUADOR. Forest.

30. CHANNEL-BILLED TOUCAN

Ramphastos vitellinus*

14" (5.5"). Mainly black; chin and sides of neck white, center of throat pale yellow deepening to orange on upper breast; pectoral band, upper and under tail coverts crimson (or with throat and upper breast orange, margined below by pale yellow; lower breast, upper belly crimson, 1). Bill black, base of culmen greenish yellow, of mandible slaty blue. Bare ocular region sealing wax red.

Tropical zone. GUIANAS, e VENEZUELA and n BRAZIL from rio Negro e to Amapá. BRAZIL s of the Amazon from Pará to Pernambuco and s to Santa Catarina, 1. Forest.

31. CITRON-THROATED TOUCAN

Ramphastos citreolaemus

18" (5.5"). Mainly black; chin and cheeks white, throat and upper breast sulphur yellow, pectoral band crimson. Upper tail coverts sulphur yellow, under tail coverts crimson. Bill black, base light blue with yellow patch on each mandible at junction with head; ridge pale yellow, greenish in center.

Tropical, occasionally subtropical zone. Nw VENEZUELA from n slopes of Andes in Táchira and Mérida w across n COLOMBIA to Gulf of Urabá. Forest.

32. YELLOW-RIDGED TOUCAN

Ramphastos culminatus

14" (5.5"). Differs from 31 in white throat and upper breast instead of yellow, and upper tail coverts cadmium yellow. Bill black, ridge and base of upper mandible greenish yellow, base of lower mandible blue.

Tropical, occasionally subtropical zone. W VENEZUELA; e COLOMBIA east of Andes from Arauca south to n BOLIVIA. W Amazonian BRAZIL e to rios Negro and Madeira and s to Mato Grosso. Forest.

33. RED-BREASTED TOUCAN

Ramphastos dicolorus

14" (4"). Mainly black; throat and sides of head pale yellow, lower throat orange; belly and lower breast crimson, separated from orange of throat by pale yellow band. Upper and under tail coverts crimson. Bill pea green narrowly bordered black at base.

Se BRAZIL from Goiás to Rio Grande do Sul; PARAGUAY; n ARGENTINA in Misiones, Corrientes, e Santa Fe and Chaco. Forest.

34. KEEL-BILLED TOUCAN

Ramphastos sulfuratus*

15" (5.5"). Mainly black; crown and mantle dark maroon, throat and upper breast deep yellow, pectoral band crimson. Upper tail coverts white, under tail coverts crimson. Upper mandible pea green with a longitudinal, wedge-shaped orange mark at cutting edge; tip crimson; lower mandible mostly light blue with crimson tip and pea green patch near base.

Tropical, lower subtropical zones. Zulia,

VENEZUELA, west across n COLOMBIA to Panama border. [Mid. Amer.] Forest.

35. CHOCO TOUCAN

Ramphastos brevis

(Considered a race of 37 in *Sp. Bds. S. Amer. cf.* Haffer).

14" (5"). Like 34 in color but smaller. Bill color quite different: culmen yellow with a green patch on center of ridge, black longitudinal patch at base of cutting edge, bordered above by green; lower mandible black.

Tropical zone. Pacific slope of COLOMBIA and nw ECUADOR. [E Panama.] Humid forest.

36. CHESTNUT-MANDIBLED TOUCAN

Ramphastos swainsonii

16" (7.7"). Like 34 in plumage color. Upper mandible mainly yellow, tinged green on ridge; dark red at base; tip of lower mandible blackish blending into dark reddish of basal portion.

Tropical, occasionally subtropical zone. COLOMBIA from middle Magdalena Valley w to Pacific coast, thence south to w ECUADOR. [Honduras southward.] Forest.

37. BLACK-MANDIBLED TOUCAN

Ramphastos ambiguus *

18" (7"). Like 34 in plumage color. Bill color differs from that of 36 by reddish chestnut replaced by black, or black slightly tinged reddish. The dark part of the upper mandible is carried forward further towards the tip of bill than in 35 or 36.

Tropical, subtropical zones. N VENEZUELA from Miranda w to COLOMBIA thence south to n Huánuco, PERU. Forest.

38. RED-BILLED TOUCAN

Ramphastos tucanus *

17" (6.5"). Like 32 in color. Bill dark red,

ridge and base of upper mandible light yellow, base of lower mandible blue gray.

Tropical zone. GUIANAS; VENEZUELA, e slope of E Andes of COLOMBIA in Arauca and Boyacá. BRAZIL n of the Amazon from Manaus eastward, and s of the Amazon east to e Pará and Maranhão. Forest, savanna, palm groves.

Fig., Title Page

39. ORANGE-BILLED TOUCAN

Ramphastos aurantiirostris

Like 37 except that dark red of bill is replaced by light orange red.

Tropical zone. GUIANAS; e VENEZUELA. Forest.

40. CUVIER'S TOUCAN

Ramphastos cuvieri *

17" (6.7"). Like 32 in color. Bill black, ridge and base of upper mandible lemon yellow, base of lower mandible blue (or similar but ridge pea green and reddish blotch near base of upper mandible, 1).

VENEZUELA in s Amazonas. E COLOMBIA from Meta s to lower río Beni, n BOLIVIA and Amazonian BRAZIL e to rios Negro and Tocantins. Upper río Beni to Santa Cruz, BOLIVIA, 1.

41. TOCO TOUCAN

Ramphastos toco *

18" (8"). Mainly black; crown dusky brown, throat and upper breast white, no red pectoral band. Upper tail coverts white, under tail coverts crimson. Bill orange crimson, fading to greenish yellow in sides of maxilla; large black oval blotch near tip of maxilla, narrow line at base of bill black.

GUIANAS; BRAZIL; PARAGUAY; n ARGENTINA from Misiones to Jujuy and Salta; n BOLIVIA from Beni to Santa Cruz. Woodland, second growth, coconut plantations, palm groves.

Family PICIDAE   WOODPECKERS, PICULETS

In habits and general appearance there is little to distinguish South American woodpeckers from those elsewhere. Their undulating flight helps distinguish them from most other birds; they are unlike tree-climbing woodcreepers because of rather raucous voices, their hammering on trees, and, in some, bright plumage and often crested heads.

Tiny piculets, about 3.5" long, are the most distinctive. Like nuthatches they often climb head downward, and like them have unstiffened tails. They usually clamber about on small. twigs at the ends of branches. They live in wooded pasturelands, dense scrub and open forests, usually in the tropical zone. They are not found in Chile. They have the same undulating flight of the larger woodpeckers and their tapping sounds seem very loud for their small size.

AID TO IDENTIFICATION

Under 5"

Underparts plain (chestnut or brown) 1a, 2b, 3b; (buffy, yellow or white) 4, 8b,

Underparts with blackish or white spots 5, 11a, 12, 20b, 21c, 22a

Underparts barred and/or streaked 9a, 10c, 13, 14, 15c, 16, 17, 19b, 20b

Underparts scaled or scalloped 6a, 7c, 18b

Over 5"

Back crimson, yellow, chestnut or cream color 31b, 39, 43, 67b, 68a

Back olive, underparts barred or spotted (inner webs of primaries plain) 32, 33, 34, 36; (inner webs of primaries barred) 35c, 59b, 61, 64, 65, 66a, 69b, 70b

Back black or black with white, (below uniform) white or pale smoky 56, 58, chestnut 76, 79b, black 47, 75c, 80b; (below barred) rump black or cream color 46, 73, 74b, 77c, rump white 48c, 49b, 50, 51, 76, 78b; (rump red) 79b

Back barred, streaked or spotted, but not black and white (uniformly dark below) 37, 38, 45; (below spotted or streaked) 23b, 27, 28, 29, 60c; (below barred or scalloped) 23b, 24b, 25, 26, 30b, 40, 41b, 42, 44b, 62b, 63c

Back barred or streaked black and white 52c, 53b, 54b, 55a, 57a, 71, 72b

Piculets

In all piculets the tail is black, the inner web of central feathers white or buff, with a diagonal band of the same across outer feathers. The crown in males is usually black; feathers of the forecrown tipped scarlet to orange scarlet, of the hindcrown dotted white. In females the crown is usually black, dotted white, otherwise the sexes are similar. These parts will not be described unless they differ from above.

1. CHESTNUT PICULET

Picumnus cinnamomeus*

3.5". Mainly chestnut. Forehead broadly white, crown black spotted with yellow (or white, ♀).

Tropical zone. Nw VENEZUELA w through Guajira Peninsula to Caribbean lowlands of COLOMBIA. Arid scrub, thickets, forest.

2. RUFOUS-BREASTED PICULET

Picumnus rufiventris*

4" (4.5", 1). Underparts and nuchal collar rufous chestnut, back and wings olive. Crown black spotted in front with red, dotted white behind (or reverse, 1).

Tropical zone. COLOMBIA south to e ECUADOR. PERU to n BOLIVIA and sw BRAZIL, 1. Forest edge.

Plate 34

3. PLAIN-BREASTED PICULET

Picumnus castelnau

3.5". Above dusky olive inconspicuously barred dusky and yellowish olive. Underparts pale yellow. ♀: Black crown.

Tropical zone. E ECUADOR and e PERU.

4. WHITE-BELLIED PICULET

Picumnus spilogaster *

3.5″. Above pale brown, barred dusky brown and whitish. Below white with a few brown spots or streaks on sides.

Tropical zone. SURINAM and FRENCH GUIANA; n VENEZUELA w to mouth of the Meta; ne BRAZIL in Roraima. Open woodland, thickets.

5. ARROWHEAD PICULET

Picumnus minutissimus

3.5″. Above grayish brown, mantle with a few white spots. Underparts whitish, feathers margined all around with black, giving scaled appearance.

Tropical zone. GUIANAS. E BRAZIL south of the Amazon, s to São Paulo, Mato Grosso and n BOLIVIA. Plantations, savanna, mangroves.

6. SCALED PICULET

Picumnus squamulatus *

3.5″. Differs from 5 mainly by olive brown back, feathers edged blackish; margins of inner remiges yellowish instead of whitish.

Tropical, lower subtropical zones. N VENEZUELA and COLOMBIA from Santa Marta s to Meta. Forest.

7. OCHRACEOUS PICULET

Picumnus limae *

(Includes *P. fulvescens* of *Sp. Bds. S. Amer.*)

3.5″. Upperparts sandy brown. Sides of head and chin yellowish white with dark flecks; throat dirty white becoming more yellowish on breast (or general plumage somewhat darker, 1).

Tropical zone. Ne BRAZIL in Ceará; in w Paraiba, se Pernambuco and n Alagoas, 1 (1 = *P. fulvescens* in *Sp. Bds. of S. Amer.*, now considered a race of *limae*).

8. OLIVACEOUS PICULET

Picumnus olivaceus *

3.5″. Upperparts olivaceous, crown brownish black spotted in front with orange, behind with white. Throat whitish, breast light olive brown, rest of underparts dull yellowish olive obscurely streaked dusky.

Tropical, subtropical zones. Nw VENE-ZUELA west through n COLOMBIA to Pacific, and s, west of W Andes to w ECUADOR. [Honduras southward.] Forest edge, cultivated lands, thickets.

9. GRAYISH PICULET

Picumnus granadensis

3.5″. Upperparts grayish brown; crown black, dotted in front with lemon yellow, behind with white. Underparts dirty white.

Upper tropical and subtropical zones. COLOMBIA in valleys of Cauca, Dagua and Patía rivers. Forest, scrub.

10. MOTTLED PICULET

Picumnus nebulosus

4.2″. Forecrown crimson; hindcrown black, feathers elongated, tipped white. Back buffy brown. Chin and throat whitish, breast sandy brown; rest of underparts buff, streaked black. ♀: Crown and nape dusky brown with white dots.

Se BRAZIL from Paraná s to URUGUAY; ne ARGENTINA in Corrientes and Misiones.

11. BLACK-DOTTED PICULET

Picumnus nigropunctatus

3.5″. Back greenish yellow, feathers with dusky subterminal bar giving scaled appearance. Below pale yellow, barred on throat and spotted on breast and belly with black.

Orinoco delta, VENEZUELA. Forest.

12. GOLDEN-SPANGLED PICULET

Picumnus exilis *

3.5″. Above olive, feathers with black subterminal spot and pale yellowish tip giving spotted appearance. Wing coverts with white terminal spots. Underparts yellowish barred with black.

Tropical zone. GUIANAS; VENEZUELA s of the Orinoco; BRAZIL in Roraima and from Maranhão and Pernambuco to Espírito Santo. Forest edge, savanna.

13. BAR-BREASTED PICULET

Picumnus borbae *

3.5″. Back and wings olive. Throat whitish; breast and belly yellowish, barred on breast and streaked on flanks and belly with black.

Tropical zone. E PERU; BRAZIL s of the

Amazon e to rio Tocantins and w Mato Grosso.

14. GOLD-FRONTED PICULET

Picumnus aurifrons *

3". Above olive, barred yellowish; below yellowish white, barred black (or barred on breast, streaked on sides and belly, 1; or above plain olive, below yellowish white, barred on breast, streaked black on sides and belly, 2). Crown dark brown finely dotted yellow or orange red in front, white behind.

Se COLOMBIA, e ECUADOR, ne PERU, n BRAZIL to rio Negro. Central and e PERU east, s of the Amazon, to Mato Grosso, BRAZIL, and rio Tapajós, 2; between the Tapajós and the Tocantins, 1. Forest and scrub.

Plate 45

15. OCHRE-COLLARED PICULET

Picumnus temminckii

3.5". Above ochre brown obscurely barred; ear coverts, sides of neck and nuchal collar bright ochraceous. Below white with broad black bars.

Se BRAZIL from São Paulo southward; PARAGUAY; ne ARGENTINA in Misiones. Forest.

16. WHITE-BARRED PICULET

Picumnus cirratus *

3.5". Above brown (or grayish brown, 1), below white barred with black (or black barred with white, 2).

Tropical, subtropical zones. GUIANAS. Ne BRAZIL from rio Tapajós eastward, 2; from Bahía to Paraná, 1. Nw Mato Grosso; PARAGUAY; n ARGENTINA; BOLIVIA. Forest, patches of woods, parks.

17. OCELLATED PICULET

Picumnus dorbygnianus *

3.5". Above grayish brown obscurely spotted with white (or dorsal feathers edged pale gray, 1); below white, feathers centered with black giving scaled appearance.

PERU in Junín and Cuzco, 1. N and e BOLIVIA; nw ARGENTINA. Forest.

18. ECUADOREAN PICULET

Picumnus sclateri *

3.5". Above brownish, obscurely barred paler. Below white, heavily barred black. Crown black dotted yellow in front, spotted white behind.

Tropical zone. W ECUADOR, nw PERU. Arid scrub.

19. SPECKLE-CHESTED PICULET

Picumnus steindachneri

3.5". Above brownish gray, feathers pale-edged. Throat whitish, breast black spotted with white, belly banded black and white.

Upper tropical and subtropical zones. Amazonas and San Martín, PERU, in drainage of río Huallaga.

20. VARZEA PICULET

Picumnus varzeae

4.5". Earthy brown, underparts sparsely dotted with white.

Ne BRAZIL on islands in the Amazon near Óbidos and on lower rio Jamundá. Swampy forest.

21. SPOTTED PICULET

Picumnus pygmaeus *

4". Differs from 20 by white spotting on upperparts and much more heavily spotted underparts, particularly on belly.

E BRAZIL in Maranhão, Piauí and Bahía. Caatinga.

22. ORINOCO PICULET

Picumnus pumilus

4". Back olive, forecrown black dotted with yellow, hindcrown pale brown dotted white. Below yellowish white barred black.

COLOMBIA on w bank of the Orinoco in Vichada. Savanna.

23. ANDEAN FLICKER

Colaptes rupicola *

14". Crown and moustachial streak gray (latter tipped red in ♂), back regularly barred black and buff; rump and underparts buff to cinnamon, lightly barred or heavily spotted with black. Tail black, outer feather lightly barred.

Subtropical to temperate zone. PERU from Amazonas s through Andes of BOLIVIA to n CHILE and w ARGENTINA to Tucumán and Catamarca. Open country, terrestrial.

24. CHILEAN FLICKER

Colaptes pitius *

13". Crown gray, cheeks and throat buffy white. Back brownish black, barred buffy white; rump white. Underparts coarsely barred black and white. Tail as in 23.

CHILE from Coquimbo to Magallanes. W ARGENTINA from Neuquén to s Santa Cruz. Open woodland, arboreal.

25. CAMPO FLICKER

Colaptes campestris *

12". Crown and throat black, sides of throat mixed red (spotted with white, ♀). Lores, area around eye white; cheeks, sides of neck and upper breast bright yellow. Back blackish barred white, underparts white, barred black. Tail as in 23.

Savanna region of s SURINAM, BRAZIL from Pará (n of the Amazon only near Monte Alegre) and Maranhão s to Paraná and Mato Grosso, PARAGUAY and n BOLIVIA. Campos, palm groves, terrestrial.

Plate 9

26. FIELD FLICKER

Colaptes campestroides

Like 25 but larger and throat white instead of black.

Se BRAZIL in Rio Grande do Sul and s Paraná (?); ARGENTINA s to Mendoza and Río Negro; URUGUAY; PARAGUAY. BOLIVIA (?). Savanna, woodland, terrestrial.

27. GREEN-BARRED WOODPECKER

Chrysoptilus melanochloros *

11". Forecrown black, hindcrown, nape and moustachial streak red (or black, dotted white, ♀), sides of head white. Back regularly barred yellowish green and black, rump brighter and yellower. Throat yellowish white finely streaked, underparts yellowish green spotted with black. Tail black, barred yellowish.

BRAZIL on Marajó I. and on Mangunça I. off coast of n Maranhão, thence south through e and central regions to Rio Grande do Sul and Mato Grosso; e PARAGUAY; URUGUAY; ne and north-central ARGENTINA in Misiones, Corrientes, Chaco and e Formosa. Palm groves, swampy woods.

Plate 9

28. GOLDEN-BREASTED WOODPECKER

Chrysoptilus melanolaimus *

Differs from 27 by black sides of neck; blacker back, barred yellowish white; breast strongly shaded orange and belly whitish.

BOLIVIA from Cochabamba and Santa Cruz e in ARGENTINA from Jujuy to Corrientes and s to Río Negro. Woodland, savanna, orchards, grassland; partly terrestrial.

29. SPOT-BREASTED WOODPECKER

Chrysoptilus punctigula *

8". Forecrown black; hindcrown, nape and moustachial streak crimson (only nape crimson, ♀). Sides of head white, throat checkered black and white. Back olive yellow, barred or spotted with black. Upper breast reddish olive to olive; rest of underparts dull yellow, spotted or dotted with black. Outer tail feathers brownish yellow, barred black.

Tropical zone. GUIANAS; n VENEZUELA; COLOMBIA west of Andes to 4°n, e of the Andes south to e PERU and n BOLIVIA; w BRAZIL east to ne Mato Grosso and n Pará. [Panama.] Open woodland, mangroves, cerrado.

30. BLACK-NECKED WOODPECKER

Chrysoptilus atricollis *

11". Forecrown gray, sides of crown, nape and moustachial streak crimson (or only nape crimson, ♀), sides of head white. Back olive, barred black. Throat and upper breast black; rest of underparts yellowish white, barred black. Outer tail feathers blackish, barred dull white.

Tropical, subtropical zones of PERU w of Andes from nw Libertad to Arequipa; subtropical to temperate zone above Marañón Valley in Piura, Libertad, Cajamarca and Ancash. Columnar cacti, open woods.

31. CRIMSON-MANTLED WOODPECKER

Piculus rivolii *

11". Uppersurface mostly crimson (crown black, ♀, or ♂ of subspecies 1), inner remiges darker, primaries margined olive. Sides of head yellowish white, moustachial streak crimson (or no moustachial streak, ♀), throat black (sometimes speckled with white). Upper breast feathers basally white with subterminal black bar and red fringe;

rest of underparts mustard yellow. Rump mustard yellow, barred black. Tail black.

Subtropical, temperate zones. Andes of w VENEZUELA and COLOMBIA to central PERU; from se PERU to n BOLIVIA, 1. Forest.

Plate 34

32. GOLDEN-OLIVE WOODPECKER

Piculus rubiginosus*

9". Crown gray; sides of crown, nape and moustachial stripe (or only nape, ♀) crimson; sides of head white, throat checkered black and white (or black, 1). Back olive, upper tail coverts barred yellowish and olive. Undersurface barred yellowish and blackish olive. Tail black, outer feathers brownish, pale-barred.

Tropical, subtropical zones. S GUYANA, VENEZUELA and COLOMBIA s (in west to nw PERU) through BOLIVIA to nw ARGENTINA. Central Andes of COLOMBIA, 1. Trinidad, Tobago. Forest, second growth, arid scrub.

33. YELLOW-THROATED WOODPECKER

Piculus flavigula*

8". Crown and moustachial streak crimson (or without moustachial streak, 1); sides of head, the throat and neck golden yellow (or with whole throat crimson, 2). Back olive; chest olive, spotted white; belly barred olive and white. Basal inner webs of remiges chestnut. Tail olive. ♀: Like male but forecrown old gold, only nape scarlet.

Tropical zone. GUIANAS; VENEZUELA s of the Orinoco; BRAZIL n of the Amazon from rio Negro eastward. COLOMBIA e of Andes, e ECUADOR, e PERU, and BRAZIL, s of the Amazon from rio Juruá and Mato Grosso e to Maranhão, 1. From Pernambuco s to Rio de Janeiro and São Paulo, 2. Forest, savanna.

34. WHITE-THROATED WOODPECKER

Piculus leucolaemus*

Like 33 except for white instead of yellow throat. ♀: Differs by white throat and yellow moustachial streak.

Tropical zone. COLOMBIA in nw Cundinamarca, and Chocó from Baudó Mts. southward; e and w ECUADOR south to n

BOLIVIA and w Amazonian BRAZIL e to rios Negro and Guaporé. Forest.

35. WHITE-BROWED WOODPECKER

Piculus aurulentus

8.5". Crown (nape only, ♀) and moustachial streak crimson; sides of head dark gray, bordered above and below by white line; throat yellow. Back olive; lowerparts evenly banded gray and white. Primaries barred chestnut and black; tail black.

Se BRAZIL from Minas Gerais and Rio de Janeiro s to Rio Grande do Sul; PARAGUAY; ne ARGENTINA. Forest.

36. GOLDEN-GREEN WOODPECKER

Piculus chrysochloros*

9". Crown and moustachial streak crimson, throat and broad line above moustachial streak yellow (or throat barred like rest of underparts, 1), sides of head dark gray. Back olive. Underparts barred dull yellow (or greenish white, 1) and olive. Inner webs of remiges cinnamon; tail blackish. ♀: Head without crimson, crown old gold (or like back, 1); otherwise like ♂.

Tropical zone. N COLOMBIA from s Córdoba to middle Magdalena Valley and e through Santa Marta to Falcón and Trujillo, VENEZUELA. BRAZIL s of the Amazon from rio Purús to n Maranhão and from Piauí and Ceará s to Rio de Janeiro and Mato Grosso; PARAGUAY; n ARGENTINA; BOLIVIA. GUIANAS, n and w BRAZIL, e PERU, e ECUADOR, se COLOMBIA and VENEZUELA in Amazonas, 1. [E Panama.] Forest savanna.

37. BLOND-CRESTED WOODPECKER

Celeus flavescens*

9". Crown and long crest buffy white; moustachial streak crimson (absent, ♀), throat buffy to yellowish. Back black, barred yellowish white (or buff with heart-shaped black spots, 1) rump yellow to buff. Underparts black (or dark brownish, 1).

BRAZIL n of lower Amazon from Óbidos to Marajó I. e to Ceará, Pernambuco and nw Bahía, 1; from Goiás to Rio Grande do Sul and Mato Grosso, PARAGUAY, e BOLIVIA in Santa Cruz and ne ARGENTINA in Misiones. Forest, groves of trees.

38. PALE-CRESTED WOODPECKER

Celeus lugubris *

9". Much like 37 but upper tail coverts chestnut, back browner and more narrowly barred, inner remiges barred with chestnut, and area around eye dusky; underparts dusky brown, feathers edged dull chestnut (or with underparts chocolate brown, 1).

BOLIVIA in Beni and Santa Cruz. W Mato Grosso, BRAZIL, PARAGUAY and nw AR-GENTINA in Formosa and Chaco, 1. Swampy forest, scrub.

39. CHESTNUT WOODPECKER

Celeus elegans *

11". Mainly chestnut. Crown and crest buffy white to buff (or chestnut like back, 1), moustachial streak crimson (absent, ♀). Rump light buffy yellowish (or dark buff, 1). Sides of body buffy white. Remiges uniform (all inner webs of remiges barred black and buff, 1). Tail black.

Tropical zone. E VENEZUELA (n of the Orinoco only in Monagas); e BRAZIL n of the Amazon w to Óbidos and the rio Branco. S VENEZUELA; COLOMBIA e of Andes south to n BOLIVIA, and Amazonian BRAZIL (except ne) south to s Amazonas, Mato Grosso and in e to Maranhão, 1. Trinidad. Forest, mangroves, savanna.

40. SCALE-BREASTED WOODPECKER

Celeus grammicus *

9". Mainly chestnut, back heavily barred black, underparts scalloped black (or lightly to virtually unbarred, 1). Moustachial streak crimson (absent, ♀). Sides of body and under wing coverts pale yellow. Primaries blackish, unbarred. Tail black.

Tropical zone. GUIANAS; VENEZUELA s of the Orinoco; e PERU; BOLIVIA in Beni. Amazonian BRAZIL in nw to rio Negro, s of the Amazon to e side of the Tapajós at Cussarí. Se COLOMBIA and e ECUADOR, 1. Forest.

41. CINNAMON WOODPECKER

Celeus loricatus *

Much like 40 (1), but much paler below and easily distinguishable by wings and tail barred chestnut and black instead of uniform. Whole throat crimson (or without crimson, ♀).

Tropical zone. Across n COLOMBIA from lower and middle Magdalena Valley to Pacific coast, thence south to nw ECUADOR. [Nicaragua through Panama.] Forest, clearings.

42. WAVED WOODPECKER

Celeus undatus *

Much like 40, but crown and crest lighter than back, tail barred black and chestnut, and rump tinged yellowish green.

Tropical zone. GUIANAS; e VENEZUELA; ne BRAZIL from rios Negro and Tocantins eastward. Forest, savanna.

43. CREAM-COLORED WOODPECKER

Celeus flavus *

10.5". Entirely canary yellow to creamy buff, except for brown to chestnut wings and dusky tail. Moustachial streak crimson, (absent, ♀).

Tropical zone. GUIANAS; VENEZUELA; e COLOMBIA; e ECUADOR; e PERU; BRA-ZIL except extreme se; n BOLIVIA in Beni. Forest, mangroves, savanna, plantations.

Plate 9

44. RUFOUS-HEADED WOODPECKER

Celeus spectabilis *

11". Head light chestnut, line from behind eye to end of crest, and moustachial streak crimson (no crimson, ♀). Back light buff, profusely marked with black heart-shaped spots; rump buff. Lower neck and upper breast brownish black, rest of underparts cinnamon buff with heart-shaped black spots. Wings mainly chestnut; tail black.

Tropical zone. E ECUADOR. PERU in Loreto and Huánuco. N BOLIVIA in Beni and Cochabamba.

45. RINGED WOODPECKER

Celeus torquatus *

9.5" (or 11.5", 1). Head cinnamon, moustachial streak crimson (no crimson, ♀). Neck, upper mantle and breast black. Back chestnut, remiges and tail lightly barred black, tail tipped black; underparts plain cinnamon buff (or back, lower breast, belly and wings barred black, 1).

Tropical zone. GUIANAS; e VENEZUELA w to río Caura, 1. E COLOMBIA (foot of Macarena Mts.); e ECUADOR; n BRAZIL in rio Negro-rio Branco region s to lower rio Tapajós, w Amazonas and Mato Grosso, and isolated population in Bahía. E PERU; n BOLIVIA in Santa Cruz.

46. LINEATED WOODPECKER

Dryocopus lineatus *

14″. Mainly black (or brownish black, 1). Crown, crest and moustachial streak crimson (or only nape crimson, ♀); sides of head gray, white line from nostril to below eye and down sides of neck; throat streaked. Scapulars white (occasionally black). Lower breast and belly barred (or spotted, 1) buff and black.

Tropical zone. GUIANAS, VENEZUELA, COLOMBIA, ECUADOR and e and nw PERU, south to s BRAZIL, n BOLIVIA, PARAGUAY and n ARGENTINA from Salta to Misiones. W ECUADOR, nw PERU, 1. Trinidad. Forest, mangroves, savanna, campos, orchards, cerradão.

Plate 9

47. BLACK-BODIED WOODPECKER

Dryocopus schulzi *

13″. Differs from 46 by being mainly black below with a few dull white bars at sides. Scapulars white or black.

PARAGUAY w of río Paraguay; ARGENTINA in Tucumán, Santiago del Estero, Chaco and Córdoba. Woodland, scrub. It has been suggested that *Dryocopus major* (Dabbene) from the Argentine chaco is a valid species.

48. HELMETED WOODPECKER

Dryocopus galeatus

12″. Forehead, sides of head and throat rufous buff, sides of head finely lined black. Ample crest, nape and malar streak crimson (no malar streak, ♀). Upper back, wings and tail black; lower back and upper tail coverts buffy white. Lower parts regularly barred black and buff.

Se BRAZIL in São Paulo, Paraná and Rio Grande do Sul; PARAGUAY; ARGENTINA in Misiones. Forest.

49. ACORN WOODPECKER

Melanerpes formicivorus *

9.5″. Forehead yellowish white, this color extending downward in front of eye, connecting with the broad yellowish white pectoral band (band across nape scarlet, ♂). Chin, throat, back, wings and tail black; rump and wing patch white. Lower breast and sides streaked black and white, abdomen white.

Subtropical, occasionally temperate zone. Andes of COLOMBIA s to head of Cauca and Magdalena Valleys. [Western US south through Mexico to w Panama.] Forest clearings.

50. YELLOW-TUFTED WOODPECKER

Melanerpes cruentatus *

8″. Mainly glossy black. Forecrown crimson (♂), stripe from above eyes white, becoming yellow posteriorly and joining across nape. Lower back white, center of belly crimson, sides barred black and white.

Tropical zone. Generally distributed e of Andes to e PERU, n BOLIVIA and Amazonian BRAZIL. Forest, burned clearings.

51. RED-FRONTED WOODPECKER

Melanerpes rubrifrons

Differs from 50 only in no white and yellow stripes on head. It is probably a color phase of 50.

Tropical zone. GUIANAS; s VENEZUELA; n BRAZIL from rio Negro eastward, s of the Amazon in e Pará. Hab. as above.

52. YELLOW-FRONTED WOODPECKER

Melanerpes flavifrons *

7.5″. Forecrown and throat bright yellow, hindcrown and nape scarlet (no scarlet, ♀). Back, wings and tail glossy black; upper back streaked, inner remiges tipped, white; lower back, rump and upper tail coverts white. Upper breast light olive, lower breast and center of abdomen scarlet, sides evenly barred black and pale yellow.

Central and s BRAZIL from Goiás and Bahía s to Rio Grande do Sul and se Mato Grosso; PARAGUAY; ne ARGENTINA in Misiones. Woodland, palm groves, parks.

53. BLACK-CHEEKED WOODPECKER

Melanerpes pucherani *

7.5″. Forehead yellow, crown and nape crimson (or mid-crown black, ♀). Back and inner remiges black, barred white; cheeks, sides of neck and wing coverts black. Throat dull white, breast smoky olive, rest of underparts barred buffy and black, center of abdomen crimson. Central tail feathers barred white on inner web.

Tropical zone. COLOMBIA in lower Cauca Valley and Pacific coast south to w ECUADOR. [Mid. Amer.] Forest.

Plate 34

54. GOLDEN-NAPED WOODPECKER

Melanerpes chrysauchen *

7.5". Forehead buffy, crown crimson (only hindcrown crimson, ♀), nape golden yellow. Black stripe through eye continued down sides of neck and back; center of back and upper tail coverts white. Throat white, rest of underparts smoky olive, barred black; center of belly scarlet. Wings and tail black, a few white spots on inner remiges and central tail feathers.

Upper tropical zone. N COLOMBIA in middle Magdalena Valley. [Sw Costa Rica and sw Panama.] Forest, coffee plantations, clearings.

55. RED-CROWNED WOODPECKER

Melanerpes rubricapillus *

6.5" (or 7.5", 1). Forehead white, crown and nape crimson (only nape crimson, ♀); back, inner remiges and central tail feathers barred black and white; rump white. Underparts light smoky gray (or generally much darker with underparts much darker and browner, 1), center of abdomen crimson orange.

Tropical, occasionally subtropical zone. GUYANA; SURINAM. VENEZUELA n of the Orinoco and in n Bolívar and n Amazonas; COLOMBIA from Guajira Peninsula to río Sinú, e of Andes in Vichada. Margarita and Patos Is. Tobago. [Bay Is.; sw Costa Rica; Panama including Pearl Is.] Scrub, cactus, palm groves, parks.

56. WHITE WOODPECKER

Leuconerpes candidus

10.5". Head, lower back and underparts white. Line across nape, a spot on breast and center of abdomen lemon yellow, (no yellow, ♀). Mantle, wings, tail and line through eye and down sides of neck all blackish brown; base of tail white.

Campos of s SURINAM and BRAZIL in Pará including Mexiana and Marajó Is. (n of

the Amazon near Óbidos), s to lower rio Madeira, Mato Grosso and São Paulo; URUGUAY; PARAGUAY; BOLIVIA; n ARGENTINA s to La Rioja, Córdoba and Santa Fe and occasionally n Buenos Aires. Cerrado, palm groves, savanna.

57. YELLOW-BELLIED SAPSUCKER

Sphyrapicus varius *

8". Crown, nape and throat crimson (♀ similar but upper throat white). Back and wings black and white, breast black; rest of underparts white, streaked and barred at sides with black; outer webs of primaries notched white.

Winter resident. Aruba, Curaçao, Bonaire. [Breeds in N Amer. In winter to w Panama and Caribbean islands.]

58. WHITE-FRONTED WOODPECKER

Trichopicus cactorum

7". Forecrown and below eye white; hindcrown and nape black with red spot on hindcrown (without red spot, ♀). Ocular region, ear coverts and wing coverts blue black. Back black with central white band, and smoky gray nuchal band. Throat golden yellow, rest of underparts pale smoky brown. Wings, rump and tail black, barred and spotted with white.

Tropical, subtropical zones. S PERU; BOLIVIA; BRAZIL in s Mato Grosso; PARAGUAY; URUGUAY; ARGENTINA s to Córdoba and Entre Ríos. Groves of trees, scrubby woods, cacti.

59. SMOKY-BROWN WOODPECKER

Veniliornis fumigatus *

7". Uniform smoky brown, crown crimson (or dark brown, ♀). Ocular region whitish. Inner webs of primaries barred white. Tail black.

Subtropical to lower temperate zone. VENEZUELA n of the Orinoco; mts. of COLOMBIA south to w and e ECUADOR; w PERU from Cajamarca s to Ancash and in e PERU; BOLIVIA in La Paz, Cochabamba and Santa Cruz. Nw ARGENTINA. [Mid. Amer.] Forest borders, plantations.

60. WHITE-SPOTTED WOODPECKER

Veniliornis spilogaster

7". Crown dark brown with red (or white,

♀) shaft streaks; broad line behind eye, moustachial streak white. Back and remiges barred olive and greenish yellow. Throat white, streaked gray; rest of underparts gray, spotted white. Tail black with broken pale bars.

Se BRAZIL from Minas Gerais s to Rio Grande do Sul; PARAGUAY; URUGUAY; ne ARGENTINA in Misiones and n Corrientes. Dry, open forest.

61. LITTLE WOODPECKER

Veniliornis passerinus *

6″. Forecrown gray, hindcrown and nape crimson (or gray, ♀), moustachial streak white. Back olive yellow, wing coverts spotted dull yellow, inner webs of primaries notched white. Underparts olive gray barred dull white. Tail black, outer feathers sometimes barred dark dull olive.

Tropical zone. GUIANAS; VENEZUELA n of the Orinoco, s of it in extreme n Amazonas and along the ríos Meta and Apure; COLOMBIA e of Andes from Meta south to n BOLIVIA, BRAZIL virtually throughout, PARAGUAY and ne ARGENTINA in Formosa, Chaco, Santa Fe and Corrientes. Forest, cerrado.

62. DOT-FRONTED WOODPECKER

Veniliornis frontalis

7″. Differs from 61 in forehead dotted white (or whole crown dotted white, ♀), back spotted with yellowish and tail dark brown barred buffy brown.

Central and e BOLIVIA; nw ARGENTINA in Jujuy, Salta and Tucumán. Forest.

63. YELLOW-EARED WOODPECKER

Veniliornis maculifrons

6.5″. Forecrown dark brown with pale shaft streaks; hindcrown crimson, bordered posteriorly to behind ear coverts with golden yellow (or crown brown with white shaft streaks, ♀). Back olive obscurely barred yellowish, feathers with pale shaft streaks. Below white, barred dusky. Tail black, barred olive brown.

E BRAZIL in Minas Gerais, Espírito Santo and Rio de Janeiro.

64. GOLDEN-COLLARED WOODPECKER

Veniliornis cassini *

6″. Crown crimson, nuchal band golden yellow (or crown brown, nuchal band golden yellow, ♀). Upperparts golden olive, wing coverts spotted white (or plain, 1), inner webs of primaries notched white. Throat spotted; rest of underparts evenly banded black and white (stained dark red on breast, 1). Tail black, feathers notched dull brown.

Tropical zone. GUIANAS; VENEZUELA in Bolívar and Amazonas; COLOMBIA at e base of E Andes in Caquetá. N BRAZIL n of the Amazon. COLOMBIA w of W Andes in Chocó and Valle and in w ECUADOR, 1. Forest, scrub.

65. RED-STAINED WOODPECKER

Veniliornis affinis *

7″. Differs from 64 by larger size, wing coverts stained dark crimson; and underparts from chin to vent barred dark olive and yellowish white.

Tropical zone. VENEZUELA in Amazonas; e COLOMBIA from Meta south to e ECUADOR, e PERU and n BOLIVIA. Amazonian BRAZIL s to rio Paraguai drainage in Mato Grosso, and in e in Maranhão and Bahía. Forest, scrub.

66. RED-RUMPED WOODPECKER

Veniliornis kirkii *

Differs from 65 by scarlet red rump and upper tail coverts.

Tropical zone. VENEZUELA n of the Orinoco, s of it only in se Bolívar. COLOMBIA on río Zulia and west of E Andes including Santa Marta, south to w ECUADOR. Trinidad and Tobago. [Sw Costa Rica and Panama.] Forest, mangroves, shrubbery.

67. SCARLET-BACKED WOODPECKER

Veniliornis callonotus *

5.5″. Above scarlet red (or crown and nape black surrounded posteriorly by white, ♀). Below dull white, finely barred on breast. Tail black, outer feathers smoky white, barred dusky.

Tropical arid zone. Sw COLOMBIA in Patía Valley. W ECUADOR s in PERU to w Lambayeque (up to 1650 m.) and e into Marañón Valley. Arid scrub, dry forest.

68. BLOOD-COLORED WOODPECKER

Veniliornis sanguineus

5.5". Above crimson (with brown pale-spotted crown, ♀); underparts dark smoky gray, barred white. Tail black.

Tropical zone. GUIANAS. Mangroves, swampy forest, plantations.

69. YELLOW-VENTED WOODPECKER

Veniliornis dignus *

7". Crown and nape crimson (or blackish with crimson nuchal band, ♀), eyebrow and moustachial streak white. Back golden olive, more or less stained crimson; wing coverts spotted yellowish white. Throat and breast barred yellowish white and blackish, belly plain mustard yellow. Central tail feathers black, outer ones barred.

Upper tropical and subtropical zones. VENEZUELA in w Táchira; Andes of COLOMBIA except e slope of E Andes. E slope of Andes of ECUADOR. PERU in e Junín. Forest.

70. BAR-BELLIED WOODPECKER

Veniliornis nigriceps *

8". Crown and nape crimson (or black, ♀). Back olive more or less stained dull crimson. Entire underparts barred dark olive and yellowish white. Tail as in 69.

Upper subtropical and temperate zones. COLOMBIA in Central Andes and in Nariño s through Andes to n BOLIVIA. Forest.

71. CHECKERED WOODPECKER

Dendrocopos mixtus *

6.5". Crown brownish black, streaked white, red spot at sides of nape (or brownish black, bordered below by white line, ♀). Back spotted, tail barred, brownish black and white. Underparts white, streaked black.

Central and s BRAZIL from Goiás, Minas Gerais and w São Paulo to Mato Grosso. URUGUAY along río Uruguay; PARAGUAY; BOLIVIA in Tarija; ARGENTINA s to borders of Chubut. Open forest.

Plate 9

72. STRIPED WOODPECKER

Dendrocopos lignarius

6.5". Crown black, speckled white in front; side of hindcrown scarlet (or no scarlet, ♀); broad line from behind eye and the moustachial streak white. Back and inner remiges barred black and white; underparts white, streaked black. Tail black, barred dark olive brown.

Subtropical to temperate zone. BOLIVIA; w ARGENTINA from Neuquén to s Santa Cruz, in winter n to Córdoba and La Rioja. CHILE from Coquimbo to Aysén, occasionally to Strait of Magellan. Forest edge, dense brush, pastures, orchards.

73. CRIMSON-CRESTED WOODPECKER

Phloeoceastes melanoleucos *

14". Crest, top and sides of head crimson; white patch at base of bill, small black and white one on ear coverts. Throat, neck, breast, back, wings, upper tail coverts and tail black. White line down sides of neck joined to white patch on upper back. Lower breast and belly barred buffy white and black. Under wing coverts and base of remiges white. ♀: Like ♂ but center of crown black, and white stripe at sides of neck begins at base of bill.

Tropical, occasionally to lower temperate zone. Generally distributed e of Andes s to n ARGENTINA. Trinidad. [Central and e Panama.] Forest, campos, swampy woods, plantations.

74. GUAYAQUIL WOODPECKER

Phloeoceastes gayaquilensis

Much like 73 but in ♂ no white at base of bill, barring of lower parts coarser, wings and tail brown, upper tail coverts barred brownish black and buff. ♀: Like 73, but browner.

Tropical zone of sw COLOMBIA (Nariño) south to nw PERU (Taulís).

75. CREAM-BACKED WOODPECKER

Phloeoceastes leucopogon *

12.5". Black, center of upper back creamy buff. Head and neck crimson except for black and white spot on ear coverts. Inner webs of remiges cinnamon. ♀: Like ♂ but crown, center of crest, space in front of and below eye to ear coverts, chin and lower malar region black; broad line from base of bill to lower ear coverts white.

BRAZIL in Rio Grande do Sul; n URU-

GUAY; PARAGUAY; e BOLIVIA; ARGEN-
TINA s to La Rioja, Córdoba, and Entre
Ríos. Forest, woods.

Plate 9

76. RED-NECKED WOODPECKER

Phloeoceastes rubricollis*

13.5". Crest, head, neck and breast crimson.
Back, wings and tail black. Lower breast,
belly, under wing coverts and inner webs of
wing feathers rufous chestnut. ♀: Like ♂ but
front and lower part of face white, outlined
in black.

Tropical zone. GUIANAS; VENEZUELA s
of the Orinoco; COLOMBIA e of Andes
from Boyacá south to e ECUADOR, e
PERU and n BOLIVIA. Forest.

77. ROBUST WOODPECKER

Phloeoceastes robustus*

14". Head and neck crimson (or head as in
76, ♀), back creamy white; underparts
barred black and buffy white. Wings and tail
black, inner remiges cinnamon rufous,
barred black.

E BRAZIL from Goiás and s Bahía s to Rio
Grande do Sul; PARAGUAY; ne ARGEN-
TINA in Misiones. Forest.

78. POWERFUL WOODPECKER

Phloeoceastes pollens*

14". Crown and crest crimson (or black, ♀);
forehead and sides of head black, latter
bordered below by broad white stripe continuing down sides of neck to join white on
back; upper mantle and tail coverts black.

Throat and upper breast black; rest of
underparts cinnamon buff, barred black.
Wings and tail black, remiges tipped white
and barred white on inner web.

Subtropical to temperate zone. VENE-
ZUELA in extreme w Táchira; COLOMBIA;
ECUADOR; e and central PERU. Forest.

79. CRIMSON-BELLIED WOODPECKER

Phloeoceastes haematogaster*

14.5". Crown, crest and hindneck scarlet;
forehead and sides of head black; narrow
line above ear coverts and a broader one
from nostril to below ear coverts buff.
Throat and foreneck black; rest of underparts, lower back and rump crimson; rest of
plumage black. Inner webs of remiges with
large white spots. ♀: Like ♂, but buff line
below eye continued down sides of neck;
breast and belly mixed dull crimson and
black, sometimes obscurely barred with
buffy.

Tropical, subtropical zones. COLOMBIA
west of W Andes s through e and w
ECUADOR and e PERU to Junín. [Pana-
ma.] Forest.

80. MAGELLANIC WOODPECKER

Campephilus magellanicus*

15.5". Head and long, curling crest crimson;
rest of plumage blue black except for
mostly white tertials, under wing coverts
and base of wing feathers. ♀: Like ♂ but area
around base of bill dark red, rest of head
black.

ARGENTINA from Neuquén and w Río
Negro to Tierra del Fuego; CHILE from
Curicó s to Magallanes. Forest.

Fig. 18. SLATE-THROATED REDSTART
Myioborus miniatus ballux
p. 365

Order PASSERIFORMES

Family DENDROCOLAPTIDAE   WOODCREEPERS

Woodcreepers are tree-climbing birds found from southern Mexico to northern Argentina. Brown, often streaked and spotted with buff, they have stiff, spiny tails to support them in climbing. Shape of the bill, not color, is a good key to sorting the genera. It varies from very small with upturned mandible, to stout and straight, or very long, thin and curved. Bills are not used like a woodpecker's, but are used for probing the bark of trees for insects. Woodcreepers start to feed at the base of trees, working upward. Superficially like creepers of northern climes, they are in no way related to them.

Woodcreepers tend to be solitary, but often join mixed bands of forest birds. Their voices are rather musical—consisting of ringing, often repeated, notes and trills.

They nest in natural cavities in trees, or use holes in trees made by other birds. They lay two or three white or greenish white, unspotted eggs.

In the following descriptions the first measurement given is the total length including bill; the second, in parentheses, is length of the bill alone.

AID TO IDENTIFICATION

Crown and back without markings

Underparts also unmarked 1b, 2, 3, 4a, 7, 11, 12, 18, 20, 21, 42b

Underparts streaked or spotted 5, 6, 8, 9, 16c, 34b, 41

Crown streaked or barred

Underparts barred or partially so 13, 14, 15c, 17c, 19, 22, 23c

Underparts streaked or spotted 10, 14, 24, 25, 26, 27, 28, 29, 30, 31, 32, 33b, 35b, 36, 37, 38b, 39c, 40c, 43, 44c, 45a, 46

Underparts plain whitish 37

Bill long 2" or more 9, 10, 14a, 18, much curved 42b, 43, 44c, 45a, 46

Bill very short 1" or less 5a, 6, 7, 8, 36a

1. TYRANNINE WOODCREEPER

Dendrocincla tyrannina*

10" (1.3"). Largest of the unstreaked wood-creepers. Olivaceous brown, duller below with inconspicuous shaft streaks on breast. Wings and tail chestnut.

Upper tropical to temperate zone. Nw VENEZUELA; COLOMBIA except Santa Marta and w Nariño; e ECUADOR; n PERU in Marañón drainage. Forest.

Plate 46

2. PLAIN-BROWN WOODCREEPER

Dendrocincla fuliginosa*

8" (1"). Much like 1 but lores and sides of head dark gray.

Tropical zone. Generally distributed e of Andes to BOLIVIA, PARAGUAY, BRAZIL to n Mato Grosso and Santa Catarina and ne ARGENTINA in Misiones. W of the Andes in COLOMBIA and ECUADOR s to Guayaquil. Trinidad, Tobago. [Honduras through Panama.] Forest.

194

3. WHITE-CHINNED WOODCREEPER

Dendrocincla merula *

7.5" (1"). Dark brown with white, sharply contrasting throat. Wings, tail and rump chestnut.

Tropical zone. GUIANAS; VENEZUELA s of the Orinoco, n PERU s to upper río Ucayali; Amazonian BRAZIL; ne BOLIVIA.

4. RUDDY WOODCREEPER

Dendrocincla homochroa *

8" (1.1"). Reddish brown, immediately distinguishable from allies by contrasting rufus cap.

Tropical, occasionally subtropical zone. Nw VENEZUELA, adjoining ne COLOMBIA and in Chocó [Mid. Amer.] Forest.

5. LONG-TAILED WOODCREEPER

Deconychura longicauda *

9" (1") [or 7.5" (.8"), 1]. Olivaceous brown, crown with pale shaft streaks. Throat and streaks (or spots, 1) on breast buffy white. Wings brown; tail chestnut, comparatively long.

Tropical zone. GUIANAS, s VENEZUELA and n COLOMBIA w of Andes, 1. From se COLOMBIA to e PERU and Amazonia BRAZIL south to s Amazonas and n Mato Grosso. [Se Honduras southward.] Forest.

Plate 15

6. SPOT-THROATED WOODCREEPER

Deconychura stictolaema *

6.5" (.7"). Rather like 5 but much smaller, rump rufous, and throat with small dark spots.

Tropical zone. FRENCH GUIANA. VENEZUELA in s Amazonas. BRAZIL n of the Amazon from Óbidos, and s of it from rio Tocantins w to ECUADOR nw and east-central PERU. Forest.

7. OLIVACEOUS WOODCREEPER

Sittasomus griseicapillus *

6.5" (.5"). Crown grayish, mantle olive brown; lower back, tertials and tail rufous. Pale band near base of inner wing feathers followed by broad black one. Underparts greenish gray to pale grayish olive (or upperparts bright olive brown, underparts bright ochraceous olive, 1).

Tropical, subtropical zones. GUIANAS, VENEZUELA and COLOMBIA, w of Andes south to nw PERU and e of them to BOLIVIA, w ARGENTINA, PARAGUAY and BRAZIL except the se. BRAZIL from s Goiás and Minas Gerais south to nw ARGENTINA and e PARAGUAY, 1. Forest.

Plate 35

8. WEDGE-BILLED WOODCREEPER

Glyphorynchus spirurus *

5.5" (.4"). Mandible upturned. Rufous brown above becoming rufous chestnut on rump. Eyebrow and throat buff, underparts dark brown with white sagittate spots (in some races shaft streaks) on breast. Band across inner webs of remiges pale cinnamon.

Tropical, subtropical zones. Generally distributed e of Andes to n BOLIVIA and BRAZIL to s Amazonas, n Mato Grosso and s Bahía. [Mid. Amer.] Forest, woodland.

Plate 46

9. SCIMITAR-BILLED WOODCREEPER

Drymornis bridgesii

12" (2.5"). Bill very long, somewhat curved. Upperparts and sides of head bright rusty rufous, broad white eyebrow and moustachial streak. Center of throat white, bordered laterally with rufous, rest of underparts with white, dark-bordered, stripes on pinkish cinnamon ground. Tail rufous chestnut.

URUGUAY from Artigas southward. ARGENTINA w of ríos Paraguay and Paraná s to La Pampa, Buenos Aires and Entre Ríos. Feeds on ground in open woodland.

Plate 15

10. LONG-BILLED WOODCREEPER

Nasica longirostris *

14" (2.5"). Bill very long, straight. Crown blackish; back, wings and tail chestnut; eyebrow, streaks on hindneck and upper mantle white. Below rufous brown broadly striped white on foreneck and breast.

Tropical zone. FRENCH GUIANA. VENEZUELA in Amazonas; e COLOMBIA south to n BOLIVIA; Amazonian BRAZIL south to n Mato Grosso, s Pará and in Maranhão. Forest.

Plate 46

11. CINNAMON-THROATED WOODCREEPER

Dendrexetastes rufigula *

9.5" (1.2"). Brown, paler below; wings and tail chestnut. A few shaft streaks on mantle and more conspicuous ones on breast white edged black; belly with a few blackish bars (or no streaks on back or bands on belly; streaks on breast much smaller, 1).

GUIANAS; BRAZIL n of the Amazon and Belém region. Se COLOMBIA through e ECUADOR to n BOLIVIA and sw BRAZIL, 1. Forest.

Plate 15

12. RED-BILLED WOODCREEPER

Hylexetastes perrotii *

12" (1.5"). Earthy brown, paler below; lower back, rump, wings and tail rufous chestnut. Throat grayish white and broad gray (or buff, 1) line from lores below eye to lower edge of ear coverts. Bill dark red, rather heavy.

GUYANA; FRENCH GUIANA; VENE-ZUELA in ne Bolívar, 1. BRAZIL n of the Amazon from rio Negro to Óbidos, s of it between rios Madeira and Tapajós; ne Mato Grosso (Serra Roncador). Forest, rarely savanna.

Plate 15

13. BAR-BELLIED WOODCREEPER

Hylexetastes stresemanni *

11" (1.3"). Rather like 12 but throat and breast with buffy white streaks, breast light rufescent brown and belly more or less barred with black. Bill red.

E PERU; w BRAZIL e to rios Negro and Purús. Forest.

14. STRONG-BILLED WOODCREEPER

Xiphocolaptes promeropirhynchus *

12" (1.5-2"). Rufescent brown, wings and tail rufous chestnut, under wing coverts barred rufous and black. Crown streaked fulvous, sometimes to upper back. Throat buff, breast broadly streaked buff (in some races reduced to shaft streaks), belly more or less barred with black. Bill grayish horn, somewhat curved.

Tropical to lower temperate zone. GUY-ANA (Acary Mts.); VENEZUELA; COLOM-BIA except W Andes and w Nariño. Sw ECUADOR and nw PERU. E ECUADOR

south to n BOLIVIA and Amazonian BRA-ZIL e to rio Xingú. [Highlands from s Mexico to w Panama.] Forest, open woodland.

Plate 35

15. WHITE-THROATED WOODCREEPER

Xiphocolaptes albicollis *

11" (1.7"). Generally like 14 but much less rufous; throat and stripe below eye white; crown blackish, streaks on crown and breast white, center of belly and under wing coverts barred black and white. Bill jet black.

E BRAZIL from Goiás and Bahía to Rio Grande do Sul; PARAGUAY; ARGENTINA in Misiones and Corrientes. Forest.

16. SNETHLAGE'S WOODCREEPER

Xiphocolaptes franciscanus

Differs from 15 by narrower bill, light gray instead of black mandible, more prominent streak below eye, and unstreaked crown.

BRAZIL in Minas Gerais (w bank of rio São Francisco).

17. MOUSTACHED WOODCREEPER

Xiphocolaptes falcirostris

Very like 15 but at once distinguishable by much slimmer horn color bill, golden buff subocular streak, cinnamon brown pileum with hair-like shaft streaks, and much paler underparts.

E BRAZIL from Maranhão to Paraiba and Bahía.

18. GREAT RUFOUS WOODCREEPER

Xiphocolaptes major *

13" (2"). Nearly uniform bright rusty rufous, crown duller and browner. Throat whitish with buffy streaks, breast with narrow white shaft streaks, belly more or less barred blackish.

BRAZIL in Mato Grosso; PARAGUAY; n and e BOLIVIA; ARGENTINA from Jujuy and Formosa s to Córdoba and Santa Fe. Feeds partly on ground. Forest edge, open woods.

19. BARRED WOODCREEPER

Dendrocolaptes certhia *

10.5" (1.3"). Brown; crown, upper back and entire undersurface regularly barred black. Lower back, wings and tail rufous chestnut.

GUIANAS; s VENEZUELA; COLOMBIA; east and nw ECUADOR; e PERU; n BOLIVIA; BRAZIL from s Amazonas to Pará, Pernambuco and Alagoas. [Mid. Amer.] Forest.

Plate 35

20. CONCOLOR WOODCREEPER

Dendrocolaptes concolor

Unbarred version of 19, sometimes with very faint bars. Under wing coverts plain ochraceous instead of barred; rump, wings and tail rufous chestnut.

BRAZIL s of the Amazon between rios Madeira and Tocantins. Forest.

21. HOFFMANNS' WOODCREEPER

Dendrocolaptes hoffmannsi

11" (1.6"). Brown, crown reddish with slight streaks in contrast to back. Foreneck and breast shaded olivaceous with inconspicuous buffy hair streaks. Bill black.

BRAZIL s of the Amazon between rios Madeira and Xingú. Forest.

22. BLACK-BANDED WOODCREEPER

Dendrocolaptes picumnus *

11" (1.6"). Crown and upper back brown streaked with buff, crown streaks expanding terminally; rump, wings and tail rufous chestnut. Throat fulvous, underparts brown, broadly streaked fulvous on breast and barred black on belly (or much more rufescent, only crown streaked and belly unbarred, 1). Bill pale bluish horn.

Tropical, subtropical zones. Generally distributed e of Andes s to BOLIVIA, PARAGUAY, and most of Amazonian BRAZIL. In w Mato Grosso, e BOLIVIA and nw ARGENTINA, 1. [Highlands of Guatemala to w Panama.] Forest.

23. PLANALTO WOODCREEPER

Dendrocolaptes platyrostris *

10.5" (1.2"). Much like 15 but smaller (or differing by crown brown like back instead of blackish, 1). Bill much smaller, horn color instead of black.

E and central BRAZIL from Piauí and n Goiás, 1; from Rio Grande do Sul and Mato Grosso to PARAGUAY, n ARGENTINA from Misiones to e Chaco. Forest.

24. STRAIGHT-BILLED WOODCREEPER

Xiphorhynchus picus *

8.5" (1.1"). Crown dusky brown spotted with fulvous, in sharp contrast to rufous chestnut back. Throat and upper breast white to buffy white, feathers edged black; lower breast brown with broad, dusky-edged, oval, buffy white spots; rest of underparts rufous brown to brown, sometimes pale-streaked. Wing coverts, wings and tail rufous chestnut. Bill very straight, flesh color to whitish horn.

Generally distributed e of Andes south to n BOLIVIA and Amazonian BRAZIL, and in Bahía. Margarita I. Trinidad. [Pacific central Panama.] Savanna, swampy woods, mangroves, plantations.

Plate 35

25. ZIMMER'S WOODCREEPER

Xiphorhynchus necopinus

Very like 24 but wing coverts brown, general color less rufescent, and streaks on underparts linear, not oval. Back more prominently streaked. Bill darker.

BRAZIL on both sides of middle and lower Amazon. Forest.

26. STRIPED WOODCREEPER

Xiphorhynchus obsoletus *

7.5". Differs from 25 in slightly smaller size, below less rufescent.

GUIANAS; VENEZUELA (n of the Orinoco only in Apure and Táchira); e COLOMBIA. Ne PERU; Amazonian BRAZIL e to rio Jamundá and upper rio Xingú. Swampy forest.

27. OCELLATED WOODCREEPER

Xiphorhynchus ocellatus *

8.5" (1.1"). Brown; crown with guttate buff spots, mantle with narrow buff streaks. Throat buff; lower throat and breast with rounded, black-edged spots becoming longitudinal streaks on lower breast. Wing coverts brown, inner remiges, lower back and tail chestnut rufous.

VENEZUELA in sw Amazonas e to base of COLOMBIAN Andes and south to n BO-

LIVIA and Amazonian BRAZIL e to rios Jamundá and Tocantins. Forest.

28. SPIX'S WOODCREEPER

Xiphorhynchus spixii *

8.5" (1"). Brown; crown blackish with guttate buff spots, back with wide black-edged buff streaks, lower back and rump plain rufous chestnut. Throat buff, underparts dull brown broadly streaked with black-edged buff stripes (or crown with small buff spots, throat whitish, lower throat and breast with dark-edged round spots; back with a few narrow buff streaks, 1). Mandible pale.

E of Andes from COLOMBIA south to n BOLIVIA. Nw BRAZIL and generally s of the Amazon to Pará and Maranhão. W of Andes in upper Magdalena Valley, COLOMBIA, 1. Forest.

29. ELEGANT WOODCREEPER

Xiphorhynchus elegans *

Very similar to 28 (1), but streaks on back drop-shaped, much wider, and spots on breast more heavily margined with black. Mandible dusky.

E PERU; n BOLIVIA in Beni; BRAZIL s of the Amazon east to n Mato Grosso and rio Tapajós. Forest.

30. CHESTNUT-RUMPED WOODCREEPER

Xiphorhynchus pardalotus *

9.5" (1.3"). Differs from 28 by large size and rusty buff instead of buffy white throat and breast streaks.

Tropical, lower subtropical zones. GUIANAS; s VENEZUELA; e Amazonian BRAZIL e from rios Negro and Tapajós. Forest, savanna.

31. BUFF-THROATED WOODCREEPER

Xiphorhynchus guttatus *

11" (1.4") [or 9.5" (1")]. Brown to russet brown; crown blackish with guttate buff spots, hindneck streaked buff; back unstreaked (or if streaked, confined to upper mantle). Throat buff, upper breast streaked buff. Wings, tail and rump rufous chestnut. Bill pale horn to black.

Generally distributed e of Andes to n BOLIVIA. Amazonian BRAZIL, also coast-ally from Paraiba to Rio de Janeiro. W of Andes in COLOMBIA, 1. Margarita I. Trinidad and Tobago. [Guatemala to Panama.] Forest, mangroves, plantations.

32. DUSKY-BILLED WOODCREEPER

Xiphorhynchus eytoni *

11" (1.6"). Not unlike 31 but upper back broadly streaked white; lower back as well as rump, rufous chestnut; throat and streaks on breast whiter; rather distinct white preocular streak. Upper mandible black, basal part of lower mandible pale.

BRAZIL n of the Amazon from rio Jamundá eastward and s of it from rio Juruá e to Maranhão and Ceará.

33. BLACK-STRIPED WOODCREEPER

Xiphorhynchus lachrymosus *

9.5" (1.3"). Strikingly streaked black and buff on head and striped on back and underparts. Throat plain buff. Lower back, rump, wings and tail rufous chestnut; wing coverts edged black.

Tropical zone. COLOMBIA west of E Andes; nw ECUADOR. [Nicaragua, Costa Rica, Panama.] Forest.

Plate 35

34. SPOTTED WOODCREEPER

Xiphorhynchus erythropygius *

9" (1.1"). Crown dark brown, upper back russet brown; lower back, wings and tail rufous chestnut; wing coverts chestnut brown. Throat buff with small ochraceous spots, rest of underparts olivaceous brown spotted with buff.

Tropical, occasionally subtropical zone. COLOMBIA from lower Cauca Valley westward, and south to w ECUADOR. Forest.

35. OLIVE-BACKED WOODCREEPER

Xiphorhynchus triangularis *

9" (1.1"). Upper parts olivaceous brown finely streaked on head and upper back with buff. Throat buff, feathers edged blackish giving scalloped look; breast similar but markings coarser, rest of underparts olivaceous spotted with buff. Lower back, wings and tail as in 34.

Tropical, subtropical zones. VENEZUELA from Miranda to sw Táchira. COLOMBIA (except Caribbean and e lowlands and w Nariño); e ECUADOR; e PERU; n BOLIVIA to Santa Cruz. Forest.

36. STREAK-HEADED WOODCREEPER

Lepidocolaptes souleyetii *

8.3" (1.1") [or 6" (.9"), 1]. Crown and nape conspicuously streaked dusky and pale buff. Back brown; rump, wings and tail rufous. Throat buffy white, underparts brown, with broad black-edged buffy white streaks.

GUYANA; VENEZUELA n of the Orinoco, s of it only in se Bolívar and bordering area of BRAZIL; COLOMBIA e of Andes to Meta and generally w of them (in Santa Marta, 1); w ECUADOR; nw PERU to Lambayeque. [Mid. Amer.] Open woods, plantations, campos, arid scrub.

Plate 25

37. NARROW-BILLED WOODCREEPER

Lepidocolaptes angustirostris *

8.5" (1.4"). Distinguishable from any other woodcreeper by broad white eyebrow. Crown and nape dusky, pale-streaked; back, wings and tail rufous. Broad eyebrow white, cheeks black. Underparts dull white more to less streaked on breast and belly according to race.

E BRAZIL s of the Amazon from rio Tapajós e to Ceará and s to Paraná and Mato Grosso; PARAGUAY; n BOLIVIA to Beni; ARGENTINA s to Buenos Aires, La Pampa and Mendoza. Campos, cerrado.

38. SPOT-CROWNED WOODCREEPER

Lepidocolaptes affinis *

8" (1"). Above brown; crown and nape spotted with buff. Wings and tail rufous. Throat white. Underparts brown to olive, with black-edged white stripes (or with drop-shaped marks, 1).

Subtropical, rarely temperate zone. Coastal mts. of VENEZUELA from Miranda to Carabobo, and from Mérida westward. Andes of COLOMBIA (Central and W Andes, 1). E and w ECUADOR; e PERU; n BOLIVIA. [S Mexico to w Panama.] Forest, open woodland.

39. SCALED WOODCREEPER

Lepidocolaptes squamatus *

8" (1"). Upperparts cinnamon rufous to olivaceous brown. Rump and tail rufous. Crown like back but pale-spotted (or crown and nape dusky, streaked buff, 1). Throat and extreme upper breast white, rest of underparts olive brown with broad black-edged white streaks.

BRAZIL in Piauí; from São Paulo to Rio Grande do Sul, e PARAGUAY and ARGENTINA in Misiones, 1. Forest.

40. LESSER WOODCREEPER

Lepidocolaptes fuscus *

7.3" (1"). Crown, nape and upper back dusky brown streaked with buff; rest of back olive brown; rump, wings and tail rufous. Throat and upper breast buffy white, rest of underparts buffy with diffused olivaceous streaks.

BRAZIL from Ceará to Santa Catarina. E PARAGUAY; ARGENTINA in Misiones. Forest.

41. LINEATED WOODCREEPER

Lepidocolaptes albolineatus *

8" (1.1"). Above uniform reddish brown, crown with or without inconspicuous dots or shaft streaks. Wings and tail rufous. Throat buff, underparts olivaceous brown streaked with black-bordered buff marks (or throat white, underparts gray streaked with black-bordered white marks, 1).

GUIANAS; s VENEZUELA; Amazonian BRAZIL, n of the Amazon from rio Jarí and s of it from rio Purús and s Amazonas e to rio Tapajós; thence east to n Maranhão, 1. E ECUADOR; e PERU; n BOLIVIA. Forest.

42. GREATER SCYTHEBILL

Campylorhamphus pucheranii

11.5" (2" chord). Earthy brown, subocular streak white. Rump, wings and tail rufous chestnut. Bill brown, long, curved, but less so than in the following species.

Upper tropical, subtropical zones. Both slopes of W Andes of COLOMBIA. E and w ECUADOR. Se PERU in Puno.

43. RED-BILLED SCYTHEBILL

Campylorhamphus trochilirostris *

12" (3" chord) [or 7.4" (2.4" chord), 1]. Bill long, curved, brown. Crown dusky, back reddish brown, both streaked fulvous. Throat whitish; underparts reddish to olivaceous brown, streaked fulvous on breast. Wings and tail rufous.

Generally distributed e of Andes from VENEZUELA and COLOMBIA s to BOLIVIA, PARAGUAY and n ARGENTINA; in e BRAZIL s to Paraná. W of Andes south to nw PERU, 1. [E Panama.] Swampy forest, woodland.

Plate 35

44. BLACK-BILLED SCYTHEBILL

Campylorhamphus falcularius

11" (2.6" chord). Bill long, curved, dusky. Crown black, streaked fulvous. Body plumage mostly olivaceous brown, paler below, streaked on breast, sides of neck, and upper mantle with fulvous. Throat whitish. Wings and tail rufous chestnut.

BRAZIL from Espírito Santo to Rio Grande do Sul; e PARAGUAY; ARGENTINA in Misiones. Forest.

45. BROWN-BILLED SCYTHEBILL

Campylorhamphus pusillus *

10" (2" chord). Bill long, curved, light brown. Dark olivaceous brown, dusky on crown; crown, upper back and breast streaked fulvous. Throat fulvous. Wings and tail rufous chestnut.

Upper tropical and subtropical zones. GUYANA; nw VENEZUELA in western Zulia and southwestern Táchira. COLOMBIA e of Andes in Boyacá, w of them generally except Santa Marta Mts. and Caribbean lowlands. [Costa Rica, w Panama.] Forest.

46. CURVE-BILLED SCYTHEBILL

Campylorhamphus procurvoides *

10.3" (2.3" chord). Bill brown. Rather like 43 but much darker, crown with narrow shaft streaks or small spots, and mantle unstreaked (or broadly streaked above and below with black-edged, pale buffy white stripes, 1).

Tropical zone. GUIANAS, s VENEZUELA in Bolívar and southwestern Amazonas. COLOMBIA along the eastern base of the E Andes from Norte de Santander southward. BRAZIL n of the Amazon from rio Negro to rio Jarí. South of the Amazon e to rio Tapajós, 1. Forest.

Family FURNARIIDAE   HORNEROS, SPINETAILS FOLIAGE-GLEANERS, ETC.

As the various names of members of this large family imply, the Furnariidae is composed of a great many species widely differing in appearance and habits, but sharing a rather somber coloration of shades of brown and russet. The sexes are similar.

Many species are terrestrial (miners, cinclodes, earthcreepers, etc.) and walk rather than hop; others live in arid cactus lands (tit-spinetails, canasteros), scrub-covered hillsides or grasslands (spinetails, canasteros), deep forest or light woodland (foliage-gleaners, treehunters), alpine meadows (miners), and open or bushy pastureland (horneros, thornbirds). They occur from sea level to snow line. Some of the forest-inhabiting species often accompany those mixed assemblages of birds which forage through forests.

Their nests are often curious: oven-like, domed mud nests (horneros) or large round, oval or tubular structures of sticks (canasteros, spinetails, thornbirds, firewood-gatherers); miners dig holes in banks and even sloping ground for nesting. Treehunters and foliage-gleaners nest in holes in banks; xenops, rayaditos and treerunners nest in holes in trees. A few species climb like woodpeckers; others clamber about bushes; some haunt reedbeds. Their voices are harsh but some have rather insignificant trilling songs. Furnariidae eat insects; some are known to eat seeds and vegetable matter as well.

The name "ovenbirds" has often been applied to this family because of the oven-like mud nests built by horneros. They, of course, are quite unrelated to the North American ovenbirds.

In this family the bill length for some species is given in parentheses following total length measurement.

AID TO IDENTIFICATION

Upperparts streaked

Streaked or scaled below (tail entirely rufous) 13b, 20b, 141b, 151b, 155b, 156, 160, 161, 164b, 165a, 191c, 192b, 193b, 195a, 198c, 199, 201; (tail other than entirely rufous) 43b, 45b, 46b, 48, 49c, 123b, 124b, 125c, 128b, 129b, 142, 152b, 200, 201

Not streaked or scaled below (tail all or partially rufous) 121b, 122b, 128b, 130c, 155b, 167b, 196b; (tail not rufous) 42, 47c, 53c, 127b, 143c

Streaked below only, not streaked above

Breast streaked or spotted (tail all or mostly rufous) 16b, 17b, 77b, 95, 101, 102, 133, 140, 144b, 148b, 150a, 160, 163, 169b, 170c, 187b; (tail not rufous) 8, 12, 23b, 25b, 26b, 27, 30b, 72a, 103b, 116b, 129b, 146b, 152b, 153a, 197b, 210

No streaking or spotting

With contrasting cap or head (cap not rufous) 33, 34, 35, 36c, 52c, 83a, 84a, 89, 99b, 100b, 157, 171c, 172a, 177; (cap rufous, tail rufous) 31c, 50b, 55c, 56b, 57a, 58b, 59, 60b, 61, 73a, 91a, 92b, 93a, 94b, 96c, 97b, 138c, 139, 186; (cap rufous, tail not rufous) 62c, 64a, 65, 66, 67, 75

No contrasting cap, tail with sharply contrasting colors, (dark terminal band) 1c, 4b, 5b, 6b, 7b, 8, 9, 11b, 21; (outer feathers differently colored from rest, or pale-tipped) 13b, 18b, 27, 27bis c, 28b, 110, 112b, 113b, 118b, 137b, 202

Upper and underparts with little contrast except for throat (throat black) 75, 109b; (throat white or grayish) 24, 32c, 68, 79b, 104a, 134b, 149b, 159, 203c, 205c, 206, 208, 210a; (throat rufous) 117, 158, 183, 207, 208; (more or less uniform below) 74, 173, 183, 185

Upper and underparts uniform but in strong contrast, wings or wing coverts in contrast to rest of plumage (with patch of color on throat) 69, 70c, 71b, 80c, 85, 111b, 119b, 121b; (no patch on throat, underparts white or ochraceous to chestnut) 29b, 76, 78b, 133, 174, 175c, 176c, 177; (below buffy or grayish) 51b, 68, 90a, 113b, 135, 138c, 177

Wings not in contrast to rest of plumage (tail bright rufous in contrast to rest of upperparts) 20b, 32c, 37, 86c, 162c, 166, 175c, 179, 180c, 181, 182b, 185, 188; (central tail feathers like back, outer ones all or mostly rufous) 14b, 15b, 19, 54c, 104a, 117b, 137b; (tail feathers much like back; above gray, brown, or foxy red; below whitish) 2b, 3b, 36, 38c, 81, 82, 87c, 98b, 136, 145b; (below gray or ashy) 22b, 79b 105b, 106b, 107b, 108b; (throat patch black) 115

Highly peculiar in color or shape of tail (forehead and throat bright yellow) 147; (central tail feathers very long, reduced to shafts with web expanding at tip) 40b; (tail very short with conspicuously protruding spines) 41b, 204b

Crested 37, 49c, 52c, 87, 142, 157, 158, 159, 180c

1. CAMPO MINER

Geobates poecilopterus

4.5". Above brown. Throat white, rest of underparts cinnamon buff streaked dusky on upper breast. Remiges banded with rufous. Tail feathers rufous with subterminal black band.

BRAZIL in campos of Minas Gerais, s Goiás, São Paulo and Mato Grosso.

2. GRAYISH MINER

Geositta maritima

5.5". Above pale sandy gray; below dull white, flanks pinkish buff. Remiges uniform dusky gray. Tail blackish, outer web of outermost feather buff.

Arid, rocky regions of w PERU from middle Ancash s to Arequipa. CHILE in Atacama and Antofagasta, interior Tarapacá. Arid littoral, interior deserts.

3. COASTAL MINER

Geositta peruviana *

Differs from 2 by sandy buff upperparts, much larger bill, and remiges pinkish buff with subterminal black band.

Arid coastal PERU from Tumbes to Ica. Sandy hillsides.

4. DARK-WINGED MINER

Geositta saxicolina

6.5". Above reddish brown. Throat white, rest of underparts pale pinkish buff. Remiges uniform dusky brown. Tail basally buff, distally blackish.

Mts. of central PERU in Lima, Junín and Huancavelica up to 15,000 ft. Stony slopes with sparse vegetation.

5. CREAMY-RUMPED MINER

Geositta isabellina

7". Above sandy brown, rump buffy white. Below dull white. Remiges ferruginous, crossed by broad blackish band. Tail basally buffy white, apically black.

Mts. of CHILE from Atacama to Talca rarely below 6000 ft. W ARGENTINA in Jujuy, Catamarca and Mendoza, where probably migrant from CHILE. Open, rocky slopes.

6. RUFOUS-BANDED MINER

Geositta rufipennis *

7". Above sandy brown. Throat white, rest of underparts pale grayish buff, sides of body rufous. Inner webs of remiges mostly rufous. Central tail feathers reddish brown with black mark toward tip, rest bright rufous with broad terminal black band.

Andes of BOLIVIA above 9500 ft. s to Santa Cruz, ARGENTINA. CHILE from Atacama to Malleco. Bushy, rocky slopes.

7. PUNA MINER

Geositta punensis

6". Differs from 6 by smaller size and paler

coloration throughout. Basal portion of outer webs of inner remiges rufous forming wing patch. Tail feathers basally cinnamon buff with broad terminal blackish band.

Andes of w BOLIVIA above 10,000 ft. W ARGENTINA to n Catamarca. W of Andes from s PERU to Atacama, CHILE. Sandy, semiarid country with dwarf vegetation.

8. COMMON MINER

Geositta cunicularia *

6.5". Earthy or grayish brown above. Breast somewhat streaked blackish. Inner remiges almost entirely rufous. Basal portion of tail buffy white (or similar but much paler, upperparts buffy gray, 1).

High plateau of s PERU (on seacoast in Arequipa and Tacna, 1) s through Andes of BOLIVIA and ARGENTINA to Tierra del Fuego. BRAZIL in Rio Grande do Sul; URUGUAY. Open sandy country, dunes, grassy punalands.

Plate 25

9. SHORT-BILLED MINER

Geositta antarctica

6". Generally like 8 but tawny area on remiges only suggested. Wings longer. Breast streaks obsolete. Bill shorter, straighter.

Breeds in Tierra del Fuego and along Strait of Magellan in CHILE and ARGENTINA; migrates n to Mendoza, ARGENTINA. Open country.

10. SLENDER-BILLED MINER

Geositta tenuirostris

7.5" (1.2"). Above sandy brown; eyebrow ochraceous. Below buffy white, mottled brown on breast. Inner primaries and secondaries chestnut with a subapical black band, wing coverts blackish edged sandy. Outer two tail feathers cinnamon rufous, next pair rufous with black subterminal blotch; central feathers blackish. Bill long, curved.

PERU from Cajamarca and Libertad s through Andes of BOLIVIA to Catamarca, ARGENTINA. Open Andean hillsides, cultivated lands, moist pastures.

11. THICK-BILLED MINER

Geositta crassirostris *

6.5". Above brown, feathers basally blackish. Eyebrow, sides of head and throat dull white, rest of underparts grayish white. Wings much as in 10, but subapical black band more pronounced. Central tail feathers like back, rest chestnut with broad black subterminal band and lightish tip. Bill rather thick, slightly curved.

W PERU from sea level to 7500 ft. in Lima and Ayacucho. Rocks, crags.

12. SCALE-THROATED EARTHCREEPER
Upucerthia dumetaria *

9" (1.2"). Bill long, curved. Above earthy brown; below buffy white, breast tinged buffy brown, feathers of throat and breast fringed blackish. Inner remiges mostly dull rufous. Central tail feathers like back, outer feathers blackish, outermost edged and tipped dull cinnamon.

Temperate zone. S PERU (Puno); w BOLIVIA in Oruro and Potosí; w ARGENTINA s to Neuquén thence e to coast and s to Tierra del Fuego; in winter to Buenos Aires and Entre Ríos; CHILE from Antofagasta s to Tierra del Fuego. Semiarid slopes, thorny brush.

Plate 25

13. WHITE-THROATED EARTHCREEPER
Upurcerthia albigula

8" (1.4"). Bill long, curved. Upperparts dark earthy brown, crown sepia. Throat white, feathers edged dark brown; rest of underparts buff becoming darker on flanks. Outer tail feathers orange cinnamon.

Puna zone of sw PERU from Arequipa to n CHILE (Tarapacá). Desert scrub, wet meadows.

14. BUFF-BREASTED EARTHCREEPER
Upucerthia validirostris *

8.5" (1.4"). Above light brown, below buffy. Central tail feathers like back; outer feathers dull, dark cinnamon.

Puna zone. W ARGENTINA from Salta and Jujuy s to Mendoza. Bushy hillsides, gravelly streambeds.

15. PLAIN-BREASTED EARTHCREEPER
Upucerthia jelskii *

7.5" (.8-1.1"). Upperparts and tail as in 14,

underparts less buffy. Throat whitish, breast feathers with indistinct dusky edges.

Puna zone of PERU from Ancash south to n CHILE. W BOLIVIA to Cochabamba and Potosí. Rocky, bushy slopes.

16. STRIATED EARTHCREEPER
Upucerthia serrana *

8" (1"). Crown dark brown, feathers of forehead with pale streaks; eyebrow white. Upper back brown shading to rufous on upper tail coverts. Throat white, rest of underparts dirty white, feathers edged laterally with grayish. Wings and tail dull rufous.

Temperate zone of PERUVIAN Andes in Cajamarca and Libertad s to Lima and Huancavelica. Stony hillsides with scattered vegetation.

17. ROCK EARTHCREEPER
Upucerthia andaecola

7.5" (1"). Upperparts, wings and tail much like 16. Throat, breast and belly white. Flank feathers edged brown.

Temperate and puna zones of BOLIVIA in La Paz, Potosí, Cochabamba and Chuquisaca; nw ARGENTINA in Jujuy and Catamarca. Rocky slopes.

18. STRAIGHT-BILLED EARTHCREEPER
Upucerthia ruficauda *

7.5" (1"). Bill only slightly curved. Crown and back light brown becoming rufescent on rump. Outer remiges basally pale rufous, distally blackish. Eyebrow and underparts white, feathers of belly and flanks edged pale buffy cinnamon. Tail light rufous, all but outermost feathers with black on inner web.

Puna zone. Sw PERU from Arequipa to Santiago, CHILE. W BOLIVIA; ARGENTINA from Jujuy to Chubut. Rocky slopes.

19. CHACO EARTHCREEPER
Upucerthia certhioides *

7" (1"). Upperparts, flanks, and under tail coverts rufescent brown (or earthy brown, 1). Lores, forehead and sides of head rufous. Throat white, rest of underparts grayish. Base of remiges rufous. Central tail feathers like back, rest dark rufous.

PARAGUAYAN chaco; ARGENTINA from

Jujuy to Corrientes and s to Córdoba; in La Rioja and Mendoza, 1. Thick scrub, dry flats.

20. BOLIVIAN EARTHCREEPER

Upucerthia harterti

6.5". Crown dark brown, eyebrow buffy white. Upper back pale brown shading to rufescent on rump. Throat white; rest of underparts grayish white, pale brown on flanks and under tail coverts. Wings and tail dull rufous.

BOLIVIA in Cochabamba, Santa Cruz and Chuquisaca between 4600 and 9300 ft.

21. BAND-TAILED EARTHCREEPER

Eremobius phoenicurus

7" (1.7"). Bill straight. Upperparts and wings light grayish brown. Lores, eyebrow, eye ring and throat white; rest of underparts dull white, vaguely streaked pale grayish. Base of tail rufous chestnut, rest of feathers black. Tail carried cocked over back.

ARGENTINA from Neuquén to s Santa Cruz, occasionally to La Rioja. Sandy, stony hillsides with thorn scrub.

22. CRAG CHILIA

Chilia melanura *

8" (.8"). Bill very straight. Crown and mantle light brown; rump, upper and under tail coverts rufous chestnut. Inner remiges basally rufous, distally brown. Throat and breast white, rest of underparts pale grayish brown. Tail blackish brown, outer web of outermost feather rufous.

Mts. of Atacama and coast and mts. of central CHILE from Aconcagua s to Colchagua. Stony outcrops, rock faces.

23. STOUT-BILLED CINCLODES

Cinclodes excelsior *

8.5" (1"). Bill curved. Upperparts and cheeks dark brown, long eyebrow buff. Underparts dirty white, whitest on throat, breast feathers edged dusky. Wing coverts dark brown, pale-edged. Basal part of inner remiges dull cinnamon. Tail dark brown, outer feathers tipped pale brown.

Páramo zone. COLOMBIA in n Central Andes and Andes of Nariño; Andes of ECUADOR. Se PERU in Puno. Open slopes.

24. BLACKISH CINCLODES

Cinclodes antarcticus *

7" (.5"). Bill straight. Uniform dusky grayish brown, throat paler.

Wollaston Archipelago and islands in Beagle Channel, CHILE; Staten I. and s Tierra del Fuego, ARGENTINA. [Falkland Is.] Clumps of coarse vegetation near rocky beaches.

25. DARK-BELLIED CINCLODES

Cinclodes patagonicus *

8" (.9"). Bill slightly curved. Upperparts dark brown. Long eyebrow white. Throat whitish, rest of underparts gray streaked white. Inner remiges with buffy bar near base. Tail dusky brown, outer feathers pale-tipped.

Rocky shores of sea and inland waters. CHILE from Aconcagua, and ARGENTINA from Mendoza to Tierra del Fuego.

26. GRAY-FLANKED CINCLODES

Cinclodes oustaleti *

6.7" (.7"). Rather like 25 but much smaller, inner primaries with pale buff basal band and rest of remiges with cinnamon basal band.

CHILE from Antofagasta and ARGENTINA from Mendoza s to Cape Horn. [Juan Fernández Is.] Rocky streams, irrigation ditches.

27. BAR-WINGED CINCLODES

Cinclodes fuscus *

7" (.8"). Above dark earthy brown. Long eyebrow white. Underparts whitish, more or less stained with brown; feathers of lower throat and breast dark-edged. Basal part of inner remiges rufescent with black median bar. Central tail feathers like back, outer feathers all rufous or only tipped rufous (or similar but wing markings pale buff, 1; or similar but back paler, underparts white, wing markings of primaries white instead of rufous, 2).

Páramo, temperate zones. W VENEZUELA; Andes of COLOMBIA and Santa Marta Mts. south to n PERU. Central PERU, w BOLIVIA s to Córdoba, ARGENTINA, 2. ARGENTINA from Mendoza, and CHILE from Atacama, s to Cape Horn, in winter n to Tucumán and URUGUAY, 1. Wags tail.

Wet pampas, corrals, rocky outcrops and streams. (27bis. Long-tailed Cinclodes, *Cinclodes pabsti*, Sick, 1969, see addenda.)

Plate 35

28. WHITE-WINGED CINCLODES

Cinclodes atacamensis *

7.7" (.8"). Differs from 27 by considerably larger size and whiter tips to outer tail feathers, outer web of outermost mostly black instead of buffy white, and white band across wing.

Puna zone. PERU from Junín and Lima s to Santiago, CHILE, and w ARGENTINA to Córdoba. Rocky slopes near streams, village outskirts.

29. WHITE-BELLIED CINCLODES

Cinclodes palliatus

8.2" (1"). Rather like 28 but no white eyebrow, grayer upperparts and pure white underparts. Size considerably larger.

Andes of PERU in San Martín, Junín, Lima and Huancavelica. Rocky slopes, streams.

30. SEASIDE CINCLODES

Cinclodes nigrofumosus *

8.5" (.9"). Dark smoky brown. Line above eye white; throat and streaks on underparts white. Patch on inner primaries cinnamon buff, base of secondaries cinnamon. Tail brownish black, outer feathers with buffy tips (or paler throughout with only chin white and streaks on underparts less conspicuous, 1).

PERU from Lima to Islay including Isla Don Martín, 1. CHILE s to Valdivia, Mocha I. Rocky seacoast at water's edge.

31. CANEBRAKE GROUNDCREEPER

Clibanornis dendrocolaptoides

8" (1.1"). Not unlike 139 but with darker underparts and shorter tail. Crown, nape and tail chestnut; postocular stripe buffy grayish, feathers edged black. Throat and sides of neck white, spotted with black; rest of underparts light brownish gray, brown on sides and under tail coverts. Tail much graduated.

Se BRAZIL in São Paulo and Paraná; e PARAGUAY; ne ARGENTINA in Misiones. Frequents bamboo stands and thickets in subtropical woodland.

32. RUFOUS HORNERO

Furnarius rufus *

7.7" (.8"). Upperparts, closed wings and tail uniform light rufous brown. Outer remiges dark brown with pale patch at base of inner web. Throat and center of abdomen white, rest of underparts light buff (or throat white, rest of underparts light pinkish brown, slightly paler than back, 1).

E BRAZIL from Goiás to São Paulo, 1; thence s to Rio Grande do Sul and west to w Mato Grosso and s to Río Negro, ARGENTINA. Groves of trees often near habitations.

33. PALE-LEGGED HORNERO

Furnarius leucopus *

6" (.9") [or 7.7" (1"), 1]. Crown smoky gray or dark reddish brown, prominent whitish eyebrow; upperparts, closed wing and tail bright cinnamon rufous. Wing as in 32. Throat white; rest of underparts mainly cinnamon, whitish on center of belly, (or underparts all white, tinged buff on breast, 1).

GUYANA, nw VENEZUELA, n COLOMBIA west to sw Bolívar. Sw ECUADOR s to Ancash, PERU, 1. E ECUADOR, e PERU, n BOLIVIA, Amazonian BRAZIL and in e from Maranhão and Ceará to Goiás and Bahía. Campos, arid coastal regions, cerrado, forest clearings, stream borders.

Plate 25

34. PALE-BILLED HORNERO

Furnarius torridus

6.5" (.8"). Very similar to 33. Crown wood brown. Best distinguishable by more extensive black bases to under tail coverts.

Ne Amazonian PERU s to lower Ucayali and s of the Amazon in w BRAZIL west to São Paulo de Olivença. Campos.

35. LESSER HORNERO

Furnarius minor

6" (.7"). Crown dull brown, postocular streak buffy. Back cinnamon brown, tail darker. Throat and center of belly white, breast and sides pale buff.

COLOMBIA in Amazonas. Ne PERU in Marañón Valley; BRAZIL s of the Amazon e to rio Tapajós, n of the Amazon from rio Jamundá to opposite mouth of rio Tapajós.

36. WING-BANDED HORNERO

Furnarius figulus *

8" (.7"). Entire upperparts, closed wing and tail bright cinnamon rufous (or with dark brown cap, 1); wide postocular streak white. Underparts white, tinged buff on breast and sides. Differs from other species by two buff bands on remiges.

BRAZIL in middle and lower Amazon Valley s to upper rio Araguaya, 1; from Maranhão to Paraiba s to Minas Gerais. Open scrub, perches on roofs and wires.

37. CRESTED HORNERO

Furnarius cristatus

6.2" (.5"). Head crested. Above light buffy brown. Throat, lores, and center of belly white; breast and sides of body pale pinkish buff. Tail rufous.

PARAGUAYAN chaco; ARGENTINA w of ríos Paraguay and Paraná to Córdoba and La Rioja, casually in Entre Ríos. Bushy, scrubby plains.

38. CURVE-BILLED REEDHAUNTER

Limnornis curvirostris

7" (1"). Bill curved, pale. Above light brown, gradually turning to russet brown on rump and upper tail coverts. Eyebrow and underparts white. Tail very much rounded, feathers rounded at tip.

Se BRAZIL in Rio Grande do Sul; se URUGUAY; ARGENTINA in s and e Entre Ríos and n Buenos Aires. Reedbeds.

Plate 25

39. STRAIGHT-BILLED REEDHAUNTER

Limnoctites rectirostris

6.7" (1"). Bill straight, mostly blackish. Above light brown, grayer on crown, narrow eyebrow white. Underparts white, sides light brown. Wings and tail cinnamon; tail much rounded, central feathers pointed.

Extreme se BRAZIL (rio Jaguarão); URU-GUAY (Deptos. Rocha; Cerro Largo; Treinta y Tres); e ARGENTINA in extreme se Entre Ríos (Paranacito). Extensive reedbeds, also dry rocky places near creeks in long spiny grass, mainly caraguatá (*Eryngium*).

Plate 25

40. DES MURS' WIRETAIL

Sylviorthorhynchus desmursii

9.5" including tail (6.5"). Reddish brown above; white, tinged brown below. Distinguishable from rest of family by extraordinary tail, feathers very narrow, central pair much the longest, the web gradually expanding toward tip, shafts thick.

CHILE from s Aconcagua to Magallanes. ARGENTINA in Neuquén and Río Negro and Santa Cruz. Humid forest in thick undergrowth and bamboo thickets.

Plate 25

41. THORN-TAILED RAYADITO

Aphrastura spinicauda *

3.9" (.3"). Crown and sides of head brownish black, forehead blackish; very long, broad superciliaries buff. Back earthy brown. Wing coverts blackish, tipped buff. Remiges blackish, base of inner primaries cinnamon; secondaries medially edged cinnamon, forming double wing bar. Underparts white (or ochre yellow, 1). Tail peculiar: Central feathers black, rest cinnamon rufous; all terminating in rather stiff, almost bare shafts about .5" long.

S ARGENTINA from Neuquén, and CHILE from Coquimbo, s to Staten I. and Tierra del Fuego. Chiloé I., CHILE, 1. Forest and clearings inland and coastally. Climbs trees.

Plate 25

42. WREN-LIKE RUSHBIRD

Phleocryptes melanops *

5.5" (.6") [or 6.1" (.6")]. Crown dark brown with pale shaft streaks. Center of back streaked black and grayish white; rump uniform brown. Underparts mostly white, breast and sides pale buffy brown. Wing much as in 41. Central tail feathers brown with median black line, outer feathers black with pale tip.

Coast of PERU from Piura to Pisco and from Arequipa s to Aysén, CHILE; PARA-GUAY; e BRAZIL from Rio de Janeiro to Rio Grande do Sul; URUGUAY; ARGENTINA s to Tierra del Fuego. PERU from Lake Junín s through w BOLIVIA to Andes of Jujuy, ARGENTINA, 1. Cattails, reedbeds.

Plate 25

Tit-Spinetails

In the genera *Leptasthenura, Schoeniophylax, Oreophylax* and *Synallaxis,* the tail is long, feathers much graduated and pointed, often as long as, and sometimes considerably longer than, the bird's body.

43. ANDEAN TIT-SPINETAIL

Leptasthenura andicola *

6.3" (.3"). Crown black, streaked rufous. Back and tail coverts dark brown, streaked white. Throat white, breast (or breast and belly, 1) buffy white, heavily streaked dusky.

Temperate, páramo zones. Nw VENEZUELA; COLOMBIA in Santa Marta Mts. and E and Central Andes, ECUADOR. PERU from Ancash south to ne BOLIVIA, 1. Matted vegetation often near streams.

Plate 35

44. STREAKED TIT-SPINETAIL

Leptasthenura striata *

Differs from 43 mainly by white underparts, throat feathers edged dusky.

W PERU (e slope in Huancavelica) from Lima s to Tarapacá, CHILE. Bushy slopes, cacti.

45. RUSTY-CROWNED TIT-SPINETAIL

Leptasthenura pileata *

Very much like 43 but gray below without buffy tinge, outer tail feathers broadly tipped gray instead of uniform. Crown rufous.

Temperate zone. PERU from Cajamarca and Libertad s to Huancavelica. Bushy and wooded places.

46. WHITE-BROWED TIT-SPINETAIL

Leptasthenura xenothorax

Differs from 45 by rufous of crown extending to upper back. Back blacker with whiter, narrower shaft stripes. Pronounced white postocular streak. Throat conspicuously black and white, sharply defined from unmarked gray underparts.

Puna zone. Urubamba Valley in Cuzco, PERU.

47. STRIOLATED TIT-SPINETAIL

Leptasthenura striolata

6.2". Crown hazel, streaked black; back paler and duller, streaked blackish brown. Narrow superciliary buffy. Below pale buff, throat dusky. Central tail feathers dark brown, next pair pale-tipped, two lateral pairs mostly rufous.

Se BRAZIL in Paraná and Rio Grande do Sul.

48. PLAIN-MANTLED TIT-SPINETAIL

Leptasthenura aegithaloides *

6". Forehead and eyebrow white. Crown and nape rufous, streaked black; back pale grayish brown, somewhat streaked white on upper mantle. Throat and upper breast white, the latter lightly streaked dusky; rest of underparts pale buffy. Wing feathers edged rufescent. Tail blackish brown, feathers margined buff.

Arid coastal to temperate zone. S PERU in Puno, and from Arequipa to Atacama and occasionally to Aysén in CHILE; w ARGENTINA to Santa Cruz, e through La Pampa to Buenos Aires. Thick brush on alkaline flats, cactus deserts, oases. Parks in winter.

49. TUFTED TIT-SPINETAIL

Leptasthenura platensis

6". Crested. Crown dark brown, forehead streaked pale cinnamon. Back pale grayish brown. Throat white, spotted with black; rest of underparts buffy. Apical portion of lateral rectrices cinnamon.

Se BRAZIL in Rio Grande do Sul; URUGUAY; ARGENTINA to Chubut. Trees in dense foliage, shrubbery.

50. BROWN-CAPPED TIT-SPINETAIL

Leptasthenura fuliginiceps *

6.2". Crown chestnut brown, back light grayish brown, rump tinged rufescent. Throat white, underparts light buff (or grayish, 1). Wings and tail cinnamon rufous.

Andes of BOLIVIA in La Paz and Santa Cruz. W ARGENTINA to Córdoba, 1. Dense scrub.

51. TAWNY TIT-SPINETAIL

Leptasthenura yanacensis

6.5". Above tawny brown, forecrown and

upper tail coverts rufous. Underparts tawny buff. Wings dark brown, remiges edged rufous basally. Tail cinnamon rufous.

Puna zone. W slope of Andes in Ancash, PERU. BOLIVIA in La Paz, Cochabamba, and Potosí. Open brush, *Polylepis* woodland.

52. ARAUCARIA TIT-SPINETAIL

Leptasthenura setaria

7" (tail very long, 4.5"). Crested; crown black, feathers with sharply defined white shaft streaks. Back bright chestnut, wing feathers broadly edged chestnut. Throat white, dotted and streaked dusky; rest of underparts dull white becoming fulvous on flanks. Central tail feathers considerably longer than rest, blackish, tipped cinnamon rufous; outermost pairs cinnamon rufous, rest mostly cinnamon rufous.

Se BRAZIL in Paraná, n Santa Catarina and Rio Grande do Sul. ARGENTINA in Misiones. Auracaria woodland.

53. CHOTOY SPINETAIL

*Schoeniophylax phryganophila**

9" (tail very long, 6"). Forehead brown, crown rufous chestnut, streaked black; back sandy brown broadly streaked black, wing coverts rufous chestnut. Chin and upper throat yellow; lower throat black, bordered below by cinnamon band; sides of neck white. Underparts light buffy brown, center of abdomen white. Tail grayish brown, much graduated, central feathers considerably longer than rest.

BRAZIL from Bahía to Rio Grande do Sul; URUGUAY; PARAGUAY; n BOLIVIA; n ARGENTINA. Sawgrass swamps with low bushes and palms, sometimes savanna.

Plate 8

54. ITATIAIA SPINETAIL

Oreophylax moreirae

7.3". Upperparts, wings and tail umber brown, somewhat darker on crown, slightly rufescent on tail. Throat ochraceous, rest of underparts soiled white.

Se BRAZIL in Minas Gerais, Espírito Santo and campos of Serra do Itatiaia between 6000 and 8000 ft. and Serra dos Orgãos in Rio de Janeiro.

55. RUFOUS-CAPPED SPINETAIL

*Synallaxis ruficapilla**

6.1". Crown and nape bright orange rufous, back reddish brown, postocular streak buffy. Wing coverts and basal margins of remiges rufous chestnut. Throat silvery gray, breast gray, belly reddish brown. Tail rather short, rufous chestnut.

E BRAZIL from Pernambuco and Alagoas w to Goiás and s to Rio Grande do Sul; URUGUAY; PARAGUAY; ne ARGENTINA in Misiones and Corrientes. Forest undergrowth.

56. BUFF-BROWED SPINETAIL

*Synallaxis superciliosa**

6.7". Upperparts, wings and tail much as in 55. Forecrown olive, long eyebrow buffy white. Feathers of lower throat black basally; underparts soiled white, brownish on flanks only.

Subtropical zone. E BOLIVIA in Santa Cruz, Chuquisaca and Tarija; nw ARGENTINA in Jujuy, Salta and Tucumán. Forest undergrowth.

57. GRAY-BROWED SPINETAIL

Synallaxis poliophrys

5.5". Forehead and upperparts brown; crown, wings and tail bright rufous, eyebrow whitish. Underparts gray, flanks brown, throat speckled with white. A short-tailed species, said to have only eight rectrices.

FRENCH GUIANA.

58. AZARA'S SPINETAIL

*Synallaxis azarae**

7". Much like 56 but with no eyebrow (or much darker and grayer below, 1). Bill longer.

Upper tropical to temperate zone. Nw VENEZUELA; COLOMBIA; ECUADOR; nw PERU. Ne PERU s to La Paz and Cochabamba, BOLIVIA, 1. Forest undergrowth.

59. SOOTY-FRONTED SPINETAIL

*Synallaxis frontalis**

6.2". Very like 57 in color but bill shorter, tail less graduated with the usual 10 instead of 8 feathers.

E BRAZIL from Maranhão to Rio Grande do Sul and Mato Grosso, w to BOLIVIA and s in ARGENTINA to Catamarca and Buenos Aires. Bushy pastures, shaded thorny scrub, cerrado, long grass.

60. DUSKY SPINETAIL

Synallaxis moesta *

6.5". Forehead olive; crown, wing coverts and margins of remiges rufous chestnut; back dark olive brown. Underparts dark olive gray (or forecrown olive, underparts dark slaty gray, 1). Tail dark rufous chestnut.

Tropical, lower subtropical zones. E slope of E Andes of COLOMBIA from Meta to Caquetá. E ECUADOR and ne PERU, 1. Scrub.

61. CABANIS' SPINETAIL

Synallaxis cabanisi *

6.5". Above much like 59. Throat feathers dusky basally with pale tips. Underparts light grayish olive to light buffy brown (or no brown on forehead, throat dusky, feathers tipped gray; underparts dark olive brown, 1).

Tropical, subtropical zones. SURINAM; FRENCH GUIANA. VENEZUELA in Bolívar, 1. From Amazonas, VENEZUELA to se COLOMBIA. E PERU to n BOLIVIA. Forest undergrowth.

62. CHICLI SPINETAIL

Synallaxis spixi

6.2". Forehead, crown, and wing coverts orange ochraceous. Back and tail light olive brown. Eyebrow, sides of head, throat and breast light gray, throat feathers black basally. Center of abdomen white, sides of body like back.

E BRAZIL from Minas Gerais s to Rio Grande do Sul; PARAGUAY; URUGUAY; ARGENTINA in Entre Ríos, Santa Fe, and n Buenos Aires and probably Misiones and Corrientes. Thickets, fern brakes.

63. CINEREOUS-BREASTED SPINETAIL

Synallaxis hypospodia

Differs from 62 by brownish gray forehead and much darker underparts.

E PERU, n BOLIVIA, adjacent BRAZIL, in e Amazonas and in Mato Grosso, and in east in Ceará, Goiás and Bahía.

64. SILVERY-THROATED SPINETAIL

Synallaxis subpudica

7". Differs from 62 by much larger size, extensively grayish forehead and grayish center of abdomen.

Subtropical, temperate zones of E Andes of COLOMBIA from Santander to Cundinamarca. Forest undergrowth.

65. PALE-BREASTED SPINETAIL

Synallaxis albescens *

Much like 62. Differs mainly by grayish or brownish crown and less extensively rufous wing coverts.

Tropical, lower subtropical zones. Generally distributed e of Andes s to central ARGENTINA. W of Andes in COLOMBIA. Margarita I., Trinidad. [Sw Costa Rica; Pacific Panama.] Clumps of grass, savanna, damp open areas.

66. SLATY SPINETAIL

Synallaxis brachyura *

6.3". Forecrown dark gray; rest of crown, wing coverts and edges to base of primaries rufous chestnut. Mantle grayish becoming olive brown on lower back. Underparts gray, throat feathers edged white. Tail long (or rather short, 1), olive brown (or darker throughout with blackish tail, 2).

Tropical zone. N COLOMBIA in middle Magdalena and lower Cauca Valleys; Pacific slope to w ECUADOR, 1. E BRAZIL in s Goiás, 2. [Honduras to Panama.] Forest, open country with low bushes and tall grass.

Plate 35

67. DARK-BREASTED SPINETAIL

Synallaxis albigularis *

Much like 66 (1) but with white upper throat.

Tropical zone. COLOMBIA e of Andes to se PERU. W BRAZIL s of the Amazon e to rio Madeira and upper rio Juruá. Grassland and scrub.

68. PLAIN-CROWNED SPINETAIL

Synallaxis gujanensis *

6.2" (or 6.8", 2). Crown grayish brown passing into olivaceous brown on back. Wings and tail bright cinnamon rufous. Throat whitish, rest of underparts clay color (or throat grayish white, rest of underparts grayish, 1; or crown brown, back rufescent cinnamon, throat white, rest of underparts cinnamon buff, 2).

Tropical zone. GUIANAS west to e CO-LOMBIA. N PERU, 1. Se PERU, n BO-LIVIA, Amazonian BRAZIL e to Maranhão and n Goiás; from s Goiás south to e and s Mato Grosso and adjacent PARAGUAY, 2.

69. WHITE-BELLIED SPINETAIL

Synallaxis propinqua

6.5″. Crown and upperparts brown, tinged rufescent; lesser wing coverts and tail rufous. Throat silvery gray, breast and sides of body ashy gray, center of abdomen white. Bill rather long for the genus: .6″.

S FRENCH GUIANA; Amazonian BRAZIL s of the Amazon; n BOLIVIA; e PERU; e ECUADOR.

70. GRAY-BELLIED SPINETAIL

Synallaxis cinerascens

5.5″. Upperparts uniform olivaceous brown. Wing coverts rufous chestnut. Tail chestnut. Throat black dotted with white, rest of underparts mostly gray.

Se BRAZIL from Rio de Janeiro s to URUGUAY; ne ARGENTINA; PARA-GUAY. Forest undergrowth.

71. BLACKISH-HEADED SPINETAIL

Synallaxis tithys

6″. Recognizable from other species by black forecrown, lores, and cheeks. Back olive brown, wing coverts light cinnamon. Tail dusky. Throat blackish, rest of underparts light gray.

Tropical zone. Sw ECUADOR from Guayas s to Tumbes and Piura, PERU. Arid scrub.

72. STRIPE-BREASTED SPINETAIL

Synallaxis cinnamomea *

6.3″. Above uniform reddish brown; eyebrow and wings mostly rufous. Throat checkered black and white; underparts reddish brown streaked with buffy white. Tail dark brown.

Upper tropical and subtropical zones. VEN-EZUELA n of the Orinoco; COLOMBIA on both slopes of E Andes from Cundinamarca northward. Trinidad, Tobago. Forest undergrowth, campos.

73. RUSTY-HEADED SPINETAIL

Synallaxis fuscorufa

7″. Head, neck, breast, wings and tail rufous. Back brownish gray. Belly buff.

Upper tropical and subtropical zones of Santa Marta Mts., COLOMBIA. Bushes, tangled thickets.

74. RUFOUS SPINETAIL

Synallaxis unirufa *

7″. More or less uniform rufous chestnut to rufous. Lores black. Tail rather long, feathers decomposed.

Subtropical, temperate zones. Nw VENE-ZUELA; COLOMBIA s through Andes to Junín, PERU. Forest undergrowth.

75. RUDDY SPINETAIL

Synallaxis rutilans *

5.8″. Upperparts rufous chestnut, in some races hindcrown and back more or less umber brown; upper tail coverts dark gray, tail black. Sides of head and most of underparts rufous chestnut, throat black (or head dark grayish, throat black, back dark olivaceous; underparts dark olivaceous gray, washed on breast with rufous; wing coverts chestnut rufous; tail black, 1).

Tropical zone. GUIANAS, s VENEZUELA, most of BRAZIL (from lower Tocantins to n Maranhão, 1), e PERU, n BOLIVIA.

76. CHESTNUT-THROATED SPINETAIL

Synallaxis cherriei *

5.5″. Much like umber-backed forms of 75 but no black on throat.

Tropical zone. E ECUADOR, n PERU. BRAZIL in nw Mato Grosso. Thick undergrowth in forest and savanna.

77. NECKLACED SPINETAIL

Synallaxis stictothorax *

5″. Forehead streaked white, crown and mantle grayish brown, rump and upper tail coverts cinnamon buff. Eyebrow white. Underparts white, streaked or spotted dusky on breast. Wing coverts cinnamon rufous. Outermost three tail feathers cinnamon, rest black; cinnamon on outer web.

Tropical zone. Sw ECUADOR s to Libertad and upper Marañón Valley, PERU. Arid scrub.

78. RUSSET-BELLIED SPINETAIL

Synallaxis zimmeri

6.3". Crown gray gradually tinged rufescent on back and turning rufous on rump and upper tail coverts. Throat gray indistinctly streaked white, rest of underparts bright pinkish cinnamon rufous. Wing coverts rufous. Central tail feathers blackish brown, rest with increasing amounts of cinnamon rufous.

Upper subtropical to temperate zone. W slope of PERUVIAN Andes in Ancash between 6000-9500 ft.

79. WHITE-BROWED SPINETAIL

Synallaxis gularis

5.5". Upperparts uniform reddish brown, short eyebrow white. Throat white, rest of underparts light cinnamon brown to gray. Tail dull chestnut brown, rather short.

Subtropical, temperate zones. Nw VENEZUELA and Andes of COLOMBIA, south to w ECUADOR. PERU in Junín. Forest undergrowth.

80. RED-SHOULDERED SPINETAIL

Gyalophylax hellmayri

6.5". Above light brownish gray, sides of breast and the neck buffy brown. Wing coverts bright hazel. Below light grayish, large dull black patch on lower throat, center of abdomen buffy.

E BRAZIL in s Piauí and n and w Bahía.

81. YELLOW-THROATED SPINETAIL

Certhiaxis cinnamomea *

5.8". Upperparts, wings and tail rufescent. Sides of head and lores grayish. Upper throat tinged pale yellow, rest of underparts white more or less stained with clay color. Tail feathers pointed.

Tropical zone. GUIANAS; n VENEZUELA south to n Amazonas and n Bolívar; n COLOMBIA; BRAZIL; n BOLIVIA; PARAGUAY; URUGUAY; n and e ARGENTINA s to Buenos Aires. Trinidad. Caatinga, marshes, mangroves.

Plate 46

82. RED-AND-WHITE SPINETAIL

Certhiaxis mustelina

5.5". Much like 81 but smaller, lores black, no yellow on throat, underparts white. Bill proportionately larger.

Ne PERU; Amazonian BRAZIL.

83. WHITE-WHISKERED SPINETAIL

Poecilurus candei *

6". Crown and nape grayish olive, sides of head and lower throat black, upper throat and sides of neck white (or virtually no white, 1). Back, breast and flanks chestnut rufous (or pale cinnamon, 2), center of belly white. Tail chestnut rufous, central feathers terminally black.

Nw VENEZUELA west to w side of Santa Marta Mts., COLOMBIA; e of Santa Marta Mts. and lower Magdalena Valley, 2; in middle Magdalena Valley, 1. Weedy pastures, thorny scrub, cacti.

84. HOARY-THROATED SPINETAIL

Poecilurus kollari

Differs from 83 by pale gray lores and cheeks, cinnamon rufous auriculars, black throat with feathers tipped silvery, and no black on end of tail.

N BRAZIL in Roraima. Campos.

85. OCHRE-CHEEKED SPINETAIL

Poecilurus scutatus *

5.7". Upperparts uniform umber brown, wings and tail rufous. Lores and eyebrow white, eyebrow becoming ochraceous behind eye; cheeks and sides of neck ochraceous. Upper throat white, lower throat black, breast and sides of body dull ochraceous, center of belly white.

BRAZIL from Maranhão and Ceará s to São Paulo. E BOLIVIA; ARGENTINA from Jujuy and w Chaco to Catamarca. Forest undergrowth, cerradão.

Plate 8

86. SULPHUR-BEARDED SPINETAIL

Cranioleuca sulphurifera

6". Upperparts light cinnamon brown, eyebrow and cheeks light cinnamon. Underparts uniform buffy cinnamon. Remiges brown, primaries edged cinnamon basally, secondaries bordered black basally. Tail rather long: 2.8″, much graduated, central feathers brown, edged rufous; rest light rufous.

BRAZIL in Rio Grande do Sul; URUGUAY; e ARGENTINA to Río Negro. Open woodland, climbs trees.

87. GRAY-HEADED SPINETAIL

Cranioleuca semicinerea *

5.5″. Head slightly crested, feathers narrow. Head and neck pale gray. Above reddish chestnut, below white, tinged gray.

E BRAZIL in Ceará, Bahía and se Goiás.

88. OLIVE SPINETAIL

Cranioleuca obsoleta

5″. Above uniform olive brown. Wing coverts and tail rufous chestnut. Eyebrow and underparts dirty buff.

Se BRAZIL, São Paulo to Rio Grande do Sul; e PARAGUAY; ne ARGENTINA in Misiones and Corrientes. Forest, climbs trees.

89. STRIPE-CROWNED SPINETAIL

Cranioleuca pyrrhophia *

5.5″. Crown strikingly streaked buffy and black, conspicuous eyebrow white. Back dull brown to pinkish brown. Underparts white. Wing coverts rufous chestnut. Tail cinnamon rufous.

Upper tropical and subtropical zones. BOLIVIA; PARAGUAY; BRAZIL in Rio Grande do Sul; URUGUAY; ARGENTINA south to n Río Negro and n Neuquén. Clearings, thickets, climbs trees.

90. CRESTED SPINETAIL

Cranioleuca subcristata *

6″. Center of crown olive, streaked blackish, bordered at sides and back with rufous. Back olivaceous brown; wings and tail cinnamon rufous. Throat whitish, rest of underparts light yellowish gray.

Tropical, subtropical zones. VENEZUELA n of the Orinoco; COLOMBIA from Norte de Santander to Boyacá. Forest.

91. STREAK-CAPPED SPINETAIL

Cranioleuca hellmayri

Differs from 90 by chestnut, black-streaked crown, whitish eyebrow and throat.

Subtropical to temperate zone of Santa Marta Mts., COLOMBIA. Forest, often among bromelias.

Plate 46

92. ASH-BROWED SPINETAIL

Cranioleuca curtata *

Differs from 91 by olivaceous forehead, unstreaked chestnut crown, gray eyebrow and darker coloration throughout, with suggestion of streaking on underparts.

Subtropical zone from head of Magdalena Valley, COLOMBIA, s to Cuzco, PERU. Forest.

93. TEPUI SPINETAIL

Cranioleuca demissa

6″. Crown, nape, shoulders and tail rufous. Wings brown, tinged cinnamon; back olive brown. Sides of head and eyebrow buffy. Chin streaked black and white, rest of underparts ashy gray.

Subtropical zone. W GUYANA; VENEZUELA in isolated mts. of Bolívar and s Amazonas; mts. along BRAZILIAN border. Forest.

94. RED-FACED SPINETAIL

Cranioleuca erythrops *

5.7″. Crown and sides of head rufous. Back olive brown with rufous tinge; wings and tail rufous. Underparts buffy brown or grayish, grayer on throat.

Upper tropical and subtropical zones. COLOMBIA from w slope of Central Andes south to w ECUADOR. [Mts. of Costa Rica and Panama.] Thickets bordering humid forests.

95. RUSTY-BACKED SPINETAIL

Cranioleuca vulpina *

6″. Upperparts, wings and tail bright rufous red. Forehead more or less streaked white and dusky. Lores and eyebrow white. Throat whitish, becoming drab white on breast and belly.

Tropical zone. VENEZUELA south to n Bolívar and n Amazonas; COLOMBIA in Vichada; BRAZIL (in east s only to Paraná); n BOLIVIA; e PERU. [Coiba I., Panama.] Pastures, thickets, near water. Climbs trees.

96. PALLID SPINETAIL

Cranioleuca pallida

5.3″. Forehead whitish spotted with black. Long eyebrow white. Crown, back, wings and tail light reddish brown. Underparts dirty white.

E BRAZIL from s Minas Gerais to São Paulo.

97. LINE-CHEEKED SPINETAIL

Cranioleuca antisiensis*

5.8″ (or 6.8″, 1). Crown, wings and tail rufous; eyebrow white. Back light olivaceous reddish brown (or gray with olive tinge, 1). Throat white, rest of underparts dirty white (or throat and breast white becoming gray on belly, 1).

Subtropical zone. W ECUADOR south on w slope of Andes to Lima, PERU. Temperate zone in PERU from Amazonas to Huánuco, 1. Woods, thickets, climbs trees.

98. MARCAPATA SPINETAIL

Cranioleuca marcapatae

6.5″. Crown, back, wings and tail rufous chestnut; crown bordered laterally by black. Sides of head buff, throat whitish, underparts light drab.

Marcapata, 10,000 ft., Cuzco, PERU.

99. LIGHT-CROWNED SPINETAIL

Cranioleuca albiceps*

6″. Crown white (or cinnamon buff, 1) bordered laterally with black, sides of head sooty. Back, wings and tail chestnut rufous. Center of throat white, underparts olivaceous gray.

Subtropical, temperate zones. BOLIVIA in La Paz; in Cochabamba, 1.

100. CREAMY-CRESTED SPINETAIL

Cranioleuca albicapilla*

6.7″. Crown buff to cinnamon, back olivaceous; wing coverts and tail rufous chestnut. Throat white, rest of underparts soiled white becoming olivaceous on flanks and crissum.

Temperate zone. Andes of PERU from Junín to Cuzco.

101. SCALED SPINETAIL

Cranioleuca muelleri

6″. Above olive brown; wings and tail rufous. Throat whitish, rest of underparts brownish olive; feathers with whitish subterminal band and narrow dark apical margin, both becoming obsolete on belly.

BRAZIL on both sides of lower Amazon and on Mexiana I.

102. SPECKLED SPINETAIL

Cranioleuca gutturata*

5.5″. Above much like 101. Chin spot yellowish, lower throat white, rest of underparts fulvous white with small black spots on breast.

Tropical zone. SURINAM across s VENEZUELA to se COLOMBIA, south through w and central Amazonian BRAZIL to e ECUADOR, e PERU, and n BOLIVIA. Forest.

103. GREAT SPINETAIL

Siptornopsis hypochondriacus

7.5″. Upperparts light earthy brown, lesser wing coverts rufous. Long eyebrow and underparts white, band of dusky streaks across breast. Tail rather long (4″), graduated. Bill black.

Subtropical, temperate zones. N and w PERU in Marañón watershed in Cajamarca, Libertad and Ancash.

Plate 8

Thistletails

Schizoeaca: Characteristics: Tail graduated, long (4″), feathers narrow, stiff, pointed; the outermost scarcely longer than tail coverts, central pair longest. Webs thin and ragged. They are inhabitants of mossy trees, shrubs, and wet grassland.

104. OCHRE-BROWED THISTLETAIL

Schizoeaca coryi

7″. Upperparts, wings and tail warm earthy brown. Long eyebrow, sides of head and the chin bright cinnamon. Underparts grayish. Tail like back.

Subtropical to páramo zone. Nw VENE-

ZUELA in Táchira, Mérida and Trujillo between 7000-12,500 ft.

105. WHITE-CHINNED THISTLETAIL

Schizoeaca fuliginosa

7.3". Upperparts, wings and tail olivaceous brown to chestnut brown. Eyebrow gray to buffy gray, eye ring white. Underparts gray to light brownish gray.

Temperate to páramo zone. VENEZUELA in Táchira; E and Central Andes of COLOMBIA south to n PERU. Tangled undergrowth.

Plate 8

106. MOUSE-COLORED THISTLETAIL

Schizoeaca griseomurina

Differs from 105 by dull sepia back and tail, and no eyebrow.

Páramo zone. S ECUADOR.

107. EYE-RINGED THISTLETAIL

Schizoeaca palpebralis

7.3". Upperparts, wings and tail chestnut; very wide, prominent white eye ring. Chin orange rufous. Underparts gray, feathers indistinctly dark-centered.

Subtropical, temperate zones of central PERU in Junín.

The following two species are better regarded as subspecies of 107. It is not impossible that all thistletails belong to one superspecies, according to C. Vaurie (*in lit.*).

108. PUNA THISTLETAIL

Schizoeaca helleri

In color between 105 and 107. Upperparts and cinnamon rufous chin spot as in 107; gray postocular streak and smoky gray underparts as in 105.

Puna zone. Se PERU in Cuzco.

109. BLACK-THROATED THISTLETAIL

Schizoeaca harterti

7.2". Upperparts, wings and tail light reddish brown. Eye ring, lores, eyebrow and chin white; throat black with white shaft streaks, rest of underparts light smoky gray.

Subtropical, temperate zones in BOLIVIA (La Paz; Cochabamba).

Canasteros

Asthenes is often distinguishable from relatives by its well-developed orange, chestnut or white-dotted black throat patch in adults; tail much graduated, feathers more or less pointed.

110. LESSER CANASTERO

Asthenes pyrrholeuca *

6.2". Above uniform dark reddish brown to light grayish brown, wing coverts pale rufescent; underparts pale grayish white, chin spot orange rufous. Central tail feathers dark brown, three outer pairs dull rufous.

Breeds in s ARGENTINA from Río Negro to Santa Cruz and in s CHILE; winters north to s BOLIVIA, PARAGUAY and URUGUAY. Scrub, stony slopes, semiarid thorny country. Nests near mountain streams and marshy meadows.

111. CREAMY-BREASTED CANASTERO

Asthenes dorbignyi *

6.3". Upperparts reddish brown; wing coverts, tertials and upper tail coverts rufous. Eyebrow gray. Underparts buffy white, rufescent on flanks and under tail coverts. Chin spot chestnut (or no chin spot, 1). Tail black, outer feathers edged chestnut.

Arid subtropical and temperate zones. PERU in Huancavelica, 1; thence s through Andes to Tarapacá, CHILE, BOLIVIA and w ARGENTINA to Mendoza. On ground among scattered bushes, often in watered valleys.

112. CHESTNUT CANASTERO

Asthenes steinbachi

6.4". Above drab brown, upper tail coverts vinaceous cinnamon. Underparts drab gray, no rufous chin spot; throat whitish, feathers edged dusky. Central tail feathers brown, outermost two pairs bright cinnamon, intervening ones mostly cinnamon.

Andean zone of w ARGENTINA to Mendoza. Hab. as in 111.

113. BERLEPSCH'S CANASTERO

Asthenes berlepschi

6.6". Like 111 (1) in color, but larger and wing coverts edged chestnut.

BOLIVIA known only from Chilcani, Monte

Illampu, and on n slope of Cordillera Real, La Paz.

114. SHORT-BILLED CANASTERO

Asthenes baeri *

6.1". Above grayish brown, tinged rufescent on rump; below whitish, grayish on breast, throat patch pale orange rufous. Four central tail feathers blackish, rest cinnamon. Bill very short.

BRAZIL in Rio Grande do Sul; URUGUAY; PARAGUAY; ARGENTINA s to Río Negro. Open scrubby forest.

115. PATAGONIAN CANASTERO

Asthenes patagonica

6.1". Above grayish brown; below grayish, tinged ochraceous on belly; throat patch black with white shaft streaks. Tail comparatively short, black, outer web of outer rectrix rufous. Bill very short.

ARGENTINA from Mendoza to Chubut. Semiarid scrub.

116. DUSKY-TAILED CANASTERO

Asthenes humicola *

6.3". Above brown, eyebrow white, wing coverts rufous. Throat white, dotted with black; breast and center of belly grayish obscurely pale-streaked, flanks and upper tail coverts cinnamon. Tail blackish, outermost feather rufous at base with rufous shaft.

CHILE from Atacama to s Maule up to 6000 ft. and Arauco; w ARGENTINA in Mendoza. Thickets, semiarid thorn scrub.

117. CORDILLERAN CANASTERO

Asthenes modesta *

6.1". Upperparts dark grayish brown to light sandy brown. Eyebrow whitish. Remiges with broad basal cinnamon band. Throat chestnut, dotted white; underparts soiled white. Tail feathers with cinnamon rufous outer webs, black inner webs.

Temperate, puna zones. Central PERU s in CHILE to Magallanes and through BOLIVIA to Santa Cruz, ARGENTINA. Semiarid land and stony slopes, sheltered valleys in winter.

118. CACTUS CANASTERO

Asthenes cactorum *

5.7". Bill long for the genus (.8"). Above sandy brown, below dirty white. Wing coverts and basal band on remiges rufous. Throat patch pale cinnamon. Four central tail feathers blackish brown, rest cinnamon.

Arid Pacific slope of PERU in Lima, Ica and Arequipa up to 7500 ft. Among columnar cacti in rocky ravines.

119. CANYON CANASTERO

Asthenes pudibunda *

6.5" (or 6", bill shorter, 1). Above dark reddish brown. Throat patch rufous chestnut or buff, dotted with white; underparts brownish gray. Tail rufous chestnut, central feathers darkest, feathers rounded (or sharply pointed, 1).

Temperate zone. W PERU from Ancash to Arequipa. BOLIVIA in La Paz and Cochabamba. Rocky cactus and brush covered hillsides. Thorn scrub, hedges, *Polylepis* woodland, 1.

120. RUSTY-FRONTED CANASTERO

Asthenes ottonis

6.5". Tail feathers narrow, central ones longer than usual in the genus. Forehead cinnamon rufous, prominent superciliary buff. Wing coverts rufous. Upperparts reddish brown, large throat patch light ochraceous. Underparts mostly buffy gray, indistinctly pale-streaked; flanks and under tail coverts bright buffy brown. Tail mostly rufous.

Temperate zone of se PERU in Huancavelica, Apurimac and Cuzco.

121. STREAK-BACKED CANASTERO

Asthenes wyatti *

6" (or 6.7", 1). Above brown streaked black. Shoulders and basal band of remiges rufous, throat with indistinct pale buffy patch, chin white. Underparts brownish gray (or buffy, 1), indistinctly spotted on breast with dusky. Central tail feathers dark brown, rest rufous, dusky along shaft.

Temperate to puna zone. W VENEZUELA. COLOMBIA in Santa Marta Mts. and n part of E Andes. Central and s ECUADOR. PERU in Lima, Junín, Huancavelica, Cuzco and Puno, 1. Shrubs and rocks, marshy areas.

122. AUSTRAL CANASTERO

Asthenes anthoides *

6.5" (or 7", 1). Upperparts sandy brown heavily streaked black (or reddish brown less heavily streaked, 1); wings much as in 121 (or with larger, paler shoulder patch, 1). Chin white, indistinct throat patch pale cinnamon. Below buffy with narrow shaft streaks on upper breast. Central tail feathers dark (or light, 1) brown, rest blackish basally, broadly tipped cinnamon.

Puna zone. PERU in Puno s through BOLIVIA to La Rioja, ARGENTINA, 1 (*punensis* group, possibly a distinct species). ARGENTINA from w Neuquén and CHILE from Aconcagua to Tierra del Fuego and Staten I. Tussocks of grass, damp meadows, open slopes.

123. CORDOBA CANASTERO

Asthenes sclateri

Very similar to 122 (1) but paler, black streaks on back smaller and tail less broadly tipped cinnamon, rectrices soft.

Mountains of Córdoba, ARGENTINA. Bushy pastures.

124. STREAK-THROATED CANASTERO

Asthenes humilis *

6.5". Above brown, back streaked dusky, basal band on remiges pale cinnamon. Narrow eyebrow white. Throat patch cinnamon rufous. Underparts fulvous white, streaked dusky on lower throat and upper breast. Tail feathers dark brown, outer ones narrowly edged cinnamon.

Arid temperate zone. Andes of PERU s to La Paz, BOLIVIA. Largely terrestrial on stony grassland.

125. HUDSON'S CANASTERO

Asthenes hudsoni

Not unlike 123. Back streaks blacker, flanks streaked instead of plain. Chin pale yellowish instead of unmarked, and central tail feathers with dark stripe along shaft instead of plain, feathers very stiff.

URUGUAY. ARGENTINA from Buenos Aires to Chubut. Thistles and weed patches, marshes with rushes.

126. JUNIN CANASTERO

Asthenes virgata

7". Upperparts brown, feathers with pale streak along shaft and edged blackish; remiges with pale cinnamon basal band. Large throat patch dull cinnamon, underparts dirty white. Four central tail feathers dark brown, rest dull cinnamon along outer web.

Páramo zone of central PERU in Junín.

127. SCRIBBLE-TAILED CANASTERO

Asthenes maculicauda

7". Forecrown chestnut. Back black, streaked with yellowish buff. Underparts soiled white, somewhat streaked on breast with dusky; no chin patch. Tail brown, irregularly lined and spotted with black.

Temperate, páramo zones. Se PERU in Puno; BOLIVIA in La Paz and Cochabamba. Nw ARGENTINA in Tucumán and Catamarca (Sierra Aconquija). Bushy pastures.

128. MANY-STRIPED CANASTERO

Asthenes flammulata *

6.7". Upperparts blackish with white streaks, crown streaked tawny, wing patch chestnut rufous. Throat white (or with deep cinnamon rufous throat patch, 1; or throat tawny buff, 2); rest of underparts whitish, lightly to heavily streaked dusky. Central tail feathers dark brown, rest more or less marked with cinnamon (or outer four pairs of tail feathers mostly dull cinnamon, 3).

Temperate, páramo zones. COLOMBIA in E Andes, 1; Central Andes s to ECUADOR, 2; PERU in Cajamarca, 3; from Amazonas to Junín. Bushy slopes.

Plate 46

129. LINE-FRONTED CANASTERO

Asthenes urubambensis *

7.5". Tail feathers narrow, very pointed. Upperparts plain chocolate brown (or narrowly streaked fulvous on crown and mantle, 1). Long eyebrow white. Underparts much as in 128. No rufous chestnut wing patch.

Temperate zone. PERU in Libertad (Marañón Valley) and Huánuco, 1; and in Cuzco and nw BOLIVIA in La Paz. Moss-covered trees, vines, thickets.

130. BAY-CAPPED WREN-SPINETAIL

Spartanoica maluroides

5.5". Forecrown rufous, upperparts light sandy brown streaked with black. Below white with ochraceous tinge. Tail feathers graduated, central ones very pointed, sandy brown, black along shaft, outer feathers with dull rufous base.

BRAZIL in Rio Grande do Sul; URUGUAY; e ARGENTINA s to Río Negro. Freshwater and tidal marshes, bushy pastures.

Softtails, Thornbirds

In the genera *Thripophaga* and *Phacellodomus* the tail is graduated, feathers broad and rounded at the tips. *Phacellodomus* builds enormous stick nests in trees.

131. STRIATED SOFTTAIL

Thripophaga macroura

7". Crown chestnut with pale shaft streaks, back reddish brown with pale shaft streaks. Throat rusty buff. Underparts brown with broad pale streaks. Tail pale tawny, feathers broad, rounded.

Se BRAZIL in e Bahía and Espírito Santo. Forest.

132. ORINOCO SOFTTAIL

Thripophaga cherriei

6.5". Above olive brown slightly rufescent on back; upper tail coverts and tail chestnut rufous. Wings bright rufous brown. Chin and upper throat bright orange rufous, rest of underparts light olive brown, front and sides of neck with buff shaft stripes.

Tropical zone. Upper Orinoco, VENEZUELA. Forest.

133. PLAIN SOFTTAIL

Thripophaga fusciceps*

7". Upperparts light olivaceous brown to rufescent brown, paler on crown. Eyebrow pale. Underparts light drab brown. Wings and tail rufous chestnut.

Tropical zone. E ECUADOR. PERU in Junín and Puno. BOLIVIA in Cochabamba. BRAZIL along upper and middle Amazon.

134. RUSSET-MANTLED SOFTTAIL

Thripophaga berlepschi

6.7". Forecrown and upper chin pale buffy; upperparts, breast, wings and tail tawny rufous, belly light olive brown.

Temperate zone of PERU in s Amazonas.

135. LITTLE THORNBIRD

Phacellodomus sibilatrix

5". Forehead narrowly chestnut; broad eyebrow light gray. Upperparts earthy brown, tinged rufescent on rump. Lesser wing coverts, base of secondaires, and lateral tail feathers cinnamon rufous. Underparts dirty white.

Central PARAGUAY; URUGUAY; ARGENTINA s to Córdoba and n Buenos Aires. Scrub.

136. RUFOUS-FRONTED THORNBIRD

Phacellodomus rufifrons*

6.6". Upperparts earthy brown, forecrown cinnamon rufous, eyebrow grayish white, wings and tail like back, bases of secondaries dull rufescent. Underparts soiled white.

Campos, tropical zone. N VENEZUELA; ne COLOMBIA. N PERU. Ne BOLIVIA. Nw ARGENTINA to n Catamarca. BRAZIL from Pernambuco to Minas Gerais and Mato Grosso. Caatinga, cerrado, grassland.

Plate 8

137. STREAK-FRONTED THORNBIRD

Phacellodomus striaticeps*

6.5". Above earthy brown, crown feathers with chestnut bases and pale tips. Below whitish. Remiges cinnamon basally. Upper tail coverts rufous; central tail feathers like back, rest cinnamon, all but outermost tipped dusky.

Temperate, páramo zones. Se PERU s through BOLIVIA to Catamarca, ARGENTINA. Open, bushy slopes.

138. RED-EYED THORNBIRD

Phacellodomus erythrophthalmus*

7.5". Above reddish brown; forehead, throat and upper breast chestnut rufous. Underparts brown, lighter than back. Tail rufous chestnut.

Coastal forests of e BRAZIL from s Bahía to Rio Grande do Sul.

139. GREATER THORNBIRD

Phacellodomus ruber

8″. Crown, wings and tail rufous chestnut; back reddish brown to rufous brown. Lores and underparts dirty white, tinged gray on breast. (Cf. 31)

S BRAZIL in Bahía and Minas Gerais west to n BOLIVIA; PARAGUAY; ARGENTINA to n Buenos Aires. Groves of mauritia palms, wet cerrado.

140. FRECKLE-BREASTED THORNBIRD

Phacellodomus striaticollis *

7″. Crown chestnut, back and wings dull earthy brown, primaries and secondaries edged dull chestnut. Throat white; breast feathers orange rufous, tipped white. Central tail feathers like back; rest dull, dark chestnut.

BRAZIL from Paraná s to URUGUAY; ARGENTINA from Misiones to Jujuy south to n Buenos Aires; e BOLIVIA. Bushy country.

141. CHESTNUT-BACKED THORNBIRD

Phacellodomus dorsalis

8″. Bill rather long: .8″. Crown dull rufous; hindneck, lower back and rump olivaceous brown; center of back, lesser wing coverts and margins of remiges chestnut. Underparts much as in 140 but whiter, throat more extensively white. Tail chestnut.

Arid and semiarid subtropical and lower temperate zones in Cajamarca, PERU.

142. LARK-LIKE BRUSHRUNNER

Coryphistera alaudina

6″. Conspicuously crested. Forecrown reddish brown, crest mostly blackish, patch below eye white; ear coverts cinnamon. Back streaked grayish buff and blackish. Underparts white, throat spotted with, and breast streaked with cinnamon rufous. Central tail feathers blackish, pale-edged; rest orange rufous with broad black tips.

BRAZIL in Rio Grande do Sul; URUGUAY; w PARAGUAY; e BOLIVIA; ARGENTINA s to Entre Ríos and Mendoza. Open scrub, thorny bushes, partly terrestrial.

143. FIREWOOD-GATHERER

Anumbius annumbi *

8.2″. Upperparts light brown, lightly streaked on crown and back with dusky. Forehead rufescent, eyebrow white; throat white, margined all around by small black spots; rest of underparts buffy. Inner remiges mostly dull chestnut brown. Central tail feathers pointed, grayish brown; rest black, tipped white.

BRAZIL in central Goiás and s Minas Gerais to URUGUAY; PARAGUAY; ARGENTINA, Misiones to central Formosa s to Chubut. Open scrub, weed and thistle patches, partly terrestrial. Builds large stick nests.

Plate 25

144. SPECTACLED PRICKLETAIL

Siptornis striaticollis

4.2″. Crown, nape and wing coverts chestnut; back and inner remiges reddish brown. Conspicuous eyebrow white. Underparts light grayish brown, streaked with white on throat and breast. Tail rufous chestnut.

Subtropical zone of slopes of E and Central Andes above middle and upper Magdalena Valley, COLOMBIA. E slope of Andes of ECUADOR (Mapoto). Forest.

Plate 46

145. DOUBLE-BANDED GRAYTAIL

Xenerpestes minlosi *

4.2″. Above dark gray, forehead blackish, lores and postocular streak white; wing coverts tipped white forming a double wing bar. Underparts creamy white. Tail gray.

Tropical zone. COLOMBIA from w Boyacá w to Pacific coast then s to río San Juan Valley. [E Panama.] Undergrowth, gleans on underside of leaves.

Plate 46

146. EQUATORIAL GRAYTAIL

Xenerpestes singularis

4.2″. Eyebrow white, forehead rufous, hindcrown streaked rufous; back olivaceous gray, wings like back but no olivaceous tinge. Below pale yellowish, streaked blackish. Tail slaty gray.

Subtropical zone. E ECUADOR (Mapoto).

147. ORANGE-FRONTED PLUSHCROWN

Metopothrix aurantiacus

4.4″. Forehead orange yellow, feathers rather stiff and plushy. Back, wings and tail olive; wing coverts pale-edged. Chin and throat orange yellow becoming buffy yellow on rest of underparts. Legs dull yellow.

Tropical zone. Se COLOMBIA to e PERU and n BOLIVIA; BRAZIL s of the Amazon e to rio Purús. Forest, clearings.

Plate 35

148. PEARLED TREERUNNER

Margarornis squamiger *

6.2". Upperparts chestnut (tinged olive on crown and hindneck, 1). Eyebrow and throat yellowish white; feathers of rest of underparts sulphur narrowly edged black (or white broadly edged black, 1), giving scaled appearance. Inner remiges and tail chestnut, tail feathers ending in bare spines.

Upper tropical to temperate zone. Nw VENEZUELA and COLOMBIA s to Cajamarca, Junín and Cuzco, PERU, 1; from Puno, PERU, to La Paz and Cochabamba, BOLIVIA. Forest.

Plate 35

149. FULVOUS-DOTTED TREERUNNER

Margarornis stellatus

6". Above uniform chestnut. Throat white, lower throat feathers edged black, rest of underparts rufous chestnut; breast feathers with white, black-encircled dots. Tail like back, ending in bare spines.

Upper tropical and subtropical zones. W slope of W Andes of COLOMBIA; nw ECUADOR. Wet, mossy forest.

150. RORAIMAN BARBTAIL

Roraimia adusta *

6". Crown and nape deep olive brown, ocular region and ear coverts black; postocular stripe, back, wings and tail dark chestnut. Throat white; breast buff, feathers margined black giving streaked appearance. Tail feathers ending in soft spines.

Subtropical zone. W GUYANA, s VENEZUELA and adjacent BRAZIL. Forest, shrubbery.

151. RUSTY-WINGED BARBTAIL

Premnornis guttuligera *

5.8". Above brown, eyebrow and streaks on hindneck buff. Throat fulvous; feathers of breast and upper belly buff, edged black giving scaled appearance. Tail rufous chestnut, feathers more or less rounded.

Subtropical zone. Extreme nw VENEZUELA; COLOMBIA west to e slope of W Andes, thence s to Cuzco, PERU. Wet, mossy forest.

152. SPOTTED BARBTAIL

Premnoplex brunnescens *

5.8". Upperparts umber brown, feathers with dusky edges (with pale shaft streaks on mantle, 1). Throat and underparts light to dark ochraceous, feathers edged black giving scaled appearance. Tail dark brown, feathers ending in soft spines.

Subtropical zone. VENEZUELA n of the Orinoco from Miranda to the Cauca Valley, COLOMBIA. E ECUADOR s to Junín, PERU; in Puno s to La Paz and Cochabamba, BOLIVIA, 1. Humid forest.

Plate 25

153. WHITE-THROATED BARBTAIL

Premnoplex tatei *

6". Crown dusky brown; back chestnut brown, feathers black-centered. Throat and breast fulvous white, belly umber brown streaked fulvous white. Tail short (2.3"), blackish brown, feathers ending in soft spines.

Upper tropical and subtropical zones. Coastal mts. of VENEZUELA e to Anzoátegui. Forest undergrowth.

154. BUFFY TUFTEDCHEEK

Pseudocolaptes lawrencii *

8". Crown and nape dusky brown with pale shaft streaks; back, rump and upper tail coverts uniform chestnut. Throat and elongated ear tufts white; upper breast feathers white, edged dusky giving scaled appearance; center of breast and belly cinnamon rufous, sides of body chestnut rufous. Tail chestnut, slightly stiffened, feathers pointed.

Upper tropical and subtropical zones. W slope of W Andes of COLOMBIA to nw ECUADOR. Forest.

155. STREAKED TUFTEDCHEEK

Pseudocolaptes boissonneautii *

Rather like 154 but crown sometimes black and back brown, streaked fulvous; wings and upper tail coverts rufous. Underparts paler, white of throat extending further down on breast, (or throat to upper belly soiled white with virtually no black markings, 1).

Subtropical, temperate zones. Andes of nw VENEZUELA and ne COLOMBIA, 1; thence south to nw PERU and La Paz and Cochabamba, BOLIVIA. Forest.

Plate 46

156. POINT-TAILED PALMCREEPER

Berlepschia rikeri

8". Head, neck and underparts streaked black and white. Back, wings and tail bright rufous chestnut. Tail feathers pointed.

Tropical zone. GUYANA; s VENEZUELA in Amazonas; locally in Amazonian BRAZIL and in Goiás. Mauritia palms; climbs trunks.

Plate 25

157. RUFOUS CACHOLOTE

Pseudoseisura cristata *

9". Crest sandy grayish, rest of plumage cinnamon rufous, paler below.

E BRAZIL from Paraiba and Piauí to Minas Gerais and w Mato Grosso; PARAGUAY; e and n BOLIVIA. Caatinga, cerrado, open woodland; climbs trees.

Plate 8

158. BROWN CACHOLOTE

Pseudoseisura lophotes *

10.5". Crest dark brown; back sandy brown, tinged rufous; rump and upper tail coverts cinnamon rufous. Throat rufous, rest of underparts rufescent, feathers edged grayish. Tail rufous.

BRAZIL in Rio Grande do Sul; URUGUAY; PARAGUAY; e BOLIVIA; ARGENTINA s to Entre Ríos, Córdoba and Mendoza. Open groves of low trees; climbs.

159. WHITE-THROATED CACHOLOTE

Pseudoseisura gutturalis *

10". Rather like 158 but much duller and browner, with brown tail and white throat.

Most of ARGENTINA from Jujuy, Salta and Tucumán on the w, and from Buenos Aires on the east s to Santa Cruz. Arid, stony, brush-covered country; climbs.

160. STRIPED WOODHAUNTER

Hyloctistes subulatus *

6.7". Upperparts pale brown with pale shaft streaks on head and mantle, wings rufous brown, rump and tail cinnamon rufous (or much darker with no streaks on mantle, 1). Throat and breast fulvous, breast feathers dark-edged, rest of underparts pale brown.

Tropical zone. Se COLOMBIA and s VENEZUELA south to w Amazonian BRAZIL and se PERU. W of Andes in w COLOMBIA and ECUADOR, 1. [Nicaragua to Panama.] Forest.

161. CHESTNUT-WINGED HOOKBILL

Ancistrops strigilatus *

7". Bill heavy, hooked. Above dark olive brown with buffy white streaks. Wings and tail rufous chestnut. Underparts yellowish buff, flammulated dusky.

Tropical zone. E COLOMBIA south to e ECUADOR, e PERU, and w Amazonian BRAZIL to rio Tapajós. Forest.

Plate 46

162. WHITE-COLLARED FOLIAGE-GLEANER

Anabazenops fuscus

7.5". Mandible somewhat upcurved. Above brown; long eyebrow, throat and nuchal collar white. Underparts pale buffy brown.

Se BRAZIL from Minas Gerais to Santa Catarina.

163. BUFF-BROWED FOLIAGE-GLEANER

Syndactyla rufosuperciliata *

7". Upperparts olivaceous brown to olive. Superciliary buff. Throat buffy white, rest of underparts streaked olive and buffy white. Tail rufous.

Subtropical zone. PERU (w slope of Andes in Cajamarca) s through BOLIVIA to PARAGUAY, se BRAZIL, and La Rioja and n Buenos Aires, ARGENTINA. Dense bushes, sometimes swamps; climbs.

164. LINEATED FOLIAGE-GLEANER

Syndactyla subalaris *

7". Crown and mantle reddish brown, finely streaked fulvous (or blackish, faintly streaked fulvous, 1); rest of back plain brown. Upper tail coverts and tail rufous chestnut. Throat buffy white. Rest of underparts olivaceous brown narrowly (or broadly, 1) streaked buffy white.

Subtropical zone. COLOMBIA in W and Central Andes and in w ECUADOR. Nw VENEZUELA, e COLOMBIA and Magdalena Valley south through Andes to se PERU, 1. [Costa Rica, Panama.] Forest.

165. GUTTULATED FOLIAGE-GLEANER
Syndactyla guttulata *

7.5". Very much like 164 but much more broadly streaked below. Crown virtually without shaft streaks. Eyebrow cinnamon buff.

Upper tropical and subtropical zones. VENEZUELA n of the Orinoco w to Yaracuy. Forest.

166. PERUVIAN RECURVEBILL
Simoxenops ucayalae

8.2". Upperparts dark ruddy brown, darker on crown; narrow, pale superciliary. Rump and upper tail coverts chestnut. Underparts amber brown. Tail bay. Mandible upcurved.

E PERU on upper río Ucayali and río Madre de Dios.

167. BOLIVIAN RECURVEBILL
Simoxenops striatus

7.5". Above reddish brown, streaks on sides of neck and hindneck cinnamon rufous, streaks on mantle fulvous. Upper tail coverts and tail rufous chestnut. Throat cinnamon rufous; rest of underparts paler, duller, becoming brownish on under tail coverts. Mandible upcurved.

Tropical zone. BOLIVIA in La Paz and Cochabamba.

Plate 25

168. SCALY-THROATED FOLIAGE-GLEANER
Anabacerthia variegaticeps *

6.2". Crown dark olive, broad superciliary bright ochraceous; back reddish brown. Throat whitish, lower throat feathers edged dusky; upper breast ochraceous, pale-streaked, fading to pale brownish on belly. Tail rufous chestnut.

Upper tropical and subtropical zones. Pacific COLOMBIA s to Loja, ECUADOR. [S Mexico to w Panama.] Forest.

169. MONTANE FOLIAGE-GLEANER
Anabacerthia striaticollis *

6.2". Crown olive brown; back, wings and tail umber brown. Narrow eyebrow and eye ring buffy white. Lores and malar streak dusky. Below olivaceous buff, streaked whitish in some races.

Upper tropical and subtropical zones. N VENEZUELA from Miranda w to Andes of COLOMBIA thence south through e ECUADOR and e PERU to n BOLIVIA. Forest.

170. WHITE-BROWED FOLIAGE-GLEANER
Anabacerthia amaurotis

6.7". Above brown, crown feathers spotted white in center and subapically margined black; broad superciliary buffy white. Throat white, underparts pale buffy brown with large white spots on foreneck and breast. Tail bright rufous.

Se BRAZIL in Rio de Janeiro and São Paulo. Ne ARGENTINA in Misiones.

171. BLACK-CAPPED FOLIAGE-GLEANER
Philydor atricapillus

6.5". Crown blackish brown, superciliary ochraceous. Mark in front of eye and ear coverts silvery white surrounded by black. Back cinnamon brown. Underparts tawny ochraceous. Tail cinnamon rufous.

E BRAZIL from Bahía to Santa Catarina; e PARAGUAY and n ARGENTINA. Forest.

172. NEBLINA FOLIAGE-GLEANER
Philydor hylobius

7". Much like 171 but ear coverts all brown and general color darker.

Subtropical zone. Mountains on VENEZUELA-BRAZIL border. Forest.

173. RUFOUS-RUMPED FOLIAGE-GLEANER
Philydor erythrocercus *

6.5". Above olive brown, lower back and rump rufous chestnut (or only upper tail coverts rufous chestnut, 1). Long eyebrow ochraceous buff. Underparts pale yellowish buff to olive buff. Tail rufous (or entirely chestnut above with crown darker, wings slaty gray instead of like back, throat buffy, rest of underparts cinnamon rufous, 2).

Tropical zone. GUIANAS; ne BRAZIL from rio Negro eastward, s of the Amazon from e PERU and n BOLIVIA in Beni e to Mato Grosso and Maranhão. Se COLOMBIA s to Puno, PERU and BOLIVIA in La Paz and Cochabamba, 1. W of Andes in COLOMBIA and ECUADOR, 2. [Panama.] Forest.

174. CINNAMON-RUMPED FOLIAGE-GLEANER

Philydor pyrrhodes

6.5". Crown and upper back rufescent olive, wings blackish. Eyebrow, lower back, tail and entire underparts bright cinnamon.

Tropical zone. GUIANAS; s VENEZUELA; e COLOMBIA; e ECUADOR; ne PERU and Amazonian BRAZIL. Forest undergrowth.

175. RUSSET-MANTLED FOLIAGE-GLEANER

Philydor dimidiatus *

Differs from 174 by much brighter cinnamon brown back. Upper tail coverts and tail dark rufous, wings russet brown (or paler throughout with upperparts light olive brown and no rufescent tinge, 1).

BRAZIL in s and central Mato Grosso; from w Minas Gerais and Goiás to Paraná and ne PARAGUAY, 1. Forest.

176. OCHRE-BREASTED FOLIAGE-GLEANER

Philydor lichtensteini

6.5". Crown and nape grayish olive, feathers basally black; back dull ochraceous brown mixed with grayish. Eyebrow and underparts dull ochraceous. Central tail feathers like back, rest dull rufous on inner web.

E BRAZIL from Goiás to Santa Catarina; w PARAGUAY; ne ARGENTINA. Forest undergrowth.

177. BUFF-FRONTED FOLIAGE-GLEANER

Philydor rufus *

7.5". Forehead, eyebrow and entire underparts ochraceous. Nape and crown from eye gray. Back and wings rufous; tail rufous brown, (or much darker throughout with

forehead tinged ochre and rest of crown and nape olivaceous like back, 1).

Subtropical zone. Coastal mts. of VENEZUELA in Carabobo and Dept. Federal; w slope of E Andes of COLOMBIA and Pacific slope to nw ECUADOR; e PERU to BOLIVIA in La Paz and Santa Cruz, 1. S BRAZIL from Bahía and Goiás to central Mato Grosso and Paraná, PARAGUAY and ne ARGENTINA. Forest.

Plate 46

178. CHESTNUT-WINGED FOLIAGE-GLEANER

Philydor erythropterus *

6.7". Upperparts gray with olive tinge, lores bright ochraceous. Underparts buffy ochraceous, brightest on throat. Wings and tail chestnut rufous.

Tropical zone. VENEZUELA in s Bolívar; e COLOMBIA south to e PERU, n BOLIVIA and BRAZIL s of the Amazon e to rio Tapajós. Forest.

179. RUFOUS-TAILED FOLIAGE-GLEANER

Philydor ruficaudatus *

7". Upperparts olive brown, wing coverts with pale edges. Eyebrow and underparts yellowish buff. Tail rufous.

GUIANAS, west across s VENEZUELA to e COLOMBIA, e ECUADOR, e PERU, n BOLIVIA and Amazonian BRAZIL (n of the Amazon only along Venezuelan border). Forest.

180. WHITE-EYED FOLIAGE-GLEANER

Automolus leucophthalmus *

7.2" (or 7.8", 1). Head crested. Upperparts reddish brown, rump and tail cinnamon rufous. Lores and throat white, rest of underparts pale ochraceous darkening to light brown on belly (or upperparts and tail much darker, back rufous chestnut, 1).

BRAZIL from Paraiba and e Bahía, 1; thence s to Santa Catarina and through s Goiás to e Mato Grosso, ne PARAGUAY and ne ARGENTINA in Misiones. Bamboo thickets.

181. OLIVE-BACKED FOLIAGE-GLEANER

Automolus infuscatus *

7.5". Upperparts and closed wing olive

brown, upper tail coverts and tail rufous. Throat white, rest of underparts dirty white with olive tinge.

Tropical zone. GUYANA and SURINAM w across VENEZUELA to e COLOMBIA thence south to n BOLIVIA. Amazonian BRAZIL. Forest undergrowth.

182. CRESTED FOLIAGE-GLEANER

Automolus dorsalis

Differs from 181 by reddish brown upperparts and buff postocular streak.

Tropical zone. Se COLOMBIA s to Puno, PERU. Forest.

183. RUDDY FOLIAGE-GLEANER

Automolus rubiginosus *

7.5". Upperparts olivaceous brown (crown rufous brown in contrast, 1), tail dark chestnut. Throat light rufous, rest of underparts light buffy brown, under tail coverts rufous (or much darker throughout, above dark bay, throat and upper breast chestnut, rest of underparts dark brown, tail black, 2).

Tropical, subtropical zones. W GUYANA, FRENCH GUIANA, s VENEZUELA, adjacent BRAZIL, COLOMBIA in Santa Marta and slopes of E Andes south to n PERU. Se PERU and n BOLIVIA, 1. Nw COLOMBIA to w ECUADOR, 2. [Mid. Amer.] Forest, second growth, tangled vines.

Plate 46

184. WHITE-THROATED FOLIAGE-GLEANER

Automolus roraimae *

7". Differs from 181 by white postocular streak and buffy white throat in sharp contrast to brown underparts.

Subtropical zone. Mts. of s VENEZUELA and bordering area of BRAZIL. Forest.

185. BUFF-THROATED FOLIAGE-GLEANER

Automolus ochrolaemus *

7.5". Above olivaceous brown, tinged rufescent; rump and tail chestnut rufous. Below dull ochraceous, paler on throat with breast indistinctly streaked dusky (or throat almost white, rest of underparts pale brown, 1).

GUIANAS w across s VENEZUELA to e

COLOMBIA then south to n BOLIVIA. Amazonian BRAZIL e to Óbidos, and rio Tapajós. COLOMBIA w of E Andes to nw ECUADOR, 1. [Mid Amer.] Forest undergrowth.

186. CHESTNUT-CROWNED FOLIAGE-GLEANER

Automolus rufipileatus *

7.5". Crown, upper tail coverts and tail chestnut; back reddish brown (or olive, 1). Wing coverts dark chestnut. Underparts pale brownish, more buffy on throat.

GUYANA, SURINAM, VENEZUELA (n of the Orinoco in Barinas and Apure), e COLOMBIA south to n BOLIVIA. BRAZIL s of the Amazon from rio Juruá e to Pará and Maranhão, 1. Forest.

187. RUFOUS-NECKED FOLIAGE-GLEANER

Automolus ruficollis *

7.3". Upperparts bright rufescent brown, eyebrow and sides of neck rufous. Throat cinnamon buff; rest of underparts pale brownish, streaked with buffy white on breast. Tail rufous.

Tropical to humid temperate zone. Sw ECUADOR and n PERU s on Pacific slope to Cajamarca and in Marañón watershed in Amazonas. Forest.

188. BROWN-RUMPED FOLIAGE-GLEANER

Automolus melanopezus

7.5". Upperparts reddish brown, lesser wing coverts dark chestnut. Sides of throat bright cinnamon rufous, center of throat paler, rest of underparts pale brownish with olive suffusion on breast and somewhat paler center of abdomen. ♀: Duller than ♂, center of abdomen almost white.

Tropical zone. Se COLOMBIA; e ECUADOR. Se PERU (Balta); w Amazonian BRAZIL on w bank of middle rio Purús. Forest.

189. HENNA-HOODED FOLIAGE-GLEANER

Hylocryptus erythrocephalus *

8.5". Head, nape, wings, tail coverts and tail bright orange rufous, palest on throat. Back light olivaceous brown. Underparts light grayish brown. Bill straight, about 1".

Tropical zone. Sw ECUADOR to nw PERU. Forest; climbs trees.

190. CHESTNUT-CAPPED FOLIAGE-GLEANER

Hylocryptus rectirostris

8.3". Above earthy brown; crown, sides of head, rump, wings and tail rufous. Below clay color. Bill straight, about 1".

E BRAZIL from s Goiás and s Bahía to Paraná w to central and s Mato Grosso. Forest.

191. PALE-BROWED TREEHUNTER

Cichlocolaptes leucophrys

8.5". Above rufous brown, feathers of crown and mantle with white shaft streaks, lower back and rump plain rufous brown. Long eyebrow and throat white; rest of underparts white, feathers edged laterally with rufous brown giving streaked look. Wings rufous brown. Tail cinnamon brown. Bill straight, about 1".

Coastal s BRAZIL from Bahía to Santa Catarina.

192. FLAMMULATED TREEHUNTER

Thripadectes flammulatus *

9.2". Crown and upper back black becoming umber brown on mantle, each feather with buff streak down center; rump, upper tail coverts and tail dark chestnut. Underparts tawny ochraceous, feathers broadly edged black giving streaked look (or throat virtually uniform deep buff, margins of feathers on rest of underparts olive brown, 1). Wings reddish brown.

Upper tropical and temperate zones. Andes of Mérida, VENEZUELA, 1. Mts. of CO-LOMBIA including Santa Marta south to w ECUADOR. Forest.

Plates 10, 46

193. STRIPED TREEHUNTER

Thripadectes holostictus *

8". Above much like 192. Throat and breast buff, feathers edged blackish; rest of underparts umber brown.

Upper tropical and subtropical zones. VENE-ZUELA in Táchira; Andes of COLOMBIA, south through e ECUADOR to n BOLIVIA. Forest.

194. BLACK-BILLED TREEHUNTER

Thripadectes melanorhynchus *

8". Above much like 192, below more uniform. Throat feathers lightly edged dusky.

Subtropical zone. E slope of COLOMBIAN Andes in Meta. E ECUADOR to se PERU. Forest.

195. STREAK-CAPPED TREEHUNTER

Thripadectes virgaticeps *

8.5". Crown and nape olive brown, feathers dusky-edged with white shaft streaks. Back plain reddish brown; rump, upper tail coverts and tail rufous chestnut. Throat cinnamon rufous, feathers edged dusky; rest of underparts cinnamon brown with olive suffusion on breast.

Upper tropical and subtropical zones. N and nw VENEZUELA, COLOMBIA south to e and w ECUADOR. Humid forest.

196. BUFF-THROATED TREEHUNTER

Thripadectes scrutator

10". Above umber brown, dusky on crown; underparts pale olive brown with obsolete buff spots in center. Throat buff, feathers conspicuously edged sooty black.

Temperate zone of central and se PERU in Junín and Cuzco.

197. UNIFORM TREEHUNTER

Thripadectes ignobilis

7.3". Upperparts, wings and tail dark chestnut brown. Underparts wood brown, throat with buffy shaft streaks. Bill somewhat shorter and thicker than in related species.

Upper tropical and subtropical zones. Pacific COLOMBIA from Antioquia s to Nariño and nw ECUADOR. Forest.

198. SHARP-BILLED TREEHUNTER

Heliobletus contaminatus

4.5". Above olive brown with pale shaft streaks on crown and broad white streaks on back. Throat white, rest of underparts pale olive brown, broadly streaked white. Tail rufous, remiges blackish with olive brown outer webs.

BRAZIL from Espírito Santo to Rio Grande do Sul; ne ARGENTINA and e PARA-GUAY. Forest; climbs trees.

199. RUFOUS-TAILED XENOPS

Xenops milleri *

4.2". Crown blackish, conspicuously pale streaked; mantle olivaceous brown, striped buffy white; rump cinnamon rufous. Upper tail coverts and tail rufous. Below pale buffy, streaked blackish olive. Primaries black with ochraceous bar; secondaries basally cinnamon and tertials mostly cinnamon.

FRENCH GUIANA and SURINAM w across s VENEZUELA to e COLOMBIA, e ECUADOR, ne PERU, Amazonian BRAZIL n of the Amazon and s of it to rio Juruá. Forest; climbs trees.

200. SLENDER-BILLED XENOPS

Xenops tenuirostris *

Rather like 199 but at once distinguishable by silvery white crescent-shaped streak on cheek, and tail in which central and two outer pairs of feathers are rufous, the intermediate ones largely black. Back streaked deeper buff, mandible slightly upturned.

SURINAM and FRENCH GUIANA, w across s VENEZUELA to se COLOMBIA thence s to extreme nw BOLIVIA. Amazonian BRAZIL s of the Amazon to se Pará. Swampy forest. Feeds at tips of branches like a titmouse.

201. STREAKED XENOPS

Xenops rutilans *

5". Rather like 200, but at once distinguishable by sharply upcurved lower mandible and much less black (or no black, 1) in tail. Considerably larger.

Tropical, subtropical zones. Generally distributed e of Andes south to n ARGENTINA; w of Andes to Piura, PERU. Santa Marta Mts. of COLOMBIA, 1. Trinidad. [Highlands of Costa Rica and Panama.] Forest; climbs trees.

202. PLAIN XENOPS

Xenops minutus *

Differs from 201 by uniform umber brown upperparts, olive brown underparts. Central tail feathers light cinnamon, next two pairs black, outermost with black only at base.

Generally distributed e of Andes, south to n BOLIVIA, s BRAZIL, PARAGUAY and ne

ARGENTINA; w of Andes to w ECUADOR. [Mid. Amer.] Forest; climbs trees.

Plate 46

203. GREAT XENOPS

Megaxenops parnaguae

6.3". Bright cinnamon rufous, paler below; throat and sides of neck white. Outer remiges brownish black. Bill heavy, mandible sharply upturned.

E BRAZIL in Ceará and Piauí and in n Bahía. Forest; climbs trees.

Plate 8

204. WHITE-THROATED TREERUNNER

Pygarrhichas albogularis *

5.5". Bill long, slender, upcurved. Tail rufous, short, ending in spines about .5" long. Upperparts dull brown mixed with rufous on lower back. Below white; sides of body with dark spots.

ARGENTINA from Neuquén, and CHILE from Santiago, to Tierra del Fuego. Small forest clearings. Climbs trees.

Leafscrapers

Sclerurus. Characteristics: Dark brown with rufous rump and whitish or rufous throat. Bill rather long, thin, straight. Terrestrial, somewhat resembling small, short-tailed thrush.

205. RUFOUS-BREASTED LEAFSCRAPER

Sclerurus scansor *

7.5". Crown, rump and upper tail coverts chestnut rufous, back dark brown. Throat white, breast rufous, belly dark brown. Tail black.

BRAZIL from Ceará to Rio Grande do Sul and through Goiás to Mato Grosso.

206. GRAY-THROATED LEAFSCRAPER

Sclerurus albigularis *

7". Much like 205 but throat light gray, and rump and upper tail coverts darker.

Upper tropical and lower subtropical zones. VENEZUELA n of the Orinoco; COLOMBIA in Santa Marta Mts. and in Meta. Se ECUADOR; ne PERU. Nw BOLIVIA. Trinidad and Tobago. [Costa Rica; w Panama.] Humid forest.

Plate 35

207. TAWNY-THROATED LEAFSCRAPER

Sclerurus mexicanus *

6.5″. Dark brown, rump dark chestnut. Throat rufous, upper breast more or less rufous chestnut. Tail black.

Tropical, subtropical zones. GUIANAS, VENEZUELA, e COLOMBIA south to n BOLIVIA. BRAZIL s of the Amazon, e to Pará and Maranhão and from Alagoas to Espírito Santo. W of Andes to sw ECUADOR. [Mid. Amer.] Forest undergrowth.

208. SHORT-BILLED LEAFSCRAPER

Sclerurus rufigularis *

6.2″. Much like 207 but duller and at once distinguishable by smaller bill (.6″ vs. 1″).

GUIANAS west across s VENEZUELA to s COLOMBIA. Amazonian BRAZIL s to Mato Grosso and n BOLIVIA. Forest.

209. BLACK-TAILED LEAFSCRAPER

Sclerurus caudacutus *

7″. Dark brown; rump dark, dull chestnut. Throat white, feathers dusky-edged, breast more or less tinged rufescent. Tail blackish.

GUIANAS west across s VENEZUELA to COLOMBIA, thence south to nw BOLIVIA. Amazonian BRAZIL and in Bahía and Espírito Santo. Forest.

210. SCALY-THROATED LEAFSCRAPER

Sclerurus guatemalensis *

Differs from 209 by having the feathers of the throat pointed and heavily margined with black; upper breast spotted with cinnamon rufous.

Tropical zone. COLOMBIA from Magdalena Valley w to Pacific, s to upper Atrato. Forest.

211. SHARP-TAILED STREAMCREEPER

Lochmias nematura *

6.2″. Dark umber brown (or chestnut brown, 1) spotted with white below (eyebrow white, 2). Tail rather short, black.

Subtropical zone. Spottily distributed. VENEZUELA on isolated mountains in Bolívar and adjacent BRAZIL, 1. COLOMBIA, e ECUADOR, e PERU to BOLIVIA. BRAZIL from Goiás and Minas Gerais to Rio Grande do Sul, PARAGUAY, URUGUAY and ne ARGENTINA, 2. [E Panama.] Mountain streambanks.

Plate 46

Family FORMICARIIDAE   ANTBIRDS

Antbirds comprise an enormous family of neotropical birds which live mostly in lower tree growth in the forest, open woodland, and sometimes fairly open places. They are found from Mexico southward through all South American countries, except Chile, to central Argentina, living mainly in tropical and subtropical zones.

Not brilliantly colored, males are often attractively clothed in shades of gray and females in various tones of brown and russet. A few species are jet black. The sexes are usually dissimilar.

Antbirds are insectivorous, and are often found among mixed bands of birds moving rapidly through forests in search of food, or following army ants to feed on the insects they disturb.

They usually nest on or near the ground or in shrubs or middle tree level, building cup-shaped nests or elaborate constructions of sticks; they sometimes use natural tree cavities.

Many antbirds have attractive songs and melodious call notes.

Among the more distinctive groups are the antshrikes, which are usually found in shrubbery and are notable for thick, hooked, shrike-like bills, and the antpittas, long-legged thrush-like inhabitants of the forest floor.

AID TO IDENTIFICATION

All gray or gray and black or all black

More or less uniform gray

Wing coverts plain 5c, 6, 23, 24b, 25, 44, 48, 49b, 70, 74, throat white 161, 162

Wing coverts edged or tipped white (marking very conspicuous) 28, 29, 30a, 31, 35b, 41; (with black cap and white eyebrow) 82, 83, 84a, 85a, 86a, 87c, 88c, 136; (wing marking inconspicuous) 21, 23, 26, 27b, 34, 41, 46b, 47, 59, 78, 79, 109, 111, 112, 117, 119b, 134, 135b, 136, 137, 138, 150; (back scalloped) 173

Gray; throat and/or breast black 37a, 45, 64, 65, 69b, 70, 71b, 72, 73, 75c, 76a, 77c, 78, 123, 125, 126, 127b, 130, 131, 134; (with white eyebrow) 124; (with white flank plumes) 68, 92c

Black

Tail black 19a, 21, 22, 23, 36b, 114, 118b, 120, 121c, 151c, 152, 153, 154b

Tail tipped white 13, 14, 31, 91, 94c, 113, 116, 117; (sides of belly white) 12a; (with chestnut crown) 14; (with bare, blue top and sides of head) 133a

Barred, streaked or spotted

Barred above and/or below

Barred above and below 1, 5c, 7, 16, 17a, 18

Barred only above or below: (above) 3, 7, 16, 160, 162b, 166, 167, 168, 169; (below) 6, 17a, 18, 31, 32c, 33, 175, 182b, 189a, 190b, 191b, 192b, 193a, 194, 197

Spotted above or below

Spotted above (over 6") 2c, 4c, 169, 173b, 176, 177b; (under 5") 103c, 127, 144c, 145c, 171, 172, 173; (on throat and breast) 40c, 98c, 118b; (on breast only) 80, 124, 125, 126, 127c, 131, 145c, 148, 170, 220b

Streaked above and/or below, no barring

Streaked above and below (under 4") 52, 54, 55, 56b, 57a; (over 5") 38b, 81, 101b, 203b, 213b

Streaked above only (under 5") 50, 51b, 52, 53a, 56b, 85; (over 5") 39, 190b, 199b, 200b

Streaked below only (large, thrush-like) 179, 180, 181, 195, 196, 201b, 202a, 203a, 214, 215b, 216, 218; (smaller, not thrush-like) 9, 19a, 42, 47, 93, 96, 99c, 102c, 104c, 113c, 115, 128, 140, 157, 220, 223a, 224b; (with conspicuous white crescent in front of eye) 225b

No bars, streaks or spots

Mainly or all gray and olive, gray and rufous, or black and rufous

Above brown or rufous, head and underparts black 120, 165, 227; (head only black) 20b, 152

With sharply contrasting rufous crown, breast patch or belly: (crown) 183, 185b, 230, 232; (breast) 36b, 116c, 134, 167; (belly) 49b

With black or checkered throat and/or black breast 63, 64, 65, 66, 67c, 94c, 142b, 147b, 148, 155b, 156, 184, 186b, 188

Gray above, below buff to bright chestnut 34, 49b, 69, 70, 73, 77c, 78, 79, 123c, 150, 159, 160b

Gray below, all or mostly brown to rufous above, wing coverts spotted 58, 66, 155b, 204a, 205b, 227, 231b

No or very little gray in plumage

Below virtually uniform very bright cinnamon, intense orange rufous to deep chestnut

Wing coverts very conspicuously spotted or margined 21, 29, 35, 58, 59, 126, 136, 137, 138, 156

Wing coverts uniform 23, 33, 39, 48, 74, 110c, 111, 112, 114, 133a, 151, 198b, 207b, 208b, 209b

Below much duller, all or mostly buff, dull ochraceous, or ochraceous olive, chestnut to olive above.

Under 5" 60c, 61, 62b, 64, 66, 67c, 68, 70, 71b, 72b, 75c, 76a, 88c, 90, 92c, 108, 126

Over 5" (below dull brown) 37a, 109, 120, 121c, 122c, 154b, 169; (below pale buff to ochraceous olive) wing coverts unmarked 15c, 24b, 25, 26, 27, 28, 39, 41, 43c, 44, 48, 94c, 211b, 217c, 221a, wing coverts marked 9, 11b, 12a, 16, 97c, 126, 134, 141, 142b, 187b

Below all or mostly white (black above) 8, 31, 90, 130, 132, 140; (brown above) 41, 70, 95, 124, 126, 127, 139b, 140; (bright rufous to chestnut above) 8, 80, 125, 158, 163, 206b; (with contrasting rufous cap) 28, 206, 229

With marked characters

All or partly pale to bright yellow below 40, 41, 50, 51, 52, 53, 54, 89b, 105, 106, 107, 128, 129, 207b

Breast black in contrast to other underparts, above brown to rufous 9, 10c, 11b, 95, 141, 143, 149, 228c, 233

Band across breast 15c, 87c, 143, 146c, 170, 207b, 210b, 212a, 219a, 220b, 221b, 226a, 230, 233, 234c

Long, silvery postocular tuft 227, 228c, 229c, 230, 231, 232b, 233, 234c

Sharply defined, checkered black and white throat patch 60c, 61, 62b, 63, 64, 65, 118b, 119b, 147b

1. FASCIATED ANTSHRIKE

Cymbilaimus lineatus *

7.1". Crown black; upperparts, wings and tail black finely banded with white. Underparts white finely banded with black. ♀: Crown rufous chestnut. Back. wings and tail black finely banded with rufous; underparts buff finely banded with black.

Tropical zone. Generally distributed e of Andes to e PERU, n BOLIVIA and Amazonian BRAZIL e to rio Jarí and ne Mato Grosso. Lower growth at forest borders.

Plate 47

2. SPOT-BACKED ANTSHRIKE

Hypoedaleus guttatus *

8.2". Upperparts, wings and tail black, spotted with white. Underparts white becoming buff on crissum. ♀: Like male but spots above tinged buff and underparts becoming light ochraceous on crissum.

E BRAZIL from Bahía and s Goiás to Santa Catarina. E PARAGUAY and ne ARGENTINA in Misiones. Forest, bamboo thickets.

3. GIANT ANTSHRIKE

Batara cinerea *

14" [or 12.5"(1)]. Head crested, crown black; back, wings and tail black finely barred white. Underparts uniform gray. ♀: Crown chestnut; back, wings and tail coarsely barred black and rufous. Throat whitish, rest of underparts pale drab (or underparts uniform drab brown, 1).

E BRAZIL from Espírito Santo to Rio Grande do Sul, PARAGUAY, n ARGENTINA, BOLIVIA in Tarija; in Santa Cruz, 1. Thick forest undergrowth.

Plate 26

4. LARGE-TAILED ANTSHRIKE

Mackenziaena leachii

10.5". Black, spotted with white except on throat, breast and tail. ♀: Crown chestnut; back and wings black, spotted with fulvous. Below black thickly spotted with whitish. Central tail feathers black sparsely barred fulvous, rest mostly black.

Se BRAZIL from Minas Gerais to Rio Grande do Sul, adjacent PARAGUAY and ARGENTINA. Bamboo thickets, forest undergrowth.

Plate 26

5. TUFTED ANTSHRIKE

Mackenziaena severa

9.5". Crested. Dark sooty gray; crown,

cheeks and throat blackish. ♀: Crown rufous; back and wings black, banded with rufous. Underparts buff, banded with black. Tail gray.

BRAZIL from Minas Gerais to Rio Grande do Sul, adjacent PARAGUAY and ARGENTINA. Thick forest undergrowth.

6. BLACK-THROATED ANTSHRIKE

Frederickena viridis

9". Crested. Crown, cheeks, throat and breast black; rest of plumage dark bluish gray. Tail faintly banded. ♀: Crown rufous chestnut. Back and wings rufous brown. Sides of head and underparts banded pale gray and black. Upper tail coverts and tail banded gray and black.

Tropical zone. GUIANAS; central and nw VENEZUELA; BRAZIL n of lower Amazon. Forest, rarely savanna.

7. UNDULATED ANTSHRIKE

Frederickena unduligera *

9". Crested. Black, waved and freckled with white. Throat black. ♀: Crown rufous brown more or less barred with black; back and wings cinnamon brown, barred with black. Underparts tawny ochraceous barred with black (or throat and breast lightly spotted with black, rest of underparts unmarked, 1.) Tail barred gray and black.

Se COLOMBIA and nw BRAZIL. E ECUADOR, e PERU and BRAZIL s of the Amazon to rio Madeira, 1. Forest.

Plate 8

8. GREAT ANTSHRIKE

Taraba major *

8". Above black, below white. Wing coverts with two white bars and outer tail feathers tipped white. ♀: Upperparts uniform chestnut to rufous. Underparts white, more or less tinged clay color.

Usually tropical zone. Generally distributed e of Andes, south to n ARGENTINA; w of Andes to nw PERU. [Mid. Amer.] Swampy forest, thickets in humid woodland.

Plates 45 (♂), 36 (♀)

9. BLACK-CRESTED ANTSHRIKE

Sakesphorus canadensis *

6.3". Crested. Crown and sides of head black, nuchal collar white, back ochraceous

brown. Wings blackish, wing coverts broadly edged white. Throat and broad line down center of breast black, rest of underparts white. Tail black, edged and tipped white. ♀: Crown rufous chestnut, back rufous brown, wing coverts tipped buff. Sides of head and throat buffy white, rest of underparts cinnamon buff, streaked with black on breast.

GUIANAS, VENEZUELA, n and e COLOMBIA, south to e PERU. N BRAZIL e to Roraima, s of the Amazon in n Mato Grosso. Mangrove undergrowth, wastelands, plantations, gardens.

Plate 46

10. SILVERY-CHEEKED ANTSHRIKE

Sakesphorus cristatus

Much like 9, chiefly distinguishable by barred tail. ♀: Unknown.

Campos of e BRAZIL in Piauí, Ceará and Bahía.

11. COLLARED ANTSHRIKE

Sakesphorus bernardi *

7.2". Much like 9 in color but with much larger bill and semiconcealed white dorsal patch. ♀: Differs from ♂ chiefly by rufous instead of mostly black tail.

Arid tropical zone. W ECUADOR s to Libertad, and in Marañón drainage in Cajamarca, PERU. Arid scrub.

12. BLACK-BACKED ANTSHRIKE

Sakesphorus melanonotus

6.2". Crown, mantle, throat, breast, center of abdomen, wings and tail black. Lower back light gray, sides of belly white. Concealed dorsal patch, edges of wing coverts, remiges, and tips of tail feathers white. ♀: Crown black, feathers edged olive brown. Back dull brown, concealed dorsal patch white. Underparts buffy. Wing coverts and inner remiges white. Tail dull rufous, outer web of outer rectrix buff.

Semiarid tropical zone. Nw VENEZUELA west to ne COLOMBIA. Thick scrub.

13. BAND-TAILED ANTSHRIKE

Sakesphorus melanothorax

7". No crest. Deep black. Lesser wing coverts white, rest of coverts with white terminal dots. Tail broadly tipped white. ♀: Upperparts bright rufous chestnut, sides of body chestnut. Sides of head, throat and breast black, belly grayish brown, tinged rufescent. Wings and tail chestnut, wing coverts with rufous tips.

SURINAM; FRENCH GUIANA; BRAZIL on w side of rio Tapajós.

14. GLOSSY ANTSHRIKE

Sakesphorus luctuosus *

7″. Crested. Deep black. Inner wing coverts and small tips to tail feathers white. ♀: Differs from male by chestnut crown and dark gray flanks.

Amazonian BRAZIL. Riparian thickets.

15. WHITE-BEARDED ANTSHRIKE

Biatas nigropectus

7″. Back reddish brown, lower breast and belly light olive brown. Cap black; cheeks, chin and nuchal collar buffy white. Large pectoral shield black. Wings and tail rufous. ♀: Differs from male by chestnut brown cap and no pectoral shield.

BRAZIL from Espírito Santo to Santa Catarina. ARGENTINA in Misiones. Thick forest undergrowth.

Plate 26

16. BARRED ANTSHRIKE

Thamnophilus doliatus *

6.5″. Above black banded with white; below white, banded with black (or center of belly unbanded, 1), throat streaked. Tail black with broken white bars. ♀: Crown rufous chestnut, sides of head streaked black and white; back, wings and tail bright rufous. Underparts buffy, throat paler (or white, tinged buffy, 1).

Tropical zone. Generally distributed e of Andes to São Paulo, BRAZIL, n ARGENTINA; PARAGUAY and BOLIVIA (in Tarija, 1). Margarita I., Trinidad and Tobago. [Mid. Amer.] Thickets, vines, savanna, riparian borders.

Plate 47

17. BAR-CRESTED ANTSHRIKE

Thamnophilus multistriatus *

Differs from 16 mainly by crown barred black and white instead of black. ♀: Upperparts, wings and tail rufous chestnut, sides of head

and nuchal collar streaked black and white, below barred black and white.

Upper tropical and subtropical zones. COLOMBIA except se. Undergrowth, forest borders.

Plate 36

18. LINED ANTSHRIKE

Thamnophilus palliatus *

Much like 16 but blacker, especially on back where white bands are very narrow (or crown black; back, wings and tail chestnut, 1). ♀: Very much like 17 but underparts more heavily barred, back averaging darker.

E COLOMBIA; e ECUADOR and n PERU s to San Martín. E PERU from Huánuco south to n BOLIVIA and BRAZIL in s Amazonas; in e from Pará to Paraiba and s to Minas Gerais and Rio de Janeiro, 1. Forest, thickets.

19. BLACK ANTSHRIKE

Thamnophilus nigriceps *

5.7″. Black; under wing coverts tipped white. ♀: Crown black streaked buffy; back, wings and tail rufous brown. Throat and breast blackish broadly streaked buffy white, becoming buffy brown on belly and rufous on under tail coverts.

Caribbean lowlands and middle Magdalena Valley, COLOMBIA. [E Panama.] Thick forest undergrowth.

20. COCHA ANTSHRIKE

Thamnophilus praecox

6.5″. ♀: Head, throat and upper breast black; front of head finely streaked white, rest of plumage tawny ochraceous. Wings and tail darker, inner remiges with cinnamon basal band. ♂: Unknown.

E ECUADOR (upper río Napo).

21. BLACKISH-GRAY ANTSHRIKE

Thamnophilus nigrocinereus *

6.5″. Crown and mantle black, lower back gray (or cap black, back all gray, 1; or all black above, 2), concealed interscapular patch white. Below gray with more or less blackish throat and breast (or all gray below, 1, 2). Upper wing coverts edged with white, under wing coverts mostly white, inner margins of primaries white. Tail black, narrowly tipped white. ♀: Top and sides of head sooty to dark gray. Back, wings and tail olive brown to rufous brown, concealed dorsal patch white. Underparts rufous brown (with sooty black throat, 2).

FRENCH GUIANA, s VENEZUELA, e COLOMBIA and nw BRAZIL, 1; sw BRAZIL, 2; both sides of middle and lower Amazon. Forest.

22. CASTELNAU'S ANTSHRIKE

Thamnophilus cryptoleucus

(Listed as a race of *T. nigrocinereus* in *Sp. Bds. S. Amer.*)

7". Shiny black; concealed dorsal patch white, flanks dark gray. Greater wing coverts edged white, under wing coverts and axillaries pure white; inner margins of remiges white, white increasing toward innermost. ♀: Differs from male only in having virtually unmarked wing coverts; axillaries and under wing coverts mixed with black.

Ne PERU from ríos Ucayali and Marañón to w Amazonian BRAZIL e to rio Negro.

23. WHITE-SHOULDERED ANTSHRIKE

Thamnophilus aethiops *

6.2". Dark gray, cap black (or without black cap, 1; with concealed white interscapular patch, 2), wing coverts lightly to strongly tipped white (or plumage entirely lustrous black, lesser and median wing coverts tipped white, 3). ♀: Rufescent brown, crown deeper and brighter; underparts paler; wings and tail slightly darker than back (or plumage deep chestnut brown, tail blackish, 3).

Tropical zone. S VENEZUELA, se COLOMBIA in Vaupés and Caquetá. Se COLOMBIA in Nariño, e ECUADOR and ne PERU, 3. Amazonian BRAZIL e to the rios Negro and Madeira. Between the rios Madeira and Tapajós s to Rondonia, 2. Between the rios Tapajós and Xingú. From the rio Tocantins east to n Maranhão and Pernambuco, 1. Forest and clearings.

24. UNIFORM ANTSHRIKE

Thamnophilus unicolor *

6.2". Uniform slaty gray. ♀: Above russet brown, brighter on crown. Lores, throat and sides of head gray. Underparts dull ochraceous brown.

Upper tropical, lower subtropical zones. COLOMBIA w of Andes and in the south-

east, and in e and w ECUADOR and ne PERU. Forest, forest border.

25. BLACK-CAPPED ANTSHRIKE

Thamnophilus schistaceus *

5.5". Uniform gray, paler below (with black cap, 1). ♀: Crown rufous, back tawny olive. Sides of head, underparts light ochraceous olive (or pale grayish olive, 2; or bright ochraceous, 3).

E COLOMBIA south to ne PERU and w Amazonian BRAZIL on upper rio Juruá, 1; from se ECUADOR south to n BOLIVIA and adjacent BRAZIL on lower rio Purús to w side of rio Madeira, 3; and from e bank east to rio Tocantins, 2. Forest undergrowth.

26. MOUSE-COLORED ANTSHRIKE

Thamnophilus murinus *

5.2". Light gray; white interscapular patch and center of abdomen. Wing coverts tipped white. Tail blackish with narrow white tip. ♀: Above reddish brown, crown rufescent. Wing coverts with slight buffy tips. Breast and sides light olivaceous brown, throat and abdomen white. Tail chestnut brown, feathers very narrowly tipped buffy.

GUIANAS; VENEZUELA s of the Orinoco; se COLOMBIA, south to ne PERU, BRAZIL n of the Amazon from rio Negro eastward, s of the Amazon e to rio Madeira. Forest undergrowth, savanna.

27. UPLAND ANTSHRIKE

Thamnophilus aroyae

5.5". Above dark slaty gray, crown blackish. Wing coverts black with large white apical spots. Concealed white dorsal patch small or absent. Below paler gray than back, feathers on center of abdomen and under tail coverts with narrow white fringes. Tail slaty black, tipped white. ♀: Crown and nape rufous; back, wings and tail reddish brown. Sides of head grayish, feathers with white hairstreaks. Below tawny olivaceous, paler and less olivaceous on center of abdomen.

Upper tropical zone. Se PERU; nw BOLIVIA.

28. SLATY ANTSHRIKE

Thamnophilus punctatus *

5.8". Crown black. Back mixed gray and

black (or gray, 1) with semiconcealed white interscapular patch, upper tail coverts black with large white tips. Underparts gray to pale gray. Wings black; wing coverts, inner remiges and scapulars conspicuously edged white. Tail black, tipped white with median white bar on outer web of outer rectrix. ♀: Crown rufous to chestnut, back reddish brown to olive brown, interscapular patch white. Below pale olivaceous brown (or white, breast tinged olivaceous, 1). Wings and tail chestnut brown with white pattern as in male.

Generally distributed e of Andes to n BOLIVIA and BRAZIL to s Mato Grosso and São Paulo (PERU in upper Marañón, and BRAZIL on e plateau, 1). W of Andes to w ECUADOR. [Guatamala southward.] Forest undergrowth, savanna, sometimes semiarid country, cerrado.

Plates 47, 36 (♀)

29. AMAZONIAN ANTSHRIKE

Thamnophilus amazonicus *

5.8". Not distinguishable in field from 28. Some forms have longer, slimmer bill. ♀: Quite different from 28. Crown chestnut rufous, sides of head and underparts cinnamon rufous (or belly white, sharply defined, 1). Back dark olive brown, interscapular patch white. Wings and tail black, patterned as in 28.

GUIANAS w across s VENEZUELA to e COLOMBIA. E PERU; n BOLIVIA; Amazonian BRAZIL (upper Orinoco, adjacent Colombia and nw Brazil, 1). Forest.

30. STREAK-BACKED ANTSHRIKE

Thamnophilus insignis *

6.2". Very like 29 but with longer tail, slimmer bill, and a larger white dorsal patch giving the back, which is blacker, a streaked look. ♀: Differs from male by white-tipped black forehead feathers, and chestnut crown surrounded by white.

Upper tropical, subtropical zones. Mts. of s VENEZUELA. Forest.

31. VARIABLE ANTSHRIKE

Thamnophilus caerulescens *

6". Bluish gray, center of back mixed with black, concealed dorsal patch white; center of abdomen with indistinct whitish bars (or underparts white, 1; or similar but throat spotted white and gray, breast whitish, belly and under tail coverts ochraceous, 2; or similar but belly and under tail coverts white, 3; or upperparts, throat and breast black, rest of underparts conspicuously barred black and white, 4; or like preceding but below all black, 5). Wings blackish, wing coverts conspicuously edged white. Upper tail coverts black; tail black, tipped white, outermost rectrix with white median patch on outer web. ♀: Upperparts wings and tail olivaceous, crown tinged rufous; wing coverts black, tipped white. Throat and breast grayish olive, rest of underparts cinnamon buff to ochraceous orange. Tail olive, marked as in male (or crown blackish, wing coverts unmarked or only slightly so, tail blackish with slight or no pale tips and no patch on outer web, 5).

Tropical to temperate zone. E PERU, 5. BOLIVIA in La Paz and Cochabamba, 4; in Santa Cruz, 3; from s Chaquisaca and Tarija to nw and n ARGENTINA and nw PARAGUAY and bordering BRAZIL, 1; and in e BRAZIL from Ceará and Pernambuco s to Rio de Janeiro and e PARAGUAY; thence s to URUGUAY and ne ARGENTINA, 2. Forest undergrowth, streambanks, scrubs, savanna.

32. RUFOUS-WINGED ANTSHRIKE

Thamnophilus torquatus

5.5". Cap black, lores whitish, back olive gray. Underparts whitish, barred on breast with black. Wings rufous chestnut; tail black, barred white. ♀: Differs from ♂ by rufous cap and tail and unbarred underparts.

E BRAZIL from se Pará, Ceará and Alagoas s to Minas Gerais and w Mato Grosso. Cerrado.

33. RUFOUS-CAPPED ANTSHRIKE

Thamnophilus ruficapillus *

7" (or 6.5", 1). Upperparts and wings reddish brown, crown strongly rufescent. Below whitish lightly barred on breast with black. Central tail feathers like back, rest barred with white on inner web (or crown chestnut, back grayish olive, wings reddish brown, underparts white, barred on chest with black, 1; or barred on chest and belly 2). ♀: Crown rufescent (or chestnut, 2), back olive brown, wings reddish brown. Underparts whitish, tinged olivaceous (or bright cinnamon buff, 1, 2). Tail like back (or dark rufous in contrast, 1, 2).

Subtropical zone. PERU from Amazonas s to La Paz and Cochabamba, BOLIVIA, 1; from e Cochabamba south to nw ARGEN-TINA, 2. BRAZIL from Minas Gerais south to e PARAGUAY and URUGUAY and ne ARGENTINA. Dense brush near water, forest undergrowth.

34. SPOT-WINGED ANTSHRIKE

Pygiptila stellaris *

5.5". Crown and nape black, back gray mixed with black, concealed white interscapular patch. Wings and tail gray, wing coverts with small white dots. Underparts uniform pale gray. ♀: Forehead, underparts and outer remiges ochraceous. Back, inner remiges and tail gray; concealed interscapular patch white.

Generally distributed e of Andes to e PERU, n BOLIVIA and Amazonian BRAZIL n of the Amazon to rio Negro and s of the Amazon to Maranhão and w Mato Grosso. Forest treetops.

Plate 46

35. PEARLY ANTSHRIKE

Megastictus margaritatus

5.5". Bluish gray, paler below. Wing coverts and inner remiges black, handsomely marked with large, round, white spots. Upper tail coverts and tail black, both tipped with white spots. ♀: Like male but ochraceous brown instead of gray, and spots on wings and tail ochraceous buff.

S VENEZUELA; se COLOMBIA; e ECUA-DOR; ne PERU; w Amazonian BRAZIL. Forest.

Plates 47 (♂), 36 (♀)

36. BLACK BUSHBIRD

Neoctantes niger

6.2". Bill narrow, compressed, lower mandible upcurved. Deep black, wings brownish black, concealed white dorsal patch. ♀: Like male but breast chestnut.

Tropical zone. Extreme se COLOMBIA to ne PERU, w Amazonian BRAZIL.

Plate 47

37. RECURVE-BILLED BUSHBIRD

Clytoctantes alixi

6.7". Bill as in 36 but larger. Lores, throat and breast black, rest of plumage dark slaty gray. ♀: Forehead, sides of head and of body chestnut, wings and tail blackish, rest of plumage brown.

Tropical zone. Extreme nw VENEZUELA w across n COLOMBIA to lower Cauca Valley. Tangled forest undergrowth.

Plate 47

38. SPECKLE-BREASTED ANTSHRIKE

Xenornis setifrons

6.5". Lower mandible slightly upturned. Forehead and sides of head dark gray; upperparts dark reddish brown, feathers with pale shaft streaks and dusky edges; wing coverts and tertials tipped ochraceous. Throat and upper breast buffy brown, feathers edged dusky giving streaked look; rest of underparts dark brown. Tail dark grayish brown. ♀: Differs from male by no gray on head.

Tropical zone. W COLOMBIA in Chocó. [E Panama.] Forest.

39. RUSSET ANTSHRIKE

Thamnistes anabatinus *

5.5". Bill heavy, hooked, shrike-like. Upperparts olive brown, crown and tail rufescent; interscapular patch orange ochraceous with black subterminal bar (no bar, ♀). Eyebrow, throat and breast yellowish ochraceous; olive on sides of body (or crown like back, upperparts with whitish shaft streaks; underparts more or less uniform bright cinnamon, 1)

Tropical, lower subtropical zones. COLOMBIA south to e and w ECUADOR. Central and se PERU s to Cochabamba, BOLIVIA, 1. [Mid. Amer.] Forest, thickets.

Plate 8

Antvireos

Dysithamnus resembles *Thamnophilus* but differs by shorter tail and thinner, finer bill.

40. SPOT-BREASTED ANTVIREO

Dysithamnus stictothorax

5.3". Crown leaden gray, postocular feathers tipped white. Back, wings and tail grayish olive; wing coverts black, tipped white. Below yellowish white, whiter on throat and upper breast, breast spotted with gray. ♀: Like male but cap bright rufous.

E BRAZIL from Bahía to Santa Catarina.

41. PLAIN ANTVIREO

Dysithamnus mentalis *

4.7". Above gray, back sometimes shaded with olive (or top and sides of head gray, back olive, 1). Throat and center of abdomen white, sometimes shaded with yellowish on belly (or throat white, rest of underparts yellow, 1; or all gray below, 2). Wings and tail like back, wing coverts pale-margined. ♀: Crown and nape dull rufous; back, wings and tail dull olive to olive brown. Throat whitish, center of belly yellowish to whitish, sides olive to brownish.

Upper tropical and subtropical zones. Generally distributed e of the Andes to ne ARGENTINA, PARAGUAY and n BOLIVIA. In BRAZIL from Bahía s to Rio Grande do Sul and s Mato Grosso, e PARAGUAY and ne ARGENTINA, 1; in se COLOMBIA and e ECUADOR, 2. W of the Andes to w ECUADOR. [Mid. Amer.] Thick forest undergrowth.

Plate 47

42. SPOT-CROWNED ANTVIREO

Dysithamnus puncticeps *

4.5". Crown black, speckled with gray; back, wings and tail gray, wing coverts spotted white. Throat and breast white, streaked with gray; center of abdomen white, sides olivaceous gray. ♀: Crown dull rufous, spotted black; back, wings and tail brown, wing coverts spotted buff. Underparts buff, streaked black on throat and breast; sides of body olivaceous brown.

Tropical zone. N and w COLOMBIA to w ECUADOR. [E Panama.] Forest.

43. RUFOUS-BACKED ANTVIREO

Dysithamnus xanthopterus

5.5". Head and mantle slaty gray, sides of head and forehead spotted white. Lower back and wings bright rufous chestnut; tail black, edged rufous. Slaty below, paler on throat and breast, flanks and belly olivaceous. ♀: Above rufous; below pale olivaceous. Wings and tail as in male.

Se BRAZIL from Espírito Santo to Paraná.

44. DUSKY-THROATED ANTSHRIKE

Thamnomanes ardesiacus *

5.2". Uniform gray, slightly darker on crown (or with black throat, 1). ♀: Above olivaceous brown, wings and tail browner. Throat whitish, rest of underparts dull ochraceous shaded olive on breast.

Tropical zone. GUIANAS, s VENEZUELA, n BRAZIL and rio Madeira region, 1. Se COLOMBIA, e ECUADOR. Forest undergrowth.

45. SATURNINE ANTSHRIKE

Thamnomanes saturninus *

Differs from 44 (1) by pure white concealed dorsal patch. ♀: Perhaps distinguishable from 44 by slightly less marked olive shading on breast.

Tropical zone. Ne PERU and w Amazonian BRAZIL to rio Tocantins.

46. WESTERN ANTSHRIKE

Thamnomanes occidentalis *

6.5". Slaty black, with concealed white interscapular patch and white-dotted wing coverts. ♀: Crown and nape chestnut; back maroon brown; wings and tail blackish brown, wing coverts spotted with white. Eyebrow, throat and breast slaty gray with white shaft streaks, rest of underparts olive brown.

Upper tropical zone. W slope of W Andes of COLOMBIA in Cauca. E ECUADOR. Forest.

47. PLUMBEOUS ANTSHRIKE

Thamnomanes plumbeus *

5.5". Dark gray; wings and tail blackish, wing coverts with narrow white apical margins, shoulder and axillaries pure white. ♀: Above dull brownish olive, bend of wing white, wing coverts margined with white. Sides of head olive gray streaked white, throat white; rest of underparts brownish gray, paler in middle (or with crown rufous; back, wings and tail reddish brown; underparts gray broadly striped white, 1).

Subtropical zone. N VENEZUELA from Miranda west to e COLOMBIA and e ECUADOR, 1. Se BRAZIL from Bahía to Espírito Santo. Forest.

48. CINEREOUS ANTSHRIKE

Thamnomanes caesius *

5.8". Much like a gray-throated 44 but bill broader at base, tail longer and general color darker (throat mottled white, 1; or with concealed white dorsal patch, 2). ♀: Above olive brown (interscapular patch as in male). Throat whitish, breast olivaceous, rest of underparts ochraceous to bright cinnamon rufous.

Tropical zone. GUIANAS w across s VENE-ZUELA to e COLOMBIA, south to ne PERU, and BRAZIL n of the Amazon to rio Jarí, 2. BRAZIL s of the Amazon from rio Purús to rio Tapajós and n Maranhão, 1; from Pernambuco to Rio de Janeiro. Forest undergrowth, clearings, savanna.

Plate 8

49. BLUISH-SLATE ANTSHRIKE

Thamnomanes schistogynus *

Much like 48 (1) but of bluish gray tint. ♀: Upperparts, breast, wings and tail like male; belly rufous chestnut, under tail coverts gray.

E PERU south to n BOLIVIA; sw BRAZIL.

Myrmotherula

These very small antwrens usually have rather short tails and resemble wrens somewhat in shape, but have shorter legs. Most live in forest undergrowth.

50. PYGMY ANTWREN

Myrmotherula brachyura *

3.2" (or 2.7", 1). Above black, streaked with white; rump gray, dorsal patch white. Throat white bordered laterally by black line, rest of underparts pale yellow. Wings black, coverts broadly edged white. Tail very short, black, pale-tipped. ♀: Differs from male by ochraceous streaks on upperparts, throat and breast tinged ochraceous.

Tropical zone. GUIANAS, s VENEZUELA and e COLOMBIA south to e ECUADOR, e PERU, and n BOLIVIA. Amazonian BRA-ZIL e to Óbidos and rio Tocantins. Nw COLOMBIA, 1. [E Panama to Canal Zone.] Lower trees at forest borders, second growth.

51. SHORT-BILLED ANTWREN

Myrmotherula obscura

Much like 50 but with less striping above, therefore blacker; malar streak wider, rump blacker. ♀: Like 50 but throat and upper breast more strongly tinged ochraceous.

Tropical zone. Se COLOMBIA s to Junín, PERU, and w Amazonian BRAZIL. Forest.

52. SCLATER'S ANTWREN

Myrmotherula sclateri *

Differs from 50 by throat yellow like rest of underparts, stripes on crown and back pale yellow, and longer tail. ♀: Like 50 but streaked yellow above; underparts yellow, streaked black.

BRAZIL s of the Amazon from rio Tapajós to rio Purús. Se PERU (Balta). Forest.

53. YELLOW-THROATED ANTWREN

Myrmotherula ambigua

Differs from 52 by crown streaks white instead of yellow and back streaks paler yellow. Throat and underparts yellow. ♀: Much like 52 but underparts unstreaked and top and sides of head streaked ochraceous buff instead of yellow.

Tropical zone. Sw VENEZUELA, bordering areas of COLOMBIA and BRAZIL. Forest undergrowth.

54. KLAGES' ANTWREN

Myrmotherula klagesi

Differs from 55 by no white interscapular patch. ♀: Above black, streaked buffy white; below buffy; breast and sides of body streaked black.

BRAZIL on both banks of lower Amazon in vicinity of rio Tapajós. Forest undergrowth.

55. STREAKED ANTWREN

Myrmotherula surinamensis *

3.5". Above streaked black and white, interscapulars pure white. Below white, streaked black. Wings black, wing coverts with broad white tips, remiges narrowly edged white. Tail black, feathers narrowly edged and tipped white. ♀: Differs from ♂ by crown and nape orange rufous striped black, mantle striped black and white, breast and sides of neck strongly tinged ochraceous (or ochraceous below without streaks, 1).

Generally distributed e of Andes from GUI-ANAS, s VENEZUELA and e COLOMBIA to e PERU and Amazonian BRAZIL to s Amazonas, n Mato Grosso and e Pará. W of Andes south to w ECUADOR, 1. Lower growth near creeks and swampy places, forest borders.

56. STRIPE-CHESTED ANTWREN

Myrmotherula longicauda *

4.3". Immediately distinguishable from 55 by no white interscapular patch, more lightly streaked underparts and much longer (1.3") tail. Also much like 54, but tail longer, underparts much less striped. ♀: Differs from 55 by mantle as well as head streaked buff, underparts much more ochraceous and virtually unstreaked.

Upper tropical zone. Se COLOMBIA s through e PERU to La Paz and Cochabamba, BOLIVIA. Forest undergrowth.

Plate 47

57. CHERRIE'S ANTWREN

Myrmotherula cherriei

Differs from 56 chiefly by throat, breast and belly heavily streaked with black. ♀: Above much like 55; below pinkish ochraceous, striped with black on throat, breast and upper belly.

VENEZUELA on upper Orinoco, adjacent BRAZIL and e COLOMBIA in s Meta. Forest.

58. RUFOUS-BELLIED ANTWREN

Myrmotherula guttata

3.5". Head, upper mantle, throat, breast and upper belly gray; lower back olive brown, concealed interscapular patch white with subterminal black bar. Wing coverts, inner remiges and tail black, handsomely tipped cinnamon. Lower belly rufous chestnut. ♀: Differs from male by crown and upper back olive brown, throat and breast light grayish brown, belly rufous chestnut.

Tropical zone. GUIANAS, s VENEZUELA, n BRAZIL from rio Negro to e Pará. Undergrowth in savanna.

59. PLAIN-THROATED ANTWREN

Myrmotherula hauxwelli *

3.5". Gray, paler below. Wing coverts and upper tail coverts black, tipped white. Con-

cealed interscapulars white. Tail black very narrowly tipped white. ♀: Much like 58 but upperparts slightly grayer, throat and breast cinnamon rufous, belly olive brown.

Tropical zone. E COLOMBIA south to n BOLIVIA. Amazonian BRAZIL s of the Amazon e to Maranhão. Forest.

60. STAR-THROATED ANTWREN

Myrmotherula gularis

4". Upperparts, flanks, under tail coverts, remiges and rectrices reddish umber brown; forehead grizzled gray. Shoulders white; wing coverts black, lesser dotted white, greater dotted buff. Throat and upper breast black spotted with white, rest of underparts gray. ♀: Similar to male but spots on throat larger.

E BRAZIL from Minas Gerais to Rio Grande do Sul.

61. BROWN-BELLIED ANTWREN

Myrmotherula gutturalis

4.3". Much like 60 but tail longer. Uppersurface much less reddish, wing coverts brown spotted with white; throat black, streaked rather than spotted with white; rest of underparts gray, shaded olive brown. ♀: Brown, buffy below; wing coverts with small fulvous spots.

GUIANAS; se VENEZUELA; ne BRAZIL, n of the Amazon, w to Óbidos. Low down in forest undergrowth.

62. CHECKER-THROATED ANTWREN

Myrmotherula fulviventris *

4.5". Above drab brown; throat white, checkered black; rest of underparts buffy brown, grayish on chest (or no grayish on chest, 1). Wings and tail brown, wing coverts blackish (or brown, 1), tipped with buff forming double wing bar. ♀: Similar to ♂ but throat buffy brown like rest of underparts.

Tropical, occasionally subtropical zone. Pacific COLOMBIA south to w ECUADOR and e to middle Cauca Valley; and from upper Sinú Valley to middle Magdalena, 1. [Honduras southward.] Forest.

63. WHITE-EYED ANTWREN

Myrmotherula leucophthalma *

4.7". Very like 62 but chest purer gray and tail longer.

Tropical zone. E ECUADOR, s to La Paz, BOLIVIA; Amazonian BRAZIL s of the Amazon.

64. STIPPLE-THROATED ANTWREN

Myrmotherula haematonota *

4". Head and nape brown, back chestnut (or upperparts all slaty gray, 1). Throat black, checkered white; rest of underparts slaty gray. Wing coverts black, tipped white or buff; wings and tail brown or slaty. ♀: Above like ♂ (or dull brown to grayish brown, 1); below buffy brown. Wings and tail like male.

Tropical zone. E ECUADOR s through east-central PERU to Junín, 1; and from Loreto, PERU, through w Amazonian BRAZIL to rios Negro and Madeira.

Plate 10

65. ORNATE ANTWREN

Myrmotherula ornata *

4". Crown, sides of head, nape, mantle, breast and belly light gray; throat black; lower back and rump chestnut (or upperparts uniform gray, 1). Wing coverts black, tipped white; wings and tail slaty. ♀: Above much like 64 or 64 (1). Throat black, checkered white; rest of underparts ferruginous brown. Wings and tail as in male.

E COLOMBIA south to ne PERU in n Loreto; Amazonian BRAZIL between rios Madeira and Tocantins to n Mato Grosso. PERU in the Huallaga and Ucayali drainage south to n BOLIVIA, 1. Forest.

66. RUFOUS-TAILED ANTWREN

Myrmotherula erythrura *

4.5". Differs mainly from 64 by gray throat, like rest of underparts, and longer tail, rufous chestnut instead of brown. ♀: Differs from 64 mainly by more olivaceous crown and mantle, and longer, rufous tail.

Tropical zone. Se COLOMBIA south to e ECUADOR and in Amazonian BRAZIL to rios Negro and Solimões. Forest.

67. BLACK-HOODED ANTWREN

Myrmotherula erythronotos

4.5". Head, neck and breast slaty black; abdomen slaty gray, sides of breast and broad margins of inner webs of remiges silky white. Back chestnut rufous. Lesser upper wing coverts white; rest black, edged white.

Wings and tail black. ♀: Above like male but head, wings and tail olive brownish. Sides of head and underparts light ochraceous, sides of breast silky white.

Se BRAZIL in Espírito Santo and Rio de Janeiro.

68. WHITE-FLANKED ANTWREN

Myrmotherula axillaris *

4.2". Above slaty gray to black, below black. Axillaries and long silky plumes springing from flanks white. Wings and tail black, wing coverts with terminal white dots. ♀: Above grayish brown to reddish brown; throat white, rest of underparts pale to dark buff, long plumes springing from flanks basally white. Wings and tail brown, wing coverts edged rufous. (Cf. 92)

Tropical zone. Generally distributed e of Andes to n BOLIVIA, Amazonian and e BRAZIL to Rio de Janeiro. W of Andes to w ECUADOR. Trinidad. [Honduras southward.] Shubbery or lower parts of forest trees.

69. SLATY ANTWREN

Myrmotherula schisticolor *

4". Dark gray, throat black. Wing and tail coverts black with white terminal spots. Tail narrowly fringed white. ♀: Above grayish olive (or bluish gray, 1), crown tinged ochraceous. Underparts ochraceous. Tail like back.

Upper tropical and subtropical zones. Mts. of n VENEZUELA w to COLOMBIA and w ECUADOR. From e COLOMBIA to se PERU, 1. Forest undergrowth.

Plate 47

70. LONG-WINGED ANTWREN

Myrmotherula longipennis *

4". Differs from 69 by paler gray plumage, considerably larger white margins to wing coverts and tips of tail feathers; shoulders gray, axillaries white (with definitely whitish eyebrow and sides of neck, 1). ♀: Rufescent brown above; eye ring, throat and breast buff; center of belly white (or much like 69 but much paler below, crown like back 1, 2).

Tropical zone. GUIANAS, s VENEZUELA; se COLOMBIA and BRAZIL n of the Amazon to opposite Santarém. E ECUADOR, e PERU, w Amazonian BRAZIL s of the Amazon, 2; from rio Madeira eastward, 1. Forest.

71. RIO SUNO ANTWREN

Myrmotherula sunensis *

3.6". Differs from 69 by much shorter tail and paler gray plumage. ♀: Above grayish olive, browner on crown; below olivaceous drab, paler on throat.

Tropical zone. Se COLOMBIA s to Junín, PERU. Forest.

72. SALVADORI'S ANTWREN

Myrmotherula minor

Much like 71 but tail longer, black of throat and breast more restricted, tail tipped white with subterminal black bar; wing coverts edged rather than tipped white. ♀: Crown ashy, shading to pale brownish olive on back. Wing coverts dusky, tipped olive buff; remiges edged olive brown, rectrices dusky brown with bright russet edges. Throat whitish, feathers indistinctly fringed dusky, rest of underparts bright olive buff.

Ne PERU. BRAZIL on rio Purús and in se from Espírito Santo to São Paulo.

73. IHERING'S ANTWREN

Myrmotherula iheringi *

Much like 72 but wing coverts blacker and tipped, instead of edged, with white. Tail gray without white tip and black subterminal bar. Bill considerably larger. Differs from 71 by larger size and longer tail. ♀: Pale slate gray above, wing coverts black with large buff apical spots; underparts pale buff.

W Amazonian BRAZIL e to rio Tapajós and n Mato Grosso.

74. ASHY ANTWREN

Myrmotherula grisea

4.2". Slaty gray, darker on head. Wing coverts unmarked. ♀: Above olive brown, below bright rufous brown; tail reddish brown.

Tropical zone. BOLIVIA in La Paz.

75. UNICOLORED ANTWREN

Myrmotherula unicolor

4". Slate gray; throat black, feathers edged slate. Differs from other black-throated

species of *Myrmotherula* (except 76) by plain gray wing coverts. ♀: Above fulvous brown, crown and nape tinged olivaceous; throat whitish, rest of underparts pale olive buff.

Se BRAZIL from Espírito Santo to Rio Grande do Sul.

76. PLAIN-WINGED ANTWREN

Myrmotherula behni *

4.5". Much like 75 but darker, black throat patch extending to upper breast. Size larger. ♀: Like 75 but much darker, especially underparts which are olivaceous.

Upper tropical and subtropical zones. GUYANA and adjacent BRAZIL; mts. of s VENEZUELA; e COLOMBIA. Forest.

77. BAND-TAILED ANTWREN

Myrmotherula urosticta

4". Gray, throat black. Wing coverts black with large white tips. Distinct from other species by distal third of tail feathers white, excepting central pair. ♀: Above clear light gray, wing coverts with large, dingy white tips. Below pale buff, throat whitish.

Se BRAZIL in Bahía, Minas Gerais and Espírito Santo.

78. GRAY ANTWREN

Myrmotherula menetriesii *

4". Light gray (or throat with varying amounts of black, 1). Wing coverts distinctive: Gray with subterminal black patch and broad white tip. Tail short. ♀: Above gray, crown tinged ochraceous; below ochraceous cinnamon. Tail gray.

Tropical zone. GUIANAS, s VENEZUELA, e COLOMBIA, e ECUADOR, PERU in Loreto, e Amazonian BRAZIL to Maranhão. E PERU, n BOLIVIA and sw BRAZIL, 1. Forest treetops.

79. LEADEN ANTWREN

Myrmotherula assimillis *

4.5". Clear light gray, paler below. Extensive concealed white patch on back. Wing coverts gray, tipped white. Tail slaty gray with small white tips to feathers. ♀: Above like male, below light cinnamon buff, throat white. Wings brownish with buff-tipped wing coverts.

Tropical zone. Ne PERU; w Amazonian

BRAZIL e to rios Jamundá and Tapajós; n BOLIVIA in Beni.

80. BANDED ANTBIRD

Dichrozona cincta *

4.8". Crown and mantle chestnut, lower back black crossed by white (or buff, ♀) crescent, upper tail coverts black, pale tipped. Wing coverts black, lesser ones tipped white (or no white, ♀), greater coverts broadly tipped buffy. Below white, breast spotted black. Tail very short (.5"), black, outer feathers white. Legs rather long.

Tropical zone. Sw VENEZUELA, e CO-LOMBIA south to n BOLIVIA. Amazonian BRAZIL e to rios Negro and Tapajós. Forest.

Plate 10

81. STRIPE-BACKED ANTBIRD

Myrmorchilus strigilatus

6.5". Above rufous chestnut broadly streaked black. wing coverts black with broad white tips; remiges black, inner ones edged chestnut. Eyebrow and moustachial streak white; throat and upper breast black; rest of underparts white, tinged buff on sides. Central tail feathers chestnut, rest black, outer ones edged and tipped white. ♀: Like male but throat white, breast fulvous, streaked black.

E BRAZIL in Paraiba, Pernambuco, Ceará and Bahía, and from sw Mato Grosso and PARAGUAY to e BOLIVIA and nw AR-GENTINA. Dense undergrowth.

82. BLACK-CAPPED ANTWREN

Herpsilochmus pileatus *

5.2". Crown black; long eyebrow white, bordered behind eye by black. Back gray, interscapulars white mixed with black. Below ashy gray, throat and center of belly white (or below grayish white, 1; tinged yellow on belly, 2). Wings black, wing coverts tipped broadly with white. Tail feathers black with white tips increasing in size to outermost, which is almost all white. ♀ Like ♂, but forehead buffy brown, crown streaked white, back olive gray.

BRAZIL along coast from Ceará to Bahía. E and central BRAZIL from Maranhão s through Goiás and Minas Gerais to São

Paulo and Mato Grosso, PARAGUAY, e BOLIVIA and nw ARGENTINA, 1. PERU in Junín and Cuzco, 2. Thick scrub, forest undergrowth and treetops.

Plate 26

83. SPOT-TAILED ANTWREN

Herpsilochmus sticturus *

4.2". Differs from 82 (1) by much shorter tail, tertials more broadly edged white, and central tail feathers with large, white, oval spots on inner web. ♀: Like ♂ but forecrown dark chestnut with white shaft streaks, hindcrown black (or crown and nape rufous with pale shaft streaks, 1). Spots on central tail feathers smaller.

GUIANAS, e VENEZUELA south to n bank of lower Amazon, BRAZIL. Se COLOM-BIA, ne ECUADOR, 1 (*dugandi*, ♂ unknown; could be distinct species). Wet savanna, forest near streams.

84. TODD'S ANTWREN

Herpsilochmus stictocephalus

4.6". Much like 83; spots on central tail feathers smaller, white margins of tertials wider. Size larger. ♀: Differs from ♂ by crown black, spotted with white; underparts white strongly tinged buff on breast.

GUYANA; FRENCH GUIANA; e VENE-ZUELA. Forest treetops.

85. SPOT-BACKED ANTWREN

Herpsilochmus dorsimaculatus

4.6". Differs from 83 mainly by back broadly striped black and white. ♀: Differs from male by forehead spotted deep ochraceous, crown with large white spots, lores ochraceous; malar region, sides of neck and the breast bright buff.

Tropical zone. S VENEZUELA, se COLOM-BIA and bordering area of BRAZIL. Forest.

86. RORAIMAN ANTWREN

Herpsilochmus roraimae

5.4". In color like 85 but tail much longer and striping of back less extensive. ♀: Like male but forehead and crown spotted white.

Upper tropical and subtropical zones. GUY-ANA; mts. of s VENEZUELA and bordering area of BRAZIL. Forest.

87. PECTORAL ANTWREN

Herpsilochmus pectoralis

5.3″. Immediately distinguishable from other black-capped, gray-backed species by black crescent on breast. ♀: Head tawny ochraceous; underparts ochraceous, darkest on breast. Above brownish olive, upper tail coverts tipped white.

BRAZIL in Maranhão and Bahía. Dry caatinga.

88. LARGE-BILLED ANTWREN

Herpsilochmus longirostris

5.8″. Distinguishable from 87 by pale gray spots instead of crescent across breast, and from other black-capped, gray-backed species by longer tail (2.3″ vs. 1.4″). ♀: Head and neck rufous; back gray. Underparts cinnamon, paler on belly. Tail coverts without white tips.

BRAZILIAN plateau from Piauí to São Paulo and Mato Grosso.

89. YELLOW-BREASTED ANTWREN

Herpsilochmus axillaris *

4.8″. Crown, nape and eyebrow black, spotted white; back olive gray. Underparts pale yellow (with white throat, 1). Wing coverts black, margined white; remiges edged olive gray. Central tail feathers like back, rest black with broad white tips. ♀: Like ♂ but crown and nape dull rufous.

Tropical, subtropical zones. W slope of W Andes in COLOMBIA, 1. E ECUADOR; e PERU to Puno. Forest.

Fig. 8, p. 54

90. RUFOUS-WINGED ANTWREN

Herpsilochmus rufimarginatus *

4.5″. Crown and nape black. Eyebrow from nostril white, postocular streak black; back mixed gray and black. Throat white, rest of underparts yellowish white. Wing coverts and inner remiges black broadly edged white, rest of remiges with bright rufous chestnut outer webs. Central tail feathers like back; rest black, tipped white. ♀: Crown chestnut. Stripe through eye black. Back olive. Underparts, wings and tail as in ♂.

Upper tropical and subtropical zones. VENEZUELA; n and ne COLOMBIA. E ECUADOR s to Puno, PERU. N BOLIVIA. Amazonian BRAZIL along rio Jarí and s of the Amazon e to Marajó I., and Pernambuco

and s to Paraná, PARAGUAY, and ne ARGENTINA. [E Panama.] Forest.

91. DOT-WINGED ANTWREN

Microrhopias quixensis *

4.2″- 4.8″. Glossy black; large semiconcealed white interscapular patch. Wing coverts and tail conspicuously tipped white. ♀: Upperparts, wings and tail as in ♂ (in some races crown and mantle dark slaty rather than black). Underparts chestnut (with black throat, 1; with black throat and belly, 2; with black belly, 3).

Tropical zone. FRENCH GUIANA, bordering area of BRAZIL. W COLOMBIA and nw ECUADOR. Se COLOMBIA, ECUADOR and ne PERU, 1. PERU in the Huallaga, upper Ucayali and Urubamba drainage, 2. PERU in Puno and Madre de Dios, and from w BOLIVIA e through Amazonian BRAZIL to rio Tapajós; between rios Tapajós and Tocantins, 3. Forest.

Plates 47 (♂), 36 (♀)

92. NARROW-BILLED ANTWREN

Formicivora iheringi

4.3″. Very like 68 in color but feathers of throat edged white, of breast edged gray. Tail longer, more graduated; bill finer. ♀: Differs from 68 by cinnamon rufous upper tail coverts, more rufescent outer tail feathers and deeper ochraceous underparts.

BRAZIL in interior of Bahía.

93. WHITE-FRINGED ANTWREN

Formicivora grisea *

4.8″. Above grayish brown, quite dark in some races (or reddish brown, 1). Below black; lengthened feathers at sides of body silky white. Wing coverts black, conspicuously spotted and edged with white. Tail graduated, black, tipped white. ♀: Above grayish brown (or reddish brown, 1). Long eyebrow white (or buff, 2). Below cinnamon buff (or deep cinnamon, 2; or whitish, tinged cinnamon on breast, 3; or more or less spotted with black on breast, 4; or heavily streaked black on throat, breast and belly, 1). Wings and tail as in male.

Tropical zone. GUIANAS, Amazonian BRAZIL from rios Negro and Madeira eastward, and s to Rio de Janeiro and Mato Grosso. N VENEZUELA and ne COLOMBIA, 4; middle Orinoco e to lower río Paragua, 1; upper

Orinoco and immediately adjacent COLOM-BIA, 2. COLOMBIA from Magdalena Valley to Bolívar, 3. Margarita I., 4. Tobago, 4. [Pearl Is., Panama.] Caatinga, campos, sandy savanna, cerradão.

94. SERRA ANTBIRD

Formicivora serrana

Rather like 95 but upperparts dark reddish brown, tertials narrowly fringed cinnamon; sides of breast and flanks smoke gray. ♀: Like 95 but underparts deeper buff.

Serras of se BRAZIL from Minas Gerais to Rio de Janeiro.

95. BLACK-BELLIED ANTWREN

*Formicivora melanogaster**

5.5". Upperparts dark slaty brown. Long eyebrow white. Below black; long, silky, gray feathers at sides, tipped white. Wings and tail as in 93. ♀: Differs from ♂ by white underparts, breast and belly lightly tinged buff.

E BRAZIL from Piauí, Ceará and Paraiba south to w São Paulo. E BOLIVIA s to Tarija. Brush and cerrado, near streams.

96. RUSTY-BACKED ANTWREN

*Formicivora rufa**

5.5". Above light cinnamon brown, crown and nape grayer. Long eyebrow white. Throat, breast and center of belly black, outlined in white; sides cinnamon brown. Wing coverts and tail brownish black, both tipped white. ♀: Above much like ♂. Below white, streaked black from throat to belly. Wings and tail as in ♂.

SURINAM; central and e Amazonian BRA-ZIL s to São Paulo and Mato Grosso, PARAGUAY and n BOLIVIA. E PERU. Savanna, campos, cerrado.

Plate 8

97. FERRUGINOUS ANTBIRD

Drymophila ferruginea

5.5". Crown and sides of head black, long eyebrow, lores and lower cheeks white. Mantle olive brown, concealed interscapular patch white with broad black subterminal band; rump chestnut. Wings olive brown, shoulders white, wing coverts black broadly tipped white. Throat and breast bright ferruginous, rest of underparts light brown. Tail strongly graduated, gray, tipped white.

♀: Like ♂ but duller, forecrown feathers tipped olive.

Se BRAZIL from Bahía to Santa Catarina; ne PARAGUAY; ARGENTINA in Misiones. Bushes.

Plate 10

98. RUFOUS-TAILED ANTBIRD

Drymophila genei

5.5". Crown black, lores and eyebrow white. Back gray mixed with black, interscapular patch white; lower back and tail rufous. Outer webs of primaries and inner remiges rufous. Wing coverts black, white tipped. Below white, streaked black on throat; breast feathers with black subapical spots; belly olive brown. ♀: Above rufous, darker on lower back, crown streaked with black, superciliary stripe yellowish buff. Wings and tail as in ♂. Below buffy, breast with indistinct black subapical spots; throat white, spotted buffy.

Se BRAZIL in Minas Gerais, Espírito Santo and Rio de Janeiro.

99. OCHRE-RUMPED ANTBIRD

Drymophila ochropyga

5". Crown black, eyebrow white. Back mixed gray and black, small white interscapular patch with subterminal black band; lower back ferruginous. Wings blackish, coverts tipped white. Throat and breast white, streaked black; belly ferruginous. Tail broadly tipped white. ♀: Similar to ♂ but duller and browner, crown spotted with brownish.

Se BRAZIL from Minas Gerais to e São Paulo.

100. STRIATED ANTBIRD

*Drymophila devillei**

5.3". Crown and upper back black, streaked white; concealed interscapular patch white, lower back chestnut rufous. Wings black, primaries edged white, tertials edged cinnamon. Below white (or ochraceous buff, 1) with a few black streaks. Sides of body cinnamon rufous. Tail blackish, tipped white, with four white spots on basal portion of inner web. ♀: Like ♂ but upperparts streaked buff.

Tropical zone. Se PERU and n BOLIVIA. BRAZIL in rio Xingú region, 1.

Plate 10

101. LONG-TAILED ANTBIRD

Drymophila caudata *

5.9". Much like 100 but larger with longer tail; tail dusky olive with black subterminal area and white tip; breast more heavily streaked, entire belly rufous chestnut. ♀: Differs from ♂ by upperparts streaked buff and black, brighter on head, and underparts buffy white to buff, only flanks buffy cinnamon.

Upper tropical and subtropical zones. VENEZUELA n of the Orinoco w to COLOMBIA and south to n BOLIVIA. Second growth, fern brakes.

102. DUSKY-TAILED ANTBIRD

Drymophila malura

5.5". Crown black, streaked gray; back dark olive with black-tipped, concealed, white interscapular patch. Wings and tail like back. Throat and breast white, streaked black; belly dull olive. ♀: Like ♂ but browner.

Se BRAZIL from Espírito Santo to Rio Grande do Sul; PARAGUAY; ARGENTINA in Misiones. Forest undergrowth.

103. SCALED ANTBIRD

Drymophila squamata *

4.8". Black above spotted with white (crown and nape unspotted, 1), concealed dorsal patch white. Below white, spotted with black. Tail black, barred white. ♀: Above brown with large round fulvous spots on lower back. Below white with narrow black streaks. Tail black, barred fulvous.

Coast regions of Bahía, 1; and from Espírito Santo to São Paulo, BRAZIL. Humid forest.

104. STREAK-CAPPED ANTWREN

Terenura maculata

4.2". Crown, nape and sides of head black, streaked white; back rufous chestnut. Wings black, remiges narrowly margined pale gray, coverts edged white. Tail light gray. Underparts white, lightly streaked on breast with black; breast and belly tinged sulphur yellow.

Se BRAZIL from Minas Gerais to Santa Catarina; PARAGUAY; ARGENTINA in Misiones. Bushes.

105. RUFOUS-RUMPED ANTWREN

Terenura callinota *

4.4". Crown black; eyebrow, nape, sides of head, the throat and breast pale gray; belly olive yellow. Mantle and upper tail coverts olive, lower back chestnut. Wing coverts black, tipped pale yellow; shoulders bright yellow. Wings and tail olive gray. ♀: Above olive, grayer on head; rump chestnut. Throat and upper breast grayish white, rest of underparts olive yellow. Wings and tail much as in male.

Subtropical zone. GUYANA. Nw VENEZUELA; COLOMBIA s to e and w ECUADOR and to Junín, PERU. [Panama.] Forest.

Plate 10

106. CHESTNUT-SHOULDERED ANTWREN

Terenura humeralis *

Not unlike 105; differs mainly by chestnut instead of yellow shoulder and pale grayish abdomen, tinged pale yellow on flanks and under tail coverts. ♀: Differs from 105 by brownish crown, dark olive green bend of wing, buffy throat and brighter olive yellow belly.

Tropical zone. E ECUADOR, e PERU, w BRAZIL s of the Amazon e to rio Purús.

107. YELLOW-RUMPED ANTWREN

Terenura sharpei

Differs from 105 by rump and stripe down back sulphur yellow bordered by black, abdomen deeper greenish yellow. ♀: Unknown.

Subtropical zone. Se PERU (Puno); n BOLIVIA (Cochabamba).

108. ASH-WINGED ANTWREN

Terenura spodioptila *

4". Crown black; upper mantle and tail coverts gray, rest of upperparts chestnut rufous. Lesser wing coverts gray (or chestnut, 1), rest blackish, tipped white; remiges externally gray. Underparts white. Tail gray narrowly tipped white. ♀: Crown and upper mantle brownish, throat and breast strongly shaded buffy brown, otherwise like male.

GUYANA; s VENEZUELA; n BRAZIL from lower rio Negro eastward; in upper rio Negro and se COLOMBIA, 1. Forest.

109. GRAY ANTBIRD

Cercomacra cinerascens *

6.3″. Uniform gray with small, concealed white interscapulars. Wing coverts with or without very small white tips (or white tips well marked, 1). Tail blackish, tipped white. ♀: Olive brown, paler below (or with back gray, 1). Wing coverts unmarked or only slightly so (or tipped white, 1, 2). Tail dusky gray, tipped white.

Tropical zone. GUIANAS w across VENE-ZUELA to e COLOMBIA, e ECUADOR and BRAZIL n of the Amazon. S of it from rio Purús eastward, 2. E PERU s of the Mara-ñón to n BOLIVIA and w BRAZIL to rio Juruá, 1. Forest undergrowth.

Plate 26

110. RIO DE JANEIRO ANTBIRD

Cercomacra brasiliana

6.5″. Differs from 109 (1) by much paler gray color; tail much longer (3″), feathers narrowly instead of broadly tipped white. Bill smaller. ♀: Differs from 109 (1) by uniform wing coverts, olivaceous brown tail and brighter underparts, more as in 111.

Se BRAZIL in Minas Gerais, Rio de Janeiro and Espírito Santo.

111. DUSKY ANTBIRD

Cercomacra tyrannina *

6″. Differs from 109 chiefly by white-edged wing coverts, and tips of tail feathers only very narrowly edged white. White dorsal patch much larger. ♀: Upperparts, wings and tail olivaceous brown; concealed inter-scapular patch white. Sides of head, under-parts and under wing coverts bright ochra-ceous orange; upper wing coverts inconspic-uously tipped buff.

Tropical, subtropical zones. GUIANAS; VENEZUELA; COLOMBIA; ECUADOR. BRAZIL n of the Amazon from rio Negro e to Amapá, and s of Amazon from rio Tocantins to Alagoas. Dense forest under-growth.

Plate 46

112. BLACKISH ANTBIRD

Cercomacra nigrescens *

6″. Dark gray to blackish gray, concealed interscapular patch white. Bend of wing white; wing coverts black, edged white. Tail like back. ♀: Forecrown, sides of head and

the underparts orange rufous. Back, wings and tail olive brown to reddish brown; concealed interscapular patch white.

Tropical zone. SURINAM; FRENCH GUI-ANA. Se COLOMBIA; e ECUADOR; e and central PERU; n BOLIVIA. Amazonian BRAZIL. Dense undergrowth in swampy forest.

113. BANANAL ANTBIRD

Cercomacra ferdinandi

6.5″. Black, with large semiconcealed white interscapular patch. Lesser wing coverts white; rest black, edged white. Tail black, tipped white; white tip increasing in size toward outermost feather. ♀: Like male but grayer. Throat somewhat blotched with white; breast with fine white streaks.

BRAZIL in w Goiás (Ilha do Bananal).

114. BLACK ANTBIRD

Cercomacra serva *

5.8″. Grayish black, blackest on throat and breast; concealed interscapular patch white. Lesser wing coverts white, rest edged white. Tail black. ♀: Very like 112. Distinguishable by only forehead instead of forecrown orange rufous.

Tropical zone. Se COLOMBIA south to n BOLIVIA. Sw Amazonian BRAZIL. Forest undergrowth.

115. JET ANTBIRD

Cercomacra nigricans *

6.2″. Black; concealed interscapular patch white. Shoulders white; wing coverts and inner margins of remiges edged white. Tail black, much graduated, tipped white. ♀: Gray, feathers of underparts barred and streaked with white except on belly. Wings and tail as in male.

Tropical zone. N VENEZUELA; COLOM-BIA; w ECUADOR. Se PERU (Balta). N BRAZIL in Roraima. [Central and e Pana-ma.] Thick forest undergrowth.

116. RIO BRANCO ANTBIRD

Cercomacra carbonaria

Nearest to 115 but differs by narrower bill and longer tail. ♀: Above grayish black; throat white, speckled with black; center breast and belly fulvous. Secondaries with small, but distinct, white apical spots.

N BRAZIL in Roraima.

117. MATO GROSSO ANTBIRD

Cercomacra melanaria

7.5". Black; interscapulars, shoulders, edges to wing coverts and tips of three outer tail feathers white. Tail much graduated. ♀: Ashy gray above, much paler below, whitish on throat and center of belly. Wings and tail as in male.

Tropical zone. N BOLIVIA in Beni and Cochabamba; BRAZIL in s and w Mato Grosso.

118. STUB-TAILED ANTBIRD

Sipia berlepschi

5". Black; interscapulars white. Tail very short (1.5"). Bill heavy. ♀: Blackish; wing coverts, throat and breast dotted with white; feathers of upper belly fringed white.

Tropical zone. Pacific COLOMBIA to nw ECUADOR. Forest.

Plate 26

119. ESMERALDAS ANTBIRD

Sipia rosenbergi

5.2". Leaden gray; rump wood brown, interscapulars white. Wing coverts black, tipped white. Tail dark gray, short (1.6"). ♀: Head and underparts leaden gray, blacker on throat which is spotted white. Back, wings and belly dark reddish brown. Lesser wing coverts dotted white, greater coverts tipped buff. Tail blackish brown.

Tropical zone. Pacific COLOMBIA to nw ECUADOR. Forest.

120. WHITE-BACKED FIRE-EYE

*Pyriglena leuconota**

7". Glossy black; large semiconcealed interscapular patch white. Iris bright red. ♀: Above tobacco brown, interscapulars white (with white eyebrow, 1); below pale grayish olive, to buffy brown, to brown; tail black (or head and tail black, interscapulars white, rest of plumage dark brown, 2; or black, interscapulars white, wings and center of back dark reddish brown, 3).

Tropical, subtropical zones. Se COLOMBIA and head of Magdalena Valley, e ECUA-

DOR, n PERU in Cajamarca, 3. Central PERU from Loreto to Junín, 2. Se PERU to n BOLIVIA, 1; between rios Tapajós and Xingú, 2; e Pará to Maranhão and Pernambuco. W ECUADOR.

Plate 8

121. FRINGE-BACKED FIRE-EYE

Pyriglena atra

7". Glossy black; feathers of white interscapular patch, with large, oval black subterminal spots. ♀: Dull brown above, paler below. Large white interscapular patch. Tail blackish.

E BRAZIL in coastal Bahía.

122. WHITE-SHOULDERED FIRE-EYE

Pyriglena leucoptera

6.8". Glossy black; concealed white interscapular patch. Lesser wing coverts white, median and greater ones fringed white. ♀: Differs from 120 by no white interscapular patch.

E and s BRAZIL from Bahía s to Santa Catarina and west to s Mato Grosso; e PARAGUAY; ARGENTINA in Misiones. Thick forest undergrowth, capoeira.

123. SLENDER ANTBIRD

Rhopornis ardesiaca

7". Uniform dark plumbeous gray above. Throat and foreneck black; sides of head and underparts gray, slightly paler than back. Median and greater wing coverts narrowly edged white. Tail long (3.5"), much graduated, black. ♀: Crown and nape ochre brown, back plumbeous gray. Throat white; rest of underparts pale gray, whitish in center of abdomen. Wings and tail as in ♂.

E BRAZIL in se Bahía (known from three specimens).

124. WHITE-BROWED ANTBIRD

*Myrmoborus leucophrys**

5.2". Forecrown and long, broad eyebrow white; sides of head and throat black, rest of plumage gray. Tail rather short. ♀: Forecrown cinnamon rufous; long, broad eyebrow cinnamon buff; sides of head black. Back, wings and tail reddish brown; wing coverts tipped buffy white. Underparts white with a few dusky spots on breast.

Tropical zone. GUIANAS w across n VENE-

ZUELA to e COLOMBIA thence south to n BOLIVIA. Amazonian BRAZIL. Undergrowth in swampy forest.

Plate 8

125. ASH-BREASTED ANTBIRD

Myrmoborus lugubris *

5.8". Forehead pale gray, sides of head and throat black. Above gray; below very pale gray or whitish in sharp contrast to black throat. ♀: Sides of head and entire upperparts, wings and tail ferruginous (or sides of head black, 1), wing coverts tipped cinnamon. Below white (breast gray, dusky spots on breast, 2).

Ne PERU in Loreto, BRAZIL, s of rio Solimões, 1, 2; n of rio Solimões and on lower rio Madeira, 1; both sides of the Amazon from rio Jamundá to rio Tocantins.

126. BLACK-FACED ANTBIRD

Myrmoborus myotherinus *

4.6". Differs from 125 by smaller size and black, white-edged (instead of plain gray) wing coverts; and by white interscapular patch. ♀: Above umber brown to olive brown; sides of head black; wing coverts black to blackish, edged buff. Below buffy cinnamon to deep cinnamon, throat white with a few blackish spots on upper breast (or uniform dark cinnamon below, 1; or white below, breast spotted black, 2); wing coverts black, edged buff to cinnamon (or edged white, 2).

Tropical zone. E COLOMBIA south to n BOLIVIA and Amazonian BRAZIL south to sw Amazonas and Mato Grosso (at Tonantins, rio Solimões, 2; s of the Amazon from rio Madeira to e Pará, 1). Forest.

127. BLACK-TAILED ANTBIRD

Myrmoborus melanurus

4.5". Head and neck blackish, rest of plumage slaty gray; wings and tail black, wing coverts margined white. ♀: Above earthy brown, sides of head olive brown. Below white, dull reddish brown on breast and sides. Wing coverts black, margined white.

Ne PERU between ríos Ucayali and Javarí.

128. WARBLING ANTBIRD

Hypocnemis cantator *

4.3". Crown black, with median line of white spots; lores and superciliary white. Mantle streaked black and white, rump rufescent. Underparts white, breast feathers edged black; sides rufous (or pale yellow below streaked black on breast, sides pale to bright rufous, 1). Bill pale. ♀: Much like male but back browner.

Tropical zone. GUIANAS; VENEZUELA in e Bolívar; BRAZIL on both sides of lower Amazon; e COLOMBIA south to e ECUADOR and PERU. Nw BRAZIL and immediately adjacent COLOMBIA and VENEZUELA, central PERU in Junín and Ayacucho, n BOLIVIA and nw Mato Grosso, BRAZIL, 1. Undergrowth in wet forest and savanna.

Plate 10

129. YELLOW-BROWED ANTBIRD

Hypocnemis hypoxantha *

Much like 128 (1) but at once distinguishable by plain olive back and much brighter yellow underparts [or underparts like 128 (1), 1]. Bill black.

Tropical zone, Se COLOMBIA to e PERU n of the Marañón and BRAZIL n of the Amazon to rio Negro; s of Amazon between rios Tapajós and Xingú, 1. Forest.

130. BLACK-CHINNED ANTBIRD

Hypocnemoides melanopogon *

4.8". Leaden gray, paler on belly; throat black; no interscapular patch. Wing coverts black, fringed white. Tail short (1.4"), black, narrowly tipped white. ♀: Differs from ♂ by white, gray-clouded underparts.

Tropical zone. GUIANAS, e and s VENEZUELA, e COLOMBIA from Meta south to ne PERU; BRAZIL in Amazonia. Undergrowth in swampy forest.

131. BAND-TAILED ANTBIRD

Hypocnemoides maculicauda *

Very like 130 but slightly larger. Black of throat more extensive, merging into gray of breast. White fringes of wing coverts and white at tip of tail broader. White interscapular patch large. ♀: Differs from ♂ by white, gray-clouded underparts.

Tropical zone. E PERU; n BOLIVIA; Amazonian BRAZIL s of the Amazon south to nw Maranhão. Riparian thickets.

132. BLACK-AND-WHITE ANTBIRD

Myrmochanes hemileucus

4.8". Crown black, somewhat crested; mantle black, white of interscapular patch showing through; rump gray. Underparts white. Wings and tail black, wing coverts and tail tipped white. ♀: Like ♂ but lores white and lower mandible pale instead of black.

Tropical zone. E ECUADOR south to n BOLIVIA. Amazonian BRAZIL s of the Amazon e to rios Madeira and Mamoré.

133. BARE-CROWNED ANTBIRD

Gymnocichla nudiceps *

6.4". Top and sides of head bare, bright, light blue. General color brownish black, fringes to wing coverts and interscapular patch white. ♀: Rufous brown above, rufous chestnut below. Top of head feathered.

Tropical zone. N COLOMBIA from nw Chocó e to middle Magdalena Valley and Santa Marta. [Guatemala southward.] Forest, second growth on or near ground.

Plate 46

134. BLACK-HEADED ANTBIRD

Percnostola rufifrons *

5.8". Leaden gray. Throat and crown black, crown with well-developed crest. Wing coverts black, fringed white. ♀: Crown and crest black, sides of head and underparts dull ferruginous. Back leaden gray. Wings brown; wing coverts black, fringed buff (or with dark brown crown, olivaceous gray back; sides of head, throat and breast bright ferruginous; rest of underparts buff, 1).

Tropical zone. GUIANAS; BRAZIL n of lower Amazon w to lower rio Negro; se COLOMBIA south to ne PERU. VENEZUELA in s Amazonas and nw BRAZIL in upper rio Negro, 1. Undergrowth in forest and savanna.

135. WHITE-LINED ANTBIRD

Percnostola macrolopha

Differs from 134 by longer crest; by much darker blackish coloration, throat and center of underparts black; and by white shoulder and under wing coverts. ♀: Unknown.

Madre de Dios and Cuzco, PERU.

136. SLATE-COLORED ANTBIRD

Percnostola schistacea

5.8". Uniform leaden gray. Wing coverts with small white terminal dots. ♀: Crown dark chestnut with pale shaft streaks, back dark reddish brown with pale shaft streaks. Wings brown, wing coverts with terminal ochraceous spots. Throat, breast and center of belly bright rufous chestnut, sides and crissum dark brown. Upper tail coverts and tail gray.

Tropical zone. Se COLOMBIA. E PERU; w Amazonian BRAZIL. Forest.

137. SPOT-WINGED ANTBIRD

Percnostola leucostigma *

5.8". Easily distinguishable from 136 by paler back, much paler underparts, black wing coverts with much larger terminal spots. ♀: Crown and sides of head gray or brown like back, back grayish brown to reddish brown. Wing coverts with large ochraceous terminal spots. Underparts deep bright rufous chestnut (or orange rufous below, chin and center of belly whitish, 1).

Tropical, subtropical zones. GUIANAS, ne BRAZIL w to rio Madeira. S VENEZUELA, e COLOMBIA, e ECUADOR, e PERU, w Amazonian BRAZIL (on upper rio Madeira, 1). Forest undergrowth, grassy or bushy savanna.

Plate 26

138. CAURA ANTBIRD

Percnostola caurensis *

7". Like darker forms of 137 but much larger. ♀: Very like ♀ of 136 but much larger and less rufescent.

Tropical zone. VENEZUELA s of the Orinoco and bordering area of BRAZIL in nw Amazonas. Forest.

139. RUFOUS-CRESTED ANTBIRD

Percnostola lophotes

6.5". Crown and crest bright cinnamon rufous, back duller and browner than crown. Bend of wing and apical spots on wing coverts cinnamon rufous. Sides of head and of breast ashy gray, center of underparts white. ♀: Similar to ♂ except for more brownish sides of neck and breast.

Tropical zone. E PERU in Loreto and Puno.

Illustrations

John R. Quinn
(Plates 1-30)

Earl L. Poole
(Plates 31-50)

PLATE 1

SICKLE-WINGED GUAN
Chamaepetes g. goudotii
Page 58

PALE-WINGED TRUMPETER
Psophia l. leucoptera
Page 64

**BLUE-THROATED
PIPING-GUAN**
Pipile pipile cumanensis
Page 58

BARE-FACED CURASSOW
Crax fasciolata pinima (♀)
Page 59

GREATER RHEA
Rhea a. americana
Page 2

RED-LEGGED SERIEMA
Cariama cristata
Page 71

RED-WINGED TINAMOU
*Rynchotus rufescens
maculicollis*
Page 7

WHITE-TIPPED DOVE
Leptotila verreauxi decolor
Page 94

PUNA TINAMOU
Tinamotis p. pentlandii (♀)
Page 8

**WHITE-THROATED
TINAMOU**
Tinamus guttatus
Page 4

SPOTTED NOTHURA
Nothura maculosa oruro (♀)
Page 8

**STRIPE-FACED
WOOD-QUAIL**
Odontophorus balliviani
Page 62

VARIEGATED TINAMOU
*Crypturellus variegatus
salvini*
Page 5

John R. Quinn

PLATE 2

PAINT-BILLED CRAKE
Neocrex erythrops
olivascens
Page 68

OCELLATED CRAKE
Micropygia s. schomburgkii
Page 68

ASHY-HEADED GOOSE
Chloephaga poliocephala
Page 32

STRIPE-BACKED BITTERN
Ixobrychus involucris (♀)
Page 25

CRESTED DUCK
Lophonetta specularioides
alticola
Page 32

WHITE-FACED
TREE-DUCK
Dendrocygna viduata
Page 31

PUNA PLOVER
Charadrius alticola
Page 75

BRAZILIAN DUCK
Amazonetta b. brasiliensis
Page 36

WHISTLING HERON
Syrigma sibilatrix
forstersmithi
Page 24

TORRENT DUCK
Merganetta armata garleppi
Page 35

GREEN IBIS
Mesembrinibis cayennensis (♀)
Page 27

MASKED DUCK
Oxyura dominica
Page 36

John R. Quinn

PLATE 3

SUNBITTERN
Eurypyga h. helias
Page 70

RINGED TEAL
Anas leucophrys
Page 35

HOATZIN
Opisthocomus hoazin
Page 63

ANDEAN FLAMINGO
Phoenicoparrus andinus
Page 29

WATTLED JACANA
Jacana j. jacana
Page 72

**CHESTNUT-BELLIED
HERON**
Agamia agami (♀)
Page 24

AZURE GALLINULE
Porphyrula flavirostris
Page 69

BUFF-NECKED IBIS
Theristicus c. caudatus
Page 27

GRAY-NECKED WOOD-RAIL
Aramides c. cajanea
Page 66

John R. Quinn

PLATE 4

MOUNTAIN PARAKEET
Bolborhynchus a. aurifrons
Page 103

SCARLET-SHOULDERED
PARROTLET
Touit huetii
Page 105

RED-FRONTED MACAW
Ara rubrogenys
Page 98

MITRED PARAKEET
Aratinga m. mitrata
Page 99

BLACK-EARED PARROT
Hapalopsittaca m. melanotis
Page 107

BLACK-HEADED PARROT
*Pionites melanocephala
pallida* (♀)
Page 106

TURQUOISE-FRONTED
PARROT
*Amazona aestiva
xanthopteryx*
Page 109

BLUE-BELLIED PARROT
Triclaria malachitacea
Page 110

ORANGE-CHEEKED
PARROT
Pionopsitta b. barrabandi
Page 106

PICAZURO PIGEON
Columba p. picazuro
Page 91

MAROON-CHESTED
GROUND-DOVE
Claravis m. mondetoura
Page 93

John R. Quinn

PLATE 5

SAW-BILLED HERMIT
Ramphodon naevius
Page 131

GREEN-FRONTED
LANCEBILL
Doryfera l. ludoviciae
Page 131

WHITE-VENTED
PLUMELETEER
Chalybura buffonii micans
Page 146

RACKET-TAILED
COQUETTE
Discosura longicauda
Page 140

VIOLET-HEADED
HUMMINGBIRD
Klais g. guimeti
Page 138

RUBY-TOPAZ
HUMMINGBIRD
Chrysolampis mosquitus
Page 137

WHITE-NECKED JACOBIN
Florisuga m. mellivora
Page 136

BLACK-THROATED MANGO
Anthracothorax nigricollis
Page 137

BLACK JACOBIN
Melanotrochilus fuscus
Page 136

AMETHYST WOODSTAR
Calliphlox amethystina
Page 161

SHORT-TAILED
WOODSTAR
Myrmia micrura
Page 162

GRAY-BELLIED COMET
Tephrolesbia griseiventris
Page 158

GRAY-BREASTED
SABREWING
*Campylopterus largipennis
aequatorialis*
Page 135

WEDGE-BILLED
HUMMINGBIRD
Schistes g. geoffroyi
Page 159

John R. Quinn

PLATE 6

RAINBOW STARFRONTLET
Coeligena iris eva
Page 152

MARVELOUS SPATULETAIL
Loddigesia mirabilis
Page 160

HORNED SUNGEM
Heliactin cornuta
Page 160

GOULD'S JEWELFRONT
Polyplancta aurescens
Page 147

COLORFUL PUFFLEG
Eriocnemis mirabilis
Page 155

**BLACK-BREASTED
HILLSTAR**
Oreotrochilus melanogaster
Page 149

**RUFOUS-BREASTED
HERMIT**
Glaucis hirsuta affinis
Page 131

HOODED VISORBEARER
Augastes l. lumachellus
Page 159

**SWALLOW-TAILED
HUMMINGBIRD**
Eupetomena m. macroura
Page 136

BOOTED RACKET-TAIL
Ocreatus underwoodii annae
Page 155

BRAZILIAN RUBY
Clytolaema rubricauda
Page 147

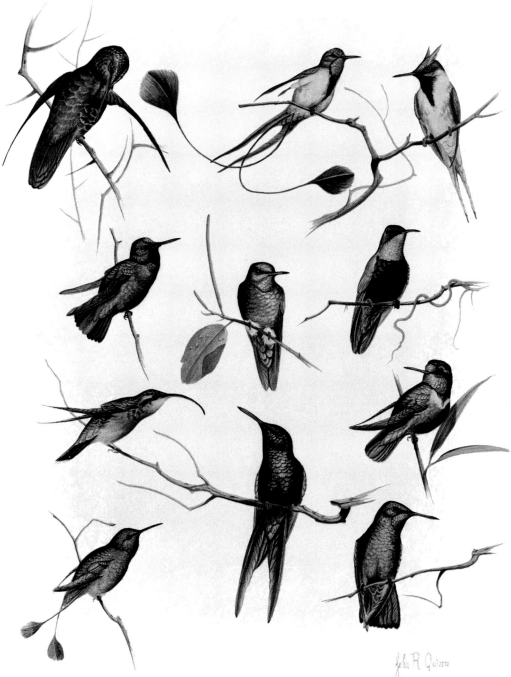

PLATE 7

BEARDED MOUNTAINEER
Oreonympha n. nobilis
Page 158

BRONZE-TAILED COMET
Polyonymus caroli
Page 156

FIERY-TAILED AWLBILL
Avocettula recurvirostris
Page 137

SPOT-THROATED
HUMMINGBIRD
Leucippus taczanowskii
Page 144

RED-TAILED COMET
Sappho sparganura sapho
Page 156

BLACK-BREASTED
PLOVERCREST
Stephanoxis l. lalandi
Page 138

OASIS HUMMINGBIRD
Rhodopis v. vesper
Page 161

SLENDER-TAILED
WOODSTAR
Microstilbon burmeisteri
Page 161

PERUVIAN SHEARTAIL
Thaumastura cora
Page 161

BLOSSOMCROWN
*Anthocephala
floriceps berlepschi*
Page 147

BLUE-TUFTED
STARTHROAT
Heliomaster furcifer
Page 160

WHITE-BELLIED
WOODSTAR
Acestrura mulsant
Page 162

BLACK-HOODED SUNBEAM
Aglaeactis pamela
Page 150

PLATE 8

WHITE-TAILED
GOLDENTHROAT
Polytmus g. guainumbi
Page 143

WHITE-CHINNED
THISTLETAIL
Schizoeaca f. fuliginosa
Page 214

GREAT XENOPS
Megaxenops parnaguae
Page 225

RUFOUS-THROATED
SAPPHIRE
Hylocharis sapphirina
Page 142

RUFOUS-FRONTED
THORNBIRD
*Phacellodomus
rufifrons sincipitalis*
Page 217

RUSTY-BACKED ANTWREN
Formicivora rufa rufatra
Page 241

GIANT HUMMINGBIRD
Patagona gigas peruviana
Page 150

WHITE-BROWED ANTBIRD
Myrmoborus l. leucophrys
Page 244

RUFOUS CACHOLOTE
*Pseudoseisura
cristata unirufa*
Page 220

VIOLET-CHESTED
HUMMINGBIRD
Sternoclyta cyanopectus
Page 149

WHITE-BACKED
FIRE-EYE
*Pyriglena
leuconota marcapatensis*
Page 244

GREAT SPINETAIL
*Siptornopsis
hypochondriacus*
Page 213

PALE-TAILED
BARBTHROAT
Threnetes l. leucurus
Page 131

CHOTOY SPINETAIL
*Schoeniophylax
phryganophila* (♀)
Page 208

SOUTHERN ANTPIPIT
Corythopis delalandi
Page 326

TOOTH-BILLED
HUMMINGBIRD
Androdon aequatorialis
Page 131

RUSSET ANTSHRIKE
*Thamnistes
anabatinus intermedius*
Page 233

CINEREOUS ANTSHRIKE
*Thamnomanes
caesius glaucus* (♀)
Page 235

MOUNTAIN AVOCETBILL
Opisthoprora euryptera
Page 158

UNDULATED ANTSHRIKE
*Frederickena
unduligera diversa* (♀)
Page 229

OCHRE-CHEEKED
SPINETAIL
Poecilurus scutatus whitii
Page 211

PLATE 9

**GREEN-BARRED
WOODPECKER**
*Chrysoptilus
melanochloros cristatus*
Page 186

**CREAM-COLORED
WOODPECKER**
Celeus flavus peruvianus
Page 188

**CREAM-BACKED
WOODPECKER**
Phloeoceastes l. leucopogon
Page 192

**GOLDEN-COLLARED
TOUCANET**
Selenidera r. reinwardtii
Page 180

LINEATED WOODPECKER
Dryocopus l. lineatus
Page 189

CHESTNUT JACAMAR
*Galbalcyrhynchus
l. leucotis* (♀)
Page 169

CHECKERED WOODPECKER
Dendrocopos m. mixtus
Page 192

GREEN KINGFISHER
*Chloroceryle
americana cabanisi*
Page 167

WHITE-FACED NUNBIRD
Hapaloptila castanea
Page 174

**BLACK-STREAKED
PUFFBIRD**
*Malacoptila
f. fulvogularis* (♀)
Page 173

LANCEOLATED MONKLET
Micromonacha lanceolata (♀)
Page 174

CAMPO FLICKER
Colaptes c. campestris
Page 186

PLATE 10

ARGUS BARE-EYE
Phlegopsis barringeri
Page 252

RUFOUS-RUMPED
ANTWREN
Terenura c. callinota
Page 242

HARLEQUIN ANTBIRD
Rhegmatorhina berlepschi (♀)
Page 250

WARBLING ANTBIRD
*Hypocnemis
cantator peruvianus*
Page 245

BICOLORED ANTBIRD
*Gymnopithys
leucaspis castanea*
Page 249

STRIATED ANTBIRD
Drymophilia d. devillei (♀)
Page 241

FLAMMULATED
TREEHUNTER
Thripadectes f. flammulatus
Page 224

STIPPLE-THROATED
ANTWREN
*Myrmotherula
haematonota amazonica*
Page 237

FERRUGINOUS ANTBIRD
Drymophila ferruginea
Page 241

BLACK-BELLIED
GNATEATER
Conopophaga melanogaster
Page 258

MARAÑON
CRESCENTCHEST
Melanopareia maranonica
Page 261

OCHRE-BREASTED
ANTPITTA
*Grallaricula
flavirostris similis* (♀)
Page 257

MOUSTACHED TURCA
Pteroptochos m. megapodius
Page 260

STRIATED ANTTHRUSH
Chamaeza nobilis rubida
Page 252

BANDED ANTBIRD
Dichrozona cincta
Page 239

PLATE 11

PALE-BELLIED
TYRANT-MANAKIN
Neopelma pallescens
Page 280

VERMILLION FLYCATCHER
Pyrocephalus r. rubinus
Page 291

KINGLET CALYPTURA
Calyptura cristata
Page 268

HOODED BERRYEATER
Carpornis cucullatus
Page 264

HELMETED MANAKIN
Antilophia galeata
Page 277

RED-RUMPED
BUSH-TYRANT
*Myiotheretes
e. erythropygius*
Page 287

SWALLOW-TAILED
COTINGA
Phibalura f. flavirostris
Page 264

SHRIKE-LIKE COTINGA
Laniisoma e. elegans
Page 264

YELLOW-CROWNED
MANAKIN
Heterocercus flavivertex
Page 280

PURPLE-THROATED
COTINGA
Porphyrolaema porphyrolaema
Page 265

MANY-COLORED
RUSH-TYRANT
*Tachuris
rubrigastra alticola*
Page 315

PIN-TAILED MANAKIN
Ilicura militaris
Page 278

John R. Quinn

PLATE 12

SOOTY-HEADED
TYRANNULET
*Phyllomyias
griseiceps pallidiceps*
Page 322

FLAMMULATED
PYGMY-TYRANT
Hemitriccus f. flammulatus
Page 311

GREENISH ELAENIA
Myiopagis v. viridicata
Page 321

TUMBES TYRANT
Tumbezia salvini
Page 292

YELLOW-BROWED TYRANT
Satrapa icterophrys
Page 292

MOUSE-COLORED
TYRANNULET
Phaeomyias m. murina
Page 321

YELLOW-CROWNED
TYRANNULET
Tyrannulus e. elatus
Page 324

BRONZE-OLIVE
PYGMY-TYRANT
*Pseudotriccus
pelzelni connectens*
Page 311

CINEREOUS TYRANT
Entotriccus striaticeps (♀)
Page 290

PATAGONIAN TYRANT
*Colorhampus
parvirostris* (♂ imm.)
Page 318

CINNAMON FLYCATCHER
Pyrrhomyias c. cinnamomea
Page 301

PALE-EYED
PYGMY-TYRANT
Atalotriccus p. pilaris
Page 310

John R. Quinn

PLATE 13

SUBTROPICAL DORADITO
Pseudocolopteryx
acutipennis
Page 314

RUFOUS-CROWNED
TODY-TYRANT
Poecilotriccus
ruficeps rufigenis (♀)
Page 309

ROUGH-LEGGED
TYRANNULET
Achrochordopus
b. burmeisteri
Page 324

GREATER
WAGTAIL-TYRANT
Stigmatura b. budytoides
Page 316

BEARDED TACHURI
Polystictus p. pectoralis
Page 314

LARGE-HEADED
FLATBILL
Ramphotrigon m. megacephala
Page 305

SHARP-TAILED TYRANT
Culicivora caudacuta
Page 315

TUFTED FLYCATCHER
Mitrephanes
phaeocercus olivaceus
Page 300

GREENISH TYRANNULET
Xanthomyias v. virescens
Page 322

HELMETED
PYGMY-TYRANT
Colopteryx galeatus (♀)
Page 310

TAWNY-CROWNED
PYGMY-TYRANT
Euscarthmus
meloryphus fulviceps
Page 313

AGILE TIT-TYRANT
Uromyias agilis
Page 316

MOTTLE-CHEEKED
TYRANNULET
Phylloscartes
ventralis angustirostris
Page 312

OCHRE-BELLIED
FLYCATCHER
Pipromorpha
oleaginea hauxwelli
Page 325

YELLOW TYRANNULET
Capsiempis f. flaveola (♀)
Page 313

SNETHLAGE'S
TODY-TYRANT
Snethlagea minor minima
Page 309

John P. Quinn

PLATE 14

MOUSTACHED WREN
Thryothorus g. genibarbis
Page 337

PALE-FOOTED SWALLOW
Notiochelidon flavipes
Page 330

RUFOUS WREN
Cinnycerthia u. unirufa
Page 336

GREEN HONEYCREEPER
*Chlorophanes
spiza caerulescens*
Page 372

RED-EYED VIREO
Vireo olivaceus chivi
Page 350

RUFOUS CASIORNIS
Casiornis r. rufa
Page 297

ROSE-BREASTED CHAT
Granatellus p. pelzelni
Page 364

CINEREOUS FINCH
Piezorhina cinerea
Page 406

ANDEAN SOLITAIRE
Myadestes r. ralloides
Page 342

GRAY-MANTLED WREN
Odontorchilus b. branickii
Page 336

GOLDEN-COLLARED
HONEYCREEPER
Iridophanes p. pulcherrima
Page 372

DWARF
TYRANT-MANAKIN
Tyranneutes stolzmanni
Page 281

GRAY-BREASTED
WOOD-WREN
*Henicorhina
leucophrys boliviana*
Page 339

PLATE 15

AUSTRAL BLACKBIRD
Curaeus c. curaeus
Page 356

SCIMITAR-BILLED
WOODCREEPER
Drymornis bridgesii
Page 195

ORIOLE BLACKBIRD
Gymnomystax mexicanus
Page 359

CASQUED OROPENDOLA
Clypicterus oseryi
Page 354

HOODED BERRYEATER
Carpornis cucullatus
Page 264

CHOPI BLACKBIRD
Gnorimopsar chopi megistus
Page 357

BAND-TAILED
OROPENDOLA
Ocyalus latirostris
Page 354

CINNAMON-THROATED
WOODCREEPER
*Dendrexetastes
rufigula devillei*
Page 196

SAFFRON-COWLED
BLACKBIRD
Xanthopsar flavus
Page 359

CHESTNUT-HEADED
OROPENDOLA
Zarhynchus w. wagleri
Page 354

RED-BILLED
WOODCREEPER
Hylexetastes p. perrotii (♀)
Page 196

SCARLET-HEADED
BLACKBIRD
Amblyrhamphus holosericeus
Page 359

OLIVE OROPENDOLA
Gymnostinops y. yuracares
Page 355

PURPLE-THROATED
FRUITCROW
Querula purpurata
Page 272

YELLOW-HOODED
BLACKBIRD
Agelaius i. icterocephalus
Page 358

CRESTED OROPENDOLA
Psarocolius d. decumanus
Page 354

RED-RUFFED FRUITCROW
Pyroderus s. scutatus
Page 272

BLACK-CAPPED
MOCKINGTHRUSH
Donacobius a. atricapillus
Page 341

LONG-TAILED
WOODCREEPER
*Deconychura
longicauda pallida*
Page 195

CAPUCHINBIRD
Perissocephalus tricolor
Page 273

COLLARED JAY
Cyanolyca viridicyana jolyae
Page 332

John R. Quinn

PLATE 16

DIADEMED TANAGER
Stephanophorus diadematus
Page 386

WHITE-TIPPED
PLANTCUTTER
*Phytotoma
rutila angustirostris*
Page 327

BUFF-BRIDLED
INCA-FINCH
Incaspiza laeta
Page 422

GREEN JAY
*Cyanocorax
yncas cyanodorsalis* (♀)
Page 333

SLATY-CAPPED
SHRIKE-VIREO
*Smaragdolanius
l. leucotis* (♀)
Page 350

SHARPBILL
Oxyruncus cristatus phelpsi
Page 326

RUFOUS-BROWED
PEPPERSHRIKE
*Cyclarhis
gujanensis cearensis*
Page 349

SWALLOW-TANAGER
*Tersina
viridis occidentalis*
Page 374

ROSE-BREASTED
THRUSH-TANAGER
Rhodinocicla rosea beebei
Page 394

BLACK-AND-RUFOUS
WARBLING-FINCH
Poospiza nigrorufa whitii
Page 424

TIT-LIKE DACNIS
Xenodacnis parina petersi
Page 374

PLUSH-CAPPED FINCH
*Catamblyrhynchus
diadema citrinifrons*
Page 399

John R. Quinn

PLATE 17

WHITE-BANDED TANAGER
Neothraupis fasciata
Page 398

BLACK-GOGGLED
TANAGER
Trichothraupis melanops
Page 394

GRAY-HOODED
BUSH-TANAGER
Cnemoscopus r. rubrirostris
Page 397

CINNAMON MANAKIN
Neopipo c. cinnamomea
Page 280

OLIVE-GREEN TANAGER
Orthogonys chloricterus
Page 391

YELLOW-BACKED
TANAGER
*Hemithraupis
flavicollis peruanus*
Page 395

GOLDEN-WINGED
MANAKIN
Masius c. chrysopterus
Page 278

BUFF-BREASTED
MOUNTAIN-TANAGER
Dubusia t. taeniata
Page 388

GRAY-HEADED TANAGER
*Eucometis
penicillata albicollis*
Page 394

ORANGE-THROATED
TANAGER
*Wetmorethraupis
sterrhopteron*
Page 387

BLUE-BACKED TANAGER
Cyanicterus cyanicterus
Page 391

DUSKY-FACED
TANAGER
Mitrospingus c. cassinii
Page 394

John R. Quinn

PLATE 18

**STRIPE-CAPPED
SPARROW**
*Aimophila
strigiceps dabbenei*
Page 421

TUMBES SPARROW
Rhynchospiza stolzmanni
Page 421

**RUFOUS-COLLARED
SPARROW**
*Zonotrichia
capensis pulacayensis*
Page 422

BLUE FINCH
Porphyrospiza caerulescens
Page 405

CRIMSON FINCH
Rhodospingus cruentus
Page 416

**MANY-COLORED
CHACO-FINCH**
Saltatricula multicolor
Page 425

GREAT PAMPA-FINCH
*Embernagra
platensis olivascens*
Page 425

**COCHABAMBA
MOUNTAIN-FINCH**
Compsospiza garleppi
Page 425

**BLACK-STRIPED
SPARROW**
*Arremonops
conirostirs striaticeps*
Page 420

COAL-CRESTED FINCH
Charitospiza eucosma
Page 416

**SULPHUR-THROATED
FINCH**
Gnathospiza taczanowskii
Page 411

**CHESTNUT-BREASTED
MOUNTAIN-FINCH**
Poospizopsis caesar
Page 425

PLATE 19

HOODED MOUNTAIN-TANAGER *Buthraupis m. montana* Page 387	MASKED CRIMSON TANAGER *Ramphocelus nigrogularis* Page 390	YELLOW CARDINAL *Gubernatrix cristata* Page 403
FAWN-BREASTED TANAGER *Pipraeidea melanonota venezuelensis* Page 379	HEPATIC TANAGER *Piranga flava lutea* Page 390	YELLOW-FACED GRASSQUIT *Tiaris olivacea dissita* Page 406
RED-CRESTED FINCH *Coryphospingus cucullatus fargoi* Page 416	WHITE-RUMPED TANAGER *Cypsnagra hirundinacea* Page 394	BLACKISH-BLUE SEEDEATER *Amaurospiza moesta* Page 410
GOLDEN-COLLARED TANAGER *Iridosornis jelskii bolivianus* Page 386	ORANGE-HEADED TANAGER *Thlypopsis s. sordida* Page 395	WHITE-WINGED DIUCA-FINCH *Diuca s. speculifera* Page 413
BLACK-CRESTED FINCH *Lophospingus pusillus* Page 415	CHESTNUT-HEADED TANAGER *Pyrrhocoma ruficeps* Page 394	SHORT-TAILED FINCH *Idiopsar brachyurus* Page 413
BLACK-THROATED FINCH *Melanodera melanodera princetoniana* Page 415	RED-CROWNED ANT-TANAGER *Habia r. rubica* Page 391	YELLOW-GREEN GROSBEAK *Caryothraustes c. canadensis* Page 403
BLUE-GRAY TANAGER *Thraupis episcopus bolivana* Page 388	CARMIOL'S TANAGER *Chlorothraupis carmioli frenata* (♀) Page 391	RED-AND-BLACK GROSBEAK *Periporphyrus erythromelas* Page 403

PLATE 20

**MAGELLANIC
DIVING-PETREL**
Pelecanoides magellani
Page 18

CAPE PETREL
Daption capense (♀)
Page 14

**BLACK-BROWED
ALBATROSS**
Diomedea m. melanophris (♀)
Page 12

GREAT SKUA
Catharacta skua chilensis (♀)
Page 83

KELP GULL
Larus d. dominicanus
Page 85

**WHITE-VENTED
STORM-PETREL**
Oceanites g. gracilis
Page 17

**AMERICAN
OYSTERCATCHER**
Haematopus p. palliatus
Page 73

MAGELLANIC PLOVER
Pluvianellus socialis
Page 76

MAGELLANIC PENGUIN
Spheniscus m. magellanicus
Page 1

SNOWY SHEATHBILL
Chionis alba (♀)
Page 83

**GRAY-BREASTED
SEEDSNIPE**
*Thinocorus
orbignyianus ingae*
Page 82

John R. Quinn

PLATE 21

OSPREY
Pandion
haliaetus carolinensis
Page 50

MAGNIFICENT
FRIGATEBIRD
Fregata magnificens
Page 22

ANHINGA
Anhinga a. anhinga
Page 22

RED-BILLED TROPICBIRD
Phaethon a. aethereus
Page 19

RED-LEGGED CORMORANT
Phalacrocorax gaimardi
Page 21

MAGUARI STORK
Euxenura maguari
Page 27

CLAPPER RAIL
Rallus l. longirostris (♀)
Page 65

FLIGHTLESS STEAMER-DUCK
Tachyeres pteneres
Page 32

MASKED BOOBY
Sula d. dactylatra
Page 20

CASPIAN TERN
Hydroprogne caspia
Page 86

INCA TERN
Larosterna inca
Page 88

LARGE-BILLED TERN
Phaetusa simplex chloropoda
Page 86

RUFOUS-CHESTED
DOTTEREL
Zonibyx modestus (♀)
Page 75

PLATE 22

WHITE-TAILED KITE
Elanus l. leucurus
Page 39

SPOT-WINGED FALCONET
Spiziapteryx circumcinctus
Page 53

ROADSIDE HAWK
*Buteo
magnirostris ecuadoriensis*
Page 44

**LESSER YELLOW-HEADED
VULTURE**
Cathartes b. burrovianus
Page 38

HOOK-BILLED KITE
Chondrohierax u. uncinatus
Page 40

BARN OWL
Tyto alba tuidara
Page 115

BOAT-BILLED HERON
Cochlearius c. cochlearius
Page 26

**CARUNCULATED
CARACARA**
Phalcoboenus carunculatus
Page 52

SUNGREBE
Heliornis fulica (♀)
Page 70

SHORT-WINGED GREBE
Centropelma micropterum
Page 11

PLATE 23

DOUBLE-STRIPED
THICK-KNEE
Burhinus
bistriatus vocifer (♀)
Page 82

CORDILLERAN SNIPE
Gallinago
stricklandii jamesoni
Page 80

TAWNY-THROATED
DOTTEREL
Oreopholus r. ruficollis
Page 75

BLACK SKIMMER
Rynchops nigra cinerascens
Page 89

LIMPKIN
Aramus guarauna carau
Page 64

SOUTH AMERICAN
PAINTED-SNIPE
Nycticryphes semicollaris (♀)
Page 72

COMMON STILT
Himantopus
himantopus mexicanus
Page 80

ANDEAN AVOCET
Recurvirostra andina
Page 81

PIED LAPWING
Hoploxypterus cayanus (♀)
Page 74

WILSON'S PHALAROPE
Steganopus tricolor (♀)
Page 81

DIADEMED
SANDPIPER-PLOVER
Phegornis mitchellii
Page 76

PLATE 24

GUIRA CUCKOO
Guira guira
Page 113

WHITE-COLLARED SWIFT
Streptoprocne z. zonaris
Page 126

**SEMICOLLARED
NIGHTHAWK**
*Lurocalis semitorquatus
rufiventris* (♀)
Page 121

**PEARLY-BREASTED
CUCKOO**
Coccyzus euleri
Page 112

SHORT-TAILED SWIFT
Chaetura b. brachyura (♀)
Page 128

SQUIRREL CUCKOO
Piaya cayana macroura (♀)
Page 112

COMMON POTOO
Nyctibius griseus cornutus
Page 121

WHITE-BANDED SWALLOW
Atticora fasciata
Page 330

BLACK-BANDED OWL
Ciccaba h. huhula
Page 118

**FERRUGINOUS
PYGMY-OWL**
*Glaucidium
brasilianum medianum*
Page 117

TROPICAL SCREECH-OWL
Otus choliba alticola
Page 116

OILBIRD
Steatornis caripensis (♀)
Page 120

PAURAQUE
*Nyctidromus
albicollis derbyianus*
Page 122

John R. Quinn

PLATE 25

COMMON MINER
Geositta
cunicularia titicacae
Page 202

BOLIVIAN RECURVEBILL
Simoxenops striatus (♀)
Page 221

POINT-TAILED
PALMCREEPER
Berlepschia rikeri
Page 220

SPOTTED BARBTAIL
Premnoplex b. brunnescens (♀)
Page 219

WREN-LIKE RUSHBIRD
Phleocryptes
melanops schoenobaenus
Page 206

PALE-LEGGED HORNERO
Furnarius
leucopus tricolor (♀)
Page 205

THORN-TAILED RAYADITO
Aphrastura s. spinicauda
Page 206

CURVE-BILLED
REEDHAUNTER
Limnornis curvirostris
Page 206

DES MURS' WIRETAIL
Sylviorthorhynchus desmursii
Page 206

FIREWOOD-GATHERER
Anumbius a. annumbi
Page 218

STREAK-HEADED
WOODCREEPER
Lepidocolaptes s. souleyetii
Page 199

SCALE-THROATED
EARTHCREEPER
Upucerthia
dumetaria hypoleuca (♀)
Page 203

STRAIGHT-BILLED
REEDHAUNTER
Limnoctites rectirostris (♀)
Page 206

John R. Quinn

PLATE 26

LARGE-TAILED
ANTSHRIKE
Mackenziaena leachii (♀)
Page 228

CHESTNUT-TAILED
ANTBIRD
Myrmeciza h. hemimelaena
Page 248

GIANT ANTSHRIKE
Batara cinerea excubitor
Page 228

GRAY ANTBIRD
*Cercomacra
cinerascens sclateri*
Page 243

BLACK-HOODED THRUSH
Turdus o. olivater
Page 344

BLACK-CAPPED ANTWREN
*Herpsilochmus
pileatus atriceps*
Page 239

STRANGE-TAILED
TYRANT
Yetapa risora
Page 289

WHITE-BEARDED
ANTSHRIKE
Biatas nigropectus
Page 230

SLATY BRISTLEFRONT
Merulaxis ater
Page 261

WHITE-THROATED
TAPACULO
Scelorchilus a. albicollis
Page 260

SILVERED ANTBIRD
Sclateria naevia argentata
Page 247

SPOT-WINGED ANTBIRD
*Percnostola
leucostigma subplumbea*
Page 246

STUB-TAILED ANTBIRD
Sipia berlepschi
Page 244

CRESTED GALLITO
Rhinocrypta l. lanceolata
Page 260

PLATE 27

WING-BARRED MANAKIN
Piprites chloris bolivianus
Page 281

SCIMITAR-WINGED PIHA
Chirocylla uropygialis
Page 269

LONG-WATTLED
UMBRELLABIRD
Cephalopterus penduliger
Page 273

WHITE-BEARDED
MANAKIN
Manacus m. manacus
Page 278

WHITE-NAPED
XENOPSARIS
Xenopsaris a. albinucha
Page 270

WHITE BELLBIRD
Procnias alba
Page 273

WHITE-RUFFED MANAKIN
Corapipo leucorrhoa altera
Page 278

SCALED FRUITEATER
Ampelioides tschudii
Page 268

BLACK-FACED COTINGA
Conioptilon mcilhennyi
Page 266

GRAYISH MOURNER
Rhytipterna simplex frederici
Page 297

BLACK MANAKIN
Xenopipo atronitens
Page 279

WHITE-CHEEKED COTINGA
Zaratornis stresemanni (♀)
Page 266

John R. Quinn

PLATE 28

DRAB WATER-TYRANT
Ochthornis littoralis
Page 292

FIRE-EYED DIUCON
Pyrope p. pyrope
Page 285

WHITE-WINGED
BLACK-TYRANT
Knipolegus a. aterrimus
Page 290

WHITE MONJITA
Xolmis i. irupero
Page 285

SHEAR-TAILED
GRAY-TYRANT
Muscipipra v. vetula (♀)
Page 291

HUDSON'S BLACK-TYRANT
Phaeotriccus hudsoni
Page 290

STREAMER-TAILED
TYRANT
Gubernetes yetapa (♀)
Page 289

SUIRIRI FLYCATCHER
Suiriri s. suiriri (♀)
Page 321

COCK-TAILED TYRANT
Alectrurus tricolor
Page 289

RUFOUS-BACKED
NEGRITO
Lessonia rufa oreas
Page 287

CHOCOLATE-VENTED
TYRANT
Neoxolmis rufiventris
Page 284

SPECTACLED TYRANT
Hymenops
perspicillata andina
Page 291

SHORT-TAILED
FIELD-TYRANT
Muscigralla brevicauda
Page 287

John R. Quinn

PLATE 29

SHINY COWBIRD
Molothrus b. bonariensis
Page 353

CEDAR WAXWING
Bombycilla cedrorum
Page 347

MASKED GNATCATCHER
Polioptila d. dumicola
Page 347

BOLIVIAN BLACKBIRD
Oreopsar bolivianus
Page 356

YELLOW-LEGGED THRUSH
*Platycichla
flavipes venezuelensis*
Page 343

CHALK-BROWED
MOCKINGBIRD
*Mimus saturninus
modulator* (♀)
Page 340

SPOTTED
NIGHTINGALE-THRUSH
Catharus dryas maculatus
Page 342

FASCIATED WREN
*Campylorhynchus
f. fasciatus* (♀)
Page 335

LONG-BILLED
GNATWREN
*Ramphocaenus
melanurus obscurus* (♀)
Page 346

WHITE-CAPPED DIPPER
Cinclus l. leucocephalus
Page 334

SHORT-BILLED PIPIT
Anthus f. furcatus
Page 348

HORNED LARK
*Eremophila
alpestris peregrina*
Page 328

PLATE 30

SLATE-COLORED
GROSBEAK
Pitylus grossus saturatus
Page 403

RED-BILLED
PIED TANAGER
Lamprospiza melanoleuca
Page 399

BLACK-HEADED
HEMISPINGUS
Hemispingus verticalis
Page 398

MAGPIE TANAGER
Cissopis l. leveriana (♀)
Page 399

BLACK-MASKED FINCH
Coryphaspiza melanotis
Page 422

BLACK-AND-WHITE
TANAGER
Conothraupis speculigera
Page 398

CARMIOL'S TANAGER
Chlorothraupis c. carmioli
Page 391

GREATER LARGE-BILLED
SEED-FINCH
*Oryzoborus maximiliani
gigantirostris*
Page 410

HOODED TANAGER
*Nemosia
pileata paraguayensis*
Page 395

SCALED DOVE
Scardafella s. squammata (♀)
Page 94

BLACK-THROATED FINCH
*Melanodera
melanodera princetoniana*
Page 415

LONG-TAILED
GROUND-DOVE
Uropelia c. campestris
Page 94

John R. Quinn

PLATE 31

SPECTACLED PARROTLET
Forpus
conspicillatus caucae
Page 104

**YELLOW-EARED
PARAKEET**
Ognorhynchus icterotis
Page 100

GOLDEN-PLUMED PARROT
Leptosittaca branickii
Page 100

**ORANGE-CHINNED
PARAKEET**
Brotogeris j. jugularis
Page 104

BLUE-HEADED PARROT
Pionus
menstruus rubrigularis
Page 107

PAINTED PARAKEET
Pyrrhura picta subandina
Page 102

IVORY-BILLED ARAÇARI
Pteroglossus
f. flavirostris
Page 179

**GRAY-BREASTED
MOUNTAIN-TOUCAN**
Andigena h. hypoglauca
Page 180

EMERALD TOUCANET
Aulacorhynchus
prasinus phaeolaemus
Page 178

**PLAIN-BREASTED
GROUND-DOVE**
Columbina m. minuta
Page 92

SAPPHIRE QUAIL-DOVE
Geotrygon
saphirina purpurata
Page 95

**OLIVE-BACKED
QUAIL-DOVE**
Geotrygon veraguensis
Page 95

E.L.Poole

PLATE 32

BUFF-TAILED
SICKLEBILL
Eutoxeres c. condamini
Page 135

FIERY TOPAZ
Topaza pyra
Page 149

VELVET-PURPLE
CORONET
Boissonneaua jardini
Page 153

VIOLET-TAILED SYLPH
Aglaiocercus c. coelestis
Page 159

WHITETIP
Urosticte b. benjamini
Page 147

TAWNY-BELLIED HERMIT
*Phaethornis
s. syrmatophorus*
Page 132

WHITE-TAILED
STARFRONTLET
Coeligena phalerata
Page 151

BEARDED HELMETCREST
Oxypogon g. guerinii
Page 158

FORK-TAILED
WOODNYMPH
*Thalurania
furcata verticeps*
Page 141

EMPRESS BRILLIANT
Heliodoxa imperatrix
Page 148

SPARKLING VIOLETEAR
Colibri c. coruscans
Page 136

RED-BILLED EMERALD
Chlorostilbon g. gibsoni
Page 140

E. L. Poole

PLATE 33

**SAPPHIRE-VENTED
PUFFLEG**
Eriocnemis l. luciani
Page 154

**SWORD-BILLED
HUMMINGBIRD**
Ensifera ensifera
Page 152

**BLACK-TAILED
TRAINBEARER**
Lesbia v. victoriae
Page 156

PERIJA METALTAIL
Metallura iracunda
Page 157

**AMETHYST-THROATED
SUNANGEL**
*Heliangelus
amethysticollis clarisse*
Page 153

PURPLE-CROWNED FAIRY
Heliothryx b. barroti
Page 159

**PURPLE-BACKED
THORNBILL**
*Ramphomicron
m. microrhynchum*
Page 156

**RAINBOW-BEARDED
THORNBILL**
Chalcostigma h. herrani
Page 158

**PURPLE-THROATED
WOODSTAR**
Philodice mitchellii
Page 161

ANDEAN EMERALD
Amazilia f. franciae
Page 145

SPANGLED COQUETTE
Lophornis stictolopha
Page 138

GREEN THORNTAIL
Popelairia conversii
Page 139

E.L.Poole

PLATE 34

GRAY-CHEEKED NUNLET
Nonnula
ruficapilla frontalis
Page 174

WHITE-TAILED TROGON
Trogon viridis chionurus
Page 165

BLUE-CROWNED MOTMOT
Momotus
momota aequatorialis
Page 168

RED-HEADED BARBET
Eubucco
bourcierii orientalis
Page 176

RUFOUS-TAILED
JACAMAR
Galbula r. ruficauda
Page 170

TOUCAN BARBET
Semnornis r. ramphastinus
Page 176

GOLDEN-HEADED
QUETZAL
Pharomachrus a. auriceps
Page 164

RUFOUS-BREASTEI
PICULET
Picumnus r. rufiventri.
Page 183

GREAT JACAMAR
Jacamerops a. aurea (♀)
Page 171

CRIMSON-MANTLED
WOODPECKER
Piculus r. rivolii
Page 186

BARRED PUFFBIRD
Nystalus radiatus
Page 172

BLACK-CHEEKED
WOODPECKER
Melanerpes p. pucherani
Page 189

E.L.Poole

PLATE 35

ORANGE-FRONTED
PLUSHCROWN
Metopothrix aurantiacus
Page 218

RED-BILLED
SCYTHEBILL
*Campylorhamphus
trochilirostris
venezuelensis*
Page 199

STRONG-BILLED
WOODCREEPER
*Xiphocolaptes
promeropirhynchus rostratus*
Page 196

OLIVACEOUS
WOODCREEPER
*Sittasomus
griseicapillus levis*
Page 195

PEARLED TREERUNNER
*Margarornis
squamiger perlatus*
Page 219

BLACK-STRIPED
WOODCREEPER
*Xiphorhynchus
l. lachrymosus*
Page 198

BARRED WOODCREEPER
*Dendrocolaptes
certhia colombianus*
Page 196

STRAIGHT-BILLED
WOODCREEPER
*Xiphorhynchus
picus picirostris*
Page 197

ANDEAN TIT-SPINETAIL
*Leptasthenura
andicola exterior*
Page 207

SLATY SPINETAIL
*Synallaxis
brachyura chapmani*
Page 209

GRAY-THROATED
LEAFSCRAPER
*Sclerurus
albigularis propinquus*
Page 225

BAR-WINGED CINCLODES
Cinclodes fuscus paramo
Page 204

E.L.Poole

PLATE 36

SLATY ANTSHRIKE
Thamnophilus
punctatus atrinucha (♀)
Page 231

WHITE-PLUMED ANTBIRD
Pithys albifrons peruviana
Page 249

BAR-CRESTED
ANTSHRIKE
Thamnophilus
m. multistriatus (♀)
Page 230

PEARLY ANTSHRIKE
Megastictus
margaritatus (♀)
Page 233

OCELLATED ANTBIRD
Phaenostictus
mcleannani chocoanus
Page 251

DOT-WINGED ANTWREN
Microrhopias
q. quixensis (♀)
Page 240

GREAT ANTSHRIKE
Taraba major
transandeanus (♀)
Page 229

RUFOUS-BREASTED
ANTTHRUSH
Formicarius
rufipectus carrikeri
Page 253

STREAK-CHESTED
ANTPITTA
Hylopezus perspicillatus
periophthalmicus
Page 256

WING-BANDED ANTBIRD
Myrmornis t. torquata
Page 253

OCELLATED TAPACULO
Acropternis o. orthonyx
Page 263

BLACK-CROWNED
ANTPITTA
Pittasoma m. michleri
Page 253

E. L. Poole

PLATE 37

BLUE COTINGA
Cotinga n. nattererii
Page 265

POMPADOUR COTINGA
Xipholena punicea
Page 265

LANCE-TAILED
MANAKIN
Chiroxiphia lanceolata
Page 277

CLUB-WINGED
MANAKIN
Allocotopterus deliciosus
Page 279

ANDEAN
COCK-OF-THE-ROCK
*Rupicola
peruviana sanguinolenta*
Page 274

BLACK-NECKED
RED-COTINGA
Phoenicircus nigricollis
Page 273

CHESTNUT-CRESTED
COTINGA
*Ampelion
rufaxilla antioquiae*
Page 266

ORANGE-BREASTED
FRUITEATER
Pipreola jucunda
Page 267

STRIPED MANAKIN
*Machaeropterus
regulus striolatus*
Page 279

WIRE-TAILED MANAKIN
Teleonema f. filicauda
Page 277

GOLDEN-COLLARED
MANAKIN
*Manacus
vitellinus viridiventris*
Page 278

GOLDEN-HEADED
MANAKIN
Pipra e. erythrocephala
Page 275

E.L.Poole

PLATE 38

FULVOUS-BREASTED
FLATBILL
Rhynchocyclus fulvipectus
Page 305

ROYAL FLYCATCHER
*Onychorhynchus
coronatus fraterculus*
Page 303

BLACK-HEADED
TODY-FLYCATCHER
Todirostrum nigriceps
Page 306

BOAT-BILLED
FLYCATCHER
Megarhynchus p. pitangua
Page 294

OLIVE-STRIPED
FLYCATCHER
*Mionectes
olivaceus hederaceus*
Page 325

SEPIA-CAPPED
FLYCATCHER
*Leptopogon
amaurocephalus faustus*
Page 325

RUSTY-MARGINED
FLYCATCHER
*Myiozetetes
cayanensis hellmayri*
Page 295

ORNATE FLYCATCHER
Myiotriccus ornatus stellatus
Page 301

ASHY-HEADED
TYRANNULET
Tyranniscus cinereiceps
Page 323

BLACK-THROATED
TODY-TYRANT
*Idioptilon
granadense lehmanni*
Page 309

SLATY-BACKED
CHAT-TYRANT
*Ochthoeca
c. cinnamomeiventris*
Page 288

BLACK-TAILED
FLYCATCHER
Myiobius a. atricaudus
Page 301

E.L.Poole

PLATE 39

RED-LEGGED
HONEYCREEPER
Cyanerpes cyaneus eximius
Page 372

BANANAQUIT
Coereba flaveola intermedia
Page 369

RUSSET-CROWNED
WARBLER
*Basileuterus
coronatus elatus*
Page 367

GOLDEN-FRONTED
REDSTART
Myioborus o. ornatus
Page 365

SCARLET-BREASTED
DACNIS
Dacnis berlepschi
Page 373

SCALE-CRESTED
PYGMY-TYRANT
*Lophotriccus
pileatus hesperius*
Page 310

BLUE-BACKED CONEBILL
Conirostrum s. sitticolor
Page 370

INDIGO FLOWER-PIERCER
Diglossa indigotica
Page 371

BLACK-BILLED
FLYCATCHER
Aphanotriccus audax
Page 301

WHITE-THROATED
TYRANNULET
*Mecocerculus
leucophrys rufomarginatus*
Page 317

RUFOUS-HEADED
PYGMY-TYRANT
Pseudotriccus ruficeps
Page 311

OLIVE-CROWNED
YELLOWTHROAT
Geothlypis s. semiflava
Page 364

E.L.Poole

PLATE 40

**ORANGE-BELLIED
EUPHONIA**
*Euphonia
xanthogaster brevirostris*
Page 377

GRASS-GREEN TANAGER
Chlorornis r. riefferii
Page 398

MOSS-BACKED TANAGER
Bangsia edwardsi
Page 388

RED-BELLIED GRACKLE
Hypopyrrhus pyrohypogaster
Page 357

**GOLDEN-CROWNED
TANAGER**
*Iridosornis
rufivertex ignicapillus*
Page 386

**CHESTNUT-BREASTED
CHLOROPHONIA**
Chlorophonia pyrrhophrys
Page 376

WHITE-CAPPED TANAGER
Sericossypha albocristata
Page 396

**SCARLET-AND-WHITE
TANAGER**
Erythrothlypis salmoni
Page 395

**BLACK-CHINNED
MOUNTAIN-TANAGER**
Anisognathus notabilis
Page 387

YELLOW-BACKED ORIOLE
Icterus chrysater giraudii
Page 359

**TAWNY-CROWNED
GREENLET**
*Hylophilus ochraceiceps
ferrugineifrons*
Page 352

**RED-BREASTED
BLACKBIRD**
Leistes militaris
Page 360

E.L.Poole

PLATE 41

PARADISE TANAGER
Tangara c. chilensis
Page 380

GLISTENING-GREEN
TANAGER
Chlorochrysa phoenicotis
Page 380

ORANGE-EARED
TANAGER
*Chlorochrysa
calliparaea bourcieri*
Page 379

YELLOW-BELLIED
TANAGER
Tangara x. xanthogastra
Page 382

SPECKLED TANAGER
Tangara guttata bogotensis
Page 381

OPAL-RUMPED TANAGER
Tangara velia iridina
Page 380

OPAL-CROWNED TANAGER
Tangara callophrys
Page 380

MULTICOLORED TANAGER
Chlorochrysa nitidissima
Page 380

E. L. Poole

PLATE 42

RED-CAPPED CARDINAL
Paroaria g. gularis
Page 404

BLUE-BLACK GROSBEAK
Cyanocompsa c. cyanoides
Page 405

YELLOW GROSBEAK
*Pheucticus chrysopeplus
chrysogaster*
Page 404

CHESTNUT-BELLIED
SEEDEATER
Sporophila castaneiventris
Page 409

OCHRE-BREASTED
BRUSH-FINCH
Atlapetes semirufus zimmeri
Page 417

BUFF-THROATED
SALTATOR
Saltator maximus iungens
Page 401

BAND-TAILED
SEEDEATER
*Catamenia
analis schistaceifrons*
Page 410

WEDGE-TAILED
GRASS-FINCH
*Emberizoides
herbicola apurensis*
Page 422

OLIVE FINCH
Lysurus castaneiceps
Page 419

SAFFRON FINCH
Sicalis f. flaveola
Page 412

TANAGER-FINCH
Oreothraupis arremonops
Page 419

ORANGE-BILLED
SPARROW
*Arremon aurantiirostris
erythrorhynchus*
Page 420

E.L.Poole

PLATE 43

WHITE HAWK
Leucopternis
albicollis williaminae
Page 45

PLUMBEOUS KITE
Ictinia plumbea
Page 41

LAUGHING FALCON
Herpetotheres
c. cachinnans
Page 51

BAT FALCON
Falco r. rufigularis
Page 54

ORNATE HAWK-EAGLE
Spizaetus ornatus vicarius
Page 48

WHITE-TAILED HAWK
Buteo albicaudatus colonus
Page 42

PEARL KITE
Gampsonyx
swainsonii leonae
Page 39

CRANE HAWK
Geranospiza
caerulescens balzarensis
Page 49

BARRED FOREST-FALCON
Micrastur
ruficollis interstes
Page 51

E.L.Poole

PLATE 44

EARED GREBE
*Podiceps
nigricollis andinus*
Page 10

NORTHERN SCREAMER
Chauna chavaria
Page 30

SPOT-FLANKED
GALLINULE
*Porphyriops
melanops bogotensis*
Page 69

CRESTED BOBWHITE
*Colinus
cristatus decoratus*
Page 61

HELMETED CURASSOW
Pauxi p. pauxi
Page 60

SLATE-COLORED COOT
Fulica ardesiaca
Page 69

TAWNY-FACED QUAIL
Rhynchortyx c. cinctus
Page 62

SALVIN'S CURASSOW
Mitu salvini
Page 60

PIED LAPWING
Hoploxypterus cayanus
Page 74

RUFOUS-SIDED CRAKE
*Laterallus
melanophaius oenops*
Page 68

CRESTED GUAN
*Penelope
purpurascens aequatorialis*
Page 56

GREATER ANI
Crotophaga major
Page 112

BROWN WOOD-RAIL
Aramides wolfi
Page 66

SPECKLED CHACHALACA
Ortalis guttata columbiana
Page 56

BANDED GROUND-CUCKOO
Neomorphus radiolosus
Page 114

PLATE 45

GOLD-FRONTED
PICULET
*Picumnus
aurifrons lafresnayi*
Page 185

WHITE-CROWNED
MANAKIN
Pipra pipra minima
Page 276

PALE-HEADED JACAMAR
Brachygalba goeringi
Page 169

SCREAMING PIHA
Lipaugus v. vociferans
Page 269

WHITE COTINGA
Carpodectes hopkei
Page 266

MASKED TITYRA
*Tityra
semifasciata columbiana*
Page 272

WHITE-FRONTED
NUNBIRD
Monasa morphoeus fidelis
Page 174

WHITE-WINGED BECARD
*Pachyramphus
polychopterus dorsalis*
Page 271

WHITE-NECKED
PUFFBIRD
*Notharchus macrorhynchus
hyperrhynchus*
Page 171

ORANGE-FRONTED
BARBET
Capito squamatus (♀)
Page 175

GREAT ANTSHRIKE
Taraba major transandeanus
Page 229

E.L.Poole

PLATE 46

TYRANNINE WOODCREEPER	**WEDGE-BILLED WOODCREEPER**	**LONG-BILLED WOODCREEPER**
Dendrocincla t. tyrannina	*Glyphorynchus spirurus sublestus*	*Nasica l. longirostris*
Page 194	Page 195	Page 195

YELLOW-THROATED SPINETAIL	**STREAK-CAPPED SPINETAIL**	**MANY-STRIPED CANASTERO**
Certhiaxis cinnamomea fuscifrons	*Cranioleuca hellmayri*	*Asthenes flammulata multostriata*
Page 211	Page 212	Page 216

SPECTACLED PRICKLETAIL	**DOUBLE-BANDED GRAYTAIL**	**STREAKED TUFTEDCHEEK**
Siptornis striaticollis	*Xenerpestes minlosi umbraticus*	*Pseudocolaptes b. boissonneautii*
Page 218	Page 218	Page 219

CHESTNUT-WINGED HOOKBILL	**BUFF-FRONTED FOLIAGE-GLEANER**	**RUDDY FOLIAGE-GLEANER**
Ancistrops s. strigilatus	*Philydor rufus riveti*	*Automolus rubiginosus rufipectus*
Page 220	Page 222	Page 223

FLAMMULATED TREEHUNTER	**PLAIN XENOPS**	**SHARP-TAILED STREAMCREEPER**
Thripadectes f. flammulatus	*Xenops minutus neglectus*	*Lochmias nematura sororia*
Page 224	Page 225	Page 226

BLACK-CRESTED ANTSHRIKE	**DUSKY ANTBIRD**	**SPOT-WINGED ANTSHRIKE**
Sakesphorus canadensis pulchellus	*Cercomacra tyrannina rufiventris*	*Pygiptila stellaris occipitalis*
Page 229	Page 243	Page 233

BARE-CROWNED ANTBIRD	**IMMACULATE ANTBIRD**	**STRIATED ANTTHRUSH**
Gymnocichla n. nudiceps	*Myrmeciza i. immaculata*	*Chamaeza nobilis rubida*
Page 246	Page 248	Page 252

PLATE 47

DOT-WINGED ANTWREN
Microrhopias q. quixensis
Page 240

SLATY ANTSHRIKE
*Thamnophilus
punctatus atrinucha*
Page 231

**STRIPE-CHESTED
ANTWREN**
*Myrmotherula
longicauda soderstromi*
Page 236

FASCIATED ANTSHRIKE
*Cymbilaimus
lineatus fasciatus*
Page 228

BARRED ANTSHRIKE
*Thamnophilus
doliatus nigricristatus*
Page 230

PLAIN ANTVIREO
*Dysithamnus
mentalis extremus*
Page 234

BLACK BUSHBIRD
Neoctantes niger
Page 233

PEARLY ANTSHRIKE
*Megastictus
m. margaritatus*
Page 233

SLATY ANTWREN
*Myrmotherula
s. schisticolor*
Page 237

UNICOLORED TAPACULO
Scytalopus unicolor latrans
Page 262

**RECURVE-BILLED
BUSHBIRD**
Clytoctantes alixi
Page 233

SPOT-BACKED ANTBIRD
Hylophylax naevia theresae
Page 251

E.L.Poole

PLATE 48

TORRENT TYRANNULET
Serpophaga c. cinerea
Page 316

TUFTED TIT-TYRANT
*Anairetes
parulus aequatorialis*
Page 315

APICAL FLYCATCHER
Myiarchus apicalis
Page 298

WHITE-CRESTED
ELAENIA
*Elaenia albiceps
griseogularis*
Page 319

YELLOW-THROATED
SPADEBILL
*Platyrinchus
f. flavigularis*
Page 304

FORK-TAILED
FLYCATCHER
Muscivora tyrannus monachus
Page 292

STREAKED FLYCATCHER
*Myiodynastes
maculatus solitarius*
Page 295

SIRYSTES
*Sirystes
sibilator albogriseus*
Page 292

LONG-TAILED TYRANT
*Colonia
colonus fuscicapilla*
Page 289

BLACK-BILLED
SHRIKE-TYRANT
Agriornis m. montana
Page 284

PIED WATER-TYRANT
Fluvicola p. pica
Page 291

PLAIN-CAPPED
GROUND-TYRANT
*Muscisaxicola
alpina quesadae*
Page 286

E.L.Poole

PLATE 49

CATTLE TYRANT
*Machetornis
rixosus flavigularis*
Page 292

TROPICAL KINGBIRD
Tyrannus m. melancholicus
Page 293

VARIEGATED
FLYCATCHER
Empidonomus v. varius
Page 293

PIRATIC FLYCATCHER
Legatus l. leucophaius
Page 294

LEMON-BROWED
FLYCATCHER
*Conopias
cinchoneti icterophrys*
Page 294

WHITE-RINGED
FLYCATCHER
Conopias parva albovittata
Page 294

SULPHURY FLYCATCHER
Tyrannopsis sulphurea
Page 293

GREAT KISKADEE
*Pitangus
sulphuratus rufipennis*
Page 296

GREATER PEWEE
Contopus fumigatus zarumae
Page 299

EULER'S FLYCATCHER
Empidonax euleri lawrencei
Page 300

RUDDY-TAILED
FLYCATCHER
*Terenotriccus
erythrurus fulvigularis*
Page 301

HANDSOME FLYCATCHER
Myiophobus p. pulcher
Page 302

CLIFF FLYCATCHER
Hirundinea f. ferruginea
Page 303

BROWNISH FLYCATCHER
Cnipodectes s. subbrunneus
Page 304

YELLOW-OLIVE
FLYCATCHER
*Tolmomyias
sulphurescens exortivus*
Page 304

SOUTHERN BENTBILL
Oncostoma o. olivaceum
Page 308

SHORT-TAILED
PYGMY-TYRANT
*Myiornis
ecaudatus miserabilis*
Page 311

MARBLED-FACED
BRISTLE-TYRANT
*Pogonotriccus
o. ophthalmicus*
Page 312

SLENDER-BILLED
TYRANNULET
Inezia tenuirostris
Page 317

PLUMBEOUS-CROWNED
TYRANNULET
Oreotriccus plumbeiceps
Page 324

YELLOW-BELLIED
TYRANNULET
*Ornithion
semiflavum dilutum*
Page 324

PLATE 50

WHITE-BROWED PURPLETUFT *Iodopleura i. isabellae* Page 268	**OCHRACEOUS ATTILA** *Attila torridus* Page 297	**THRUSH-LIKE MANAKIN** *Schiffornis turdinus furvus* Page 281
BROAD-BILLED MANAKIN *Sapayoa aenigma* Page 281	**MUSICIAN WREN** *Cyphorhinus arada phaeocephalus* Page 339	**BLACK SOLITAIRE** *Entomodestes coracinus* Page 342
GIANT CONEBILL *Oreomanes f. fraseri* Page 370	**FULVOUS SHRIKE-TANAGER** *Lanio fulvus peruvianus* Page 392	**TAWNY-CRESTED TANAGER** *Tachyphonus d. delatrii* Page 393
SCARLET BROWED TANAGER *Heterospingus x. xanthopygius* Page 393	**RUFOUS-CRESTED TANAGER** *Creurgops verticalis* Page 393	**COMMON BUSH-TANAGER** *Chlorospingus ophthalmicus jacqueti* Page 396
BLACK-FACED TANAGER *Schistochlamys melanopis aterrima* Page 399	**SOLITARY BLACK CACIQUE** *Cacicus solitarius* Page 356	**VELVET-FRONTED GRACKLE** *Lampropsar t. tanagrinus* Page 357
GREATER LARGE-BILLED SEED-FINCH *Oryzoborus maximiliani occidentalis* Page 410	**BLUE-BLACK GRASSQUIT** *Volatinia jacarina splendens* Page 405	**HOODED SISKIN** *Spinus magellanicus capitalis* Page 426
PLUMBEOUS SIERRA-FINCH *Phrygilus unicolor geospizopsis* (♀) Page 414	**SLATY FINCH** *Haplospiza r. rustica* Page 415	**YELLOW-BROWED SPARROW** *Myospiza a. aurifrons* Page 421

140. SILVERED ANTBIRD

Sclateria naevia*

5.8″. Bill rather long (.9″), and slender; feet pale. Above leaden gray, wings and tail darker, wing coverts with white apical spots. Below white, flammulated with gray. ♀: Like male but brown instead of gray with dull rufous spots on wing coverts (or grayish sepia brown above; below white, sides of neck and body rufous chestnut, 1).

Tropical zone. GUIANAS; both banks of lower Amazon s to Maranhão and w to rios Xingú and Negro; e and central VENEZUELA. Se COLOMBIA, bordering area of VENEZUELA s through w BRAZIL to e PERU and n BOLIVIA, 1. Trinidad. Coastal mangroves, swampy forest.

Plate 26

141. WHITE-BELLIED ANTBIRD

Myrmeciza longipes*

5.6″. Upperparts, wings and tail rufous chestnut. Long eyebrow gray. Throat and breast black, rest of underparts white, cinnamon on flanks and crissum. ♀: Above like ♂ (or crown and nape gray, 1). Throat and breast bright cinnamon, center of belly white. Wing coverts with black subterminal bar.

Tropical zone. GUYANA; VENEZUELA; n COLOMBIA from Meta west to n Bolívar (in upper Magdalena Valley, 1); n BRAZIL n of lower Amazon and in Roraima. Trinidad. [Central and e Panama.] On or near the ground in woodland undergrowth or second growth, especially near streams.

142. CHESTNUT-BACKED ANTBIRD

Myrmeciza exsul*

5.6″. Crown, nape and upper throat blackish gray. Back, wings and tail sepia brown; wing coverts with (or without, 1) apical white spots. Below leaden gray, brown on flanks and crissum. ♀: Like ♂ above; upper throat gray, rest of underparts rufous chestnut.

Tropical zone. N COLOMBIA e to middle Magdalena Valley (on w shore of Gulf of Urabá, 1), s along Pacific slope to Prov. del Oro, ECUADOR. [Nicaragua s through Panama.] Forest, sometimes swampy, undergrowth.

143. FERRUGINOUS-BACKED ANTBIRD

Myrmeciza ferruginea*

5.5″. Upperparts, wings and tail chestnut; wing coverts black broadly fringed cinnamon. Line from behind eye white. Sides of head, throat and breast black; lower breast feathers broadly edged white. Belly and flanks chestnut brown. ♀: Much like ♂ but throat white, black of breast forming broad pectoral band.

Tropical zone. GUIANAS, BRAZIL n of the Amazon w to rio Negro, s of Amazon between rios Tapajós and Madeira. Forest, mostly terrestrial.

144. SCALLOPED ANTBIRD

Myrmeciza ruficauda*

5.4″. Crown and nape olive brown, bordered laterally with gray. Feathers of mantle black broadly edged buffy concealing white interscapular patch. Lower back, wings and tail reddish brown; wing coverts with broad subterminal black patch and cinnamon fringe. Throat and breast black, breast feathers broadly edged white giving scaled look; belly reddish brown. ♀: Above much like ♂. Throat and breast pale buff, feathers slightly edged black.

E BRAZIL from Pernambuco and Paraiba to Santa Catarina. Forest.

145. SQUAMATE ANTBIRD

Myrmeciza squamosa

6″. Rather like 144 but tail much longer, eyebrow white; wing coverts black, fringed white; mantle feathers without buffy edges, and lower breast white. ♀: Much like ♂.

Se BRAZIL from Rio de Janeiro southward.

146. WHITE-BIBBED ANTBIRD

Myrmeciza loricata

6″. Above much like 145 but eyebrow very much wider. Throat black; rest of underparts white with broad band of black, white-edged feathers across breast. ♀: Above like ♂. Eyebrow and throat buff; band across breast black, feathers edged buff; rest of underparts white.

E BRAZIL from Bahía s to São Paulo. Humid forest.

147. DULL-MANTLED ANTBIRD

Myrmeciza laemosticta *

5.2". Crown and nape dark leaden gray. Back, wings and tail reddish brown (or deep umber brown, tail blackish, 1). Concealed white interscapular patch. Wing coverts brown (or black, 1) with apical white spots. Below leaden gray, flanks umber brown. ♀: Like ♂ but throat feathers with white subterminal bar (or spot, 1).

Nw VENEZUELA w across n COLOMBIA to Pacific, thence s to río Dagua. In sw COLOMBIA and nw ECUADOR, 1. Forest.

148. GRAY-BELLIED ANTBIRD

Myrmeciza pelzelni

5". Lores and sides of head grayish white. Back, wings and tail rufous brown. Wing coverts black with large buff apical spots. Throat and breast black, belly leaden gray. No interscapular patch. ♀: Differs from male by white throat and breast, breast streaked lightly with black.

Tropical zone. Se VENEZUELA and immediately adjacent COLOMBIA and BRAZIL. Forest.

149. CHESTNUT-TAILED ANTBIRD

Myrmeciza hemimelaena *

4.7". Crown and nape dark gray. Back, wings and tail reddish brown; interscapular patch white with black subterminal band. Throat and breast black, rest of underparts white. Wing coverts black with terminal white spots. ♀: Upperparts, wings and tail much as in male. Throat and breast cinnamon buff, rest of underparts mostly buffy white.

Tropical zone. Se COLOMBIA south to n BOLIVIA and Amazonian BRAZIL e to rio Xingú and s Mato Grosso. Forest.

Plate 26

150. PLUMBEOUS ANTBIRD

Myrmeciza hyperythra

7". Uniform dark leaden gray. Wings and tail blackish, wing coverts with small terminal white spots. ♀: Differs from ♂ by uniform bright orange rufous underparts.

Tropical zone. Se COLOMBIA. E PERU; n BOLIVIA; sw Amazonian BRAZIL e to rio Purús. Forest.

151. GOELDI'S ANTBIRD

Myrmeciza goeldii

7.7". Uniform deep black. Bend of wing and large semiconcealed interscapular patch white. ♀: Upperparts bright cinnamon rufous. Forehead and eyebrow dark gray. Interscapular feathers white basally. Wings and tail rufous brown. Cheeks and throat white, rest of underparts bright ochraceous cinnamon.

Tropical zone. Sw BRAZIL on upper rio Purús; se PERU (Balta). Forest.

152. WHITE-SHOULDERED ANTBIRD

Myrmeciza melanoceps

7.4". Differs from 151 by no white interscapular patch; shoulder extensively white. ♀: Head, throat and upper breast black, rest of plumage rufous, paler below.

Tropical zone. E COLOMBIA south to e PERU and w Amazonian BRAZIL.

153. SOOTY ANTBIRD

Myrmeciza fortis *

6.5". Head, throat and breast black; rest of plumage dark, dull gray. Bend of wing white. ♀: Crown chestnut. Sides of head and underparts light gray. Back, wings, tail and crissum sepia brown.

Tropical zone. E COLOMBIA south to e PERU and w Amazonian BRAZIL. Forest.

154. IMMACULATE ANTBIRD

Myrmeciza immaculata *

7.5". Differs from 151 by no white interscapular patch and from 152 by only the bend of wing being white. ♀: Upperparts dark chestnut brown; underparts dull brown mixed with gray in center of abdomen (or chin blackish, underparts much like back, 1). Tail black.

Upper tropical and subtropical zones. Nw VENEZUELA, w in COLOMBIA to Cauca Valley. COLOMBIA on Pacific slope south to w ECUADOR, 1. [Costa Rica and Panama.] Forest.

Plate 46

155. GRAY-HEADED ANTBIRD

Myrmeciza griseiceps

5.4". Top and sides of head and upper mantle dull leaden gray. Back umber brown with large semiconcealed white interscapular patch, feathers subterminally black. Wing coverts black with apical white spots. Throat and breast black; belly gray; crissum brown. Tail dark gray, tipped white. ♀: Upperparts, wings and tail much like ♂ but crown paler gray. Throat and breast gray, feathers black basally.

Subtropical zone. Sw ECUADOR and nw PERU. Forest.

156. BLACK-THROATED ANTBIRD

*Myrmeciza atrothorax ***

5.3''. Upperparts umber brown, interscapular patch white, rump and upper tail coverts blackish (or above mostly slaty gray, lower back tinged brownish olive, 1). Wing coverts blackish, dotted white. Throat and breast black, rest of underparts slaty gray. Tail black. ♀: Olive brown above. Sides of head gray, throat white, breast and sides of body orange rufous, center of abdomen buffy white. Wing coverts dotted buffy white. Tail black.

Tropical zone. GUIANAS, VENEZUELA s of the Orinoco, e COLOMBIA; Amazonian BRAZIL; n BOLIVIA. E ECUADOR, ne PERU, 1. Undergrowth in forest and savanna.

157. SPOT-BREASTED ANTBIRD

Myrmeciza stictothorax

Much like 156, differs mainly by more restricted black of throat and breast, breast somewhat streaked with white. ♀: Very much like 156.

Tropical zone. Known only from w bank of rio Tapajós, BRAZIL.

158. YAPACANA ANTBIRD

Myrmeciza disjuncta

5''. Upperparts blackish gray, crown and nape tinged brown. Concealed white interscapular patch; wing coverts narrowly tipped white. Sides of head gray, chin white; rest of underparts white, strongly tinged ochraceous buff; center of abdomen white. ♀: Like ♂ but wing coverts tipped dusky ochraceous buff.

Known only from central Amazonas, VENEZUELA. Forest.

159. WHITE-PLUMED ANTBIRD

*Pithys albifrons ***

4.3''. Long plumes springing from forehead and chin white, the former swept backward to form two long "horns," the latter forming a beard. Crown, sides of head and lower throat black. Back and wings gray; nuchal collar, underparts, rump and tail chestnut.

Tropical zone. GUIANAS, s and nw VENEZUELA, e COLOMBIA, south to e PERU and Amazonian BRAZIL e to middle Amazon. Savanna and forest, mostly terrestrial.

Plate 36

160. WHITE-MASKED ANTBIRD

Pithys castanea

6''. Crown, ear coverts, lower cheeks and upper throat black; lores, sides of head and chin white; rest of plumage, including wings and tail, chestnut. No plumes.

Tropical zone. Ne PERU on lower río Pastaza. Known from one specimen.

161. WHITE-THROATED ANTBIRD

*Gymnopithys salvini ***

6''. Gray; eyebrow and throat white. Tail black, barred white. ♀: Crown blackish; forehead, sides of head, nape and throat chestnut. Back umber brown, feathers with subterminal black bar and cinnamon rufous fringe. Wing coverts black broadly edged chestnut. Breast chestnut brown turning to umber on flanks and crissum. Tail chestnut, barred black.

Tropical zone. E PERU from río Ucayali e to río Madeira, BRAZIL; n BOLIVIA in Beni and Cochabamba.

162. LUNULATED ANTBIRD

Gymnopithys lunulata

Differs from 161 chiefly by black tail without white bars. ♀: Throat and superciliary streak white. Back rather like 161 but fringes of feathers buff instead of cinnamon rufous. Tail dusky brown, only inner web of feathers with three or four white bars. Underparts brownish olive.

Tropical zone. Se ECUADOR to PERU, chiefly in río Ucayali Valley.

163. BICOLORED ANTBIRD

*Gymnopithys leucaspis ***

5.5''. Upperparts, wings and tail reddish

brown; crown in some races brighter. Post-ocular region gray, lower cheeks black. Throat and center of underparts white; sides of neck and breast black (or brown, 1).

Tropical zone. Nw COLOMBIA from río Sinú w to Pacific coast, s to Cauca, 1; and from Nariño to w ECUADOR. E of Andes from Meta, COLOMBIA, south to n PERU and e to rio Negro, BRAZIL. Forest undergrowth.

Plate 10

164. RUFOUS-THROATED ANTBIRD

Gymnopithys rufigula *

5.5″. Upperparts, wings and tail olive brown. Cheeks and throat rufous chestnut, breast buffy ochraceous darkening to olive brown on sides. Concealed interscapular patch white (or semiconcealed and bright pinkish ochraceous, ♀).

Tropical zone. GUIANAS; s VENEZUELA; n BRAZIL from rio Negro n of the Amazon e to Óbidos. Undergrowth in forest and savanna, partly terrestrial.

165. BARE-EYED ANTBIRD

Rhegmatorhina gymnops

6″. Head crested. Head and underparts black, flanks brownish. Back, wings and tail umber brown. ♀: Much like male but sides of body brown. No crest. In *Rhegmatorhina* the ocular region is bare, pale blue, pale green in 168. All inhabit humid forest.

BRAZIL s of the Amazon between rios Tapajós and Xingú.

166. HARLEQUIN ANTBIRD

Rhegmatorhina berlepschi

6.2″. Head crested. Center of crown dark chestnut, hindcrown bright chestnut. Forehead, sides of head and the throat black. Breast rufous chestnut, rest of underparts light gray. Back olive brown, sides and tail chestnut brown. ♀: Differs from ♂ by feathers of upper back and wing coverts with broad black subterminal band and ochraceous fringe. Breast chestnut, lower breast and abdomen buff, banded with black.

Known only from w bank of lower rio Tapajós, BRAZIL.

Plate 10

167. CHESTNUT-CRESTED ANTBIRD

Rhegmatorhina cristata

Differs from 166 by bright rufous chestnut neck and breast; back somewhat lighter. ♀: Very different from 166. Like male with a shorter crest and a few black spots on mantle.

Known only from rio Uaupés in BRAZIL and COLOMBIA.

168. WHITE-BREASTED ANTBIRD

Rhegmatorhina hoffmannsi

6.2″. Lores, crown and crest deep black; cheeks, throat, foreneck and upper breast white, rest of underparts dull gray. Back light dull olive. ♀: Crown dark chestnut with black shaft streaks. Back, wings and tail more rufescent than in ♂, feathers of upper back and wing coverts with broad black subterminal band and narrow cinnamon fringe. Cheeks and breast white; belly ochraceous broadly banded black.

Sw BRAZIL along the east bank of the rio Madeira.

169. HAIRY-CRESTED ANTBIRD

Rhegmatorhina melanosticta *

6.3″. Crown and crest pale smoky gray, feathers whitish basally; lores and sides of head black. Back and wings reddish brown, tail dusky brown. Underparts olive brown spotted on throat with black. ♀: Like ♂ but feathers of upper back and wing coverts with ochraceous-edged black spots.

Tropical zone. Se COLOMBIA, e ECUADOR south to nw BOLIVIA and BRAZIL s of the Amazon e to rios Madeira and Mamoré.

170. SPOTTED ANTBIRD

Hylophylax naevioides *

4.2″. Tail very short. Crown and sides of head dark gray, tinged brownish. Back chestnut with concealed white interscapular patch. Throat black, rest of underparts white with band of black spots across breast. Wing coverts black, lesser ones tipped white, rest as well as tertials with broad black terminal band. Tail olive with broad black subterminal band and buffy tip. ♀: Upperparts, wings and tail much like ♂. Below fulvous white with dusky pectoral band.

Tropical zone. Caribbean lowlands of CO-

LOMBIA w to Pacific and south to w ECUADOR. [Nicaragua southward.] Forest.

171. SPOT-BACKED ANTBIRD

Hylophylax naevia *

4.2". Top and sides of head gray; mantle black, spotted with buff. Concealed interscapular patch white, rump buffy olive. Below like 170, but belly buffy ochraceous. Wing coverts black, tipped white. Tail brown or gray, with dusky subterminal area and pale-tipped. ♀: Differs from ♂ mainly by white throat, cinnamon buff breast and belly, breast spotted black.

Tropical zone. GUIANAS; VENEZUELA s of the Orinoco; e COLOMBIA south to n BOLIVIA and n and w Amazonian BRAZIL. Forest.

Plate 47

172. DOT-BACKED ANTBIRD

Hylophylax punctulata *

3.9". Crown and upper back olive, lores and sides of head whitish; lower back black, spotted white; concealed interscapular patch white. Throat black, rest of underparts white with broad band of black spots across breast. Wing coverts and tertials black broadly tipped white. Tail black with small white tip. ♀: Differs from ♂ by white center of throat and buffy belly.

Tropical zone. VENEZUELA s of the Orinoco; central Amazonian BRAZIL; ne PERU. Forest.

173. SCALE-BACKED ANTBIRD

Hylophylax poecilonota *

5". Leaden gray (with black throat, 1) feathers of lower back and wing coverts, with broad black subterminal bar and white fringe giving scaled look. Tail black, with a median row of white spots and a white tip. ♀: Crown, nape, sides of head and chin orange ochraceous; back reddish brown, a few feathers in center of back and the wing coverts black with ochraceous fringe. Underparts light gray. Tail black, marked as in male (or plain reddish brown above, light gray below, throat whitish; tail brown with black subterminal band and white tip, 2; or forehead and sides of head ochraceous chestnut, crown and upper back reddish brown; feathers of center of back black,

fringed white; underparts orange ochraceous to dull brown, 3).

Tropical zone. GUIANAS; VENEZUELA s of the Orinoco (except the sw); BRAZIL n of lower Amazon; also se PERU, BRAZIL s of the Amazon from e bank of rio Purús to e bank of rio Madeira, in n and central Mato Grosso and n BOLIVIA in Beni. BRAZIL s of the Amazon from e of rio Madeira to n Maranhão, 1, 2. E COLOMBIA, sw VENEZUELA in sw Amazonas south to e ECUADOR, PERU to Junín and w BRAZIL east to e side of rio Negro, 3; s of the Amazon to rio Juruá, 1, 3. Undergrowth in savanna.

174. OCELLATED ANTBIRD

Phaenostictus mcleannani *

7.5". Orbital skin violet blue. Crown and nape grayish brown, throat black, upper breast and nuchal collar rufous chestnut. Upperparts and wing coverts sandy brown, feathers broadly black subapically and fringed buff. Below similar but feathers fringed cinnamon. Tail rather long (3.7"), grayish black.

Tropical zone. COLOMBIA from lower Cauca Valley w to Pacific and south to nw ECUADOR. [Nicaragua southward.] Forest undergrowth.

Plate 36

175. PALE-FACED BARE-EYE

Skutchia borbae

(Called *Phlegopsis borbae* in *Sp. Bds. S. Amer.*)

7.5". Yellowish bare patch behind eye. Patch of elongated whitish feathers on lores and black patch of stiffened feathers above eye. Head dark rufous shading to cinnamon rufous on throat and breast, belly dull brownish with a band of dusky white-barred feathers between breast and belly. Back greenish chestnut with slight black spots, rump dull brownish. Tail distally blackish.

Known from e side of lower rio Madeira to rio Tapajós, BRAZIL. Forest undergrowth.

176. BLACK-SPOTTED BARE-EYE

Phlegopsis nigromaculata *

7". Orbital skin red. Head, neck, breast and upper belly black. Back and wing coverts olive brown spotted with black, belly olive brown. Remiges and tail rufous chestnut.

Tropical zone. E COLOMBIA e of Andes to n BOLIVIA. Amazonian BRAZIL s of the Amazon east to e Pará and Maranhão, n of the Amazon in Amapá. Forest undergrowth.

177. ARGUS BARE-EYE

Phlegopsis barringeri

7.5". Orbital skin red. Head, throat, breast and center of belly glossy black. Back and wing coverts reddish brown, feathers subterminally black, surrounding round buff spot. Upper and under tail coverts mostly chestnut. Remiges externally chestnut, primaries with black speculum. Basal half and tip of tail feathers chestnut, distal half black. ♀: Unknown.

Known only from se Nariño, COLOMBIA. Undoubtedly ne ECUADOR. Forest undergrowth. Known from one specimen.
Plate 10

178. REDDISH-WINGED BARE-EYE

Phlegopsis erythroptera *

6.7". Orbital skin red. Mostly black, back feathers fringed white; wing coverts terminally, and basal part of primaries, chestnut. ♀: Chestnut brown above, orange rufous below. Wings and tail blackish; double wing bar and spot on outer web of remiges buff.

Tropical zone. S VENEZUELA; w and central BRAZIL; se COLOMBIA; e ECUADOR; e PERU. Forest undergrowth.

179. SHORT-TAILED ANTTHRUSH

Chamaeza campanisona *

8.3". Upperparts, wings and tail uniform olive brown, tail with blackish subterminal area and pale tip. Postocular streak white. Below white, more or less suffused with buffy particularly on breast and sides; feathers heavily margined laterally with blackish giving streaked look. Under tail coverts buff.

Tropical, subtropical zones. GUYANA; mts. of VENEZUELA. COLOMBIA south to n BOLIVIA. E BRAZIL from Bahía to Rio Grande do Sul, Misiones, and Corrientes, ARGENTINA. Bamboo thickets, forest.

180. STRIATED ANTTHRUSH

Chamaeza nobilis *

9.2". Much like 179 but bill heavier, crown blackish, upperparts darker, and underparts whiter, with lateral dark edges to feathers blacker and wider. Postocular streak much reduced.

Tropical zone. E COLOMBIA south to se PERU; Amazonian BRAZIL s of the Amazon e to lower rio Tapajós. Forest floor.
Plates 10, 46

181. RUFOUS-TAILED ANTTHRUSH

Chamaeza ruficauda *

8.3". Differs from 179 by smaller bill, no black subterminal patch on tail, and by white feathers of sides having broad black median stripe and narrowly margined black laterally; back more reddish brown. Postocular streak white, prominent.

Subtropical zone. Mts. of coastal VENEZUELA from Miranda to Yaracuy. COLOMBIA in Andes above Magdalena Valley. Se BRAZIL from Rio de Janeiro to Rio Grande do Sul. Forest.

182. BARRED ANTTHRUSH

Chamaeza mollissima *

8". Above uniform chestnut brown, below narrowly barred blackish and fulvous white. Postocular feathers somewhat elongated, barred black and white.

Subtropical, temperate zones. Andes of COLOMBIA; e ECUADOR. N BOLIVIA in La Paz. Forest.

183. RUFOUS-CAPPED ANTTHRUSH

Formicarius colma *

7". Crown and nape bright cinnamon rufous (or with black forehead, 1). Lores, sides of head, throat and breast black becoming olive gray on belly. Back olive. Bend of wing and base of remiges cinnamon. Tail black. ♀: Differs from ♂ by white, black-spotted throat (or like ♂, 2).

Tropical zone. GUIANAS, e VENEZUELA, BRAZIL n of the Amazon e of rio Negro. BRAZIL s of the Amazon from rio Madeira e to Maranhão and south to w Mato Grosso and Rio Grande do Sul, 2. E COLOMBIA and upper Orinoco, VENEZUELA, south to e ECUADOR, e PERU and w Amazonian BRAZIL w of rios Negro and Madeira, 1. Terrestrial in forest undergrowth. Coastal forest in e Brazil.

184. BLACK-FACED ANTTHRUSH

Formicarius analis *

7.5″. Upperparts uniform olivaceous brown to reddish brown. Ear coverts in some races chestnut brown. Upper tail coverts usually more reddish than back. Throat blackish, rest of underparts light to dark gray, center of abdomen pale buffy in some races. Under tail coverts light to dark chestnut, tail blackish.

Tropical zone. Generally distributed e of Andes, south to n Maranhão, n Mato Grosso, n BOLIVIA and se PERU. W of Andes in COLOMBIA. Trinidad. [Mid. Amer.] Forest, terrestrial.

Fig. 17, p. 166

185. RUFOUS-FRONTED ANTTHRUSH

Formicarius rufifrons

Not unlike 184 but easily distinguishable by bright orange rufous forehead and bright cinnamon axillaries, under wing coverts and inner margins of remiges.

Known from two females from Madre de Dios, se PERU.

186. BLACK-HEADED ANTTHRUSH

Formicarius nigricapillus *

6.5″. Head, upper mantle, throat and breast dull black. Back and wings dark olive brown, becoming dark chestnut on upper tail coverts; flanks and belly dark olive, under tail coverts chestnut. Under wing coverts and base of remiges ochraceous.

Tropical, subtropical zones. COLOMBIA w of the Western Andes south to w ECUADOR. [Costa Rica; Panama.] Forest and scrub.

187. RUFOUS-BREASTED ANTTHRUSH

Formicarius rufipectus *

7″. Crown, nape, breast, upper and under tail coverts chestnut, back dark olive or dark grayish olive; belly dark olivaceous. Tail blackish (or with blackish crown, upper tail coverts like back, 1).

Upper tropical and temperate zones. COLOMBIA in the Central and Western Andes; w ECUADOR. E ECUADOR, e PERU, 1. [Costa Rica; Panama.] Forest.

Plate 36

188. WING-BANDED ANTBIRD

Myrmornis torquata *

6″. Crown chestnut, back feathers gray, broadly margined chestnut; black patch in center of back, the feathers with hidden white bases. Wing coverts black, lesser ones margined chestnut, rest buff. Area behind eye white, feathers edged black. Throat and upper breast black irregularly outlined in white (or no white outline, 1), rest of underparts gray; under tail coverts ochraceous orange. Tail very short, rufous chestnut. ♀: Differs from ♂ by ochraceous throat and upper breast.

Tropical zone. Generally distributed e of Andes s to ECUADOR and Amazonian BRAZIL, n of the Amazon in rio Negro region and s of it from rio Madeira eastward and south to n Mato Grosso. W of Andes in n COLOMBIA, 1. [Se Nicaragua and Panama.] Forest undergrowth.

Plate 36

Antpittas

Antpittas look like long-legged thrushes with very short tails. Terrestrial, they are difficult to see due to the thick cover which they haunt.

189. BLACK-CROWNED ANTPITTA

Pittasoma michleri *

7.5″. Crown black, back olive brown somewhat streaked and spotted with black. Wing coverts with small terminal buffy white spots. Ear coverts chestnut. Throat black, spotted with white; rest of underparts barred black and white. ♀: Much like ♂, but underparts barred buff and black.

Tropical zone. Nw COLOMBIA in nw Chocó. [Costa Rica and Panama.] Forest.

Plate 36

190. RUFOUS-CROWNED ANTPITTA

Pittasoma rufopileatum *

6.5″. Crown rufous chestnut, lores and long broad superciliary deep black, back and wings much as in 189. Throat and cheeks ochraceous with black shaft streaks; rest of underparts white, barred black (or ochraceous almost plain to lightly barred black, 1).

Tropical zone. Pacific slopes of COLOMBIA

from Baudó Mts. southward, 1. Nw ECUA-DOR. Forest.

191. UNDULATED ANTPITTA

*Grallaria squamigera ***

9". Upperparts, wing and tail coverts oliva-ceous, hindcrown and nape ashy (or entire upperparts, wings and tail gray, 1). Center of throat white, margined black laterally; rest of underparts ochraceous, banded with black.

Subtropical, temperate zones. Nw VENE-ZUELA, Andes of COLOMBIA and ECUA-DOR. Andes of PERU to n BOLIVIA, 1. Forest.

192. GIANT ANTPITTA

*Grallaria gigantea ***

10.5". Above much like 191 but darker and browner with rufous forehead. Underparts deep orange rufous, barred with black.

Upper subtropical to temperate zone. CO-LOMBIA on e slope of Central Andes in Huila. E and w ECUADOR. Forest.

193. GREAT ANTPITTA

*Grallaria excelsa ***

10.5". Much like 191 but considerably larger, above darker and more brownish olive. Inner web of remiges margined with ochraceous at base.

Subtropical zone. Nw VENEZUELA. Forest.

194. VARIEGATED ANTPITTA

*Grallaria varia ***

7.5". Forecrown and back olive brown; hindcrown and nape gray, feathers edged black with pale shaft streaks. Lores and moustachial streaks buffy white. Throat and breast dark reddish brown, feathers with buffy white shaft streaks; buffy white patch on center of lower throat, lower breast buffy brown gradually turning to plain ochraceous buff, lower breast broadly streaked buffy white (belly barred with dusky, 1). Under wing coverts bright cinna-mon.

Tropical zone. GUIANAS, s VENEZUELA, Amazonian BRAZIL n of the Amazon. From rio Madeira e to Pernambuco, thence to Rio Grande do Sul, e PARAGUAY, ne ARGENTINA, 1. Bamboo thickets, forest.

195. MOUSTACHED ANTPITTA

Grallaria alleni

8". Crown and nape slate gray, malar streak white edged black. Back and wings dark olivaceous brown. Upper throat russet brown, bordered below by a white bar; breast olive brown streaked with white, belly white. Flanks under wing- and under tail coverts ochraceous. Tail ochraceous orange.

Subtropical zone. W slope of Central Andes of COLOMBIA. Forest.

196. SCALED ANTPITTA

*Grallaria guatimalensis ***

7". Rather like 195 but somewhat smaller, malar streak buffy and breast and belly light to dark ochraceous. Tail olivaceous brown.

Upper tropical and subtropical zones. S VENEZUELA; bordering area of BRAZIL; COLOMBIA south on the east to se PERU, on the west to nw PERU. Trinidad. [Mid. Amer.] Tangled forest undergrowth, often near streams.

197. TACHIRA ANTPITTA

Grallaria chthonia

7". Rather like 196 but decidedly darker and more olive above. Upper breast buffy brown with white shaft streaks; lower breast and sides whitish, barred with gray.

Subtropical zone in nw Táchira, VENE-ZUELA. Forest.

198. PLAIN-BACKED ANTPITTA

*Grallaria haplonota ***

7.5". Above rather like 196. Throat white bordered by black moustachial streak, rest of underparts dull ochraceous brightest on under tail coverts (or throat hardly different from breast, crown rufous, 1).

Upper tropical and subtropical zones. VEN-EZUELA n of the Orinoco. W ECUADOR, 1. Forest.

199. OCHRE-STRIPED ANTPITTA

Grallaria dignissima

(Called *Thamnocharis dignissima* in *Sp. Bds. S. Amer.*)

7". Above reddish brown, tinged grayish on crown; lower back with a few white streaks. Throat and breast ferruginous red; belly white, streaked black on sides, feathers much lengthened. Tail very short, concealed by feathers of lower back.

Tropical zone. Se COLOMBIA in Putumayo, e ECUADOR, extreme ne PERU. Forest.

200. ELUSIVE ANTPITTA

Grallaria eludens[1]

Differs from 199 by less reddish upperparts, white throat, and buff to pinkish buff breast.

Tropical zone. Known only from vicinity of Balta, río Curanja, se Loreto, PERU.

201. CHESTNUT-CROWNED ANTPITTA

*Grallaria ruficapilla**

8″. Crown and nape orange rufous; back, wings and tail olive brown (crown and back with pale shaft streaks, 1). Below white with blackish to olive streaks, sometimes with slight rufous admixture. Flank feathers considerably lengthened.

Upper tropical and subtropical zones. Nw VENEZUELA; COLOMBIA (except Santa Marta) south to nw ECUADOR and e and central PERU. In sw ECUADOR and nw PERU, 1. Forest, comes into open early morning and evening.

202. SANTA MARTA ANTPITTA

Grallaria bangsi

7″. Crown and nape dull ashy gray; back, wings and tail ashy olive, wings somewhat browner. Throat ochraceous, rest of underparts white heavily streaked on breast and sides with ashy olive. Flank feathers lengthened.

Subtropical zone of Santa Marta Mts., COLOMBIA. Tangled forest undergrowth.

203. STRIPE-HEADED ANTPITTA

*Grallaria andicola**

7″. Conspicuous eye ring white. Upperparts olive brown, streaked fulvous on forecrown (or entire upperparts, except rump, streaked fulvous, 1). Throat buffy white; rest of underparts buffy white, feathers very broadly margined black giving scaled or streaked look.

Temperate zone. Andes of PERU s to

Huancavelica; in Puno and nw BOLIVIA, 1. Fern brakes, dense bushes under stunted trees.

204. BICOLORED ANTPITTA

Grallaria rufocinerea

7″. Sides of head, upperparts, wings and tail uniform dark reddish brown; below uniform dark gray, tinged rufous on throat.

Upper tropical and lower temperate zones of Central Andes of COLOMBIA in Antioquia and Caldas. Forest.

205. CHESTNUT-NAPED ANTPITTA

*Grallaria nuchalis**

8″. Crown, nape and sides of head chestnut rufous; back dark reddish brown; wings rufous brown. Underparts dark gray, blackish on throat.

Upper subtropical to lower temperate zone. COLOMBIA on w slope of E Andes in Cundinamarca and both slopes of Central Andes; e and w ECUADOR. Forest.

206. WHITE-THROATED ANTPITTA

Grallaria albigula

8″. Above much like 205 but back more olivaceous. Below mostly white; breast, sides of body and crissum pale gray.

Subtropical zone. S PERU in Puno; e BOLIVIA in Santa Cruz.

207. BAY-BACKED ANTPITTA

*Grallaria hypoleuca**

(Includes *przewalski* (2), *erythroleuca* (3) and *capitalis* (4) of *Sp. Bds. S. Amer.*)

7″. Upperparts and sides of head chestnut brown; below white, tinged gray on sides and breast (or below primrose yellow, sides chestnut brown, 1; or throat pale buff, middle of breast and abdomen ashy, sides rufous brown, 2; or throat and center of abdomen white, breast and sides rufous brown, 3; or underparts nearly uniform orange rufous, 4).

Subtropical zone. COLOMBIA on slopes of Andes above Magdalena Valley. W slope of W Andes to w ECUADOR, 1 (*flavotincta*).

[1]Lowery and O'Neill, Auk, 1969, *86*, 1, p.1. (Balta, río Curanja, 10°8's, 71°13'w, Loreto, Peru).

PERU in Amazonas and Loreto, 2. In Cuzco, 3. In Junín, 4. Forest, often near streams.

208. GRAY-NAPED ANTPITTA

Grallaria griseonucha *

6″. Above rufous brown, band around nape dark gray. Below bright rufous.

Upper tropical and temperate zones. Andes of Mérida and Táchira, VENEZUELA. Forest.

209. RUFOUS ANTPITTA

Grallaria rufula *

5.5″. Uniform rufous brown to olive brown above. Uniform ochraceous brown to dull ochraceous below.

Subtropical, temperate zones. Nw VENE-ZUELA s through Andes to n BOLIVIA. Forest undergrowth, meadows in early morning.

210. RUFOUS-FACED ANTPITTA

Grallaria erythrotis

7.5″. Upperparts, wings and tail olivaceous; sides of head and neck orange rufous, throat and center of abdomen white; breast streaked orange rufous, sides olivaceous.

Subtropical zone. N BOLIVIA in La Paz and Cochabamba. Forest.

211. TAWNY ANTPITTA

Grallaria quitensis *

6.5″. Upperparts, wings and tail olive to grayish olive. Below buffy ochraceous, more or less intermixed with dull white.

Upper tropical and temperate zones. E and Central Andes of COLOMBIA and through e and w ECUADOR to n PERU. Forest.

212. BROWN-BANDED ANTPITTA

Grallaria milleri

5.5″. Upperparts, wings, tail, sides of head, breast band and flanks dark olivaceous brown. Lores, throat and center abdomen dull white.

Temperate zone. W slope of Central Andes of COLOMBIA in Caldas. Forest.

213. STREAK-CHESTED ANTPITTA

Hylopezus perspicillatus *

(This and the next four were placed in *Grallaria* in *Sp. Bds. S. Amer.*)

5.5″. Crown dark gray, back olive, lightly streaked with buff. Wing coverts tipped with buff, primaries brown with orange rufous at base. Lores and conspicuous eye ring buff to orange rufous. Underparts white, malar streak black; breast and sides buffy, streaked with black.

Tropical zone. COLOMBIA w of E Andes and w ECUADOR. [Nicaragua southward.] Forest.

Plate 36

214. SPOTTED ANTPITTA

Hylopezus macularius *

6″. Differs from 213 by unstreaked back and plain ochraceous flanks.

Tropical zone. GUIANAS; VENEZUELA s of the Orinoco; se COLOMBIA in Amazonas. Ne PERU in Loreto. BRAZIL along rio Negro and s of the Amazon from rio Madeira eastward; BOLIVIA on upper rio Madeira. Forest.

215. FULVOUS-BELLIED ANTPITTA

Hylopezus fulviventris *

Differs from 214 by blackish crown, much darker upperparts, no orange at base of primaries, and breast and sides much darker ochraceous. No eye ring; wing coverts unspotted.

Tropical zone. Pacific slopes of COLOMBIA and e of Andes from Caquetá south to e and w ECUADOR. [Nicaragua southward.] Forest.

216. AMAZONIAN ANTPITTA

Hylopezus berlepschi *

5.5″. Upperparts including crown, wings and tail olive. Malar streak black. Below white, tinged buff (or dark ochraceous, 1) on breast and sides, streaked with black. No eye ring.

Tropical zone. BRAZIL s of the Amazon, e to rio Xingú; n BOLIVIA in Beni and Cochabamba. Se PERU in Junín, 1.

217. SPECKLE-BREASTED ANTPITTA

Hylopezus ochroleucus *

5.5''. Back and wings plain brownish olive; below pale ochraceous, the black markings on breast confined to sides (or on breast as well, 1) and more like spots than streaks.

E BRAZIL from Ceará to São Paulo; thence to Rio Grande do Sul, e PARAGUAY and ne ARGENTINA in Misiones, 1. Bamboo thickets, forest.

218. THRUSH-LIKE ANTPITTA

Myrmothera campanisona *

5.6''. Upperparts, wings and tail reddish brown to olive brown. Below white, streaked on breast with olive.

Tropical zone. GUIANAS; VENEZUELA s of the Orinoco; e COLOMBIA from Meta south to e PERU; Amazonian BRAZIL e to Amapá and rio Tapajós. Forest.

219. BROWN-BREASTED ANTPITTA

Myrmothera simplex *

5.6''. Upperparts, wings and tail chestnut brown. Breast and sides ashy gray. Throat, sharply outlined, and belly white.

Upper tropical and subtropical zones. Mts. of s VENEZUELA and bordering area of n BRAZIL. Forest.

Grallaricula

These are a small edition of *Grallaria*; they live in the undergrowth of forests rather than on the ground.

220. OCHRE-BREASTED ANTPITTA

Grallaricula flavirostris *

4.7''. Above olive brown, crown shaded gray in some races. Throat and breast ochraceous to ochraceous orange, streaked on breast and sides with black; belly white (or center of throat white, breast buffy, feathers heavily scalloped with black, 1).

Tropical, subtropical zones. COLOMBIA; e and w ECUADOR; n PERU south to n BOLIVIA. [Costa Rica, Panama.] Forest undergrowth.

Plate 10

221. RUSTY-BREASTED ANTPITTA

Grallaricula ferrugineipectus *

4.7''. Olive brown above; below ochraceous,

crescent across lower throat and center of abdomen white (or above rufous brown, brightest on crown, below darker, 1).

Subtropical zone. Nw VENEZUELA from Dist. Federal west to Mérida and Lara; COLOMBIA in Santa Marta Mts. (in Cundinamarca and Perijá Mts., 1). N PERU in Amazonas. Undergrowth in humid forest.

222. SLATE-CROWNED ANTPITTA

Grallaricula nana *

4.2''. Crown dark gray; back russet brown to olivaceous. Underparts ochraceous orange, center of belly white; white crescent across throat in some races.

Upper tropical and temperate zones. Mts. of n VENEZUELA and in Bolívar. Locally in COLOMBIA and ECUADOR. Forest undergrowth.

223. SCALLOP-BREASTED ANTPITTA

Grallaricula loricata

4.2''. Crown and nape deep rufous, back olive brown. Underparts white, feathers of breast and sides edged with black, throat sometimes tawny. Lower mandible yellow.

Subtropical zone. Mts. of n VENEZUELA from Dist. Federal to Yaracuy. Forest undergrowth.

224. PERUVIAN ANTPITTA

Grallaricula peruviana

Very similar to 223 but crown and back duller, and lower mandible blackish instead of yellowish.

Subtropical zone. N PERU in Piura.

225. CRESCENT-FACED ANTPITTA

Grallaricula lineifrons

5.2''. Crown and sides of head slaty black; long, broad white crescent in front of eye; back, wings and tail brownish olive. Below buffy white, broadly streaked olivaceous brown.

Temperate zone of ne ECUADOR.

226. HOODED ANTPITTA

Grallaricula cucullata *

4.7''. Head orange rufous; back, wings and tail olive brown. Breast and sides of body ashy gray; center of abdomen and patch at base of throat white.

Subtropical zone. VENEZUELA in sw Táchira. COLOMBIA on e slope of Central Andes and e slope of W Andes. Forest undergrowth.

Gnateaters

The Gnateaters were placed in a separate family (Conopophagidae) in *Sp. Bds. S. Amer.* They are inhabitants of the undergrowth and forest floor where they reveal their presence by melodious whistles. Their legs are rather long and their tails short. Males are usually characterized by a silvery white postocular tuft of feathers.

227. BLACK-BELLIED GNATEATER

Conopophaga melanogaster

5.7". Head and underparts black, postocular tuft white. Back, wings and tail chestnut. ♀: Forecrown dark gray, hindcrown and nape dark brown, long eyebrow pale gray. Throat and center of belly whitish, rest of underparts pale gray. Back and wings like ♂.

BRAZIL s of the Amazon from rio Madeira to rio Tocantins; n BOLIVIA in Beni.

Plate 10

228. HOODED GNATEATER

Conopophaga roberti

5". Head, throat and breast black; postocular tuft white. Center of belly white, sides of body gray. Back, wings and tail rufous brown. ♀: Crown rufous like back. Throat, breast and sides of body pale gray; center of abdomen white.

E BRAZIL from e Pará to Maranhão and w Ceara. Forest undergrowth, capoeira.

229. BLACK-CHEEKED GNATEATER

Conopophaga melanops *

5". Crown and wing coverts bright orange rufous, sides of head, lores and forehead black (or forehead orange rufous, 1), postocular tuft white. Back grayish brown (or ochraceous brown, 1), feathers edged laterally with black. Throat and center of underparts white, sides of body gray. Wings and tail grayish (or brown, 1). ♀: Above olive brown, mantle feathers edged laterally with black; postocular tuft white. Wing coverts

like back with buff terminal spots. Throat, breast and sides of body ferruginous; center of belly white.

E BRAZIL from Paraiba to Bahía, 1; thence southward to São Paulo. Forest.

230. ASH-THROATED GNATEATER

Conopophaga peruviana

5.2". Crown dark brown, long silvery white postocular tuft. Mantle gray, feathers laterally edged black; rump olivaceous brown. Wings and tail dark brown, wing coverts with terminal white spots. Throat whitish, breast gray, abdomen white, flanks olivaceous brown. ♀: Above like ♂; throat and belly white, breast dark ferruginous red. Postocular tuft present.

Tropical zone. E ECUADOR, e PERU and sw Amazonian BRAZIL e to upper rio Purús.

231. SLATY GNATEATER

Conopophaga ardesiaca *

5.2". Upperparts, wings and tail dark olive brown; dorsal feathers inconspicuously margined black. Forehead slaty gray, long silvery white postocular tuft. Below either uniform dark gray or with white center to abdomen. ♀: Upperparts, wings and tail reddish brown; forehead orange rufous. Below like ♂, but under tail coverts and flanks ochraceous brown. No postocular tuft.

Upper tropical and subtropical zones. Se PERU from Cuzco s to Chuquisaca, BOLIVIA.

232. CHESTNUT-CROWNED GNATEATER

Conopophaga castaneiceps *

5.2". Rather like 231 but at once distinguishable by light orange rufous forecrown and chestnut brown hindcrown. ♀: Like ♂ above, but browner with white postocular tuft. Throat, sides of head and the breast orange rufous; belly gray, flanks olive.

Upper tropical and subtropical zones. COLOMBIA; e ECUADOR; n and e PERU. Forest undergrowth.

233. CHESTNUT-BELTED GNATEATER

Conopophaga aurita *

5.2". Crown chestnut brown, postocular tuft silvery white. Lores and sides of head and throat (also breast, 1) black. Back, wings and tail olivaceous brown, mantle feathers more or less edged black. Breast orange rufous (except 1), center of belly white, sides pale olivaceous (or underparts except breast light pinkish cinnamon, 1). ♀: Upperparts, wings and tail like ♂ but browner. Lores whitish, postocular tuft present. Throat whitish, breast bright orange rufous, center of abdomen whitish, sides olivaceous.

Tropical zone. GUIANAS. Se COLOMBIA south to e PERU. BRAZIL n of the Amazon to Amapá and s of it to rio Tocantins (on rio Tapajós, 1). Forest undergrowth.

234. RUFOUS GNATEATER

Conopophaga lineata *

4.5". Upperparts, wings and tail uniform umber brown. Lores and eyebrow bluish gray, postocular tuft white. Throat and breast cinnamon rufous, white crescent across lower throat. Abdomen white, flanks olivaceous. ♀: Differs from ♂ by gray instead of white postocular tuft.

E BRAZIL from Ceará s to Rio Grande do Sul, e Mato Grosso, PARAGUAY and ne ARGENTINA in Misiones. Caatinga, bamboo thickets.

Family RHINOCRYPTIDAE   TAPACULOS

Members of this interesting family are found only in the New World, from Costa Rica southward, and reach their highest development in Chile. Usually birds of cool regions, they are found high in the Andes or on the plateau and mountains of central and eastern Brazil, only reaching lowlands in southern South America. A few species however do inhabit tropical regions.

Tapaculos vary in size from that of a wren to a very large thrush and are best recognized by their peculiar erect tail carriage. They are almost exclusively terrestrial, rarely fly, and run swiftly on exceptionally large feet. They are very timid and seldom seen, but their loud and wierd notes often reveal their presence. They inhabit dense forests or open brushlands and live almost entirely on insects.

Members of the *Scytalopus* group are reminiscent of wrens, particularly in the banded, brown immature plumage. Most species resemble each other closely, often seeming to grade into each other, and are very difficult to tell apart even in the hand. Slight differences in the shape of the bill are helpful in distinguishing them. They inhabit cool humid forests, mostly in western South America, and are probably not found below 4000 ft.

AID TO IDENTIFICATION

Not wren-like

Slaty black and chestnut, or ferruginous, or olive brown (chestnut) 1b, 2b; (olive brown) 14b, 15b; (ferruginous) 15b; (barred below) 3b, 4b, 5b

Mostly pale grayish or cinnamon (with crest)6; (without) 7.

Spotted white above and below 28

Band across breast 8, 9, 10, 11, 12

Small, wren-like

Dotted white above, dotted black below, 13c

Mostly dark to pale gray with rufous rump and flanks (flanks and rump unbarred) 16b,

17b, 18b, 19c, 23b, 26b; (barred) 18b, 20b, 21b, 22b, 23b, 24c

Throat and breast white 25c, 27b

1. CHESTNUT-THROATED HUET-HUET

Pteroptochos castaneus

10". Hindcrown, hindneck and back slaty black; lower back shaded dark chestnut and barred with black and buff, upper tail coverts similar but brighter. Wings blackish, outer wing coverts tipped yellowish white. Tail smoky black. Forecrown, eyebrow, throat and upper breast rufous chestnut; belly and flanks darker and barred with black and yellowish white.

Central CHILE from Colchagua to río Bío-Bío. Forest.

2. BLACK-THROATED HUET-HUET

Pteroptochos tarnii

10". Crown chestnut; sides of head, neck all around and back dark slaty gray. Rump, breast and rest of underparts chestnut, barred on belly and under tail coverts with black and buff. Wings and tail black. Variable shade of rufous on lower parts.

S CHILE from río Bío-Bío s to Messier Channel, Magallanes. ARGENTINA from Neuquén to Santa Cruz. Heavy beach forest, bamboo thickets.

3. MOUSTACHED TURCA

Pteroptochos megapodius *

9.2". Above light smoky brown becoming rufescent on rump; narrow superciliary and very broad moustachial streak buffy white. Center of throat smoky brown, upper breast dull chestnut; lower breast and belly buffy white, banded dusky and dull chestnut. Wings like back. Tail dull rufescent (or smaller, much paler with virtually no chestnut shades, 1).

N CHILE in coastal mts. of Freirina and Vallenar and cordillera of Copiapó in Atacama, 1; central provinces from Coquimbo to Concepción. Bush-covered hillsides on seacoast, in interior up to 7000 ft.

Plate 10

4. WHITE-THROATED TAPACULO

Scelorchilus albicollis *

8". Above rufous brown, wings and tail more rufous. Lores, eyebrow and throat dirty white; rest of underparts buffy white

crossed by narrow, irregular, dark brown bars (or with light brownish gray upperparts, tail cinnamon rufous, 1).

CHILE in Atacama and Coquimbo, 1; and from Santiago to Curicó. Hab. same as 3. In semiarid country, 1.

Plate 26

5. CHUCAO TAPACULO

Scelorchilus rubecula *

7". Above dark brown inclining to rufous in old birds. Rump, flanks and tail rufous. Lores, throat and breast orange rufous; rest of underparts gray, irregularly barred with black and white.

CHILE from Colchagua to Aysén and Mocha I. ARGENTINA from w Neuquén to Chubut. Dense beach forest, thickets, bamboo.

6. CRESTED GALLITO

Rhinocrypta lanceolata

9". Crown, conspicuous crest, nape and sides of head rufous with white shaft streaks. Back olivaceous gray. Tail blackish. Throat and breast pale gray, sides of body conspicuously bright chestnut, abdomen white.

E BOLIVIA in Santa Cruz; w PARAGUAY; w ARGENTINA s to Río Negro and extreme s Buenos Aires. Dry, open brush.

Plate 26

7. SANDY GALLITO

Teledromas fuscus

6.7". Above pale cinnamon brown, forehead rufescent, eyebrow whitish. Below whitish, tinged cinnamon; central tail feathers like back, rest blackish, outermost tipped white.

W ARGENTINA from sw Salta and Tucumán s to Río Negro. Open brush, dry gravelly hillsides.

8. RUSTY-BELTED TAPACULO

Liosceles thoracicus *

8". Crown and nape dark grayish brown, narrow eyebrow white. Back and wings dark reddish brown, tail darkest. Sides of neck and of breast gray, edged by black line. Throat and breast white, breast crossed by yellow-shaded rufous band sometimes incomplete; rest of underparts black, barred with rufous and white.

Tropical zone. Se COLOMBIA; e ECUADOR; e PERU; w BRAZIL e to rios Içá and Tapajós. Forest.

Fig. 13, p. 110

9. COLLARED CRESCENTCHEST

Melanopareia torquata *

5″. Crown grayish brown (or rufous brown, 1; or black, 2). Superciliary white, sides of head black. Broad nuchal collar cinnamon rufous. Back bright russet brown (or brownish olive, 2). Throat buffy; pectoral band black, edged white above; rest of underparts tawny, buff in center of abdomen.

E BRAZIL in Bahía and Piauí; from Goiás and Minas Gerais to São Paulo and Mato Grosso, 1. E BOLIVIA, 2. Open cerrado in association with anthills.

10. OLIVE-CROWNED CRESCENTCHEST

Melanopareia maximiliani *

6″. Above olive brown. Superciliary and throat buff. Sides of head and pectoral band black, rest of underparts chestnut to tawny ochraceous. Wings and tail like back. Concealed interscapulars white.

Subtropical zone. N and e BOLIVIA; w PARAGUAY; w ARGENTINA e to Chaco and s to Córdoba. Bushes, sawgrass.

11. MARAÑON CRESCENTCHEST

Melanopareia maranonica

6.2″. Crown, nape, sides of head and broad pectoral band black. Eyebrow buff; throat buff at sides, white in center. Back olive brown. Breast and belly tawny ochraceous. Wing coverts and margins of outer remiges, white. Tail black, feathers edged olive brown.

Tropical zone. N PERU in arid parts of Marañón Valley in Cajamarca.

Plate 10

12. ELEGANT CRESCENTCHEST

Melanopareia elegans *

5.5″. Crown, nape, sides of head and broad breast band black. Eyebrow and throat buffy white. Back grayish olive. Breast chestnut shading to cinnamon buff on rest of underparts. Outer remiges broadly edged silvery, wing coverts and inner remiges broadly edged chestnut. Tail black. ♀: Similar to ♂ (or with crown scarcely different from back, 1).

Tropical zone up to 4500 ft. W ECUADOR from Manabí southward. Nw PERU s to Cajamarca, 1. Arid scrub.

13. SPOTTED BAMBOOWREN

Psilorhamphus guttatus

5.3″. Wren-like. Tail long, much graduated. Crown, nape and upper back gray; lower back and rump rufous brown. Throat and breast white, belly rufous buff. Above dotted white, below dotted black. Tail reddish brown, notched buff and tipped white. ♀: Differs from ♂ by rufous brown upperparts and buffy underparts, dotted like ♂.

Se BRAZIL from Minas Gerais to Paraná. Ne ARGENTINA in Misiones. Bamboo thickets.

14. SLATY BRISTLEFRONT

Merulaxis ater

7.5″. Slaty black; lower back, flanks and belly dark olive brown. Loral plumes long, stiff, narrow, pointed. ♀: Earthy brown above. Throat, breast and middle of belly cinnamon brown.

Se BRAZIL from s Bahía to Paraná. Forest.

Plate 26

15. STRESEMANN'S BRISTLEFRONT

Marulaxis stresemanni

Like 14 in color, but considerably larger. ♀: Above dark brown with slaty cast; below intense ferruginous. Wings and tail dark brown.

E BRAZIL in coastal Bahía. Forest.

16. OCHRE-FLANKED TAPACULO

Eugralla paradoxa

5″. Slaty gray, paler below; rump and flanks rufous. Upper mandible blackish, lower yellowish. Differs from *Scytalopus* by oval base of culmen encroaching on forehead.

CHILE from Maule to Chiloé and Mocha Is. ARGENTINA in Río Negro. Thick forest undergrowth.

17. ASH-COLORED TAPACULO

Myornis senilis

5". More or less uniform ashy gray. Tail 2.4". Much like *Scytalopus* but at once separable by long tail.

Temperate zone. COLOMBIA in Central and E Andes and probably immediately adjacent Venezuela. Forest undergrowth.

18. UNICOLORED TAPACULO

Scytalopus unicolor

6". Uniform blackish (1) to silvery gray, with flanks and crissum pale to dark brown (lightly barred, 2) with intermediates between the two extremes. ♀: Similar to ♂ (1) or with rump, flanks and crissum reddish brown more or less barred dusky, back shaded brownish.

Upper subtropical to temperate zone. W VENEZUELA, COLOMBIA, e ECUADOR and n PERU in w Cajamarca, 1. Sw ECUADOR, w PERU to w Lambayeque. N PERU in s Cajamarca and Libertad, 2. PERU in Amazonas s through San Martín and Puno to La Paz, w BOLIVIA. Mossy forest.

Plate 47

19. MOUSE-COLORED TAPACULO

Scytalopus speluncae

4.5". Dark slaty gray, remarkably like 1 (1) in color. ♀: Dark brown; wings and underparts barred dusky.

Se BRAZIL from Minas Gerais to Rio Grande do Sul. Ne ARGENTINA in Misiones. Thick forest undergrowth.

20. LARGE-FOOTED TAPACULO

Scytalopus macropus

6". Largest species. Dark ashy gray, upper tail coverts, flanks and crissum brown, barred black. Tail comparatively long (2"). Feet very large.

Upper subtropical zone in Amazonas, Libertad, Huánuco and Junín, PERU. Moss-covered vegetation and rocks along mountain torrents.

21. RUFOUS-VENTED TAPACULO

Scytalopus femoralis *

5". Crown and upper back blackish gray, lower back dark brown. Tail 2". Below gray, paler than crown; flanks and belly

chestnut brown, barred black. ♀: Differs from ♂ by browner upperparts and wings.

Upper tropical to temperate zone. COLOMBIA on w slope of Central Andes s through W Andes to w ECUADOR. [E Panama.] Mossy forest.

22. PALE-THROATED TAPACULO

Scytalopus panamensis *

5". Very like 21 but tail much shorter (or differing additionally by white eyebrow, 1).

Upper tropical to temperate zone. COLOMBIA on e slope of Cerro Tacarcuna, 1. The W Andes s to Nariño and east to w slope of Central Andes. ECUADOR. [E Panama.] Mossy forest.

23. BROWN-RUMPED TAPACULO

Scytalopus latebricola *

5". Rather light ashy gray; rump, flanks and crissum cinnamon rufous with only traces of dark bars (or much darker, with conspicuous dark bars on flanks, 1). ♀: Upperparts and wings browner than ♂.

Subtropical to temperate zone. Santa Marta Mts. of COLOMBIA. Nw VENEZUELA s through central and E Andes of COLOMBIA to ECUADOR, 1. Open woodland, dense thickets.

24. BRASILIA TAPACULO

Scytalopus novacapitalis

5". Above slaty blue gray; throat and breast pale gray sharply defined from darker upperparts. Upper tail coverts and flanks rusty brown, barred dusky. Legs brownish yellow.

Known only from Distrito Federal, Goiás, BRAZIL.

25. WHITE-BREASTED TAPACULO

Scytalopus indigoticus

5". Above slaty blue black tinged reddish brown on lower back. Throat and center of underparts white, sides of body slaty; flanks reddish brown, barred dusky. ♀: Above dark brown, below like ♂.

Se BRAZIL from Bahía to Rio Grande do Sul.

26. ANDEAN TAPACULO

Scytalopus magellanicus *

4.5-5". A species exhibiting various styles of

coloration from very dark, almost uniform slaty gray (1) to pale silvery gray with cinnamon flanks, and rump barred dusky (or unbarred, 2); with or without pale gray superciliaries. In southern races sometimes a white crown spot.

Temperate zone. Nw VENEZUELA. Santa Marta Mts. of COLOMBIA, 2. Andes of COLOMBIA south to to n BOLIVIA. W AR- GENTINA from Mendoza, and CHILE from Atacama, s to Tierra del Fuego and Cape Horn, 1. [The Falkland Is.] Dark forest ravines, thickets, often near streams.

27. WHITE-BROWED TAPACULO

Scytalopus superciliaris *

5". Eyebrow and throat white (or pale silvery gray, 1). Back slaty (or brownish, 1), barred black and rufous on upper tail coverts. Breast and belly slaty gray, flanks and crissum barred brown and black.

Temperate zone. BOLIVIA in Chuquisaca, 1. W ARGENTINA in Salta, Jujuy and Tucumán. Alder thickets.

28. OCELLATED TAPACULO

Acropternis orthonyx *

9". Forehead, sides of head, neck, throat and upper breast, lower back, flanks and under tail coverts chestnut rufous. Hind- crown, mantle, wing coverts and underparts black with large round white spots. Tail blackish. Hind claw very long (1"), straight.

Upper tropical to temperate zone. Nw VENE- ZUELA; COLOMBIA in E and Central Andes; Andes of ECUADOR to about 2° s. Forest.

Plate 36

Family COTINGIDAE   COTINGAS

Included in this very diverse family are some of the gaudiest, most beautiful and most peculiar South American birds. Cotingas vary in size from the tiny Kinglet Calyptura, actually of kinglet size, to the Umbrella Bird, as large as a crow. Some species exhibit enamel-like blue and purple colors, others are plain gray, and still others are bright green, crimson, snow white or wine red. Some are adorned with crests and wattles, others have bare heads or necks. In addition some, such as bell-birds and the Screaming Piha, emit the most astounding sounds.

The family is found from the southern border of the United States southward to southern Brazil, northern Argentina and Bolivia, but not in Chile. Cotingas are most abundant in the tropics, usually living in thick forest, rarely ascending the mountains as high as the subtropical zone. They feed on fruit and insects and are rather solitary in habits.

AID TO IDENTIFICATION

With crimson or blue or purple in plumage

Blue and purple 7b, 8, 9, 10, 11c

With white in plumage (wings white) 12, 13, 14c; (below mostly white) 6; (with purple pectoral tufts) 33c, 34a, 35

Underparts mostly bright crimson 62, 71, 72

Throat or band across breast crimson (below yellow) 27b (below green) 29b; (below black or gray) 30a, 40a, 58, 63

Back bright grass green 21b, 22b, 23b, 24b, 25b, 26b, 27b, 28a, 29b

Back olive green

> Over 7" (below streaked, banded or scalloped) 1, 5c, 30a, 31b, 32b, 69, 70c, 71; (plain below) 3c, 41b, 42b
>
> Under 6" (bright yellow below) 36c; (with yellow breast band) 46; (yellowish below) 47, 53, 54, 55b

Back not olive green

> Barred, streaked, spotted or scalloped below (tail forked) 2c; (belly yellow or ochraceous streaked black) 18b, 19b; (throat olive yellow, breast barred) 46; (brown, paler below, feathers scalloped whitish) 8, 9, 10, 11c
>
> Not barred etc., below brown 8, 20b, 56c, belly and nuchal collar bright yellow 4c
>
> Body plumage white or grayish white (wings and tail white) 15b, 69, 70c; (wings black, tail grayish white) 71; (crown, wings and tail black) 59, 60, 61; (streaked black below) 59
>
> Plumage all or partially rufous to tawny ochraceous 43b, 49b, 50, 51, 52b, 56, 57b, 58, above black 64b, wings and tail black 67
>
> Plumage all or mostly black 53, 63, 65, 66b (with orange or crimson throat) 58, 63, 64; (yellow wing patch) 3c; (wings gray) 68; (wings and tail white) 13; (below gray) 53, 56
>
> Plumage all or mostly gray 12, 13, 14c, 15b, 16b, 17, 37b, 38, 39c, 49b, 54, 55, 68; (under tail coverts magenta or chestnut) 40a, 44; (with contrasting cap) 45, 49b, 50, 54, 56, 57b
>
> ·Gray or black above, white below 45, 48, 50, 55; (streaked blackish) 59, 60, 61

1. SHRIKE-LIKE COTINGA

Laniisoma elegans*

7". Lores, crown and nape black (or like back, ♀). Back, wings and tail olive green. Below yellow, lightly barred black.

Tropical zone. Nw VENEZUELA; e COLOMBIA, e ECUADOR. Nw BOLIVIA. Se BRAZIL from Bahía to São Paulo. Forest.

Plate 11

2. SWALLOW-TAILED COTINGA

Phibalura flavirostris*

9". Tail long, deeply forked, blue black. Center of crown and sides of head glossy blue black, sides of crown ashy olive. Semiconcealed occipital crest maroon red. Back olive green, feathers with black subterminal band and yellow fringe. Wings blue black with whitish patch on innermost tertials. Chin and throat bright yellow; breast white, barred black; belly pale yellow, spotted black. ♀: Much like ♂ but duller. Crown and hindneck grayish olive, no occipital crest.

Se BRAZIL from s Goiás to Rio Grande do Sul; n PARAGUAY; ne ARGENTINA; nw BOLIVIA. Forest treetops.

Plate 11

3. BLACK-AND-GOLD COTINGA

Tijuca atra

11". Deep black, outer webs of remiges bright yellow forming conspicuous patch. Bill orange yellow. ♀: Dull olive green; yellowish on belly, under tail coverts and outer webs of remiges.

Se BRAZIL in coastal mts. of Espírito Santo and Rio de Janeiro to n São Paulo.

4. HOODED BERRYEATER

Carpornis cucullatus

9". Head, neck and breast black. Collar on hindneck yellow, mantle bay, lower back olive. Lower breast and belly bright yellow. Wings and tail black, edged olive; wing coverts black, edged yellow. ♀: Differs from ♂ by greenish head, neck and breast.

Se BRAZIL from Espírito Santo to Rio Grande do Sul.

Plates 11, 15

5. BLACK-HEADED BERRYEATER

Carpornis melanocephalus

8". Head and neck black. Back and upper breast dull olive; rest of underparts yellower, lightly banded with dusky. Wings and tail blackish, edged olive. ♀: Like ♂ but duller.

Coastal se BRAZIL from Bahía to São Paulo. Forest.

6. PURPLE-THROATED COTINGA

Porphyrolaema porphyrolaema

6.5". Upperparts, wings and tail black; dorsal feathers fringed white; inner wing coverts and tertials broadly edged white. Throat deep plum color. Upper breast white, stained plum; rest of underparts white. ♀: Above dull blackish, speckled and barred light brown; below ferruginous brown narrowly barred black.

Tropical zone. S COLOMBIA south to e PERU; w BRAZIL e to rios Negro and lower Purús. Forest.

Plate 11

7. BLUE COTINGA

Cotinga nattererii

7.5". Shining, enamel-like turquoise blue; throat and belly deep purple. Wings and tail black, edged turquoise blue. ♀: Above dark brown with faint bluish cast, feathers edged buff; below ochraceous buff, breast feathers with dark brown centers; under tail coverts cinnamon.

Tropical zone. Nw VENEZUELA; COLOMBIA w of E Andes; nw ECUADOR. [Central and e Panama.] Forest.

Plate 37

8. PLUM-THROATED COTINGA

Cotinga maynana

7.5". Brilliant, shining turquoise blue, feathers of crown and lores narrow, pointed and rather stiff. Throat plum color. Body feathers basally white with subterminal purple band showing through here and there. Wings and tail black, inner webs of remiges largely white. ♀: Differs from 7 by paler back with less conspicuous pale edges to feathers. Greater wing coverts narrowly and inconspicuously edged buff instead of conspicuously edged cinnamon. Underparts much paler, less cinnamon, dark centers of breast feathers ill-marked.

Tropical zone. Se COLOMBIA south to e PERU and nw BOLIVIA thence through w BRAZIL to rios Negro and Purús. Forest.

9. SPANGLED COTINGA

Cotinga cayana *

8.5". Shining, enamel-like turquoise blue, feathers of crown and back with conspicuous black bases showing through. Throat and upper breast reddish purple. Wings and tail black. ♀: Much darker and blacker above, grayer and much darker below than preceding two; feathers with narrow, sharp whitish edges.

Tropical zone. GUIANAS, VENEZUELA and e COLOMBIA south to e PERU, n BOLIVIA and BRAZIL s to Mato Grosso and mouth of the Amazon. Forest, savanna, open woods.

10. PURPLE-BREASTED COTINGA

Cotinga cotinga

7.5". Upperparts and flanks enamel-like, shining purplish blue; throat breast and center of abdomen rich reddish purple. Wings and tail black. ♀: Very like 9 but much blacker above, underparts blacker with wider pale fringes to feathers.

Tropical zone. GUIANAS; s VENEZUELA; BRAZIL n of the Amazon w to rio Uaupés and s of Amazon to rio Tapajós. Forest.

11. BANDED COTINGA

Cotinga maculata

8". Much like 10 but with purplish blue band across breast. ♀: Much like 10.

Coastal mts. of se BRAZIL from s Bahía to Minas Gerais and Rio de Janeiro. Forest.

12. POMPADOUR COTINGA

Xipholena punicea

8". Shining crimson purple, including tail. Remiges white, tipped black. Inner wing coverts much lengthened, narrow, stiff, and crimson purple with white shafts. ♀: Back gray, inner wing coverts and inner remiges edged white. Throat and breast gray, paler than back, fading to whitish, tinged pinkish on belly and strongly so on under tail coverts.

Tropical zone. GUIANAS; VENEZUELA s of the Orinoco; extreme se COLOMBIA; e ECUADOR; BRAZIL n of the Amazon, s of it between rios Juruá and Madeira. Forest.

Plate 37

13. WHITE-TAILED COTINGA

Xipholena lamellipennis *

8". Deep blackish purple, feathers, except those of belly, stiff and enamel-like; wing coverts as in 12. Wings and tail white. ♀: Brownish, paler below, inner wing coverts edged white.

Ne BRAZIL s of the Amazon from w bank of rio Tapajós e to Belém and n Maranhão. Forest, palms.

14. WHITE-WINGED COTINGA

Xipholena atropurpurea

8". Intermediate in color and texture of feathers between 12 and 13. Wing coverts only slightly lengthened and of nearly normal form. Wings white, tail brownish purple. ♀: Much like preceding two.

Coastal BRAZIL from Paraiba and Pernambuco to Rio de Janeiro. Forest.

15. WHITE COTINGA

Carpodectes hopkei

9.5". White; small black spot at tip of wing feathers and central tail feathers. Iris orange; bill black. ♀: Back ashy gray, throat and breast pale gray, belly white. Wings and tail blackish, wing coverts and inner remiges margined white.

Tropical zone. Pacific slope of COLOMBIA south to nw ECUADOR. [E Panama.] Forest and scrub.

Plate 45

16. BLACK-FACED COTINGA

Conioptilon mcilhennyi

8". Head black; normal feathers interspersed with narrow stiff, shiny feathers. Back gray, becoming blackish on upper tail coverts. Below pale gray with black shaft streaks; under tail coverts white. Wings and tail black.

Tropical zone. Se PERU in Loreto at headwaters of rio Purús (río Curanja).

Plate 27

17. RED-CRESTED COTINGA

Ampelion rubrocristatus

8". Mostly darkish gray. Head blackish with long narrow flat maroon occipital crest. Lower back and under tail coverts white, streaked black; all but central tail feathers

with large white subterminal patch on inner web.

Upper subtropical to temperate zone. W VENEZUELA and COLOMBIA s in Andes to nw BOLIVIA and on w slope s to Lima, PERU. Edge of forest, open woods.

18. CHESTNUT-CRESTED COTINGA

Ampelion rufaxilla *

9". Forecrown gray, center of crown black; long, ample, flat mahogany red crest. Back olive gray, feathers with dusky centers. Throat, sides of neck and ear coverts orange rufous; upper breast gray, lower breast and belly pale yellow broadly striped black. Wings and tail black, wing coverts mahogany red.

Subtropical zone. COLOMBIA in E and Central Andes. N and central PERU. Nw BOLIVIA. Forest.

Plate 37

19. WHITE-CHEEKED COTINGA

Zaratornis stresemanni

8". Crown black, sides of head white. Back streaked black and ochraceous buff. Chin, throat and upper breast grayish brown; rest of underparts boldly streaked ochraceous cinnamon, and black. Wings and tail dusky brownish.

Humid temperature zone. W PERU in Ancash and Lima. Mountain woodland.

Plate 27

20. BAY-VENTED COTINGA

Doliornis sclateri

8.2". Crown and nape black with concealed mahogany red crest. Throat, sides of head and upper back gray becoming brownish gray on lower back. Breast and belly mouse brown; under tail coverts pale mahogany red.

Temperate zone of PERU in Junín (Maraynioc).

21. GREEN-AND-BLACK FRUITEATER

Pipreola riefferii *

8". Top and sides of head greenish black to shiny black. Throat and upper breast dark moss green to blackish green, these dark areas margined by narrow yellow line. Back, wings and tail grass green, inner remiges with narrow terminal white band. Belly yellow, more or less heavily mixed with green. ♀: Similar but head and breast green like back. In this genus bill and feet are yellow to orange yellow.

Upper tropical to lower temperate zone. N and w VENEZUELA, COLOMBIA (except Santa Marta Mts.), e and w ECUADOR s to San Martín and Amazonas, PERU. Forest.

22. BAND-TAILED FRUITEATER

Pipreola intermedia

Much like 21 but slightly larger, head and breast glossy black with no green tint, line surrounding these parts brighter and deeper yellow. Tail with black subterminal bar and narrow white tip. ♀: Differs from 21 by blue green crown, bluer green back and white-tipped tail.

Subtropical zone. N and central PERU in Libertad, Junín, s San Martín, Cuzco and Puno to nw BOLIVIA.

23. BLACK-CHESTED FRUITEATER

Pipreola lubomirskii

6.7″. Head, neck, throat and center of breast glossy black. Sides of breast, back, wings and tail grass green. Center of underparts clear, bright yellow; sides of body green, somewhat spotted with black. ♀: Head, back, wings and tail grass green, below streaked green and yellow.

Subtropical zone. COLOMBIA at head of Magdalena Valley. E ECUADOR; n PERU. Forest.

24. ORANGE-BREASTED FRUITEATER

Pipreola jucunda

7″. Head and upper throat black; lower throat and upper breast orange, continued upward behind ear coverts; sides of breast green, almost meeting on center of breast where divided by yellow which expands on rest of underparts; sides of body, back, wings and tail grass green. ♀: Head, back, wings and tail grass green; below streaked green and yellow.

Subtropical zone. Pacific slope of COLOMBIA from lower río San Juan s to Guayaquil, w ECUADOR. Forest.

Plate 37

25. MASKED FRUITEATER

Pipreola pulchra

Not unlike 24; differs mainly by dusky green instead of glossy black head and upper throat; yellow of abdominal area much paler and less extensive. ♀: Upperparts, wings and tail grass green. Throat and belly yellow, streaked green; breast green, streaked yellow.

Subtropical zone. PERU mostly on e side of central Andes in San Martín, Huánuco and Junín.

26. GOLDEN-BREASTED FRUITEATER

Pipreola aureopectus *

6.7″. Back, wings and tail grass green, sometimes strongly shaded with blue. Chin green, throat and breast bright yellow (yellow extending up behind ear coverts in narrow line, 1); rest of underparts green, streaked yellow. ♀: Much like 24 but inner remiges and outer rectrices narrowly edged yellowish white.

Upper tropical and subtropical zones. Nw VENEZUELA. COLOMBIA in Santa Marta Mts., 1; E Andes, possibly also on w slope of the W Andes and in Nariño. Heavy forest.

27. SCARLET-BREASTED FRUITEATER

Pipreola frontalis *

6.5″. Forehead blackish; rest of upperparts, wings and tail grass green (or head much darker than back, 1); inner remiges tipped yellowish white. Throat yellow mixed with scarlet, patch on center of breast scarlet, rest of underparts bright yellow. ♀: Narrow frontlet and throat yellow; rest of plumage grass green, mixed with yellow on lower breast and belly.

Upper tropical and subtropical zones. Se ECUADOR, 1. Central PERU in San Martín, Junín and Puno. N BOLIVIA.

28. HANDSOME FRUITEATER

Pipreola formosa *

6.5″. Head and throat glossy black. Upperparts, wings and tail grass green; inner tertials with large white terminal spots. Underparts yellow inclining to orange on breast. ♀: Above grass green; throat green, patch on lower throat yellow, rest of underparts barred green and yellow.

Upper tropical and subtropical zones. N

VENEZUELA from Paria Peninsula w to Yaracuy. Forest.

29. FIERY-THROATED FRUITEATER

Pipreola chlorolepidota

4.8". Throat and breast scarlet, rest of plumage grass green, belly yellowish green, inner remiges tipped white. ♀: Like 28 but much smaller and throat yellow, barred with green.

Tropical zone. E ECUADOR. Central PERU from San Martín s to Junín and Pasco. Sight record from se COLOMBIA. Thick forest.

30. RED-BANDED FRUITEATER

Pipreola whitelyi *

7". Above dull grayish green, forecrown and eyebrow dull orange; below gray with broad orange scarlet pectoral band and orange under tail coverts. Wings and tail orange brown. ♀: Upperparts, wings and tail dull green, wings and tail shaded olive. Below yellowish white boldly streaked with black.

Subtropical zone. Mts. of Bolívar, VENE-ZUELA, and immediately adjacent GU-YANA.

31. BARRED FRUITEATER

Pipreola arcuata *

9". Head, neck, throat and breast glossy black. Back olivaceous green; wing coverts and remiges green on outer webs, black at tips, with yellowish white subterminal spot on outer web. Lower breast, belly and under tail coverts barred greenish yellow and black. Upper tail coverts with black subterminal spot and yellow tip. Tail black, central feathers like back, all pale-tipped (or mostly green with black subterminal band and pale tip, 1). ♀: Differs from ♂ by green crown and sides of head; throat and breast barred like rest of underparts.

Subtropical to temperate zone. Nw VENE-ZUELA s through Andes to central PERU. Se PERU to n BOLIVIA, 1. Forest.

32. SCALED FRUITEATER

Ampelioides tschudii

8". Crown, nape and sides of head glossy black (or green like back, ♀); lores yellowish white. Yellowish line from gape continued around hindneck to form narrow nuchal collar. Back black, each feather broadly

margined with olive green giving scaled look (or olive green with black centers, ♀). Throat whitish, spotted black; rest of underparts greenish yellow, feathers edged olive (or black, ♀) giving scaled look. Wings and tail black. Bill blackish.

Upper tropical and subtropical zones. Nw VENEZUELA; COLOMBIA in Macarena Mts., and on w slope of E and W Andes. E ECUADOR; n and central PERU s to Junín. Thick forest.

Plate 27

33. BUFF-THROATED PURPLETUFT

Iodopleura pipra *

3.5". Above gray (rump band white, 1). Throat, upper breast and under tail coverts pinkish ochraceous. Pectoral tufts purple (or absent, ♀); rest of underparts white, barred black.

Tropical zone. GUYANA, 1. Se BRAZIL from Minas Gerais to se São Paulo. Forest edge, capoeira.

34. DUSKY PURPLETUFT

Iodopleura fusca

4.2". Above slaty black, rump white; below smoky brown, middle of belly white. Pec-toral tufts violet blue (or white, ♀).

Tropical zone. GUIANAS, VENEZUELA in s Bolívar. Forest treetops, forest edge.

35. WHITE-BROWED PURPLETUFT

Iodopleura isabellae *

4.7". Above very dark brown, crown glossed blue black, rump white. Lores, crescent before eye, stripe behind eye and spot at gape white. Throat and center of underparts white, sides of body dark brown, pectoral tufts violet (or white, ♀).

Tropical zone. S VENEZUELA and CO-LOMBIA e of Andes south to e PERU, n BOLIVIA and Amazonian BRAZIL to Mato Grosso. Forest, second growth.

Plate 50

36. KINGLET CALYPTURA

Calyptura cristata

3". Olive green above, rump yellow. Fore-head yellow; center crown scarlet bordered laterally by black, feathers somewhat length-ened forming crest. Below yellow. Wing coverts and inner remiges tipped white. Tail very short.

BRAZIL in Espírito Santo and mts. of Rio de Janeiro. Vines and bromelias in forest and second growth.

Plate 11

37. DUSKY PIHA

Lipaugus fuscocinereus[1]

13″. Entirely ashy gray, purer gray on throat; breast and belly tinged brownish. Tail rather long (7″).

Subtropical to temperate zone. COLOMBIA on E, Central, and n part of W Andes. E ECUADOR. Forest.

38. SCREAMING PIHA

*Lipaugus vociferans**

10.5″. Very similar to 37 but considerably smaller and tail not conspicuously long. Emits very loud three-note call preceded by low gurgling sound unmistakable when once heard.

Tropical, occasionally subtropical zone. GUIANAS, VENEZUELA and COLOMBIA e of E Andes south to e PERU, n BOLIVIA and Amazonian BRAZIL to n Mato Grosso, and in e from Maranhão to Alagoas and s coastally to Bahía and Espírito Santo. Forest, often near streams, savanna.

Plate 45

39. CINNAMON-VENTED PIHA

Lipaugus lanioides

10.5″. Head and throat gray, rest of plumage brownish gray becoming browner on upper tail coverts. Throat and breast with white shaft streaks. Wings and tail dull brownish.

Se BRAZIL from Minas Gerais and Espírito Santo s to Santa Catarina.

40. ROSE-COLLARED PIHA

Lipaugus streptophorus

8.5″. Above dark gray, below pale gray. Broad magenta band across lower throat continued backward joining narrow magenta nuchal collar. Under tail coverts magenta. Wings and tail blackish. ♀: No magenta collar; under tail coverts rufous.

Upper tropical and subtropical zones. Nw GUYANA, VENEZUELA in mts. of se Bolívar and immediately adjacent BRAZIL. Forest.

41. GRAY-TAILED PIHA

Lipaugus subalaris

9″. Upperparts bright olive green, semiconcealed black patch on center of crown (no patch in ♀). Throat and breast grayish olive green becoming pale gray on belly and under tail coverts. Under wing coverts sulphur yellow. Tail pale pearl gray.

Upper tropical zone. E ECUADOR. Central and e PERU to Junín.

42. OLIVACEOUS PIHA

*Lipaugus cryptolophus**

9″. Above dark olive green, semiconcealed black crest, feathers basally white (or rufous, 1). Below olive green becoming bright olive yellow on center of abdomen. Under wing coverts sulphur yellow. Tail dark grayish, broadly edged olive green.

Upper tropical and subtropical zones. COLOMBIA on the w slope of W Andes in Cauca and Nariño, and nw ECUADOR. In the upper Magdalena Valley and e ECUADOR to central PERU in Huánuco, 1. Heavy forest.

43. RUFOUS PIHA

*Lipaugus unirufus**

9″. Rufous brown, paler below, particularly on throat (see also *Rhytipterna holerythra*, 107 of Tyrannidae).

Tropical zone. COLOMBIA from Sinú Valley w to Pacific and south to w ECUADOR. Forest.

44. SCIMITAR-WINGED PIHA

Chirocylla uropygialis

10.5″. Above dark gray, below paler. Rump, upper and under tail coverts and sides of body chestnut red. Wings abnormal; tips of primaries narrow, twisted, curved inward. ♀: Similar but primaries less modified.

Subtropical zone. N BOLIVIA in La Paz and Cochabamba.

Plate 27

---

[1]The genera *Attila, Pseudattila, Casiornis, Laniocera* and *Rhytipterna*, usually listed here in this family, are more properly placed in the Tyrannidae.

45. WHITE-NAPED XENOPSARIS

Xenopsaris albinucha *

5″. Crown and nape lustrous black (or brown, ♀). Forehead, lores, sides of head, concealed patch on nape and the underparts white. Back gray; wings and tail dull brown, wing coverts edged white.

Tropical zone. VENEZUELA in n Bolívar, w Apure and ne Lara. E BRAZIL in Piauí, Ceará and w Bahía; PARAGUAY; n ARGENTINA to Buenos Aires; n BOLIVIA. Thickets, reedy riverbanks, treetops.

Plate 27

46. GREEN-BACKED BECARD

Pachyramphus viridis *

6″. Forehead and lores white, crown lustrous black. Back bright olive green with (or without, 1, 2) gray nuchal collar. Sides of head and throat gray (or yellow, 1, 2). Broad breast band greenish yellow (or no breast band, 1). Center of throat, breast and belly white. Wing coverts grayish green (or black, edged greenish yellow, 1, 2). ♀: Like male but crown green like back, wing coverts mostly chestnut.

Tropical zone. GUYANA, VENEZUELA in Bolívar, 1. E ECUADOR, e PERU, 2. E and s BRAZIL from Marajó I. s to Rio Grande do Sul, PARAGUAY, n ARGENTINA and e BOLIVIA. Forest treetops.

47. BARRED BECARD

Pachyramphus versicolor *

5″. Crown and mantle glossy black, rump and tail gray. Sides of head, neck and throat light greenish yellow; rest of underparts dull white, finely barred grayish black. Wings black, wing coverts and secondaries edged white. ♀: Crown dusky gray, back dull olive green. Underparts yellowish white to yellow, finely barred dusky. Wings blackish, coverts and secondaries broadly edged chestnut. Tail brownish gray.

Subtropical zone. Nw VENEZUELA; COLOMBIA from w slope of E Andes west to W Andes and south to nw ECUADOR. E Andes and south to nw ECUADOR. E PERU from Amazonas s to Puno and sw Cajamarca. BOLIVIA in Cochabamba. [Costa Rica; w Panama.] Forest borders, ravines.

48. GLOSSY-BACKED BECARD

Pachyramphus surinamus

5.7″. Above glossy black, crown spangled with steel blue. Large patch on each side of neck, base of scapulars and all underparts white. Tail black, outer rectrices tipped white. ♀: Crown dark bay, mantle gray, lower back and entire underparts white, throat and breast with a slight grayish tinge. Wings black, wing coverts and inner remiges broadly edged chestnut. Upper tail coverts brown, tail black, feathers edged dark brown, outer feathers with white tips.

Tropical zone. SURINAM; FRENCH GUIANA; e BRAZIL n of Amazon. Forest treetops.

49. SLATY BECARD

Pachyramphus spodiurus

5.5″. Crown and nape black, only slightly glossed; lores gray. Back dark gray mixed with dull black; below gray, paler than back. Wing coverts and remiges narrowly edged white. Tail dark gray. ♀: Upperparts and edges to wing coverts and remiges ochraceous tawny. Narrow supraloral line buffy. Underparts uniform ochraceous.

Tropical zone. From Esmeraldas, nw ECUADOR, s to Piura, nw PERU. Forest, open woods.

50. CINEREOUS BECARD

Pachyramphus rufus *

5″. Crown and nape black, forehead and lores white. Back pearl gray. Wings and tail black, wing coverts and remiges narrowly edged white. Below white, tinged gray on sides of neck and breast. Upperparts, edges of wing coverts and remiges cinnamon rufous. Below white to buffy. Tail cinnamon rufous.

Tropical zone. GUIANAS; n and e VENEZUELA; COLOMBIA w to Cauca Valley. E ECUADOR; ne PERU; Amazonian BRAZIL e to islands in mouth of the Amazon. [Central and e Panama.] Savanna, undergrowth, plantations, mangroves, flooded forest.

51. CHESTNUT-CROWNED BECARD

Pachyramphus castaneus *

5.5″. Crown dark chestnut broadly margined, except in front, with gray. Back and tail rufous chestnut. Underparts tawny ochraceous, center of belly whitish. Primaries black, inner webs partially cinnamon, second primary half the length of first. ♀: Similar but second primary normal.

Tropical, subtropical zones. VENEZUELA and se COLOMBIA south to n BOLIVIA, n ARGENTINA and BRAZIL to Santa Catarina. Forest.

52. CINNAMON BECARD

Pachyramphus cinnamomeus *

5.5″. Upperparts, wings and tail chestnut rufous, line above lores whitish. Below pale cinnamon (or white, washed cinnamon, 1).

Tropical zone. W VENEZUELA across n COLOMBIA to lower río Sinú and lower Cauca Valleys, 1; from upper río Sinú w to Pacific, thence south to nw ECUADOR. [Mid. Amer.] Forest.

53. WHITE-WINGED BECARD

Pachyramphus polychopterus *

6″. Crown black, spangled with glossy blue black. Mantle black, lower back gray, gray nuchal collar in some races (or all glossy black above, 1). Below pale to dark slaty gray (or all to almost all black, 1). Wings black, coverts broadly edged white, remiges more narrowly so. Tail much graduated, black, broadly tipped white. ♀: Above dull, light olive; darker and grayer or browner on crown. Below light yellow. Wings brown, coverts and remiges broadly edged cinnamon buff. Central tail feathers like back, with dark subterminal area and pale tip; rest black broadly tipped cinnamon buff.

Tropical, subtropical zones. GUIANAS; VENEZUELA and BRAZIL s to URUGUAY, PARAGUAY, e BOLIVIA. Se COLOMBIA, e ECUADOR, e PERU, nw BOLIVIA, 1. [Guatemala southward.] Mangroves, plantations, campos, treetops in open woods.

Plate 45

54. BLACK-CAPPED BECARD

Pachyramphus marginatus *

5.2″. Much like 53 but smaller, back mixed black and gray; below much paler gray. ♀: Differs from 53 by smaller size and rufous crown.

Tropical zone. GUIANAS, VENEZUELA and e COLOMBIA s to São Paulo and Mato Grosso, BRAZIL, e BOLIVIA and e PERU. Flooded forest, savanna, clearings.

55. BLACK-AND-WHITE BECARD

Pachyramphus albogriseus *

5.2″. Crown glossy blue black, lores and narrow frontlet white. Back gray; throat and breast much paler gray, belly white. Wings and tail as in 53. ♀: Crown ochre brown margined at sides and back with black; narrow line above eye white. Sides of head gray, throat white, rest of underparts yellow. Back olivaceous. Wings and tail as in 53.

Tropical zone. N VENEZUELA w to Santa Marta, COLOMBIA, thence s to Piura, Cajamarca and San Martín, PERU. [W Nicaragua southward.] Forest.

56. CRESTED BECARD

Platypsaris rufus *

7.5″. Head with flat, black crest. Crown glossy black; back, wings and tail grayish black. Concealed white dorsal patch. Entire underparts smoky brownish (or gray, 1). ♀: Crown dark grayish; back, wings and tail rufous; below buff.

Tropical zone. Se PERU, 1. N and e BOLIVIA; n ARGENTINA. E and s BRAZIL from Marajó I., Pará, s to Mato Grosso and Rio Grande do Sul. Scattered trees, tall shrubs, campos in e Brazil.

57. ONE-COLORED BECARD

Platypsaris homochrous *

6″. Rather like 56 but much smaller. Back, wings and tail much lighter gray, below purer gray. ♀: Differs in color from 56 by rufous instead of gray crown.

Tropical zone. Nw VENEZUELA w across n COLOMBIA to Pacific, thence s to Piura, nw PERU. [E Panama.] Treetops in open woods.

58. PINK-THROATED BECARD

Platypsaris minor

6.5″. Above, including tail, black; concealed dorsal patch white. Below dark gray with rosy crimson patch on lower throat. ♀: Crown gray; mantle rufous, tinged gray; lower back, rump and tail rufous. Wing coverts rufous, tipped black. Below buff.

Tropical zone. GUIANAS; VENEZUELA s

of the Orinoco; COLOMBIA e of Andes from Meta south to e PERU and n BOLIVIA. Amazonian BRAZIL e to Maranhão. Treetops in forest, forest borders, clearings, shrubbery.

59. BLACK-TAILED TITYRA

Tityra cayana*

8.2''. Pale, pearly gray to grayish white. Crown, sides of head, wings and tail black. Bare skin around eye and base of bill reddish flesh color. ♀: Like ♂ but back dark gray, back and breast streaked black (or crown and sides of head gray, streaked black; entire underparts streaked black, 1). Soft parts as in ♂.

Tropical zone. GUIANAS, VENEZUELA and COLOMBIA e of Andes south to n and e BOLIVIA. E and s BRAZIL from Piauí s to Rio Grande do Sul, PARAGUAY and ne ARGENTINA, 1. Open woods, burned areas, tops of tall dead trees.

60. MASKED TITYRA

Tityra semifasciata*

8.2''. Pale, pearly gray to grayish white. Forecrown, ocular region, chin and wings black. Basal half of tail pale gray, distal half black. Bare skin around eye and base of bill red. ♀: Top and sides of head dark grayish brown. Back gray to brownish gray. Throat and belly whitish. Breast pale gray. Tail black, basally gray. Soft parts as in ♂.

Tropical, lower subtropical zones. GUIANAS; VENEZUELA n of the Orinoco; COLOMBIA; e and w ECUADOR; central and e PERU; Amazonian BRAZIL east to n Maranhão; north and e BOLIVIA. [Mexico southward.] Open woods, tops of tall, dead trees.

Plate 45

61. BLACK-CROWNED TITYRA

Tityra inquisitor*

7.3''. Back pearl gray; below white, tinged gray on breast. Top and sides of head (or top only, 1) black. Wings black, tail all black to white with broad black subterminal band. No bare ocular skin. Bill dark with no red. ♀: Much like other species but at once distinguishable by rufous sides of head.

Tropical zone. GUIANAS, VENEZUELA and COLOMBIA south to s BRAZIL, ne

ARGENTINA, PARAGUAY, n and e BOLIVIA. In w and se COLOMBIA, e and w ECUADOR, and e PERU, 1. [Mid. Amer.] Treetops, forest edge, dead trees.

62. CRIMSON FRUITCROW

Haematoderus militaris

15''. Shining crimson red above and below, feathers, except on belly, narrow and elongated. Wings and tail dusky brown. ♀: Dark brown above, head crimson; underparts pinkish crimson.

Tropical zone. GUIANAS; BRAZIL on both sides of lower Amazon. Forest treetops.

63. PURPLE-THROATED FRUITCROW

Querula purpurata

12''. Glossy black with (without, ♀) large shiny crimson throat patch. Bill light grayish blue.

Tropical zone. GUIANAS; VENEZUELA in Bolívar; COLOMBIA; e and w ECUADOR; e PERU; Amazonian BRAZIL; n BOLIVIA. [Costa Rica, Panama.] Forest, forest edge; usually in small flocks.

Plate 15

64. RED-RUFFED FRUITCROW

Pyroderus scutatus*

17''. Throat, breast and sides of neck reddish orange, feathers shiny, stiff and somewhat crimped. Chin and rest of plumage black, breast more or less spotted with chestnut (or breast and belly solid chestnut, 1).

Upper tropical and subtropical zones. Nw VENEZUELA. E and Central Andes of COLOMBIA; ECUADOR; e and central PERU, GUYANA; north-central VENEZUELA and n Bolívar. W. COLOMBIA and w ECUADOR, 1. Se BRAZIL from se Bahía to Rio Grande do Sul, se PARAGUAY and ne ARGENTINA. Forest.

Plate 15

65. AMAZONIAN UMBRELLABIRD

Cephalopterus ornatus

19''. Black, glossed with blue. Tall upstanding crest of silky hair-like feathers, shafts white at base. Flat, short, wide wattle feathered in front, at base of neck. ♀: Similar but duller with smaller wattle. Crow-like. Iris white or light gray.

Tropical zone. GUIANAS; VENEZUELA s of the Orinoco, COLOMBIA e of Andes from Boyacá south to e PERU and n BOLIVIA. Amazonian BRAZIL s to upper rio Paraguai. Forest, often on islands in larger rivers.

66. LONG-WATTLED UMBRELLABIRD

Cephalopterus penduliger

Much like 65 but somewhat smaller, crest not as tall and rounder, neck wattle much longer (up to 18"), cylindrical instead of flat and feathered all around. ♀: Duller with shorter wattle. Iris dark brown.

Upper tropical and subtropical zones. Pacific slopes of COLOMBIA from Cauca south to w ECUADOR. Forest.

Plate 27

67. CAPUCHINBIRD

Perissocephalus tricolor

14". Top and sides of head bare, grayish black. Plumage chestnut rufous; wings dark brown, tail black. ♀: Similar but head less bare.

Tropical zone. GUIANAS; VENEZUELA in Bolívar and sw Amazonas; BRAZIL n of the Amazon from rio Uaupés eastward. Forest treetops.

Plate 15

68. BARE-NECKED FRUITCROW

Gymnoderus foetidus

15". Crown, hindneck and chin covered by short, dense, black plush-like feathers. Neck similarly feathered but very sparsely so, the skin black, tinged blue. Above and below black with grayish powdery bloom. Wings mostly silvery gray. Tail grayish, central feathers black. ♀: Smaller than ♂ and wings like back with no gray. General plumage grayer, less blackish.

Tropical zone. GUIANAS; VENEZUELA s of the Orinoco; COLOMBIA e of Andes from Meta south to e PERU, n BOLIVIA and Amazonian BRAZIL s to upper rio Paraguai. Forest, campos.

69. WHITE BELLBIRD

Procnias alba

10.5". White, throat feathered. Long, sparsely feathered cylindrical wattle hanging from forehead. ♀: Upperparts, wings and tail olive green. Throat and upper breast olive green, pale-streaked; rest of underparts yellowish white, streaked olive.

Tropical zone. GUIANAS; se VENEZUELA; n BRAZIL in rio Negro region. Trinidad. Forest treetops.

Plate 27

70. BARE-THROATED BELLBIRD

Procnias nudicollis

10.5". White. Ocular region and throat bare, greenish, covered with black bristles. ♀: Like 69 but head black.

Se BRAZIL from n Bahía s to Rio Grande do Sul; PARAGUAY; ne ARGENTINA. Forest treetops.

71. BEARDED BELLBIRD

Procnias averano *

10". Silvery gray. Top and sides of head light cinnamon brown. Wings black. Throat black, bare, thickly covered by long narrow string-like caruncles. ♀: Much like 69 but throat gray, pale-streaked; underparts yellower, more lightly streaked.

Tropical, lower subtropical zones. Sw GUYANA; n and e VENEZUELA; COLOMBIA in Perijá Mts. and possibly middle Magdalena Valley. BRAZIL in Roraima and in s Maranhão, n Ceará, and Alagoas. Trinidad. Heavy forest.

72. GUIANAN RED-COTINGA

Phoenicircus carnifex

8.5". Crown crimson. Sides of head and back blackish crimson, rump bright crimson. Throat and breast deep purplish crimson. Inner remiges brownish red. Tail bright crimson, tipped dark red. ♀: Crown and tail dull red, back and wings olivaceous. Throat and breast grayish, belly dull crimson.

Tropical zone. GUIANAS; VENEZUELA in e Bolívar; Amazonian BRAZIL from rios Negro and Madeira to Amapá and e Pará. Forest.

73. BLACK-NECKED RED-COTINGA

Phoenicircus nigricollis

9.5". Slightly crested, crown crimson, feathers silky. Sides of head, throat, mantle, inner remiges and tip of tail velvety black;

rest of plumage crinson. ♀: Top and sides of head dull red. Back and wings olive. Throat olive brown; rest of underparts crimson, lighter and duller than in ♂. Tail dull red, tipped blackish.

Tropical zone. VENEZUELA in sw Amazonas; se COLOMBIA; ne ECUADOR; ne PERU; Amazonian BRAZIL e to rios Negro and Xingú. Forest.

Plate 37

Family RUPICOLIDAE   COCKS-OF-THE-ROCK

These magnificent birds are found only in the forests of northern South America. They are remarkable for their habit of clearing a piece of ground on which to "dance" and display in the breeding season. Only females build the nests of mud and saliva, plastered to walls of caves or to rock faces in precipitous ravines over mountain streams. Males do not participate in caring for the young. Cocks-of-the-Rock live on fruit and insects.

1. GUIANAN COCK-OF-THE-ROCK
Rupicola rupicola

11". Brilliant orange. Head decorated by tall compressed crest stretching from bill-tip to nape, crest edged narrowly with purplish red. Wings and tail brownish black, edged and tipped pale orange. Wing speculum white. ♀: Dull brown, crest scarcely developed.

Tropical, subtropical zones. GUIANAS; VENEZUELA s of the Orinoco; e COLOMBIA in Vichada and Vaupés; Amazonian BRAZIL n of the Amazon. Forest and second growth. Nests in caves.

2. ANDEAN COCK-OF-THE-ROCK
Rupicola peruviana *

11". Intense orange to scarlet orange. Crest extending from base of bill to hindcrown, compressed but rather bushy. Wings and tail black, inner remiges pearl gray. ♀: Generally, including tail, orange brown to mahogany red. Inner remiges grayish brown, outer remiges brown to mahogany red. Crest smaller than in ♂.

Upper tropical and subtropical zones. Nw VENEZUELA. Andes of COLOMBIA s through e and w ECUADOR, e and s PERU to n BOLIVIA in La Paz and Cochabamba. Precipitous, rocky ravines, usually above streams.

Plate 37

Family PIPRIDAE   MANAKINS

Manakins, found only in tropical America, are mostly small, brightly colored birds which inhabit chiefly tropical forests and woodlands. Females are usually solitary, while males are remarkable for their often communal display consisting of rather elaborate "dancing" usually accompanied by snapping and rasping noises, some produced by their curiously modified wing feathers.

Manakins live on small berries and insects. Females generally differ in color from males—usually some shade of green—and the species are difficult to tell apart.

AID TO IDENTIFICATION

Mostly or all black above and/or below

Entirely black 31, 32b

Body black (crown and sides of head red) 2, 3b, 4b, 5; (yellow) 1; (forecrown and throat yellow) 22b; (crown, crest and mantle red) 18c; (crown white) 6, 7b; (crown blue) 8b, 9; (throat white) 24a, 25b

Partly black above (yellow to crimson below) 15, 16, 17; (white below) 23c, 26; (back blue) 19a, 20

With no black in body plumage. Above olive green, below olive and/or yellow, or gray, crown different from back

Crown glistening opal or gold 11, 12; (white) 13; (blue) 8b, 9; (gray) 6; (crown or coronal streak yellow) 35b, 40c, 41, 42, 43, 44, 48b

Above olive green, below striped; crown yellow and/or red 28, 29

Above olive or grass green, crown like back

Wing bars prominent 47

No wing bars (grass green above) 7b, 8b, 9, 10, 11, 13, 14; (olive green above) central tail feathers protruding or filamentous 17, 19a, 21c, 23c, tail normal (size 3"-4.5") 1, 2, 3b, 4b, 6, 15, 16, 17, 20, 26, 27b, 28, 29, 30b, 45 (size 5"-7") 5, 18c, 31, 32b, 33a, 34b, 35b, 48b, with brown wings and tail 50c and 51

Below all or mostly chestnut to cinnamon

Back olive 37, 38, 39b

Back chestnut to cinnamon (tiny) 36; (large) 49, 51; (crown crimson) 30b; (crown black) 46c

Blue above and below 21c

1. GOLDEN-HEADED MANAKIN

Pipra erythrocephala *

3.5". Glossy blue black; top and sides of head golden yellow; under wing coverts black; thighs scarlet. ♀: Olive green, belly whitish yellow; under wing coverts white.

Tropical, lower subtropical zones. GUI-ANAS, VENEZUELA and COLOMBIA south to ne PERU and n side of the Amazon, BRAZIL. Trinidad. Undergrowth at forest border.

Plate 37

2. RED-HEADED MANAKIN

Pipra rubrocapilla

4". Differs from 1 chiefly by scarlet top and sides of head, under wing coverts white, tail longer and softer. ♀: Above dark olive; below dull gray, tinged olive on breast.

Tropical zone. Ne PERU from central Loreto s to lower rio Huallaga. BRAZIL s of the Amazon east to w Mato Grosso and to e Pará, and from Maranhão to Alagoas s to

Rio de Janeiro. N BOLIVIA in Beni. Forest undergrowth and tops of fruiting trees.

3. RED-CAPPED MANAKIN

Pipra mentalis *

4". Differs from 2 mainly by yellow thighs and under wing coverts. ♀: Differs chiefly from 1 by yellow under wing coverts and longer tail.

Tropical zone. Pacific slope of COLOMBIA to nw ECUADOR. [Mid. Amer.] Forest undergrowth.

Fig. 21, p. 436

4. ROUND-TAILED MANAKIN

Pipra chloromeros

4.3". Very like 3 in color but under wing coverts black. Tail stiff, shorter, rounded instead of square. ♀: Like 1 in color but center of abdomen yellower.

Upper tropical, lower subtropical zones. Ne PERU from Amazonas south to n BOLIVIA. Thick forest.

5. SCARLET-HORNED MANAKIN

Pipra cornuta

5″. Glossy blue black. Entire head and long, recumbent, bilobed crest crimson; thighs crimson. ♀: Very like 2 in color but much larger with much longer tail.

Upper tropical and subtropical zones. GUYANA; mts. of s VENEZUELA; immediately adjacent BRAZIL s to the Amazon at Óbidos. Forest.

6. WHITE-CROWNED MANAKIN

Pipra pipra *

3.5″-4″. Glossy blue black; top of head white, in some races the feathers long, extending to upper back. ♀: Distinguishable from any other ♀ *Pipra* by blue gray crown and nape. Back olive green; underparts gray, or gray with olive breast band, or with bright yellowish olive underparts.

Tropical, subtropical zones. Generally distributed e of Andes to e PERU and BRAZIL s to upper rio Juruá, Mato Grosso and Rio de Janeiro. Undergrowth in forest and savanna.

Plate 45

7. BLUE-RUMPED MANAKIN

Pipra isidorei *

3.2″. Velvety black. Top of head white with faint bluish cast. Rump and upper tail coverts sky blue. ♀: Top of head yellowish olive, back bluish green, rump emerald green. Below dull green, center of abdomen pale yellow.

Tropical zone. E COLOMBIA from Meta s to Huánuco, PERU. Forest.

8. CERULEAN-CAPPED MANAKIN

Pipra caeruleocapilla *

3.5″. Velvety black. Top of head sky blue, rump and upper tail coverts darker blue. ♀: Above green, bluish green on rump and upper tail coverts; below like 7.

Upper tropical zone. Central and e PERU in Huánuco, Junín, Cuzco and Puno. Forest.

9. BLUE-CROWNED MANAKIN

Pipra coronata *

3.5″. Dull black to deep velvety black (or dull black with middle of breast and abdomen dingy olive, sides dark green, 1; or back grass green, throat and breast darker, middle of breast and belly pale yellow, 2). Crown sky blue to purplish blue. ♀: Upperparts, including crown, grass green to bluish green; throat dull yellowish gray, breast dull green, abdomen pale yellow.

Tropical zone. VENEZUELA s of the Orinoco; e and w COLOMBIA; e and nw ECUADOR; ne PERU n of the Marañón. E and central PERU from San Martín and s Loreto to n BOLIVIA. W BRAZIL along s bank of the Amazon to lower rio Purús, 1. W BRAZIL on middle rio Purús and upper Juruá e to the w bank of rio Madeira, 2. [Costa Rica; Panama.] Forest.

10. WHITE-FRONTED MANAKIN

Pipra serena *

3.8″. Black; forehead white; upper tail coverts bright blue. Belly orange (or with belly and spot on breast bright yellow, 1). ♀: Forecrown blue, rest of upperparts green becoming blue green on rump. Throat whitish, breast and sides dull green; abdomen and under tail coverts yellow.

Tropical zone. GUYANA, nw and s VENEZUELA, immediately adjacent BRAZIL in Roraima. SURINAM, FRENCH GUIANA and immediately adjacent Amapá, BRAZIL, 1. Forest and forest edge.

11. OPAL-CROWNED MANAKIN

Pipra iris *

3.8″. Crown glistening, pale, silvery opalescent. Above grass green. Throat and breast darker and duller, belly yellow. ♀: Similar, but crown like back.

E Amazonian BRAZIL from e bank of lower rio Tapajós e to Belém region and ne Mato Grosso. Forest.

12. GOLDEN-CROWNED MANAKIN

Pipra vilasboasi

3.8″. Differs from 11 mainly by crown and nape glistening golden yellow. ♀: Unknown.

Known only from headwaters of rio Tapajós, BRAZIL. Forest.

13. SNOW-CAPPED MANAKIN

Pipra nattereri

3.5″. Crown, nape, lower back and rump snowy white; back, throat and upper breast dull green; rest of underparts yellow. ♀: Differs from ♂ by bluish green cap, and all-green back.

Central Amazonian BRAZIL from e bank of rio Madeira east to w bank of lower rio Tapajós and rio Xingú. Forest.

14. SICK'S MANAKIN

Pipra obscura

3.8". ♀: Not unlike 13 but darker green above; wing coverts bluish green instead of olive. ♂ ad.: Unknown.

Range as in 12.

15. CRIMSON-HOODED MANAKIN

Pipra aureola *

4". Forehead and throat golden yellow; crown, nape, upper mantle, breast and center of abdomen crimson. Back, flanks, wings and tail black; bases of remiges white. ♀: Olive green, paler and yellower below. Under wing coverts white.

Tropical zone. GUIANAS; e VENEZUELA; central and e Amazonian BRAZIL from rios Negro and Madeira e to Amapá and e Pará. Undergrowth in swampy forest, open woods.

16. BAND-TAILED MANAKIN

Pipra fasciicauda *

4.2". Forehead and throat golden yellow, rest of underparts scarlet, yellow on lower belly (or underparts golden yellow, orange on breast, 1, 2). Crown, nape and mantle scarlet. Back and wings black; wings with white patch forming a band on inner web of feathers. Tail black with variable white median band on outer feathers (or with solid white median band, 2). ♀: Like 15, but slightly larger.

Tropical zone. E PERU between the Huallaga and the Marañón. E PERU on the Ucayali w to rio Madeira, BRAZIL, 1. Se PERU and n BOLIVIA, 2. BRAZIL from rio Tapajós e to Ceará and s to Mato Grosso, n São Paulo, PARAGUAY and ne ARGENTINA. Thick forest, capoeira.

17. WIRE-TAILED MANAKIN

Teleonema filicauda

4.3" (excluding filaments). Much like 16 in color: forehead, sides of head and entire underparts golden yellow. Crown, nape and upper back scarlet. Lower back, wings and tail velvety black; inner remiges with white patch on inner web. Tail black, feathers ending in long black hair-like filaments. ♀: Upperparts dull olive, throat and breast paler; rest of underparts dull yellow. Tail feathers ending in filaments.

Tropical zone. VENEZUELA n of the Orinoco; e COLOMBIA s to lower río Huallaga in ne PERU. W BRAZIL e to rios Juruá and Branco.

Plate 37

18. HELMETED MANAKIN

Antilophia galeata

6". Velvety black. Projecting frontal crest, crown, nape and mantle crimson. ♀: Dull olive green, paler and grayer below. Frontal crest small, olive.

Tableland of central and s BRAZIL from Maranhão and Piauí s to Paraná, n Mato Grosso and ne PARAGUAY. Swampy forest and capoeira.

Plate 11

19. LANCE-TAILED MANAKIN

Chiroxiphia lanceolata *

5.2". Sooty black; crown crimson; mantle and lower back light blue. Central tail feathers narrow, pointed, protruding about .5" beyond rest. ♀: Olive green above, paler below center of abdomen whitish. Tail shaped as in ♂.

Tropical zone. VENEZUELA n of the Orinoco; Caribbean lowlands of COLOMBIA. Margarita I. [Sw Costa Rica; Panama, Coiba I.] Lower trees in second growth and open woodland.

Plate 37

20. BLUE-BACKED MANAKIN

Chiroxiphia pareola *

5". Much like 19 but deep black instead of sooty (or with golden yellow crown patch, 1). Tail of normal shape. ♀: Above olive green, below paler, center of abdomen pale yellowish to pale greenish.

Tropical zone. Generally distributed e of Andes from GUIANAS, s VENEZUELA and se COLOMBIA to e PERU and n BOLIVIA. BRAZIL to s bank of the Amazon, east to Pará, (between rios Javarí and Tapajós, 1), and in the e from Pernambuco to Rio de Janeiro. Dense undergrowth at forest edge and woodland borders.

21. SWALLOW-TAILED MANAKIN

Chiroxiphia caudata

6". Crown scarlet; sides of head, throat and nape, wings and outer tail feathers black; rest of plumage pale blue. Central tail feathers blue, lengthened, tapering to a point 1" beyond rest. ♀: Olive green, paler below, central tail feathers lengthened.

Se BRAZIL from s Bahía to Rio Grande do Sul; PARAGUAY; ne ARGENTINA in Corrientes and Misiones. Forest treetops and mid level.

22. GOLDEN-WINGED MANAKIN

Masius chrysopterus *

4.3". Velvety black; curled frontal crest and forecrown golden yellow; recumbent crest on hindcrown scale-like, orange red (or tobacco brown, 1). Center of throat and extreme upper breast pale yellow. Wings and tail black, inner webs of both yellow. ♀: Olive green. Throat and extreme upper breast and center of abdomen greenish yellow.

Upper tropical and subtropical zones. Nw VENEZUELA, COLOMBIA except Santa Marta. West of W Andes and w ECUADOR, 1. E ECUADOR and ne PERU. Forest.

Plate 17

23. PIN-TAILED MANAKIN

Ilicura militaris

5". Forecrown deep crimson; rest of crown, nape, mantle and wing coverts velvety black; wings pale brown, tertials olive. Rump and upper tail coverts scarlet. Sides of head, throat and breast very pale gray; lower breast and belly white. Tail black; central feathers thin, pointed, protruding 1" beyond rest. ♀: Above bright olive green. Sides of head, throat and breast gray; rest of underparts whitish, tinged olive. Tail shaped as in ♂.

Se BRAZIL from Minas Gerais and Espírito Santo s to Santa Catarina. Forest treetops, capoeira.

Plate 11

24. WHITE-THROATED MANAKIN

Corapipo gutturalis

3.5". Glossy blue black, throat feathers white extending down in point to upper breast. Three inner secondaries largely white. ♀: Above bright olive; below white, band across breast and sides of body yellowish olive.

Tropical zone. GUIANAS; s VENEZUELA; immediately adjacent BRAZIL and in Amapá. Forest.

25. WHITE-RUFFED MANAKIN

Corapipo leucorrhoa *

3.7". Glossy blue black; throat white, feathers at sides of throat lengthened to form a ruff. Under tail coverts yellowish white. Outermost primary nearly as long as next (or only about half as long, 1). ♀: Olive green. Throat and sides of head gray. Center of abdomen and under tail coverts yellowish.

Tropical, subtropical zones. Nw VENEZUELA; COLOMBIA e of Andes in Arauca and west of E Andes w to Cauca and río Dagua; from Panama border to Baudó Mts., 1. [Se Honduras southward.] Forest.

Plate 27

26. WHITE-BEARDED MANAKIN

Manacus manacus *

3.7"-4.2". Crown, mantle, wings and tail black. Sides of head, throat, beard, breast, and broad collar on hindneck (to upper back in some races) white; rump dark gray; belly pale gray (or upper mantle, throat and breast yellowish white; rump and abdomen olive gray, 1). ♀: Olive green, grayish on throat; belly greenish yellow to yellowish green.

Tropical zone. Generally distributed e of Andes to ne PERU, ne BOLIVIA, PARAGUAY and ne ARGENTINA; BRAZIL s to se Mato Grosso, n São Paulo and n Paraná. West of E Andes in COLOMBIA (in Magdalena Valley, 1), south to w ECUADOR. Undergrowth in forest and woodland.

Plate 27

27. GOLDEN-COLLARED MANAKIN

Manacus vitellinus *

4". Much like 26 in pattern but white parts of plumage bright golden yellow, belly yellowish olive and rump dark olive. ♀: Olive green above, below paler, yellowish olive on center of abdomen.

Tropical zone. COLOMBIA in lower Cauca and Sinú valleys, and Pacific slope s to

Guapí, Cauca. [Costa Rica, Panama.] Forest.

Plate 37

28. FIERY-CAPPED MANAKIN

Machaeropterus pyrocephalus *

3.5''. Crown and nape golden yellow with median scarlet stripe; ear coverts olive. Lores and entire back rosy chestnut. Wings olive, inner remiges gray with round black spot near tip of outer web. Below pinkish white, streaked rosy plum color. Tail reddish brown. ♀: Above olive; below much paler, grayish on throat, yellowish on breast and abdomen.

Tropical zone. VENEZUELA in nw Bolívar. E PERU south to nw BOLIVIA. BRAZIL n of the Amazon in Amapá, s of it in sw Pará, n and central Mato Grosso and s Goiás. Forest.

29. STRIPED MANAKIN

Machaeropterus regulus *

3.5''. Crown and nape crimson. Sides of head and neck, and entire back olive green. Throat dull white; rest of underparts pinkish chestnut striped with white, more or less stained scarlet on breast. Inner remiges with white inner webs. Tail short, grayish brown, feathers broad and stiff. ♀: Above olive green; below whitish with more or less distinct brownish breast band. Wings and tail as in ♂.

Tropical zone. VENEZUELA; COLOMBIA; e ECUADOR; ne PERU; w and central BRAZIL s of the Amazon and in n e in Bahía, Espírito Santo and Rio de Janeiro. Forest.

Plate 37

30. CLUB-WINGED MANAKIN

Allocotopterus deliciosus

4''. Crown scarlet. Back, sides of head, throat and upper breast rufous chestnut; rump and lower breast dark chestnut deepening almost to black on belly. Wings and tail black; bend of wing yellow, under wing coverts white. Inner remiges peculiar: shafts white, very thick, curved and club-like at extremity. ♀: Olive green; throat white, bordered laterally by chestnut. Center of belly and bend of wing yellow; under wing coverts white. Inner remiges white on inner web.

Upper tropical zone. Pacific COLOMBIA from Valle south to nw ECUADOR.

Plate 37

31. BLACK MANAKIN

Xenopipo atronitens

5.5''. Glossy blue black. Wings and tail brownish black, pale brown on underside. ♀: Dark green above, paler and more yellowish below, head tinged grayish. Wings and tail as in ♂.

Tropical zone. GUIANAS; s VENEZUELA; e COLOMBIA in Meta and Vaupés; Amazonian BRAZIL s to rio Madeira and n Mato Grosso. Thick bushes in savanna, cerradão.

Plate 27

32. JET MANAKIN

Chloropipo unicolor *

5''. Glossy blue black, becoming dull black on belly; white lengthened feathers at sides of breast. Wings blackish brown; tail blue black. ♀: Dark green, crown darker, throat and belly tinged grayish; feathers at sides of breast as in ♂. Remiges and rectrices margined green.

Upper tropical and subtropical zones. N and central PERU in Cajamarca, San Martín and Junín.

33. OLIVE MANAKIN

Chloropipo uniformis *

5.5''. Above olive; throat grayish, breast olive, belly considerably paler; feathers at sides of breast somewhat lengthened, dull grayish olive.

Upper tropical and subtropical zones. W GUYANA; mts. of s VENEZUELA; immediately adjacent BRAZIL. Forest.

34. GREEN MANAKIN

Chloropipo holochlora *

5''. Above olive green to bluish green. Throat and breast olive green, tinged grayish on throat. Center of belly olive yellow to yellow, much brighter and sharper in contrast to breast than in 33.

Tropical zone. COLOMBIA; e and w ECUADOR; e PERU. Forest.

35. YELLOW-HEADED MANAKIN

Chloropipo flavicapilla

5''. Crown and ample, flat crest extending

over nape bright yellow; back olive yellow. Throat and breast olive, breast and belly pale yellow. ♀: Like ♂ but top of head olive yellow like back.

Subtropical zone of Central and W Andes of COLOMBIA and head of Magdalena Valley. Forest.

36. CINNAMON MANAKIN

Neopipo cinnamomea *

3.5''. Crown gray, semiconcealed median stripe orange rufous or yellow. Upper back gray, lower back light rufous becoming bright cinnamon rufous on rump and tail. Throat buffy white, rest of underparts pinkish cinnamon.

Tropical zone. GUIANAS. VENEZUELA in s Amazonas; se COLOMBIA south to se PERU. Amazonian BRAZIL s of the Amazon east to w Pará. Forest.

Plate 17

37. FLAME-CROWNED MANAKIN

Heterocercus linteatus

5.7''. Top and sides of head black with orange scarlet spot in center of crown. Back dark, dull olive gray. Throat silky white, feathers at sides lengthened to form ruff. Sides of breast like back, center of breast chestnut, rest of underparts cinnamon. Tail like back, much rounded. ♀: Crown and sides of head olive, throat and ruff grayish white, otherwise like ♂.

Tropical zone. Ne PERU. Amazonian BRAZIL s of the Amazon.

38. YELLOW-CROWNED MANAKIN

Heterocercus flavivertex

5.7''. Like 37 but back brighter and greener, crown green like back with central yellow stripe, sides of head grayish. ♀: Like 37 but back lighter and greener.

Tropical zone. VENEZUELA in Amazonas, immediately adjacent COLOMBIA, n BRAZIL from rio Uaupés e to rio Jamundá. Forest.

Plate 11

39. ORANGE-CROWNED MANAKIN

Heterocercus aurantiivertex

Much like 38 but crown stripe orange; breast not chestnut but cinnamon like belly. ♀: Much like 38 but underparts paler.

Tropical zone. E ECUADOR; ne PERU n of río Marañón south to e bank of río Huallaga.

40. WIED'S TYRANT-MANAKIN

Neopelma aurifrons *

5''. Flycatcher-like. Coronal streak golden yellow to orange depending on light. Upperparts, wings and tail olive green. Throat grayish white, breast and sides grayish olive, center of belly yellow. ♀: Similar but coronal streak less developed.

E BRAZIL from Bahía and e Minas Gerais to São Paulo. *Neopelma* is superficially like *Myiopagis*. (Cf. p. 320.)

41. SULPHUR-BELLIED TYRANT-MANAKIN

Neopelma sulphureiventer

Much like 40 but bill much larger, belly clearer yellow.

Tropical zone. E PERU from río Huallaga south to n BOLIVIA and immediately adjacent BRAZIL.

42. SAFFRON-CRESTED TYRANT-MANAKIN

Neopelma chrysocephalum

Differs from 41 by much more extensive yellow crown forming a crest reaching nape; sides of crown and head gray.

Tropical zone. GUIANAS, s VENEZUELA, n BRAZIL in rio Negro region and immediately adjacent COLOMBIA. Rather open savanna, forest.

43. PALE-BELLIED TYRANT-MANAKIN

Neopelma pallescens

5.5''. Coronal patch sulphur yellow. Back dull olive. Throat whitish streaked gray, breast gray, belly white.

BRAZIL n of lower Amazon in Pará and s of the Amazon from rio Tapajós e to Maranhão and Pernambuco, thence south to w Mato Grosso and São Paulo. Campos, cerradão.

Plate 11

44. TINY TYRANT-MANAKIN

Tyranneutes virescens

3.1''. Above olive, semiconcealed coronal

patch yellow. Throat whitish faintly streaked grayish, breast and sides grayish olive, center of belly yellowish white. ♀: Similar but coronal patch much smaller.

Tropical zone. GUYANA; SURINAM; VENEZUELA in e Bolívar. N BRAZIL from lower rio Negro e to Amapá. Undergrowth in forest.

45. DWARF TYRANT-MANAKIN

Tyranneutes stolzmanni

3.5″. Upperparts olive. Throat and breast grayish olive, streaked white; belly pale yellow. Tail considerably longer than in 44.

Tropical zone. VENEZUELA s of the Orinoco east to e COLOMBIA thence south to se PERU and nw BOLIVIA. Amazonian BRAZIL e to rio Negro, Belém region and ne Mato Grosso. Forest.

Plate 14

46. BLACK-CAPPED MANAKIN

Piprites pileatus

5″. Cap black; back rich maroon chestnut. Remiges black, edged yellowish white, with white patch at base of primaries. Central tail feathers brownish black, outer three cinnamon rufous. Throat, breast and sides cinnamon buff; center of belly pale yellow.

Coastal se BRAZIL from Espírito Santo to ne Santa Catarina. ARGENTINA in Misiones. Forest treetops.

47. WING-BARRED MANAKIN

Piprites chloris *

5″-5.5″. Above olive green, nape gray; inner remiges and greater wing coverts broadly tipped yellowish white. Throat, breast and sides yellowish olive; belly bright yellow (or throat yellowish olive, rest of underparts gray, 1; or lower breast and sides gray, 2). Tail blackish, tipped whitish.

Tropical, subtropical zones. GUIANAS; VENEZUELA n of the Orinoco in Carabobo and s of it in Bolívar and Amazonas; extreme e COLOMBIA; n BRAZIL from rios Negro and Madeira eastward, and in Maranhão, 1. Nw VENEZUELA, e COLOMBIA (w of Andes in Antioquia), e ECUADOR, e PERU; nw BRAZIL e to rio Negro

and in se from Espírito Santo to Paraná; PARAGUAY and nw ARGENTINA in Misiones. N BOLIVIA and immediately adjacent BRAZIL, 2. Forest treetops.

Plate 27

48. BROAD-BILLED MANAKIN

Sapayoa aenigma

6.2″. Bill flat and wide. Oily olive green; paler and yellower below. Semiconcealed yellow coronal stripe (none ♀).

Tropical zone. W COLOMBIA from upper Sinú Valley w to Pacific, thence south to nw ECUADOR. [E Panama.] Forest.

Plate 50

49. GREATER MANAKIN

Schiffornis major *

6″. More or less uniform cinnamon rufous, lower breast and belly paler. Wings blackish; tail like back.

Tropical zone. VENEZUELA in s Amazonas. E PERU; nw BOLIVIA; Amazonian BRAZIL on both sides of the Amazon e to rio Tapajós. Forest.

50. GREENISH MANAKIN

Schiffornis virescens

6″. Dull olive, paler below; wings and tail reddish brown.

Se BRAZIL from s Bahía southward; se PARAGUAY; ne ARGENTINA in Misiones. Forest, capoeira.

51. THRUSH-LIKE MANAKIN

Schiffornis turdinus *

6.5″. Generally similar to 50 but varies in color according to locality between dull olive with brown wings and tail, to bronzy brown with olivaceous belly. Bill larger than in 50.

Tropical, upper tropical zones. GUIANAS, VENEZUELA and COLOMBIA south to w ECUADOR and e of Andes to n BOLIVIA and s BRAZIL to s Amazonas, n Mato Grosso and Espírito Santo. [Mid. Amer.] Undergrowth in forest and woodland.

Plate 50

Family TYRANNIDAE   TYRANT-FLYCATCHERS

Tyrant-Flycatchers form the largest family of birds found in the Americas: as many as 384 species range from Alaska to Tierra del Fuego. No less than 315 of these occur in South America. Most numerous in the tropics, only 30 species occur regularly north of the Mexican border, and no more than 7 reach Alaska. In the far south only 10 species go as far as Tierra del Fuego.

The tropical species are usually sedentary, but birds nesting in high latitudes are often migratory. Birds breeding in the Andes migrate vertically.

Tyrant-Flycatchers are mostly arboreal, and live chiefly on insects often caught on the wing. Many species eat considerable amounts of berries and other wild fruit. A few *(Muscisaxicola, Lessonia)*, found mostly in western and southern South America, are terrestrial and catch insects on the ground much in the manner of pipits. Many forest inhabiting species glean among the leaves, like vireos.

The family for the most part is dull-colored, with shades of grays, browns and olives predominating. The sexes are usually similar, but many have a red or yellow crest or coronal streak, which is most marked in the male. A few species are brightly colored, often with lemon or golden yellow underparts. A few have long or curiously formed tails; one has an enormous red and blue fan-shaped crest. The bill is usually rather flat, hooked, and bristled at the base.

Although not notable for their songs, many species have loud calls so distinctive that some have been named from their notes (pewee, kiskadee, etc.).

Nesting is very varied: most usual is an open, cup-shaped nest, but some species build round or domed structures with entrances at side or bottom, and a few nest in crevices or in tree holes.

AID TO IDENTIFICATION

Plumage black and white, black and rufous to cinnamon, or all black, no streaking

Black and white 8c, 10c, 43, 56, 60, 61, 62, 171, with much lengthened tail 44, 46, 47c

Rufous and black 27, 49c, 192

All black 48c, 49c, 50, 51, 53c, 55, 56

Above gray or brownish gray, underparts dark or pale gray to white, no contrasting colors in tail, or if so white only. No streaking

Andean, terrestrial, hindcrown often with patch of brown to cinnamon 15b, 16b, 17b, 18b, 19, 20b, 21b, 22b, 23b, 24b, 25

Dark gray above, all or mostly so below 51, 54, 59c, 103, 105, 118, 119, 120, 121, 122, 237b, 265, with black crown and yellow crest 78

Gray above, pale gray to white below 6, 7, 14b, 68, 70, 72, 126b, 243b, 245, 247, 276, 280, 282, tail very long 79, tail very short 26b

Cinnamon, rufous or chestnut in body plumage but no yellow and no streaking on body

7″ or over (more or less uniform rufous) 94, 95, 98, 99b, 101, 104b, 107b; (with top and sides of head gray) 33b, 96c, 97, 100; (with inner webs of remiges largely rufous) 5, 31b, 145; (with grayish brown back) 108b; (with conspicuous red or orange crest) 146

Under 7″ (above dark gray or grayish) 34b, 38b, 39b, 129; (above dull brown to cinnamon) 35b, 38b, 129, 135b, 143, 147, 231c; (above olive green) 135b, 173a, 311, 312, 313c

Streaks somewhere in plumage

No olive or green in plumage (only throat streaked) 1b, 2, 3a, 11, 28b, 29b, 86b; (throat white, breast streaked) 12, 58, 63, 77, 79, 84, 85, 143; (throat and breast and sometimes even belly streaked) 51, 53, 57, 85, 94, conspicuous crest 234b, 235b, 236b, 238b; (streaked on back only) 232

Olive or green in plumage (5" to 8.5") 87, 94, 158, 159b, 161, 162, 266, 309b, 310; (3" to 4.5") conspicuous crest 193, 194, 195, 196; no crest 165, 169, 181, 182, 185, 187, 188c, 189a, 198, 205

All or mostly bright deep yellow below

Size large 6"-9" (all yellow below) 66, 67, 80, 81, 82; (throat white) 67a, 74, 75, 76, 82a, 83, 87, 88, 89, 90, 91a, 92, 93

Size small 3.5"-5.5" (crown not in contrast to olive back) 65b, 157, 168, 220c, 223, 226, 228, 229, 233, 304b, all black above 166b; (crown in contrast to back) gray 167c, 206c, 211a, black 164b, 165, 166b, 227, rufous 191

Breast gray, tawny or olive; belly yellow, *sharply demarcated*

Breast olive or tawny 71, 134b, 142b, 151, 160b

Breast light gray 73b, 106, 109, 110b, 111, 112b, 113, 114, 115a, 116, 208, 281, 282, 283

Tawny buff to chestnut on head, face, or throat, size small under 5" 150, 151, 152b, 171, 172, 173a, 174, 175, 177c, 180, 184c, 186b, 191b, 192, 193, 201, 202b, 212a, 213c, 221a, 222c, 224, 230, 231

With none of the characters given above

With wing bars

Belly yellow, breast olive to grayish, breast color *gradually shading* into yellow of belly (wing bars ochraceous, cinnamon or rufous) 42b, 136b, 137b, 140b, 141b, 144, 153, 155, 158, 159b, 163, 184c, 209b, 216a, 225c, 252b, 256b, 305, 306, 307b, 308b; (with gray or olive wing bars) 128, 270; (with yellow wing bars) 5.5"-6" 154, 155, 285, 3.5"-5" 156, 157, 178a, 199, 207b, 208b, 210b, 215, 276, 278, 279, 286c, 294a, 296b, 297, 298b, 299b, 300c, 302; (with white or whitish wing bars) 5.5"-7" 252b, 259, 261, 267, 269, 271b, 272, 274, 281, 3.5"-5" 130a, 190, 244, 249, 275, 284, 290b, 292b, 301, 303

Belly whitish, or greenish or yellowish white, breast pale gray, brownish or pale olive (buff to rufous wing bars) 36b, 37b, 40b, 41b, 123, 125, 127, 138b, 246, 252b, 253b, 254, 255b, 258, 282, 291, 311; (yellow or olive wing bars) 170, 176, 183, 197a, 199, 214a, 217a, 276, 288c; (white to grayish white wing bars) 118, 119, 124, 248c, 250a, 251, 257b, 260, 262, 263, 264c, 268, 281a, 273a, 281, 282, 288c, 293b

Without wing bars

Belly yellow; breast grayish, brownish or pale olive shading into yellow of belly (with yellow rump patch) 131b, 132, 133; (no yellow rump patch) size 5.5"-7" 102c, 277b, 313, size 3.5"-4.7" 42b, 102, 139, 149, 150, 189, 200b, 218c, 289, 295

Belly white to greenish or grayish white (size 6"-7") 36b, 117b, 153; (size 4"-5") 40b, 148c, 179c, 186b, 203c, 204c, 219c, 242, 283b, 287

Breast and belly uniform (white) 61, 62, 239b; (sandy gray) 64; (dusky) 27, 63; (fawn) 184c; (ochraceous) 312; (vermilion) 63

With easily identifiable characters

Outer tail feathers all or mostly white or black and white, or with distinctive pattern 3b, 4b, 7, 65b, 234b, 237b, 240, 241, 253b, 255b

Outer tail feathers cinnamon to rufous 13b, 28b, 32b, 33b, 50, 52, 53, 54, 55, 113, 115, 134, 145

Tail very long or deeply forked 44, 45, 46, 47, 59c, 69, 177c

Conspicuous wing pattern in flight (white) 6, 7, 8c, 9, 50, 56, 58; (cinnamon to rufous) 5, 12c, 13, 28b, 29a, 30b, 31b, 32b, 45, 58, 88, 92, 135b, 145

Prominent breast band 39b, 45, 46, 47, 314, 315

Vermilion underparts or pink belly 63

1. GREAT SHRIKE-TYRANT

Agriornis livida *

11". Above dark brownish, obscurely streaked dusky on head. Throat white conspicuously streaked black, rest of underparts light smoky brown, sides somewhat tinged rufescent; under tail coverts cinnamon. Wings like back, feathers narrowly pale-edged. Tail blackish, external web of outer rectrix white.

Coast and mts. up to 6000 ft. ARGENTINA from Neuquén, and CHILE from Atacama, s to Tierra del Fuego. Scrub, fields.

2. GRAY-BELLIED SHRIKE-TYRANT

Agriornis microptera *

10". Very much like 1 but smaller, paler, and chiefly distinguishable by narrow white eyebrow.

Lowlands and Andes up to 13,500 ft. Se PERU; BOLIVIA; PARAGUAY to Santa Cruz, ARGENTINA, and Iquique, CHILE. Bushy country.

3. BLACK-BELLIED SHRIKE-TYRANT

Agriornis montana *

9". Above dark ashy brown, narrow eyebrow buffy. Throat whitish narrowly streaked dusky. Breast ashy brown becoming paler on abdomen and white on under tail coverts. Central tail feathers like back, rest with apical half white to all white. Bill black.

Temperate, páramo zones of Andes of se COLOMBIA, ECUADOR, PERU, BOLIVIA, nw ARGENTINA s to Córdoba, Buenos Aires and Santa Cruz. CHILE s to Magallanes. Rocky slopes, villages.

Plate 48

4. WHITE-TAILED SHRIKE-TYRANT

Agriornis albicauda *

10". Much like white-tailed form of 3 but larger with longer tail, throat streaks much wider. Bill with pale lower mandible.

Temperate zone of Andes. ECUADOR s through PERU and BOLIVIA to nw ARGENTINA and n CHILE. Open scrub.

5. CHOCOLATE-VENTED TYRANT

Neoxolmis rufiventris

9". Smoky gray above, sides of head blackish. Wing coverts mostly buffy white; remiges mostly cinnamon, innermost like back. Throat and breast pale smoky gray with faint striations. Belly, under tail coverts and wing coverts cinnamon rufous. Tail black, outer web of outer feather white.

Nests in s ARGENTINA and CHILE from Magallanes s to Tierra del Fuego. Winters in ARGENTINA n to Córdoba, Entre Ríos and URUGUAY. Open scrub.

Plate 28

6. GRAY MONJITA

Xolmis cinerea *

9". Above ashy gray, forehead and short eyebrow white. Moustachial streak black; throat and belly white, sharply contrasted from gray breast. Wings black; base of remiges, under wing coverts and edges to tertials white. Tail black, base of feathers white, tips of feathers grayish white.

SURINAM (Sipaliwini). BRAZIL s of the Amazon from rio Tapajós to Marajó I. and Mato Grosso; URUGUAY; PARAGUAY, e BOLIVIA and ARGENTINA to n Buenos Aires and Tucumán. Open country often near water, towns, cerrado.

7. WHITE-RUMPED MONJITA

Xolmis velata

8". Forehead and eyebrow white, crown pale gray, back brownish gray. Rump and underparts white. Tail basally white, distally black. Remiges black, basally white; tertials mostly white.

E BRAZIL n of the Amazon from e Pará to Mexiana and Marajó Is. s to São Paulo and Mato Grosso; PARAGUAY and e and n BOLIVIA. Scrub, campos.

8. BLACK-AND-WHITE MONJITA

Xolmis dominicana

8". White. Wings and tail black, distal third of primaries white.

Se BRAZIL in Paraná and Rio Grande do Sul; URUGUAY; PARAGUAY; e ARGENTINA s to Buenos Aires. Open scrub.

9. BLACK-CROWNED MONJITA

Xolmis coronata

8.2". Forehead white, crown black surrounded by broad white band; ear coverts dark brown. Back brownish gray, underparts white. Wings brownish black, wing coverts broadly edged white, inner webs of primaries basally white. Tail black narrowly tipped white.

Breeds in s ARGENTINA in La Pampa and Río Negro. Winters north to se BRAZIL, PARAGUAY and e BOLIVIA. Open scrub.

10. WHITE MONJITA

Xolmis irupero *

7.2". White. Primaries and band at tip of tail black; primaries basally white.

E BRAZIL from Ceará s to Mato Grosso and Rio Grande do Sul; URUGUAY; PARAGUAY; e BOLIVIA; ARGENTINA s to Buenos Aires and Córdoba. Open country, often near habitations.

Plate 28

11. MOUSE-BROWN MONJITA

Xolmis murina

7.7". Above light grayish brown, below much paler becoming whitish on belly. Throat white, streaked dusky. Wings blackish, coverts and inner remiges broadly edged grayish white. Tail black narrowly tipped white, outer rectrix edged white.

Breeds in s ARGENTINA from Neuquén to Río Negro. Winters n to PARAGUAY and e BOLIVIA. Open scrub.

12. RUSTY-BACKED MONJITA

Xolmis rubetra

7.7". Broad eyebrow white. Crown and remiges rufous, back duller. Sides of head and underparts white, streaked black except on throat and center of belly. Upper wing coverts and inner remiges mostly light grayish, primaries black; inner webs, under wing coverts and sides of body cinnamon rufous. Tail black, outer web of outermost feathers white.

Breeds in w ARGENTINA from Mendoza to Chubut; winters n to Santa Fe and Tucumán. Open scrub.

13. RUFOUS-WEBBED TYRANT

Xolmis rufipennis

8.5". Upperparts and breast dark ashy gray, throat paler, belly white. Closed wing and tail like back; inner webs of remiges basally cinnamon; inner webs of rectrices mostly cinnamon, outer feather edged white.

Subtropical, temperate zones. PERU from Amazonas s to BOLIVIA in Potosí, Oruro and Cochabamba. Brushland, *Polylepis* woodland, grasslands.

14. FIRE-EYED DIUCON

Pyrope pyrope *

8.5". Above ashy gray, breast paler, throat whitish narrowly streaked gray, belly whitish. Wings blackish. Tail gray with narrow blackish streak along shaft, outer web whitish near base. Iris red.

Breeds from Atacama, CHILE, and Neuquén, ARGENTINA, to Tierra del Fuego. [Falkland Is.] Open woodland.

Plate 28

Ground-Tyrants

Birds belonging to genus *Muscisaxicola* all look alike with upperparts light grayish to brownish, dirty white below, black upper tail coverts and tails, and white outer web to outermost tail feathers. They are best differentiated by head pattern and size. The birds are terrestrial and have a habit of flicking their wings and tails. They live on open, often stony, hillsides mostly high in the Andes.

15. RUFOUS-NAPED GROUND-TYRANT

Muscisaxicola rufivertex *

6.5". Forecrown grayish like back, hindcrown cinnamon to chestnut, short eyebrow white. Back pale gray.

Temperate, puna zones. N PERU s to

Colchagua, CHILE, Potosí, BOLIVIA and Córdoba, ARGENTINA. Southern birds migrate northward.

16. WHITE-BROWED GROUND-TYRANT

Muscisaxicola albilora

7". Forecrown brown, tinged rufescent; hindcrown orange rufous. Long, narrow white eyebrow. Back strongly brownish.

Breeds in Andes of CHILE from Aconcagua to Magallanes and ARGENTINA from Neuquén s to Santa Cruz. Migrates n to ECUADOR.

17. PUNA GROUND-TYRANT

Muscisaxicola juninensis

6.5". Much like 15 but back browner and darker.

Puna zone. PERU from Junín south to n CHILE, w BOLIVIA and n ARGENTINA in Jujuy.

18. OCHRE-NAPED GROUND-TYRANT

Muscisaxicola flavinucha *

8". Large species with broadly white forehead, prominent white eyebrow and subocular region. Patch on hindcrown buffy cinnamon.

Breeds in ARGENTINA from Neuquén, and CHILE from Arica, s to Cape Horn Archipelago. Winters north to n PERU, BOLIVIA and n ARGENTINA.

19. CINNAMON-BELLIED GROUND-TYRANT

Muscisaxicola capistrata

7". Forecrown and ocular region black, hindcrown chestnut. Belly pale pinkish cinnamon.

Breeds in ARGENTINA from s Santa Cruz, and CHILE from Magallanes s to Tierra del Fuego. Winters n to BOLIVIA and to Puno, PERU.

20. BLACK-FRONTED GROUND-TYRANT

Muscisaxicola frontalis

7.2". Lores white; forecrown black, black running backward narrowly over center of hindcrown.

Breeds in ARGENTINA in Mendoza, Neuquén and Río Negro, in CHILE from Anto-

fagasta to Colchagua. Winters n to BOLIVIA and s PERU.

21. WHITE-FRONTED GROUND-TYRANT

Muscisaxicola albifrons

9". Much the largest species. Forehead and preocular streak white, lores dusky.

Andes of PERU from Lima and Junín south to nw BOLIVIA and n CHILE to Tarapacá.

22. PLAIN-CAPPED GROUND-TYRANT

Muscisaxicola alpina *

7". Above smoky brown (or gray, 1), lores dusky, eyebrow white. Whole crown dull rufescent brown (or gray like back, 1).

Temperate, páramo zones. COLOMBIA in E and Central Andes; ECUADOR. N PERU from Cajamarca s to BOLIVIA and n CHILE to Tarapacá and w ARGENTINA to Mendoza, 1.

Plate 48

23. DARK-FACED GROUND-TYRANT

Muscisaxicola macloviana *

6.2". Sides of head sooty black, crown dark reddish brown, back grayish in contrast.

Breeds from Neuquén, ARGENTINA, and from Llanquihue, CHILE, s to Cape Horn Archipelago. Winters n to coast and Andes of PERU, and in n ARGENTINA; URUGUAY (sight).

24. SPOT-BILLED GROUND-TYRANT

Muscisaxicola maculirostris *

5.7". Pipit-like. Above light brownish; eyebrow whitish; below buffy white (or below warm buffy cinnamon, 1). Tail black. Base of mandible yellow.

Temperate zone. COLOMBIA in E Andes; ECUADOR, 1. N PERU from Cajamarca s to BOLIVIA, n CHILE to Magallanes and ARGENTINA to Santa Cruz.

25. LITTLE GROUND-TYRANT

Muscisaxicola fluviatilis

5.4". Pipit-like. Above brownish gray. Throat and breast pale sandy buff, belly white. Tail black.

Tropical to temperate zone. E PERU from n bank of the Marañón south to n BOLIVIA; sw Amazonian BRAZIL. Riverbanks, sandbars, rocks.

26. SHORT-TAILED FIELD-TYRANT

Muscigralla brevicauda

4.2". Legs long; tail very short. Above brownish gray; occipital stripe yellow, two pale wing bars. Rump band pinkish white. Upper tail coverts chestnut; tail black, tipped pinkish white. Underparts whitish, ashy on breast. ♀: Like ♂ but tail without white tip.

Sw ECUADOR s coastally probably to n CHILE. Arid scrub, grass and weed patches, roadsides. Flicks tail, terrestrial.

Plate 28

27. RUFOUS-BACKED NEGRITO

Lessonia rufa *

5". Black; back rufous. ♀: Crown and nape grayish grading into brown back. Underparts grayish white, darkest on breast. Wings and tail black (or crown and nape dusky in contrast to rufescent back; underparts dusky, whitish on throat, 1).

Temperate zone. PERU from Huánuco south to w BOLIVIA, n CHILE to Antofagasta and w ARGENTINA in Jujuy, 1. CHILE from Copiapó, ARGENTINA from Salta and Formosa, s to Tierra del Fuego. Southern breeders migrate n to URUGUAY, PARAGUAY, se BRAZIL and BOLIVIA. Terrestrial. Damp, open lands near water.

Plate 28

28. STREAK-THROATED BUSH-TYRANT

Myiotheretes striaticollis *

9". Upperparts earthy brown. Sides of head and throat, and the upper breast white, streaked black; rest of underparts cinnamon. Inner webs of remiges mostly cinnamon. Outer tail feathers cinnamon, tipped blackish; central pair blackish, rest cinnamon on inner web with dark tip.

Temperate, rarely subtropical zone. Nw VENEZUELA; mts. of COLOMBIA s through Andes to nw ARGENTINA. Shrubby ravines, haciendas.

29. SANTA MARTA BUSH-TYRANT

Myiotheretes pernix

7.5". Differs from 28 by cinnamon parts of plumage much deeper, dark ferruginous; tail dusky, only outer web of outer rectrix furruginous.

Temperate zone of Santa Marta Mts., COLOMBIA. Shrubby ravines.

30. SMOKY BUSH-TYRANT

Myiotheretes fumigatus *

8". Dark smoky brown, wings and tail darker; basal half of inner web of remiges cinnamon; wing coverts edged clay color.

Temperate, páramo, rarely subtropical zone. Nw VENEZUELA s through Andes of COLOMBIA to Junín, PERU. Shrubby hillsides.

31. RUFOUS-BELLIED BUSH-TYRANT

Myiotheretes fuscorufus

7.5". Earthy brown above, dull cinnamon below, throat buffy white. Wings dusky with two broad rufous wing bars; inner remiges edged rufous and basal half of inner webs of remiges rufous. Tail blackish, outer web of outermost feathers and margins of inner webs pale cinnamon.

Temperate zone. Se PERU; w BOLIVIA. Shrubby hillsides.

32. JELSKI'S BUSH-TYRANT

Myiotheretes signatus

5.5". Dark olive gray above, darker on crown. Throat and center of abdomen pale yellowish, under tail coverts reddish brown; rest of underparts olive gray, paler than back. Inner webs of tail feathers reddish brown.

Andes of central PERU in Junín. Shrubby hillsides.

33. RED-RUMPED BUSH-TYRANT

Myiotheretes erythropygius

9". Forecrown grayish white, hindcrown gray, back dark ashy gray, rump rufous. Throat whitish, streaked gray; breast gray, belly rufous. Wings blackish with white patch at base of inner remiges. Central tail feathers black, rest rufous with dusky apical band.

Temperate, páramo zones. COLOMBIA in Santa Marta Mts. and in Nariño s through Andes to nw BOLIVIA. Shrubby slopes, ravines.

Plate 11

34. D'ORBIGNY'S CHAT-TYRANT

Ochthoeca oenanthoides *

6" (or 6.7", 1). Above pale (or dark, 1) grayish brown. Forehead and broad long eyebrow white. Wings dark brown, wing coverts and inner remiges edged buffy (or plain, 1). Throat grayish, rest of underparts cinnamon buff (or cinnamon rufous, 1). Tail dark brown, outer web of outer tail feather white.

Temperate, páramo zones. PERU from Libertad to Puno, 1. N and w BOLIVIA; nw ARGENTINA to La Rioja; n CHILE in Arica. Bushy hillsides, steep wooded valleys near streams.

35. BROWN-BACKED CHAT-TYRANT

Ochthoeca fumicolor *

6.5". Differs from 34 by being much browner above, eyebrows buffy white; wing bars conspicuous, deep rufous; no white on outer tail feather.

Upper subtropical to páramo zone. Nw VENEZUELA s through Andes of COLOMBIA to n BOLIVIA. Thickets.

36. WHITE-BROWED CHAT-TYRANT

Ochthoeca leucophrys *

5.7". Above smoky brown, forehead and long wide eyebrow white. Two broad rufous wing bars (or no wing bars, 1). Throat and breast light gray, belly white. Tail feathers blackish with white outer web on outermost.

Temperate zone. N Peru s to nw CHILE, 1. N and w BOLIVIA; nw ARGENTINA to La Rioja. Fields, hedgerows; in Peru descends to coast.

37. PIURA CHAT-TYRANT

Ochthoeca piurae

4.8". Very much like 36 but much smaller, darker and browner above with wing bands deeper in color.

Subtropical, lower temperate zones. Nw PERU from Piura to Ancash. Shrubby hillsides, arid regions.

38. RUFOUS-BREASTED CHAT-TYRANT

Ochthoeca rufipectoralis *

5.5". Above dark sooty brown to brown, crown darker; white eyebrows very long and prominent. Throat grayish, breast rufous, belly white to grayish white. Very well marked rufous wing bar (or no wing bar, 1). Tail feathers blackish, outer web of outermost white.

Upper subtropical to temperate zone. Nw VENEZUELA, s through Andes of COLOMBIA to s PERU. Nw BOLIVIA, 1. Forest. Bushy hillsides usually near springs and brooks.

39. SLATY-BACKED CHAT-TYRANT

Ochthoeca cinnamomeiventris *

5". Sharp white streak from nostril to above eye. General plumage dark slaty gray; lower breast and belly dark chestnut (or all slaty gray below, 1; or slaty gray with dark chestnut band across breast, 2).

Subtropical to temperate zone. VENEZUELA in Mérida and n Táchira, 1. S Táchira s through Andes of COLOMBIA to e ECUADOR. N PERU s to n BOLIVIA, 2. Forest.

Plate 38

40. CROWNED CHAT-TYRANT

Ochthoeca frontalis *

5". Stripe from nostril to above eye yellow, turning to white posteriorly (or forehead and eyebrow white, 1). Crown, sides of head and the back dark brown; underparts ashy gray, under tail coverts rusty. Wings and tail dark brown (or with two conspicuous rufous wing bars, 2).

Temperate zone. Northern E Andes of COLOMBIA, 1. From Central Andes s through ECUADOR to n PERU. From central PERU south to nw BOLIVIA, 2. Shrubby hillsides.

41. GOLDEN-BROWED CHAT-TYRANT

Ochthoeca pulchella *

Very like 40 (2) with prominent wing bars but back more reddish brown, markedly so on rump; olivaceous brown, not gray, sides of both head and breast; whiter belly.

Subtropical, temperate zones. Se ECUADOR south in w PERU to Lima and in the east to nw BOLIVIA. Shrubby hillsides.

42. YELLOW-BELLIED CHAT-TYRANT

Ochthoeca diadema *

4.5"-5". Forehead and long eyebrow yellow. Back olivaceous brown, darker on crown. Throat and belly greenish yellow, breast strongly shaded with olive. Wings with narrow to broad rufous double wing bars (or no bars, 1).

Subtropical, temperate zones. W VENEZUELA, COLOMBIA in Santa Marta Mts. and northern E Andes, 1. From Central and W Andes s through ECUADOR to Junín, PERU. Shrubby hillsides.

43. BLACK PHOEBE

Sayornis nigricans *

7.5". Sooty black, blackest on head and breast; center of belly white. Inner remiges and wing coverts broadly edged white. Outer web of outer tail feather white.

Tropical, chiefly subtropical, occasionally temperate zone. VENEZUELA n of the Orinoco w to COLOMBIA and s to PERU, BOLIVIA and nw ARGENTINA. [Western US southward.] Riverbanks, especially rapid rocky streams.

44. LONG-TAILED TYRANT

Colonia colonus *

5". Central tail feather much lengthened, up to 8" long. Black; cap grayish white to gray; rump white (also center of back white, 1).

Tropical zone. COLOMBIA w of E Andes to w ECUADOR, 1. GUIANAS; VENEZUELA in e and s Bolívar. E COLOMBIA s through e ECUADOR to n BOLIVIA. BRAZIL s of the Amazon to PARAGUAY and ne ARGENTINA. [S Honduras southward.] Forest and scrub. Slender dead trees at forest edge often near water.

Plate 48

45. STREAMER-TAILED TYRANT

Gubernetes yetapa

8" (17" including very long, much graduated tail). Above pale gray with dark shaft streaks, eyebrow and throat white. Sides of neck and pectoral band chestnut. Breast and sides gray, belly white. Wings and tail blackish, basal half of outer web of primaries rufous.

N and e BOLIVIA; s BRAZIL in Mato Grosso e to Minas Gerais and s to São Paulo; n and central ARGENTINA from Misiones to e Formosa and s Buenos Aires and San Luis. Open woodland.

Plate 28

46. COCK-TAILED TYRANT

Alectrurus tricolor

5.5" (8" including lengthened tail feathers). Above black, rump gray. Forehead, eyebrow and underparts white; incomplete breast band black. Lesser wing coverts white, rest broadly margined gray. Tail very peculiar: outer feathers black, lengthened (2.5"), very broad, often held erect. ♀: Brown above, rump and wing coverts paler; below dirty white, incomplete breast band brown. Tail normal.

N and e BOLIVIA; s BRAZIL from Mato Grosso and Minas Gerais s to PARAGUAY and ne ARGENTINA. Brush country, woodland.

Plate 28

47. STRANGE-TAILED TYRANT

Yetapa risora

6" (14" including lengthened tail feathers). Above black, rump gray. Scapulars, wing coverts and margins of remiges white. Below white with broad black breast band. In breeding season throat bare, skin salmon. Tail very peculiar: outer feathers much lengthened (8"), black, basal part of shaft bare, rest with inner web very broad in center, outer web absent. ♀: Above brown, feathers edged rufescent buff; rump plain buff. Below buffy white, pectoral band dark brown, tail as in ♂ but shorter.

S BRAZIL; PARAGUAY; URUGUAY; ARGENTINA from Misiones to e Formosa, s to Buenos Aires and San Luis. Grasslands and marshes, shrubbery.

Plate 26

48. CRESTED BLACK-TYRANT

Knipolegus lophotes

8". Conspicuously crested, crest feathers pointed. Glossy blue black; base of outer remiges white. Bill black. ♀: Like ♂ but smaller.

S BRAZIL from Minas Gerais and Goiás s to Mato Grosso, Rio Grande do Sul and URUGUAY. *Knipolegus* inhabits forest borders and thickets, often near water; reedbeds.

49. VELVETY BLACK-TYRANT

Knipolegus nigerrimus

7.2". Much like 48 but crest shorter,

feathers rounded at tip. Bill bluish. ♀: Like ♂ but throat dark cinnamon, streaked black.

Se BRAZIL from Minas Gerais to São Paulo.

50. WHITE-WINGED BLACK-TYRANT

Knipolegus aterrimus*

7". Differs from 49 by dull black rather than glossy black plumage; white band across base of primaries. Bill bluish white to leaden blue. ♀: Above grayish brown, rump bright cinnamon rufous. Below brownish buff, throat and belly paler, breast obscurely streaked. Wings black with two broad buff to white wing bars. Tail feathers cinnamon buff with broad blackish apical band, central pair mostly black; in some races less extensive cinnamon buff.

Subtropical zone. N PERU from Cajamarca s to BOLIVIA and ARGENTINA w of río Paraná s to Chubut.

Plate 28

51. RIVERSIDE TYRANT

Knipolegus orenocensis*

6". Dark slaty gray with olive tinge; crown and lores blackish, (or no olive tinge, 1; or sooty black with slight gloss above, 2). ♀: Like ♂ but much paler (or below buffy white, clouded with gray, 1; or upperparts dark brown, below buffy streaked gray, 2).

Tropical zone. VENEZUELA along ríos Orinoco and Apure. BRAZIL s of the Amazon from n Goiás w to rio Madiera, 1. Ne PERU and immediately adjacent BRAZIL, 2.

52. RUFOUS-TAILED TYRANT

Knipolegus poecilurus*

6". Not unlike ♀ of 50. Differs mainly by rump much like back; tail feathers, except central pair, cinnamon on inner webs; breast and throat grayer with pale fawn patch on lower throat. Sexes similar.

Tropical to temperate zone. VENEZUELA; n BRAZIL n of the Amazon to Roraima. Andes of COLOMBIA south to n BOLIVIA. Trinidad and Tobago.

53. BLUE-BILLED BLACK-TYRANT

Knipolegus cyanirostris

6". All black, no white at base of primaries. Bill blue. ♀: Crown and nape dull chestnut, streaked black on forecrown; back black,

upper tail coverts rufous. Below yellowish white, heavily streaked black. Wings brownish black with two buff wing bars. Tail dark brown, inner webs of feathers cinnamon.

BRAZIL from se Minas Gerais and Rio de Janeiro w to Mato Grosso and s to PARAGUAY, URUGUAY, and e ARGENTINA to Buenos Aires and La Pampa.

54. PLUMBEOUS TYRANT

Knipolegus cabanisi

6.3". Slaty gray; abdomen light gray; wings and tail blackish. Not unlike 51 but at once distinguishable by white base to inner webs of primaries. ♀: Above grayish brown with olive cast, upper tail coverts rufous. Throat whitish, streaked olive gray; breast olive gray, belly white, under tail coverts pale cinnamon. Two whitish wing bars. Tail dusky, cinnamon on inner web.

Tropical to lower temperate zone. Se PERU; e BOLIVIA; nw ARGENTINA to n Cajamarca.

55. AMAZONIAN BLACK-TYRANT

Phaeotriccus poecilocercus

5.2". Glossy black; three outer primaries narrow, pointed. ♀: Above dull olive, tail coverts and margins of tail feathers cinnamon. Two buffy wing bars. Below pale buff, streaked dusky on throat and breast. Primaries as in ♂.

Tropical zone. GUYANA; w VENEZUELA; Amazonian BRAZIL; ne PERU. Forest.

56. HUDSON'S BLACK-TYRANT

Phaeotriccus hudsoni

6". Like 55 but at once distinguishable by white base of inner webs of remiges. ♀: Much like ♀ of 50 but outer wing feathers pointed and narrow. Size smaller. Differs readily from 55 by cinnamon tail with blackish subterminal band.

Breeds in s ARGENTINA in Buenos Aires and Río Negro. Winters n to BOLIVIA, PARAGUAY and ne Mato Grosso, BRAZIL. Open scrub.

Plate 28

57. CINEREOUS TYRANT

Entotriccus striaticeps

4.7". Dark olivaceous gray, blackish on head. Wing coverts and inner remiges edged gray. Outer primaries narrow, pointed. Tail black. Iris scarlet. ♀: Above olivaceous, browner on head and rump, crown streaked blackish. Below whitish, streaked dusky. Two whitish wing bars. Tail blackish; inner webs of feathers rufous, tipped dusky.

Breeds in nw ARGENTINA from Tucumán and Santiago del Estero to Córdoba and La Rioja. Winters north to s and e BOLIVIA and s Mato Grosso, BRAZIL. Open scrub.

Plate 12

58. SPECTACLED TYRANT

Hymenops perspicillata *

5.6″. Bill and conspicuous wattle around eye yellow. Plumage black, primaries white with black tip and base. ♀: Above dark brown, feathers edged lighter. Remiges chestnut with dark brown tips. Wing coverts dark brown, pale-tipped. Below buffy white, streaked dusky on breast.

Breeds in ARGENTINA from Entre Ríos and Córdoba s to Chubut, and in CHILE from Atacama to Aysén. Winters north to n and e BOLIVIA, Mato Grosso, BRAZIL; and URUGUAY. Reedbeds, swamps.

Plate 28

59. SHEAR-TAILED GRAY-TYRANT

Muscipipra vetula

9″. Dark gray; wings and tail black; tail conspicuously forked, rather long.

Se BRAZIL from Espírito Santo and Minas Gerais s to Rio Grande do Sul. Ne ARGENTINA in Misiones; PARAGUAY. Scrub.

Plate 28

60. PIED WATER-TYRANT

Fluvicola pica *

4.5″ (or 5.5″, 1). Forecrown, sides of head and underparts white. Hindcrown, center of back, wings and tail black; scapulars, lower back and rump white (or hindcrown and back dark ashy brown, narrow rump band white, 1). ♀: Like ♂ but tail tipped white.

Tropical zone. GUIANAS, VENEZUELA, COLOMBIA (except Pacific slope) south to n BRAZIL. E PERU and BRAZIL s of the Amazon to BOLIVIA, central ARGENTINA and URUGUAY, 1. Trinidad. [E Panama.] Riverbanks, marshes.

Plate 48

61. MASKED WATER-TYRANT

Fluvicola nengeta *

5.5″. Head, rump and underparts white; long black stripe from lores through eye. Back pale sandy gray; wings and tail black, tail rounded, broadly tipped white.

Arid tropical zone. Sw ECUADOR, immediately adjacent PERU. E BRAZIL from Maranhão and Ceará s to Bahía. Riverbanks, marshes, parks.

62. WHITE-HEADED MARSH-TYRANT

Arundinicola leucocephala

4.6″. Black; head white. ♀: Forecrown and underparts white. Back and wings ashy gray; tail black. Bill black, base of mandible yellow.

Generally distributed e of Andes south to e BOLIVIA, PARAGUAY and n ARGENTINA. W of Andes in Santa Marta region and Caribbean lowlands of COLOMBIA. Marshes, wet pastureland, riverbanks.

Fig. 9, p. 63

63. VERMILION FLYCATCHER

Pyrocephalus rubinus *

5.5″-6.2″. Cap and underparts vermilion. Sides of head, back, wings and tail sooty brown to sooty black. ♀: Above dark grayish brown; throat and breast white, breast streaked dusky brown; lower breast and belly pinkish vermilion, amount and shade varying (according to race) to only pale pinkish on lower belly and under tail coverts. (A melanistic phase also exists among normally colored birds in which both sexes are uniform dark ashy brown, sometimes with a few vermilion feathers scattered about, 1).

Tropical to temperate zone in arid, semiarid and scrubby areas; campos, wet cerrado. GUYANA; VENEZUELA; n BRAZIL in Roraima; n and central COLOMBIA; w ECUADOR s through w PERU (from Lima to Arequipa, 1) to n CHILE. Central PERU. PARAGUAY; URUGUAY; n and central ARGENTINA to Río Negro. Southern breeders migrate across BOLIVIA and BRAZIL and winter in e PERU, e ECUADOR and e COLOMBIA. [Sw United States s to Nicaragua. Galápagos Is.]

Plate 11

64. DRAB WATER-TYRANT

Ochthornis littoralis

5.5". Pale sandy brown, paler below. Eyebrow white; streak through eye dusky, bordered by white below.

Tropical zone. GUYANA; FRENCH GUIANA; VENEZUELA s of the Orinoco; e COLOMBIA and e ECUADOR south to n and w BOLIVIA. Ne BRAZIL n of the Amazon from Roraima eastward, and s of it from e PERU east to n Mato Grosso and w Pará. Sandy riverbanks.

Plate 28

65. TUMBES TYRANT

Tumbezia salvini

5.5". Forehead, broad eyebrow and underparts lemon yellow. Sides of head and crown dusky gray, back slightly paler with olive cast. Wings blackish with conspicuous white double wing bars. Tail blackish, outer web of outer feathers and narrow tip white. ♀: Like ♂ but crown like back, and outer rectrix largely white.

Nw PERU in arid littoral from Tumbes to Libertad.

Plate 12

66. YELLOW-BROWED TYRANT

Satrapa icterophrys

6.5". Upperparts olive, becoming lighter on rump. Long, conspicuous eyebrow yellow; sides of head dusky. Underparts bright yellow, sides of breast olive. Wings and tail blackish; double wing bar gray. Outer web of outer rectrix white.

E and central BRAZIL from Maranhão s to Mato Grosso and Rio Grande do Sul; URUGUAY; PARAGUAY; n and e BOLIVIA; ARGENTINA s to Buenos Aires. In winter some migrate to VENEZUELA. Woodland, cultivated lands.

Plate 12

67. CATTLE TYRANT

Machetornis rixosus *

8". Crown and nape light gray, concealed crest orange scarlet. Back light olive brown, throat creamy white (or yellow, 1), rest of underparts yellow. Tail brown, two outermost pairs of feathers with pale patch at tip of inner web.

Tropical zone. VENEZUELA n of the Orinoco and s of it in n Bolívar; n COLOMBIA to Caribbean lowlands, 1. E and central BRAZIL from Maranhão and Ceará s to URUGUAY, PARAGUAY, n and e BOLIVIA and ARGENTINA to La Rioja and Buenos Aires. Pasturelands, often on ground.

Plate 49

68. SIRYSTES

Sirystes sibilator *

7". Somewhat crested. Crown and nape black, back gray obscurely streaked dusky (or with rump white, 1; or back gray, tinged yellowish, unstreaked, rump white, 2). Throat and breast gray becoming grayish white to pure white on belly. Wings black, wing coverts edged gray (or white, 2). Inner remiges edged white. Tail black (with white tip, 2).

Tropical zone. Nw VENEZUELA in s Táchira and e COLOMBIA from Meta south to e PERU and w BRAZIL, east, n of the Amazon, to e Pará and s of it to rio Purús. N BOLIVIA, 1. E BRAZIL from Bahía s to Rio Grande do Sul and Mato Grosso; PARAGUAY; ne ARGENTINA in Misiones. West of Andes in nw Chocó, COLOMBIA, 2. [E Panama, 2.] Forest treetops, cerradão.

Plate 48

69. FORK-TAILED FLYCATCHER

Muscivora tyrannus *

16". Tail black, very long 11", deeply forked, much graduated. Top and sides of head black, semiconcealed crest yellow. Above gray, rump black. Below white. ♀: Similar, but tail a little shorter than ♂.

Tropical to temperate zone. Breeds locally e of Andes to URUGUAY, PARAGUAY, BOLIVIA and ARGENTINA to Río Negro. W of Andes in COLOMBIA. Curaçao. Trinidad, Tobago. Highly migratory. [Mid. Amer. Acc. Falkland Is. Antilles. Bermuda. New Jersey, US] Semiarid pastures, savanna, woodland and towns.

Plate 48

70. EASTERN KINGBIRD

Tyrannus tyrannus

8.5". Above dark gray, concealed crest fiery orange. Below white, tail tipped white.

Winter resident (Oct.-May) from COLOM-BIA to nw ARGENTINA. Straggler to e VENEZUELA, GUYANA, Mato Grosso, BRAZIL and CHILE in Arica. [Breeds in Canada and US. Migrant in Central America, winters in Panama. Casual in Cuba, Swan I., San Andrés.] Campos, savanna.

71. TROPICAL KINGBIRD

Tyrannus melancholicus *

9″. Upperparts, throat and breast light gray, belly yellow. Concealed crest orange. Wings blackish, wing coverts and inner remiges edged grayish white. Tail blackish, notice-ably forked.

Tropical to temperate zone. Generally dis-tributed w of Andes to Ica, PERU, and e of them to Río Negro, ARGENTINA. Aruba to Trinidad and Tobago. Southern breeders are migratory. [Breeds from Arizona south-ward. Grenada. Vagrant, Cuba.] Savanna, parks.

Plate 49

72. GRAY KINGBIRD

Tyrannus dominicensis *

8.5″. Above ashy gray, crown and sides of head dusky; concealed crown patch orange, feathers basally white. Throat and breast whitish gray, belly white. Wings dusky, coverts and remiges pale-edged. Tail black-ish, slightly forked.

Winter resident (Oct.-April). GUIANAS, n VENEZUELA, n and w COLOMBIA. Aruba to Trinidad and Tobago. [Se US; the Ba-hamas, Antilles, Cozumel. Winters in Pana-ma.] Savanna.

73. SNOWY-THROATED KINGBIRD

Tyrannus niveigularis

7.5″. Looks much like 112, but darker. Crown gray with partially concealed yellow crest, black streak through eye. Back gray strongly tinged yellowish olive, upper tail coverts and tail black. Throat white, breast pale gray, belly bright yellow. Wings black, coverts edged gray, inner remiges edged white.

Tropical zone from sw Nariño, COLOMBIA, s to Ancash, w PERU. Arid scrub. Perches low down in bushes instead of on top as does 112.

74. WHITE-THROATED KINGBIRD

Tyrannus albogularis

7″. Crown and nape light gray, concealed crest orange. Throat white; rest of under-parts bright yellow, clouded olive on chest. Back light olive. Wings grayish brown, wing coverts and remiges narrowly edged olive. Tail black, somewhat forked.

Tropical zone. W GUYANA; sw SURINAM; s VENEZUELA in Bolívar. Both sides of the Amazon from e PERU east to w Pará and s to Mato Grosso, Goiás, Minas Gerais and São Paulo. Savanna, forest edge, wet ce-rrado.

75. SULPHURY FLYCATCHER

Tyrannopsis sulphurea

7.5″. Crown, nape, sides of head, neck and breast dark ashy gray; center of throat and upper breast white, rest of underparts yel-low. Wings and tail olive brown; tail com-paratively short, square.

Tropical zone. GUIANAS; ne VENEZUELA in Bolívar and w Amazonas. COLOMBIA in Meta; e ECUADOR; e PERU; Amazonian BRAZIL e to Amapá, Maranhão and e Goiás. Open forest and sandy areas near Mauritia palms.

Plate 49

76. DUSKY-CHESTED FLYCATCHER

Tyrannopsis luteiventris *

6″. Above, including wings and tail, dark brown; concealed crest orange (♀, no crest). Throat white, streaked dusky; underparts bright yellow, sides of breast olive, center of breast streaked olive. Bill very much smaller (.3″) than in 75 (.75″).

Tropical zone. S SURINAM. VENEZUELA in central Bolívar. Se COLOMBIA in Putu-mayo. E PERU near Iquitos; w Amazonian BRAZIL e to rios Negro and Tapajós. Forest edge.

77. VARIEGATED FLYCATCHER

Empidonomus varius *

7.5″. Crown and sides of head brownish black, occipital crest yellow; long broad eyebrow, joining across nape, and moustachial streak dull white. Back dusky brown, feathers pale-edged giving streaked look. Upper tail coverts and tail dusky brown broadly edged rufous chestnut. Underparts yellowish white boldly streaked dusky except on throat. Wings dusky, coverts and inner remiges edged white.

Tropical sometimes subtropical zone. Generally distributed e of Andes s to La Pampa, ARGENTINA. Southern breeders migrate n as far as e COLOMBIA, VENEZUELA and Trinidad. Open woodland.

Plate 49

78. CROWNED SLATY-FLYCATCHER

Empidonomus aurantioatrocristatus *

7". Cap black. concealed crest yellow. Upperparts, wings and tail brownish gray; below pure gray, lighter and slightly yellowish on crissum and under tail coverts.

Tropical zone. Breeds in e BRAZIL s of the Amazon from e bank of the Tapajós e to Maranhão and Piauí. PARAGUAY; URUGUAY; ARGENTINA s to La Pampa. Migrates north to n BRAZIL, e ECUADOR and se COLOMBIA. Open brushy areas, forest edge, cerrado.

79. PIRATIC FLYCATCHER

Legatus leucophaius *

6". Not unlike 77 in color, but smaller. Back uniform and browner, breast less densely streaked, sides of body and under tail coverts yellower, tail coverts and tail olive brown edged with reddish brown. Bill much broader.

Tropical zone. Generally distributed w of Andes to nw ECUADOR, and e of them to n ARGENTINA. Trinidad. Open woodland, generally up high.

Plate 49

80. THREE-STRIPED FLYCATCHER

Conopias trivirgata *

6". Top and sides of head sooty black; long, broad eyebrow white. Back dull olive; wings and tail brownish black. Below yellow, strongly tinged olive on breast.

Tropical zone. Once in VENEZUELA (Bolívar). Once in e PERU (Loreto). W Amazonian BRAZIL from rio Japurá e to Óbidos and Santarém; in e BRAZIL from Bahía to Paraná; e PARAGUAY; ne ARGENTINA in Misiones. Open woodland, often in colonies

of icterids. Appropriates nests of other species.

81. LEMON-BROWED FLYCATCHER

Conopias cinchoneti *

6.7". Upperparts and sides of head olive green. Pale yellow long, broad eyebrows meeting across nape. Underparts all bright yellow. Wings and tail dark brown.

Upper tropical and subtropical zones. Extreme nw VENEZUELA; Andes of COLOMBIA, e ECUADOR and central PERU to Cuzco. Forest.

Plate 49

82. WHITE-RINGED FLYCATCHER

Conopias parva *

6.2". Crown and nape brownish black completely surrounded by broad white band; concealed yellow crest. Sides of head brownish black. Back, wings and tail dark olive brown. Underparts yellow (with white throat, 1).

Tropical zone. GUIANAS; VENEZUELA s of the Orinoco; se COLOMBIA, n BRAZIL in upper rio Negro region. Pacific COLOMBIA to w ECUADOR, 1. [Costa Rica; Panama.] Forest.

Plate 49

83. BOAT-BILLED FLYCATCHER

Megarhynchus pitangua *

9". Bill very large, broad, flat. Crown dark brown completely surrounded by white band. Concealed crest yellow, or orange or tawny orange. Sides of head blackish, throat white, rest of underparts bright yellow. Back olive brown to brown; wings darker, inconspicuously to conspicuously margined rufous (see no. 92).

Tropical, lower subtropical zones. Generally distributed e of Andes to BOLIVIA, PARAGUAY, BRAZIL to Paraná and w of Andes to nw PERU. [Mid. Amer.] Forest edge, clearings, usually high up in trees, cerrado.

Plate 38

84. SULPHUR-BELLIED FLYCATCHER

Myiodynastes luteiventris *

8.5". Forehead, eyebrow and malar region white; back dark brown, streaked olive buff. Rump and tail mostly cinnamon rufous. Throat white, rest of underparts sulphur yellow with black streaks on sides of neck, on breast and sides of body. Wing with two white wing bands. Bill black.

Migrant. Transient through COLOMBIA and e ECUADOR, wintering in PERU and n BOLIVIA. [Breeds from se Arizona to Costa Rica; migrates through Mid. Amer.] Open woodland, clearings.

85. STREAKED FLYCATCHER

Myiodynastes maculatus *

Very like 84; best distinguished by whitish instead of yellow underparts and pale lower mandible (or much darker, blackish above streaked buffy white; below white, heavily streaked black, 1).

Tropical, lower subtropical zones. Generally distributed w of Andes to nw PERU, e of Andes to La Pampa, ARGENTINA, (birds breeding in e BRAZIL from Piauí to Rio Grande do Sul, URUGUAY, PARAGUAY, e BOLIVIA and ARGENTINA s to La Pampa are migratory, 1). Trinidad, Tobago. [Mid. Amer.] Mangroves, clearings, forest edge, plantations, open woodland, cerrado.

Plate 48

86. BAIRD'S FLYCATCHER

Myiodynastes bairdi

9″. Forehead and lores velvety black becoming brownish black behind eye; eyebrow pale sandy, concealed crest lemon yellow. Back pale brown with olive cast, rump rufous. Throat white, streaked gray; upper breast pale ochraceous, rest of underparts light yellow. Wings and coverts dusky, feathers very broadly edged bright rufous. Tail largely rufous.

Tropical zone. Coastal ECUADOR from Manabí to n Lima, PERU. Arid coastal area.

87. GOLDEN-CROWNED FLYCATCHER

Myiodynastes chrysocephalus *

8.5″. Crown dusky becoming ashy on nape, crest yellow, sides of head blackish with white line above and below eye. Back dull olive to grayish olive. Chin white, throat cinnamon buff; rest of underparts yellow, streaked olive on breast. Wings and tail dusky; coverts, outer remiges and tail edged rufous.

Upper tropical and subtropical zones. VEN-

EZUELA n of the Orinoco; COLOMBIA; e and w ECUADOR; central and e PERU to Puno. [E Panama.] Forest edge, generally near streams.

88. RUSTY-MARGINED FLYCATCHER

Myiozetetes cayanensis *

7″. Crown and sides of head blackish brown, concealed crest yellow, long eyebrow white. Back dark brown to olive brown. Primaries edged exteriorly, and more broadly on inner web with rufous (or basal half of primaries rufous on both webs, 1). Throat white, rest of underparts yellow. Tail dark brown (feathers margined rufous, 1).

Tropical, subtropical zones. GUIANAS; VENEZUELA in mouth of the Orinoco, Bolívar, Amazonas and the nw. Rest of VENEZUELA, 1. COLOMBIA; w ECUADOR. BRAZIL from rios Negro and Tapajós e to Roraima and Maranhão, south to n Minas Gerais, Mato Grosso and e BOLIVIA. BRAZIL in Rio de Janeiro and s Minas Gerais, 1. [E Panama.] Forest and open country near rivers and ponds, plantations. In *Myiozetetes* the bill is noticeably small.

Plate 38

89. VERMILION-CROWNED (or Social) FLYCATCHER

Myiozetetes similis *

Very like 88 but crown not noticeably darker than back, concealed crest vermilion instead of yellow, back greener, little or no rufous on exterior part of wing, and inner webs of remiges margined buffy instead of rufous.

Tropical zone. Generally distributed e of Andes from VENEZUELA and COLOMBIA s to BOLIVIA, PARAGUAY and ne ARGENTINA; w of Andes to Tumbes, PERU. [Mid. Amer.] Open woodland often near water, clearings.

90. GRAY-CAPPED FLYCATCHER

Myiozetetes granadensis *

Much like 89 but no eyebrow, forehead white, crown gray, back greener. Concealed crest orange vermilion. ♀: No crest.

Tropical zone. VENEZUELA and COLOMBIA south to n BOLIVIA and w BRAZIL e to Rondonia. W of Andes to Tumbes, PERU. [Nicaragua southward.] Clearings, isolated trees.

91. WHITE-BEARDED FLYCATCHER

Myiozetetes inornatus

6". Rather like 88 but much smaller.

Tropical zone. Central n coast of VENE-ZUELA s on the llanos to río Apure and n Bolívar. Savanna, llanos, often near water.

92. GREAT KISKADEE

Pitangus sulphuratus *

8"-10". Crown and sides of head black, crest yellow, crown surrounded by white band. Back and wings brown, coverts and remiges edged rufous, in some races rufous on both webs basally. Tail dark brown, edged rufous. Throat white, rest of underparts bright yellow. Remarkably like 83 in color but bill quite different: narrow and sharply ridged instead of broad and flat.

Tropical zone. Generally distributed e of Andes to La Pampa, ARGENTINA. West of E Andes in COLOMBIA, except Pacific slope. Once in CHILE (Bío-Bío). [Texas, Mid. Amer.]. Open woodland, parks, gardens, clearings.

Plate 49

93. LESSER KISKADEE

Pitangus lictor *

7". Almost exactly like 92 in color but much smaller with relatively longer, more slender bill.

Tropical zone. GUIANAS, VENEZUELA south to n Bolívar and n Amazonas w to Caribbean lowlands of COLOMBIA and south to s BRAZIL and n BOLIVIA. [Panama.] Mangroves, pond and river borders, campos, plantations, always near water.

94. BRIGHT-RUMPED ATTILA

Attila spadiceus *[1]

7"-8". Very variable in color but in any phase differs from other attilas (except 95) by contrasting bright yellow to tawny buff rump and upper tail coverts. Upperparts olive green, to tawny olive, to rufous. Throat and breast olive-yellow to olive-brown, streaked dusky; belly white; sides of body olive yellow, to tawny olive, to rufous; or throat and breast rufous, rest of underparts buff. Wings dark brown to olive, wing coverts with two olive to rufous bars. Tail dark brown to rufous. Bill rather large with prominent hook in all attilas.

Tropical, subtropical zones. E of Andes south to Rio de Janeiro, BRAZIL, n BOLIVIA and PERU. W of Andes to w ECUADOR. Trinidad. [Mid. Amer.] Forest, savanna.

95. DULL-CAPPED ATTILA

Attila bolivianus *

8.5". Crown and nape dull brown gradually passing into rufous brown on back and cinnamon on rump. Throat and breast rufous passing into tawny rufous on belly. Primaries blackish brown, inner remiges like back. Tail cinnamon rufous. Rather like a rufous 94 but no wing bars and crown dull brown instead of rufous chestnut.

Tropical zone. E PERU, n BOLIVIA, sw BRAZIL e to upper rio Xingú. Forest.

96. GRAY-HOODED ATTILA

Attila rufus *

9". Crown and upper mantle gray with black shaft streaks on crown. Back rufous chestnut becoming cinnamon rufous on rump and tail. Throat grayish white, streaked gray (or chin and sides of neck grayish white, center of throat cinnamon rufous, 1); breast rufous, belly cinnamon rufous. Remiges black.

Se BRAZIL in se Bahía, 1; thence s through the mountains of Rio de Janeiro to Santa Catarina.

97. CITRON-BELLIED ATTILA

Attila citriniventris

7". Crown, nape, sides of head and chin leaden gray obscurely streaked dusky. Back brown with slight olive tinge, becoming chestnut rufous on lower back and cinnamon on tail coverts. Wings blackish, inner remiges like back. Throat and breast chestnut brown obscurely streaked gray, rest of underparts cinnamon rufous, yellowish in center of belly.

---

[1] The genera *Attila, Pseudattila, Casiornis, Laniocera* and *Rhytipterna* were place in the Cotingidae in *Sp. Bds. S. Amer.*

Tropical zone. VENEZUELA in central and s Amazonas; e ECUADOR; ne PERU; nw BRAZIL along rio Uaupés, and s of the Amazon at Tefé. Forest.

98. CINNAMON ATTILA

Attila cinnamomeus

7.2". Bright chestnut brown above, somewhat lighter on rump. Throat and breast cinnamon brown, belly lighter. Inner remiges like back, rest black; lesser wing coverts like back, rest blackish edged with chestnut brown.

Tropical zone. GUIANAS; VENEZUELA; e COLOMBIA in Meta. E ECUADOR; ne PERU. Nw BOLIVIA in Beni; Amazonian BRAZIL and in Maranhão. Mangroves, swampy forest, plantations.

99. OCHRACEOUS ATTILA

Attila torridus

8.2". Rather like 98 but much larger and much paler, center of belly yellowish. Wing coverts black with two cinnamon wing bars.

Tropical to lower subtropical zone. W ECUADOR from Esmeraldas s to Peruvian border. Forest.

Plate 50

100. RUFOUS-TAILED ATTILA

Pseudattila phoenicurus

Like 98 but top and sides of head brownish gray.

Tropical zone. VENEZUELA in Amazonas. Central and s BRAZIL between rios Purús and Tapajós and from s Goiás to Paraná and Mato Grosso. PARAGUAY. ARGENTINA in Misiones. Forest treetops.

101. RUFOUS CASIORNIS

Casiornis rufa*

7". Above chestnut rufous, darker and redder on crown. Throat and breast cinnamon, belly yellowish white. Wings and tail like back, greater wing coverts tipped black.

E and central BRAZIL n of the Amazon in Pará and s of it from Maranhão, Goiás and w Minas Gerais to São Paulo and Mato Grosso; PARAGUAY; n and e BOLIVIA; n ARGENTINA. Open or dense scrub, campos.

Plate 14

102. ASH-THROATED CASIORNIS

Casiornis fusca

7". Differs from 101 mainly by back brown in contrast to rufous cap and rump. Belly yellower.

BRAZIL from rio Tapajós e to Maranhão and Paraiba and south to n Bahía. Scrub, caatinga.

103. CINEREOUS MOURNER

Laniocera hypopyrrha

8.5". Ashy gray, paler below, a few feathers of underparts rufous with black tips. Pectoral tufts orange rufous. Wing coverts and inner remiges tipped with large round cinnamon spot, surrounded by black. Under tail coverts rufous, tipped black. Tail tipped cinnamon. ♀: Similar but cinnamon markings smaller and pectoral tufts and under tail coverts barred gray and white.

Tropical zone. GUIANAS; e and s VENEZUELA; e COLOMBIA south to n BOLIVIA, Amazonian BRAZIL and in s Bahía and Espírito Santo. Lower stages of forest and undergrowth.

104. SPECKLED MOURNER

Laniocera rufescens*

8". Above dark rufous brown, below paler, a few feathers of underparts tipped black. Pectoral tufts yellow. Wings brown, wing coverts with large round black-edged cinnamon tips. ♀: Differs from ♂ by less intense markings.

Tropical zone. COLOMBIA from middle Magdalena w to Pacific and south to nw ECUADOR. Forest. [Guatemala southward]

105. GRAYISH MOURNER

Rhytipterna simplex*

9". Gray with slight greenish cast, belly palest with definite yellowish green cast. Head slightly crested.

Tropical zone. GUIANAS west to e COLOMBIA and s to BOLIVIA and s BRAZIL, in e to Rio de Janeiro. Open forest.

Plate 27

106. PALE-BELLIED MOURNER

Rhytipterna immunda

8.5". Grayish brown above, browner on upper tail coverts and tail. Throat and breast gray becoming dirty yellow on lower breast and abdomen, latter tinged rusty. Wings grayish brown, wing coverts pale-edged, primaries edged rusty. Looks much like a *Myiarchus* but hindpart of upper tarsus strongly serrated, which is characteristic of *Rhytipterna.*

Tropical zone. SURINAM; FRENCH GUIANA; n BRAZIL from rio Negro to se COLOMBIA on río Guainía. Bushy savanna.

107. RUFOUS MOURNER

Rhytipterna holerythra *

8″. More or less uniform rufous, slightly paler below; lower mandible pale. (See 43 of Cotingidae)

Tropical zone. COLOMBIA from middle Magdalena Valley w to Pacific and south to nw ECUADOR. Forest. [Guatemala southward]

Myiarchus

The genus *Myiarchus* is composed of a group of flycatchers very similar to each other in appearance (except for 108) and difficult to tell apart. The head is more or less crested, the back grayish brown or grayish with an olive tinge, to olive. Throat and breast are pale gray, rest of the underparts pale yellow. Most species show two well-marked wing bars. In the following descriptions only distinguishing characters are given.

108. RUFOUS FLYCATCHER

Myiarchus semirufus

7″. Upperparts, sides of head and neck dull dark grayish brown; upper tail coverts rufous; below uniform cinnamon. Wing coverts and margins of remiges rufous. Tail mostly rufous, central feathers with black along shaft.

Coastal PERU from Tumbes to n Lima. Arid coast and foothills.

109. SHORT-CRESTED FLYCATCHER

Myiarchus ferox *

8″. Above dull dark olive, upper tail coverts browner. Wing bars dull gray, not very prominent. Bill black.

Tropical zone. Generally distributed e of Andes s to URUGUAY and ARGENTINA to Tucumán and Córdoba. Tobago. [Sw Costa Rica and Panama.] Trees or thickets in savanna, edge of mangroves, campos and riparian thickets.

110. APICAL FLYCATCHER

Myiarchus apicalis

8″. Differs from any other *Myiarchus* by large, pale area at tip of all but central tail feathers.

Arid tropical, subtropical zones. Suitable localities in central and w COLOMBIA w of E Andes. Arid scrub.

Plate 48

111. PALE-EDGED FLYCATCHER

Myiarchus cephalotes *

8″. Wing bars very light gray to whitish. Outer web of outer tail feathers grayish white.

Subtropical zone. N VENEZUELA. COLOMBIA on slopes above Magdalena and Cauca valleys; e of Andes in se Nariño south to n BOLIVIA. Forest.

112. SOOTY-CROWNED FLYCATCHER

Myiarchus phaeocephalus *

8″. Forehead and lores ashy gray, crown black (or dusky brown, 1) in contrast to back; upper mantle gray increasingly tinged olive toward rump. Tail with small grayish tip. (Cf. 73)

Arid tropical zone. W ECUADOR s to Piura, PERU; e slope in Cajamarca and in nw Amazonas, 1. Arid scrub.

113. BROWN-CRESTED FLYCATCHER

Myiarchus tyrannulus *

8″. Crown dull brown. All but central tail feathers with rufous inner margins of inner web. Primaries narrowly edged rufous; wing bars whitish. Throat paler gray than breast.

Tropical zone. GUIANAS; VENEZUELA and n COLOMBIA. BRAZIL n of the Amazon w of rio Negro and s of the Amazon from e PERU to Pará and s to Mato Grosso and Paraná, PARAGUAY, e and n BOLIVIA. Aruba to Trinidad. [S Arizona and sw New Mexico south to nw Costa Rica. Bay Is.] Mangroves, forest and second growth, cerrado.

114. SWAINSON'S FLYCATCHER

*Myiarchus swainsoni**

8". Differs from other species by reddish brown instead of black lower mandible.

Tropical zone. GUIANAS, VENEZUELA and COLOMBIA s to BOLIVIA, PARAGUAY, URUGUAY and La Pampa and Buenos Aires, ARGENTINA. Trinidad. Mangroves, bushy savanna, cerrado. Southern birds migrate n into territory of northern breeders.

115. GREAT-CRESTED FLYCATCHER

*Myiarchus crinitus**

8.3". Much like 113 but slightly larger with almost entire inner web of all but central tail feathers rufous. Throat not paler than breast.

Winter resident in COLOMBIA w of Andes (Nov.-May). Casual in VENEZUELA. [Breeds in e N Amer.; winters from Florida southward.] Open woodland.

116. DUSKY-CAPPED FLYCATCHER

*Myiarchus tuberculifer**

6.5"-7.5". Recognizable by small size, olive green back and contrasting black to dark brown cap. Margins of remiges rufescent.

Tropical, subtropical zones. GUIANAS, VENEZUELA, COLOMBIA, e and w ECUADOR s to BOLIVIA, PARAGUAY, BRAZIL to Rio de Janeiro and Mato Grosso. Nw ARGENTINA. [Sw US southward.] Arid or moist woodlands, pastures. Southern breeders are migratory.

117. OLIVE-SIDED FLYCATCHER

Nuttallornis borealis

7.5". Above dark brownish gray. Throat and narrow line down center of breast and expanding on belly, white. Sides of breast and body olive. Wings and tail dusky, gray wing bars inconspicuous. Tuft of mostly concealed silky white feathers at sides of lower back.

Winters (Aug.-May) in mts. of n VENEZUELA and COLOMBIA to s PERU. Bonaire. Trinidad. [Breeds in N Amer. Migrates through Mid. Amer.] Pasturelands and woods.

118. WOOD PEWEE

*Contopus virens**

6". Dark brownish gray above, wings and tail darker; two gray wing bars. Throat and abdomen whitish, breast gray, paler than back. Partial eye ring.

Tropical to temperate zone. Winters (Sept.-Apr.) from VENEZUELA and COLOMBIA to PERU and w BRAZIL. [Breeds from Alaska and Canada s to Guatemala; migrates through Mid. Amer.] Forest and woodland.

119. TROPICAL PEWEE

*Contopus cinereus**

5.5". Very like 118 but smaller, lores whitish instead of dusky, and crown dusky to blackish. Wing formula different.

Tropical, occasionally to temperate zone. GUIANAS; n VENEZUELA and in s Amazonas; COLOMBIA. Arid sw ECUADOR s to Ica and Junín, PERU. N BRAZIL along Venezuelan border and from s Maranhão to Paraná and s Mato Grosso; PARAGUAY; e and s BOLIVIA; n ARGENTINA. Trinidad. [Mid. Amer.] Open woodland and scrub.

120. WHITE-THROATED PEWEE

Contopus albogularis

4.7". Dark gray; large, irregular white throat patch.

Tropical zone. FRENCH GUIANA (Maripasoula). Forest, known from one specimen.

121. BLACKISH PEWEE

*Contopus nigrescens**

5". Virtually uniform dark gray with no white on belly or under tail coverts. Cap black to dark gray. No wing bars in ad. but whitish double wing bars in imm.

Upper tropical zone. S GUYANA (Acary Mts.). E ECUADOR; ne PERU. Forest.

122. GREATER PEWEE

*Contopus fumigatus**

7". Large all-gray flycatcher with dusky to brownish cap, (center of belly yellowish white in some races). Wing bars inconspicuous if present.

Upper tropical to temperate zone. GUYANA; n VENEZUELA from Miranda w, and in s Bolívar and Amazonas; Andes of COLOMBIA; e and w ECUADOR; nw PERU south to n and e BOLIVIA and nw ARGEN-TINA. Trinidad. [Arizona south to w Pana-ma.] Forest.

Plate 49

Empidonax

Empidonax looks much like a small, pale-bellied *Contopus* with an eye ring. The wings reach only to the base of the tail instead of covering the basal third as they do in *Contopus*, and the inner remiges are characteristically marked by outer webs being black basally, cinnamon or silvery medially.

123. ACADIAN FLYCATCHER

Empidonax virescens

5.5". Much like 119 but olive green above and belly strongly suffused with yellow. Double wing bars buffy white instead of gray. Eye ring conspicuous. Inner remiges distinctively edged blackish basally, silvery medially.

Winter resident (Oct.-Apr.). Tropical to tem-perate zone. Nw VENEZUELA; COLOM-BIA west of E Andes and in Putumayo; w ECUADOR to El Oro. [Breeds from n US and se Canada s to Gulf Coast and Florida. Migrates through Mid. Amer.]. Woodland, swampy woods.

124. TRAILL'S FLYCATCHER

Empidonax traillii*

Virtually indistinguishable in color from 118, but bend of wing buffy instead of gray, back very slightly tinged olive, white eye ring present and wing bars much whiter (except in imm.) and more prominent. Inner remiges marked as in 123.

Winter resident (Aug.-Apr.) in tropical zone from nw VENEZUELA and COLOMBIA s through ECUADOR, PERU and BOLIVIA to n ARGENTINA. [Breeds in Alaska and Canada s to California and Virginia. Winters in Mid. Amer.] Thickets near streams, swamps.

125. EULER'S FLYCATCHER

Empidonax euleri*

5"-5.7". Olive brown to brown above. Throat and belly whitish to yellow, breast olive brown. Eye ring white. Double wing bar buffy cinnamon. Inner remiges distinc-tively edged black basally and cinnamon medially.

Tropical, subtropical zones. SURINAM; VENEZUELA; e COLOMBIA south to n and e BOLIVIA; Amazonian and e BRAZIL to Rio Grande do Sul; PARAGUAY; ARGEN-TINA to Buenos Aires. [Grenada I.] Open woods and clearings, parks.

Plate 49

126. GRAY-BREASTED FLYCATCHER

Empidonax griseipectus

5". Above olive gray, grayer on crown; double wing bars white. Throat grayish white; breast pale gray, sharply contrasting with white belly. Prominent eye ring white.

Tropical zone. Sw ECUADOR to Lambay-eque, PERU. Arid scrub.

127. FUSCOUS FLYCATCHER

Cnemotriccus fuscatus*

6". Upperparts and sides of head grayish brown to reddish or dark brown; lores and long superciliary buffy white. Throat grayish white, breast grayish to grayish brown; belly white to yellowish white, or even pale yellow. Two buffy cinnamon to clay color wing bars. Tail brown.

Tropical zone. GUIANAS, VENEZUELA, n COLOMBIA. Ne PERU, Amazonian BRA-ZIL and from Maranhão and Pernambuco s to Rio Grande do Sul and Mato Grosso; n and e BOLIVIA; PARAGUAY; ne ARGEN-TINA to Corrientes. Trinidad, Tobago. Dense undergrowth in forest, often swampy; plantations, capoeira, cerradão.

128. TUFTED FLYCATCHER

Mitrephanes phaeocercus*

5.2". Crested, eye ring pale. Upperparts and sides of head dull olive, crown browner (or above bright olive, 1). Throat and breast buffy olive (or yellowish olive, 1), belly yellow. (Two gray wing bars, wings and tail grayish, 1).

Tropical, subtropical zones. Nw COLOM-BIA and Atrato Valley; nw ECUADOR. Ne PERU south to n BOLIVIA, 1. [Mid. Amer.] Open woodland.

Plate 13

129. RUDDY-TAILED FLYCATCHER

Terenotriccus erythrurus *

4". Crown and nape olive gray to cinnamon brown, gradually turning to bright cinnamon on rump; closed wings and tail cinnamon rufous. Throat and sides of head grayish to cinnamon, rest of underparts bright cinnamon.

Tropical zone. GUIANAS; VENEZUELA, n and e COLOMBIA south to n BOLIVIA. Amazonian BRAZIL to n Mato Grosso. [Mid. Amer.] Lower stages of forest.

Plate 49

130. BLACK-BILLED FLYCATCHER

Aphanotriccus audax

5". Above olive green, tinged grayish on crown. Eye ring and line above lores white. Throat yellowish white, breast olive, belly yellow. Wings olive brown with two pale wing bars, basal portion of inner webs of inner remiges white. Tail olive brown. Rictal bristles prominent.

Tropical zone. Nw COLOMBIA in Córdoba. [E Panama.] Forest.

Plate 39

131. TAWNY-BREASTED FLYCATCHER

Myiobius villosus *

5.5". Above very dark olive, rump pale sulphur yellow, upper tail coverts and tail brownish black; semiconcealed yellow (or reddish brown, ♀) crest. Throat light grayish, breast and sides ochraceous brown, center of belly dull yellow. *Myiobius* has notably long, abundant rictal bristles.

Upper tropical and subtropical zones. Nw VENEZUELA, COLOMBIA, w and e ECUADOR south to nw BOLIVIA. [E Panama.] Forest trails, open woods.

132. SULPHUR-RUMPED FLYCATCHER

Myiobius barbatus *

5". Above olive green, rump sulphur yellow, upper tail coverts and tail blackish. Semiconcealed crown patch bright yellow, (or no crown patch, ♀). Throat yellowish white, breast olivaceous, belly yellow (or much like 131 but smaller, breast much brighter ochraceous, belly brighter yellow, 1).

Tropical zone. GUIANAS, VENEZUELA, e COLOMBIA and in Lebrija Valley south to e ECUADOR, e PERU; BRAZIL n of the

Amazon. BRAZIL s of the Amazon and in the east s to Santa Catarina, 1. COLOMBIA west of W Andes to w ECUADOR, 1. [Mid. Amer.] Forest.

133. BLACK-TAILED FLYCATCHER

Myiobius atricaudus *

5". Very like 132 but tail longer, as long as wing instead of shorter and much more rounded. Rump patch somewhat larger, breast tinged with buffy olive.

Tropical zone. VENEZUELA in n Bolívar. COLOMBIA west of E Andes. Sw and se ECUADOR; nw and e PERU s to Junín; BRAZIL s of the Amazon e to Maranhão and s to São Paulo. [Sw Costa Rica; Panama.] Forest.

Plate 38

134. ORNATE FLYCATCHER

Myiotriccus ornatus *

4.2" (or 4.7", 1). Lores and forehead white, crown black with concealed yellow crown patch, throat and sides of head gray. Back and breast olive, rest of underparts golden yellow. Rump yellow. Tail blackish with rufous base (or all light cinnamon rufous, 2).

Upper tropical and subtropical zones. COLOMBIA on the west slope of the E Andes and the north portion of the Central Andes, 1. W Andes to w ECUADOR. From se COLOMBIA s to Puno, se PERU, 2.

Plate 38

135. CINNAMON FLYCATCHER

Pyrrhomyias cinnamomea *

5". Concealed crest golden yellow. Upperparts brownish olive, narrow rump band cinnamon buff, upper tail coverts and tail dusky brown (or upperparts chestnut, narrow rump band cinnamon chestnut, tail chestnut with dark subterminal area, 1). Throat and breast chestnut rufous becoming cinnamon rufous on belly. Primaries blackish with chestnut inner webs basally, inner remiges chestnut on both webs basally forming a wing patch.

Subtropical zone. N VENEZUELA and Santa Marta Mts. of COLOMBIA, 1. Andes of COLOMBIA and ECUADOR s to BOLIVIA and nw ARGENTINA. Clearings in thick forest.

Plate 12

136. FLAVESCENT FLYCATCHER

*Myiophobus flavicans**

4.8". Above olive brown (or olive, 1), concealed coronal patch yellow to orange (♂ only). Eye ring yellow; below yellow, shaded olive on breast and ochraceous on sides (or no ochraceous shading, 1). Wings with ochraceous wing band. Tail grayish brown.

Subtropical zone. N VENEZUELA; Andes of COLOMBIA s through ECUADOR to e PERU (in Junín, 1). Forest.

137. ORANGE-CRESTED FLYCATCHER

*Myiophobus phoenicomitra**

Differs from 136 by darker and greener upperparts; paler, sulphur yellow underparts, and orange cinnamon (or yellow or mixed cinnamon and yellow, 1) coronal patch in both sexes.

Tropical zone. COLOMBIA on w slope of W Andes and nw ECUADOR, 1. E ECUADOR. Forest.

138. OLIVE-CHESTED FLYCATCHER

Myiophobus cryptoxanthus

5". Upperparts and tail earthy brown. Concealed coronal patch yellow (slightly indicated, ♀). Wings dark brown with double, buffy white wing bar. Throat whitish, upper breast grayish brown, lower breast and belly pale yellow, lower breast streaked grayish brown. Tail grayish brown.

Tropical zone. E ECUADOR; ne PERU in Loreto and s San Martín.

139. UNADORNED FLYCATCHER

Myiophobus inornatus

Very like 136 but upperparts more brownish olive, yellow of lowerparts paler and olive of breast streaked pale yellow. Wings with no or not very obvious wing bars and remiges edged cinnamon brown. Eye ring yellow, very well marked. Crown patch yellow in both sexes.

Subtropical zone. Se PERU; nw BOLIVIA.

140. HANDSOME FLYCATCHER

*Myiophobus pulcher**

4.2". Concealed crown patch orange (small or absent ♀). Upperparts, wings and tail olive brown to dull olive; wings black, double wing bar and outer margins of inner remiges buffy white (or cinnamon, 1). Throat and breast yellow, lightly (to very heavily, 1) washed with orange buff. Tail grayish brown.

Subtropical zone. COLOMBIA on E and Central Andes, 1; from w slope of W Andes south to w ECUADOR and in Cuzco and Puno, PERU. Forest, often in dense creepers.

Plate 49

141. ORANGE-BANDED FLYCATCHER

Myiophobus lintoni

4.8". Differs from 140 by larger size, longer tail, much darker and browner upperparts. Below more greenish yellow, no ochraceous shade on breast. Wing coverts with drop-shaped cinnamon mark on outer web of feathers instead of on both webs.

Subtropical zone. Inter-Andean plateau in s Azuay and n Loja, ECUADOR.

142. OCHRACEOUS-BREASTED FLYCATCHER

Myiophobus ochraceiventris

5.2". Above dark brownish olive; semi-concealed but extensive crown patch golden yellow. Throat, breast and sides of neck light orange ochraceous; belly bright yellow. Wings dusky with two white, ochraceous-tinged wing bars and edges to inner remiges. Tail dusky, edged dark olive brown. ♀: Differs from ♂ by chestnut rufous crown patch.

Subtropical zone. Central PERU from Junín to La Paz, BOLIVIA.

143. BRAN-COLORED FLYCATCHER

*Myiophobus fasciatus**

4.5"-5". Upperparts grayish brown to reddish brown; concealed crown patch yellow to orange rufous (absent or ill-marked in ♀). Double wing bar whitish to cinnamon. Throat whitish, breast streaked and strongly shaded grayish, or buff streaked dusky; belly plain white (or pale yellow, 1; or all underparts plain cinnamon, 2).

Tropical, subtropical zones. GUIANAS, n VENEZUELA, COLOMBIA w of E Andes, w ECUADOR. Coast and foothills of w PERU from Libertad to Arequipa and CHILE in Arica, 2. Central and e PERU from Moyobamba to Cuzco, 1. E and central BRAZIL from e Pará s to Rio Grande do Sul and Mato Grosso; PARAGUAY; e and n BOLIVIA; URUGUAY; ARGENTINA s to Córdoba and Buenos Aires. Trinidad. [Costa Rica, Panama.] Undergrowth in forest and savanna, bushy pastures, cerrado.

144. RORAIMAN FLYCATCHER

Myiophobus roraimae *

4″. Above olive brown to reddish brown with concealed orange rufous crest (♂ only). Wings dark brown, wing coverts rufous (or blackish with double cinnamon rufous bar, remiges margined rufous, 1). Throat and belly pale yellow, breast grayish olive. Tail brown, outer web of outermost feather somewhat rufescent.

Tropical, subtropical zones. W GUYANA; isolated mts. in Bolívar and Amazonas, VENEZUELA; se COLOMBIA in Vaupés. PERU in Puno, 1. Forest.

145. CLIFF FLYCATCHER

Hirundinea ferruginea *

7.2″. Upperparts, including rump, sooty brown; forehead and sides of head grizzled white (or upperparts sooty brown to brown, rump and upper tail coverts cinnamon to light chestnut, no white on head, 1). Underparts chestnut. Closed wing blackish with chestnut patch; outer remiges with inner web mostly chestnut, inner remiges with both webs chestnut basally. Tail feathers blackish, all but central pair with basal 2/3 of inner web chestnut (or tail chestnut with terminal black bar, 1).

Tropical zone. GUYANA; FRENCH GUIANA; VENEZUELA s of the Orinoco; immediately adjacent BRAZIL. E COLOMBIA. E PERU. BRAZIL s of the Amazon from Pará s to Paraná and Mato Grosso, PARAGUAY, n and e BOLIVIA, URUGUAY and ARGENTINA to La Rioja and Córdoba, 1. Ravines, rock faces, arid hillsides, towns, open woodland. Swallow-like in flight.

Plate 49

146. ROYAL FLYCATCHER

Onychorhynchus coronatus *

6.5″-7″. Unmistakable by enormous fan-shaped vermilion (or yellow, ♀) crest, the feathers over 1″ long terminating in black spot and fringed shiny greenish blue. In display the crest is raised and spread. Upperparts brown; tail and underparts mostly cinnamon.

Tropical zone. GUIANAS; VENEZUELA s of the Orinoco, and in extreme ne and nw; n and e COLOMBIA; e and w ECUADOR; ne and nw PERU; n BOLIVIA; Amazonian BRAZIL to Maranhão and from e Minas Gerais to Paraná. [Mid. Amer.] Savanna and forest undergrowth, often near streams.

Plate 38

Spadebills

Spadebills are squat, large headed little flycatchers with short tails and broad stubby flat bills.

147. WHITE-CRESTED SPADEBILL

Platyrinchus platyrhynchos *

4.5″. Crown and sides of head gray, long semiconcealed coronal streak and throat white. Back, wings and tail olive brown; breast and belly warm buffy to brownish buff.

Tropical zone. GUIANAS; s VENEZUELA. E ECUADOR south to n BOLIVIA. Amazonian BRAZIL to s Amazonas and Pará. Low bushes at forest edge.

148. RUSSET-WINGED SPADEBILL

Platyrinchus leucoryphus

5″. Above dull olivaceous; large coronal streak, spot before eye and eye ring white. Below white, sides of breast extensively olive brown. Wing coverts and inner remiges rufous, primaries edged rufous. Tail like back.

Se BRAZIL from Espírito Santo to São Paulo. E PARAGUAY. Forest.

149. WHITE-THROATED SPADEBILL

Platyrinchus mystaceus *

4″. Above olive brown, browner on wings and tail. Large coronal patch bright yellow (♂ only). Eye ring and center of ear coverts buffy white, streak above ear coverts and moustachial streak blackish brown. Throat buffy to white, breast and sides of body brownish, center of belly buff to white.

Upper tropical, lower subtropical zones.

GUIANAS, VENEZUELA and COLOMBIA south to n BOLIVIA, PARAGUAY, and ne ARGENTINA. E and central BRAZIL from Maranhão south to s Mato Grosso and Rio Grande do Sul. [Mid. Amer.] Forest undergrowth, second growth, thickets.

150. GOLDEN-CROWNED SPADEBILL

Platyrinchus coronatus *

4". Upperparts olive green. Crown yellow bordered laterally by chestnut; broad eyebrow black. Underparts primrose yellow. ♀: Crown chestnut bordered laterally by black, eyebrow buffy white, otherwise like ♂.

Tropical zone. GUIANAS; VENEZUELA s of the Orinoco; COLOMBIA; e and w ECUADOR; e PERU. Amazonian BRAZIL from rio Negro and rio Purús e to rio Xingú. Forest undergrowth.

151. CINNAMON-CRESTED SPADEBILL

Platyrinchus saturatus

4". Dark olive brown, crown patch orange cinnamon. Throat whitish, sides of breast olive brown, center of breast and underparts pale yellow. ♀: Similar but crown patch small or absent.

Tropical zone. GUIANAS; VENEZUELA s of the Orinoco; se COLOMBIA. Ne PERU; n Amazonian BRAZIL e to Amapá, and n Maranhão. Forest.

152. YELLOW-THROATED SPADEBILL

Platyrinchus flavigularis *

4". Crown and nape reddish brown; coronal patch white, feathers tipped black. Back, wings and tail olive. Throat yellow, breast olive, belly pale yellow.

Tropical zone. Nw VENEZUELA. COLOMBIA in Magdalena Valley. Ne ECUADOR. PERU from Amazonas to Junín. Forest undergrowth.

Plate 48

153. BROWNISH FLYCATCHER

Cnipodectes subbrunneus *

7". Upperparts and breast dark brown. Throat grayish; belly grayish white, tinged yellow. Wings blackish, coverts and remiges edged rufescent. Tail rufescent brown. Primaries stiff, twisted in adult males.

Tropical zone. Nw and se COLOMBIA. W ECUADOR. Ne PERU from Loreto to Huánuco. W BRAZIL e to rios Negro and Madeira. [Panama.] Lower forest growth.

Plate 49

Tolmomyias

The genus *Tolmomyias* forms a group of small to medium-sized, large-headed, flat-billed flycatchers resembling each other in their olive yellow coloration. They are difficult to tell apart.

154. YELLOW-OLIVE FLYCATCHER

Tolmomyias sulphurescens *

6". Largest species. Olive above with crown and nape olive to olive gray to gray; line above lores white. Underparts olive yellow, yellow on center of belly; in some races throat grayish (or with throat gray, breast grayish olive, 1). Wings blackish, remiges edged olive yellow, double wing bar yellowish white or yellow.

Tropical, subtropical zones. Generally distributed e of Andes to e BOLIVIA, n ARGENTINA and BRAZIL to Rio Grande do Sul. West of E Andes in COLOMBIA, 1. W ECUADOR to nw PERU. Trinidad. [Mid. Amer.] Upper levels of forest and light woodland.

Plate 49

155. YELLOW-MARGINED FLYCATCHER

Tolmomyias assimilis *

5.5". Very similar to 154, but distinguished by white outer webs on outer primaries just below wing coverts, which form an inconspicuous speculum. In some races the wing bars have an ochraceous tinge.

Tropical, subtropical zones. GUIANAS; VENEZUELA s of the Orinoco; COLOMBIA; nw and e ECUADOR; e PERU; nw BOLIVIA; Amazonian BRAZIL south to sw Amazonas, n Mato Grosso and n Maranhão. [Costa Rica; Panama.] Forest.

156. GRAY-CROWNED FLYCATCHER

Tolmomyias poliocephalus *

5": Much like preceding two but much

smaller; darker above, with crown and nape dark slaty gray.

Tropical zone. GUIANAS; VENEZUELA s of the Orinoco; COLOMBIA east of E Andes south to n BOLIVIA; nw and s Amazonian BRAZIL e to rio Negro and Maranhão, and in the east s to Bahía and Espírito Santo. Lower stages of forest, savanna, plantations.

157. YELLOW-BREASTED FLYCATCHER

Tolmomyias flaviventris *

5". Bright yellowish olive above with no grayish tinge on crown; below bright olive yellow, clear yellow in center of belly; breast in some races washed olive or gamboge yellow. Lores yellowish.

Tropical zone. GUYANA; SURINAM; VENEZUELA; n and e COLOMBIA; e ECUADOR; e PERU; n BOLIVIA; Amazonian and e BRAZIL east to e Pará and Maranhão and from Pernambuco to e Minas Gerais and Rio de Janeiro. Trinidad and Tobago. Mangroves, swampy woodland, plantations, capoeira, cerradão.

Rhynchocyclus

Rhynchocyclus differs from *Tolmomyias* by being larger, breast obscurely streaked, and bill even broader and flatter.

158. OLIVACEOUS FLATBILL

Rhynchocyclus olivaceus *

6.5". Above olive green; tail grayish, edged green. Throat and breast light grayish olive, streaked pale yellow; belly pale yellow. Wing coverts and remiges edged pale yellow.

Tropical zone. GUIANAS; VENEZUELA; n and e COLOMBIA south to n BOLIVIA. E Amazonian BRAZIL, and from Maranhão and Pernambuco s to Rio de Janeiro and e Minas Gerais. [Central and e Panama.] Swampy forest and savanna.

159. EYE-RINGED FLATBILL

Rhynchocyclus brevirostris *

Much like 158 but upperparts and breast darker and greener; lower breast and belly darker yellow, streaked olive on lower breast; wing coverts edged tawny olive;

remiges edged olive, tawny olive on distal part of inner remiges; tail somewhat browner. Eye ring white.

Tropical zone. W COLOMBIA from n Chocó south to nw ECUADOR, [Mid. Amer.] Middle stages of forest.

160. FULVOUS-BREASTED FLATBILL

Rhynchocyclus fulvipectus

6.8". Above olive; throat and breast tawny ochraceous, belly yellow. Wing coverts and inner remiges broadly margined ochraceous.

Tropical, subtropical zones. COLOMBIA west of E Andes to nw ECUADOR. E ECUADOR south to n BOLIVIA. Forest.

Plate 38

161. RUFOUS-TAILED FLATBILL

Ramphotrigon ruficauda

6.5". Above dull olive, tail bright rufous. Wing coverts with two broad rufous bars, remiges broadly edged rufous. Throat and breast grayish olive, pale-streaked; lower breast and belly yellow, streaked olive; under tail coverts pale rufous. Bill in this genus narrower than in *Rhynchocyclus*.

Tropical zone. GUIANAS; central and s VENEZUELA; e COLOMBIA. E PERU; n BOLIVIA. Amazonian BRAZIL and on upper rio Paraguai. Forest undergrowth, savanna.

162. DUSKY-TAILED FLATBILL

Ramphotrigon fuscicauda

Differs from 161 by blackish wings and tail, narrowly edged buffy citrine; wing coverts tipped cinnamon forming two wing bars. Underparts dull yellow, streaked dusky.

Tropical zone. Ne ECUADOR; e PERU; n BOLIVIA. Forest undergrowth.

163. LARGE-HEADED FLATBILL

Ramphotrigon megacephala *

6". Above olive; eye ring and narrow eyebrow yellowish white surmounted by blackish brown stripe. Wings blackish with two broad cinnamon wing bands. Throat yellowish, breast brownish olive, rest of underparts yellow.

Tropical zone. N VENEZUELA and in s Amazonas; e COLOMBIA. PERU in se Loreto; BOLIVIA in Beni. BRAZIL in upper rio Negro region, in w Amazonas, and from e Minas Gerais to São Paulo. Ne ARGENTINA; e PARAGUAY. Forest undergrowth, bamboo thickets.

Plate 13

Tody-Flycatchers

Todirostrum forms a group of very small flycatchers with rather long, rather wide flat bills, and narrow tails. They inhabit shrubby places, gardens and plantations and sometimes the edges of mangroves.

164. BLACK-HEADED TODY-FLYCATCHER

Todirostrum nigriceps

3.7". Top and sides of head glossy black; throat white. Back olive yellow; underparts bright yellow. Wings black with yellow double bar, remiges edged yellow. Tail black, feathers edged yellow.

Tropical zone. Nw VENEZUELA w to lower río Atrato in Pacific COLOMBIA. W ECUADOR. [Costa Rica; Panama.] Forest and scrub.

Plate 38

165. PAINTED TODY-FLYCATCHER

Todirostrum chrysocrotaphum *

3.5". Distinguishable from 164 by broad yellow postocular stripe and yellow instead of white throat (or with white throat and black malar streak, 1; or all yellow below, spotted black on sides of neck and across breast, 2; or spotted like 2 but no yellow postocular stripe, 3). (See also 169)

Tropical zone. GUIANAS, e and s VENEZUELA and immediately adjacent BRAZIL to Amapá, 3. E COLOMBIA, BRAZIL on río Uaupés and lower río Negro, ne PERU, 2. Ne BRAZIL s of the Amazon from río Tapajós to Maranhão, 1. Extreme n PERU south to n BOLIVIA and in BRAZIL in w Amazonas to río Negro.

166. GOLDEN-WINGED TODY-FLYCATCHER

Todirostrum calopterum *

3.5". Top and sides of head black, throat white, rest of underparts bright yellow. Back olive (or black, 1); lesser wing coverts chestnut, middle coverts yellow, inner remiges broadly edged yellowish white. Tail black.

Tropical zone. Se COLOMBIA, e ECUADOR. E PERU, 1.

167. GRAY-HEADED TODY-FLYCATCHER

Todirostrum poliocephalum

3.7". Forecrown slaty gray becoming paler posteriorly. Large loral spot bright yellow. Back bright yellowish green; below bright yellow. Double wing bar and edges to remiges yellow. Rectrices grayish brown, edged yellowish green.

Tropical zone. Se BRAZIL from e Minas Gerais to Santa Catarina. Forest edge, gardens, towns.

168. COMMON TODY-FLYCATCHER

Todirostrum cinereum *

3.7". Crown blackish, often with a few white spots in center. Back gray, to olive gray to olive. Underparts bright yellow (throat white, 1). Remiges and wing coverts edged yellow. Rectrices black with broad white tips.

Tropical, lower subtropical zones. GUIANAS, VENEZUELA, COLOMBIA, e and w ECUADOR (in w Ecuador and sw Colombia, 1); nw and e PERU; n and e BOLIVIA. BRAZIL virtually throughout s to Paraná and s Mato Grosso. [Mid. Amer.] Clearings, scattered trees, tree lined streams, arid country, campos, parks, wet cerrado.

169. SPOTTED TODY-FLYCATCHER

Todirostrum maculatum *

4". Crown blackish to leaden gray, spotted black; back bright olive green. Throat white; rest of underparts yellow, spotted with black except on center of belly. Remiges, wing coverts and rectrices black, edged yellow. Not unlike 165(3) except for white throat.

Tropical zone. GUIANAS; delta of the Orinoco, VENEZUELA; Amazonian BRAZIL; e PERU; n BOLIVIA. Trinidad. Often in mangroves, along creeks, gardens, bushes, campos.

170. SMOKY-FRONTED TODY-FLYCATCHER

Todirostrum fumifrons *

3.5″. Forehead smoky grayish, ocular region buffy white; crown and back olive green. Throat white; rest of underparts pale yellow, brighter on center of abdomen. Wings and tail blackish, feathers edged olive yellow, two prominent yellowish white wing bars.

Tropical zone. SURINAM; FRENCH GUIANA. E BRAZIL from rio Xingú to Maranhão and s Bahía. Bushes, edge of savanna.

171. BLACK-AND-WHITE TODY-FLYCATCHER

Todirostrum capitale *

3.7″. Upperparts, sides of head and neck and the breast black. Center of throat and rest of underparts white (with black pectoral band, 1). Wings and tail black. Bend of wing and under wing coverts yellow, inner remiges edged yellow. Tail with white tip to outermost feather. ♀: Crown chestnut, back olive. Sides of throat and breast gray, center of throat and belly white. Wings olive, bend of wing and inner remiges yellow. Tail grayish with dusky terminal area.

Tropical zone. Se COLOMBIA to ne PERU. Sw BRAZIL in nw Rondonia, 1. Forest.

172. WHITE-CHEEKED TODY-FLYCATCHER

Todirostrum albifacies

Superficially like ♀ of 171 but sides of head white instead of gray, conspicuous black nuchal collar, and primaries and rectrices with olive edges. ♂: Unknown.

Known from a ♀ from mouth of río Colorado, Madre de Dios, se PERU.

173. RUDDY TODY-FLYCATCHER

Todirostrum russatum

4″. Forecrown, sides of head, throat, breast and thighs dull orange rufous; belly gray. Back dark olive. Wings with two rufous bars, remiges edged olive yellow.

Subtropical zone. VENEZUELA in se Bolívar and immediately adjacent n BRAZIL. Forest.

174. OCHRE-FACED TODY-FLYCATCHER

Todirostrum plumbeiceps *

3.8″. Crown dark gray to olive gray; lores, sides of head, eyebrow and throat cinnamon buff (or pale buff, 1); patch on lower throat white, breast and sides gray (or buffy olivaceous, 1); center of belly white. Back olive; wings blackish with two yellowish to buff bars. Rectrices grayish brown, edged olive.

Subtropical zone. Se PERU; n and e BOLIVIA; nw ARGENTINA. S BRAZIL in Mato Grosso and in the east from se Minas Gerais to São Paulo; from Paraná to Rio Grande do Sul and ne ARGENTINA, 1.

175. RUSTY-FRONTED TODY-FLYCATCHER

Todirostrum latirostre *

4″. Upperparts olive green, darker and browner on crown; lores and ocular region ochraceous. Throat white, faintly streaked gray; breast and sides of body clouded with olive; belly white. Wings black with two well-marked ochraceous wing bands, remiges conspicuously edged light yellow. Tail grayish, edged olive.

Tropical zone. Se COLOMBIA to n BOLIVIA; Amazonian BRAZIL south to w São Paulo and PARAGUAY. Scrub.

176. SLATE-HEADED TODY-FLYCATCHER

Todirostrum sylvia *

4.3″. Upperparts olive green, crown and nape dark gray, lores and ocular ring white to buffy. Throat and breast pale gray, palest on throat; belly white, sides of body tinged greenish yellow. Wings black; bend of wing, two wing bands and narrow edges to remiges yellow. Rectrices grayish brown, edged olive.

Tropical zone. GUYANA; FRENCH GUIANA; VENEZUELA; COLOMBIA s to Valle and Meta. N BRAZIL in Roraima and from se Pará to Maranhão and Piauí. [Mid. Amer.] Low, tangled thickets.

177. FORK-TAILED PYGMY-TYRANT

Ceratotriccus furcatus

4″. Unmistakable. Tail forked, outer

feathers curving outward; tail gray, feathers edged olive basally with broad black subapical band and diagonal silky white tip. Head and throat dull rufous, latter edged white below; breast and sides gray, belly white. Back olive green. ♀: Like ♂ but tail much less forked.

Se BRAZIL in Espírito Santo, Rio de Janeiro and e São Paulo.

178. SOUTHERN BENTBILL

Oncostoma olivaceum *

3.5". Uniform olive above; throat and breast dull olive yellow, faintly streaked gray; belly dull, pale yellow. Wing coverts and inner remiges edged olive yellow. Bill very thick with high decurved ridge.

Tropical zone. N COLOMBIA from Santa Marta region w to Chocó. [E Panama.] Plantations, open woodland near small streams.

Plate 49

Idioptilon

Idioptilon comprises a large group of small flycatchers differing slightly from *Todirostrum* by shorter, narrower, more pointed bills. They inhabit the lower stages of humid forest. Perhaps best included in *Todirostrum*.

179. HANGNEST TODY-TYRANT

Idioptilon nidipendulum *

3.6" (or 4.2", 1). Above uniform olive green. Wing coverts and remiges edged olive, bend of wing pale yellow. Throat and breast pale olive gray, belly creamy white.

Se BRAZIL in Bahía; in Rio de Janeiro and São Paulo, 1.

180. BUFF-THROATED TODY-TYRANT

Idioptilon rufigulare

4.7". Upperparts olive green, eye ring buff. Breast and sides of neck dull, light buffy brown, indistinctly streaked gray; belly white. Under wing coverts creamy yellow. Wings unbanded.

Upper tropical zone. Se PERU; nw BOLIVIA.

181. STRIPE-NECKED TODY-TYRANT

Idioptilon striaticolle *

4.4". Above like 180, tail shorter. Throat yellowish white, sides of breast olive, rest of underparts bright yellow, throat and breast sharply streaked black.

Tropical zone. E COLOMBIA (Meta). N PERU; Amazonian and central BRAZIL s of the Amazon east to n Maranhão and s to Mato Grosso, Goiás and Bahía; n BOLIVIA (Beni).

182. YUNGAS TODY-TYRANT

Idioptilon spodiops

4.2". Above olive green, preocular area grayish buff surmounted by narrow, inconspicuous black line. Neck, throat and breast grayish olive, streaked whitish; paler area at base of throat; belly yellowish white. Wings dusky with two narrow olive wing bars, inner remiges margined olive. Rectrices edged olive.

Upper tropical zone. N BOLIVIA in La Paz and Cochabamba.

183. ZIMMER'S TODY-TYRANT

Idioptilon aenigma

4". Above dark olive green, crown obscurely streaked dusky brown. Chin and upper throat whitish with prominent dusky shaft streaks; lower throat, breast and sides yellowish olive buff indistinctly streaked dusky; center of belly yellowish white. Wings with two broad yellowish white bars. Tail dusky, edged olive.

Tropical zone. E bank of lower rio Tapajós, BRAZIL.

184. BUFF-BREASTED TODY-TYRANT

Idioptilon mirandae *

4". Above olive, crown duller washed buff, forehead light buffy brown. Sides of head, throat and breast bright, light fawn, paler on belly and pale yellow on flanks; no wing bars (or much browner above, yellowish buff below, belly strongly yellow; two pronounced buffy wing bars, 1).

E BRAZIL in n Ceará, Pernambuco and Alagoas; in ne Santa Catarina, 1. Caatinga.

185. PEARLY-VENTED TODY-TYRANT

Idioptilon margaritaceiventer *

4.2". Above dull olive, grayer on crown (or

dull brown above, 1), lores and ocular ring white. Throat and breast white conspicuously streaked gray; belly silky white. Bend of wing and under wing coverts pale yellow; two whitish to gray wing bars. Remiges and rectrices dusky, edged olive.

Tropical zone. Arid littoral of VENEZUELA from Margarita I. w to Santa Marta region and lower Magdalena Valley, COLOMBIA. Central and s PERU; e BOLIVIA; e and central BRAZIL from Maranhão south to n São Paulo; PARAGUAY; ne ARGENTINA. Forest, cerrado.

186. BLACK-THROATED TODY-TYRANT

Idioptilon granadense *

4". Back bright olive green, lores and ocular region white (or buff, 1). Throat and sides of head black, patch at base of throat white, breast gray, belly white. Bend of wing yellow, inner remiges and rectrices edged olive.

Subtropical to temperate zone. VENEZUELA in Distrito Federal, 1; in Zulia and Táchira. COLOMBIA in Santa Marta Mts., 1; in the three Andean ranges s through e ECUADOR to Amazonas and Cuzco, PERU. In Puno, PERU, 1. Humid forest.

Plate 38

187. WHITE-EYED TODY-TYRANT

Idioptilon zosterops *

4.2". Underparts olive green. Supraloral streak and eye ring white. Throat and breast whitish, streaked gray or olivaceous; belly white, tinged greenish yellow at sides. Wings blackish with two narrow yellowish wing bars, remiges narrowly edged pale yellow. Tail grayish brown, feathers edged olive.

Tropical zone. SURINAM; FRENCH GUIANA; sw VENEZUELA; se COLOMBIA south to n BOLIVIA. BRAZIL s of the Amazon to Pernambuco and n of it to nw Pará. Forest.

188. EYE-RINGED TODY-TYRANT

Idioptilon orbitatum

4.5". Broad eye ring white, dusky preocular spot. Above olive; throat white, streaked dusky; breast grayish brown, streaked yellowish; center of belly yellow. Tarsi flesh color. No wing bars, inner remiges broadly

edged white giving effect of stripe on each side of back.

Se BRAZIL in Espírito Santo and e Minas Gerais to São Paulo.

189. BOAT-BILLED TODY-TYRANT

Microcochlearius josephinae

4.7". Upperparts, wings and tail olive green. Lores and upper throat grayish, breast olive shading into pale yellow on lower breast and abdomen. Under tail coverts ochraceous yellow. No wing bars. Bill rather long and broad.

Tropical zone. GUYANA on the Supenaan River. Known from one specimen. (Possibly better included in *Todirostrum*.)

190. SNETHLAGE'S TODY-TYRANT

Snethlagea minor *

3.7". Above dull olive. Throat and breast pale yellowish, streaked grayish olive; belly yellowish white. Wings with two yellowish white bars and edges to remiges. ♀: Differs from ♂ by slightly smaller size, brighter and greener upperparts, yellower wing bars and belly. Bill proportionally broader than in *Idioptilon*, and nostrils round and exposed.

Tropical zone. Sw SURINAM; Amazonian BRAZIL n of the Amazon on lower rio Negro, south of it from rio Jurúa to rio Tocantins and south to n Rondonia and w Mato Grosso. Forest.

Plate 13

191. RUFOUS-CROWNED TODY-TYRANT

Poecilotriccus ruficeps *

4". Crown rufous chestnut bordered behind by black line (also at sides, 1), nape gray. Back bright olive green. Cheeks rufous buff (or white, 1), bordered below by black moustachial streak; throat white (or no moustachial streak, throat rufous buff like cheeks, 2). Upper breast white separated from bright yellow belly by ill-marked dusky line. Wing coverts black with two well-marked yellowish white to buffy white bars.

Upper tropical and subtropical zones. Nw VENEZUELA, E Andes of COLOMBIA and e COLOMBIA, 1; Central Andes and upper

Cauca Valley, w Nariño and nw ECUADOR, 2. N PERU. Forest.

Plate 13

192. BLACK-CHESTED TYRANT

Taeniotriccus andrei *

4.6". Forehead and sides of head chestnut, throat cinnamon buff. Back, breast and tail black (or tail dark olivaceous, 1); belly gray (or olive gray, 1), thighs black. Wings black; bend of wing, under wing coverts, base of remiges which form conspicuous band (or no band, 1), and the outer webs of innermost tertials yellowish white. Bill black; base of mandible, feet and legs flesh color. ♀: Head and wings as in ♂; back olive; breast gray, center of belly white, sides of belly and under tail coverts yellowish olive.

Tropical zone. VENEZUELA in n and central Bolívar and Delta Amacuro, 1. BRAZIL on lower rio Tapajós. Forest.

193. SCALE-CRESTED PYGMY-TYRANT

Lophotriccus pileatus *

4.2". Head crested, feathers black broadly edged tawny chestnut giving scaled look; back olive green. Sides of neck and the breast grayish; underparts whitish to pale yellow, conspicuously streaked gray on throat and breast. Wings with two narrow, inconspicuous olive bars.

Upper tropical and subtropical zones. N VENEZUELA from Aragua w to Andes of COLOMBIA; e and w ECUADOR south to e PERU and sw BRAZIL. [Costa Rica; Panama.] Forest.

Plate 39

194. DOUBLE-BANDED PYGMY-TYRANT

Lophotriccus vitiosus *

Much like 193 with yellow, gray-streaked underparts but crest feathers edged pale gray (or yellow, 1) instead of tawny chestnut.

Tropical zone. GUIANAS. Se COLOMBIA; e ECUADOR; e PERU; BRAZIL n of the Amazon. S of the Amazon from the Solimões to upper rio Juruá and ne Mato Grosso, 1. Forest undergrowth.

195. LONG-CRESTED PYGMY-TYRANT

Lophotriccus eulophotes

Differs from 194 by unbanded wings, somewhat darker green back; white, dark-streaked underparts yellowish only on flanks, and conspicuous buffy eye ring.

BRAZIL on rio Purús (Hiutanaã). Se PERU (Balta). Bamboo thickets.

196. HELMETED PYGMY-TYRANT

Colopteryx galeatus

4". Head crested; feathers black, pointed, edged olive. Back olive. Upper throat and breast olive, streaked whitish. White patch at lower throat; belly white, tinged yellowish. Wings and tail dusky; wing coverts, remiges and rectrices edged olive.

Tropical zone. GUIANAS; VENEZUELA; COLOMBIA e of Andes. E Amazonian BRAZIL from rios Negro and Tapajós east to n Maranhão. Undergrowth in forests and plantations.

Plate 13

197. PALE-EYED PYGMY-TYRANT

Atalotriccus pilaris *

3.7". Uncrested, but otherwise much like 196 (or with crown gray in contrast to back, 1); underparts whiter. Sides of head buff. Four outer primaries very short, narrow, pointed. Iris yellowish white or pale gray.

Tropical zone. GUYANA; VENEZUELA s of the Orinoco, 1. N VENEZUELA w to Córdoba, COLOMBIA. [Pacific Panama.] Thickets, forest undergrowth, often near streams.

Plate 12

198. EARED PYGMY-TYRANT

Myiornis auricularis *

3.5" (or 3.2", 1). Crown and back olive green, crown tinged brown. Broad (or narrow, 1) postocular streak and nape pale gray, sides of head cinnamon buff (or buff, 1). Very conspicuous auricular spot black (or less conspicuous and gray, 1). Upper throat white, streaked black; lower throat white; rest of underparts bright yellow (or white, sides and under tail coverts yellow, 1), streaked dusky on breast. Double wing bar and edges of inner remiges greenish yellow. Tail feathers edged olive.

Tropical zone. Central PERU in Huánuco

and Junín, n BOLIVIA from La Paz to Santa Cruz, 1. E PARAGUAY; e BRAZIL from Bahía to Rio Grande do Sul; ne ARGENTINA in Misiones. Forest undergrowth, forest edge.

199. SHORT-TAILED PYGMY-TYRANT

Myiornis ecaudatus *

2.9″. Lores and conspicuous eye ring white. Crown gray (or black, 1). Back bright olive green, tail very short (.4″). Underparts white, yellowish green at sides (or throat white gradually changing to yellowish green on breast and belly, 1).

Tropical zone. Pacific COLOMBIA south to nw ECUADOR, 1. E of Andes from GUIANAS to e COLOMBIA and south to e PERU, n BOLIVIA, Amazonian BRAZIL. Trinidad. [E Costa Rica; Panama.] Shrubbery and open forest.

Plate 49

200. BRONZE-OLIVE PYGMY-TYRANT

Pseudotriccus pelzelni *

4.6″. Upperparts, wings and tail dark, dull olive green; throat, breast and sides of body dull olive; center of belly creamy yellowish (or much browner throughout, dark bronzy brown above, crown darker, throat whitish, breast and sides reddish olive brown, center of belly pale creamy yellowish, 1). Rictal bristles long.

Upper tropical and subtropical zones. Pacific COLOMBIA south to w ECUADOR, 1. E COLOMBIA s to Puno, PERU. [E Panama.] Upper levels of open forest, lianas.

Plate 12

201. HAZEL-FRONTED PYGMY-TYRANT

Pseudotriccus simplex

4.3″. Like 200 but forecrown and sides of head hazel brown, as are edges of remiges, rectrices and thighs.

Subtropical zone. Se PERU (Puno) and nw BOLIVIA (La Paz).

202. RUFOUS-HEADED PYGMY-TYRANT

Pseudotriccus ruficeps

4.5″. Head and throat rufous chestnut; wings, tail and upper tail coverts chestnut. Back dark olive, breast and sides pale olive, center of abdomen creamy yellow.

Subtropical to temperate zone. Andes of COLOMBIA south through e and w ECUADOR to nw BOLIVIA. Forest.

Plate 39

203. DRAB-BREASTED PYGMY-TYRANT

Hemitriccus diops

4.7″. Conspicuous white preocular spot. Above olive green including edges of remiges and rectrices; below gray with slight pinkish cast, base of throat and center of belly white.

Se BRAZIL from Bahía s to Rio Grande do Sul; e PARAGUAY; ne ARGENTINA in Misiones. Forest undergrowth.

204. BROWN-BREASTED PYGMY-TYRANT

Hemitriccus obsoletus *

Differs from 203 by brownish olive upperparts, buffy preocular spot; buffier sides of head, throat and breast; and buffy white instead of white base of throat and center of belly. Flanks and under tail coverts buffy yellow.

Se BRAZIL in mts. of Rio de Janeiro, se São Paulo, Paraná and Rio Grande do Sul.

205. FLAMMULATED PYGMY-TYRANT

Hemitriccus flammulatus *

Differs from 203 by broader bill, grayish preocular stripe, and white-streaked throat and breast.

Tropical zone. Se PERU, n BOLIVIA and immediately adjacent Mato Grosso, BRAZIL.

Plate 12

206. SOUTHERN BRISTLE-TYRANT

Pogonotriccus eximius

4.5″. Extensive preocular area, eye ring and line behind eye white; sides of crown gray, center of crown and entire back bright olive green. Ear coverts yellowish green, bordered behind by black crescent. Underparts yellowish green becoming bright yellow on belly. Wing coverts, remiges and rectrices edged olive yellow.

Se BRAZIL from Minas Gerais to Rio Grande do Sul and Mato Grosso; e PARAGUAY; ne ARGENTINA in Misiones. Forest.

207. MARBLED-FACED BRISTLE-TYRANT

Pogonotriccus ophthalmicus *

4.8''. Crown gray; lores, sides of head, mystacial region and upper throat marbled gray and white; ear coverts mostly black. Back bright olive green; breast pale olive, rather sharply defined from yellow breast and belly (or underparts mainly grayish white, 1). Wings with pale yellow double bar. (See 299)

Subtropical zone. N VENEZUELA; central COLOMBIA south through e and w ECUADOR to Junín, PERU; from Puno to La Paz and Cochabamba, BOLIVIA, 1. Forest.

Plate 49

208. ECUADOREAN BRISTLE-TYRANT

Pogonotriccus gualaquizae

4.5''. Crown grayish olive. Supraloral streak and eye ring white. Ear coverts pale yellowish surrounded by dusky line reaching to below eye. Back dull olive. Throat and breast pale olivaceous white, belly pale yellow. Wing coverts with two conspicuous pale yellow bands. Margins of tail feathers dull olive.

Subtropical zone. E ECUADOR s to San Martín, PERU.

209. VARIEGATED BRISTLE-TYRANT

Pogonotriccus poecilotis *

Much like 208 but instantly separable from it and any other *Pogonotriccus* by two very broad bright ochraceous wing bars.

Subtropical zone. Nw VENEZUELA; n COLOMBIA from w slope of E Andes westward and south to sw Cauca. E and nw ECUADOR. N PERU s to Pasco. Forest.

210. SPECTACLED BRISTLE-TYRANT

Pogonotriccus orbitalis

4.2''. Crown gray, back dull olive. Conspicuous eye ring white. Below yellow. Wing coverts with two well-marked yellowish white bars, outer webs of inner remiges broadly whitish.

Subtropical zone. E ECUADOR. Central PERU from s San Martín to Puno. N BOLIVIA in Cochabamba.

211. VENEZUELAN BRISTLE-TYRANT

Pogonotriccus venezuelanus

4.2''. Crown grayish, forehead and lores yellowish, black crescent on hindpart of ear coverts. Below lemon yellow. Wing coverts with terminal yellowish white spots forming two wing bars.

Lower subtropical zone. Coastal mts. of VENEZUELA from Dist. Federal to Carabobo, and in interior in Arauca. Forest.

212. YELLOW-BELLIED BRISTLE-TYRANT

Pogonotriccus flaviventris

4.7''. Lores, short eyebrow and eye ring rufous. Crown and back dull olive green. Wing coverts tipped pale yellow forming two conspicuous wing bars. Underparts clear, light yellow. Tail feathers edged olive.

Upper tropical zone. Coastal mts. in Dist. Federal, in the interior chain in Miranda, and the Andes of Mérida, VENEZUELA. Forest.

213. BAY-RINGED TYRANNULET

Leptotriccus sylviolus

4.5''. Lores and ocular region chestnut. Upperparts bright yellowish green, edges of wings and tail feathers bright olive; underparts white; throat, breast and sides washed greenish yellow. Bill small, black.

Se BRAZIL from Espírito Santo to Santa Catarina; se PARAGUAY; ne ARGENTINA in Misiones. Forest.

214. OLIVE-GREEN TYRANNULET

Phylloscartes virescens

5''. Above dull olive. Lores dusky, eye ring yellowish white. Throat grayish yellow; rest of underparts pale, dull yellow flammulated with olive on breast. Double wing bar pale yellowish white.

Tropical zone. GUIANAS. Forest treetops.

215. MOTTLE-CHEEKED TYRANNULET

Phylloscartes ventralis *

5''. Above dull olive. Lores dusky, eye ring pale yellow. Throat grayish yellow, rest of underparts dull yellow flammulated with olive on breast. Double wing bar pale yellow.

Subtropical zone. Central PERU from San

Martín south to n and e BOLIVIA; PARA-
GUAY; ne and nw ARGENTINA; e BRA-
ZIL from Minas Gerais s to Rio Grande do
Sul and URUGUAY. Forest treetops.

Plate 13

216. CHAPMAN'S TYRANNULET

Phylloscartes chapmani *

4.5''. Forehead and conspicuous eyebrow
white, mottled blackish olive. Chin light
gray; below pale greenish yellow, yellower
in center of abdomen. Broad double wing
bar ochraceous.

Subtropical zone. VENEZUELA on isolated
mts. in Bolívar and Amazonas. Forest treetops.

217. BLACK-FRONTED TYRANNULET

Phylloscartes nigrifrons

5.5''. Broad frontal band black, slightly
bordered white in front and behind; cap
gray; back drab olive green. Throat and
breast gray, flammulated with white; belly
white, under tail coverts pale yellow. Wing
coverts black with two yellowish white
bands.

Upper tropical and subtropical zones. VEN-
EZUELA on isolated mts. of Bolívar and
Amazonas. Forest treetops.

218. OUSTALET'S TYRANNULET

Phylloscartes oustaleti

4.7''. Conspicuous eye ring yellow, auricular
spot black. Above olive green; below pale
yellowish, tinged olive. Tertials with suggested apical spot. No wing bars. Tail
brownish, broadly edged yellowish olive.

Se BRAZIL from Espírito Santo to Santa
Catarina. Forest treetops.

219. SERRA DO MAR TYRANNULET

Phylloscartes difficilis

5''. Above bright yellowish green, eye ring
white, sides of head mottled and streaked
whitish. Throat and breast pale grayish,
mottled white; abdomen white; under tail
coverts pale yellow. No wing bars. Wings
and tail edged yellowish green.

BRAZIL in coastal mts. from Espírito Santo
to Rio Grande do Sul.

220. SÃO PAULO TYRANNULET

Phylloscartes paulistus

4.5''. Frontal band and eyebrow yellowish;
auriculars dusky. Above light olive green;
below uniform deep yellow. No wing bars.

Se BRAZIL from Espírito Santo s to Santa
Catarina and west to se Mato Grosso and e
PARAGUAY.

221. RUFOUS-BROWED TYRANNULET

Phylloscartes superciliaris *

5''. Crown grayish black to gray, lores and
short eyebrow rufous, sides of head mottled
gray and white. Throat and breast pale gray,
belly lemon yellow to white. Back olive
green; wings and tail feathers edged olive
green, no wing bars.

Tropical, subtropical zones. COLOMBIA
("Bogotá") and probably humid forest in
Caribbean lowlands; nw VENEZUELA.
[Costa Rica; Panama.] Forest.

222. MINAS GERAIS TYRANNULET

Phylloscartes roquettei

4''. Forehead, lores and ocular region rufous. Above bright olive green; below bright
yellow, clouded with olive on breast. Wing
coverts with two pale yellow bands.

Known only from Brejo Januaria, Minas
Gerais, BRAZIL.

223. YELLOW TYRANNULET

Capsiempis flaveola *

4.5''. Above olive to olive citrine, to brownish olive; eyebrow yellow (or white, 1).
Underparts bright yellow with ochraceous
tinge on breast. Double wing bars yellowish.
Wing and tail feathers margined olive yellow. Tail rounded rather than square as in
Phylloscartes (cf. 226).

Tropical zone. GUIANAS, VENEZUELA, n
and e COLOMBIA (in Magdalena Valley, 1)
s to BOLIVIA, PARAGUAY, ne ARGEN-
TINA, north-central and se BRAZIL. [Nica-
ragua to Panama.] Shrubbery, campos, dense
capoeira. Behaves like a vireo.

Plate 13

224. TAWNY-CROWNED PYGMY-TYRANT

Euscarthmus meloryphus *

4.5'' (or 4'', 1). Above brown with semiconcealed ochraceous orange crest; lores and

sides of head buffy white (or cinnamon buff, 1). Underparts dirty white. Wings and tail like back (or with two buffy wing bars, 1). Tail rounded.

Tropical zone. N VENEZUELA and ne Bolívar; COLOMBIA in Santa Marta and Magdalena Valley. E PERU from Marañón Valley south to n and e BOLIVIA, PARAGUAY, n ARGENTINA. E BRAZIL from Maranhão s to Paraná and Mato Grosso and URUGUAY. West of Andes from sw ECUADOR to Lima, PERU, 1. Near ground in dry scrub or in swampy woods, cerrado.

Plate 13

225. RUFOUS-SIDED PYGMY-TYRANT

Euscarthmus rufomarginatus *

4.8". Above earthy brown, feathers of center of crown edged cinnamon basally. Throat white, rest of underparts pale yellow, deepening to ochraceous on sides and under tail coverts. Wings with two ochraceous bars. Tail longer, more graduated than in 224. Tail feathers very narrow.

SURINAM (Sipaliwini). E BRAZIL from Maranhão to São Paulo and s Mato Grosso. Open cerrado, savanna.

226. DINELLI'S DORADITO

Pseudocolopteryx dinellianus

3.6". Slightly crested. Crown earthy brown, feathers edged rusty buff, sides of head and the back dull greenish. Below bright yellow. Three pale wing bands. Fourth and fifth primary in ♂ very short, very narrow, pointed.

Subtropical zone. N ARGENTINA in Tucumán and Santa Fe, s PARAGUAY, se BOLIVIA where perhaps a migrant. Open scrub.

227. CRESTED DORADITO

Pseudocolopteryx sclateri

4". Prominent crest of black, yellow-edged feathers. Back dull olivaceous, mottled dusky. Below uniform bright yellow. Two grayish wing bars. Primaries as in 226.

Tropical zone. GUYANA. E BRAZIL from Bahía to Rio Grande do Sul and Mato Grosso; n PARAGUAY; n ARGENTINA from Formosa and Entre Ríos to n Buenos Aires. Trinidad (breeding). Bogs, mangrove swamps.

228. SUBTROPICAL DORADITO

Pseudocolopteryx acutipennis

4.5". Dark olive green above, bright yellow below. Wings with two dull grayish olive bars. Inner primaries narrow, pointed, most pronounced on sixth and seventh. Looks much like 223 but bill much more slender. Imm.: Narrow yellow eyebrow and flesh color lower mandible.

Subtropical zone. Central Andes of COLOMBIA south through e ECUADOR to n BOLIVIA and w ARGENTINA to Córdoba. Shrubbery, clumps of wiry grass.

Plate 13

229. WARBLING DORADITO

Pseudocolopteryx flaviventris

4.8". Upperparts, wings and tail dull brown; crown feathers somewhat lengthened, edged reddish brown; cheeks blackish brown. Below dull yellow. Primaries normal.

Se BRAZIL from São Paulo to Rio Grande do Sul; URUGUAY; PARAGUAY; n and central ARGENTINA to Chubut. CHILE from Santiago to Valdivia. Scrub near water, swamps, rushes.

230. BEARDED TACHURI

Polystictus pectoralis *

4". Crested: crown gray, feathers elongated, white at base, supraloral streak white. Chin white, upper throat mottled gray and white; lower throat, center of breast and entire belly white; sides of breast cinnamon (or all underparts rufous, 1). Back grayish brown, rump dull cinnamon. Wings with two buffy bands, primaries remarkably wide. Tail feathers very narrow, edged white on outer web. ♀: Differs from ♂ by dark brown crest, throat all buffy white, sides of breast and body cinnamon, wing bars buffier.

Tropical zone in GUYANA; SURINAM; s and w VENEZUELA; immediately adjacent BRAZIL (Roraima). Tropical, subtropical and temperate zones in Meta, Cundinamarca and Valle, COLOMBIA, 1. Se BRAZIL in São Paulo, Rio Grande do Sul and Mato Grosso; PARAGUAY; e BOLIVIA; ne ARGENTINA s to Buenos Aires and La Pampa. Marshes, open bushy country.

Plate 13

231. GRAY-BACKED TACHURI

Polystictus superciliaris

4.1". Crown and sides of head gray, superciliary white; crown feathers somewhat lengthened, white at base. Back brownish gray; underparts cinnamon, buffy white on center of abdomen and under tail coverts. Two faint pale gray wing bars. Axillaries cinnamon buff. Tail dusky, outer feathers narrowly edged buffy white.

E BRAZIL, campos on borders of Minas Gerais and Bahía.

232. SHARP-TAILED TYRANT

Culicivora caudacuta

4.8". Above sandy brown, streaked black. Crown and sides of head blackish, lores and eyebrow white. Below pale sandy, brownish on sides. Tail feathers narrow, pointed; central feathers much longer (1.9") than outermost (1.3").

S BRAZIL in São Paulo, Paraná and Mato Grosso; PARAGUAY; e BOLIVIA; nw ARGENTINA from Misiones to Chaco and n Santa Fe. Brush.

Plate 13

233. MANY-COLORED RUSH-TYRANT

Tachuris rubrigastra *

4.7" (or 4", 1). Crown black, central stripe scarlet; long, broad eyebrow golden yellow (bluish white, 1; or greenish yellow, 2); sides of head deep blue. Back moss green, flecked yellow (or mostly dark bluish green, 1, 2). Below golden buff (or white, tinged buff, 1; or throat white, breast and belly golden buff, 2) with incomplete black pectoral band. Under tail coverts orange (or pink, 1). Wing bar and broad edges to innermost remiges white. Upper tail coverts and tail black, outer tail feathers white, next two mostly white.

Tropical, temperate zones. Littoral of PERU from Piura to n Ica, 1. Highlands of PERU in Junín and Puno, n and w BOLIVIA, nw Jujuy and Tucumán, ARGENTINA. PARAGUAY along río Paraná, coastal se BRAZIL from São Paulo s to URUGUAY and e ARGENTINA south to Santa Cruz, 2. Marshes, reedbeds.

Plate 11

234. TUFTED TIT-TYRANT

Anairetes parulus *

4.3". Long, narrow, recurved black median crest. Crown black, front of crown slightly streaked white, eyebrow white. Back smoky gray, tinged olive on rump. Below pale yellow, streaked black. Wings black with two white bars. Tail black, outer feather edged white. Bill black, iris white.

Subtropical to páramo zone. COLOMBIA from s Central Andes s through Andes to Tierra del Fuego. Bushes, semiarid hillsides.

Plate 48

235. YELLOW-BILLED TIT-TYRANT

Anairetes flavirostris *

4.3". Differs from 234 by crown extensively white basally; breast streaks coarser, ending abruptly on breast. Wing bars white, very well marked. Base of mandible orange, iris brown.

Temperate zone. W and s central PERU south to n CHILE and BOLIVIA. ARGENTINA from Córdoba and Buenos Aires s to Río Negro, migrating in winter to nw ARGENTINA. Thickets often near streams, cultivated terraces.

236. PIED-CRESTED TIT-TYRANT

Anairetes reguloides *

5.5" (or 4.5", 1). Long crest black, hindcrown white; back black, streaked white. Below white heavily streaked black except on belly (or throat and sides of head virtually solid black, 1). Double wing bar white. Tail feathers black, outermost with white outer web, rest tipped white. Mandible flesh color. ♀, 1: Differs from male by streaked throat.

Temperate zone of PERU above Marañón Valley from Cajamarca to Ancash and above the Huallaga in Huánuco. Littoral of PERU from Ancash to Arica, CHILE, 1. Scrubby hillsides often near streams, bushes in cultivated fields.

237. ASH-BREASTED TIT-TYRANT

Anairetes alpinus *

5.5". Mostly dark gray, blackish on lower back; belly white. Long crest black, center of hindcrown white. Wings black with double white bar, inner remiges edged and minutely tipped white. Tail black, outer feathers mostly white.

W slope of PERUVIAN Andes above 13,000 ft. in Ancash. BOLIVIA in La Paz.

238. AGILE TIT-TYRANT

Uromyias agilis

5". Center of crown black; long crest black, tipped cinnamon buff; band at sides of crown whitish, expanding posteriorly and becoming pale cinnamon. Back brown, streaked dusky; below straw yellow narrowly streaked dark brown on throat and breast. Tail long (2.7", outermost feather 2"), much more rounded than in *Anairetes*.

Subtropical, temperate zones. Nw VENEZUELA, (Táchira). E Andes of COLOMBIA and n ECUADOR. Forest.

Plate 13

239. UNSTREAKED TIT-TYRANT

Uromyias agraphia

5". Differs from 238 by white, unstreaked underparts, plain black crest, white superciliaries, and unstreaked back.

Known only from Idma, above Urubamba Valley, Cuzco, PERU.

240. GREATER WAGTAIL-TYRANT

Stigmatura budytoides *

5.7". Upperparts grayish olive. Eyebrow and underparts pale yellow, more or less tinged buff on breast. Wing bar white; tail long (3.2"), graduated, with median white band and broad white tip (no band, 1).

Ne BRAZIL in Pernambuco and Bahía. PARAGUAY; n and e BOLIVIA; w ARGENTINA s to Córdoba and La Rioja; from Mendoza to Río Negro, 1. Southern birds migrate northward. Scrub. Jerks tail, often carried cocked above back.

Plate 13

241. LESSER WAGTAIL-TYRANT

Stigmatura napensis *

5.4". Differs from 240 by browner back; shorter tail, white at base.

Tropical zone. E ECUADOR. W Amazonian BRAZIL from rios Madeira and Negro e to the Tapajós and Jamundá, and in Pernambuco and Bahía. Scrub.

242. RIVER TYRANNULET

Serpophaga hypoleuca *

4.5". Above grayish brown, browner on rump. Crest brownish black, white basally. Below white, washed with gray on breast. Wings like back, unbanded. Tail blackish brown.

Tropical zone. VENEZUELA along middle Orinoco, lower Apure and lower río Meta. PERU in Loreto, e Pasco and n Cuzco. W BRAZIL s of the Amazon to rio Tocantins. Open spaces along rivers.

243. TORRENT TYRANNULET

Serpophaga cinerea *

4.5". Crown black, somewhat crested, feathers with white bases; back pale, clear gray. Below grayish white, white on center of abdomen. Wings and tail black, wing coverts pale yellow. (Cf. 251)

Subtropical zone. Nw VENEZUELA; Santa Marta Mts. and Andes of COLOMBIA s to n BOLIVIA. [Costa Rica; w Panama.] Rocky streams. Flicks tail.

Plate 48

244. WHITE-CRESTED TYRANNULET

Serpophaga subcristata *

4.3". Above gray with definite green wash, crest feathers streaked black with white base. Lores and eye ring white. Wings dusky with two yellowish white bands. Throat white, breast gray, belly and under wing coverts pale yellow. (Cf. 251)

Tropical, subtropical zones. E BRAZIL from Pernambuco and Piauí s to Mato Grosso and URUGUAY; PARAGUAY; n and e BOLIVIA; ARGENTINA s to Río Negro. Scrub and forest.

245. WHITE-BELLIED TYRANNULET

Serpophaga munda

4.4". Back pure gray, belly and under wing coverts white, otherwise like 244, but white of crown more extensive.

Upper tropical and subtropical zones. S BRAZIL in w Mato Grosso and Rio Grande do Sul; PARAGUAY; n, central and e BOLIVIA; ARGENTINA s to La Pampa. Thickets, weed patches.

246. GRAY-CROWNED TYRANNULET

Serpophaga griseiceps

4". Crown and nape gray, eyebrow and eye ring white; back olivaceous gray; wings with two ochraceous wing bars. Throat and breast grayish white; belly white, washed yellow.

Subtropical zone. Cochabamba, BOLIVIA.

247. SOOTY TYRANNULET

Serpophaga nigricans

5". Above dark gray, below paler gray. Semiconcealed coronal patch white. Wings and tail blackish, wing coverts with two pale gray bars.

Se BRAZIL from Minas Gerais s to Rio Grande do Sul; URUGUAY; PARAGUAY; BOLIVIA in Tarija; ARGENTINA s to Río Negro. Scrub.

248. BANANAL TYRANNULET

Serpophaga araguayae

4.5". Above light slaty gray, washed olivaceous on rump; crown slightly darker, but purer gray indistinctly streaked black; feathers in center of crown white basally; sides of head and ear coverts streaked white. Throat grayish white, breast and sides light slaty gray, center of belly white. Two white wing bars, inner remiges broadly edged white. Tail dusky.

Ilha do Bananal in rio Araguaya, Goiás, BRAZIL.

249. PALE-TIPPED TYRANNULET

Inezia subflava *

5". Upperparts brownish olive to brown (or ochraceous brown, 1). Eyebrow and eye ring white; malar region whitish; ear coverts dusky, crossed medially by narrow silvery white line. Below dull yellow, paler on throat, breast more or less clouded olive (or with rusty breast, 1). Wings and tail brown, wing coverts with white (or yellowish, 1) double bar, inner remiges bordered white on outer web. Tail rounded, tipped white (or ochraceous, 1).

Tropical zone. GUIANAS, VENEZUELA in Bolívar, Monagas, Anzoátegui, Guárico and Apure and in n BRAZIL, 1. VENEZUELA n of río Apure and in upper Orinoco and río Casiquiare regions. COLOMBIA in ne and se.

Amazonian BRAZIL from rios Negro and Madeira e to rios Jamundá and Tapajós. Mangroves, savanna at edge of forest. Often carries tail cocked.

250. SLENDER-BILLED TYRANNULET

Inezia tenuirostris

3.7". Upperparts, wings and tail dull grayish brown. Lores, eye ring white. Throat white, breast tinged grayish, belly pale sulphury yellow. Wings with two white bars.

Tropical zone. Nw VENEZUELA from coast of Falcón s to Lara and w to Santa Marta region, COLOMBIA. Desert county and humid woodland.

Plate 49

251. PLAIN TYRANNULET

Inezia inornata

4.3". Crown and nape ashy gray, back olive gray; lores, eye ring and shaft streaks on ear coverts white. Throat and upper breast mixed grayish and white, lower breast white, belly pale sulphur yellow. Wings and tail grayish brown, wing coverts with two white bars. ♀: Head and nape like back, otherwise like ♂. Much like 244, but no crest.

Upper tropical zone. N and e BOLIVIA; PARAGUAY in Chaco; BRAZIL in Mato Grosso; nw ARGENTINA in Salta. Scrub.

252. WHITE-THROATED TYRANNULET

Mecocerculus leucophrys *

5"-6". Above brown to olive brown (or dark reddish brown, 1); short eyebrow and eye ring white. Throat whitish, breast grayish (or brownish, 1), belly yellowish white to pale sulphur yellow. Wings dusky with two prominent white to buffy (or deep rufous, 1) wing bars and margins to inner remiges. Tail rather long, grayish brown (or dark brown, 1).

Subtropical, temperate zones. Mts. of VENEZUELA and immediately adjacent BRAZIL. COLOMBIA in Santa Marta Mts.; Eastern, n Central and W Andes. S Central Andes of COLOMBIA s through ECUADOR to PERU, to Ancash in the w and Junín and Cuzco in the e, 1. Extreme s PERU s to BOLIVIA and ne ARGENTINA to Tucumán. Forest, forest edge, scrub.

Plate 39

253. WHITE-TAILED TYRANNULET

Mecocerculus poecilocercus

4.5". Differs from other species of the genus by pale sulphur upper tail coverts, and by white inner webs to tail feathers excepting central pair. Eyebrow white. Wing coverts with two whitish, occasionally ochraceous, bands; remiges similarly margined; secondaries deep black on outer web forming a black patch. Back olive green. Throat and breast pale gray, rest of underparts yellowish white.

Subtropical, temperate zones. Andes of COLOMBIA and ECUADOR, s to Junín and Cuzco, PERU. Forest.

254. BUFF-BANDED TYRANNULET

Mecocerculus hellmayri

4.5". Differs from 253 by tail and upper tail coverts pale brownish olive, tail with no white.

Subtropical zone. Se PERU (n Puno); BOLIVIA in Cochabamba, Santa Cruz and Chaquisaca; ARGENTINA in Jujuy.

255. RUFOUS-WINGED TYRANNULET

Mecocerculus calopterus

4.7". Differs from other species of the genus by rufous chestnut margins to inner remiges and white outermost pairs of tail feathers. Crown gray, lores and conspicuous eyebrow white. Back olive. Wing coverts with two buffy white bars. Below like 253. Central four tail feathers like back.

Subtropical zone. W ECUADOR from 2°s, south to w San Martín, PERU. Forest.

256. SULPHUR-BELLIED TYRANNULET

Mecocerculus minor

4.7". Differs from other species of the genus by bright yellow lower breast and belly. Above olive, crown and nape grayish. Below yellow, clouded olive on throat and breast. Double wing bar ochraceous buff, inner remiges margined same. Tail grayish.

Subtropical zone. VENEZUELA in w Táchira. COLOMBIA e of Andes in Norte de Santander, and at head of Magdalena Valley in Huila. Nw PERU in central Cajamarca. Forest.

257. WHITE-BANDED TYRANNULET

Mecocerculus stictopterus *

5". Above olive to olive brown; long, prominent eyebrow white. Throat and breast pale gray, belly white, flanks and under tail coverts pale yellowish. Wing coverts and base of inner remiges black, two well-marked white wing bars, inner remiges edged buffy white. Tail grayish.

Subtropical, temperate zones. Nw VENEZUELA. Andes of COLOMBIA s through ECUADOR to Cochabamba, BOLIVIA. Forest.

258. PATAGONIAN TYRANT

Colorhamphus parvirostris

5.5". Dark grayish brown above, gradually turning to sepia on rump; below dark gray becoming lighter and tinged with yellow on abdomen. Double wing bar and edges to inner remiges cinnamon rufous. Tail brownish gray. Bill very small.

ARGENTINA from Neuquén, and CHILE from Valdivia, s to Tierra del Fuego. Winters n to Buenos Aires and Aconcagua. Forest treetops.

Plate 12

Elaenias

Elaenias are notoriously difficult to tell apart. Most are some shade of olive above, with yellowish to grayish underparts. Wings and tail are like back, and wing coverts usually have two well-marked pale bars. The head is somewhat crested, usually in the genus *Elaenia* with a mostly concealed white coronal patch (in the allied genus *Myiopagis* it is usually yellow). The lower mandible is flesh color basally. Only distinguishing characters will be mentioned below.

259. YELLOW-BELLIED ELAENIA

Elaenia flavogaster *

6". Above olive. Throat and sides of neck grayish white deepening to pearl gray on upper breast, rest of underparts pale yellow. Crest with white center, conspicuous.

Tropical, subtropical zones. GUIANAS; VENEZUELA and COLOMBIA south, e of

Andes, to n ARGENTINA and w of Andes to nw PERU. Trinidad, Tobago. [Mid. Amer. Lesser Antilles.] Open savanna, gardens, campos, cerrado. Very noisy.

260. CARIBBEAN ELAENIA

Elaenia martinica *

6.2". Grayish olive above, throat and breast pale gray gradually merging with pale yellow abdomen.

Aruba, Curaçao, Bonaire. Dense scrub, mangroves. [Caribbean islands.]

261. LARGE ELAENIA

Elaenia spectabilis *

7". Much like 259 in color but considerably larger. Wing bars somewhat narrower.

Tropical zone. Se COLOMBIA. Ne PERU; BRAZIL; e and s BOLIVIA; n ARGENTINA. Birds from n BRAZIL and PERU possibly are migrants. Forest treetops, riparian thickets.

262. WHITE-CRESTED ELAENIA

Elaenia albiceps *

6". Dark olive above. Throat and breast gray, tinged olive; sides of body olive, center of abdomen white, flanks and under tail coverts pale yellowish.

Subtropical, temperate zones. COLOMBIA s through Andes to Tierra del Fuego. Southern breeders migrate n through URUGUAY, PARAGUAY and w Pará, BRAZIL, to breeding grounds of northern birds. Scrub, open mountain slopes.

Plate 48

263. SMALL-BILLED ELAENIA

Elaenia parvirostris

6". Differs from 260 by greener upperparts and by well-marked white eye ring.

Breeds in BOLIVIA, PARAGUAY, URUGUAY and s BRAZIL s to central ARGENTINA. Migrates n to GUYANA, SURINAM, VENEZUELA and e COLOMBIA. Treetops in open woodland, forest edge.

264. OLIVACEOUS ELAENIA

Elaenia mesoleuca

6". Above olive. Throat pale gray; breast grayish, tinged olive; sides of body pale olive; center of abdomen white; flanks and under tail coverts pale greenish yellow. Wing bars narrow.

Se BRAZIL from ne Mato Grosso, Goiás and Bahía s to Rio Grande do Sul; PARAGUAY and ne ARGENTINA to Santa Fe. Forest treetops.

265. SLATY ELAENIA

Elaenia strepera

6.3". Differs from other species by dark, pure gray general coloration. Center of belly white. Wings with two narrow inconspicuous gray wing bars. Tail dusky, edged olive.

Breeds in s BOLIVIA and nw ARGENTINA. Winters to e Pasco, PERU, e COLOMBIA and e VENEZUELA. Forest treetops.

266. MOTTLE-BACKED ELAENIA

Elaenia gigas

7.8". Above brown, feathers edged olive. Throat whitish; upper breast brownish gray becoming streaked with yellow on lower breast, and pure light yellow on abdomen. Tail narrowly tipped whitish.

Tropical zone. Eastern base of E Andes of COLOMBIA s through ECUADOR to PERU and nw BOLIVIA. Forest.

267. BROWNISH ELAENIA

Elaenia pelzelni

8". Above dull, dark brown with no olive tinge; center of throat whitish, breast and sides pale brown, lower breast and belly white; two narrow grayish white wing bars. Males with white at base of crown feathers; females without.

Tropical zone. Ne PERU; w and central Amazonian BRAZIL from rios Negro and Juruá e to rios Jamundá and Tapajós.

268. PLAIN-CRESTED ELAENIA

Elaenia cristata *

5.5". Above brownish gray with only slight olive tinge. Throat whitish, upper breast pale gray; lower breast and abdomen pale sulphur yellow, white in worn plumage. No white crown patch. Crest feathers rather long, narrower than in most species, darker and browner than back. Wing bars white, conspicuous.

Tropical zone. GUIANAS; VENEZUELA, except nw; BRAZIL n of the Amazon in

Roraima and s of it from Pará s to São Paulo and n Mato Grosso. Open country, savanna, cerradão.

269. LESSER ELAENIA

Elaenia chiriquensis*

5.5"-6". Much like 268 but white crown patch present; crest feathers not as narrow, and same color as back; outer webs of inner remiges more broadly edged white.

Tropical, subtropical zones. GUIANAS; VENEZUELA; COLOMBIA; nw ECUADOR. E PERU; n BOLIVIA; nw ARGENTINA in Jujuy; PARAGUAY; BRAZIL (except forested parts) s to São Paulo and Mato Grosso. [Sw Costa Rica and Panama.] Rather dry, open woods, cerrado, thickets in open areas.

270. RUFOUS-CROWNED ELAENIA

Elaenia ruficeps

6". Distinguishable from other elaenias by orange rufous crown patch. Above dark brown with slight olive tinge; below pale yellow, streaked gray on throat and breast. Wing bars conspicuous pale gray; tail narrowly tipped white.

Tropical, lower subtropical zones. GUIANAS; s VENEZUELA; e COLOMBIA; n BRAZIL from rio Negro eastward and on lower rio Madeira. Forest.

271. MOUNTAIN ELAENIA

Elaenia frantzii*

5.5". No white crown patch; otherwise much like 269, but wing bars tinged grayish or yellowish, not pure white as in 269. More olive, less grayish above and below.

Subtropical, temperate zones. Mts. of nw VENEZUELA; mts. of COLOMBIA. [Guatemala to w Panama.] Forest clearings, forest edge.

272. HIGHLAND ELAENIA

Elaenia obscura*

7.8". Reminiscent of 266 but no white crown patch. Back uniform dark, dull olive to olive brown; throat and breast pale greenish, throat paler, center of abdomen yellow.

Upper tropical and subtropical zones. PERU from Cajamarca and Amazonas south to n

and e BOLIVIA, n ARGENTINA, e PARAGUAY. E and s BRAZIL from Minas Gerais to Rio Grande do Sul and s Mato Grosso. Forest.

273. GREAT ELAENIA

Elaenia dayi*

8". Crown blackish without white, back dark brown. Two prominent whitish wing bars. Throat whitish to grayish; breast and sides grayish olive slightly tinged yellow, becoming pale yellowish white on lower belly. Tail blackish, narrowly tipped whitish.

Subtropical zone. VENEZUELA on mts. of se Bolívar and Amazonas. Forest.

274. SIERRAN ELAENIA

Elaenia pallatangae*

6". Above olivaceous (or olivaceous brown, 1). Concealed crown patch white. Throat and breast grayish yellow, yellower on throat; belly bright pale yellow (or throat and breast pale olive gray, belly pale greenish yellow, 1). Wings dusky with two pale yellowish (or white, 1) wing bars and edges to inner remiges.

Subtropical zone. W GUYANA and mts. of VENEZUELA s of the Orinoco, immediately adjacent n BRAZIL, 1. COLOMBIA from head of the Magdalena to Pacific slope, thence south through the Andes to n BOLIVIA. Forest clearings.

275. FOREST ELAENIA

Myiopagis gaimardii*

5". Crown and nape gray with a semi-concealed white to yellowish white (or canary yellow, 1) crest and poorly defined white eyebrow. Back dull olive. Throat whitish; rest of underparts bright pale yellow, clouded with gray on breast. Wings with two yellowish white wing bars.

Tropical zone. Generally distributed e of Andes south to n BOLIVIA and BRAZIL to Mato Grosso and São Paulo. West of Andes in n COLOMBIA from Santa Marta westward, 1. Trinidad. [Central and e Panama.] Forest borders and humid woodland. The genus *Myiopagis* can be confused with *Neopelma* (Pipridae). (Cf. p. 280).

276. GRAY ELAENIA

Myiopagis caniceps *

4.5"-5". Rather variable in color: either gray crown, nape and upper mantle with bright olive green back, or all gray above; with white crown patch. Below whitish, grayer on breast; under tail coverts pale yellow. ♀ or imm.: Above like green-backed ♂, but crown patch often light yellow. Throat gray, underparts bright yellow. Wings in both sexes and phases black with white or pale yellow wing bars and edges.

Tropical zone FRENCH GUIANA; s and nw VENEZUELA; COLOMBIA in Chocó and Vaupés; e and w ECUADOR; PERU in Loreto and Pasco. W Amazonian BRAZIL and from Maranhão to Paraná and Mato Grosso. BOLIVIA, PARAGUAY, n ARGENTINA in Jujuy, Salta, Misiones. [E Panama.] Woodland.

277. PACIFIC ELAENIA

Myiopagis subplacens

6.2". Crown grayish brown with semiconcealed bright yellow crest. Eyebrow mottled white and dusky. Back dull, pale olive. Throat and breast pale dove gray, streaked with white; rest of underparts pale sulphur yellow. Wings dusky, coverts and edges to remiges pale yellow. Tail pale brownish, edged olive. ♀: Like ♂ but smaller with less developed crest.

Arid tropical zone. W ECUADOR from Esmeraldas to nw PERU. Dry scrub.

278. YELLOW-CROWNED ELAENIA

Myiopagis flavivertex

5". Above dull olive green; crown darker, with semiconcealed golden yellow crest. Throat and breast grayish olive, belly pale yellow. Wings and tail brownish; double wing bar and edges of inner remiges pale yellow.

Tropical zone. SURINAM; FRENCH GUIANA; VENEZUELA in Delta Amacuro and Amazonas; ne PERU in ne Loreto; Amazonian BRAZIL. Forest.

279. GREENISH ELAENIA

Myiopagis viridicata *

5"-5.5". Upperparts olive green (or dull green, 1). Crown like back (or with sides of crown and nape gray, 1) with semiconcealed golden or orange yellow crest. Throat

whitish, breast grayish olive, rest of underparts pale yellow. Wings dusky, coverts and edges of inner remiges pale greenish yellow. Tail brownish, edged olive.

Tropical zone. VENEZUELA and e and w COLOMBIA south, e of Andes, to n ARGENTINA. In w ECUADOR, 1. Woodland near streams.

Plate 12

280. SUIRIRI FLYCATCHER

Suiriri suiriri *

6.8" (6", 1). Above gray, supraloral streak white. Throat white, breast pale grayish, belly sulphur yellow (or white, 1). Wings and tail black, wing coverts and inner remiges broadly edged pale gray; outer web of outer rectrix and base of all but central tail feathers broadly whitish, broad tips to tail feathers gray (or tail all black except for white outer web of outermost rectrix, 1).

BRAZIL on both sides of lower Amazon southward in the e through Maranhão to Rio Grande do Sul and Mato Grosso. URUGUAY, PARAGUAY, e BOLIVIA and ARGENTINA s to Buenos Aires and La Pampa, 1. Open scrub, mangroves, cerrado.

Plate 28

281. SCRUB FLYCATCHER

Sublegatus modestus *

5.7". Head somewhat crested, forehead grizzled with white. Above brownish gray; throat whitish, breast pale to dark gray, belly sulphur yellow, sides gray, center of abdomen pale gray. Wings and tail dark brown, coverts edged grayish white forming three bars, inner remiges broadly edged grayish white. Very like 259 but no white crown patch. Bill blacker, flatter, broader.

Tropical to temperate zone. GUIANAS, VENEZUELA, COLOMBIA and PERU, BRAZIL, s to URUGUAY, PARAGUAY and ARGENTINA s to Mendoza and La Pampa. Southern birds migrate to n Brazil and Peru. Aruba to Trinidad. [Pacific Costa Rica and Panama.] Mangroves, dry scrub, open forest, cerrado.

282. MOUSE-COLORED TYRANNULET

Phaeomyias murina *

5". Lores white; eyebrow pale, poorly marked. Above mouse brown; throat whitish, breast pale gray, belly pale yellow to yellowish white (or breast pale brown, belly buffy white, 1). Double wing bar and margins to inner remiges whitish (or cinnamon, 2). Tail like back.

Tropical zone. GUIANAS, VENEZUELA, COLOMBIA, BRAZIL n of the Amazon. Sw ECUADOR, w PERU s to Tumbes and upper Marañón, 2; in Lambayeque and Libertad, 1, 2. BRAZIL s of the Amazon s to São Paulo, PARAGUAY, BOLIVIA, e PERU and nw ARGENTINA. Trinidad. [Pacific central Panama.] Open country with trees and bushes, gardens, cerrado.

Plate 12

283. GRAY-AND-WHITE TYRANNULET

Phaeomyias leucospodia *

5″. Much like a dark 281, but at once distinguishable by semiconcealed white crown patch, pale sulphur instead of pale buff under wing coverts and under tail coverts, and shorter tail.

Arid littoral of sw ECUADOR to Libertad, PERU. Arid scrub.

284. SOUTHERN BEARDLESS TYRANNULET

Camptostoma obsoletum *

4.5″. Above olive; crown gray to brownish gray to brown; lores and narrow eyebrow white. Throat and breast yellow, tinged gray or olive on throat and breast. Double wing bar white or buff, (or upperparts grayish with no olive tinge; underparts white, tinged yellow at sides, double wing bar buff to cinnamon, 1).

Tropical, subtropical zones. GUIANAS, VENEZUELA, COLOMBIA, e PERU, BRAZIL, URUGUAY, PARAGUAY, n ARGENTINA, e BOLIVIA. W ECUADOR, PERU e to Marañón Valley and s to Lima, nw BOLIVIA, 1. [Costa Rica; Panama.] Bushes, arid scrub, woodland, gardens, campos, cerrado.

285. GREENISH TYRANNULET

Xanthomyias virescens *

5.6″. Rather bright olive green above. Lores and eye ring white (with ashy forehead, 1). Throat whitish, breast bright olive flammulated with yellow, rest of underparts primrose yellow. Wing coverts with drop-shaped yellow spot on outer web of feathers forming two bars, remiges edged olive green. Tail rather long, feathers edged olive green.

Upper tropical zone of ne VENEZUELA, 1. E and central BRAZIL from Goiás and Minas Gerais s to Rio Grande do Sul and Mato Grosso; PARAGUAY; ne ARGENTINA in Misiones. Forest treetops.

Plate 13

286. REISER'S TYRANNULET

Xanthomyias reiseri

Much like 285 (1), but smaller, back clearer yellowish green; wing bars broader.

E BRAZIL in s Piauí and in ne PARAGUAY.

287. SCLATER'S TYRANNULET

Xanthomyias sclateri

5″. Upperparts, wings and tail as in 285 (1). Eyebrow and eye ring white. Throat and breast grayish white, flammulated with yellow; sides of body, under wing coverts and under tail coverts greenish yellow; belly white, flammulated with yellow.

Subtropical zone. Se PERU in Cuzco; n and e BOLIVIA; nw ARGENTINA. Forest.

288. PLANALTO TYRANNULET

Phyllomyias fasciatus *

4.2″ (or 4.7″, 1). Above light grayish or brownish olive; crown gray, feathers with dusky centers; throat whitish, chest olivaceous yellow with gray tinge, belly pale yellow. Two whitish wing bars (or larger; darker above; below yellower, tinged olive on breast; wing bars yellower, 1).

E BRAZIL from Ceará and Maranhão to Goiás and Mato Grosso; from Minas Gerais and Espírito Santo s to Rio Grande do Sul, e PARAGUAY and ne ARGENTINA, 1. Forest.

289. SOOTY-HEADED TYRANNULET

Phyllomyias griseiceps *

4″. Crown and nape dark gray (or black, 1), supraloral streak white. Back olive. Wings and tail dusky, feathers edged grayish olive. Throat whitish, rest of underparts pale yellow, tinged olive on breast.

Tropical zone. GUYANA; VENEZUELA n of the Orinoco and in Bolívar. N and central COLOMBIA (in Cauca Valley, 1). E and w

ECUADOR s to Junín, PERU. BRAZIL n of the Amazon. [E Panama.] Shrubbery.

Plate 12

290. BLACK-CAPPED TYRANNULET

Tyranniscus nigrocapillus *

4.5". Crown black (or sepia brown, 1). Eyebrow white (or yellow, 1). Back olive green. Wings blackish with yellowish white double wing bar and yellow edges to inner remiges. Chin and throat yellowish white, breast light olive, rest of underparts yellow (or all yellow below, 1). Tail grayish brown, edged olive.

Subtropical, temperate zones. Nw VENE-ZUELA and Santa Marta Mts. of COLOM-BIA, 1. Andes of COLOMBIA, ECUADOR and PERU to Junín. Thick forest.

291. TAWNY-RUMPED TYRANNULET

Tyranniscus uropygialis

4.7". Crown dark brown, eyebrow white; back brown gradually turning to ochraceous on rump and upper tail coverts; tail light brown, edged dull ochraceous. Sides of head, neck and upper breast light gray; yellowish white on sides of body and under tail coverts, center of belly white. Wings black with two buffy bars, secondaries edged yellowish, tertials edged white.

Subtropical, temperate zones. Nw VENE-ZUELA in Mérida. COLOMBIA in Andes south to ECUADOR, nw PERU and n and central BOLIVIA. Forest.

292. ASHY-HEADED TYRANNULET

Tyranniscus cinereiceps

4.3". Crown blue gray; forehead, lores and ocular region grizzled with white, black spot on ear coverts. Back light moss green. Throat and breast greenish yellow, rest of underparts bright yellow. Wings black with light yellow double wing bars and edges to inner remiges. Tail light brown, edged olive.

Subtropical zone. Andes of COLOMBIA s through ECUADOR to Cuzco, PERU.

Plate 38

293. OLROG'S TYRANNULET

Tyranniscus australis[1]

4.5". Above pale olive gray, crown darker in contrast to back, rump olive. Tail brownish gray, edged light olive. Remiges edged yellow, two whitish wing bars. Throat and breast pale gray, belly pale yellowish (perhaps a subspecies of 292).

Nw ARGENTINA in Jujuy (Yuto).

294. PALTRY TYRANNULET

Tyranniscus vilissimus *

4.8". Forehead, eyebrow and eye ring white (no white at forehead, 1); lores and crown dusky olive, back olive green. Throat whitish, breast light gray obscurely streaked yellow, rest of underparts light yellow. Wings blackish, coverts and inner remiges edged greenish yellow. Tail grayish brown, edged yellowish olive.

Tropical, subtropical zones. Coastal mts. of VENEZUELA from Miranda westward, 1. COLOMBIA from Santa Marta Mts. w to Chocó. [Mid. Amer.] Forest edge, open forest.

295. BOLIVIAN TYRANNULET

Tyranniscus bolivianus *

5". Above uniform olive green; below pale yellow, palest on throat, breast overlaid with gray. Wings dusky, coverts and inner remiges edged yellow. Tail dusky brown, edged olive.

Subtropical zone. Se PERU. BOLIVIA in La Paz and Cochabamba.

296. RED-BILLED TYRANNULET

Tyranniscus cinereicapillus

5". Differs from 295 mainly by crown grayish olive, underparts much brighter yellow and lower mandible purplish flesh color instead of black.

Tropical zone. Ne ECUADOR. Central PERU in Ayacucho and Junín.

297. SLENDER-FOOTED TYRANNULET

Tyranniscus gracilipes *

4.5". Crown dark slaty gray, back olive, wings and tail dusky. Wing coverts and inner remiges sharply but narrowly edged yellow.

[1] Olrog and Contino, Inst. Mig. Lillo y Facult. Cienc. Nat.; 1966, (Dec. 1); *12*, no. 39, p. 113.

Below yellowish olive, clear pale yellow on center of abdomen.

Tropical, subtropical zones. GUIANAS; s VENEZUELA; e COLOMBIA south to n BOLIVIA and Amazonian BRAZIL e to Pará, and in Maranhão and Ceará. Treetops in forest and savanna.

298. GOLDEN-FACED TYRANNULET

Tyranniscus viridiflavus*

4.8". Forehead and lores yellow, crown olive like back, wings and tail as in 297. Chin yellow, throat whitish, breast light gray, center of belly yellowish white (or differing from 296 only in yellow forehead and lores and black mandible, 1).

Tropical, subtropical zones. VENEZUELA n of the Orinoco; COLOMBIA; e and w ECUADOR; n PERU s to Piura and San Martín. In Huánuco and Junín, PERU, 1. Forest and scrub.

299. PLUMBEOUS-CROWNED TYRANNULET

Oreotriccus plumbeiceps

4.8". Much like 207. Crown pale gray; eyebrow, ocular region and posterior edge of ear coverts white; spot on ear coverts black. Back bright olive green. Wings blackish with two yellow bars, inner remiges edged yellow. Chin and upper throat whitish, turning to light olive yellow on breast and bright yellow on belly. Tail grayish brown margined olive.

Subtropical zone. Andes of COLOMBIA s to central and s PERU in Cuzco. Forest.

Plate 49

300. GRAY-CAPPED TYRANNULET

Oreotriccus griseocapillus

4.5". Crown, nape and sides of head grayish brown sharply demarcated from olive green back. Throat and upper breast pale smoky gray, line down center abdomen white; sides of body bright greenish yellow. Double wing bar and broad edges to inner remiges yellow. Tail grayish.

Se BRAZIL from Minas Gerais to Espírito Santo s to Santa Catarina.

301. YELLOW-CROWNED TYRANNULET

Tyrannulus elatus*

4". Sides of crown grayish black to black; large, semiconcealed golden yellow crest. Back light grayish olive. Wings and tail dark brown; double wing bar and broad edges to inner remiges yellowish white. Upper throat grayish; rest of underparts pale yellow, tinged olive on breast.

Tropical zone. GUIANAS, VENEZUELA, COLOMBIA, nw ECUADOR, e PERU, n BOLIVIA, Amazonian BRAZIL and in Maranhão. [Panama.] Forest, open woodland, clearings, gardens.

Plate 12

302. ROUGH-LEGGED TYRANNULET

Acrochordopus burmeisteri*

4.5". Forehead and ocular region whitish, crown dark gray (or olive like back, 1). Above olive, below yellow, throat and breast tinged gray. Wings blackish, coverts and inner remiges narrowly edged yellow. Tail brown, margined olive. Bill rather thick, lower mandible flesh color.

Upper tropical, lower subtropical zones. VENEZUELA n of the Orinoco and in Bolívar. COLOMBIA in Meta. Se and sw ECUADOR. Se PERU in Cuzco. E BOLIVIA, e PARAGUAY, n ARGENTINA and se BRAZIL from Espírito Santo to Rio Grande do Sul, 1. [Costa Rica; w Panama.]

Plate 13

303. WHITE-LORED TYRANNULET

Ornithion inerme

3.5". Crown dark slaty gray, narrow but very sharply marked white eyebrow, line below eye white. Back dark, dull olive. Wings blackish, coverts tipped with yellowish white spots forming two wing bars. Throat whitish, rest of underparts greenish yellow, greener on breast and sides of body.

Tropical zone. GUIANAS, VENEZUELA s of the Orinoco, and e COLOMBIA s to Pasco, PERU. BRAZIL on rio Negro, and from rio Tapajós to e Pará, possibly in Bahía. Forest, scrub.

304. YELLOW-BELLIED TYRANNULET

Ornithion semiflavum*

3.5". Crown sepia brown, eyebrow white. Back dull olive; underparts bright yellow, tinged olive on breast. No wing bars.

Tropical zone. N VENEZUELA from Miranda west to n and w COLOMBIA; nw

ECUADOR. [Mid. Amer.] Forest, humid woodland borders.

Plate 49

305. SLATY-CAPPED FLYCATCHER

Leptopogon superciliaris *

5.2". Crown dark slaty gray; forehead, lores, and cheeks marbled black and white; spot on ear coverts black. Back olive green. Wings blackish, coverts with two prominent ochraceous buff (or white, 1) bars, inner remiges conspicuously margined buffy olive (or whitish olive, 1). Throat and breast olive (or pale gray, tinged olive, 1), belly yellow (or yellowish white, 1).

Upper tropical and subtropical zones. VENEZUELA n of the Orinoco and in s Amazonas; Andes of COLOMBIA south through e and w ECUADOR to Junín, PERU; from Puno south to n BOLIVIA, 1. [Costa Rica; Panama.] Forest.

306. SEPIA-CAPPED FLYCATCHER

Leptopogon amaurocephalus *

Much like 305 but easily distinguishable by sepia brown instead of gray crown and nape.

Tropical zone. GUYANA; VENEZUELA; n and e COLOMBIA, south to e ECUADOR, e PERU, n and e BOLIVIA, PARAGUAY; n ARGENTINA. BRAZIL in w Amazonas and in the e from Maranhão and Pernambuco through Goiás to Mato Grosso and Santa Catarina. [Mid. Amer.] Forest and scrub.

Plate 38

307. RUFOUS-BREASTED FLYCATCHER

Leptopogon rufipectus *

5.3". Crown olivaceous gray, lores and ocular region rufous. Throat and breast rufous, belly yellow. Back olive green; tail brown, edged olive. Wings dusky, coverts edged buffy forming two bars; inner remiges margined light olive.

Subtropical zone Nw VENEZUELA. COLOMBIA on w slope of E Andes and both slopes of Central Andes. Ne ECUADOR. Forest.

308. INCA FLYCATCHER

Leptopogon taczanowskii

Differs from 307 by gray lores, ocular region and throat; much paler and duller breast, and much deeper tawny ochraceous wing bars and margins to remiges. Crown with little gray tinge.

Subtropical zone. Central Andes of PERU from s Amazonas to Cuzco.

309. STREAK-NECKED FLYCATCHER

Mionectes striaticollis *

5.8". Crown and nape gray (or like back, 1), back bright olive green. Wings and tail brown, edged olive. Sides of head gray with white shaft streaks; throat and breast gray narrowly streaked white (or sides of head, throat and breast olive, narrowly streaked white, 2). Lower breast and belly yellow, streaked olive; belly yellow. Second primary from outside, narrow and pointed in ad. ♂.

Subtropical zone. Central and E Andes of COLOMBIA south through e ECUADOR to n BOLIVIA. COLOMBIA on w slope of W Andes in Caldas, 2; in w Nariño and nw ECUADOR, 1, 2. Forest, shrubbery.

310. OLIVE-STRIPED FLYCATCHER

Mionectes olivaceus *

5.8". Very like 309 (1, 2), but sides of head and throat lighter olive, pale streaking generally wider; in some races, buffy double wing bar. Second primary from outside, narrowed in center of inner web, rounded and blunt at tip in ad. ♂.

Tropical, lower subtropical zones. VENEZUELA n of the Orinoco; COLOMBIA in Santa Marta Mts. and south through Andes of e and nw ECUADOR to Puno, PERU. [Costa Rica; Panama.] Forest, shrubbery.

Plate 38

311. OCHRE-BELLIED FLYCATCHER

Pipromorpha oleaginea *

5". Above bright olive green; below tawny ochraceous, tinged olive on throat and upper breast. Wings and tail brownish, double wing bar and edges to inner remiges tawny buff.

Tropical zone. GUIANAS, VENEZUELA and COLOMBIA south to w ECUADOR and e of Andes to BOLIVIA. Amazonian BRAZIL and in the e from Alagoas to Espírito Santo. Trinidad, Tobago. [Mid. Amer.] Forest, shrubbery.

Plate 13

312. McCONNELL'S FLYCATCHER

Pipromorpha macconnelli *

5". Chiefly distinguishable from 311 by plain wings without buffy bars or edges to inner remiges.

Tropical, subtropical zones. GUYANA and FRENCH GUIANA; VENEZUELA s of the Orinoco. Central PERU in Junín. N and nw BOLIVIA; Amazonian BRAZIL.

313. GRAY-HOODED FLYCATCHER

Pipromorpha rufiventris

5.6". Differs chiefly from 312 by throat and sides of head ashy gray instead of tawny olive, and crown and nape gray with olive tinge.

Se BRAZIL from Espírito Santo and e Minas Gerais to Rio Grande do Sul.

314. RINGED ANTPIPIT

Corythopis torquata *

5.5". Above dark reddish brown, sides of head dark gray to dark brown. Below white with broad black pectoral band breaking up into black streaks on lower edge. Under wing coverts dusky gray.

Tropical zone. GUIANAS; VENEZUELA s of the Orinoco; se COLOMBIA; e ECUADOR; e PERU and Amazonian BRAZIL e to Amapá and n Maranhão, Wet forest, near streams. Walks wagging tail.

315. SOUTHERN ANTPIPIT

Corythopis delalandi

5.5". Very like 314 but back and sides of head lighter, tinged olive. Under wing coverts white.

E BRAZIL from s Maranhão s to Santa Catarina and Mato Grosso; PARAGUAY; e BOLIVIA; ne ARGENTINA. Thick undergrowth in forest.

Plate 8

The last two species have usually been placed in the family Conopophagidae. Recently it has been suggested that they belong more properly to the Tyrannidae (probably in subfamily Tyranninae). As the exact systematic position of *Corythopis* remains to be established it is placed here at the end of the family.

Family OXYRUNCIDAE   SHARPBILLS

The exact position of the Sharpbill is yet to be determined. Some regard it as an aberrant member of the Tyrant-Flycatchers but usually it is placed in a family of its own. It is a solitary inhabitant of humid forests and feeds on fruit. Little is known of its habits despite its wide, but curiously discontinuous, range.

SHARPBILL

Oxyruncus cristatus *

7". Above bright olive green; median crest golden yellow to scarlet, narrowly bordered laterally by black; side of crown and forehead barred black and olive or black and yellowish white. Below pale yellow to white, profusely spotted with black. Wings and tail blackish, coverts and inner remiges edged yellowish white.

Tropical, subtropical zones. Mts. of GUYANA and s VENEZUELA. E PERU in Junín, 4000 ft. Amazonian BRAZIL on rio Tocantins and near Belém, and (chiefly in the mountains) from Espírito Santo and s Minas Gerais to Santa Catarina; e PARAGUAY. [Mts. of Costa Rica and Panama.] Tall forest treetops.

Plate 16

Family PHYTOTOMIDAE   PLANTCUTTERS

Plantcutters resemble stocky, thick-billed finches. They are found only in western and southern South America, usually in small, loose flocks in bushy country or low woodland. Sometimes also found in orchards and cultivated lands, where they can do considerable damage to fruits, buds and tender leaves which they cut up, wastefully, with their finely serrated bills.

Plantcutters have an undulating flight and perch on top of shrubs to deliver a peculiar song said to resemble the rubbing together of two sticks and the croaking of frogs! Their relationship is obscure, but are thought by some to be affiliated with the Cotingas.

1. WHITE-TIPPED PLANTCUTTER

Phytotoma rutila *

7.5". Slightly crested. Forecrown and underparts deep cinnamon rufous; back gray, streaked black. Wings dusky brown with prominent white wing bar; tail blackish, all but central feathers tipped white. ♀: Sparrowlike. Above dark brown, streaked white; rump gray, streaked black. Below white, becoming buffy on lower abdomen, streaked everywhere with black. Wings and tail as in ♂. Young birds are much browner than adults.

Highlands of BOLIVIA from La Paz to Santa Cruz and s to Potosí and Tarija; PARAGUAY; URUGUAY; ARGENTINA s to Río Negro.

Plate 16

2. RUFOUS-TAILED PLANTCUTTER

Phytotoma rara

7.8". Crown chestnut; back olive brown heavily streaked black. Wings black; median coverts broadly, greater coverts narrowly, edged white. Sides of head black; patch on lower ear coverts and the moustachial streak white. Below deep cinnamon rufous. Central tail feathers dusky, rest with outer web and broad tip black, rest of inner webs chestnut. ♀: Sparrow-like. Above olive brown, streaked black. Throat buff; rest of underparts buff, streaked black. Wings with narrow buffy double bar. Tail as in ♂.

CHILE from Atacama to Aysén; ARGENTINA from Neuquén to Río Negro. [Acc. Falkland Is.]

3. PERUVIAN PLANTCUTTER

Phytotoma raimondii

7.2". Forehead rufous chestnut; back gray, middle of back spotted black. Below pale gray, center of abdomen and under tail coverts cinnamon rufous. Wings black with broad double wing bar and edges to inner remiges white. Tail as in 1. ♀: Sparrow-like. Above blackish brown, streaked white; below buffy white, streaked blackish brown. Wings and tail as in ♂.

Coastal nw PERU from Tumbes to n Lima.

Family ALAUDIDAE   LARKS

The only American member of the lark family, essentially an Old World group, is the Horned Lark. It is widespread in North America from Alaska to Mexico and reappears, after a gap of about 2000 miles, in the northwest corner of South America in the Eastern Andes of Colombia.

Horned Larks are birds of open fields and swampy meadows where they walk, rather than hop, in search of insects.

HORNED LARK

Eremophila alpestris *

6". Forehead and eyebrow white, forecrown and line above eyebrow black, line prolonged backward to form two "horns." Lores and broad stripe turning downward below eye blackish, the stripe bordering the straw yellow throat. Breast band black; rest of underparts white, tinged rufous just below breast band. Hindcrown to upper mantle, sides of breast, upper tail coverts and wing coverts cinnamon rufous. Tail feathers black, outer web of outermost feather white.

Temperate zone of n part of E Andes of COLOMBIA. [Breeds in N Amer., s Mexico; Eurasia, n Africa; winters south to n Mexico and Florida, n Africa, n India, s China.]

Plate 29

Family HIRUNDINIDAE   SWALLOWS, MARTINS

Swallows are of virtually worldwide distribution, and although superficially like swifts, are in no way related to them.

They are easily distinguishable from swifts by much slower flight; less rasping, more twittering, notes; and by perching readily on wires, trees and other exposed places. Many species live near man, nesting in barns, under eaves, in church belfries and other suitable places. Some species nest in hollow trees and in burrows which they dig in banks.

Swallows live on insects caught on the wing; birds nesting in cold climates are migratory.

AID TO IDENTIFICATION

Above glossy blue-black or glossy greenish black

Below blue black 7, 10, with center of abdomen white 8a, with white band across chest 14

Below entirely white (rump like back) 1a, 12; (rump white) 2b, 3, 4, 5

Below white with blue black pectoral band 15

Below all or partly ashy 7, 8a, 9, 10, 11b, 21b

Throat buff to chestnut 13b, 20, 22, 23b

Above brown

With broad brown band across breast 1a, 6, 19

With underparts uniform grayish brown 16

With cinnamon buff throat 17, 18

1. TREE SWALLOW

Tachycineta bicolor

5". Above shining bluish green, below white. Wings and tail blue black. Tail forked. Imm.: Closely resembles 19 but larger and darker above, breast band paler.

Migrant from N Amer. Acc. in GUYANA (Apr.). Temperate e Nariño, COLOMBIA (Feb.). Off Trinidad (Apr.). [Breeds in N Amer. s to Mid-Atlantic states and California. Winters s to Honduras, irregularly Panama.]

2. MANGROVE SWALLOW

Tachycineta albilinea *

4.7". Above shiny, oily green; rump grayish white with dusky shaft streaks. Below grayish white, darkest on breast, breast with narrow dusky streaks. Wings blackish, innermost remiges narrowly edged white. Tail blackish, forked.

Coastal PERU from Piura to Libertad. [Mid. Amer.]

3. WHITE-WINGED SWALLOW

Tachycineta albiventer

5.5". Above shiny bluish green (old birds are very blue); rump and underparts white. Wings black, greater wing coverts and inner remiges very broadly edged white so as to form large white patch on closed wing. Tail black, slightly forked, basal part of inner web of outer feathers white.

Widespread throughout the humid regions e of Andes to n ARGENTINA. West of the Andes in n COLOMBIA to the Atrato Valley. Trinidad. Wooded rivers, marshes.

4. WHITE-RUMPED SWALLOW

Tachycineta leucorrhoa

Very like 3 but at once distinguishable by white supraloral streak, no white in wing or tail.

Se BRAZIL from Minas Gerais to Rio Grande do Sul and w across Mato Grosso to n BOLIVIA and central PERU, s to La Pampa and Buenos Aires, ARGENTINA. Open woodland, pastures.

5. CHILEAN SWALLOW

Tachycineta leucopyga

5". Above shiny deep ultramarine blue; rump and underparts white. Wings and tail blackish. Innermost remiges with narrow white apical edge. Tail slightly more forked than in 4.

Breeds in Atacama, CHILE, and Neuquén and Río Negro, ARGENTINA, s to Tierra del Fuego. Winters north to s BRAZIL and BOLIVIA. [Casual, Falkland Is.] Woodland, sometimes nests in towns and villages.

6. BROWN-CHESTED MARTIN

Phaeoprogne tapera *

7". Above smoky brown, wings and tail darker. Below white with well-marked smoky brown breast band (with drop-shaped smoky brown spots below breast band, 1). Tail forked (see 19).

Tropical zone. GUIANAS; VENEZUELA; n and e COLOMBIA south to nw PERU, Amazonian BRAZIL and in the e to Bahía.

BRAZIL from Minas Gerais and s Mato Grosso, PARAGUAY and BOLIVIA s to Buenos Aires and Mendoza, ARGENTINA, migrating n to COLOMBIA, VENEZUELA, GUIANAS and Trinidad, 1. [Migrant to Panama.] Open woodland, towns.

7. PURPLE MARTIN

Progne subis *

7.5". Shiny dark purplish blue; wings and tail blackish. Tail rather deeply forked. ♀: Above much duller blue than ♂, forehead and narrow collar on hindneck whitish; pale patch at sides of neck. Throat grayish, feathers with dark centers; breast smoky brown, feathers edged white; rest of underparts white with dark shaft streaks.

Winter resident (Sept.-Apr.). GUYANA, SURINAM, VENEZUELA and COLOMBIA south to n BOLIVIA and s BRAZIL. Curaçao; Trinidad? [Breeds from s Canada s to Baja California and Florida, migrating through Mid. Amer.] Open country.

8. CARIBBEAN MARTIN

Progne dominicensis *

Differs from 7 by slightly smaller size and largely blue underparts, but with pure white center of belly and under tail coverts. ♀: Bluer above than 7, throat paler, upper breast plain ashy brown, sides and flanks browner, rest of underparts white without dark shaft streaks.

Tobago, may breed. [Breeds in W Indies and w Mexico.] Frequents towns, cliffs.

9. GRAY-BREASTED MARTIN

Progne chalybea *

6.8" (or 8", southern breeders). Much like ♀ of 8, but forecrown blue instead of ashy, throat darker, sides of chest glossy blue. ♀: Much like 8, but forecrown darker, dusky brown; throat dark like breast, ashy of breast grading gradually into white of underparts instead of sharply defined from brownish sides and breast.

Generally distributed south, w of the Andes to nw PERU and e of Andes in the lowlands to Buenos Aires and Córdoba, ARGENTINA. Southern breeders migrate to VENEZUELA, SURINAM and Curaçao; Trinidad. [Breeds in Mid. Amer. Causal in Texas.] Towns, open lands and open woodland.

10. SOUTHERN MARTIN

Progne modesta*

6.5" (or 8", 1). Dark, somewhat glossy blue; wings and tail blackish, tail deeply forked (or with shorter, less deeply forked tail, 1). ♀: Steel blue above; throat, breast and sides of body smoky brown, feathers broadly edged white; center of abdomen white; under tail coverts white with dusky shaft streaks (or upperparts mouse gray; center of back, scapulars, lesser wing coverts and longest upper tail coverts steel blue; below mouse gray, under tail coverts fringed whitish, 1).

Coast of PERU from Piura to Ica, casually south to n CHILE, 1. BOLIVIA, PARAGUAY, URUGUAY and ARGENTINA s to Chubut, migrating north to nw BRAZIL, SURINAM and e PERU. [Galápagos Is. Casual to e Panama. Once Florida.] Rocky coasts, in cultivated lands, open woodland, villages.

11. BROWN-BELLIED SWALLOW

Notiochelidon murina*

5.5". Above steely green (or steely blue, 1); below smoky grayish brown. Wings and tail dark brown, tail rather deeply forked.

Upper subtropical to temperate zone. Nw VENEZUELA and mts. of COLOMBIA s to Arequipa, PERU. BOLIVIA in La Paz, 1. Cliffs, open mountain slopes.

12. BLUE-AND-WHITE SWALLOW

Notiochelidon cyanoleuca*

5". Upperparts and under tail coverts glossy steel blue; underparts white. Tail forked. Feet dusky. Imm. has buffy throat.

Tropical to temperate zone. Generally distributed s to Tierra del Fuego. Southern birds migratory. [Mid. Amer., breeder and migrant.] Open country near rivers, lakes and pastures. Towns.

13. PALE-FOOTED SWALLOW

Notiochelidon flavipes

4.8". Above dull, dark blue with little gloss. Throat and upper breast pinkish buff, sides of body blackish, center of breast and of belly white; under tail coverts blue black. Wings and tail black. Feet pinkish white.

Upper subtropical zone. Central Andes of COLOMBIA in Caldas and Tolima. PERU in Junín.

Plate 14

14. WHITE-BANDED SWALLOW

Atticora fasciata

6". Deep, glossy steel blue, band across lower breast and the thighs white. Tail long, deeply forked.

Tropical zone. GUIANAS; ne and s VENEZUELA; e COLOMBIA south to ne BOLIVIA. Amazonian BRAZIL s to Mato Grosso. Forested rivers.

Plate 24

15. BLACK-COLLARED SWALLOW

Atticora melanoleuca

5.5". Upperparts, sides of head and neck, and under tail coverts dark steely blue. Below white with dark blue band across breast. Tail long, deeply forked.

Tropical zone. GUYANA; SURINAM; s VENEZUELA; se COLOMBIA; Amazonian BRAZIL and in Goiás and Bahía. Forested rivers, particularly near rocky outcrops, waterfalls.

16. WHITE-THIGHED SWALLOW

Neochelidon tibialis*

5" (or 4.6", 1). Above dark brown with slight greenish gloss, rump pale smoky brown (or drab brown above with virtually no green gloss, rump not lighter than back, 1). Below smoky grayish brown, thighs white. Wings and tail blackish brown, tail rather long, forked.

Tropical zone. SURINAM (Sipaliwini); s VENEZUELA and se COLOMBIA south, e of Andes, to se PERU and Amazonian s BOLIVIA, PARAGUAY, and n ARGEN-Janeiro. West of E Andes in COLOMBIA and ECUADOR, 1. [Central and e Panama.] Forest and scrub.

17. TAWNY-HEADED SWALLOW

Alopochelidon fucata

5". Forehead, sides of head, throat, upper breast and nuchal collar tawny ochraceous; crown feathers black, edged tawny. Lower breast, belly and under tail coverts white. Back, wings and tail grayish brown, feathers pale-edged. Tail slightly forked.

Tropical, subtropical zones. VENEZUELA in mts. of Dist. Federal, Cumaná and e Bolívar. Extreme n BRAZIL in Roraima and in s from Minas Gerais to Rio Grande do Sul and Mato Grosso; URUGUAY; PARAGUAY; n and e BOLIVIA; se PERU; ARGENTINA s to Córdoba and Mendoza. Open hill country.

18. ROUGH-WINGED SWALLOW

Stelgidopteryx ruficollis *

5.3". Upperparts glossy brown, darker on crown, paler on rump. Throat cinnamon, breast and sides grayish brown, center of abdomen pale yellow. Wings and tail blackish; innermost remiges like back, edged whitish. Tail square.

Virtually throughout (except in Chile) to n Buenos Aires and Catamarca, ARGENTINA. Trinidad. [Breeds in N and Mid. Amer.] Open country, usually along rivers.

19. BANK SWALLOW

Riparia riparia *

5.2". Upperparts and sides of head smoky brown. Below white with smoky brown pectoral band and line down center of lower breast. Wings and tail blackish brown. Tail forked. [See 1 (imm.) and 6.]

Winter resident (Sept.-Apr.). Spottily recorded in GUYANA, VENEZUELA, COLOMBIA, w ECUADOR, e PERU, BRAZIL, s BOLIVIA, PARAGUAY, and n ARGENTINA. Curaçao, Bonaire. Trinidad. [Migrates through Mid. Amer. Breeds in temperate zone of N Hemisphere. Winters to Africa, India, Borneo and the Philippines.] Lakes, ponds, rivers, marshes.

20. BARN SWALLOW

Hirundo rustica *

6". Upperparts, sides of head and breast shiny ultramarine blue. Throat and breast chestnut, rest of underparts buffy white to cinnamon. Wings blackish; tail black, all but central feathers with median white blotch on inner web; outer feathers lengthened and narrowed apically.

Winter resident (Aug.-May). Occurs throughout from tropical to temperate zones to Tierra del Fuego. [Extralimital range much as in 19.] Pasturelands, marshlands.

21. ANDEAN SWALLOW

Petrochelidon andecola *

5.8". Glossy greenish to bluish black above, brownish on upper tail coverts. Throat and upper breast ashy gradually turning to pale grayish white on lower breast and belly. Wings and tail dusky. Tail slightly forked.

Puna zone. Central and s PERU; n CHILE; w, central and e BOLIVIA. Open mountain country.

22. CLIFF SWALLOW

Petrochelidon pyrrhonota *

5.8". Forehead buffy white, crown glossy blue black. Sides of head and neck, nuchal collar and upper throat chestnut, center of lower throat and of breast blue black, sides of lower breast buffy, rest of underparts white. Back glossy blue black, streaked white; rump rufous. Wings and tail dusky, tail square.

Transient, COLOMBIA, VENEZUELA. Winters from s BRAZIL s to Tucumán and Buenos Aires, ARGENTINA. Casual in CHILE to Tierra del Fuego. Aruba to Bonaire. [Breeds from Canada s to Mexico.] Open country, often along rivers.

23. CAVE SWALLOW

Petrochelidon fulva *

5.3". Forehead dull chestnut brown; crown and back glossy blue black, back streaked grayish; nuchal band and rump chestnut. Throat and sides of head white, tinged buff; pectoral band and streaks on sides dull chestnut, rest of underparts buffy white. Wings and tail dusky, tail square.

Tropical zone. Sw ECUADOR in Loja. W PERU in coastal Lima [S Texas; Mexico; Greater Antilles.] Cultivated lands, pastures.

Family CORVIDAE   JAYS

Jays belong to the crow family and are usually brightly colored in contrast to typical crows, which are not found in South America.

Jays inhabit wooded country and savanna and are gregarious, moving about in small flocks or family groups. They are found in all South American countries except Chile. They feed on insects, fruit, and even small mammals and reptiles.

AID TO IDENTIFICATION

Belly blue, more or less like back 3b, with pectoral band 1b, 2b, with throat and breast black 4c, 5, 6, 8a

Belly white (without moustachial streaks) 7c; (with white moustachial streak) 9a, 13b; (with blue moustachial streak) 10a, 11, 12c, 14

Belly bright yellow 14

1. COLLARED JAY

Cyanolyca viridicyana *

13". General plumage dark greenish blue to purplish blue. Forehead and mask black, forecrown and narrow band across lower throat silvery white to bluish white (or forecrown like back, throat band black, 1). Tail long, much graduated.

Subtropical, temperate zones. Nw VENE-ZUELA, Central and E Andes of COLOM-BIA and e and w ECUADOR, 1. E and central PERU to n BOLIVIA in Cocha-bamba. Forest.

Plate 15

2. TURQUOISE JAY

Cyanolyca turcosa

12.5". Resembles 1 (1), but much lighter and purer, less purplish blue, particularly on crown and throat.

Subtropical, temperate zones. COLOMBIA on both slopes of Andes of Nariño; e and w ECUADOR; nw PERU in Piura. Forest.

3. BEAUTIFUL JAY

Cyanolyca pulchra

10.5". Forehead and mask black. Crown milky bluish white becoming purplish blue on nape; mantel dusky purplish brown; lower back, rump, wings and tail purplish blue. Throat purplish blue, breast dusky blue, rest of underparts purplish blue.

Upper tropical and subtropical zones. Pacific COLOMBIA from upper río San Juan south to nw ECUADOR (Milpe). Forest.

4. AZURE JAY

Cyanocorax caeruleus

15". Bright blue; head, throat and breast black.

Se BRAZIL from São Paulo to Rio Grande do Sul; e PARAGUAY; ne ARGENTINA west to e Formosa and Chaco. Forest.

5. PURPLISH JAY

Cyanocorax cyanomelas

13". Forehead and lores black, hindcrown and nape blackish brown with violet tinge; throat and breast dull black; rest of plumage dull violet; tail violet blue.

Tropical, subtropical zones. Se PERU; BO-LIVIA except sw; PARAGUAY; Mato Grosso, BRAZIL; ne ARGENTINA from Misiones to Santa Fe, e Chaco and e Formosa. Groves of trees, tall trees in stream beds.

6. VIOLACEOUS JAY

Cyanocorax violaceus

13". Head, throat and breast black; hind-crown and sides of neck milky bluish white rapidly deepening into violet blue; below violet blue, paler than back. Wings and tail dark violet blue.

Tropical zone. GUYANA; VENEZUELA; e COLOMBIA; e ECUADOR; e PERU; w BRAZIL e to Roraima and the rio Purús. Forest, clearings.

7. CURL-CRESTED JAY

Cyanocorax cristatellus

12″. Forecrown and frontal crest, sides of head, throat and breast black; lower breast and rest of underparts white. Hindcrown and upper mantle violaceous brown; back and wings purplish blue. Basal third of tail blue, distal two-thirds white.

Tableland of BRAZIL from sw Pará, Maranhão and Piauí s to Mato Grosso and São Paulo. Cerrado.

8. AZURE-NAPED JAY

Cyanocorax heilprini

14″. Forecrown, sides of head and neck, the throat and breast black; forecrown feathers stiff and upstanding. Hindcrown, nape and short moustachial streak milky bluish white; rest of plumage light violet blue, fading to white on under tail coverts. Tail tipped white.

Tropical zone. W VENEZUELA from nw Amazonas s to immediately adjacent BRAZIL and COLOMBIA along ríos Guainía and Vaupés. Forest, savanna.

9. CAYENNE JAY

Cyanocorax cayanus

13″. Forecrown, sides of head and neck, throat and breast black; blue spot above and below eye; moustachial streak white. Hindcrown, nape, sides of breast and rest of underparts white. Back violet brown, rump white. Wings and tail violet blue, tail broadly stripped white.

Tropical zone. GUIANAS; VENEZUELA from Bolívar s to rio Branco-rio Negro region of BRAZIL. Treetops in forest and savanna; sometimes frequents fruit trees in settlements.

10. BLACK-CHESTED JAY

*Cyanocorax affinis**

13.5″. Head, sides of neck, throat and breast black; large spot above eye, smaller one below it, and conspicuous moustachial streak bright blue. Nape and rump blue, back violet blue. Lower breast and belly white to creamy white. Wings and tail deep blue; tail tipped white.

Tropical, subtropical zones. Nw VENEZUELA; COLOMBIA from Santa Marta region s to Bogotá and across Caribbean lowlands to Pacific, thence s to middle río San Juan in Chocó. [Costa Rica; Panama.] Woodland.

11. PLUSH-CRESTED JAY

*Cyanocorax chrysops**

14″. Head, sides of neck, throat and breast black; crown feathers plush-like, lengthened at nape; spot above eye bright silvery blue, spot below eye and moustachial streak deep blue. Band across nape milky bluish white becoming dark violet blue on back. Lower breast and belly creamy white. Wings and tail deep blue, tail broadly tipped creamy white.

BRAZIL s of the Amazon from e bank of rio Madeira e to upper rio Tapajós in se Pará; also in Alagoas, and from São Paulo to Rio Grande do Sul and se Mato Grosso; PARAGUAY; URUGUAY; n and e BOLIVIA; n ARGENTINA. Hab. as in 5, also cerrado and cerradão.

12. WHITE-NAPED JAY

Cyanocorax cyanopogon

14″. Not unlike 11 but bluish white of nape extending to upper back; back dark purplish brown. Breast and belly pure white. Wings and tail black, tail broadly tipped pure white.

BRAZIL from se Pará and Maranhão to Paraiba and south to w Paraná and e Mato Grosso. Forest.

13. WHITE-TAILED JAY

Cyanocorax mystacalis

13″. Head, sides of neck, throat and breast black; spot above eye and a broad moustachial streak which curves up to reach lower eyelid both milky bluish white. Nape, hindneck, upper mantle and underparts pure white. Back and wings bright blue. Central tail feathers blue, rest white.

Arid tropical zone. S ECUADOR from Guayas s to Libertad, PERU. Dry scrub.

14. GREEN JAY

*Cyanocorax yncas**

12.5″. The only South American jay with bright green back and bright yellow breast, belly and outer tail feathers. Forecrown with more to less prominent, upstanding crest; spot above eye and wide patch on cheeks bright deep blue. Sides of head, throat and breast black. Hindcrown to upper mantle white to pale blue depending on race. Central tail feathers green.

Tropical, subtropical zones. VENEZUELA n of the Orinoco; COLOMBIA except Santa Marta; e ECUADOR; e and central PERU; n BOLIVIA in La Paz and Cochabamba. [Se Texas to Honduras.] Forest.

Plate 16

Family CINCLIDAE   DIPPERS

Dippers are the only truly aquatic passerine birds. They are chunky, short-tailed terrestrial birds related to wrens. Living among boulders and along banks of mountain streams, they swim and dive easily and are able to walk submerged along the bottom. They fly swiftly, close over the water, and usually for short distances.

They live on mollusks, small fish, worms and some vegetable matter. Dippers also occur in North America and Eurasia.

1. WHITE-CAPPED DIPPER

*Cinclus leucocephalus**

6". Crown, nape, center of back and underparts white (or white confined to head and throat, 1, 2); sides of head and rest of plumage blackish brown (or much more grayish, 1). Basal part of remiges white.

Subtropical, temperate zones. Santa Marta Mts., COLOMBIA, 1. Nw VENEZUELA,

Andes of COLOMBIA s to ECUADOR. N PERU south to n BOLIVIA, 2.

Plate 29

2. RUFOUS-THROATED DIPPER

Cinclus schultzi

6". General color dark leaden gray; throat and sides of neck cinnamon.

Subtropical zone of nw ARGENTINA south to n Catamarca.

Family TROGLODYTIDAE   WRENS

Wrens are members of an essentially New World family—only one of its 39 species is found outside of the Americas. They live for the most part in low, tangled undergrowth and around treefalls, and seem to like the vicinity of water. Few species live inside forests. Grass wrens are fond of swampy fields and grassland; a few other kinds live in semidesert cactus scrub.

In South America wrens are found from the shores of the Caribbean to Cape Horn and up mountain slopes to snow line.

Almost all wrens are fine singers; their song is remarkably loud for their size. Both sexes sing and their plumage is similar. They feed chiefly on insects.

AID TO IDENTIFICATION

With spots, bars or streaks on underparts
> Throat only spotted or streaked 16b, 19a, 22b, 34
> Breast and belly spotted 2b, 3, 4a, 5b, 6a, 20b

Breast and belly or belly only barred 15b, 20b, 21b, 35, 36a, with white bar on wing 37

Underparts plain, unspotted and unbarred

Underparts all or mostly white 1a, 2b, 3, 7, 8b, 11, 18, 23a, 24a, 26b, 30, 33, 35

Underparts pale gray 17, 18, 29, 34

Underparts all or partly brown, chestnut, cinnamon or buff 9b, 10b, 11, 12a, 13a, 14b, 17a, 18a, 22b, 25, 26b, 27, 28c, 30, 31b, 32a, 35, 38b, 39

1. BICOLORED WREN

Campylorhynchus griseus *

7'' (or 8.5'', 2). Crown, nape and postocular streak dark brown; long broad eyebrow and entire underparts white; back rufescent brown (or brownish black like crown and nape, 2). Wings unbarred, blackish, edged (or not, 1) rufescent. Tail blackish, outer feathers more or less barred and tipped white (or all but central feathers distally white with narrow black tip, 2).

Tropical zone. W GUYANA; VENEZUELA s of the Orinoco and immediately adjacent BRAZIL. VENEZUELA n of the Orinoco; Caribbean lowlands of COLOMBIA, and e of Andes s to Meta, 1; drier parts of Magdalena Valley, 2. Forest edge and clearings, semiarid scrub, savanna.

2. WHITE-HEADED WREN

Campylorhynchus albobrunneus *

7.5''. Head and underparts white (or head variably clouded dusky; below dusky, sometimes with a few spots or bars or whitish clouded grayish, 1.) Upperparts, wings and tail dark chocolate brown (with traces of pale bars, 1).

Tropical zone. Pacific COLOMBIA s to Baudó Mts.; in sw Nariño, 1 (possibly hybirds of this species and 6 or possibly 3). [Central and e Panama.] Humid forest edge and clearings.

3. THRUSH-LIKE WREN

Campylorhynchus turdinus *

8''. Above grayish brown to brownish gray, the feathers with dusky centers. Below white lightly to heavily spotted with dusky brown (or virtually unspotted, 1). Wings and tail dark brown, the outer webs of primaries more or less notched paler.

Tropical zone. COLOMBIA e of the Andes south to n BOLIVIA. Amazonian BRAZIL s of the Amazon and in the east s to Espírito Santo. E BOLIVIA and w Mato Grosso, 1.

4. STRIPE-BACKED WREN

Campylorhynchus nuchalis *

7''. Above black, broadly striped white; suggestion of rufescent nuchal collar. Below white, lightly to heavily spotted black. Wing and tail feathers black, notched white.

Tropical zone. N VENEZUELA south to the s bank of the Orinoco. COLOMBIA e to upper río Sinú. Dry woodland, forest edge, usually near streams and lagoons.

5. FASCIATED WREN

Campylorhynchus fasciatus *

7.5''. Rather like 4 but upperparts banded instead of striped.

Tropical semiarid zone of sw ECUADOR s in PERU to Ancash, and in n interior valleys of the ríos Marañón and Huallaga from Piura to central Huánuco and Lima. Thorny scrub, cactus.

Plate 29

6. BAND-BACKED WREN

Campylorhynchus zonatus *

Much like 4 with similar rufescent nuchal collar, but back banded instead of striped, and white bands tinged buff; lower breast and abdomen cinnamon buff instead of white; tail feathers barred instead of notched.

Tropical zone. N COLOMBIA from Santa Marta Mts. to Córdoba. Nw ECUADOR. Dry forest and clearings.

7. TOOTH-BILLED WREN

Odontorchilus cinereus

4.5''. Above mouse gray, crown tinged dark brown, eyebrow buffy. Below dirty white. Tail gray, banded black.

Amazonian BRAZIL s of the Amazon from río Xingú to Tapajós, and on upper río Madeira.

8. GRAY-MANTLED WREN

Odontorchilus branickii *

4.5". Above bluish slaty gray, crown and nape brown, paler on forehead, sides of head streaked white. Below white. Tail barred black and gray (or four middle feathers virtually uniform gray, 1).

Tropical, lower subtropical zones. COLOMBIA in upper Magdalena Valley. E ECUADOR s to Junín and Cuzco, PERU. Nw ECUADOR, 1.

Plate 14

9. RUFOUS WREN

Cinnycerthia unirufa *

7". Uniform rufous chestnut (or chestnut brown, 1), lores black. Wing feathers with very narrow wavy black lines. Tail with suggestion of barring.

Subtropical to temperate zone. Nw VENEZUELA and n part of E Andes of COLOMBIA; Central Andes of COLOMBIA and Andes of ECUADOR, 1. Forest.

Plate 14

10. SEPIA-BROWN WREN

Cinnycerthia peruana *

5.5" (or 6.5", 2). Reddish sepia brown, postocular streak grayish (or with broad buffy white eyebrow, 1); wings and tail with numerous narrow black bars (or darker and browner throughout with no postocular streak, but often with buffy white patch on forecrown, 2).

Subtropical, temperate zones. Andes of COLOMBIA and ECUADOR, 2. PERU in Junín. From Puno and Cuzco south to n BOLIVIA, 1.

11. GRASS WREN (or Short-billed Marsh-Wren)

Cistothorus platensis *

4". Crown brown, streaked black in some races; short eyebrow buffy white. Mantle black broadly streaked buffy white. Inner remiges and tail rufescent, barred black. Underparts buffy to white.

Tropical to temperate zone. GUYANA, VENEZUELA and COLOMBIA s through ARGENTINA and CHILE to Tierra del Fuego [Falkland Is., s Canada, US south locally to w Panama.] Grasslands, wet meadows, tidal marshes.

12. PARAMO WREN

Cistothorus meridae

Differs from 11 mainly by very broad white eyebrow reaching sides of the neck.

Temperate, páramo zones in Trujillo and Mérida, nw VENEZUELA. Grassland.

13. APOLINAR'S MARSH-WREN

Cistothorus apolinari

5". Differs from 11 by much larger size, broader black bands on tail, and gray instead of white eyebrow.

Temperate zone of northern E Andes of COLOMBIA, near Bogotá and the Páramo de Sumapaz. Marshy meadows.

14. SOOTY-HEADED WREN

Thryothorus spadix

6". Crown dark smoky gray; throat and sides of head black, ear coverts streaked white; rest of plumage chestnut. Center of belly buffy gray with a few blackish bars. Tail broadly barred black.

Upper tropical, lower subtropical zones in río San Juan Valley, w COLOMBIA. [E Panama.] Forest undergrowth.

15. BLACK-BELLIED WREN

Thryothorus fasciatoventris *

6". Upperparts rufous. Eyebrow, throat and upper breast white; lower breast black, belly black with narrow white bars, sides tinged rusty. Tail barred black.

Tropical zone. N COLOMBIA from Santa Marta w to the lower Cauca, and lower Atrato and s to río San Juan. [Costa Rica; Panama.] Undergrowth in semideciduous forest and forest edge.

16. PLAIN-TAILED WREN

Thryothorus euophrys *

6.5". Forecrown grayish brown to blackish, upperparts rufous including unbarred tail. Eyebrow white, streak through eye and moustachial streaks black. Throat and breast white coarsely and heavily (or lightly, 1) spotted black, rest of underparts buffy (or with center of underparts whitish gray, 1).

Upper subtropical zone. Sw COLOMBIA and w ECUADOR. E ECUADOR and ne PERU, 1. Forest.

17. MOUSTACHED WREN

Thryothorus genibarbis *

6.5". Crown, nape and upper mantle gray to dusky brownish gray; sides of head gray, streaked white on ear coverts; eyebrow and throat white to buff with prominent moustachial streaks. Breast grayish, belly buffy to brown. Tail rufous or buffy gray or olive brown, barred black (or uniform bright rufous, 1).

Upper tropical and subtropical zones. N VENEZUELA in Dist. Federal, Carabobo, Miranda and Aragua, 1. Nw VENEZUELA; COLOMBIA; e ECUADOR; e PERU; n BO-LIVIA; Amazonian BRAZIL s of the Amazon, and in the e and center from Maranhão and Ceará s to Rio de Janeiro and Mato Grosso. Forest edge, capoeira, cerrado.

Plate 14

18. CORAYA WREN

Thryothorus coraya *

Rather like 17 but somewhat smaller and at once distinguishable by lower cheeks solid black without moustachial streaks. Throat white, rest of lowerparts grayish buff, or rufous or white. Tail barred (or tail unbarred, 1).

Tropical, subtropical zone. GUIANAS; VENEZUELA s of the Orinoco; e COLOMBIA; e ECUADOR; e PERU; BRAZIL n of the Amazon; s of it between rios Tapajós and Tocantins, 1. Savanna and forest undergrowth.

19. RUFOUS-BREASTED WREN

Thryothorus rutilus *

5.5". Above light reddish brown to olive brown, crown more rufescent than back. Throat and sides of head checkered black and white, upper breast orange rufous (lightly spotted black, 1), sides of body light cinnamon brown, center of underparts white, under tail coverts barred black. Tail barred gray and black.

Tropical, subtropical zones. VENEZUELA n of the Orinoco. COLOMBIA in the Santa Marta region, 1; east slope of E Andes s to Meta, west slope in s Magdalena. Trinidad, Tobago. [Sw Costa Rica to Panama.] Woodland undergrowth, tangled vines, treefalls.

20. SPOT-BREASTED WREN

Thryothorus maculipectus *

5.5". Upperparts and tail much as in 19. Underparts and sides of head white, profusely spotted and barred black (or similar but belly dull ochraceous, unspotted, 1).

Subtropical zone. COLOMBIA on w slope of Central Andes in Valle, and possibly w slope of E Andes in Tolima. Arid tropical zone of w ECUADOR south to Piura, nw PERU; in upper tropical and subtropical Marañón Valley in Cajamarca, 1. [Mexico to Costa Rica.]

21. BAY WREN

Thryothorus nigricapillus *

5.5". Crown and nape deep black, sides of head mixed black and white. Back rufous chestnut. Tail barred chestnut and black. Throat and upper breast barred black and white, belly reddish brown barred black (or throat and upper breast white, belly only tinged reddish brown, barred black, 1).

Tropical, lower subtropical zones. W CO-LOMBIA from Gulf of Urabá s along Pacific slope to río Dagua, middle Cauca and middle Magdalena valleys; from the río Dagua south through w ECUADOR to Peruvian border, 1. [Nicaragua to Panama.]

22. STRIPE-THROATED WREN

Thryothorus thoracicus *

4.5". Above earthy brown to grayish brown, wings and tail barred black. Throat and sides of head streaked black and white; underparts light reddish brown (or grayish brown, 1).

Tropical zone. COLOMBIA in Córdoba and n Chocó, 1; thence s along Pacific lowlands to nw ECUADOR. [Nicaragua southward.]

23. RUFOUS-AND-WHITE WREN

Thryothorus rufalbus *

6". Above deep rufous-chestnut (or light rufous chestnut, 1), wings and tail barred black. Below white, sides rufescent, under tail coverts barred black. Lores and eyebrow white, postocular streak chestnut, cheeks and sides of neck streaked black and white. Rump feathers with small concealed white subapical spots.

Tropical, lower subtropical zones. N VENE-ZUELA from Paria Peninsula to Falcón and s to the e llanos of Guárico. Interior nw

VENEZUELA from Cojedes west in ne COLOMBIA to Cartagena, e of Andes to Macarena Mts., 1. [Mid. Amer.] Tangled growth, often near streams.

24. NICEFORO'S WREN

Thryothorus nicefori

6.5". Differs from 23 by crown and mantle olive brown, becoming somewhat rufescent on lower back; subapical white spots on rump larger, rounder and edged black. Below white, sides grayish.

Upper tropical zone. W slope of E Andes in Santander, COLOMBIA. Woodland, coffee plantations.

25. BUFF-BREASTED WREN

Thryothorus leucotis *

5.6". Above reddish brown becoming rufous on upper tail coverts. Wings and tail barred black. Eyebrow white, postocular streak dusky; lores and sides of head white, latter lightly streaked dusky. Throat white gradually changing through buff on breast to rufous on belly. Not unlike 22 but easily separated by color of underparts.

Tropical zone. GUIANAS, VENEZUELA and n COLOMBIA s to Junín, PERU, and through Amazonian BRAZIL to Mato Grosso and Amazonas, in the e from Maranhão s through Piauí, Goiás and w Minas Gerais to w São Paulo. [Central and e Panama, Pearl Is.] Shrubbery and undergrowth, tangled vines near lagoons and wet places.

26. FAWN-BREASTED WREN

Thryothorus guarayanus

Very like 25 but distinguishable by darker, grayer, less reddish back and more strongly streaked cheeks. Probably a subspecies of 25.

N BOLIVIA east to w Mato Grosso, BRAZIL.

27. SUPERCILIATED WREN

Thryothorus superciliaris *

6". Differs from 25 mainly by white unstreaked sides of head, broader white eyebrow and unbarred rufous under tail coverts.

Arid coastal area from Manabí, ECUADOR to Ancash, PERU. Arid scrub.

28. LONG-BILLED WREN

Thryothorus longirostris *

Very like 25 in color but bill much longer (1" vs .6").

Interior e BRAZIL from Piauí, Ceará and Pernambuco s to Bahía, and coastally from Espírito Santo to Santa Catarina. Forest edge, caatinga.

29. GRAY WREN

Thryothorus griseus

5". Distinct from other species by very short (1.3") tail. Above light grayish brown, tail neutral gray irregularly barred black. Superciliaries dull white. Below smoky gray, somewhat darker on flanks; under tail coverts with faint dusky bars.

BRAZIL in sw Amazonas.

30. HOUSE WREN

Troglodytes aedon *

4.7". Above reddish brown to gray brown, the back sometimes with a few narrow black bars. Lores whitish; eyebrow narrow, inconspicuous, whitish to buffy. Wings and tail barred with black, tail like back or rufous in some races. Below drab white to pinkish white to light cinnamon, under tail coverts barred or not.

Tropical to temperate zone throughout. Trinidad and Tobago. [Falkland Is.; s Canada s through Mid. Amer.; W Indies.] Mangroves, plantations, forest clearings, savanna, gardens, habitations, arid scrub, cerrado.

31. MOUNTAIN WREN

Troglodytes solstitialis *

Not unlike 30 but smaller and at once distinguishable by broad conspicuous white to buff eyebrow and black-barred white under tail coverts.

Subtropical to páramo zone. Nw VENEZUELA and mts. of COLOMBIA s through Andes to nw ARGENTINA. Bushes and shrubs.

32. TEPUI WREN

Troglodytes rufulus *

4.5". Entire upperparts, wings and tail rufous brown; wings and tail narrowly barred black. Eyebrow, throat and cheeks pale chestnut; center of underparts whitish, sides rufous brown (or underparts more whitish, flanks and belly lighter reddish brown, 1; or underparts uniform gray, 2).

Subtropical zone. VENEZUELA on isolated peaks in Bolívar; in Amazonas, 1, on Cerro La Neblina, 2. Immediately adjacent BRAZIL in Roraima. Woodland undergrowth, campos.

33. WHITE-BREASTED WOOD-WREN

Henicorhina leucosticta *

4". Crown, nape and sometimes upper mantle black (or chestnut like back, 1); conspicuous eyebrow white, broad postocular stripe black, lower cheeks streaked black and white. Back chestnut, wings and tail strongly barred black. Throat, breast and center of belly white; flanks chestnut brown.

Tropical, lower subtropical zones. GUYANA; SURINAM; VENEZUELA s of the Orinoco; e COLOMBIA w across Caribbean lowlands to n Chocó; from lower río San Juan to nw ECUADOR, 1. E of the Andes s to Huánuco, PERU. N BRAZIL on upper río Negro and in Amapá. [Mid. Amer.] Thick undergrowth in forest and savanna near fallen trees.

34. GRAY-BREASTED WOOD-WREN

Henicorhina leucophrys *

4.2". Very like 33 but distinguishable by lighter chestnut back, throat and breast pale gray instead of white, and much less heavily barred wings and tail. Size slightly larger, tail longer, bill smaller.

Upper tropical and subtropical zones. N VENEZUELA e to Miranda; COLOMBIA; e and w ECUADOR; e and central PERU, n BOLIVIA. [Mid. Amer.] Forest undergrowth often near fallen trees.

Plate 14

35. NIGHTINGALE WREN

Microcerculus marginatus *

4.5". Bill rather long; tail very short, hardly longer than tail coverts. Above deep reddish brown, wings and tail unbarred. Throat and breast white, sides of body like back. Young birds are at first dark brown below with whitish throat; later with white, dark-barred underparts, bars disappearing as bird matures.

Tropical, lower subtropical zones. N VENEZUELA e to Aragua and south to w Amazonas; COLOMBIA; e and w ECUADOR; e PERU; Amazonian BRAZIL (n of the Amazon e only to rio Negro); w BOLIVIA. [Mid. Amer.] Forest undergrowth.

36. FLUTIST WREN

Microcerculus ustulatus *

4". Chestnut brown; throat tawny, breast and belly dark brown to grayish brown with some dusky edges to feathers.

Subtropical zone. W GUYANA. Mts. of VENEZUELA s of the Orinoco. BRAZIL in Roraima. Forest undergrowth.

37. WING-BANDED WREN

Microcerculus bambla *

4.3". At once distinguishable from other wrens by broad white wing band formed by tips of wing coverts. Upperparts and belly dark brown, feathers edged blackish; throat and breast pale gray, finely barred with wavy lines.

Tropical zone. GUIANAS; VENEZUELA s of the Orinoco; BRAZIL n of the Amazon; e ECUADOR. Forest undergrowth.

38. CHESTNUT-BREASTED WREN

Cyphorhinus thoracicus *

6". Culmen elevated at base. Upperparts, wings and belly dark umber brown; tail black; throat, breast and sides of head chestnut rufous.

Upper tropical and subtropical zones. COLOMBIA in Central and W Andes; e ECUADOR s to Puno, PERU. Forest.

39. MUSICIAN WREN

Cyphorhinus arada *

5". Forehead orange rufous, darkening to chestnut on crown; broad black, white-spotted collar from sides of neck across upper back; back brown; wings and tail barred black. Throat and breast orange rufous, lower breast and belly whitish; under tail coverts barred, (or much darker with no black and white collar, the back dark brown, throat and breast light to dark chestnut, belly grayish or dark brown; southern races with rufous eyebrow, 1). In nw birds often show little to considerable white on throat.

Tropical zone. GUIANAS; VENEZUELA in the Gran Sabana, Bolívar; n BRAZIL e to rio Negro. COLOMBIA, e and w ECUADOR, e PERU, n BOLIVIA and BRAZIL s of the Amazon e to rio Tapajós, 1 (*phaeocephalus** from west of Andes may be a distinct species). [Honduras southward.] Thick forest undergrowth. Riverbanks.

Plate 50

Family MIMIDAE   MOCKINGBIRDS, THRASHERS

Mockingbirds form a small, exclusively American family. The typical species are rather slender with longish tails extensively tipped white, or with white outer tail feathers. Their backs are gray or brown, underparts usually whitish (spotted in young birds). They are found in more or less open, sometimes arid country and feed on insects. Most species are notable for their song and agressive habits.

The rather aberrant mockingthrush differs from others in preferring marshy habitats; it is the only species of the group with cinnamon buff underparts.

1. TROPICAL MOCKINGBIRD

*Mimus gilvus**

10". Above pale gray; below white. Cheeks dusky, eyebrow white. Wings and tail black; tail much graduated, broadly tipped white.

Tropical, subtropical zones. GUIANAS; VENEZUELA; n COLOMBIA. BRAZIL in Roraima and from e Pará, Ceará and Pernambuco s to Bahía and Rio de Janeiro. Aruba to Trinidad. [S Mexico to El Salvador. Introduced Panama.] Campos, arid scrub, gardens, bushy pastures.

2. CHILEAN MOCKINGBIRD

Mimus thenca

11". Upperparts dull brown; underparts pale brownish gray, streaked dusky on belly. Broad eyebrow and throat white; conspicuous moustachial streaks and stripe through eye blackish. Wings and tail dusky, wing coverts and tail tipped white.

CHILE from Atacama s to Valdivia. Bush-covered hillsides.

3. LONG-TAILED MOCKINGBIRD

*Mimus longicaudatus**

11". Feathers of crown and back dusky brown, broadly edged pale gray. Broad eyebrow white, stripe through eye black, lower cheeks white encircled by broad blackish moustachial streak; patch at sides of neck white. Throat and belly white; breast brownish gray, feathers edged white.

Wings and tail dusky brown. Greater wing coverts largely white, forming conspicuous patch. Tail broadly tipped white.

Tropical zone. Sw ECUADOR south to Arequipa, PERU, and in upper Marañón Valley. Arid scrub, often near streams.

4. CHALK-BROWED MOCKINGBIRD

*Mimus saturninus**

10". Above dark brown, feathers edged dull gray, below white. Broad eyebrow white, stripe through eye black. Wings and tail brownish black, wing coverts and remiges edged white, tail broadly tipped white.

E and s BRAZIL from the lower Amazon e to Maranhão and Paraíba, s to Mato Grosso and Rio Grande do Sul, URUGUAY, PARAGUAY, n BOLIVIA and n ARGENTINA. Campos, bushy pastures, cerrado.

Plate 29

5. PATAGONIAN MOCKINGBIRD

Mimus patagonicus

9". Above plain brownish gray. Eyebrow white. Throat white with narrow, indistinct moustachial streaks. Breast grayish brown, paler than back; center of belly whitish; sides dull, pale cinnamon. Wings and tail black, wing coverts and remiges edged white; tail tipped white.

ARGENTINA s to Santa Cruz. CHILE from Aysén to Tierra del Fuego. Bushy hillsides, pastures.

6. WHITE-BANDED MOCKINGBIRD

Mimus triurus

9". Crown and mantle grayish brown, changing to rufous brown on rump. Eyebrow white. Wings black; wing coverts and inner remiges largely white, forming wing stripe. Underparts dirty white, buffy on sides and under tail coverts. Four central tail feathers black, rest mostly white.

S BRAZIL in w Rio Grande do Sul and s Mato Grosso. URUGUAY; PARAGUAY; e and n BOLIVIA; n and central ARGENTINA. Acc. in CHILE. Bushy pastureland.

7. BROWN-BACKED MOCKINGBIRD

Mimus dorsalis

11". Upperparts chocolate brown, rufous brown on tail coverts. Eyebrow and underparts soiled white. Wings black, remiges basally white forming conspicuous wing patch. Tail as in 6.

Temperate, puna zones. BOLIVIA from La Paz and Cochabamba s to Potosí and Tarija. ARGENTINA in Jujuy. Bushy hillsides.

8. BLACK-CAPPED MOCKINGTHRUSH

Donacobius atricapillus *

8". Top and sides of head black. Back dark chocolate brown to blackish brown. Underparts deep cinnamon buff finely barred black on sides, these marks very variable and sometimes absent. Wings black, base of remiges white. Tail black, tipped white.

Tropical, lower subtropical zones. GUIANAS, VENEZUELA and COLOMBIA south through e ECUADOR and BRAZIL to BOLIVIA, PARAGUAY and ne ARGENTINA from Chaco eastward. [E Panama.] Riparian swampy scrub, marshes.

Plate 15

9. PEARLY-EYED THRASHER

Margarops fuscatus *

11". Upperparts, wings and tail dusky brown, feathers pale-edged; throat white, streaked reddish brown; breast and sides reddish brown, feathers edged white; center of belly white. Bill yellowish, iris white.

VENEZUELA on La Horquilla I.; Bonaire. [The Bahamas. Puerto Rico. The Lesser Antilles.] Scrub, woodland.

Family TURDIDAE   THRUSHES, SOLITAIRES

Thrushes form a very large family of birds found virtually throughout the world. Famous as songbirds, they are rather dull in color. South American species do not differ appreciably from thrushes found elsewhere; they are easily recognizable as thrushes, some even closely resembling the familiar American Robin or European Blackbird. Most species are largely terrestrial and feed on insects and berries.

The forest-inhabiting solitaires, which are also found in western North America, differ from typical thrushes by stubby, rather wide bills, short legs and purely arboreal habits.

AID TO IDENTIFICATION

Breast spotted or throat streaked

Breast spotted 7b, 8, 9a, 10, 19b

Throat streaked (with pure gray back) 16, 17b; (with rufous belly or sides) 20b, 21, 27c, 32c; (with conspicuous white patch at base of throat) 24, 25, 32; (size very large, 13") 14b; (nondescript) 11, 16, 22b, 23, 25, 26, 27, 28, 29a, 30, 31

Underparts without spots or streaks

With black in plumage (cheeks pure white) 3b, 4b; (all black) 11a, 12, 13b, 14b, 15; (with black head and breast) 11, 18; (head only black) 20b

No black in plumage (gray or grayish white below) 1a, 5a, 6b, over 12" 14 b; (brown or brownish below) 2, 12, 13b, 14b, 15, 18

1. ANDEAN SOLITAIRE

Myadestes ralloides *

6.5". Bill short and wide, lower mandible yellow. Above rufous brown becoming more rufous toward rump. Forehead and fore-crown gray in some races. Below leaden gray. Tail dark brown, outer feathers with white on inner web.

Subtropical zone. Nw VENEZUELA and Andes of COLOMBIA south to n BOLIVIA. [Costa Rica; Panama.] Forest treetops.

Plate 14

2. RUFOUS-BROWN SOLITAIRE

Myadestes leucogenys *

9". Upperparts, wings and tail reddish brown. Throat ochraceous tawny, breast reddish brown; belly pale grayish, tinged brown; under tail coverts ochraceous orange (or buff, 1).

Lower subtropical zone. W GUYANA; VEN-EZUELA in se Bolívar. Nw ECUADOR. Central PERU. Coastal BRAZIL in se Bahía and Espírito Santo, 1. Forest.

3. WHITE-EARED SOLITAIRE

Entomodestes leucotis

9.5". Crown and nape black (dark brown, ♀). Broad streak below eye white. Upper-parts and inner remiges rufous chestnut, lowerparts glossy black. Primaries black with white patch on inner web near base. Tail black, outer two feathers broadly tipped white.

Subtropical zone. PERU from Libertad to Puno; n BOLIVIA in La Paz and Cocha-bamba. Forest.

4. BLACK SOLITAIRE

Entomodestes coracinus

9". Jet black. Broad cheek patch, axillaries, patch on inner web of inner remiges and distal part of outer tail feathers white.

Upper tropical and subtropical zones. W Andes of COLOMBIA to nw ECUADOR. Dense humid forest, treetops.

Plate 50

5. ORANGE-BILLED NIGHTINGALE-THRUSH

Catharus aurantiirostris *

6.5". Above light reddish brown (or oliva-ceous brown, 1; with crown grayish, 2). Throat and center of underparts white, breast and sides light gray. Bill and legs orange.

Upper tropical and subtropical zones. VEN-EZUELA n of the Orinoco w to Santa Marta Mts. of COLOMBIA; in E Andes and upper Magdalena Valley, 1; in upper Cauca and Patía Valleys and Nariño, 2. Trinidad [Mexi-co to w Panama.] Dense second growth, forest edge, bamboo thickets.

6. SLATY-BACKED NIGHTINGALE-THRUSH

Catharus fuscater *

7.2". Upperparts and sides of head dark leaden gray, blacker on crown and nape (or dark brownish gray, 1). Throat, breast and sides lighter gray than back; center of abdomen white. Wings and tail like back. Bill and legs orange.

Subtropical zone. Nw VENEZUELA w to Santa Marta Mts. and northern E Andes of COLOMBIA; e and w ECUADOR. Central PERU to n BOLIVIA, 1. [Costa Rica; Panama.] Thick forest.

7. SPOTTED NIGHTINGALE-THRUSH

Catharus dryas *

6". Top and sides of head black; back, wings and tail olive. Underparts apricot yellow, throat and breast spotted dusky. Bill crim-son; eye ring and legs orange red. Olive and yellow tints in the plumage quickly fade in skins, back becomes gray, underparts buffy white.

Upper tropical zone. Nw VENEZUELA; COLOMBIA e of Andes and head of Magda-lena Valley; e and w ECUADOR south to n and e BOLIVIA and nw ARGENTINA. [S Mexico; Guatemala; Honduras.] Forest.

Plate 29

8. VEERY

Catharus fuscescens

7". Upperparts, wings and tail reddish brown. Throat and upper breast buffy lightly spotted on sides of neck and upper breast with dusky, rest of underparts white.

Winter resident (Oct.-Apr.). GUYANA; VENEZUELA; n COLOMBIA. BRAZIL s to lower Amazon and in w Mato Grosso. Acc. Curaçao. [Breeds in s Canada and US. Migrates through Mid. Amer. Rare transient W Indies.] Forest edge.

9. GRAY-CHEEKED THRUSH

Catharus minimus *

Not unlike 8 but back and sides of head olive, sides of body strongly shaded grayish and spots on breast blacker and more prominent.

Winter resident (Sept.-May). GUYANA; VENEZUELA; n COLOMBIA; ECUADOR; ne PERU; nw BRAZIL. Curaçao. Trinidad. [Breeds in e Siberia and N Amer. Migrates through W Indies and Mid. Amer.] Open woodland, semiarid scrub.

10. SWAINSON'S THRUSH

Catharus ustulatus *

Very like 9; best distinguished by buffy eye ring and cheeks.

Winter resident (Oct.-Apr.). GUYANA; VENEZUELA and COLOMBIA south to w ARGENTINA, PARAGUAY and w BRA-ZIL. [Breeds in N Amer. Migrates and winters through Mid. Amer.] Woodland.

11. YELLOW-LEGGED THRUSH

Platycichla flavipes *

8.5". Head, throat, breast, wings and tail black; rest of plumage bluish gray (or all black, 1). Iris dark brown; bill and legs yellow. ♀: Upperparts, wings and tail oliva-ceous brown; underparts pale brown, streaked dusky on throat; center of abdo-men paler. Iris brown, eye ring yellow. Bill blackish, ridge yellow; legs yellow.

Upper tropical and subtropical zones. W GUYANA; VENEZUELA n of the Orinoco and in Bolívar; immediately adjacent n BRAZIL; COLOMBIA in Santa Marta Mts. and e slope of Andes in Norte de Santander. E BRAZIL in Paraíba and from s Bahía to Rio Grande do Sul; e PARAGUAY and ne ARGENTINA. Trinidad. Tobago, 1. Forest, parks.

Plate 29

12. PALE-EYED THRUSH

Platycichla leucops

8.5". Glossy black. Iris greenish white; bill and legs orange yellow. ♀: Dark umber brown above including wings and tail. Throat and breast brown, belly pale gray. Bill black; legs yellowish brown. Iris brown.

Subtropical zone. Nw GUYANA; VENE-ZUELA; COLOMBIA; e and w ECUADOR; PERU; n BOLIVIA; BRAZIL in Roraima. Treetops in very humid forest.

13. CHIGUANCO THRUSH

Turdus chiguanco *

11". Pale ashy brown, (or dark sooty, 1). Bill orange red, legs pale yellow.

Coast and mts. from s ECUADOR south to n CHILE; from BOLIVIA s to Córdoba, ARGENTINA, and acc. in CHILE, 1. Shady woodland near streams, orchards.

14. GREAT THRUSH

Turdus fuscater *

13". From dark to light brownish or grayish olive like 13; distinguishable in field only by larger size; also shorter bill (with streaked throat in ♂, 1). Bill orange yellow, legs yellow.

Subtropical to páramo zone. Nw VENE-ZUELA s through Andes of COLOMBIA (including Santa Marta Mts.) to se PERU. BOLIVIA in La Paz and Cochabamba, 1. Grassland with stunted trees and bushes.

15. GLOSSY-BLACK THRUSH

Turdus serranus *

10". Similar to 12 but considerably larger, has orange eye ring, and iris brown instead of greenish white. Bill orange red, legs orange yellow. ♀: Differs from 12 by larger size and brown belly, uniform with breast instead of contrasting gray.

Subtropical, temperate zones. N VENE-ZUELA, Andes of COLOMBIA; e and w ECUADOR; PERU (on the west s to Caja-marca) south to n and se BOLIVIA. Forest.

16. SLATY THRUSH

Turdus nigriceps *

9". Top and sides of head black, back and wings dark gray, tail black. Throat white sharply streaked black; breast and sides gray, center of belly white; under wing coverts gray (or paler throughout with top and sides of head gray, white under wing coverts, 1). Bill and legs yellow. ♀: Like ♂ in pattern but umber brown instead of gray.

Subtropical zone. Se ECUADOR, PERU (on the west, south to s Cajamarca) s to BOLIVIA and w ARGENTINA to Córdoba. E and s BRAZIL from Goiás s to Paraná, PARAGUAY and ne ARGENTINA, 1. Forest.

17. PLUMBEOUS-BACKED THRUSH

Turdus reevei

9.5″. Upperparts, wings and tail blue gray; throat white, narrowly but sharply streaked black; rest of underparts grayish white, tinged buffy on sides of body. Iris bluish white; bill dusky, tipped yellow; legs pale brown.

Arid tropical zone. W ECUADOR s to Lambayeque, PERU. Dry forest, arid scrub.

18. BLACK-HOODED THRUSH

Turdus olivater *

9.2″. Entire head and upper breast black (or throat grayish, streaked black, 1); back and wings olive brown, tail blackish. Underparts pale sandy buff. Bill yellow. Under wing coverts pale cinnamon. Bill dusky brown (or yellow, 1). ♀: Like ♂ but no black.

Upper tropical and subtropical zones. Nw GUYANA; mts. of VENEZUELA and immediately adjacent Roraima, BRAZIL. COLOMBIA in Santa Marta Mts., e slope of Andes in Santander. W slope of Central COLOMBIAN Andes in s Cauca, 1. Forest, sometimes coffee plantations.

Plate 26

19. MARAÑON THRUSH

Turdus maranonicus

8.5″. Upperparts, wings and tail olive brown; feathers of back indistinctly edged darker. Underparts white, profusely spotted with dark olive brown. Bill blackish; legs leaden horn color.

Subtropical zone. N PERU in valley of upper río Marañón and tributaries. Dry woodland.

20. CHESTNUT-BELLIED THRUSH

Turdus fulviventris

10″. Head and tail black; back and wings dark gray. Breast and under tail coverts pale gray, rest of underparts orange rufous.

Subtropical zone. Nw VENEZUELA; COLOMBIA on both slopes of E Andes; e ECUADOR; n PERU in Cajamarca. Forest.

21. RUFOUS-BELLIED THRUSH

Turdus rufiventris *

10″. Upperparts, wings and tail olive brown; throat white, streaked brown; breast pale grayish, rest of underparts orange rufous. ♀: Paler below than ♂.

E BRAZIL from Maranhão to Paraiba and s to Rio Grande do Sul and Mato Grosso; URUGUAY; PARAGUAY; e BOLIVIA; ARGENTINA s to La Rioja and Buenos Aires. Parks, thickets, woodland often near streams, grassland.

22. AUSTRAL THRUSH

Turdus falcklandii *

10″. Top and sides of head blackish; throat white, streaked black; upper breast pale brownish, lower breast and belly buff. Back and wings olive brown; tail black.

CHILE from Atacama, and ARGENTINA from Neuquén and Río Negro, s to Cape Horn [Falkland Is.; Juan Fernández Is.] Pastures, groves of willows.

23. PALE-BREASTED THRUSH

Turdus leucomelas *

9.5″. Upperparts olive brown, distinctly grayer on crown and sides of head; ear coverts with white shaft streaks; throat white, streaked brown. Upperparts pale grayish to pale brownish, center of abdomen white. Under wing coverts and axillaries bright orange rufous. Bill blackish brown; legs dark horn color.

Tropical, lower subtropical zones. GUIANAS; VENEZUELA; COLOMBIA w to Magdalena Valley and from Perijá Mts. to the Llanos del Meta. Ne PERU. N and e BRAZIL from Roraima and rio Tapajós eastward and s to Paraná and Mato Grosso; PARAGUAY; n BOLIVIA; ne ARGENTINA. Gardens, bushy savanna, plantations, open woodland near streams.

24. CREAMY-BELLIED THRUSH

Turdus amaurochalinus

9.5". Upperparts, wings and tail dark olive brown, lores dusky. Throat white, streaked blackish; patch at base of throat white; breast and sides pale smoky gray, center of belly and the under tail coverts white. Under wing coverts pale cinnamon. Bill yellow with black tip (all black or blackish, ♀).

Tropical, subtropical zones. E, central and s BRAZIL s of the Amazon s to URUGUAY, PARAGUAY, n and e BOLIVIA, se PERU in Puno, n and central ARGENTINA to Río Negro. Acc. in CHILE. Parks, orchards, thickets, thick woodland.

25. BLACK-BILLED THRUSH

Turdus ignobilis *

Very like 24. Distinguishable by less sharply streaked throat, pure white lower throat in some races, grayer tone of underparts and duller under wing coverts. Bill black in both sexes.

Subtropical, tropical zones. GUYANA; VENEZUELA; COLOMBIA (except Santa Marta); e ECUADOR south to n BOLIVIA; w Amazonian BRAZIL e to rio Tapajós and Itacoatiara. Forest edge, savanna.

26. LAWRENCE'S THRUSH

Turdus lawrencii

9". Above dark smoky brown, wings and tail darker. Underparts light smoky brown, throat streaked black, center of belly and under tail coverts white. Under wing coverts bright cinnamon rufous. Bill yellow with black tip.

Tropical zone. S VENEZUELA; e ECUADOR; ne PERU in Loreto; w Amazonian BRAZIL e to middle rio Solimões and nw Mato Grosso. Forest.

27. COCOA THRUSH

Turdus fumigatus *

9". Rufous brown, paler below; center of belly white, under tail coverts rufous brown (or paler throughout, more ochraceous brown, 1). Throat whitish, streaked dark brown. Under wing coverts orange rufous. Bill pale horn color.

Tropical zone. GUIANAS; VENEZUELA n of the Orinoco, s of it in w Amazonas. E COLOMBIA s to Vichada. BRAZIL almost throughout; e BOLIVIA. Trinidad, 1. Forest often near streams, savanna.

28. PALE-VENTED THRUSH

Turdus obsoletus *

Very like 27 above and 27 (1) below. Best distinguished by pure white under tail coverts and black bill.

Tropical, subtropical zones. VENEZUELA in Amazonas; COLOMBIA in w Chocó s to upper Cauca and Patía valleys and in Vaupés. W ECUADOR. E PERU; n BOLIVIA. W BRAZIL n of rio Solimões and from rio Juruá to e bank of the Madeira. [Costa Rica; Panama.] Forest.

29. CLAY-COLORED THRUSH

Turdus grayi *

9.5". Not unlike 24 but underparts virtually uniform pale sandy brown including under tail coverts, instead of grayish with white belly and under tail coverts; throat somewhat inconspicuously, instead of strongly, streaked dusky. Under wing coverts pale cinnamon as in 24. Bill yellowish olive instead of yellow.

Tropical zone of Caribbean COLOMBIA. [Mid. Amer. Casual, Texas.] Open woodland near streams.

30. BARE-EYED THRUSH

Turdus nudigenis *

Very like 25 in color, but with bare orange skin around eye and olive yellow bill.

Tropical, occasionally subtropical zone. GUIANAS; n BRAZIL from Roraima to s bank of the lower Amazon. W of Andes in sw ECUADOR and nw PERU. Margarita and Patos Is.; Trinidad, Tobago. Gardens, plantations, savanna, dry forest.

31. UNICOLORED THRUSH

Turdus haplochrous

9.5". Rather like 30 but browner throughout. Under wing coverts pale brownish instead of dull cinnamon, under tail coverts brownish olive instead of white.

E BOLIVIA in Santa Cruz (río San Julián).

32. WHITE-NECKED THRUSH

Turdus albicollis *

9.5". Upperparts and wings dark brown, tail

blackish (or grayish, 1). Throat white conspicuously streaked dark brown, patch at base of throat pure white. Breast and sides pale grayish brown (or rufous brown, 1; or dark brown, 2). Under wing coverts clay color to deep ochraceous. Center of belly and under tail coverts white.

Tropical, lower subtropical zones. GUI-ANAS; VENEZUELA; COLOMBIA in Santa Marta and e of Andes south through e ECUADOR to n BOLIVIA. Amazonian BRAZIL and in the e from Maranhão s to Bahía, thence s to Rio Grande do Sul, sw Mato Grosso, PARAGUAY and ne ARGENTINA, 1. COLOMBIA west of W Andes south to nw ECUADOR, 2. Trinidad, Tobago. Forest, woodland, gardens.

Family SYLVIIDAE   GNATCATCHERS, GNATWRENS

Gnatwrens and gnatcatchers form two American groups of birds of doubtful affinities. The former were at one time placed with antbirds, while gnatcatchers have usually been included among Old World warblers (Sylviidae). Gnatwrens are inhabitants of humid forest undergrowth; gnatcatchers are more partial to open, sometimes dry forest and thickets. Both live on insects.

1. COLLARED GNATWREN

Microbates collaris *

4.2" including bill of .8". Upperparts, wings and tail earthy brown. Long eyebrow white. Ear coverts white, enclosed by black line curving down from behind eye to wide black moustachial streak. Throat and breast white, crossed by conspicuous black pectoral band. Sides of body olive brown, center of belly white.

Tropical zone. SURINAM; FRENCH GUIANA; s VENEZUELA; se COLOMBIA; BRAZIL n of the Amazon.

2. HALF-COLLARED GNATWREN

Microbates cinereiventris *

4" including bill of .7". Above reddish brown to olive brown. Cheeks and ear coverts cinnamon rufous (with dusky postocular line, 1). Throat white, moustachial streaks black. Underparts mostly gray, streaked black on upper breast. Tail very short, reddish brown becoming black at tip (or tipped white, 2).

Tropical zone. COLOMBIA on Pacific slope south to w ECUADOR, 1; from lower Cauca and middle Magdalena valleys to e base of Andes in Cundinamarca, 2. From se COLOMBIA s to Puno, PERU. [S Nicaragua through Panama.] Forest.

Fig. 1, p. x

3. LONG-BILLED GNATWREN

Ramphocaenus melanurus *

5" including bill of .9". Crown reddish brown, sides of head ochraceous cinnamon; back grayish brown; tail narrow, black. Below buffy white to light cinnamon buff, throat mottled with black.

Tropical zone. GUIANAS; VENEZUELA; e and n COLOMBIA; e ECUADOR; e PERU. Amazonian and e BRAZIL south to n Mato Grosso and Santa Catarina. [Mid. Amer.] Dense forest undergrowth, dry forest.

Plate 29

4. TROPICAL GNATCATCHER

Polioptila plumbea *

4.5". Crown, nape and sides of head to lower eyelid black, (or crown and nape black, eyebrow and sides of head white, 1). Back gray; underparts white, shaded with gray on breast and sides. Inner remiges very broadly, to narrowly, edged white. Central tail feathers black, rest with increasing white toward outermost. ♀: Like ♂ but no black on head, (or crown and nape black, eyebrow and sides of head white, 2).

Tropical zone. GUIANAS; VENEZUELA. Western and northern COLOMBIA, w ECUADOR, and nw PERU, 1. E COLOMBIA in Norte de Santander and Vichada. W and central PERU (in subtropical Marañón Valley and tributaries, 2). BRAZIL on both sides of lower Amazon and in e from Maranhão to Bahía. [Mid. Amer.] Arid scrub, mangroves, plantations.

5. CREAM-BELLIED GNATCATCHER

Polioptila lactea

4.2". Lores and eyebrow white; crown glossy black; back slaty gray, sides of head and underparts creamy white. Central tail feathers black, outer three increasingly white, outermost all white. ♀: No black cap.

Se BRAZIL from Espírito Santo to Paraná; e PARAGUAY; ne ARGENTINA in Misiones. Shrubbery.

6. GUIANAN GNATCATCHER

Polioptila guianensis *

4". Upperparts blackish gray; narrow eye ring and supraloral streak white; throat and neck slate gray, upper throat variegated with white, rest of underparts white. Central tail feathers black, outermost three pairs almost all white (or outermost white, next two pairs with considerable black, 1).

Tropical zone. GUIANAS. VENEZUELA in Amazonas, immediately adjacent upper rio Negro, BRAZIL and s of the lower Amazon from rio Tapajós eastward, 1.

Forest treetops, often with mixed bands of birds.

7. SLATE-THROATED GNATCATCHER

Polioptila schistaceigula

4". Slaty gray; belly white. Tail black, outermost feather very narrowly tipped white.

Tropical zone. N COLOMBIA in middle Magdalena and lower Cauca valleys, w slope of W Andes in Valle, e of Andes in Cundinamarca. Nw ECUADOR. [E Panama.] Forest.

8. MASKED GNATCATCHER

Polioptila dumicola *

4.7". Mask black, crown and upperparts blue gray. Below blue gray, slightly paler than back; belly grayish white (or throat and belly white, breast pale dove gray, 1). ♀: Like ♂ but lores white, black of face not as deep.

Tableland of BRAZIL from s Pará s to Minas Gerais and n São Paulo, Mato Grosso except sw, lowlands of n BOLIVIA, 1. S BRAZIL in Rio Grande do Sul and sw Mato Grosso; URUGUAY; PARAGUAY; highlands of n and e BOLIVIA; ARGENTINA s to Buenos Aires, La Rioja and Córdoba. Cerrado, shrubbery.

Plate 29

Family BOMBICILLIDAE   WAXWINGS

These birds, characteristic of coniferous and birch forests of the Northern Hemisphere reach only northermost South America as stragglers in winter. They are gregarious and fly in rather compact flocks, uttering a soft, lisping note. They feed on berries and insects.

CEDAR WAXWING

Bombycilla cedrorum

7". Head with long crest. Mask black, outlined in white. General plumage soft, dull, cinnamon or brown; throat blackish, center of belly dull lemon yellow. Rump, wings and tail gray; tips of inner remiges sometimes terminating in bright red sealing-

wax-like appendages. Tail tipped bright yellow.

Acc. winter visitor. COLOMBIA in Chocó (once Feb.); VENEZUELA in the Perijá Mts. (once). [Winters irregularly southward to central Panama; the Greater Antilles; Bahamas. Breeds in northern N Amer.] Open woodland, scrub.

Plate 29

Family MOTACILLIDAE   PIPITS

The seven species of pipits found in South America look very much alike. Terrestrial birds of pastures and open slopes, they run along the ground in search of insects.

Feathers of upperparts are dusky-centered, edged reddish or sandy brown, giving a streaked look; below they vary from buffy white to cinnamon buff, the breast streaked dusky. The tail is blackish, feathers pale-edged, outer feathers white. Rather than describe each species, only the distinguishing characters of each are given. The family includes Old World wagtails as well as pipits.

1. SHORT-BILLED PIPIT

Anthus furcatus*

6". Differs from other species by breast cinnamon buff, heavily streaked, *sharply* demarcated from white belly; sides of body scarcely streaked. Feathers of back edged sandy all around giving a somewhat scaled look. Outer tail feathers mostly pure white.

Puna zone of PERU from Huánuco south to w and s BOLIVIA, n and central ARGENTINA to Río Negro, PARAGUAY, URUGUAY and BRAZIL in Rio Grande do Sul.

Plate 29

2. HELLMAYR'S PIPIT

Anthus hellmayri*

5.6". Differs from other species by mostly brownish white instead of pure white outer tail feathers.

Subtropical, temperate zones. From Puno, PERU, s through ARGENTINA from Mar del Plata and Entre Ríos to Chubut and Río Negro. CHILE in Cautin. E BRAZIL from Espírito Santo s to URUGUAY.

3. YELLOWISH PIPIT

Anthus lutescens*

5.1". Differs from other species by small size and yellow-tinged underparts.

Tropical zone. GUIANAS, the llanos of VENEZUELA and COLOMBIA south, e of Andes, to n ARGENTINA. Coast of PERU from Trujillo south to n CHILE. [Pacific slope of Panama.]

4. CHACO PIPIT

Anthus chacoensis

Much like 3 but streaks on back whiter, less buffy; underparts less yellowish, more buffy.

PARAGUAY and n ARGENTINA in Formosa and Chaco.

5. CORRENDERA PIPIT

Anthus correndera*

6". Richly colored species with back boldly striped black and cinnamon rufous in fresh plumage, becoming sandier with wear. Sides of body boldly streaked on cinnamon buff, or white, background.

Highlands of PERU in Junín, Cuzco and Puno. BOLIVIA in Potosí. CHILE and ARGENTINA s to Tierra del Fuego. Coast of se BRAZIL from São Paulo s through URUGUAY.

6. OCHRE-BREASTED PIPIT

Anthus nattereri

6". Bill rather thick; tail feathers very pointed. Throat whitish; breast bright ochraceous yellow, streaked dusky. Above ochraceous, streaked dusky.

Se BRAZIL n to São Paulo; PARAGUAY; ne ARGENTINA in Misiones and Corrientes.

7. PARAMO PIPIT

Anthus bogotensis*

6". Best distinguished from other species by uniform buffy underparts with usual dusky streaking on breast, and by rufous brown shoulders.

Temperate, páramo zones. Nw VENEZUELA and E Andes of COLOMBIA s through Andes to w ARGENTINA to Catamarca.

Fig. 3, p. 2

Family VIREONIDAE

VIREOS, PEPPERSHRIKES, SHRIKE-VIREOS

Vireos form a family of New World birds, some of which resemble warblers. In South America four distinct groups are found: peppershrikes, distinguishable by their curious bills which are high, very narrow and somewhat parrot-like; shrike-vireos, notable for bright green and blue, or golden yellow and olive, coloring; ordinary vireos, dull in color with rather thick, hooked bills, some of which migrate to South America from North and Middle America; and finally greenlets, small and warbler-like with thin, sharply pointed bills.

Vireos feed on insects and some fruit, and live in forest or scrub growth. They weave pretty, deep, cup-shaped nests which are suspended by the rim from the crotch of a branch.

AID TO IDENTIFICATION

Conspicuous gray, white, yellow or rufous eyebrows, (eyebrow rufous) 1, 2b; (eyebrow yellow) 3a, 4, 5a; (eyebrow white) 6, 8b; (eyebrow gray) 7

Without eyebrows

Crown conspicuously different from back (ochraceous to chestnut) 1, 9, 16, 17a, 21; (gray) 11, 12, 13a, 14

Crown not different from back (upperparts bright greenish yellow) breast lemon yellow 10, breast white 22b; (upperparts olive) 17a, 18, 19b, 20a, 21; (upperparts brown) 15

1. RUFOUS-BROWED PEPPERSHRIKE

Cyclarhis gujanensis *

6". Bill high, narrow, hooked. Forehead and broad eyebrow rufous to chestnut; crown and nape gray to greenish gray (or crown ochraceous to chestnut, 1; or bright yellowish olive like back, 2). Cheeks and ear coverts gray to white. Throat and belly white, belly tinged ochraceous in some races (or throat and belly gray, 3). Lower throat and breast tinged yellow to bright yellow (or olive like back, 3). Back olive green (or bright yellowish olive, 2). Wings and tail like back. Bill pale brown.

Tropical, subtropical zones. GUIANAS, VENEZUELA in s Bolívar, se COLOMBIA in Vaupés, Amazonian BRAZIL, e PERU and nw BOLIVIA, 3. VENEZUELA except se; ne COLOMBIA; BOLIVIA except extreme nw and se; w PARAGUAY; w ARGENTINA. Tableland of BRAZIL from Maranhão, Ceará and Piauí s to Mato Grosso, URUGUAY, e PARAGUAY and e ARGENTINA to Buenos Aires, temperate zone of central PERU, 1. Arid zone of w ECUADOR and immediately adjacent

PERU, 2. [Mid. Amer.]. Forest edge, clearings, capoeira, brushy pastures.

Plate 16

2. BLACK-BILLED PEPPERSHRIKE

Cyclarhis nigrirostris *

6". Forehead and narrow eyebrow deep chestnut. Crown, back, wings and tail olive green. Throat and sides of body gray, upper breast olive yellow, center of abdomen whitish. Bill black, shaped as in 1.

Upper tropical and subtropical zones. COLOMBIA w of E Andes (not in Santa Marta); e and w ECUADOR. Forest edge, clearings.

3. GREEN SHRIKE-VIREO

Smaragdolanius pulchellus *

5.5". Crown bright blue (or bluish green, 1); long narrow eyebrow and spot below eye bright yellow. Back, wings and tail grass green. Throat yellow, gradually turning to yellowish green on rest of underparts (under tail coverts bright yellow, 1).

Tropical zone. Nw VENEZUELA and CO-

LOMBIA e of Andes in Boyacá and w of them in Santander; in Bolívar and Córdoba, 1. [Mid. Amer.] Forest treetops.

4. SLATY-CAPPED SHRIKE-VIREO

Smaragdolanius leucotis *

6". Crown, nape and sides of head gray; long broad eyebrow and spot below eye bright yellow (with diagonal white streak below eye, 1). Back, wings and tail olive green. Underparts bright yellow.

Tropical, subtropical zones. GUIANAS, s VENEZUELA, se COLOMBIA, e ECUADOR and BRAZIL n of the Amazon, 1. W COLOMBIA and w ECUADOR. Amazonian BRAZIL s of the Amazon; e and central PERU; n BOLIVIA. Tops of tall forest trees, sometimes with mixed bands of birds.

Plate 16

5. YELLOW-THROATED VIREO

Vireo flavifrons

5.5". Crown and mantle olive; lower back, rump and upper tail coverts gray. Narrow eyebrow, eye ring, throat and breast yellow; rest of underparts white. Wings blackish, double wing bar and broad edges to inner remiges white. Tail blackish, outer feathers edged white all around.

Winter resident (Nov.-March). N VENEZUELA; n COLOMBIA, also once in Vaupés. Tobago. [Breeds in e N Amer. from s Canada to Florida and e Texas. Winters in Mid. Amer.] Forest edge, open woodland.

6. RED-EYED VIREO

Vireo olivaceus *

5.5". Crown and nape dull gray; broad eyebrow white or grayish white, bordered black above. Back dull olive green. Below white, tinged gray (or olive to bright olive yellow in some races) on breast and sides; under tail coverts yellow. Wings and tail dusky, feathers edged olive.

Migrant and resident. Found throughout s to Buenos Aires, ARGENTINA, acc. in CHILE. [Migrants breed in N and Mid. Amer.] Open woodland, forest edge, thickets, capoeira, cerrado.

Plate 14

7. BLACK-WHISKERED VIREO

Vireo altiloquus *

5.5". Much like 6 but distinguishable at once by much larger bill, narrow black moustachial streaks, much shorter tail.

Breeds in Dutch and VENEZUELAN Caribbean islands, possibly in Trinidad. Winter resident (Aug.-Apr.) in GUYANA, SURINAM, VENEZUELA, ne COLOMBIA, Amazonian BRAZIL s to lower rios Madeira and Tapajós. Ne PERU (?) [Breeds in s Florida, the Bahamas and Antilles, Providencia and San Andrés.] Open woodland, gardens, plantations, mangroves.

8. WARBLING VIREO

Vireo gilvus *

4.6". Crown and nape dark brown to grayish brown; back olive brown to brown, but paler than crown. Eyebrow white. Throat white, rest of underparts primrose yellow to yellowish white.

Upper tropical to temperate zone. Mts. of n VENEZUELA and COLOMBIA s through Andes to La Paz and Cochabamba, BOLIVIA. [N and Mid. Amer. Northern birds winter to Nicaragua.] Open woodland.

9. RUFOUS-CROWNED GREENLET

Hylophilus poicilotis *

5". Crown and nape bright cinnamon ochraceous. Ear coverts dusky with white shaft streaks. Back, wings and tail yellowish olive green. Throat and upper breast light grayish, sides of body olive yellow, center of lower breast and belly creamy white. Under wing coverts and axillaries bright yellow.

E BRAZIL from Piauí, Ceará and Paraiba s to Rio Grande do Sul and sw Mato Grosso. E PARAGUAY; n BOLIVIA; ne ARGENTINA. Forest treetops.

10. LEMON-CHESTED GREENLET

Hylophilus thoracicus *

5". Upperparts, wings and tail yellowish olive green; crown, and especially nape, tinged gray. Breast lemon yellow, throat and belly white to grayish. Under wing coverts and axillaries bright yellow.

Tropical zone. GUIANAS; VENEZUELA in Bolívar. COLOMBIA probably in Meta. Central and e PERU. BRAZIL except extreme se. Forest near streams, capoeira, gardens.

11. GRAY-CHESTED GREENLET

Hylophilus semicinereus *

4.5″. Hindcrown and nape gray; forecrown, back, wings and tail yellowish olive green. Throat, upper breast and sides of body gray; lower breast mixed gray and olive, center of abdomen whitish. Under wing coverts and axillaries pale yellow.

Tropical zone. FRENCH GUIANA; s VENE-ZUELA; Amazonian BRAZIL. Forest.

12. ASHY-HEADED GREENLET

Hylophilus pectoralis

4.5″. Differs from 11 mainly by lemon yellow breast and white throat and belly. Under wing coverts and axillaries bright yellow.

Tropical zone. GUIANAS; n, central and e Amazonian BRAZIL and from Maranhão and Alagoas to Goiás and Mato Grosso. Ne BOLIVIA. Plantations, gardens, mangroves, scrub, riparian thickets.

13. TEPUI GREENLET

Hylophilus sclateri

Very like 12 but forehead and lores buff, crown and nape purer gray. Wings and tail gray instead of olive green. Under wing coverts and axillaries yellowish white.

Upper tropical and subtropical zones. GUY-ANA; VENEZUELA in Bolívar and Ama-zonas. BRAZIL in Roraima. Forest.

14. BUFF-CHESTED GREENLET

Hylophilus muscicapinus *

4.1″. Above olive; crown gray, forehead, lores and sides of head buff (or forehead gray like crown, 1). Below white, tinged buff on breast and throat. Axillaries and under wing coverts pale yellow, under tail coverts lemon yellow. Wings and tail olive.

Tropical zone. GUIANAS; s VENEZUELA; Amazonian BRAZIL. Forest treetops.

15. BROWN-HEADED GREENLET

Hylophilus brunneiceps *

4.5″. Crown and back brown, rump, upper tail coverts and tail olive green. Underparts whitish, washed on throat and breast with buffy brown (or throat and breast grayish white, rest of underparts washed yellowish

green, 1). Under wing coverts and axillaries yellowish white.

Tropical zone. VENEZUELA in w Ama-zonas, se COLOMBIA in Vaupés; nw BRA-ZIL. S of the Amazon between rios Tapajós and Tocantins, 1. Forest.

16. RUFOUS-NAPED GREENLET

Hylophilus semibrunneus

5″. Crown and nape rufous chestnut, lores and ocular region white. Back olive green. Throat grayish white, pectoral band pale buff, belly white; under tail coverts, under wing coverts and axillaries pale yellow.

Upper tropical and subtropical zones. Nw VENEZUELA; COLOMBIA west of E Andes excepting Santa Marta and Nariño. E ECUADOR. Forest.

17. GOLDEN-FRONTED GREENLET

Hylophilus aurantiifrons *

4.5″. Forehead and lores dull yellow; crown and nape pale, dull reddish brown; back pale brownish olive becoming clearer and more yellowish olive on rump and upper tail coverts. Wings and tail olive. Throat whitish, rest of underparts creamy yellow; under tail coverts and wing coverts yellow.

Tropical zone. VENEZUELA n of the Ori-noco; Caribbean and ne COLOMBIA. Trini-dad. [Panama.] Scrub, lower growth of open woods.

18. DUSKY-CAPPED GREENLET

Hylophilus hypoxanthus *

5″. Crown brown, back olive brown, olive on rump. Throat grayish white, rest of underparts olive yellow, bright yellow on center of underparts (or paler above and below, 1). Wings and tail like back.

Tropical zone. VENEZUELA in w Ama-zonas; se COLOMBIA; e ECUADOR; e and central PERU (in Ayacucho, 1); n BO-LIVIA; w Amazonian BRAZIL e to rios Negro and Xingú. Forest.

19. OLIVACEOUS GREENLET

Hylophilus olivaceus

5″. Above dull olive, more yellowish on forehead. Below yellowish olive, yellower on abdomen. Under wing coverts and axil-laries pale yellow.

Subtropical zone. E ECUADOR s to Junín, PERU.

20. SCRUB GREENLET

Hylophilus flavipes *

4.5". Above light yellowish olive with brownish wash, particularly on crown. Throat whitish, rest of underparts pale yellow washed with buff on breast.

Tropical zone. VENEZUELA except Amazonas; n COLOMBIA w to Gulf of Urabá and s to Huila. Margarita I.; Tobago. [Costa Rica; Panama.] Light woods, shrubbery.

21. TAWNY-CROWNED GREENLET

Hylophilus ochraceiceps *

4.5". Crown bright orange rufous becoming tinged with olive on hindcrown (or only forehead and lores orange rufous or buffy, crown olive, 1). Back dark olive green.

Throat gray, breast olivaceous to yellowish olive, belly gray (or throat and breast buffy, abdomen whitish to yellowish, 1). Wings olive, tail olive (or dull rufous, 1).

Tropical zone. GUIANAS, immediately adjacent VENEZUELA, south in e BRAZIL to Belém and west, s of the Amazon, to rio Madeira, 1. VENEZUELA in Amazonas; e and w COLOMBIA; e and nw ECUADOR south to n BOLIVIA and w Amazonian BRAZIL. [Mid. Amer.] Forest, woodland.

Plate 40

22. LESSER GREENLET

Hylophilus minor *

4". Upperparts bright yellowish olive green, duller and darker on crown. Below white, sides of body and under tail coverts lemon yellow.

Tropical zone. COLOMBIA from middle Magdalena Valley w to Pacific, thence south to w ECUADOR. [Mid. Amer.] Woodland.

Family ICTERIDAE   AMERICAN ORIOLES AND BLACKBIRDS

In addition to the well-known yellow and black orioles, this family comprises an assortment of birds ranging from forest-inhabiting oropendolas and caciques to the more familiar grackles, cowbirds and meadowlarks. Conspicuous and aggressive, they inhabit all types of country. The family, found only in the New World, is not related to the Old World orioles and perhaps would be better called icterids.

The 63 species in South America are often so different from each other that the only shared characteristic is the rather long, conical, sharply pointed bill. The sexes are often similar, but males are often larger than females.

Orioles feed on fruit and insects, and many species construct beautifully woven, purse-shaped nests.

AID TO IDENTIFICATION

All black or glossy purplish or bluish black (bill black) 1, 2c, 5, 26b, 27a, 28b, 29b, 30c, 31b, 35, 36, 39, 40b; (bill pale) 23b, 24, 25b

Black and yellow or orange

Mostly black (axillaries yellow) 33a; (upper wing coverts yellow) 37, 41; (rump yellow) 22b; (upper wing coverts and rump yellow) 17, 20b, 21, 22b; (with yellow head or crown) 41, 43

Mostly yellow to orange (back black) 45a, 46a, 48a, 50b, 51b, 52; (back yellow or orange) 46, 47a, 49a, 53c

Yellow on underparts but no black in plumage (upperparts unstreaked) throat and breast yellow 44a, 48a, throat and breast dark olive brown 55c, 56c; (upperparts streaked) 39c, 41, 53c, 62

With crimson or scarlet in plumage

Upperparts all or partly black (lower back or rump crimson) 18, 19; (belly scarlet) 32a; (head and breast scarlet) 52c; (throat and breast crimson) 57a, 58, 59b, 60c, 61

Upperparts streaked, breast pinkish crimson or stained pinkish crimson 57a, 58, 59b, 60c, throat white 61

With chestnut or maroon in plumage

With yellow in tail (no olive in plumage) 6b, 7b, 9, 13a, 14a, 15c; (with olive or olive green in plumage) 8b, 10, 11, 12, 16

With no yellow in tail (wing coverts chestnut) 42; (crown and breast chestnut) 38; (underparts chestnut) 44a; (axillaries chestnut) 34a; (wings chestnut) 3c

With none of the preceding color combinations

Streaked above, sparrow-like 37, 57a, 58, 63

Unstreaked above (size large, uniform buffy brown below) 28b; (size small, gray below) 1, 27a; (shiny bronzy brown) 4; (black below) 63

1. SHINY COWBIRD

Molothrus bonariensis*

7"-8.5". Head, neck, breast and upper back black shot with shining purple or purple blue; lower back and abdomen less purplish, more blue. Wings and tail shining blue with greenish cast. ♀: Grayish brown above, much lighter grayish brown below, throat and eyebrow whitish (or dark brown above and below, back with slight bluish gloss, 1).

Tropical, subtropical zones. Virtually throughout, east of Andes, s to Chubut, ARGENTINA, and Llanquihue, CHILE. In sw COLOMBIA, w ECUADOR and n PERU, 1. [E Panama. Lesser Antilles.] Marshes, cultivated fields, pastures, cerrado. A brood parasite, laying eggs in other birds' nests to be reared by them.

Plate 29

2. SCREAMING COWBIRD

Molothrus rufoaxillaris

7". Silky black with purplish blue gloss. Axillaries with small chestnut spot (sometimes without).

Se BRAZIL in Rio Grande do Sul; URUGUAY; PARAGUAY; se BOLIVIA in Tarija; ARGENTINA s to La Rioja and Buenos Aires. Bushy pastures, marshes. A brood parasite on 3.

3. BAY-WINGED COWBIRD

Molothrus badius*

8". Upperparts grayish brown, below paler and grayer. Wings mostly rufous chestnut; tail blackish.

Tropical to temperate zone. E and s BRAZIL from Piauí, Ceará and Pernambuco s to Rio Grande do Sul and s Mato Grosso; URUGUAY; BOLIVIA; ARGENTINA s to La Pampa. Acc. CHILE. Bushy pastures; open, low forest. Not a brood parasite, but often uses abandoned nests.

4. BRONZE-BROWN COWBIRD

Molothrus armenti

8.5". Lustrous, bronzy brown.

Tropical zone. Leticia on the Amazon, COLOMBIA. Savanna. Old records supposedly from Cartagena.

5. GIANT COWBIRD

Scaphidura oryzivora*

14". Shiny bluish purple. Wings and tail blue black. Feathers at sides of neck elongated, forming a sort of ruff. ♀: Smaller, duller, feathers at sides of neck less elongated.

Tropical, subtropical zones. Virtually throughout, e of Andes, south to PERU, n BOLIVIA, PARAGUAY and ne ARGENTINA in Misiones. W of Andes to w ECUADOR. Trinidad. Tobago (introduced?). [Mid. Amer.] Forest, clearings, pastures and plantations. A brood parasite, laying eggs in the nests of colonial oropendolas and caciques.

6. BAND-TAILED OROPENDOLA

Ocyalus latirostris

12.5". Crown, sides of neck and upper mantle maroon chestnut; back and underparts velvety black. Wings and central tail feathers shiny greenish black, outer tail feathers bright yellow with black tips. Bill bluish gray; base broadened, flattened and rounded to cover forehead. ♀: Similar but smaller.

Tropical zone. E ECUADOR; ne PERU in lower Ucayali, Marañón and Huallaga drainages. W BRAZIL on rio Juruá. Forest.

Plate 15

7. CHESTNUT-HEADED OROPENDOLA

*Zarhynchus wagleri **

14", ♀ 11". Whole head, long narrow crest feathers, upper mantle and breast maroon; middle of back, lower breast and center abdomen glossy greenish black; lower back, rump, sides of body and under tail coverts chestnut. Wings and central tail feathers black, rest of tail feathers bright yellow. Bill shaped like 6 but much longer, and pale greenish ivory. ♀: Like ♂, but black plumage duller.

Tropical zone. COLOMBIA from middle Magdalena and lower Cauca valleys w to Pacific and south to nw ECUADOR. [Mid. Amer.] Forest.

Plate 15

8. CASQUED OROPENDOLA

Clypicterus oseryi

15", ♀ 13". Bill as in 7 but shorter, more swollen at forehead. Mainly chestnut; throat and breast olive yellow. Four central tail feathers and outer web of outermost dusky olive; rest bright yellow.

Tropical zone. E ECUADOR s to Puno, PERU. Forest.

Plate 15

9. CRESTED OROPENDOLA

*Psarocolius decumanus **

17", ♀ 13". Bill ivory white. General plumage including thin occipital crest brownish black (or deep black, 1; or brownish black irregularly spotted yellowish white, 2). Rump, upper and under tail coverts chestnut. Central tail feathers black, rest bright yellow.

Tropical, subtropical zones. GUIANAS; VENEZUELA except nw; e and central COLOMBIA south through e ECUADOR to ne PERU and BRAZIL n of the Amazon. E PERU south to n and e BOLIVIA, BRAZIL s of the Amazon, PARAGUAY, and n ARGENTINA, 2. COLOMBIA w of E Andes, 1. Trinidad; Tobago. [Panama.] Open forest with scattered trees, forested rivers, forest edge.

Plate 15

10. GREEN OROPENDOLA

*Psarocolius viridis **

17", ♀ 14.5". Bill ivory, somewhat swollen at forehead. General plumage including thin occipital crest olive yellow. Rump, upper and under tail coverts, sides of body and lower belly chestnut. Central pair of tail feathers dusky olive, rest yellow.

Tropical zone. GUIANAS; s VENEZUELA; se COLOMBIA; e ECUADOR; e PERU; Amazonian BRAZIL. Forest.

11. DUSKY-GREEN OROPENDOLA

Psarocolius atrovirens

15.5", ♀ 14". Bill pea green, not swollen at forehead. Differs from 10 by much darker olive green general color, chestnut plumage paler, no occipital crest, and the four central and the outermost tail feathers olive, the rest yellow, tipped olive.

Subtropical zone. Se PERU; n BOLIVIA in La Paz and Cochabamba.

12. RUSSET-BACKED OROPENDOLA

*Psarocolius angustifrons **

17", ♀ 14". Bill and forehead or forecrown yellow. Upperparts chestnut, paler on rump and shaded olive on hindcrown and nape; underparts chestnut to olivaceous (or bill black, head and throat olivaceous; rest of plumage dull dark chestnut, shaded olivaceous below, 1). Crest feathers short and rather broad, not filamentous. Central tail feathers dusky; next pair dusky on inner web, yellow on outer; rest yellow with dusky tips.

Tropical, subtropical zones. N VENEZUELA; COLOMBIA in W, Central and E Andes, on e slope in subtropical Meta; w ECUADOR. E of Andes from tropical Meta s through e ECUADOR to n BOLIVIA and w Amazonian BRAZIL, 1. Forest.

13. BLACK OROPENDOLA

Gymnostinops guatimozinus

18″, ♀ 15″. Skin on cheeks bare, dusky red; bill black with red tip. Head, nape, mantle and underparts black, glossed greenish on upperparts; lower back, scapulars, rump, upper and under tail coverts dark maroon chestnut. Remiges all black; two central tail feathers black, rest yellow.

Tropical zone. N COLOMBIA from lower Atrato Valley e to middle Magdalena. [E Panama.] Forest, forest edge.

14. CHESTNUT-MANTLED OROPENDOLA

Gymnostinops cassini

Differs from 13 by less extensively flesh-colored cheeks; black of upperparts without green gloss and extending only to extreme upper mantle; back much brighter chestnut, outer webs of remiges chestnut like back, tertials all chestnut instead of black; flanks chestnut, thighs black.

Tropical zone. Nw COLOMBIA in lower Atrato Valley s to río Atratro-río Baudó watershed. Forest, forest edge.

15. PARA OROPENDOLA

Gymnostinops bifasciatus

18″. Differs from 14 by lower breast, belly and thighs chestnut; black of head brownish black rather than deep black.

BRAZIL in extreme lower Amazonia from rio Tocantins to Belém region. Forest.

16. OLIVE OROPENDOLA

Gymnostinops yuracares *

20″, ♀ 16″. Bright olive yellow. Back, wings, belly and under tail coverts chestnut. Two central tail feathers olive, rest bright yellow.

Tropical zone. VENEZUELA s of the Orinoco; e COLOMBIA from Meta south to n BOLIVIA; Amazonian BRAZIL e to rios Negro and Xingú. Forest.

Plate 15

17. YELLOW-RUMPED CACIQUE

Cacicus cela *

11″, ♀ 9.5″. Bill yellowish green (or dusky green, 2). Glossy black; inner wing coverts, lower back, upper and under tail coverts bright golden yellow (or orange yellow, 1); basal half of tail yellow, distal half black (or only base of tail yellow, 1, 2).

Tropical zone. GUIANAS, VENEZUELA, e COLOMBIA south to n BOLIVIA, and Amazonian and e BRAZIL south to s Bahía. Central and n COLOMBIA from n Chocó e to Santa Marta and middle Magdalena Valley, 1. W ECUADOR; nw PERU, 2. [Central and e Panama.] Open woodland, edge of mangroves and riverbanks.

18. RED-RUMPED CACIQUE

Cacicus haemorrhous *

10″, ♀ 8″. Glossy blue black; rump and lower back crimson. Bill ivory white.

Tropical zone. GUIANAS, s VENEZUELA and e COLOMBIA south to e PERU and Amazonian BRAZIL, and from Pernambuco to Paraná; thence to PARAGUAY and ne ARGENTINA west to e Chaco and n Santa Fe. Forest edge, forested riverbanks; not in open country.

19. SCARLET-RUMPED CACIQUE

Cacicus uropygialis *

11″, ♀ 10″ (or 9″, ♀ 8″, 1). Slightly crested. Blue black, rump flame scarlet (or flame orange, 1). Bill greenish white.

Tropical, subtropical zones. Nw VENEZUELA; ne COLOMBIA in Norte de Santander and generally w of Andes (in tropical zone of Pacific Colombia, 1) south to e ECUADOR and ne PERU. [Nicaragua, Costa Rica, Panama.] Forest.

20. SELVA CACIQUE

Cacicus koepckeae

9″. Glossy jet black; rump bright yellow. Head moderately crested. Bill bluish gray with pale tip.

Tropical zone. E PERU in Loreto (Balta, río Curanja). Forest.

21. GOLDEN-WINGED CACIQUE

Cacicus chrysopterus

8″. Differs from 20 by extensively yellow wing coverts.

S BRAZIL from Mato Grosso and Espírito Santo to URUGUAY, PARAGUAY, e BOLIVIA and ARGENTINA to Buenos Aires and Tucumán. Forest.

22. MOUNTAIN CACIQUE

Cacicus leucorhamphus *

11", ♀ 9". Glossy jet black; wing coverts, rump and upper back golden yellow (or with black wing coverts, 1).

Subtropical, temperate zones. Nw VENE-ZUELA, Andes of COLOMBIA, e PERU s to Junín; thence s to BOLIVIA in La Paz and Cochabamba, 1. Forest.

23. ECUADOREAN BLACK CACIQUE

Cacicus sclateri

7.5", ♀ 7". Dull black; wings with brownish cast. Bill bluish gray with white tip, expanded and rounded at forehead. Much like 25, differing by shape of bill and much less rounded wing.

Tropical zone. E ECUADOR. Forest.

24. SOLITARY BLACK CACIQUE

Cacicus solitarius

10.5", ♀ 9.5". Blue black, head somewhat crested. Bill yellowish white.

Tropical zone. Nw VENEZUELA, e CO-LOMBIA from Arauca s through e ECUA-DOR and Amazonian and e BRAZIL to n ARGENTINA and w URUGUAY. Dense scrub, forest, woodland, campos.

Plate 50

25. YELLOW-BILLED CACIQUE

Cacicus holosericeus *

8.5", ♀ 7". Dull black. Bill yellowish white, not expanded on forehead (see 23).

Tropical to temperate zone. N VENE-ZUELA; n and w COLOMBIA; w and se ECUADOR; nw and e PERU s to Cocha-bamba, BOLIVIA. [Mid. Amer.] Forest.

26. SCRUB BLACKBIRD

Dives warszewiczi *

9" (or 12", 1). Glossy blue black. Bill black. ♀: Slightly smaller, duller.

Semiarid coastal region from río Chone, w ECUADOR to Tumbes, PERU; from Liber-tad to Ica, 1.

27. CARIB GRACKLE

Quiscalus lugubris *

10", ♀ 8.5". Glossy purplish black, wings and tail glossy bluish green. Tail wedge-shaped. Bill black. ♀: Uniform brownish black (or grayish brown above, lighter and grayer below, 1).

Tropical zone. GUIANAS; n VENEZUELA; e COLOMBIA s to Meta; ne BRAZIL in Amapá. Trinidad; Margarita I. On Los Frailes, Los Testigos and Los Hermanos Is., 1. [Lesser Antilles.] Farmyards, gardens, coastal marshland.

28. GREAT-TAILED GRACKLE

Cassidix mexicanus *

18", ♀ 13". Shiny blue black, shot with violet. Wings and tail greenish black; tail long, wedge-shaped. ♀: Bronzy brown above, crown browner, eyebrow buffy. Underparts pale buffy brown, paler on throat, blackish on under tail coverts.

Tropical zone. Nw VENEZUELA in Zulia; Caribbean COLOMBIA and s along Pacific coast to nw PERU. [Arizona, Texas and Louisiana s through Mid. Amer.] Low wet areas, pastures, villages, riverbanks.

29. AUSTRAL BLACKBIRD

Curaeus curaeus *

11". Glossy black; feathers of crown, nape and sides of head narrow and pointed, with stiff shiny black shafts. Bill black (1.2"), very pointed; culmen flattened. ♀: Browner and duller than ♂.

ARGENTINA from w Neuquén and w Río Negro, and CHILE from Atacama s to Cape Horn Archipelago. Bushy hillsides, forest edge, cultivated fields.

Plate 15

30. FORBES' BLACKBIRD

Curaeus forbesi

(Called *Agelaius forbesi* in *Sp. Bds. S. Amer.*)

9.5", ♀ 8.5". Very like 29 but somewhat smaller; shafts of head feathers glossier, therefore more striking; tail feathers more graduated.

E BRAZIL in interior Pernambuco and se Minas Gerais.

31. BOLIVIAN BLACKBIRD

Oreopsar bolivianus

9". Dull brownish black; wings dark, dull brown. Bill short (.9"), black.

Highlands of BOLIVIA in Cochabamba, Chuquisaca and Potosí. Trees in dry inter- montaine basins.

Plate 29

32. RED-BELLIED GRACKLE

Hypopyrrhus pyrohypogaster

12″, ♀ 10.5″. Black; belly and under tail coverts crimson. Feathers of top and sides of head narrow and pointed, with shiny black shafts.

Subtropical zone. COLOMBIA, e of Andes in Caquetá, w of them to Magdalena and Cauca Valleys and w slope of W Andes in Caldas. Forest, moist scrubland.

Plate 40

33. GOLDEN-TUFTED GRACKLE

Macroagelaius imthurni

11″. Blue black; dorsal feathers with some- what glossy edges; rump feathers with white bases; lengthened axillaries golden yellow. Tail rather long (5″), rounded. Bill short (.6″).

Tropical, subtropical zones. GUYANA, immediately adjacent VENEZUELA and BRAZIL. Forest.

34. MOUNTAIN GRACKLE

Macroagelaius subalaris

12″. Silky blue black; rump feathers with dark gray bases. Lengthened axillaries chest- nut. Tail rounded; bill short (.6″).

Subtropical, temperate zones. W slope of E Andes of COLOMBIA from Santander to Cundinamarca. Forest.

35. VELVET-FRONTED GRACKLE

Lampropsar tanagrinus *

11″ (or 9″, 1). Silky blue black (or violet black, 2); forehead feathers dense, plush- like. Tail rounded; bill short (.6″).

Tropical zone. N GUYANA and the Orinoco Valley west to n Amazonas, VENEZUELA. Se COLOMBIA, e ECUADOR, ne PERU, amazonian BRAZIL e to Itacoatiara and rio Madeira (on the rio Guaporé in w Mato Grosso, 2). N BOLIVIA in Beni, 1. Man- groves, forest edge near water.

Plate 50

36. CHOPI BLACKBIRD

Gnorimopsar chopi *

10″. Glossy blue black; feathers of crown and nape narrow, pointed. Distinguishable from other black icterids by ridge and groove at base of lower mandible.

E and central BRAZIL from Maranhão and Ceará s to URUGUAY, PARAGUAY, n and e BOLIVIA and ARGENTINA to Salta, Santa Fe and Buenos Aires. Marshy mead- ows, reedbeds, cultivated lands.

Plate 15

37. YELLOW-WINGED BLACKBIRD

Agelaius thilius *

7.2″. Black, feathers edged sandy, edges disappearing with wear when bird becomes all black. Shoulders, under wing coverts and axillaries yellow. ♀: Above blackish, streaked sandy brown; below sandy, streaked black. Axillaries and under wing coverts yellow. Eyebrow whitish.

Temperate zone. S BRAZIL in Rio Grande do Sul; URUGUAY. N and central BO- LIVIA. Se PERU in Puno and Cuzco. CHILE from Atacama to Valdivía; ARGEN- TINA s to Chubut. Salt and freshwater marshes.

38. CHESTNUT-CAPPED BLACKBIRD

Agelaius ruficapillus *

7″. Crown, throat and breast tawny rufous to chestnut; rest of plumage glossy blue black. ♀: Throat and foreneck chamois to light tawny olive; rest of plumage streaked black and sandy brown or olivaceous brown.

FRENCH GUIANA; e and central BRAZIL s to Rio Grande do Sul and Mato Grosso; URUGUAY; PARAGUAY; e BOLIVIA; n ARGENTINA. Marshes.

39. UNICOLORED BLACKBIRD

Agelaius cyanopus *

9″. Silky, glossy black. ♀: Crown sandy brown, streaked black; back streaked chest- nut and black; rump dark olivaceous gray. Wings and tail black, inner remiges edged chestnut. Below yellow faintly streaked gray; sides olivaceous heavily streaked black.

Ne BRAZIL n of the Amazon in Amapá, in nw Maranhão, in coastal Rio de Janeiro and in rio Paraná drainage; PARAGUAY; BO-

LIVIA; ne ARGENTINA w to Santiago del Estero and s to Buenos Aires. Marshes, cultivated lands.

40. PALE-EYED BLACKBIRD

Agelaius xanthophthalmus [1]

9". Black, with slight green blue gloss especially on breast and back. Iris pale orange.

Upper tropical zone. PERU in Huánuco (near Tingo María). Marshes.

41. YELLOW-HOODED BLACKBIRD

Agelaius icterocephalus *

7". Head and upper breast bright light yellow; ocular region and rest of plumage blue black. ♀: Crown and nape olive yellow; back olive, streaked black. Eyebrow and throat bright yellow turning to olive yellow on breast and grayish olive on belly.

Tropical to temperate zone. GUIANAS; VENEZUELA; COLOMBIA. N PERU; Amazonian BRAZIL. PARAGUAY. Trinidad. Marshes, grassy swamps.

Plate 15

42. EPAULET ORIOLE

Icterus cayanensis *

8". Deep black; shoulder chestnut, tawny or yellow (with yellow upper and under wing coverts, axillaries and tibia, 1).

Tropical zone. SURINAM; FRENCH GUIANA; most of BRAZIL (from Maranhão to Ceará s through Bahía to Rio de Janeiro, 1); COLOMBIA on the Amazon; e PERU; n and e BOLIVIA; PARAGUAY; URUGUAY; ARGENTINA s to Buenos Aires and La Rioja. Open woodland.

43. MORICHE ORIOLE

Icterus chrysocephalus

Like 42 (1) but mid-crown to nape, golden yellow. Intermediates or hybrids with 42 are found in the Guianas and nw Brazil.

Tropical zone. GUIANAS, VENEZUELA, e COLOMBIA s to BRAZIL n of the Amazon, e ECUADOR and ne PERU. Forest treetops, savanna forest often near Moriche palms, gardens.

44. ORCHARD ORIOLE

Icterus spurius *

6.5". Head, breast and upper back black; lower back and rest of underparts chestnut. Wings and tail black, remiges edged white. ♀: Upperparts and tail light yellowish olive, underparts greenish yellow; wings brownish, feathers edged whitish. ♂ imm.: Like ♀ but throat black.

Winter resident (Aug.-Mar.). Nw VENEZUELA; n COLOMBIA [Breeds in N Amer. Winters in Mid. Amer.] Open woodland.

45. ORANGE-CROWNED ORIOLE

Icterus auricapillus

7.5". Top and sides of head orange; forehead, ocular region, throat, upper breast, center of back, wings and tail black. Shoulders, lower breast, belly and lower back golden yellow.

Tropical zone. VENEZUELA n of the Orinoco and in n Bolívar. N COLOMBIA from Catatumbo lowlands west to n Chocó. [E Panama.] Scrub, second growth.

46. TROUPIAL

Icterus icterus *

9". Whole head, throat and upper breast black (or with crown, except forehead, orange like back, 1). Upper mantle, underparts and lower back orange yellow; mantle black (or with black band across upper back, 2; or back all orange, 1). Wings and tail black. Shoulders yellow, inner wing coverts and broad edges to inner remiges white (or with only small patch of white at base of inner remiges, 1).

Tropical zone. N VENEZUELA from Paria Peninsula westward (in sw Apure, 2); n COLOMBIA to lower Magdalena Valley. Sw COLOMBIA, e ECUADOR, Amazonian and e BRAZIL s to Espírito Santo, Mato Grosso, PARAGUAY, and nw BOLIVIA, 1. Aruba to Trinidad. [Introduced into Puerto Rico, St. Thomas.] Woodland near rivers.

47. YELLOW ORIOLE

Icterus nigrogularis *

8.5". Lemon yellow. Ocular region, throat,

[1] Short, Occ. Pap. Mus. Zool., Louisiana State U., no. 36, p. 1, March, 1969 (15 km. n of Tingo María, 2150 ft., Huánuco, Peru).

wings and tail black; greater wing coverts and inner remiges edged white.

Tropical zone. GUIANAS; n VENEZUELA south to n Bolívar and n Amazonas; n BRAZIL in Roraima; n and ne COLOMBIA s to Meta. Aruba to Trinidad. Mangroves, clearings, gardens.

48. BALTIMORE ORIOLE

Icterus galbula

7.7″. Whole head, throat and upper back black; rest of plumage orange. Wings black, lesser coverts orange, greater coverts and inner remiges broadly edged white. Central tail feathers black, rest mostly yellow. ♀: Above grayish, tinged yellow on crown and lower back. Throat, upper breast and upper and under tail coverts dull orange, center of belly white, sides grayish. Wings as in ♂: tail dull brownish orange.

Winter resident (Oct.-May). Nw VENE-ZUELA, (Perijá Mts.); n COLOMBIA w to Pacific. Acc. Trinidad. [Winters in Mid. Amer. Breeds in e N Amer.] Open woodland.

49. YELLOW-BACKED ORIOLE

Icterus chrysater *

8.5″. Orange yellow. Forehead, ocular region, sides of head, throat, upper breast, wings and tail black.

Tropical to temperate zone. Mts. of n VENEZUELA; COLOMBIA, except Santa Marta. [Mid. Amer.] Forest and open woodland.

Plate 40

50. WHITE-EDGED ORIOLE

Icterus graceannae

8″. Forehead, ocular region, throat, upper breast, mantle, wings and tail black; rest of plumage rich yellow. Lesser wing coverts yellow, inner remiges edged white, outer tail feathers tipped white.

Tropical zone. W ECUADOR from Manaví s to Libertad, PERU. Desert scrub.

51. YELLOW-TAILED ORIOLE

Icterus mesomelas *

9″. Differs from 49 by bright yellow outer tail feathers, yellow wing coverts and narrower white margins to wing feathers (without white margins, 1).

Tropical zone. Nw VENEZUELA; n and

central COLOMBIA and Pacific slope of Nariño, 1. W ECUADOR s to Piura and Libertad, PERU. [Mid. Amer.] Forest.

52. ORIOLE BLACKBIRD

Gymnomystax mexicanus

12″. Golden yellow; back, wings and tail black. Ocular region black, bare.

Tropical zone. GUYANA; FRENCH GUI-ANA; n VENZUELA and n Amazonas; e COLOMBIA; e ECUADOR; e PERU; BRA-ZIL n of the Amazon, s of it between rios Tapajós and Tocantins. Gardens, campos, savanna.

Plate 15

53. SAFFRON-COWLED BLACKBIRD

Xanthopsar flavus

8.5″. Head, entire underparts, rump, shoulders and under wing coverts bright golden yellow. Lores, back, wings and tail glossy black. ♀: Upperparts brown, darkest on crown, feathers with dark centers giving streaked look; rump yellow. Eyebrow and underparts yellow to dull orange yellow. Wings and tail brown, shoulders and under wing coverts yellow.

BRAZIL in Rio Grande do Sul; URUGUAY; PARAGUAY; n BOLIVIA; e ARGENTINA west to e Formosa and south to n Buenos Aires. Reedbeds, marshes.

Plate 15

54. SCARLET-HEADED BLACKBIRD

Amblyramphus holosericeus

9.5″. Black; head, breast and thighs scarlet.

S BRAZIL in Rio Grande do Sul and s Mato Grosso; URUGUAY; PARAGUAY; n BO-LIVIA; e ARGENTINA west to e Formosa, south to n and e Buenos Aires. Reedbeds, marshes.

Plate 15

55. YELLOW-RUMPED MARSHBIRD

Pseudoleistes guirahuro

9.5″. Crown and breast blackish brown, back similar but feathers edged olivaceous; rump, upper and under wing coverts and lower parts bright yellow. Wings and tail dark brown.

E BRAZIL from s Goiás and Minas Gerais s to Rio Grande do Sul and s Mato Grosso; URUGUAY; e PARAGUAY; e ARGEN-

TINA w to Formosa and south to n Buenos Aires. Pastures and cultivated lands, usually near water.

56. BROWN-AND-YELLOW MARSHBIRD

Pseudoleistes virescens

9". Much like 55 but rump and flanks brown, and yellow of wing coverts more restricted. Bill longer.

BRAZIL in Rio Grande do Sul; URUGUAY; ARGENTINA from Corrientes to Tucumán and s to Buenos Aires and Córdoba. Wooded pastures, usually near water.

57. RED-BREASTED BLACKBIRD

Leistes militaris

7.5". Black; throat and breast and lesser wing coverts bright red. In nonbreeding plumage, black parts broadly margined sandy brown, giving these parts a brown look. ♀: Upperparts dark brown with the feathers edged sandy and chestnut, giving a streaked appearance. Eyebrow and coronal streak buffy. Below buffy, stained red on breast, streaked dusky at sides of belly.

Tropical zone. GUIANAS; VENEZUELA mainly n of the Orinoco; e and n COLOMBIA s to Meta and w to the upper Cauca Valley. Trinidad, Tobago. [Panama.] Bushy pastures, wet grassland, swampy places.

Plate 40

58. WHITE-BROWED BLACKBIRD

Leistes superciliaris

(Called *Leistes militaris superciliaris* in *Sp. Bds. S. Amer.*)

Differs from 57 mainly by long buffy white postocular stripe and shorter bill. ♀: Differs from 57 mainly by shorter, thicker bill.

BRAZIL from Pernambuco and Ceará s to Santa Catarina and Mato Grosso; PARAGUAY; URUGUAY; ARGENTINA s to Córdoba and Buenos Aires; n and e BOLIVIA; se PERU. Hab. as in 57.

59. PERUVIAN RED-BREASTED[1] MEADOWLARK

Sturnella bellicosa

(Considered a race of *Pezites militaris* (= *Sturnella loyca*) in *Sp. Bds. S. Amer.*)

8". Upperparts, sides and belly blackish, the feathers edged grayish brown; under wing coverts and thighs white; throat and breast bright red. Eyebrow red before eye, white behind it. Much like 60 but smaller with a shorter bill, and thighs white instead of dark; breast more intensely colored. ♀: Above streaked blackish and grayish brown; below whitish, speckled black on upper breast; lower breast and abdomen tinged pinkish.

Tropical, subtropical zones. Sw ECUADOR s through w PERU to Tarapacá, n CHILE. Farmlands, fields.

60. LESSER RED-BREASTED MEADOWLARK

Sturnella defilippi

(Called *Pezites defilippi* in *Sp. Bds. S. Amer.*)

Chiefly distinguishable from 59 by its black under wing coverts and thighs and by its more slender bill.

Se BRAZIL from Paraná s to URUGUAY and La Pampa and se Buenos Aires, ARGENTINA. Grasslands.

61. LONG-TAILED MEADOWLARK

Sturnella loyca*

(Called *Pezites militaris,* Greater Red-breasted Meadowlark, in *Sp. Bds. S. Amer.*)

10". Largest of the red-breasted group of meadowlarks; differs from 59 by much longer tail and larger bill. Under wing coverts white as in 59. ♀: Chiefly distinguishable from 59 by long tail and conspicuously white throat, bordered by black at sides.

Nw ARGENTINA from Jujuy s to Mendoza, and from se Buenos Aires and CHILE from Atacama, s to Tierra del Fuego. [Falkland Is.] Fields, farmlands.

---

[1] For changes in the nomenclature of this group of meadowlarks see Short, Amer. Mus. Novit., no. 2349, Oct. 1968.

62. EASTERN MEADOWLARK

Sturnella magna*

10". Crown dark brown; eyebrows, coronal stripe and cheeks buffy white. Back chestnut brown, feathers variegated with black and edged laterally with buffy white. Throat, center of breast and belly yellow; pectoral collar black; sides of body buff to buffy white, streaked dark brown. Inner remiges and central tail feathers brown, barred blackish; outer tail feathers mostly white.

Tropical to temperate zone. GUYANA; SURINAM; VENEZUELA; n COLOMBIA from s slope of Santa Marta Mts. to head of Magdalena Valley, the e llanos in Meta and Vichada. N BRAZIL in Roraima, on Marajó I., and on lower rio Tocantins. [N Amer. e of Rockies southward locally through Mid. Amer. Cuba.] Open country, savanna, fields.

63. BOBOLINK

Dolichonyx oryzivorus

5.7". Head, neck, underparts, wings and tail black; hindneck cinnamon buff; mantle black, streaked buffy; lower back and rump whitish; scapulars white. In winter plumage resembles female. ♀: Sparrow-like. Upperparts streaked blackish, buff and brown. Broad eyebrow buffy, coronal streak light brown. Throat and breast buff; rest of underparts yellowish buff, streaked dusky on sides of body.

Winter resident. PERU, BOLIVIA and s BRAZIL s to Córdoba and Buenos Aires, ARGENTINA. Transient through n South America and islands from Aruba to Trinidad. [Breeds in N Amer. Migrates chiefly through the West Indies, in small numbers through Mid. Amer. Irregular, Galápagos Is.] Open fields.

Family PARULIDAE   WOOD-WARBLERS

This large family of small, often brightly colored, birds is found only in the New World. Most species are forest and woodland inhabitants, living high up in trees. However, ovenbirds, water thrushes and those birds belonging to the genus *Basileuterus* are terrestrial or mostly so.

Wood-warblers feed on insects and berries, the North American species spending winters in Middle and South America. Males, brightly colored in breeding plumage, assume the dull plumage of females when wintering. Before departing for the north they reassume their bright breeding plumage.

AID TO IDENTIFICATION

Underparts all or partly bright yellow or orange

Below all yellow or orange yellow (crown olive like back) 2a, 6, 17, 18b, 32b, 33, 34; (crown or crown patch yellow) 2a, 23b, 26a, 35, 45b; (crown patch chestnut) 24b, 25a, 28, 29a, 42a; (crown patch ochraceous to orange) 35, 36b, 40, 45b; (crown gray) 5, 18b; (crown black) 14a, 17, 24b, 27a, 30a, 31b

Below partly yellow or orange (throat, or breast band or spots black) 16a, 20, 22; (throat and breast gray or grayish) 15, 16a, 38, 39b, 43a, 44b; (throat white, bordered black) 37a; (throat and breast ochraceous, or chestnut or streaked chestnut) 5, 6a; (throat and upper breast orange or yellow) 8

No bright yellow or orange below

Underparts waxy or buffy yellow 7, 32b, 38

Underparts spotted or streaked 1a, 10, 11a, 12, 13a, 38

Underparts white or grayish to dingy pale olivaceous (back streaked) 1, 7, 9a, 10; (back not streaked) bright greenish yellow 4a, dull olive with black crown stripes 41c, 44b, 47c, 48c

Underparts buffy, back brownish olive 49c, with cinnamon buff rump 49b

With red, yellow or chestnut in plumage (with orange or yellow in wings) 3a, 21; (with rose red underparts) 19; (breast chestnut) 9a

1. BLACK-AND-WHITE WARBLER

Mniotilta varia

4.5". Streaked black and white (see also 10). ♀: Like ♂ but underparts white, scarcely streaked.

Winter resident (mid-Aug.-Apr.). Mts. of n VENEZUELA, COLOMBIA and e ECUADOR. Curaçao, Trinidad. [Breeds in N Amer. Winters in Mid. Amer. and West Indies.] Woodland. Creeps on branches and trunks of trees.

2. PROTHONOTARY WARBLER

Protonotaria citrea

4.8". Golden yellow, back olive yellow; rump and wings blue gray; outer tail feathers white on inner web. ♀: Differs from ♂ by top and sides of head yellowish olive like back.

Winter resident (Sept.-Apr.). Mts. of n VENEZUELA; n COLOMBIA. Casual in GUYANA, SURINAM and w ECUADOR. Curaçao, Trinidad, Tobago. [Breeds in N Amer. Winters in Mid. Amer., West Indies.] Wooded swamps.

3. GOLDEN-WINGED WARBLER

Vermivora chrysoptera

5". Crown and wing coverts golden yellow; throat and broad stripe through eye black; narrow eyebrow and broad moustachial streak white; rest of plumage blue gray, paler below, white on center of belly. ♀: Differs from ♂ by grayish black ocular streak and throat.

Winter resident (Sept.-Mar.). Mts. of n VENEZUELA and of COLOMBIA, e of Andes s to Meta. [Breeds in N Amer. Winters southward from Guatemala through Panama.] Forest and woodland.

4. TENNESSEE WARBLER

Vermivora peregrina

4.2". Crown, nape and sides of head gray; lores and eyebrow white. Back, wings and tail olive green; greater wing coverts edged yellowish. Below whitish. ♀: Differs from male by olive crown and nape.

Winter resident (Sept.-May). Mts. of n VENEZUELA w across n COLOMBIA. [Breeds in N Amer. Winters in Mid. Amer.] Forest and woodland.

5. TROPICAL PARULA

Parula pitiayumi *

3.7"-4.3". Upperparts and sides of head blue gray, yellowish olive on center of back; ocular region blackish. Wings and tail gray; double wing bar and patch on outer tail feathers white. Below bright yellow, throat and breast burnt orange in some races.

Tropical, subtropical zones. GUYANA, VENEZUELA, COLOMBIA, e and w ECUADOR, nw and e PERU, BOLIVIA, n BRAZIL in Roraima, and tableland from Maranhão s to PARAGUAY, URUGUAY and to Buenos Aires and Córdoba, ARGENTINA. Margarita I.; Trinidad; Tobago. [Breeds from s Tex. s through Panama.] Forest, thickets.

6. YELLOW WARBLER

Dendroica petechia *

5". Crown chestnut (or yellow, 1); forehead, sides of head and underparts golden yellow; breast streaked chestnut (or entire head and breast chestnut, lower breast streaked chestnut, 2). Back greenish yellow. Inner webs of tail feathers yellow. ♀: Like ♂ but no chestnut on crown (or like ♂ but duller, 1; or like ♂ but no chestnut head and breast, 2).

Resident. Coastal VENEZUELA in Sucre and Anzoátegui west to e Falcón; from Paraguaná Peninsula w across n COLOMBIA to Cartagena, 2; from Nariño, COLOMBIA, s to Tumbes and possibly Lima, PERU. Aruba to Trinidad and Tobago. Coastal mangroves and thickets. Winter resident (Aug.-May), chiefly inland south to the Amazon, 1. [N and Mid. Amer., West Indies, Caribbean is., Galápagos Is.] Clearings, parks.

7. CERULEAN WARBLER

Dendroica cerulea

4.7". Above grayish blue, streaked black; double wing bar and underparts white. All but central tail feathers with white patch on inner web. ♀: Crown greenish blue; back light olive with blue cast; eyebrow and underparts yellowish white. Wings and tail as in ♂.

Winter resident (Sept.-Mar.). VENEZUELA and COLOMBIA south to n BOLIVIA. [Breeds in N Amer. Migrates through West Indies, Mid. Amer.] Woodland.

8. BLACKBURNIAN WARBLER

Dendroica fusca

5″. Long eyebrow, crown patch, throat and upper breast orange; upperparts and sides of head black; mantle streaked white. Lower breast and belly yellowish white, streaked black at sides. Wings and central tail feathers black, inner wing coverts and outer tail feathers mostly white. ♀: Washed-out version of ♂ with back brown instead of black.

Winter resident (Sept.-April). VENE-ZUELA; COLOMBIA chiefly w of E Andes; ECUADOR to central PERU. Casual Tobago. Transient Curaçao, Bonaire. [Breeds in N Amer. Winters from Guatemala southward.] Woodland.

9. BAY-BREASTED WARBLER

Dendroica castanea

5.5″. Forehead and sides of head black; large patch at sides of neck creamy buff; crown, nape, throat and sides of body chestnut; center of underparts white. Back olive, streaked black. Wings and tail black; double wing bar and patch on inner web of two outer tail feathers white. ♀: Upperparts yellowish olive narrowly streaked black. Underparts whitish, flanks sometimes with suggestion of chestnut; feet dark. Wings and tail as in ♂. In spring, a dull replica of ♂.

Winter resident (Nov.-May). Nw VENE-ZUELA. COLOMBIA w of E Andes s to 4°n. Tortuga I. Curaçao (casual). [Breeds in N Amer. Winters from Panama southward.] Woodland.

10. BLACKPOLL WARBLER

Dendroica striata

5.5″. Crown black; back grayish olive, streaked black. Cheeks white, bordered black below; underparts white, streaked black on sides. Wings and tail much as in 9. ♀: Above much like 9 but less greenish. Below yellowish white. Feet pale.

Winter resident (Sept.-Apr.). GUIANAS; VENEZUELA; COLOMBIA e of E Andes, casual w of them; e PERU; BRAZIL n of the Amazon. Casual in ARGENTINA. Acc. in CHILE. Transient in Curaçao, Bonaire; Trinidad and Tobago. [Breeds in N Amer. Migrates through West Indies; casually Mexico; Panama.] Woodland.

11. OVENBIRD

Seiurus aurocapillus *

6″. Upperparts, wings and tail olive brown. Crown orange rufous, bordered at each side by conspicuous black line. Underparts white, moustachial streak and conspicuous spots on breast black.

Winter resident (Oct.-Apr.). N VENEZUELA in Aragua and Falcón; casual in COLOMBIA. Curaçao. [Breeds in N Amer. Winters in Mid. Amer. and West Indies.] Terrestrial, woodland.

12. NORTHERN WATERTHRUSH

Seiurus noveboracensis *

5.5″. Upperparts, wings and tail dark ashy brown. Eyebrow yellowish. Below including throat, yellowish white, streaked black.

Winter resident (Sept.-Apr.). GUIANAS; VENEZUELA; COLOMBIA; e and nw ECUADOR; ne PERU. Aruba to Trinidad and Tobago. [Breeds in N Amer. Winters in Mid. Amer., West Indies.] Terrestrial, swampy woods, stream borders, mangroves. Teeters like a sandpiper.

13. LOUISIANA WATERTHRUSH

Seiurus motacilla

5.5″. Much like 12, but bill longer, eyebrow and underparts white without yellow tinge; often tinged brownish on flanks, throat unstreaked, streaks on breast not as black.

Winter resident (Oct.-Jan.). Nw VENE-ZUELA; ne COLOMBIA in Santa Marta and Meta. Trinidad. [Breeds in N Amer. Winters in Mid. Amer., W Indies.] Terrestrial. Habits like 12, especially borders of rapid streams.

14. KENTUCKY WARBLER

Geothlypis formosus

(This, 15 and 16 were placed in *Oporornis* in *Sp. Bds. S. Amer.*)

5″. Upperparts, wings and tail dull olive. Black forecrown and broad stripe from below eye down side of neck. Eyebrow, eye ring and underparts bright yellow.

Winter resident (Oct.-May). Nw VENE-ZUELA; ne COLOMBIA. [Breeds in N Amer. Winters in Mid. Amer.] Forest undergrowth.

15. CONNECTICUT WARBLER

Geothlypis agilis

5". Conspicuous eye ring white, sides of head gray. Upperparts, wings and tail dull olive. Throat grayish white deepening to dove gray on breast, rest of underparts dull yellow. ♀: Differs from ♂ by whitish throat deepening to brownish on breast.

Winter resident (Oct.-May). N and w VENE-ZUELA; ne and e COLOMBIA; w Amazonian BRAZIL. Aruba, Curaçao. [Breeds in N Amer. Migrates through West Indies. Casual in Panama.] Woodland.

16. MOURNING WARBLER

Geothlypis philadelphia

5". Head gray; throat and breast black, throat feathers broadly edged gray; rest of underparts yellow. Back, wings and tail dull olive. ♀: Differs from 15 by much brighter yellow underparts, no white eye ring.

Winter resident (Oct.-May). Nw VENE-ZUELA; COLOMBIA; e ECUADOR. Curaçao. [Breeds in N Amer. Winters from Nicaragua southward to w Panama.] Woodland.

17. MASKED YELLOWTHROAT

Geothlypis aequinoctialis *

5.2". Crown gray; back, wings and tail olive green. Forehead, lores, ocular region and anterior ear coverts black. Entire underparts bright yellow. ♀: Differs from ♂ by no black at sides of head; crown like back or grayish.

Tropical zone. GUIANAS; VENEZUELA; COLOMBIA w to Magdalena Valley; e BRAZIL s to URUGUAY; PARAGUAY; e BOLIVIA; se PERU; ARGENTINA s to Buenos Aires and Córdoba. W ECUADOR from río Chone s to Lima and upper Marañón Valley, PERU. [Sw Costa Rica; w Panama.] Freshwater marshes, cerrado.

18. OLIVE-CROWNED YELLOWTHROAT

Geothlypis semiflava *

5.2". Differs from 17 mainly by forecrown and sides of head extensively black. ♀:

Differs from 17 mainly by yellowish olive forecrown.

Tropical zone. Pacific lowlands and upper Cauca Valley in COLOMBIA; w ECUADOR s to El Oro. [Honduras to ne Panama.] Fresh-water marshes.

Plate 39

19. ROSE-BREASTED CHAT

Granatellus pelzelni *

5". Crown (or forecrown only, 1), sides of head and neck, breast wings and tail black; postocular streak white. Back bluish slate; throat white, narrowly outlined with black; rest of underparts rosy red, bordered (or not, 1) at sides of body by silky white. ♀: Upperparts slaty blue; eyebrow, throat and sides of head buff; breast and belly duller rosy red than in ♂.

Tropical zone. GUYANA; SURINAM; s VENEZUELA; Amazonian BRAZIL w to rios Branco and Madeira (in Pará, e of rio Tocantins, 1) south to n Beni, BOLIVIA. Forest.

Plate 14

20. CANADA WARBLER

Wilsonia canadensis

5.2". Upperparts, wings and tail light gray; crown spotted black. Eye ring white. Black line at sides of throat joining band of black spots across breast. Lores and underparts bright yellow, under tail coverts white. ♀: Differs from ♂ by olive gray upperparts, line at sides of throat, and pectoral spots grayish instead of black.

Winter resident (Sept.-May). Nw and s VENEZUELA and COLOMBIA s to Roraima BRAZIL; e ECUADOR; se PERU. [Breeds in N Amer. Migrates mostly through Mid. Amer.] Woodland.

21. AMERICAN REDSTART

Setophaga ruticilla *

5". Upperparts, throat, breast, wings and tail black; patch at base of remiges, sides of breast and basal half of all but central tail feathers orange. Belly white. ♀: Like ♂ in pattern but orange replaced by yellow. Crown gray, back brownish; underparts all white.

Winter resident (end of Aug.-May). GUY-ANA; SURINAM; VENEZUELA; COLOM-

BIA; nw and e ECUADOR; PERU (Moyobamba); nw BRAZIL. Aruba to Trinidad and Tobago. [Breeds in N Amer. Winters in Mid. Amer. and W Indies.] Woodland, mangroves.

22. SLATE-THROATED REDSTART

Myioborus miniatus *

5". Upperparts slaty gray, crown patch chestnut. Sides of neck gray, throat blackish; breast and belly bright yellow, more or less ochraceous on upper breast. Tail blackish, outer feathers and under tail coverts white.

Upper tropical and subtropical zones. Nw GUYANA, VENEZUELA and COLOMBIA s through nw BRAZIL and ECUADOR to La Paz and Cochabamba, BOLIVIA. [Mid. Amer.] Forest.

Fig. 18, p. 193

23. GOLDEN-FRONTED REDSTART

Myioborus ornatus *

5". Crown lemon yellow, chin and sides of head white (or forecrown, chin and sides of head orange yellow, 1); hindcrown, rear auriculars and sides of neck black. Back dark olivaceous gray. Underparts lemon yellow (or orange yellow, 1). Tail as in 22.

Tropical zone. Nw VENEZUELA; COLOMBIA in E Andes; in Central and W Andes, 1. Forest.

Plate 39

24. SPECTACLED REDSTART

Myioborus melanocephalus *

5.5". Crown and sides of head black; forehead, lores and ocular region yellow (or crown patch chestnut surrounded by black, ocular ring yellow, 1—some individuals with varying amounts of yellow on forehead and lores, little or no black on crown, a variant of 1, this type is found only in Colombia); nape black, back dark gray; underparts bright yellow. Tail as in 22.

Subtropical, temperate zones. Andes of Nariño, COLOMBIA, e and w ECUADOR and nw PERU in Piura and Cajamarca, 1. E PERU s to La Paz and Cochabamba, BOLIVIA. Forest.

25. WHITE-FRONTED REDSTART

Myioborus albifrons

5.3". Forehead, lores and ocular region pure white; crown black, center feathers cinnamon rufous, tipped black. Back dark gray; below bright yellow. Tail black, outer three pairs of feathers white.

Upper subtropical and temperate zones. Nw VENEZUELA in Trujillo, Táchira and Mérida. Forest.

26. YELLOW-CROWNED REDSTART

Myioborus flavivertex

5.5". Front and sides of crown black, center of crown bright yellow, loral spot buffy. Nape and sides of head black, back moss green. Underparts bright yellow, deepest on throat and breast. Tail as in 22.

Subtropical, temperate zones. Santa Marta Mts., COLOMBIA. Forest treetops.

27. WHITE-FACED REDSTART

Myioborus albifacies

5.7". Chin and sides of head pure white, crown black; back brownish gray. Underparts bright orange. Tail as in 22.

Upper tropical and subtropical zones. VENEZUELA in mts. of Amazonas. Forest.

28. BROWN-CAPPED REDSTART

Myioborus brunniceps *

5.2". Crown rufous chestnut, narrow eyebrow and eye ring white. Sides of both head and neck, upper mantle and wings gray; center of back olive. Underparts bright yellow. Tail as in 25 (or similar but back brownish olive, 1; with orange underparts, 2; both with tail as in 22).

Subtropical zone. Nw GUYANA, s VENEZUELA (on Mt. Duida, 2) and BRAZIL in Roraima, 1. N and e BOLIVIA south in w ARGENTINA to s La Rioja. Forest.

29. YELLOW-FACED REDSTART

Myioborus pariae

Differs from 28 (1), mainly by yellow eye ring, supraloral streak and narrow frontlet, back grayish with yellowish olive cast, and more white on outer tail feathers.

Subtropical zone. Paria Peninsula in VENEZUELA. Forest.

30. SAFFRON-BREASTED REDSTART

Myioborus cardonai

5.2". Crown and area before and below eye black; eye ring and chin white. Back dark gray; underparts orange yellow. Tail as in 22 but less white.

Subtropical zone. Cerro Guaiquinima, Bolívar, VENEZUELA. Forest.

31. BLACK-CRESTED WARBLER

Basileuterus nigrocristatus

5.7". Crown and preocular spot black, eye ring yellow. Back, wings and tail olive green; underparts yellow, olivaceous at sides.

Subtropical, temperate zones. N VENEZUELA; COLOMBIA; e and w ECUADOR; n PERU s to Ancash. Forest undergrowth.

32. CITRINE WARBLER

Basileuterus luteoviridis *

5.7". Upperparts, wings and tail olive citrine; eyebrows pale yellowish white to bright yellow. Below dull waxy yellow to bright yellow, brightest in southern birds; flanks olive citrine.

Subtropical, temperate zones. Andes from w VENEZUELA and COLOMBIA s through e ECUADOR to La Paz and Cochabamba, BOLIVIA. Forest undergrowth.

33. PALE-LEGGED WARBLER

Basileuterus signatus *

5.2". Much like brighter examples of 32 but smaller, more olive above; yellow eyebrow bordered blackish above. Feet pale.

Subtropical zone. COLOMBIA in Cundinamarca. Central PERU from Junín to La Paz and Cochabamba, BOLIVIA; ARGENTINA in Jujuy. Thickets.

34. FLAVESCENT WARBLER

Basileuterus flaveolus

5.5". Upperparts, wings and tail bright olive green; lores, cheeks and underparts bright yellow. Only species of this type with pale bill.

Tropical zone. N VENEZUELA; COLOMBIA e of Andes in Santander, possibly in Cauca Valley. Ne BOLIVIA; PARAGUAY; e BRAZIL from Maranhão, Piauí and Ceará s through Goiás to São Paulo and Mato Grosso. Forest undergrowth. Wags tail.

35. TWO-BANDED WARBLER

Basileuterus bivittatus *

5.7". Upperparts, wings and tail olive. Central crown feathers all yellow, or with yellow bases and orange rufous tips, or all orange rufous, bordered laterally by broad, black stripe; eyebrow olive to olive yellow, lores dusky. Underparts yellow, shaded with olive.

Upper tropical and subtropical zones. W GUYANA; s VENEZUELA, immediately adjacent BRAZIL in Roraima. Se PERU; n and e BOLIVIA; nw ARGENTINA in Jujuy and Salta. Undergrowth.

36. GOLDEN-BELLIED WARBLER

Basileuterus chrysogaster *

5". Differs from 35 by smaller size, crown stripe orange.

Tropical zone. COLOMBIA from w slope of W Andes in Cauca s to Chimbo, w ECUADOR. Central and s PERU from Junín to Puno. Undergrowth.

37. SANTA MARTA WARBLER

Basileuterus basilicus

6". Top and sides of head black; coronal streak and eyebrow curving downward to enclose ear coverts, white; lores, eye ring and upper throat white; rest of underparts bright yellow. Back, wings and tail olive green.

Lower temperate zone. COLOMBIA in Santa Marta Mts. Shrubbery.

38. THREE-STRIPED WARBLER

Basileuterus tristriatus *

5.2". Head pattern much as in 37, but stripes dull buffy white. Back, wings and tail dull olive; underparts waxy white to bright yellow, sides olive; some races have indistinctly spotted breast.

Upper tropical zone. N VENEZUELA; COLOMBIA except Santa Marta; e ECUADOR; e PERU south to n BOLIVIA. [Costa Rica; Panama.] Thickets.

39. THREE-BANDED WARBLER

Basileuterus trifasciatus *

5". Top and sides of head gray, tinged yellowish on center of crown; stripe through eye and two broad stripes from base of bill along sides of crown to nape, black. Back, wings and tail dull grayish olive, brighter and greener on rump and upper tail coverts. Throat and upper breast grayish white, rest of underparts bright yellow.

Subtropical zone. Sw ECUADOR from El Oro s to Libertad, PERU. Forest undergrowth.

40. GOLDEN-CROWNED WARBLER

Basileuterus culicivorus *

5″. Center of crown yellow to orange rufous, feathers tipped olive or gray; two broad stripes at sides of crown and another through eye black, eyebrow white. Back, wings and tail olive to gray; underparts yellow.

Upper tropical and subtropical zones. GUYANA; VENEZUELA n of the Orinoco; s of the Orinoco in e and n Bolívar and Amazonas; COLOMBIA e of the Andes s to Meta and from the Santa Marta Mts. w to Pacific and s to río Patía. N BRAZIL in Roraima and in e and central parts from Maranhão, Piauí and Ceará to URUGUAY, PARAGUAY, e BOLIVIA and ARGENTINA to Entre Ríos and Córdoba. [Mexico to w Panama.] Forest undergrowth, thickets. Wags tail.

41. WHITE-BELLIED WARBLER

Basileuterus hypoleucus

5″. Crown orange rufous, feathers gray-tipped; two broad black stripes at sides of crown; lores and long eyebrow white. Back, wings and tail olive gray. Underparts white, clouded gray; under tail coverts pale yellow.

South-central BRAZIL in Goiás, Minas Gerais, São Paulo and Mato Grosso; PARAGUAY. Forest undergrowth.

42. RUFOUS-CAPPED WARBLER

Basileuterus rufifrons *

4.7″. Crown and ear coverts chestnut, lores dusky, eyebrow white. Nape grayish olive; back, wings and tail olive green. Underparts bright yellow.

Upper tropical zone. Nw VENEZUELA; COLOMBIA in Santa Marta Mts. s in Magdalena Valley to Huila. [Mid. Amer., where belly white in northern races.] Woodland shrubbery.

43. GRAY-THROATED WARBLER

Basileuterus cinereicollis *

5.5″. Top and sides of head gray; semi-concealed coronal patch yellow, bordered by ill-marked black lateral stripes; back, wings and tail dark dull olive. Throat grayish white, breast light gray; rest of underparts yellow, olive at sides.

Upper tropical and subtropical zones. Nw VENEZUELA; COLOMBIA in n portion of Sierra de Perijá and in E Andes from Norte de Santander to Cundinamarca and Meta. Forest undergrowth.

44. RUSSET-CROWNED WARBLER

Basileuterus coronatus *

5.8″. Crown patch light to dark rufous, bordered laterally by black stripe; stripe through eye black; ocular ring and supraloral streak white (or absent, 1). Sides of head and neck and the nape gray. Back, wings and tail greenish to brownish olive. Throat grayish white, rest of underparts bright yellow (or all underparts grayish white, 1).

Subtropical, temperate zones. Nw VENEZUELA; Santa Marta Mts. and Andes of COLOMBIA. Sw and e ECUADOR s to BOLIVIA in La Paz and Cochabamba. Thickets, fern brakes.

Plate 39

45. GRAY-AND-GOLD WARBLER

Basileuterus fraseri *

5.8″. Crown patch lemon yellow (or orange ochraceous, 1) bordered laterally by broad, deep black stripe; supraloral streak white. Sides of head, back, wings and tail blue gray, tinged yellowish olive on center of back. Underparts bright yellow.

Arid tropical zone. W ECUADOR from Manaví to Guayaquil and Puná I., 1; from Santa Rosa s to Tumbes and Piura, PERU.

46. GRAY-HEADED WARBLER

Basileuterus griseiceps

5.4″. Top and sides of head slaty gray; forehead and lateral crown stripes slaty black; eye ring and lores white. Back yellowish olive; underparts bright yellow.

Subtropical zone. VENEZUELA in coastal mts. of Sucre, Monagas and Anzoátegui. Forest.

47. WHITE-STRIPED WARBLER

Basileuterus leucophrys

6.5″. Head slaty gray with obsolete black crown stripes and broad white eyebrow. Back olive; underparts white, sides of breast ashy, flanks and under tail coverts ochraceous.

Central BRAZIL in nw São Paulo and s Mato Grosso.

48. WHITE-BROWED WARBLER

Basileuterus leucoblepharus

5.7". Differs from 47 by blacker crown stripes, narrow white eyebrow, brighter and greener back, olivaceous flanks and ochraceous yellow under tail coverts.

Se BRAZIL from Espírito Santo s through e São Paulo to URUGUAY; PARAGUAY; e ARGENTINA w to Formosa and Chaco and s to Buenos Aires. Forest undergrowth.

49. RIVER WARBLER

Basileuterus rivularis *

5". Upperparts olive brown, grayish on crown. Supraloral streak and short eyebrow buffy to cinnamon; underparts white, slightly to heavily clouded with buff to solid cinnamon buff. Upper tail coverts brighter and tinged rufescent, tail like back (or upper tail coverts and basal two-thirds of tail cinnamon buff, 1).

Tropical zone. GUIANAS; ne and s VENEZUELA; e BRAZIL s to Rio Grande do Sul and w to rios Branco and Tapajós; PARAGUAY; n and e BOLIVIA; ne ARGENTINA. COLOMBIA w of E Andes and e of them from Meta south through e and w ECUADOR to nw and e PERU, and w Amazonian BRAZIL e to rio Madeira, 1 (B. fulvicauda, Buff-rumped Warbler, sometimes considered a distinct species). [Honduras southward, 1]. Borders of forest streams.

Family COEREBIDAE   HONEYCREEPERS

Honeycreepers form a composite family of groups of birds much unlike each other, some related to tanagers, others to wood-warblers and some perhaps even to finches.

They share the habit of feeding on the pollen and nectar of flowers, as well as on berries, small seeds and insects. They are found from tropical lowland forests to temperate Andean slopes.

Main groups in the family are: flower-piercers, characterized by curiously upturned, hooked bills used to pierce the corolla of flowers to secure nectar; honeycreepers, with long curved bills and bright colors, sometimes confused with hummingbirds but unlike them never hovering in front of flowers; conebills, dull-colored with short, conical, pointed bills; and finally dacnis, with similar bills but brilliant plumage.

AID TO IDENTIFICATION

All or virtually all black or gray (with chestnut or buff under tail coverts) 2, 3a, 6b, 15b, 19a; (with chestnut moustachial streak or pectoral band) 14b; (under tail coverts black or gray) 12b, 14b, 15a, 16a, 17b, 18a

All, including wings and tail, dark blue 10b, 12b, 20b, 21b, 22b, 37b; (with white cap) 10b

Blue and black

Blue, wings and tail black; bill long, curved 23, 24, 25a

Blue, back partly black (bill long, curved) 26; (bill short straight, pointed) 29, 30c, 31, 36, underparts black 34b

All or mainly green

Breast streaked, bill curved 23, 24, 25a, 26

More or less uniform grass green 27, crown blue 29

Yellowish green below 32a, 36

Glistening green, top and sides of head black 27, back black 32a

Below all or mostly chestnut to rufous to buff (below uniform) 7b, 8a, 11b, 13b, 17b; (with throat, or throat and breast black) 9b, 14b; (with belly grayish) 37b

Below mostly yellow or crimson

Below yellow (throat gray) crown blackish 1, crown blue 10b; (throat black) 33; (sides of body blue or olive) 31b

Lower breast crimson 35b

Different from above catagories

Head and back black, center of back opalescent 28b

Below dull whitish or grayish or buffy (back green) 2; (back olive) 4, 6b, 13b, 31, 33; (back gray or blue) 3a, 4, 5, 6b, 34a

1. BANANAQUIT

Coereba flaveola *

4.5". Upperparts sooty gray to sooty brown to blackish, rump yellow to olive yellow; long eyebrow, wing speculum and under tail coverts white. Throat pale gray, rest of underparts bright lemon yellow. Bill curved (.5").

Mainly tropical but occasionally to temperate zone. Widely distributed e of Andes to e PERU, BOLIVIA, PARAGUAY, Rio Grande do Sul, BRAZIL (not recorded from sw Amazonia), and ne ARGENTINA. W of Andes s to Ancash, PERU. [Mid. Amer. Bahamas; acc. Florida. Islands of Caribbean.] Gardens, parks, clearings, plantations, capoeira.

Plate 39

2. CHESTNUT-VENTED CONEBILL

Conirostrum speciosum *

4.5". Dark blue gray above, paler below; center of abdomen white, under tail coverts chestnut. ♀: Top and sides of head bluish green, back green. Wings and tail yellowish green. Below whitish, buffy on breast; under tail coverts buff to yellowish. Bill straight, sharply pointed.

Tropical zone. Widely distributed e of Andes to e PERU, BOLIVIA, Amazonian and e BRAZIL s to PARAGUAY and n ARGENTINA. Swampy forest, capoeira, campos, lake borders.

3. WHITE-EARED CONEBILL

Conirostrum leucogenys *

4". Crown and nape black; eye patch from below eye to ear coverts white. Back dark blue gray, rump white. Underparts blue gray, paler than back, white on center of abdomen. Under tail coverts mostly chestnut. Wings and tail black, small white speculum. ♀: Differs from ♂ by pale yellowish underparts, brightest on center of abdomen, grayish on sides.

Tropical zone. W and n VENEZUELA; COLOMBIA e to Santa Marta, and s in Magdalena Valley to Huila. [E Panama.] Tangled woodland.

4. BICOLORED CONEBILL

Conirostrum bicolor *

4". Above blue gray; below pale grayish with buffy wash. Bill and feet pale. Young are grayish green above, dull yellow below.

Tropical zone. GUIANAS; coastal VENEZUELA; COLOMBIA in delta of the Magdalena. Coastal BRAZIL s to São Paulo and up the Amazon, and lower course of larger tributaries, to e PERU. Mangroves, flooded forest.

5. PEARLY-BREASTED CONEBILL

Conirostrum margaritae

4". Very similar to 4; distinguishable by lighter gray upperparts and purer gray underparts without buff wash.

Tropical zone. Ne PERU in Loreto; w Amazonian BRAZIL to rio Madeira, n of the Amazon to Pará border. Flooded forest.

6. CINEREOUS CONEBILL

Conirostrum cinereum *

5". Above leaden gray to olivaceous brownish gray. Forehead and broad eyebrow white, crown blackish. Below pale gray, center of abdomen buffy white. Wings and tail slaty black, wing coverts and speculum white.

Chiefly temperate zone. Andes of s COLOMBIA south to n CHILE and nw BOLIVIA; in PERU found also in arid coastal zone from Piura south. Shrubby hillsides, plantations, occasionally gardens and parks.

7. WHITE-BROWED CONEBILL

Conirostrum ferrugineiventre

5". Crown black, broad eyebrows white. Back, sides of head and neck gray; underparts bright chestnut rufous, chin whitish.

Temperate zone. PERU from Huánuco, Junín and Cuzco to Cochabamba, BOLIVIA. Open bushy slopes with stunted trees.

8. RUFOUS-BROWED CONEBILL

Conirostrum rufum

5.3". Above dark gray. Forecrown, eyebrow and all underparts chestnut rufous. Wings and tail slaty black, inner remiges edged whitish.

Upper subtropical to temperate zone. COLOMBIA in Santa Marta Mts. and E Andes s to Bogotá. Open slopes with low, stunted trees.

9. BLUE-BACKED CONEBILL

Conirostrum sitticolor *

5.5". Head, neck and upper breast black; eyebrow and back bright blue (or upper breast dull blue, eyebrow very broad, 1). Underparts cinnamon rufous. Wings and tail black.

Subtropical, temperate zones. Nw VENEZUELA from Mérida to Táchira, and Andes of COLOMBIA (not Santa Marta) s through ECUADOR to nw PERU from Piura to s Cajamarca; thence south to n BOLIVIA, 1. Forest edge, shrubby slopes.

Plate 39

10. CAPPED CONEBILL

Conirostrum albifrons *

5.5". Dark purplish blue to blackish above, brighter and bluer on lower back and inner wing coverts. Below purplish to bluish black. Crown and lores white (or glossy

ultramarine blue, 1). ♀: Crown blue; back and sides of neck, throat and breast gray. Back, wings and tail yellowish olive green. Lower breast and belly greenish yellow.

Subtropical to temperate zone. N VENEZUELA in Aragua, 1; from Táchira west to E and Central Andes of COLOMBIA. From e slope of W COLOMBIAN Andes s through ECUADOR to n BOLIVIA, 1.

11. GIANT CONEBILL

Oreomanes fraseri *

7.2". Above light gray, below chestnut. Eyebrow chestnut, cheeks and ear coverts white. Bill (.8") straight and pointed.

Temperate zone of Andes in *Polylepis* woodland from sw COLOMBIA (?) south through ECUADOR and PERU to La Paz, Cochabamba and Potosí, BOLIVIA. Climbs trees.

Plate 50

12. BLUISH FLOWER-PIERCER

Diglossa caerulescens *

5.6". Dull blue to grayish blue above, below paler (or underparts pale gray, 1). Lores and forehead narrowly black. ♀: Like ♂ but duller. Bill not as sharply upturned as is usual in *Diglossa*.

Andes of COLOMBIA south to n PERU; from Cajamarca to nw BOLIVIA, 1. Forest.

13. SLATY FLOWER-PIERCER

Diglossa baritula *

5". Top and sides of head, back, wings and tail bluish gray (or forehead and sides of head blackish, 1). Underparts cinnamon. ♀: Olive brown above; pale, dull buffy below.

Subtropical, occasionally upper tropical zone. N VENEZUELA and COLOMBIA in Santa Marta Mts.; in Colombian Andes, 1. ECUADOR s to BOLIVIA and nw ARGENTINA. [Mexico to w Panama.] Shrubby hillsides. (If the South American birds are considered as a species distinct from the Middle American group, their name would be *D. sittoides*, Rusty Flower-Piercer.)

14. GLOSSY FLOWER-PIERCER

Diglossa lafresnayii *

6.2". Glossy black, shoulders blue gray (or with slaty rump, underparts light rufous, throat slaty, 1; or with broad white moustachial streaks and broad pectoral band, center of belly and under tail coverts chestnut, 2; or with long broad light-to-dark cinnamon moustachial streaks and under tail coverts and no pectoral band, 3).

Temperate zone. Nw VENEZUELA, E and Central Andes of COLOMBIA s to Cajamarca, PERU. COLOMBIA at n end of W Andes, 1. Central PERU from Amazonas to Junín, 2. Se PERU from Cuzco to La Paz, BOLIVIA, 3. (Sometimes considered as distinct species are no. 1, *D. gloriosissima*, Chestnut-bellied Flower-Piercer, and nos. 2 and 3, *D. mystacalis*, Moustached Flower-Piercer.)

15. CARBONATED FLOWER-PIERCER

Diglossa carbonaria *

5.2"-5.8". Head, throat, upper breast, back, wings and tail dull black; short eyebrow and shoulders blue gray; rump slaty gray; lower breast and belly chestnut rufous (or glossy black, wing coverts blue gray, rump slate gray, 1; or glossy black, rump slate gray, 2; or entirely glossy black, 3; or glossy black above; eyebrow, shoulders and lower back blue gray; below rufous chestnut, center throat black, 4; or glossy black; shoulders, rump, breast and belly blue gray, under tail coverts chestnut, 5).

Temperate, páramo zones. VENEZUELA in Trujillo and Mérida. Extreme w VENEZUELA and n part of E Andes of COLOMBIA, 1; Santa Marta Mts., 2; Central Andes s through ECUADOR to nw PERU, 3. N part of Central Andes in COLOMBIA, PERU except nw, south to nw BOLIVIA and n CHILE (Putre), 4; in Cochabamba, BOLIVIA, 5. (Sometimes grouped as a distinct species are nos. 1, 2 and 3, *D. humeralis*, Black Flower-Piercer.)

16. VENEZUELAN FLOWER-PIERCER

Diglossa venezuelensis

5.8". Coal black; axillaries, under wing coverts and patch at sides of breast white. ♀: Upperparts and sides of head dull yellowish olive, brighter and greener on forehead; back dark gray, feathers with dark centers and olivaceous edges. Malar region olive buff; underparts dull gray, washed buffy.

Subtropical zone. N VENEZUELA in mts. of Monagas and Sucre.

17. WHITE-SIDED FLOWER-PIERCER

Diglossa albilatera *

5.2". Blackish slaty gray to bluish slaty gray; under wing coverts and patch at sides of breast white. ♀: Olive brown above; rufescent brown below, abdomen buffy, patch at sides of body white.

Subtropical, temperate zones. N VENEZUELA from Aragua w to mts. of COLOMBIA and south to w Cajamarca and Huánuco, PERU. Forest edge, shrubby hillsides.

18. SCALED FLOWER-PIERCER

Diglossa duidae *

6". Top of head black; back dark slate gray. Sides of head sooty black; rest of underparts slaty, becoming slaty gray on sides. Feathers of underparts centered pale gray, giving slightly scaled look; under tail coverts edged white.

Subtropical zone. Mountains of s Amazonas, VENEZUELA and immediately adjacent BRAZIL (Cerro Uei-tepui). Shrubby hillsides.

19. GREATER FLOWER-PIERCER

Diglossa major *

7". Dark blue gray, feathers, particularly of upperparts with pale blue shaft streaks. Forehead, lores and ear coverts black, the latter bordered below with whitish; under tail coverts chestnut.

Subtropical zone. VENEZUELA in the mountains of central and s Bolívar, and adjacent BRAZIL in Roraima. Shrubby hillsides.

20. INDIGO FLOWER-PIERCER

Diglossa indigotica

4.5". Shining indigo blue; margins of remiges greenish blue; lores black.

Upper tropical and subtropical zones. W slope of W Andes in COLOMBIA from upper río San Juan south in w ECUADOR to Pichincha. Forest.

Plate 39

21. DEEP-BLUE FLOWER-PIERCER

Diglossa glauca *

4.8". Dark, dull indigo blue to purplish blue; lores and forehead narrowly black.

Subtropical zone. Se COLOMBIA s through Andes to n BOLIVIA.

22. MASKED FLOWER-PIERCER

Diglossa cyanea *

6". Dark purplish blue; forecrown, throat and sides of head black. ♀: Similar but duller.

Subtropical to temperate zone. N VENEZUELA from Miranda and Aragua w to COLOMBIA s through e and w ECUADOR to Cajamarca in w PERU and through Andes to n BOLIVIA. Forest.

23. SHORT-BILLED HONEYCREEPER

Cyanerpes nitidus *

4.2" (bill curved, .4"). Cornflower blue; lores, throat, upper breast, wings and tail black; legs yellow. ♀: Upperparts and sides of head grass green. Forehead, eye ring and malar streak blue. Breast and sides of body grass green, streaked with white. Throat and center of abdomen buffy white.

Tropical zone. S VENEZUELA; se COLOMBIA s to Junín, PERU. W Amazonian BRAZIL e to rio Negro and to n Mato Grosso and n Goiás. Forest.

24. PURPLE HONEYCREEPER

Cyanerpes caeruleus *

4.2" (bill curved, .7"). Much like 23, but only throat black; forecrown and sides of head distinctly paler and purer blue. Legs bright yellow. ♀: Forehead, lores and ocular region tawny buff. Upperparts, wings and tail grass green, forecrown narrowly streaked buffy. Throat buff, malar streak blue; rest of underparts green, streaked yellowish; center of abdomen and under tail coverts plain yellowish.

Tropical zone. GUIANAS, VENEZUELA and COLOMBIA s through e and w ECUADOR to se PERU, Amazonian BRAZIL and n BOLIVIA. Trinidad. Forest, capoeira, coffee plantations.

25. SHINING HONEYCREEPER

Cyanerpes lucidus *

4.5" (bill curved, .7"). Very like 24 but bluer with lighter, almost azure blue sides of head; black of throat has a rounded instead of a truncated outline on the chest. ♀: Differs from 24 by no tawny forehead

and lores; crown grayish blue; breast blue streaked whitish, instead of green streaked yellowish; throat paler buff.

Tropical zone. Nw COLOMBIA in Chocó. [Mid. Amer.] Treetops in open forest and forest edge.

26. RED-LEGGED HONEYCREEPER

Cyanerpes cyaneus *

5.5" (bill curved, .7"). Center of crown enamel-like, brilliant turquoise blue; forehead, lores, stripe through eye, and upper back black; rest of body plumage purple blue. Wings black, inner webs of feathers canary yellow. Tail and under tail coverts black. Legs red. ♀: Dark green above; eyebrow and throat greenish white; rest of underparts pale green, streaked yellowish white; center of belly and under tail coverts plain yellowish.

Tropical zone. Generally distributed e of Andes to PERU in San Martín; n BOLIVIA, and Amazonian and e BRAZIL to Santa Catarina. West of the Andes from COLOMBIA s to Manaví, ECUADOR. Bonaire (once). Margarita I. Trinidad. [Mid. Amer.] Forest, second growth, parks.

Plate 39

27. GREEN HONEYCREEPER

Chlorophanes spiza *

5.5" (bill almost straight, .5"). Shining emerald to bluish green. Top and sides of head and neck black. Mandible yellow. ♀: Grass green, more to less yellow on throat and center of belly.

Tropical zone. South America generally e of the Andes s to BOLIVIA and s BRAZIL (in the e to Santa Catarina). W of the Andes south to nw PERU. Trinidad. [Mid. Amer.] Forest, forest edge.

Plate 14

28. GOLDEN-COLLARED HONEYCREEPER

Iridophanes pulcherrima *

5.2". Tanager-like. Head, upper mantle and upper tail coverts black, golden yellow collar on hindneck; center of back shiny, opalescent greenish straw color. Breast and sides of body greenish straw color, lower breast and abdomen whitish. Wing coverts shining purplish blue; remiges and rectrices black, edged blue; outer rectrix sometimes with white patch.

Subtropical zone. COLOMBIA (head of Magdalena Valley?). E and w ECUADOR. PERU in Huánuco, Junín and Cuzco. Orange groves, forest.

Plate 14

29. BLUE DACNIS

Dacnis cayana*

5.5" (bill straight, very pointed, .4"). Mainly turquoise blue, to blue, to dark purplish blue. Forehead, lores, throat, center of back, wings and tail black. ♀: Grass green; crown blue, throat gray.

Tropical zone. Generally distributed s to PERU, BOLIVIA, BRAZIL, PARAGUAY and ne ARGENTINA; w of Andes s to Río del Oro, w ECUADOR. [Nicaragua southward.] Open forest, capoeira, orange trees, parks.

30. BLACK-LEGGED DACNIS

Dacnis nigripes

4.7". Much like 29 with which it occurs only in e Brazil. Differs by less black on back and throat, shorter tail and stouter, wider bill. ♀: Quite unlike that of 29, rather like 34. Brownish olive above, crown and rump tinged blue; underparts pale ochraceous.

E BRAZIL in Minas Gerais, Espírito Santo, Rio de Janeiro, and Santa Catarina.

31. BLACK-FACED DACNIS

Dacnis lineata*

4.8". Glossy sky blue (or verditer blue, 1). Forehead, sides of head and neck, mantle, wings and tail glossy blue black. Center of abdomen, under wing coverts and tail coverts white (or golden yellow, 1). ♀: Above light olive brown (with bluish cast, 1); below pale greenish, center of abdomen whiter (or bright golden yellow, 1). Wings and tail brown.

Tropical zone. Widely distributed e of Andes south to e PERU, n BOLIVIA and s Amazonian BRAZIL. W of Andes from Magdalena and Cauca valleys, COLOMBIA, to Chimbo, w ECUADOR, 1. Hab. as in 29.

32. VIRIDIAN DACNIS

Dacnis viguieri

4.8". Mainly shining blue green, bluer on rump and underparts, sky blue on upper tail coverts. Forehead, lores, triangular patch on upper back, wings and tail black. Inner remiges and wing coverts shining, bright olive green. ♀: Above pale olive; below pale greenish, center of abdomen pale buff. Wings and tail brown, feathers edged olive.

Tropical zone. COLOMBIA from Córdoba w to nw Chocó. [E Panama.] Forest edge, shrubbery.

33. YELLOW-BELLIED DACNIS

Dacnis flaviventer

5". Crown and nape bluish olive green. Forehead, lores, sides of head, center of throat, mantle, wings and tail black. Scapulars, lower back, underparts and malar streak golden yellow, breast feathers with black bases giving somewhat mottled effect. ♀: Above dull olivaceous brown, below pale grayish buff slightly mottled on breast; center of abdomen and under tail coverts buff.

Tropical zone. S VENEZUELA and se COLOMBIA, e ECUADOR and e PERU south to n BOLIVIA; w Amazonian BRAZIL e to rios Negro and Xingú. Forest.

34. SCARLET-THIGHED DACNIS

Dacnis venusta*

5.2". Turquoise blue above, sides of mantle black. Forecrown, lores, eye ring and all underparts black. Thighs scarlet. ♀: Greenish blue above, much brighter and lighter on lower back and rump. Below buffy brown, center of underparts fawn; under tail coverts cinnamon buff.

Tropical zone. COLOMBIA from middle Magdalena Valley west and south to nw ECUADOR. [Costa Rica; Panama.] Humid forest and borders, occasionally coffee plantations.

35. SCARLET-BREASTED DACNIS

Dacnis berlepschi

4.8". Head, throat, upper breast and back dark blue; back bright blue narrowly streaked everywhere with glistening silvery blue; lower back plain silvery blue. Lower breast flame scarlet, rest of underparts golden buff. ♀: Underparts, wings and tail brown. Throat and breast light brown, band across lower breast flame orange; rest of underparts golden buff, brownish on sides.

Tropical zone. Sw COLOMBIA (La Guayacana) and nw ECUADOR (Esmeraldas, Imbabura). Forest.

Plate 39

36. WHITE-BELLIED DACNIS

Dacnis albiventris

4.8″. Shiny purple blue; forehead, sides of head, wings and tail black; center of lower breast, the abdomen and under tail coverts white. Wings black, coverts edged purplish blue. ♀: Above green, brighter on rump; underparts greenish yellow, yellow in center of lower belly.

Tropical zone. Se COLOMBIA south to ne PERU. BRAZIL in s Pará (rio Cururú). Forest.

37. TIT-LIKE DACNIS

Xenodacnis parina *

4.8″-5.5″. Bill small, sharply pointed. Purplish blue; brighter on head and rump (narrowly streaked everywhere with glistening prussian blue, 1). ♀: Top and sides of head blue (or forecrown and ocular region blue, 1). Back ashy brown, wing coverts and upper tail coverts blue. Below dull ferruginous, buffy yellow on center of abdomen.

Temperate zone. PERU in Ancash and Amazonas, 1; in Cuzco and Arequipa and probably immediately adjacent Chile. *Polylepis* woodland, shrubbery.

Plate 16

Family TERSINIDAE   SWALLOW-TANAGERS

The one member of this family, sometimes included among tanagers, differs from them by its very wide, flat bill and long, swallow-like wings.

Swallow-tanagers are gregarious birds of more or less open, often dry, forests and they have the peculiar habit of nesting in holes in banks, trees or even walls of houses. They feed on insects and fruit.

SWALLOW-TANAGER

Tersina viridis *

5.8″. Mainly purple blue when seen against the light, bluish green with the light. Mask, throat, bars at sides of body black. Belly and under tail coverts white. ♀: Mainly grass green. Face and throat mottled grayish brown; center of abdomen and bars on flanks pale yellow.

Tropical, lower subtropical zones. Generally distributed s to PERU, BOLIVIA, PARAGUAY, ne ARGENTINA and BRAZIL to Rio Grande do Sul; west of Andes south to nw ECUADOR. Trinidad. [E Panama.]

Plate 16

Family THRAUPIDAE   TANAGERS

Tanagers form a very large heterogeneous family of primarily neotropical birds related to finches, honeycreepers, wood-warblers and icterids. Essentially birds of the forest canopy and forest edge, they are found from the tropical lowlands to the temperate slopes of the high Andes. They feed on fruit and some insects; euphonias, however, subsist mainly on mistletoe berries.

Tanagers are among the most beautiful of birds, clothed in brilliant hues of green, red, blue and opalescent shades of silvery green and gold. Females usually resemble males, but are somewhat duller. In such an enormous family, including no less than 222 species, it is not surprising that some are garbed in more sober colors. Euphonias form a distinctive group of small tanagers, males glossy blue black above, all or mostly yellow below, with a small bullfinch-like bill.

For the most part tanagers are poor singers, although euphonias bear a certain reputation as songbirds.

Tanagers, like many other neotropical birds, often join mixed bands of birds seeking food through the forest canopy or undergrowth.

AID TO IDENTIFICATION

Underparts mostly bright yellow to ochre yellow

Throat and/or breast black (back glossy blue black to purple black) 4, 5, 6a, 7b, 8, 9a, 10a, 11a, 12b, 13, 16, 22c; (back black) 86a; (back blue) 81b, 90b; (back green) 83; (back olive yellow or ochraceous yellow) 80b, 82b, 121; (back dary gray) 135b

Throat and/or breast blue 55, 97, 111

Throat and/or breast greenish gray or gray 8, 21, 45b, 69a, 129, 134, 161b

Throat and/or breast green 1, 2b, 3b, 19

Throat and/or breast red or orange 84b, 103b, 110b

Underparts all pale yellow to ochraceous yellow

Back with black in it (back glossy blue black to purple black) 14, 15; (back black) crown yellow 79b, rump yellow 104b; (back streaked black and yellow) 44b

Back olive to yellowish olive (crown yellow) 79b; (tail short, bill stubby, size 5" or less) 10a, 11a, 12b, 13, 14, 15, 19, 20, crown blue 4; (size over 5") 106, 107, 109b, 128, 143, 144, 147, 163a, 164b, 173, wings black 108, top and sides of head rufous 151b, top and sides of head black 162b

Back bluish gray to blue 21, 77a, 78b, 111

Underparts not yellow

Back olive (underparts gray to white with throat or pectoral band yellow or greenish yellow) 8, 9a, 19, 144a, 154b, 156b, 157b, 158b; (below gray, sides greenish yellow) 5, 6, 17c, 18c, 20, 22c, 159b; (below buffy to ochraceous) 5, 7b, 115b, 124, 125, 126, 145b, 165b; (below olive to yellowish olive) 95, 108, 112c, 113b, 165b, 179; (below gray to bluish gray) 96, throat yellow 114b, throat gray 136a

Body plumage all or mostly all black, black and gray, or gray and white

Black 122, 123c, 130b, 152c, rump ochraceous 124, 126, rump bright yellow 104b, 131b, 144

Black and white 125, 129, 172, 173b, 176, 177

Black and gray 179, underparts white 141, 160b, 168b, 176, with straw-colored pectoral band 56b

Gray above, whitish below 127, 164b, 169b, with blue wing coverts 57b

With buff, rufous, ochraceous or chestnut in plumage

Above brown to ochraceous or rufous, below buff to rufous or brown 24a, 116, 117a, 120, 121, 122, 123c, 124, 130b, 166b, 175c, center of underparts black 63c, below ochraceous brown 125, 126

Above gray to olive gray (below uniform buff to chestnut) 132b, 148b, 166b, 167a; (with head or crown rufous to chestnut in contrast to body) 133a, 140c, 146a, 147

Above blue (below buff) 23, 89b; (breast buff, belly white) 141; (throat yellow) 71b; (ear coverts yellow) 72b

Crown and mantle coppery chestnut 61c, 62c, crown only chestnut 63

Head yellow 44a

Above blue black, black, or grayish black (shiny blue black) 16, 18c; (black with buff or white rump) 55, 128, 139; (back grayish black) 137a

Above olive (below buff to cinnamon buff) 97, 138, 170b; (breast rufous) 142c, 143

Above pale shining green, head and throat coppery 67b

With red, scarlet or magenta in plumage

All red 106, 107, 116, 117a, 119a

Body red, wings and tail black 98c, 99, 100b, 101a, 105b, 108b, 109

Back all or partly black (throat red) 99b, 152c, 153b; (rump red) 30, 102, 103b; (rump blue) 76b

Back dark gray (throat and crest red) 118; (below mostly magenta) 137a

Red; flanks white 145b

All blue or mostly blue

Pale silvery blue 91, 92, 93c

Dark blue 65b, throat yellow 70b, crown yellow 73b, nape yellow or rufous 54b, 74b, crown red and white 75c, wing coverts yellow 94c

Blue below (mantle black, rump blue) 24a, 50b; (rump silvery) 28, 29; (back black, rump yellow and red) 30; (back olive or green) 58b, 96a

Mainly green (grass green) 25b, 26b, 38b, 58a, 174b; (olive, spot on chest yellow) 87b, 88a; (shiny light green above, grayish green below) 66b, 68b

Spotted below (back green, spotted black) 39, 40a, 41, 42; (back mainly black) 43b, 54, 64b

With highly colorful and variegated pattern, size 5″-6″

Mantle black (head green) 30; (head blue) 31c, 32c, 52, 53; (head yellow to orange) 48c; (head or sides of head red) 33c; (head coppery gold) 33b

Mantle yellow (head yellow) 27a; (head red) 59b

Mantle green (rump and ear coverts orange) 26b; (ear coverts rufous) 49a; (lores and hindcrown black) 51b

Mantle silvery blue or straw color 63, 66b, 67b, 68, 69a

Mantle finely streaked (green and black) 33c, 35c, 36, 37b, 38b, 46b, 47b; (gold and black) 34c, 35c, 44b

1. BLUE-NAPED CHLOROPHONIA

Chlorophonia cyanea *

4.5″. Head, throat and breast bright grass green, yellower on crown. Eye ring and back bright blue, belly golden yellow (or with yellow forehead, blue nuchal collar, rump and upper tail coverts, and green back, 1). ♀: Like respective ♂ but duller; lower parts olive yellow.

Upper tropical and subtropical zones. GUYANA, s VENEZUELA and from Sucre w to Lara and to the Santa Marta Mts. in COLOMBIA, 1. VENEZUELA in Perijá Mts. s through Andes of COLOMBIA and e ECUADOR to n BOLIVIA, PARAGUAY and ne ARGENTINA. E BRAZIL from Bahía s to Rio Grande do Sul. Forest.

2. YELLOW-COLLARED CHLOROPHONIA

Chlorophonia flavirostris *

4″. Bright grass green; collar on hindneck, eye ring, center of breast and belly golden yellow; narrow chestnut band separating the yellow from green of breast. Upper and under tail coverts yellow. Bill and feet yellow or salmon. Iris white. ♀: Similar but no yellow.

Tropical zone. COLOMBIA in sw Nariño (La Guayacana); nw ECUADOR (below Gualea, 3500 ft.). Forest.

3. CHESTNUT-BREASTED CHLOROPHONIA

Chlorophonia pyrrhophrys

4.5″. Crown and nape purplish blue; forehead and eyebrow black; back, wings and tail grass green; rump yellow. Throat, sides of head and neck, bright emerald green; narrow breast band black. Sides of body golden yellow; center of breast and belly, and under tail coverts chestnut. ♀: Differs from ♂ by maroon red forehead and eyebrow, green instead of yellow rump, no black breast band, and olive yellow underparts.

Subtropical, temperate zones. Nw VENEZUELA; Andes of COLOMBIA and e ECUADOR. Forest.

Plate 40

4. BLUE-HOODED EUPHONIA

Euphonia musica *

(*Euphonia* replaces *Tanagra* of *Sp. Bds. S. Amer.*)

4.5". Forehead black (or deep yellow, 1); crown and nape light blue to purplish blue; back glossy blackish purple or blackish blue; rump deep yellow. Throat and sides of head black, rest of underparts deep yellow. Wings and tail like back. Many Euphonias have wing feathers with a white base which does not show when the bird is perched or in flight. ♀: Forehead ochraceous, crown and nape blue, back olive, underparts bright to dull olive yellow.

Tropical, subtropical zones. SURINAM; VENEZUELA n of the Orinoco and in se Bolívar; ne COLOMBIA s to Meta and w of Andes to río Patía; e and w ECUADOR (in temperate se ECUADOR, 1), nw and e PERU, BOLIVIA south to n ARGENTINA and PARAGUAY. BRAZIL n of lower Amazon and from Bahía s to Rio Grande do Sul. Trinidad. [Mexico to w Panama. West Indies.] Forest treetops.

5. ORANGE-BELLIED EUPHONIA

Euphonia xanthogaster *

4.5". Crown yellow (or light rufous to chestnut, 1). Back glossy blue black, purplish on nape. Throat and sides of head purple black, rest of underparts deep yellow. Wings and tail like back, outermost tail feather with large white patch on inner web. ♀: Above bronzy olive, grayish on nape, forecrown yellowish olive to rufescent. Center of throat and underparts pinkish gray (or dull cinnamon, 2); sides of body bright olive yellow.

Tropical, subtropical zones. GUYANA; VENEZUELA; COLOMBIA (except Santa Marta); e and w ECUADOR; e PERU s to Junín; in Cuzco and Puno, 1; in La Paz and Cochabamba, BOLIVIA, 1, 2. [E Panama.] Forest, often in mixed bands of birds.

Plate 40

6. TAWNY-CAPPED EUPHONIA

Euphonia anneae *

4.5". Very like 5 (1) but rufous crown patch more extensive, back much more purplish, under tail coverts white instead of yellow. ♀: Above dusky olive; below dull olive, brighter on belly.

Upper tropical zone. N Chocó, COLOMBIA near Gulf of Urabá. [Costa Rica; Panama.]

7. FULVOUS-VENTED EUPHONIA

Euphonia fulvicrissa *

4". Back glossy purplish blue black including wings and tail; forecrown, breast and belly deep yellow; under tail coverts rufous. ♀: Forecrown rufous; rest of upperparts dark olive, glossed bluish, particularly on crown; underparts olive yellow, center of belly ochraceous.

Tropical zone. COLOMBIA west of E Andes (except Santa Marta); nw ECUADOR. [Central and e Panama.]

8. WHITE-VENTED EUPHONIA

Euphonia minuta *

4". Glossy blue black; forecrown, breast and belly yellow; center of abdomen and under tail coverts white. Inner webs of outer three tail feathers mostly white. ♀: Above olive; throat, center of belly and under tail coverts grayish white; breast and sides of body greenish yellow.

Tropical zone. Generally distributed s to BOLIVIA and Amazonian BRAZIL; w of Andes to w ECUADOR. [Mid. Amer.]

9. TRINIDAD EUPHONIA

Euphonia trinitatis

Differs from 8 mainly by paler, more extensive yellow crown patch, yellow center of belly and under tail coverts. ♀: Differs from 8 by yellowish throat and sides of body, yellow under tail coverts.

Tropical zone. N VENEZUELA south to n Bolívar and n Amazonas; n COLOMBIA. Trinidad; Tobago (casual ?). Forest treetops.

10. FINSCH'S EUPHONIA

Euphonia finschi

4". Glossy steel blue, including wings and tail; cheeks and throat strongly purple. Forecrown and upper breast deep yellow darkening to ochraceous yellow on lower breast, belly and under tail coverts. ♀: Yellowish olive green above; sides of head and underparts greenish yellow.

Upper tropical zone. GUIANAS; VENEZUELA (Mt. Roraima); BRAZIL in e Roraima. Shrubbery, savanna.

11. VELVET-FRONTED EUPHONIA

Euphonia concinna

4″. Differs from 10 by black forehead and paler crown patch, breast and belly with little ochraceous tinge. ♀: Olive above, forehead and supraloral streak dull yellow; below dull yellow, brighter on center of abdomen.

Tropical zone. COLOMBIA in Magdalena Valley from Tolima south.

12. ORANGE-CROWNED EUPHONIA

Euphonia saturata

4.3″. Steely purple; becoming steely blue on lower back and upper tail coverts, wings and tail. Crown deep yellow; breast and belly ochraceous yellow, darkest on belly and under tail coverts. ♀: Olive green above; olive yellow below, center of belly yellow.

Upper tropical zone. COLOMBIA on both slopes of W Andes from Valle s to extreme nw PERU. Forest.

13. PURPLE-THROATED EUPHONIA

Euphonia chlorotica *

4.5″. Differs from 12 by lemon yellow crown and underparts and by having the inner webs of the two outer pairs of tail feathers white. ♀: Virtually similar to 12 but underparts slightly paler.

Tropical zone. Widely distributed e of the Andes s to central ARGENTINA. Forest.

14. THICK-BILLED EUPHONIA

Euphonia laniirostris *

5.″. Forecrown and entire underparts bright yellow to light ochraceous yellow. Upperparts, sides of head and neck, wings and tail steely blue; purplish on sides of head and nape. Tail like back, with inner web of outer two pairs of tail feathers largely white (or no white, 1). ♀: Loral spot white. Above olive, below olive yellow, brighter on center of abdomen.

Tropical, lower subtropical zones. N VENEZUELA; n COLOMBIA s to upper Cauca and Magdalena valleys; w ECUADOR; nw and se PERU; n and e BOLIVIA and immediately adjacent Mato Grosso and upper rio Madeira, BRAZIL. Se COLOMBIA, e ECUADOR, n PERU and w and central Amazonian BRAZIL, 1. [Costa Rica; Panama.] Open woodland.

15. VIOLACEOUS EUPHONIA

Euphonia violacea *

Differs from 14 by much deeper yellow forecrown reaching only the eye instead of covering whole crown; much more white on outer two tail feathers, tail shorter. ♀: Best distinguished from 14 by shorter tail and white patch on inner web of outer feather.

Tropical zone. GUIANAS; VENEZUELA except w; Amazonian and e BRAZIL w to rio Madeira and s to Rio Grande do Sul, e PARAGUAY and Misiones, ARGENTINA. Trinidad, Tobago. Forest, edge of mangroves, coffee plantations.

16. RUFOUS-BELLIED EUPHONIA

Euphonia rufiventris

4.5″. Glossy steel blue including wings and tail. Breast and belly rufous ochraceous, deepening to chestnut on under tail coverts; sides of breast golden yellow. ♀: Above olive, chin, flanks and belly olive yellow; under tail coverts ochraceous rufous, center of underparts gray.

Tropical zone. S VENEZUELA; e COLOMBIA s to Puno, PERU; Amazonian BRAZIL e to rios Negro and Xingú and south to e BOLIVIA. Forest, among parasitic plants.

17. GOLDEN-SIDED EUPHONIA

Euphonia cayennensis

4.5″. Steel blue, patch at sides of breast orange yellow. ♀: Differs from 16 mainly by gray instead of ochraceous under tail coverts.

Tropical zone. GUIANAS; se VENEZUELA; e Amazonian BRAZIL from rio Negro to Amapá, Belém region and n Maranhão. Forest and savanna.

18. CHESTNUT-BELLIED EUPHONIA

Euphonia pectoralis

4.8″. Differs from 17 by lower breast, belly and under tail coverts dark chestnut. ♀: Differs from 16 by lower breast and belly olive yellow, only small area on center of belly gray.

Se BRAZIL from s Goiás and Minas Gerais to Rio Grande do Sul, e PARAGUAY and Misiones, ARGENTINA. Forest treetops.

19. BRONZE-GREEN EUPHONIA

Euphonia mesochrysa *

4". Upperparts, wings and tail somewhat glossy bronzy olive, glossier and greener on crown; forehead yellow. Throat and sides of body olive, breast and belly intense ochraceous yellow. ♀: Differs from ♂ by breast and belly pale gray, forehead without yellow. Much like ♀ of 16, 17, 18 but differs by entire throat yellowish olive instead of chin only.

Subtropical zone. COLOMBIA in upper Magdalena Valley and in Meta. E ECUADOR s to Puno, PERU and BOLIVIA in La Paz and Cochabamba. Forest.

20. GOLDEN-BELLIED EUPHONIA

Euphonia chrysopasta *

4.6". Lores and chin white, forecrown and sides of head olive; crown and nape gray, back somewhat glossy bronzy olive, tail coverts olive yellow. Underparts golden yellow, inconspicuously mottled dusky on breast. ♀: Differs from ♂ by pale gray underparts with olive flanks and yellow under tail coverts.

Tropical zone. GUIANAS; VENEZUELA; e COLOMBIA south to n BOLIVIA. Amazonian BRAZIL n of the Amazon from rio Negro eastward, s of the Amazon from rio Solimões east to nw Mato Grosso. Shrubbery in open forest.

21. PLUMBEOUS EUPHONIA

Euphonia plumbea

3.6". Upperparts, throat and sides of head glossy gray blue; underparts orange yellow. ♀: Crown and nape gray, throat and sides of head much paler gray. Back olive; breast and belly yellow, tinged olivaceous on sides.

Tropical zone. GUYANA; SURINAM; s VENEZUELA; BRAZIL from upper rio Negro e to Amapá. Forest.

22. GREEN-THROATED EUPHONIA

Euphonia chalybea

5". Upperparts, throat and sides of head,

wings and tail shiny bronze green, somewhat bluer on top of head. Frontal band and underparts bright yellow. ♀: Very like 17 but back darker green, bill thicker and more massive.

Se BRAZIL from Espírito Santo to Rio Grande do Sul; e PARAGUAY; ne ARGENTINA in Misiones. Forest treetops.

23. FAWN-BREASTED TANAGER

Pipraeidea melanonota *

6". Crown, nape and rump bright, light blue; back darker blue to blue black. Forehead and mask black. Underparts buff to ochraceous buff. ♀: Like ♂ but duller.

Upper tropical to lower subtropical zone. From mts. of n VENEZUELA and COLOMBIA s to Lima, PERU, w of Andes; e of Andes s through PERU to n ARGENTINA. BRAZIL in rio Negro region and in the e from se Bahía to Rio Grande do Sul and URUGUAY. Forest borders, clearings.

Plate 19

24. TURQUOISE DACNIS-TANAGER

Pseudodacnis hartlaubi

4.5". Forehead, throat, sides of head, mantle, wings and tail blue black. Crown, rump, upper tail coverts, breast and belly turquoise blue. Looks much like a dacnis but has a thicker bill. ♀: Lores and sides of head light olive brown; upperparts dull brown, the feathers edged greenish. Underparts grayish buff, yellowish white in center.

Upper tropical zone. COLOMBIA on the w slope of the Western Andes (Cisneros, Las Pavas, La Cumbre) and "Bogotá." Forest.

25. ORANGE-EARED TANAGER

Chlorochrysa calliparaea *

5.2". Upperparts shining emerald green; spot in center crown yellow. Lower back and upper tail coverts verditer blue, rump orange. Conspicuous tuft at sides of neck burnt orange (or orange, 1), throat black; sides of breast, body and under tail coverts emerald green; lower breast and belly shining blue or blue green (or throat, breast and line down center of belly dark blue; sides of body extensively grass green, 1). ♀: Like ♂ but much duller.

Subtropical zone. Upper Magdalena Valley, COLOMBIA, s through e ECUADOR to Junín, PERU; from Puno to Cochabamba,

BOLIVIA, 1. Forest edge, forest among parasitic plants.

Plate 41

26. GLISTENING-GREEN TANAGER

Chlorochrysa phoenicotis

5.2". Glistening emerald green. Small patch of glistening gray enamel-like feathers at sides of head, bordered behind by small orange tuft. Wing coverts glistening gray.

Upper tropical, lower subtropical zones. From headwaters of río San Juan in Pacific COLOMBIA south to nw ECUADOR. Creepers on forest trees.

Plate 41

27. MULTICOLORED TANAGER

Chlorochrysa nitidissima

5". Forecrown and sides of head golden yellow; patch on ear coverts black; upper throat orange yellow, feathers of lower throat white basally with dusky subterminal bar and golden yellow fringe; patch at sides of neck glistening chestnut. Hindcrown and nape grass green; triangular patch on mantle glistening lemon yellow; lower back, rump and upper tail coverts shining blue green. Breast, belly and under tail coverts glistening blue; center of both belly and lower breast velvety black. Wings and tail grass green. ♀: Differs from ♂ mainly by green breast and belly, yellowish green patch on mantle.

Upper tropical and subtropical zones. COLOMBIA from w slope of Central Andes in Caldas west to w slope of the Western Andes from Antioquia to Cauca.

Plate 41

28. OPAL-RUMPED TANAGER

Tangara velia *

6". Forecrown purple blue (margined behind by silvery, 1). Throat, sides of head and underparts purple blue (or silvery blue, 2); center of belly and under tail coverts chestnut. Crown, upper back, wings and tail black; wing coverts, remiges and rectrices edged purple blue. Lower back silvery opalescent, upper tail coverts blue. ♀: Like ♂ but sides of head lighter blue, with turquoise cast.

Tropical zone. GUIANAS; s VENEZUELA; e COLOMBIA s through e ECUADOR to Puno, PERU; n Amazonian BRAZIL. S of

Amazon on Marajó I. and in Pará, 1; from Pernambuco coastally to Rio de Janeiro, 1, 2. Forest treetops.

Plate 41

29. OPAL-CROWNED TANAGER

Tangara callophrys

6". Forehead purple blue, forecrown and sides of crown glistening opalescent. Back, wings and tail as in 28. Underparts and sides of head shining purple blue, center of belly and under tail coverts black.

Tropical zone. Se COLOMBIA in Caquetá and Putumayo; e ECUADOR; e PERU to Puno; w Amazonian BRAZIL s of the Amazon e to río Purús. Forest clearings.

Plate 41

30. PARADISE TANAGER

Tangara chilensis *

6". Top and sides of head covered with scale-like yellowish green feathers; eye ring black. Upper back, sides of neck, wings and tail velvety black; lower back and rump crimson (or lower back crimson or orange, rump yellow, 1). Throat, upper breast, edges of primaries purple blue; breast, belly and wing coverts brilliant turquoise blue to purple blue; center of belly and under tail coverts black.

Tropical zone. GUIANAS, VENEZUELA s of the Orinoco, Amazonian BRAZIL e to the río Branco—río Negro regions, 1. COLOMBIA e of the Andes, e ECUADOR, e PERU, w Amazonian BRAZIL south to w Mato Grosso and n BOLIVIA. Forest.

Plate 41

31. SEVEN-COLORED TANAGER

Tangara fastuosa

6". Forehead and chin black, rest of head shining turquoise blue; mantle, lower throat and upper breast black; lower breast turquoise blue; belly violet blue. Lesser wing coverts turquoise blue, greater ones violet blue. Tail black.

E BRAZIL in Pernambuco and Alagoas. Forest and capoeira.

32. GREEN-HEADED TANAGER

Tangara seledon

6". Head and upper throat blue green, lower throat black; mantle and sides of neck shining golden green, center of back black, rest of back orange yellow, upper tail coverts green. Below shining blue, flanks bright green. Wing coverts purple blue, primaries edged turquoise blue, inner remiges edged shining green. Tail black.

Se BRAZIL from s Bahía s to Santa Catarina; e PARAGUAY; ARGENTINA in Misiones. Forest.

33. RED-NECKED TANAGER

Tangara cyanocephala *

5.7". Forehead, lores, chin and mantle black; cap and throat blue, eye ring cerulean blue. Cheeks, ear coverts and nuchal collar scarlet. Underparts, lower back, edges to remiges and to rectrices grass green to bluish. Wing coverts black, edged orange yellow. ♀: Differs from ♂ by mantle streaked with green.

E BRAZIL from Ceará s to Rio Grande do Sul; e PARAGUAY; ARGENTINA in Misiones. Forest.

34. GILT-EDGED TANAGER

Tangara cyanoventris

6". Above streaked black and gold. Forehead and throat black, sides of head gold. Below shining blue, green on center abdomen. Wings and tail black, feathers edged grass green.

Se BRAZIL from Bahía to São Paulo.

35. BRASSY-BREASTED TANAGER

Tangara desmaresti

6". Forehead black; forecrown and eye ring sky blue. Upperparts streaked gold and black when seen against the light, shining emerald green and black with the light. Sides of head moss green. Throat and breast ochre yellow, patch on center of throat black. Center of belly and under tail coverts dull yellow, sides of body grass green. Wings black, feathers edged green. Tail dark green.

Coastal se BRAZIL from Rio de Janeiro to Paraná.

36. GREEN-AND-GOLD TANAGER

Tangara schrankii *

6". Forehead, chin and sides of head black. Crown, rump and center of breast and belly golden yellow. Mantle streaked grass green and black; throat and sides of body grass

green. Wing coverts, outer remiges and rectrices black, edged blue; inner remiges edged green. ♀: Differs from ♂ by green and black streaked crown.

Tropical zone. Amazonian COLOMBIA; e ECUADOR; e PERU; w Amazonian BRAZIL; n BOLIVIA. Forest.

37. EMERALD TANAGER

Tangara florida *

6". Above much like 36. Forehead and ear coverts black, ocular region and underparts grass green, center of abdomen pale yellow. ♀: Differs from ♂ by no yellow crown patch.

Upper tropical zone. Pacific COLOMBIA from upper río San Juan s to Nariño. [Costa Rica; Panama.] Forest.

38. BLUE-WHISKERED TANAGER

Tangara johannae

6". Forehead, throat and sides of head black, bordered by blue. Short moustachial streak blue. Back streaked golden green and black; rump golden yellow. Below bright shiny grass green, yellowish in certain lights. Wings and tail as in 36.

Tropical zone. Pacific COLOMBIA from upper río Atrato south to n Los Ríos, w ECUADOR.

39. SPOTTED TANAGER

Tangara punctata *

5". Crown black, edged blue green. Above green, spotted black; below white, spotted black; sides of breast and body greenish yellow. Wings and tail black, feathers edged green.

Tropical, subtropical zones. GUIANAS; VENEZUELA s of the Orinoco; e ECUADOR; e PERU; nw BOLIVIA; n and e Amazonian BRAZIL.

40. SPECKLED TANAGER

Tangara guttata *

5.5". Much like 39 but slightly larger, crown much yellower, sides of head yellow instead of greenish, back greener, and sides of body white, instead of yellowish green, spotted with black.

Subtropical zone. VENEZUELA; COLOMBIA on e slope of E Andes s to Meta and e slope of Central Andes in Tolima. N BRA-

ZIL in n Roraima. [Costa Rica; Panama.] Forest.

Plate 41

41. DOTTED TANAGER

Tangara varia

4.5″. Head, rump and underparts grass green somewhat spotted with black below, mantle tinged blue. Wings and tail light blue.

Tropical zone. SURINAM; FRENCH GUIANA; s VENEZUELA. BRAZIL on lower río Negro and lower río Tapajós.

42. YELLOW-BELLIED TANAGER

Tangara xanthogastra *

5″. Head, throat and breast green, spotted with black. Mantle and upper tail coverts black, feathers broadly edged verditer blue; rump green. Center of belly bright yellow, sides of body yellow green.

Tropical zone. VENEZUELA s of the Orinoco east to e COLOMBIA; nw BRAZIL; e ECUADOR; e PERU; nw BOLIVIA. Forest.

Plate 41

43. RUFOUS-THROATED TANAGER

Tangara rufigula

5.1″. Top and sides of head black, throat rufous. Back black, feathers edged golden green giving scaled look; rump pale opalescent green. Feathers of breast and sides black, broadly edged opalescent green or golden green depending on light. Center of belly buffy white, under tail coverts buff. Wings and tail black, feathers edged opalescent green.

Upper tropical and subtropical zones. Pacific COLOMBIA from upper río San Juan s to El Oro, w ECUADOR. Forest.

44. GOLDEN TANAGER

Tangara arthus *

6″. Top and sides of head yellow, ear coverts and lores black, underparts chestnut (or with throat and center of belly golden yellow, 1; or with underparts golden yellow to amber yellow, 2; or with black chin, throat and breast chestnut to ochraceous yellow; rest of underparts yellow, 3). Back streaked black and gold, rump golden yellow. Wings and tail black.

Upper tropical, subtropical zones. N VENEZUELA from Miranda to Falcón, Barinas

and Táchira. COLOMBIA in Macarena Mts. and w slope of E Andes in Santander, 1. Perijá Mts. of VENEZUELA, w slope of E Andes in Magdalena, COLOMBIA, s through Andes to w ECUADOR, 2. E ECUADOR s through Andes to n BOLIVIA, 3. Forest.

45. SILVER-THROATED TANAGER

Tangara icterocephala *

5.5″. Top and sides of head golden yellow, throat silvery green separated from yellow by black line. Back striped greenish gold and black; rump golden yellow. Underparts golden yellow, greenish yellow at sides. Wings and tail black, feathers edged green.

Upper tropical and subtropical zones. Pacific COLOMBIA from Antioquia south to nw ECUADOR. [Costa Rica; Panama.] Humid forest.

46. SAFFRON-CROWNED TANAGER

Tangara xanthocephala *

5.5″. Crown and sides of head golden yellow (or crown orange, sides of head golden yellow, 1). Mask, upper throat and nuchal collar black. Back striped greenish blue and black; rump and breast opalescent green blue; belly buffy. Wings and tail black, feathers edged blue.

Upper tropical and subtropical zones. N VENEZUELA from Miranda w to COLOMBIA and south to w and e ECUADOR and central PERU; from se PERU to n BOLIVIA, 1. Forest, light woodland.

47. GOLDEN-EARED TANAGER

Tangara chrysotis

6″. Forehead and eyebrow glistening opalescent gold; ear coverts glistening golden copper. Crown, lores, broad band below cheeks black. Mantle black, finely streaked glistening golden green; lower back, rump, throat, breast and sides of body glistening opalescent golden green to blue depending on light. Center of underparts chestnut. Wings and tail black, feathers edged opalescent green.

Subtropical zone. COLOMBIA in upper Magdalena Valley and e slope of Andes in Caquetá. E ECUADOR south to n BOLIVIA. Forest.

48. FLAME-FACED TANAGER

Tangara parzudakii *

6″. Forecrown and cheeks scarlet, hindcrown and nape orange yellow, (or forecrown and cheeks yellow like crown, 1). Ocular region, ear coverts and upper throat black; lower back and underparts opalescent silvery green, pale cinnamon on belly and under tail coverts. Mantle, wings and tail black. Wing coverts opalescent.

Upper tropical and subtropical zones. Nw VENEZUELA in sw Táchira, COLOMBIA on w slope of E Andes from Cundinamarca and e slope in Nariño s through e ECUADOR to Cuzco, PERU. Pacific COLOMBIA from upper río San Juan south to w ECUADOR, 1. Forest.

49. RUFOUS-CHEEKED TANAGER

Tangara rufigenis

6″. Cheeks, ear coverts and upper throat rufous. Crown and rump glistening blue green, back dark green. Lower throat, breast and sides of body shining pale silvery green to bluish depending on the light. Center of belly pale buff deepening to cinnamon on under tail coverts. Remiges black, edged olive yellow; rectrices black, edged green.

Upper tropical and subtropical zones. Coastal mts. of VENEZUELA from Dist. Federal to Carabobo and Lara. Forest.

50. BLUE-BROWED TANAGER

Tangara cyanotis *

5″. Top and sides of head, back, wings and tail black (or with dusky blue back and dark blue cheeks, 1). Long eyebrow, rump, throat, breast, sides of body and wing coverts glistening verditer blue to silvery green depending on the light. Center of abdomen and the under tail coverts cinnamon buff.

Subtropical zone. COLOMBIA in upper Magdalena Valley, s through e ECUADOR to se PERU. Nw BOLIVIA in La Paz and Cochabamba, 1. Forest.

51. METALLIC-GREEN TANAGER

Tangara labradorides *

5.2″. Shining silvery green or blue according to the light. Forehead, lores, center of hindcrown and nape, scapulars, wings and tail black. Center of abdomen grayish, under tail coverts cinnamon buff. Lesser wing coverts glistening purplish blue; greater wing coverts, margins of wing and tail feathers shining green.

Upper tropical and subtropical zones. COLOMBIA w of E Andes; nw ECUADOR; n PERU s to San Martín.

52. BLUE-NECKED TANAGER

Tangara cyanicollis *

5.3″. Head turquoise blue, throat purplish in some races; rest of plumage mainly black, belly more or less dark blue (or all black below, 1). Rump, under tail coverts, wing coverts, margins to remiges and to rectrices opalescent green to gold depending on the light.

Upper tropical, lower subtropical zones. Mts. of n VENEZUELA from Carabobo w to Zulia and Táchira and e slope of COLOMBIAN Andes in Norte de Santander, 1. COLOMBIA (except N de Sant.); e and w ECUADOR south to nw BOLIVIA; BRAZIL in central Mato Grosso. Forest.

53. MASKED TANAGER

Tangara nigrocincta *

5.5″. Head and nape pale silvery violet blue, cheeks pale green, forehead and mask black (or with forecrown and ocular region purplish blue, bordered by silvery blue; rest of head metallic golden copper, 1). Breast, mantle, wings and tail black. Center of belly white, sides of body light blue. Rump and upper tail coverts blue. Wing coverts blue, inner remiges broadly edged silvery blue green, outer remiges edged blue (or very narrowly edged silvery green, 1).

Tropical zone. GUYANA; s VENEZUELA; COLOMBIA e of Andes; e ECUADOR; e PERU; w Amazonian BRAZIL e to rios Negro and Madeira; n BOLIVIA. COLOMBIA west of E Andes to w ECUADOR, 1. [Mid. Amer., 1.] Forest, plantations, clearings.

54. GOLDEN-NAPED TANAGER

Tangara ruficervix *

5.5″. Mainly turquoise blue (or purplish blue, 1). Forehead, chin and mask black; forecrown blue, hindcrown golden straw separated from blue by black bar, nuchal band black (or forecrown blue like back, hindcrown orange rufous, 1). Center of belly white, under tail coverts cinnamon buff. Wings and tail black, feathers edged blue.

Upper tropical and subtropical zones. CO-LOMBIA w of E Andes; e and w ECUA-DOR; n PERU. PERU from Junín south to nw BOLIVIA, 1.

55. TURQUOISE TANAGER

Tangara mexicana *

5.5". Forehead, hindcrown, lores, back, wings and tail black; center of crown, sides of head, throat, breast, sides of body and rump cornflower blue (or pale silvery blue, 1). Lower breast, belly and under tail coverts yellow (or white, 1). Wing coverts purplish blue to turquoise (or silvery, 1).

Tropical, lower subtropical zones. Widely distributed e of Andes s to Amazonian BRAZIL, e PERU and n BOLIVIA. Se BRAZIL from s Bahía to Rio de Janeiro, 1. Trinidad. Open woodland.

56. GRAY-AND-GOLD TANAGER

Tangara palmeri

6.3". Mask black, crown pearl gray, throat white. Mantle pale silvery green, rump pale gray, tail coverts dark gray; feathers of breast with black bases fringed silvery green to golden straw depending on the light. Center of belly white, sides pale gray. Wings and tail black, wing coverts and broad margins to remiges pale gray.

Tropical zone. Pacific COLOMBIA south to nw ECUADOR. [E Panama.] Forest.

57. PLAIN-COLORED TANAGER

Tangara inornata *

5". Upperparts, throat and breast gray, lower breast and belly white. Wings and tail black; wing coverts bright blue.

Tropical zone. N COLOMBIA from the middle Magdalena westward. [Se Costa Rica; Panama.] Forest.

58. BAY-HEADED TANAGER

Tangara gyrola *

5"-5.5". Species varies much throughout its vast range, the races grading into each other; always recognizable by reddish chestnut head; bright green back, wings and tail; and green or bright blue underparts. Some races have blue rump, or yellow or rufous shoulders, or yellow nuchal band; intermediate races are found between the two extremes. Generally speaking, northern birds are greenest; southern and western birds bluest.

Tropical, lower subtropical zones. Generally distributed from the GUIANAS, VENE-ZUELA and COLOMBIA s to Amazonian BRAZIL, e PERU, n BOLIVIA and w ECUADOR. [Costa Rica, Panama.] Forest, forest edge, cocoa plantations, bushes.

59. RUFOUS-WINGED TANAGER

Tangara lavinia *

5". Not unlike 58 but at once distinguishable by bright yellow hindneck and upper back and orange rufous wings. Underparts bright green, center of throat and center of belly narrowly bright blue.

Tropical zone. The Pacific lowlands of COLOMBIA (including Gorgona I.), and nw ECUADOR to Esmeraldas. [Guatemala through Panama.] Forest.

60. SCRUB TANAGER

Tangara vitriolina

6". Crown rufous, sides of head black. Above dull silvery green, below paler silvery green or grayish, depending on the light. Center of belly and the under tail coverts buff.

Upper tropical and subtropical zones. CO-LOMBIA from upper Magdalena Valley westward and south to nw ECUADOR. Dry, scrubby country.

61. CHESTNUT-BACKED TANAGER

Tangara preciosa

6.5". Top and sides of head, nape and mantle bright coppery chestnut; wing coverts and lower back silvery ochraceous, greenish in certain lights. Underparts silvery bluish green, under tail coverts coppery chestnut. Remiges and rectrices edged blue. ♀: Crown and nape coppery chestnut; back, wings and tail green; below pale silvery green.

Se BRAZIL from São Paulo s to URU-GUAY, e PARAGUAY, and e ARGENTINA south to n Buenos Aires.

62. BLACK-BACKED TANAGER

Tangara peruviana

6". Differs from 61 in color by black center of back. ♀: Like 61.

Se BRAZIL from Espírito Santo s to Santa Catarina. Forest treetops.

63. BURNISHED-BUFF TANAGER

Tangara cayana *

6". Crown rufescent, rest of upperparts silvery straw color with greenish tinge in certain lights (or upperparts shiny ochraceous yellow, 1). Facial area black, throat and center of breast dark bluish, rest of underparts pale tawny buff with a blue shine in certain lights (or sides of head, throat, breast and center of abdomen black, sides of body shiny ochraceous, 1). Wings and tail feathers black, edged blue. ♀: Like ♂ but much duller and greener, throat whitish, rest of underparts buffy white with a greenish tinge; under tail coverts buff. Wings and tail bluish green.

Tropical zone. GUIANAS, VENEZUELA, COLOMBIA e of Andes. N PERU in San Martín. N and w BRAZIL e to rios Tapajós and Branco. E BRAZIL from Marajó I. s to Goiás and Paraná, central Mato Grosso, BOLIVIA in Beni, and PARAGUAY, 1. Bushy savanna, cerrado, gardens.

64. BERYL-SPANGLED TANAGER

Tangara nigroviridis *

5.3". Crown, nape and lower back silvery blue or silvery green depending on the light; mantle, forehead and chin black. Underparts and sides of head black, profusely spotted with silvery green or blue; throat bluer. Wings and tail black, feathers edged dark blue.

Tropical, subtropical zones. Mts. of n VENEZUELA from Miranda w to COLOMBIA (not Santa Marta); e and nw ECUADOR south to nw BOLIVIA. Open forest, treetops.

65. BLUE-AND-BLACK TANAGER

Tangara vassorii *

6". Uniform shining purple blue (or with crown and nape shining pale silvery greenish blue in contrast to back, 1; or with head like 1 but with shining silvery straw-colored nuchal patch, black mantle and spots on underparts, 2). Wings and tail black.

Subtropical, temperate zones. Nw VENEZUELA, Andes of COLOMBIA, e and w ECUADOR, nw PERU to sw Cajamarca. E PERU s to Libertad, 1; from Huánuco s to Cochabamba, BOLIVIA, 2. Forest and second growth.

66. BLACK-CAPPED TANAGER

Tangara heinei

5.2". Crown black; sides of head, throat and upper breast shining silvery green; back, wings and tail pale shining silvery violet blue; breast and belly similar but duller. ♀: Top and sides of head, throat and upper breast shining silvery green, paler and duller than in ♂. Back and sides of body, wings and tail bright yellowish green; center of underparts pale gray.

Upper tropical and subtropical zones. N VENEZUELA from Dist. Federal west to e and w COLOMBIA; ne ECUADOR. Forest clearings.

67. SILVERY TANAGER

Tangara viridicollis *

5.5". Throat and sides of head shining silvery greenish straw color (or shining golden coppery, 1). Crown, nape and most of underparts black, back and flanks shining silvery gray with bluish (or greenish, 1) cast. Wings and tail black, feathers edged dull blue. ♀: Crown dull brown (or reddish brown, 1). Throat and sides of head shining greenish, breast pale silvery green (or throat and sides of head shining pale coppery gold, breast duller and greener, 1). Back, wings and tail shining bluish green (or golden green, 1). Belly gray, flanks green. Wings and tail green.

Subtropical zone. Sw ECUADOR, n PERU s to Amazonas and sw Cajamarca, 1; in the s from Huánuco to Puno. Woodland and second growth.

68. GREEN-THROATED TANAGER

Tangara argyrofenges *

5". Crown, most of underparts, scapulars, lesser wing coverts, inner remiges and tail black. Cheeks and throat silvery green. Back and flanks silvery straw color. ♀: Feathers of crown edged dull green; throat and breast pale silvery green; belly gray. Back and flanks shining yellowish green. Wings and tail green.

Subtropical zone. E PERU in Amazonas and San Martín. BOLIVIA in La Paz, Cochabamba and Santa Cruz.

69. BLACK-HEADED TANAGER

Tangara cyanoptera *

5". Shining opalescent silvery greenish straw color; head black. Wings and tail black, feathers edged dark blue. ♀: Head and nape grayish blue. Throat and breast grayish, streaked bluish; belly yellow, clouded with green. Back yellowish green. Wings and tail feathers edged green.

Tropical, subtropical zones. Nw GUYANA; VENEZUELA; ne COLOMBIA in Santa Marta Mts. and Norte de Santander. BRAZIL in n Roraima. Forest.

70. PURPLISH-MANTLED TANAGER

Iridosornis porphyrocephala

6". Purplish blue, becoming greenish blue on rump and belly; center of belly buff. Throat bright yellow. Wings and tail black, broadly edged blue.

Upper tropical and subtropical zones. COLOMBIA from w slope of Central Andes westward and south to w ECUADOR, e slope in Loja. Forest.

71. YELLOW-THROATED TANAGER

Iridosornis analis

Differs from 70 mainly by yellow of throat reaching upper breast, and underparts tawny buff becoming chestnut on under tail coverts.

Upper tropical and subtropical zones. Se ECUADOR s to Puno, PERU. Forest, thickets in ravines.

72. GOLDEN-COLLARED TANAGER

Iridosornis jelskii *

6". Forehead, face and throat black. Crown, nape and sides of neck golden yellow. Breast and belly dull chestnut; back, wings and tail blue.
Temperate zone. PERU from Huánuco s to La Paz, BOLIVIA.

Plate 19

73. GOLDEN-CROWNED TANAGER

Iridosornis rufivertex *

7". Head black, center of crown rich yellow; upperparts shining purplish blue; underparts similar but darker, belly and under tail coverts chestnut (or blue, 1).

Temperate zone. Extreme w Táchira, VENEZUELA; COLOMBIA except Santa Marta (on n part of Central and W Andes, 1); e and w ECUADOR. Forest.

Plate 40

74. YELLOW-SCARFED TANAGER

Iridosornis reinhardti

6.5". Differs from 73 (1) by black crown and broad golden yellow band extending across nape to ear coverts.

Upper subtropical and temperate zones. E PERU from Santa Martín to Junín, PERU. Forest.

75. DIADEMED TANAGER

Stephanophorus diadematus

7.7". Forecrown, lores and center of throat black; center of crown snow white with crimson patch in center; sides of crown and rest of plumage shining dark purplish blue. ♀: Differs from ♂ by duller, less distinctly marked crown.

Coastal se BRAZIL from Minas Gerais s to URUGUAY, e PARAGUAY and e ARGENTINA south to n Buenos Aires. Forest treetops, also shrubbery, dense thickets.

Plate 16

76. SCARLET-BELLIED MOUNTAIN-TANAGER

Anisognathus igniventris *

7.5". Black; wing coverts and rump shining blue; patch on ear coverts, lower breast, belly and under tail coverts orange to crimson (with black belly and/or under tail coverts, 1).

Upper subtropical, temperate zones. Extreme w Táchira, VENEZUELA; Andes of COLOMBIA and ECUADOR, 1. N and central PERU s to La Paz and Cochabamba, BOLIVIA. Thickets, open woodland.

77. BLACK-CHEEKED MOUNTAIN-TANAGER

Anisognathus melanogenys

7.5". Sides of head black; crown and nape glossy cornflower blue; upperparts, wings and tail dull greenish blue. Underparts and small spot below eye golden yellow.

Subtropical, temperate zones of Santa Marta Mts., COLOMBIA. Forest.

78. LACRIMOSE MOUNTAIN-TANAGER

Anisognathus lacrymosus*

7''. Above dark dull dusty blue to blackish; brighter and bluer on rump (or above light grayish blue, 1). Forehead, sides of head and neck blackish (or olive yellow, 1). Spot below eye and behind ear coverts bright yellow. Underparts bright yellow to ochraceous orange. Wings and tail blackish, feathers edged blue; wing coverts bright shiny purplish blue.

Subtropical, temperate zones. Nw VENE-ZUELA in Zulia, 1; from Trujillo and Táchira to COLOMBIA (except Santa Marta and w slope of W Andes) and e and sw ECUADOR south to s Cajamarca and Junín, PERU. Forest.

79. BLUE-WINGED MOUNTAIN-TANAGER

Anisognathus flavinucha*

7''. Above black, or black with olive rump or with entirely olive back depending on race (with black back and shining blue rump, 1). Center of crown to nape, and entire underparts golden yellow. Wing coverts shining purplish blue, remiges edged shining purplish blue to turquoise blue.

Subtropical zone. Coastal mts. of VENE-ZUELA west to E and Central Andes of COLOMBIA, thence s to central PERU. From se PERU to La Paz and Cochabamba, BOLIVIA, 1. Forest.

80. BLACK-CHINNED MOUNTAIN-TANAGER

Anisognathus notabilis

8''. Top and sides of head, upper throat and sides of neck black; patch on hindcrown yellow. Back yellowish olive, rump yellower. Underparts yellow ochre. Wings and tail black, feathers edged blue.

Upper tropical and subtropical zones. Pacific COLOMBIA from upper río San Juan south to nw ECUADOR and e of Andes at Loja.

Plate 40

81. HOODED MOUNTAIN-TANAGER

Buthraupis montana*

8.5''. Head and throat black; back glistening purplish blue (with silvery azure blue nuchal band, 1). Underparts golden yellow, thighs black. Wings and tail black, feathers edged purplish blue.

Subtropical, temperate zones. Nw VENE-ZUELA in Zulia and Táchira s through COLOMBIA and e ECUADOR to se PERU. BOLIVIA in La Paz and Cochabamba, 1. Forest.

Plate 19

82. MASKED MOUNTAIN-TANAGER

Buthraupis wetmorei

8.5''. Above mostly bright yellowish olive. Mask black, encircled by bright yellow. Sides of throat and breast black, bright yellow of undersurface extending in a point to upper throat. Wings and tail black, wing coverts violet blue.

Temperate zone. W slope of s Central Andes, COLOMBIA. South-central ECUADOR. Forest.

83. BLACK-CHESTED MOUNTAIN-TANAGER

Buthraupis eximia*

8.5''. Crown and nape blue; throat, breast and sides of head black; lower breast and belly golden yellow. Back moss green (with blue rump and upper tail coverts, 1). Shoulders blue, inner remiges broadly edged moss green; primaries and rectrices black.

Subtropical, temperate zones. Nw VENE-ZUELA in Táchira. E Andes of COLOMBIA from Norte de Santander to Cundinamarca. North portion of W and Central Andes and east slope of E Andes in Nariño, south to e and w ECUADOR, 1. Forest.

84. ORANGE-THROATED TANAGER

Wetmorethraupis sterrhopteron

7.5''. Upperparts, chin, sides of neck, breast and body, wings and tail velvety black. Throat and upper breast bright orange, rest of underparts apricot yellow. Wing coverts and edges of inner remiges shining violet blue.

Upper tropical zone. Ne PERU in upper Marañón Valley. Forest canopy.

Plate 17

85. GOLDEN-CHESTED TANAGER

Bangsia rothschildi

6.5". Mainly blue black, tinged purplish below. Band across foreneck, under wing coverts and under tail coverts yellow.

Tropical zone. W slope of W Andes of COLOMBIA in Chocó south to nw ECUADOR. Forest.

86. BLACK-AND-GOLD TANAGER

Bangsia melanochlamys

6.5". Mainly black. Shoulders and rump blue; center of breast and belly golden yellow, tinged orange on breast.

Lower subtropical zone. W slope of n part of Central Andes and west slope of W Andes near the sources of the río San Juan, Chocó, COLOMBIA. Forest.

87. MOSS-BACKED TANAGER

Bangsia edwardsi

6.5". Crown and lores black, sides of head blue, back and tail moss green; throat greenish black, rest of underparts olive green, patch on breast yellow. Wings mostly dull slaty blue.

Tropical, lower subtropical zones. Pacific COLOMBIA from Dagua Valley, Valle, south to nw ECUADOR. Forest.

Plate 40

88. GOLD-RINGED TANAGER

Bangsia aureocincta

6.5". Differs from 87 mainly by broad golden yellow band from eye encircling ear coverts, thence running below green cheeks to base of lower mandible.

Subtropical zone. Known only from sources of río San Juan, Chocó, COLOMBIA. Forest.

89. CHESTNUT-BELLIED MOUNTAIN-TANAGER

Dubusia castaneoventris *

6.5". Above blue, silvery on crown, particularly at sides; below chestnut. Sides of head and moustachial streak black. Wings and tail blue.

Temperate zone. PERU from Huánuco s to La Paz and Cochabamba, BOLIVIA. Open or cultivated lands with scattered woods.

90. BUFF-BREASTED MOUNTAIN-TANAGER

Dubusia taeniata *

7.5". Head, throat and upper mantle black; forecrown, long eyebrow and streaks behind ear coverts silvery blue; upper breast buffy white (or with crown dark blue; throat buff, streaked black; breast cinnamon buff, 1); lower breast and belly golden yellow; under tail coverts buff. Wing coverts silvery blue. Edges to wing and tail feathers blue.

Subtropical, temperate zones. Andes of VENEZUELA s through COLOMBIA, (in Santa Marta Mts., 1), and e and w ECUADOR to Cuzco, PERU. Forest.

Plate 17

91. BLUE-GRAY TANAGER

Thraupis episcopus *

(Called *T. virens* in *Sp. Bds. S. Amer.*)

7". Mainly pale blue, darkest on back. Wings and tail much darker blue than rest of plumage. Shoulder purplish blue, violet or white depending on race. Some white shouldered races have white wing bar.

Tropical, subtropical zones. Widely distributed south to nw PERU and e of the Andes south to n BOLIVIA and Amazonian BRAZIL e to Maranhão. Trinidad and Tobago. [Mid. Amer.] Parks, clearings, plantations, towns.

Plate 19

92. SAYACA TANAGER

Thraupis sayaca *

Very like duller races of 91 with blue shoulders, but still duller and grayer with edges of remiges light greenish blue rather than purplish blue (or with throat and sides of head very pale gray in contrast to bright greenish blue breast and sides of body, latter color becoming violet when seen against the light, 1).

Tropical zone. Dry Caribbean coast and inland in n VENEZUELA w to Bolívar, COLOMBIA, 1. E and s BRAZIL from Maranhão and Ceará s to URUGUAY, PARAGUAY, n and e BOLIVIA and ne ARGENTINA to Buenos Aires. Margarita I. Arid scrub, woodland, capoeira, parks.

93. AZURE-SHOULDERED TANAGER

Thraupis cyanoptera

7.8". Much like 91 but larger; back bluer

with head darker and bluer than back instead of paler; wing coverts shiny dark violet blue.

Coastal se BRAZIL from Espírito Santo to Rio Grande do Sul; e PARAGUAY. Forest treetops.

94. GOLDEN-CHEVRONED TANAGER

Thraupis ornata

7.2". Head and underparts violet blue, bluer on crown. Mantle dull dark blue turning to dull dark olive on rump. Greater wing coverts fringed bright yellow; inner remiges and rectrices edged yellowish green, primaries edged bluish green. ♀: Similar to ♂ but much duller; back and underparts grayish, only tinged violet blue.

Se BRAZIL from Bahía to Santa Catarina. Parks, capoeira.

95. PALM TANAGER

Thraupis palmarum *

7". Top and sides of head glossy light greenish, throat grayer; back darker and browner; underparts glossy olive (heavily glossed violet above and below, 1). Wings and tail dark brown; wing coverts and speculum pale light grayish green.

Tropical, lower subtropical zones. GUIANAS; VENEZUELA and COLOMBIA e of Andes s to BOLIVIA, PARAGUAY and Rio Grande do Sul, BRAZIL. COLOMBIA w of E Andes, w ECUADOR, 1. Margarita and Patos Is.; Trinidad. [Nicaragua through Panama, 1.] Forest edge, parks, capoeira, cerrado, mixed bands of birds, palms.

96. BLUE-CAPPED TANAGER

Thraupis cyanocephala *

7". Crown and nape shiny bright blue; underparts gray to greenish blue (or with head and underparts uniform shiny bright blue, 1). Back olive to yellowish olive. Thighs and under tail coverts yellow.

Subtropical, occasionally to temperate zone. VENEZUELA n of the Orinoco (in coastal mts. from Aragua to Miranda, 1); COLOMBIA s through e and w ECUADOR and e PERU to La Paz and Cochabamba, BOLIVIA. Trinidad. Forest.

97. BLUE-AND-YELLOW TANAGER

Thraupis bonariensis *

7". Head blue, lores black. Underparts and lower back orange yellow; mantle black (or olive, 1). Wings and tail black, feathers heavily margined with blue. ♀: Top and sides of head bluish; back grayish olive, dull yellowish on rump; underparts buff.

Temperate zone. Andes of ECUADOR south to nw BOLIVIA and n CHILE, 1. E BOLIVIA e to PARAGUAY, se BRAZIL, and n ARGENTINA to Buenos Aires and La Pampa. Bushy pastures, gardens and parks.

98. BRAZILIAN TANAGER

Ramphocelus bresilius *

7.5". Scarlet, somewhat darker on mantle. Wings and tail black. Base of mandible conspicuously silvery. ♀: Head and neck dull brown, back reddish brown, rump and underparts dull crimson. Wings and tail brownish black.

E BRAZIL from Paraiba south to e São Paulo and Santa Catarina. Forest edge, capoeira.

99. SILVER-BEAKED TANAGER

Ramphocelus carbo *

7". Above blackish maroon to velvety black; throat and breast deep crimson, rest of underparts black (or very dark crimson above; below dark crimson, brightest on throat and breast, 1). Wings and tail black. Base of mandible silvery. ♀: Rosy rufous, browner on back, brighter on rump (or blackish, belly mixed with rusty rufous, 2).

Tropical zone. GUIANAS; e and s VENEZUELA; se COLOMBIA; Amazonian BRAZIL and in the e from Maranhão and Piauí s to Paraná, s Mato Grosso and PARAGUAY. N VENEZUELA from Miranda west to w Falcón, Táchira and COLOMBIA from Arauca to Meta, 1. E PERU, 1; nw BOLIVIA, 1, 2. Trinidad. Brushland, plantations, open woodland, campos, towns.

100. BLACK-BELLIED TANAGER

Ramphocelus melanogaster *

7". Differs mainly from 99 (1) by bright crimson rump; lower breast and belly have black line down center. ♀: Differs mainly from 99 by bright rosy red forehead, ocular region and upper throat.

Tropical, subtropical zones. E PERU in Huallaga watershed in San Martín and Huánuco. Hab. as in 99.

101. CRIMSON-BACKED TANAGER

Ramphocelus dimidiatus *

7". Differs from 99 by darker crimson throat and upper breast, but mainly by center of underparts extensively black. ♀: Head and throat blackish; back dull crimson; rump, breast and belly rather bright rosy crimson.

Tropical zone. Nw VENEZUELA in Mérida, Zulia and n Táchira; COLOMBIA e of Andes in Santander and generally w of them, except Nariño. [Panama.] Brushland, plantations, open woods.

102. MASKED CRIMSON TANAGER

Ramphocelus nigrogularis

7.5". Crimson; throat, mask, mantle, center of belly, wings and tail, velvety black. Base of mandible silvery. ♀: Similar but duller.

Tropical zone. Se COLOMBIA from Caquetá south to e PERU and w in Amazonian BRAZIL n and s of the Amazon to w Pará. Forest, second growth near streams.

Plate 19

103. FLAME-RUMPED TANAGER

Ramphocelus flammigerus

8". Velvety black; lower back, rump and upper tail coverts flame scarlet. ♀: Top and sides of head, mantle, wings and tail brownish black. Breast, rump and upper tail coverts orange; lower breast and belly lemon yellow.

Upper tropical and subtropical zones. COLOMBIA from middle Cauca Valley westward to sw Nariño. Clearings, second growth.

104. YELLOW-RUMPED TANAGER

Ramphocelus icteronotus

Differs from 103 by lower back, rump and upper tail coverts lemon yellow. ♀: Differs from 103 by bright yellow rump and underparts.

Tropical, subtropical zones. COLOMBIA from middle Magdalena Valley w to the lower Atrato and south to nw ECUADOR. [Panama.] Damp clearings. Hybrids between 103 and 104, with lower back in varying shades of orange, are not unusual.

105. VERMILION TANAGER

Calochaetes coccineus

6.7". Shining, bright vermilion; mask, throat, wings and tail black. ♀: Like ♂ but duller.

Tropical zone. Se COLOMBIA from Caquetá s to Junín, PERU. Forest.

106. HEPATIC TANAGER

Piranga flava *

7". Dark crimson red to light orange red depending on race; lighter and brighter below. Bill dark with conspicuous notch on upper mandible. ♀: Olive yellow above, dull to bright yellow below. Wing- and tail feathers dusky, conspicuously edged olive yellow.

Tropical, subtropical zones. Widely distributed s to Lima, PERU, in the west, and e of Andes to Córdoba and Buenos Aires, ARGENTINA. [Sw US and highlands of Mid. Amer.] Open woodland, plantations, cerrado.

Plate 19

107. SUMMER TANAGER

Piranga rubra *

6.5". Much like 106 but smaller, general tone of plumage rosier; bill smaller, light in color and without notch. ♀ and ♂ in winter: Best distinguishable from 106 by smaller size and pale, unnotched bill. Males in transition plumage are irregularly blotched rosy red.

Winter resident (Sept.-May). Tropical to lower temperate zone. GUYANA; VENEZUELA, COLOMBIA and e and w ECUADOR, south to nw BOLIVIA and w Amazonian BRAZIL. Acc. in CHILE. Curaçao. Trinidad. [Breeds in N Amer. s to Florida and Mexico. Winters Mexico southward.]

108. SCARLET TANAGER

Piranga olivacea

7". Scarlet; wings and tail black. In winter olive above, yellow below; wings and tail black. ♀: Olive, yellower below; wings and tail brown.

Winter resident (Oct.-May). COLOMBIA s through ECUADOR to PERU and nw BOLIVIA. Casual in Aruba, Curaçao. [Breeds in N Amer. e of Rocky Mts. s to Gulf States. Transient Mid. Amer.]

109. WHITE-WINGED TANAGER

Piranga leucoptera *

5.5". Crimson; wings and tail black, wing coverts with two broad white bars. ♀: Olive above, yellow below. Wings and tail grayish black, wings with two white bars.

Upper tropical and subtropical zones. N VENEZUELA and in se Bolívar and immediately adjacent BRAZIL; COLOMBIA south to nw BOLIVIA. [Mexico to w Panama.] Forest and scrub.

110. RED-HOODED TANAGER

Piranga rubriceps

7.5". Whole head, throat and breast scarlet; rest of underparts bright yellow. Back olive yellow, yellower on rump. Wings black, wing coverts bright yellow. Tail dusky olive, feathers edged olive. ♀: Differs from ♂ by less extensive scarlet on head and breast.

Subtropical to lower temperate zone. COLOMBIA from w slope of E Andes west to e slope of W Andes, e of them in Nariño; e ECUADOR; n PERU s to San Martín. Forest.

111. BLUE-BACKED TANAGER

Cyanicterus cyanicterus

6.5". Upperparts, throat, upper breast, wings and tail purplish blue; lower breast and belly bright yellow. Bill large. ♀: Greenish blue above; yellow below. Wings and tail blue.

Tropical zone. GUIANAS; VENEZUELA in e Bolívar (río Yurúan); n BRAZIL on lower rio Negro. Savanna, forest treetops.

Plate 17

112. OLIVE-GREEN TANAGER

Orthogonys chloricterus

8". Lores, upperparts, wings and tail dark oily olive green; underparts olive yellow. Bill slender.

Coastal regions of se BRAZIL from Espírito Santo to Santa Catarina.

Plate 17

113. CARMIOL'S TANAGER

Chlorothraupis carmioli *

6.5". Upperparts, wings and tail olive; lores and underparts yellowish olive; throat yel-

lower, lightly streaked olive. Bill rather thick.

Tropical zone. Se COLOMBIA in Nariño. E PERU from Huánuco s to Puno and Cuzco; nw BOLIVIA in La Paz and Cochabamba. [Nicaragua, Costa Rica, Panama.] Forest.

Plates 19, 30

114. LEMON-BROWED TANAGER

Chlorothraupis olivacea

Differs from 113 by darker coloring, more sharply defined yellow of throat and middle of belly, and mainly by bright yellow lores and eye ring.

Tropical zone. COLOMBIA from middle Magdalena Valley w to Pacific, thence south to nw ECUADOR. [E Panama.] Forest.

115. OCHRE-BREASTED TANAGER

Chlorothraupis stolzmanni *

7". Upperparts, sides of head, wings and tail dark olive (or crown and sides of head dusky olive, 1). Underparts ochraceous buff, olive at sides of body.

Tropical zone. W COLOMBIA from upper río San Juan south to west Nariño, 1. W ECUADOR to Chimbo. Forest.

116. RED-CROWNED ANT-TANAGER

Habia rubica *

6.7"-8". Slightly crested. Dull rosy red to carmine red, brightest on throat and breast. Broad coronal stripe flame scarlet. ♀: Brown above; coronal stripe cinnamon buff, yellowish or buffy orange. Wings and tail reddish brown.

Tropical zone. VENEZUELA n of the Orinoco; n and e COLOMBIA; e ECUADOR; e PERU s to Ayacucho. N BOLIVIA; BRAZIL s of the Amazon; PARAGUAY; ne ARGENTINA. Trinidad. [Mid. Amer.] Forest undergrowth, swampy woods.

Plate 19

117. RED-THROATED ANT-TANAGER

Habia fuscicauda *

Much like 116 but with dusky red tail, blackish chin and mystacal region. ♀: Differs from 115 by no pale crown stripe and by throat buffy white in contrast to rest of underparts.

Tropical zone. Caribbean COLOMBIA from

Atlántico westward. [Mid. Amer.] Forest undergrowth, woodland.

118. SOOTY ANT-TANAGER

Habia gutturalis

7.7". Mostly slaty gray. Crest flame scarlet; sides of crown and head and throat black; center of throat rosy scarlet becoming dark, dull crimson on extreme upper breast.

Tropical zone. COLOMBIA in middle Magdalena Valley and in valleys of ríos Ité and Nechí in Santander, Tolima and Antioquia. Dense forest.

119. CRESTED ANT-TANAGER

Habia cristata

7.5". Much like a cardinal. Sides of head, back, wings and tail crimson red. Conspicuous crest, throat and breast bright scarlet; lower breast and belly dull crimson, tinged gray.

Upper tropical and subtropical zones. COLOMBIA on both slopes of W Andes from Antioquia to s Cauca. Forest on steep slopes.

120. FULVOUS SHRIKE-TANAGER

*Lanio fulvus**

6.8". Head, wings and tail black; breast dull chestnut; rest of plumage ochraceous yellow, yellowest on upper mantle, most ochraceous on under tail coverts. ♀: Upperparts ochraceous brown, below brighter and paler; upper and under tail coverts ochraceous rufous. Wings brown, tail rufescent.

Tropical zone. GUIANAS; VENEZUELA; COLOMBIA e of Andes; e ECUADOR; ne PERU; BRAZIL n of the Amazon. Forest treetops, in mixed bands of birds.

Plate 50

121. WHITE-WINGED SHRIKE-TANAGER

*Lanio versicolor**

7.5". Center of forecrown olive yellow, rest of crown and sides of head black; throat dusky olive, rest of underparts bright yellow. Mantle ochraceous, rump yellow. Wings and tail black, wing coverts extensively white. ♀: Much like 120 in color, but with center of abdomen yellow.

Tropical zone. E PERU from río Marañón

south to n BOLIVIA; Amazonian BRAZIL s of the Amazon. Hab. as in 120.

122. WHITE-LINED TANAGER

Tachyphonus rufus

7". Silky blue black; axillaries and under wing coverts white. ♀: Uniform rufous.

Chiefly tropical zone. GUIANAS; VENEZUELA; COLOMBIA; e and nw ECUADOR; ne and se PERU; e and south-central BRAZIL to São Paulo and Mato Grosso; PARAGUAY; e ARGENTINA to n Buenos Aires. Trinidad and Tobago. [Costa Rica; Panama.] Capoeira, forest edge, roadsides.

123. RUBY-CROWNED TANAGER

Tachyphonus coronatus

6.7". Silky blue black; coronal stripe scarlet; axillaries and under wing coverts white. ♀: Crown grayish brown; back, wings and tail reddish brown. Throat whitish; rest of underparts ochraceous, streaked grayish on throat and breast.

Se BRAZIL from Minas Gerais s to Rio Grande do Sul and Mato Grosso; PARAGUAY and ne ARGENTINA in Misiones. Forest undergrowth.

124. FLAME-CRESTED TANAGER

*Tachyphonus cristatus**

6.5". Black; throat and rump buff; shoulders narrowly white. Flat crest scarlet to orange, bordered buff in front and at sides. Under wing coverts white. ♀: Upperparts, wings and tail rufous brown (or olivaceous brown, 1), tinged ashy on forehead and nape. Throat whitish; rest of underparts ochraceous, tinged ashy on breast.

Tropical zone. GUYANA and ne VENEZUELA, 1; thence w to COLOMBIA, w ECUADOR and generally e of Andes to n BOLIVIA, and BRAZIL to n Mato Grosso, Pará and w Goiás. Capoeira, open woodland, cocoa plantations.

125. NATTERER'S TANAGER

Tachyphonus nattereri

6". Glossy blue black, shoulder extensively white, rump suffused with dull orange rufous. Flat crest orange rufous. Under wing coverts white. ♀ (?): Differs from 124 by more rufescent underparts; rump and upper tail coverts much more rufous.

Sw BRAZIL (e bank of upper rio Paraguai) and ne Rondonia. Known from a male and (possibly) a female.

126. FULVOUS-CRESTED TANAGER

Tachyphonus surinamus *

6". Glossy blue black, shoulders extensively white. Crest, pectoral tufts, and rump pale ochraceous; flanks chestnut (or crest, rump and flanks rufous chestnut, pectoral tufts white, 1). Under wing coverts white. ♀: Top and sides of head gray, back olive, underparts fawn to cinnamon buff.

Tropical zone. GUIANAS; VENEZUELA; COLOMBIA e of Andes; e ECUADOR; e Amazonian BRAZIL. E PERU, w Amazonian BRAZIL, 1. Forest treetops, often in mixed bands of birds.

127. RED-SHOULDERED TANAGER

Tachyphonus phoenicius

6.5". Glossy black; inner lesser wing coverts and under wing coverts white, point of shoulder orange scarlet. ♀: Dusky brownish gray above, tail blackish. Throat and belly dull white, breast gray.

Tropical zone. GUIANAS; s VENEZUELA; e COLOMBIA. Ne PERU; Amazonian BRAZIL e to rios Negro and Araguaya. Savanna.

128. YELLOW-CRESTED TANAGER

Tachyphonus rufiventer

6". Black above, rump buff. Crest yellow; sides of head, neck, breast, narrow pectoral band and sides of body black; center throat buffy white; center of breast and underparts and the under tail coverts chestnut; sides of belly paler, more buffy. Inner and under wing coverts white. ♀: Dull citrine above, upper tail coverts tinged ochraceous. Sides of head grayish, throat white; rest of underparts ochraceous yellow, ochraceous on under tail coverts.

Tropical zone. E PERU s of the Marañón; nw BOLIVIA in La Paz. BRAZIL on upper rio Juruá.

129. WHITE-SHOULDERED TANAGER

Tachyphonus luctuosus *

5". Glossy black; very extensive white shoulder patch, white under wing coverts. ♀: Head and neck gray, palest on throat. Back olive citrine, wing coverts edged yellowish. Underparts yellow, tinged olive on breast.

Tropical, subtropical zones. GUYANA; SURINAM; VENEZUELA; COLOMBIA; e and w ECUADOR; e PERU; n BOLIVIA; Amazonian BRAZIL. Trinidad. [Honduras southward.] Forest, shady woodland.

130. TAWNY-CRESTED TANAGER

Tachyphonus delatrii *

5.5". Black, including under wing coverts; crest orange yellow. ♀: Dusky olivaceous brown, blackish on lower back and upper tail coverts. Tail black.

Tropical zone. COLOMBIA from middle Magdalena Valley w to Pacific and south to nw ECUADOR. [Nicaragua southward.] Forest; keeps fairly low in trees.

Plate 50

131. SCARLET-BROWED TANAGER

Heterospingus xanthopygius *

6.5". Black; scarlet tuft of feathers springing from behind eye; shoulders and rump bright yellow, pectoral tufts white. ♀: Grayish black above, rump yellow. Below dark gray, pectoral tufts white.

Range as in 130. [Pacific e Panama.] Forest.

Plate 50

132. RUFOUS-CRESTED TANAGER

Creurgops verticalis

6.5". Upperparts, wings and tail gray. Coronal patch and entire underparts rufous ochraceous. ♀: No coronal patch.

Subtropical, humid temperate zones. Nw VENEZUELA from Táchira s through Andes of COLOMBIA to e ECUADOR and se PERU. Forest.

Plate 50

133. SLATY TANAGER

Creurgops dentata

6". Slaty gray; crown rufous chestnut, bordered laterally by black. ♀: Slaty gray above, crown blackish. Eyebrow and eye ring grayish white. Center of throat whitish; sides of neck, cheeks, breast and sides of body orange rufous, center of belly white.

Subtropical zone. Se PERU in Puno; n BOLIVIA from La Paz to Santa Cruz.

134. GRAY-HEADED TANAGER

Eucometis penicillata *

7". Crested. Top and sides of head gray, throat white (or head and throat gray, 1; or top and sides of head grayish olive, throat buffy white, 2). Back, wings and tail bright olive yellow. Breast and belly bright yellow.

GUIANAS, n Amazonian BRAZIL west to e ECUADOR, e PERU and se COLOMBIA. N VENEZUELA, ne COLOMBIA and generally w of E Andes, 1. E BOLIVIA, n PARAGUAY, ne ARGENTINA and s BRAZIL from Mato Grosso and Goiás to São Paulo, 2. [Mid. Amer.] Forest undergrowth, shady woodland, often swampy. Follows army ants.

Plate 17

135. DUSKY-FACED TANAGER

Mitrospingus cassinii *

7.2". Forehead and sides of head blackish; crown olive, back dark gray, upper tail coverts tinged olive. Throat ashy gray, underparts oily olive yellow, under tail coverts rufescent.

Tropical zone. Pacific COLOMBIA e to middle Cauca Valley; nw ECUADOR. [Costa Rica; Panama.] Forest, shady second growth.

Plate 17

136. OLIVE-BACKED TANAGER

Mitrospingus oleangineus *

7.5". Much like 135 but forehead and sides of head slaty gray, crown and back yellowish olive, throat paler gray, underparts much brighter and yellower (or with duller underparts, 1).

Tropical, subtropical zones. W GUYANA and VENEZUELA on Cerro Roraima; on isolated mountains in Bolívar, and immediately adjacent BRAZIL in Roraima, 1. Humid forest.

137. ROSE-BREASTED THRUSH-TANAGER

Rhodinocicla rosea *

8". Upperparts, wings and tail dusky grayish or dusky olive. Throat, breast, center of abdomen, under tail coverts and bend of wing rosy magenta. Superciliary stripe magenta in front of eye, white behind it. ♀:

Differs from ♂ in that ochraceous orange replaces magenta coloring.

Upper tropical, lower subtropical zones. N VENEZUELA in coastal mts. of the Dist. Federal and Carabobo; in interior mts. from Miranda west to w slope of Andes of COLOMBIA in Tolima and Cundinamarca. [W Mexico. Sw Costa Rica, Panama.] Woodland, dense second growth; forages on ground.

Plate 16

138. BLACK-GOGGLED TANAGER

Trichothraupis melanops

6.5". Forehead, ocular region, wings and tail deep black; crown with broad yellow recumbent crest. Above olive gray; below buff, deepest on under tail coverts. Basal patch on inner web of remiges white. ♀: Differs from ♂ by no black or yellow on head.

Upper tropical and subtropical zones of e PERU in w San Martín and Junín; BOLIVIA in Cochabamba and Santa Cruz; PARAGUAY; ne ARGENTINA; s BRAZIL from s Bahía south to s Mato Grosso and Rio Grande do Sul. Shrubbery.

Plate 17

139. WHITE-RUMPED TANAGER

Cypsnagra hirundinacea

6". Upperparts, wings and tail black; rump, outer wing coverts and wing speculum white. Throat and sides of neck chestnut, fading to buffy on breast and becoming white on rest of underparts; flanks buffy.

Campos of e and central BRAZIL from s Maranhão s to Minas Gerais and Mato Grosso west to e bank of rio Madeira; n PARAGUAY; n BOLIVIA. Cerrado.

Plate 19

140. CHESTNUT-HEADED TANAGER

Pyrrhocoma ruficeps

5". Forehead, lores and chin black; head and throat chestnut, rest of plumage dark gray. ♀: Head cinnamon, lighter on throat. Above olive; below yellowish with grayish flanks.

SE BRAZIL from Espírito Santo s to Rio Grande do Sul; PARAGUAY; ne ARGENTINA. Shrubbery, forest undergrowth.

Plate 19

141. HOODED TANAGER

Nemosia pileata *

5.3″. Top and sides of head, and sides of neck and breast black; lores white. Back, wings and tail blue gray; underparts white. Legs yellow. ♀: Lores white; upperparts blue gray. Below white, tinged pinkish buff on throat and breast. Legs yellow.

Tropical zone. GUIANAS; n VENEZUELA and in e Bolívar; n COLOMBIA. Ne PERU. N and se BOLIVIA; PARAGUAY; Amazonian BRAZIL and in the e from Maranhão to Alagoas and south to w São Paulo and w Mato Grosso. N ARGENTINA. Coastal mangroves, coffee plantations, woodland, forest treetops.

Plate 30

142. RUFOUS-HEADED TANAGER

Hemithraupis ruficapilla *

5″. Top and sides of head orange rufous, throat paler; breast dark ochraceous; rest of underparts gray, yellowish in center; under tail coverts yellow. Crescent at sides of neck yellow. Back, wings and tail olive green; rump ochraceous. ♀: Olive green above, grayish on crown. Sides of head and underparts dingy white, under tail coverts yellow.

Se BRAZIL from s Bahía south to Santa Catarina. Forest edge, parks.

143. GUIRA TANAGER

Hemithraupis guira *

5.3″. Throat and sides of head black. Forehead and broad eyebrow bright yellow; eyebrow curves downward and broadens posteriorly to enclose ear coverts, where it forms a patch. Upperparts bright yellowish green, rump ochraceous. Breast ochraceous, center of belly and under tail coverts yellow, sides of body gray. ♀: Olive green above, remiges and rectrices edged yellowish. Below pale to bright yellow.

Tropical zone. N VENEZUELA and in e and s Bolívar; COLOMBIA e of Andes and in middle and upper Magdalena and Cauca valleys; e and sw ECUADOR; ne PERU. N and se BOLIVIA; PARAGUAY; n ARGENTINA. BRAZIL virtually throughout. Forest treetops, parks.

144. YELLOW-BACKED TANAGER

Hemithraupis flavicollis *

5.5″. Crown and upper back, wings (with yellow-tipped wing coverts, 1) and tail brownish black to black. Wing speculum white. Lower back, throat and under tail coverts light yellow (or dark yellow, 2; with center of throat white, sides of throat yellow, 3). Breast, mottled blackish in some races, and belly white. ♀: Rather like 143 but upperparts duller, olive; underparts all bright yellow (or throat, upper breast and under tail coverts yellow, center of belly white, sides grayish, 2).

Tropical zone. GUIANAS; VENEZUELA; COLOMBIA (along e base of E Andes, 1; in Magdalena, Cauca and Sinú valleys, 3; in extreme nw Chocó, 2). E ECUADOR and ne PERU, 1. E COLOMBIA in Vaupés, se PERU, n BOLIVIA, Amazonian BRAZIL and in the e from Pernambuco to Rio de Janeiro. [E Panama, 2.] Forest treetops, forest edge, parks, cerrado.

Plate 17

145. SCARLET-AND-WHITE TANAGER

Erythrothlypis salmoni

5″. Flame scarlet, flanks white. ♀: Above bronzy olive brown, dirty white below.

Tropical zone. Pacific COLOMBIA from Baudó Mts. south to nw ECUADOR. Forest.

Plate 40

146. FULVOUS-HEADED TANAGER

Thlypopsis fulviceps *

5.7″. Head and throat orange rufous (or chestnut rufous, 1). Above gray, below pale gray, belly white, under tail coverts pale buff. ♀: Like ♂ but throat whitish, back tinged olive.

Subtropical zone. N VENEZUELA. Both slopes of E Andes, COLOMBIA, 1. Forest.

147. ORANGE-HEADED TANAGER

Thlypopsis sordida *

6.7″. Crown and nape orange rufous; lores, ocular region and throat yellow. Above gray, tinged olive; below white, tinged gray or buff. ♀: Above yellowish, underparts butter yellow.

Tropical zone. VENEZUELA in Bolívar and Anzoátegui. Se COLOMBIA; e ECUADOR to n BOLIVIA; PARAGUAY; sw and e Amazonian BRAZIL e to Maranhão and s to Paraná and Mato Grosso; n ARGENTINA. Forest edge, parks, open woodland.

Plate 19

148. BUFF-BELLIED TANAGER

Thlypopsis inornata

5.7". Crown orange rufous, sides of head and the underparts cinnamon buff. Back, wings and tail gray.

Subtropical zone. Andes of n PERU chiefly w of the Marañón.

149. RUFOUS-CHESTED TANAGER

Thlypopsis ornata *

5.4". Differs from 148 chiefly by darker cinnamon rufous underparts and pure white center of belly.

Subtropical, humid temperate zones. CO-LOMBIA on s Central Andes. E and w ECUADOR. PERU south to w Lima and Cuzco. Open woodland.

150. BROWN-FLANKED TANAGER

Thlypopsis pectoralis

5.2". Head, throat and breast orange rufous; lower breast and center of belly white, flanks grayish brown. Back, wings and tail gray.

Humid temperate zone. Central PERU in Huánuco and Junín. Bushy mountain slopes along streams.

151. RUST-AND-YELLOW TANAGER

Thlypopsis ruficeps

5.2". Top and sides of head orange rufous; back, wings and tail olive green. Below bright yellow, olivaceous at sides.

Subtropical, temperate zones. S PERU from Apurimac s to central and n BOLIVIA; nw ARGENTINA to Tucumán. Open woods, alder groves.

152. SCARLET-THROATED TANAGER

Sericossypha loricata

9". Glossy blue black; throat and center of upper breast scarlet. Feathers of lower back and lengthened flank feathers with con-cealed white bases. ♀: Glossy blue black.

Interior dry regions of e BRAZIL from Maranhão to Alagoas and s to Goiás and Bahía.

153. WHITE-CAPPED TANAGER

Sericossypha albocristata

10". Crown and lores snow white. Throat and upper breast crimson. Body velvety black; wings and tail glossy blue black. ♀: Like male but throat and upper breast dusky crimson.

Subtropical, lower temperate zones. Nw VENEZUELA. E slope of E Andes and w slope of s Central Andes, COLOMBIA; e ECUADOR; e PERU s to Junín. Open forest.

Plate 40

154. COMMON BUSH-TANAGER

Chlorospingus ophthalmicus *

5.7". Crown, nape and sides of head brown-ish to slaty gray to black; white eye ring in some races. Back, wings and tail olive green. Underparts dingy white; pectoral band, sides of body and under tail coverts greenish yellow. Throat more or less spotted with blackish (or throat yellow, breast greenish yellow, 1).

Upper tropical to lower temperate zone. N VENEZUELA and COLOMBIA (on Mt. Tacarcuna, 1) s through Andes to BOLIVIA and nw ARGENTINA. [Mid. Amer.] Forest and woodland, chiefly lower and middle growth.

Plate 50

155. YELLOW-GREEN BUSH-TANAGER

Chlorospingus flavovirens

5.5". Top and sides of head dark slaty gray, blackish on forecrown. Back olive green. Throat and breast dull yellow, tinged green-ish on breast; center of abdomen dull lemon yellow, sides of body yellowish olive green. Under tail coverts yellow.

Upper tropical zone. Nw ECUADOR in Pichincha.

156. YELLOW-THROATED BUSH-TANAGER

Chlorospingus flavigularis *

6.5". Upperparts yellowish olive. Throat yellow (or only sides of throat yellow, 1). Preocular region, chin, breast and belly gray; sides and under tail coverts greenish yellow.

Tropical, lower subtropical zones. COLOM-BIA on E and Central Andes (on W Andes and w ECUADOR, 1) south through e ECUADOR to e PERU and nw BOLIVIA. [Highlands of w Panama.] Forest.

157. SHORT-BILLED BUSH-TANAGER

Chlorospingus parvirostris *

6". Very like 156 (1) but back duller, pre-ocular region olive instead of gray; and yellow at sides of throat deeper, feathers extending backward almost like a tuft, to below ear coverts.

Subtropical zone. COLOMBIA on e slope of E Andes, at head of Magdalena Valley and through e ECUADOR to nw BOLIVIA. Forest.

158. ASH-THROATED BUSH-TANAGER

Chlorospingus canigularis *

Very like 154 (gray-crowned type) but at once distinguishable by pale gray unspotted throat and narrow white postocular streak.

Subtropical zone. VENEZUELA in sw Táchira; Andes of COLOMBIA; e and w ECUADOR. PERU in Cajamarca. [Caribbean Costa Rica.] Forest edge.

159. DUSKY-BELLIED BUSH TANAGER

Chlorospingus semifuscus *

5.5". Crown and nape dusky brownish gray. Back, wings and tail dark olive. Underparts dull gray (center of abdomen whitish, 1), breast suffused with brownish. Sides of body and under tail coverts olive.

Upper tropical and subtropical zones. COLOMBIA on w slope of W Andes; from Nariño to w ECUADOR, 1. Forest.

160. BLACK-BACKED BUSH-TANAGER

Urothraupis stolzmanni

6.7". Above black, blackest on head; below white, mottled and clouded with dark gray. Flanks and under tail coverts ashy gray. Tail black, rather long, rounded.

Humid temperate zone. Central Andes of COLOMBIA and e slope of Andes of ECUADOR. Forest.

161. GRAY-HOODED BUSH-TANAGER

Cnemoscopus rubrirostris *

6.7" (or 6", 1). Head, nape, throat and breast gray (or throat and breast grayish white, 1). Back, wings and tail olive; lower breast and belly bright yellow. Bill light brown or reddish brown (or black, 1).

Subtropical, temperate zones. Nw VENE-ZUELA, Andes of COLOMBIA and ECUA-DOR. E PERU to Junín, 1. Forest.

Plate 17

162. BLACK-CAPPED HEMISPINGUS

Hemispingus atropileus *

7" (or 6"). Top and sides of head black. Long eyebrow white to buffy white (or very wide, bright ochraceous orange, 2). Back olive green. Underparts dull oily olive yellow, tinged ochraceous on breast (or throat and breast ochraceous yellow, center of belly bright yellow, 1).

Tropical to temperate zone. Nw VENE-ZUELA, Andes of COLOMBIA, and e and w ECUADOR. From Amazonas, PERU, s to Puno, 1. Nw BOLIVIA in La Paz, 1, 2. Forest.

163. GRAY-CAPPED HEMISPINGUS

Hemispingus reyi

6". Cap gray; back, wings and tail olive. Underparts bright yellow, olive yellow on flanks and under tail coverts.

Subtropical, temperate zones. Nw VENE-ZUELA in Trujillo, Mérida and e Táchira. Forest.

164. SUPERCILIARIED HEMISPINGUS

Hemispingus superciliaris *

6". Forecrown gray to blackish, eyebrow white (or forecrown olive, eyebrow yellow, 1). Upperparts, wings and tail olive (or gray, 2). Below bright yellow (or white, tinged gray on breast, 2). Iris brown.

Subtropical, temperate zones. Andes of nw VENEZUELA, 1. E and Central Andes of COLOMBIA s through e and w ECUADOR to nw PERU in Urubamba Valley and nw BOLIVIA. Central PERU from Jaén to Junín, 2. Forest.

165. OLEAGINOUS HEMISPINGUS

Hemispingus frontalis *

6". Above olive green to grayish olive with ill-marked yellowish olive eyebrow (or well-marked ochraceous eyebrow, 1). Below oily olive, yellower on center of abdomen (or dull pale ochraceous, 1).

Subtropical, temperate zones. Nw VENE-ZUELA from Lara w to Perijá Mts., 1. Andes of COLOMBIA s to Cuzco, PERU. Forest.

166. BLACK-EARED HEMISPINGUS

Hemispingus melanotis *

6". Above gray to grayish olive, sides of head black (or dusky, 1); no eyebrow (or long white eyebrow, 2, 3). Point of chin black (or upper throat black, 2; or crown and upper throat black, 3). Throat, breast, and under tail coverts cinnamon buff; center of abdomen whitish, flanks dull pale brown (or breast and under tail coverts orange rufous, belly buff, 2; or entire underparts orange rufous, 3). Wings and tail brown, remiges pale-edged.

Subtropical zone. Nw VENEZUELA in Táchira, Central and E Andes of COLOMBIA and e ECUADOR. Sw COLOMBIA, nw ECUADOR, 1. Nw PERU s to Cajamarca, 3. E PERU south to nw BOLIVIA, 2. Forest.

167. SLATY-BACKED HEMISPINGUS

Hemispingus goeringi

Much like 166 (3) but crown black, long eyebrow white. Back, wings and tail slaty gray; below orange rufous; tarsi very much longer than in 166.

Temperate zone. Nw VENEZUELA in Mérida and Táchira. Forest.

168. BLACK-HEADED HEMISPINGUS

Hemispingus verticalis

5.7". Throat and sides of head black. Center of crown pale grayish brown. Back gray, wings and tail blackish. Below gray, much paler than back; center of lower breast and belly white.

Temperate, lower páramo zones. VENEZUELA in w Táchira. COLOMBIA on E and Central Andes and in Nariño. Forest.

Plate 30

169. DRAB HEMISPINGUS

Hemispingus xanthophthalmus

6". Above gray, below grayish white. Much like 164 (2) but upperparts, wings and tail browner; no eyebrow. Iris straw yellow instead of brown.

Humid temperate zone. Central PERU from Amazonas to Cuzco.

170. THREE-STRIPED HEMISPINGUS

Hemispingus trifasciatus

5.7". Upperparts, wings and tail olive brown. Sides of crown, sides of head, and the neck black, long eyebrow buffy white. Underparts ochraceous tawny, paler on center of abdomen.

Humid temperate zone. Se PERU from Junín s to La Paz and Cochabamba, BOLIVIA.

171. WHITE-BANDED TANAGER

Neothraupis fasciata

6.7". Upperparts bluish gray. Lores and sides of head black. Inner and outer wing coverts black, middle wing coverts white. Wings and tail grayish brown, breast and sides white, washed pale gray.

Campos of e and central BRAZIL from s Maranhão s to São Paulo and s Mato Grosso. E BOLIVIA in Santa Cruz.

Plate 17

172. CONE-BILLED TANAGER

Conothraupis mesoleuca

5.7". Black, somewhat glossy above. Concealed white patch on throat; center of breast and belly, base of primaries, under wing coverts and thighs also white. ♀: Unknown.

Known only from near Cuyabá, Mato Grosso, BRAZIL. Dry open woodland.

173. BLACK-AND-WHITE TANAGER

Conothraupis speculigera

7". Glossy blue black; rump gray. Bases of slightly elongated feathers of hindcrown, under wing coverts, wing speculum, lower breast and belly white. ♀: Upperparts, wings and tail light olive, central crown feathers dusky gray. Underparts and under wing coverts light yellow, olivaceous on breast.

Upper tropical zone. Sw ECUADOR; PERU in Piura and Lambayeque, San Martín, and from n Loreto s to río Curanja. Dry scrub and weedy pastures.

Plate 30

174. GRASS-GREEN TANAGER

Chlorornis riefferii *

8.5". Bright grass green; shoulders shiny bluish green. Mask, center of abdomen and under tail coverts chestnut.

Upper tropical to humid temperate zone. COLOMBIA s through Andes to Cochabamba, BOLIVIA, w of Andes to w ECUA-DOR. Forest.

Plate 40

175. BROWN TANAGER

Orchesticus abeillei

7.2″. Hazel brown above, forehead and eyebrow rufous. Below ochraceous, browner on sides. Wings and tail rufous brown, wing coverts ochraceous.

Se BRAZIL from e Bahía s to Paraná.

176. RED-BILLED PIED TANAGER

Lamprospiza melanoleuca

6.2″. Upperparts, wings, tail and thighs glossy blue black; throat and center of breast blue black ; rest of underparts white with two broad bands from center of breast crossing diagonally to sides of body. Bill scarlet. ♀: Differs from male by blue gray nape and back.

Tropical zone. GUIANAS, BRAZIL in lower and middle Amazon and nw Mato Grosso. Se PERU in Puno. Bushy savanna.

Plate 30

177. MAGPIE TANAGER

Cissopis leveriana *

11″. Black and white with long, much graduated, white-tipped tail feathers. Head, throat, breast and upper mantle glossy blue black; feathers pointed. Lower back, lower breast and belly white; black feathers of back and breast encroaching raggedly on upper back and to a point on lower breast.

Wings and tail dull black, wing coverts white, inner remiges broadly edged white.

Tropical, subtropical zones. GUYANA; FRENCH GUIANA. N VENEZUELA to n Bolívar and n Amazonas. E COLOMBIA south to n BOLIVIA, w Amazonian BRA-ZIL and from Pernambuco to Santa Cata-rina and Mato Grosso; PARAGUAY; ne ARGENTINA in Misiones. Forest edge.

Plate 30

178. CINNAMON TANAGER

Schistochlamys ruficapillus *

6.7″. Mask black, crown and nape reddish brown to drab brown; sides of head, throat, breast and under tail coverts light pinkish cinnamon; belly white. Upperparts, thighs, wings and tail blue gray. ♀: Similar but duller. Bill bullfinch-like.

E and central BRAZIL from Maranhão and Pernambuco s to Paraná and e Mato Grosso. Capoeira, dry scrub, caatinga, cerrado.

179. BLACK-FACED TANAGER

Schistochlamys melanopis *

7″. Gray, paler below; forecrown, sides of head, throat and center of upper breast black. Tail blackish, narrowly tipped white. ♀: Olive green, paler below; center of abdomen yellowish.

Tropical, lower subtropical zones. The GUI-ANAS, VENEZUELA, n COLOMBIA; n, central and s PERU; n BOLIVIA; n, e and central BRAZIL, south in the e to São Paulo. Savanna, woodland, cerrado.

Plate 50

Family CATAMBLYRHYNCHIDAE   PLUSH-CAPPED FINCHES

The Plush-capped Finches are inhabitants of open woodland and shrubby mountain slopes. Little is known of their habits. The single species forming the family has been placed by some ornithologists with the tanagers, by others with the finches. Specimens collected recently in Colombia were found to have eaten insects.

PLUSH-CAPPED FINCH

Catamblyrhynchus diadema *

5.5″. Feathers of forecrown plushlike, deep yellow; lores, hindcrown and nape black. Sides of head and all underparts rich chest-nut. Back, wings and tail dark gray. Bill stubby.

Subtropical to temperate zone. N VENE-ZUELA from Dist. Federal to Zulia; Santa Marta Mts. and Andes of COLOMBIA south to n BOLIVIA and nw ARGENTINA; w of Andes s to Lambayeque, PERU.

Plate 16

Family FRINGILLIDAE   FINCHES, GROSBEAKS, ETC.

Finches form a very large family of small to medium-sized birds found virtually everywhere except in the East Indies east of the Wallace line, Australia and the Pacific Islands. It is composed of three distinct groups, but there is still disagreement as to their composition.

Most nearly related to tanagers are the cardinal finches (Cardinalinae), including cardinals, saltators and certain grosbeaks.

The buntings (Emberizinae), many of which are called sparrows in America, contain among others the seedeaters, brush-finches, yellow-finches and the ubiquitous Rufous-collared Sparrow. Inhabitants of open and bushy country, most northern species are migratory but very few reach South America.

The third group is composed of siskins and goldfinches (Carduelinae), probably most nearly related to, and sometimes included in, the mainly Old World weaver-finches (Ploceidae)—mostly African—to which family the House Sparrow belongs.

The food of finches is usually seeds, but some eat fruit and buds. They build open, cup-shaped nests, live in all sorts of habitats from sea level to the upper limits of the Andes, but usually prefer open or bushy country or forest edge. Many are excellent singers and are often kept as cage birds.

AID TO IDENTIFICATION

Goldfinch- or Siskin-like

Olive above, all or partly yellow below (cap black) 175a, 176, 186; (head black) 178, 179, 180, 181b, 182

Black and yellow (all yellow below) 187; (lower breast and belly yellow) 183, 185b; (belly yellow) 184b

Olive above, gray or olive below, patch in wings and tail bright yellow 175a, 176, 177, 178, 179, 180, 181b, 182, 183, 185, 186, no yellow in wings or tail 187

Upperparts conspicuously streaked

Under parts all or partly yellow 25, 75, 77b, 83, 84, 85b, with black crest 18c, with black lower throat 31a, with yellow breast band 31a, 83, with yellow upper throat 74b

Upperparts all or partly gray 72b, 93b, 96 with white in tail 71b, 97b, 146b, 150b

Below streaked 27, 66b, 71b, 72b, 83, 92b, 93b, 96b, 98

Sparrow-like, whitish below 141, 142, 143b, 144b, 145, with chestnut sides of neck 151, with long, pointed tail 152

Rose patch on breast 27

Black throat and breast 92b, 98

Black breast band 160b

Below pure white, wings olive yellow 153c

Below dusky grayish brown, under tail coverts chestnut 73a

Below tawny buff; tail long, pointed 155c

Upperparts unstreaked

Underparts mostly yellow (back partly black) 25, 26, 113b; (above olive to yellow or cinnamon) 15c, 76b, 79b, 82, 99, 114a, 115a, 120, head or face black or gray 13, 15c, 48, 89b, 90b; (above brownish gray or grayish) 78b, 80b, 81, 100b; (with crown different from back) orange 82, chestnut 111a, 112b, 113, 117a, 118b, 119a, yellow 116, black 110a

Underparts solid cinnamon to chestnut (back like underparts) 57c, 64c; (back gray) 56, 58b, 59, 62, 63, 165, 166b, 171

Underparts partly cinnamon to chestnut (breast band black) 7, 45c; (throat and breast black) 60, 68, 105c; (throat chestnut or orange rufous) 66b, 170b; (throat white, breast cinnamon or chestnut) 157, 161, 169b; (below chestnut to orange rufous) center belly gray 132b, center belly white 164; (flanks only cinnamon or chestnut) 5a, 158b, 159b, 168c, 172; (belly chestnut rufous) large 11b, small 61c

Black, gray and white in various combinations (black and white) 38, 44, 46, 47b, 53; (gray and white) throat white 16, 43, 86b, 87, 95b, bill yellow 37b, 40c, 41, 42a, 53; (black, gray and white) 49c, 162, 163c, pectoral band black 9b, 16, 51, 52c, 138b, 160b, 161; (gray and black) bill red 7, 17c

Uniform dark blue or black or gray (dark blue) 28, 29, 30c, 32c, 69b, 70c; (black) 33, 36, 67, 67bis, 68a; (gray) bill red 17c, bill yellow 71b, 72b, 73a, bill black 88b, 93b, 101, 102c

With red in plumage (head black) 15c, 177a; (head red) 19, 20c, 21, 22c, 23; (all dark or light red) 24a, 106; (with red crest) 24a, 107; (with black back) 108b

Above olive, underparts not yellow or chestnut

Top and sides of head black (bill black) 34a, 35a, 36, 130a, with white eyebrow 2b, 138b; (bill yellow) 136a, chin and eyebrow yellow 34a

Top and sides of head black with gray median coronal band, below mostly white 129, 134, with black pectoral band 135, 137b

Top and sides of head gray, two broad black coronal stripes 140a

Crown chestnut 128b, 133b

Crown gray, throat checkered black and white 14

Crown olive like back (throat white or cinnamon buff, bordered black) 1, 4c; (underparts streaked) 12b; (throat and breast gray to buff) 34a, 35a, 36, 173, 174

Back black, gray, grayish brown or brown; below whitish, buffy, gray or olive

Back gray (crown rufous or chestnut) 121b, 122b, 123b, 124b; (with black coronal stripe) 139a; (throat yellow) 109a; (throat white, bordered black; or black pectoral collar) 3, 6c, 7

Back brown or rufous, throat black, 10, 147b, 148b, 149, 150b

Back grayish brown (breast band gray) 94b; (face or head white) 126b, 127b; (chin black) 125b; (crested, outer tail feather white) 103

1. BUFF-THROATED SALTATOR

Saltator maximus *

8.5". Upperparts, wings and tail bright olive green. Narrow streak above lores white, sides of head gray. Moustachial streaks black, center of throat cinnamon buff. Breast and sides of body gray, center of belly buff, under tail coverts cinnamon buff.

Tropical zone. Widely distributed e of Andes south to e PERU, w BOLIVIA and PARAGUAY, Amazonian BRAZIL and interior planalto and in the east s to Rio de Janeiro. W of Andes south to w ECUADOR.

[Mid. Amer.] Clearings, swampy areas, trees bordering streams, cerradão.

Plate 42

2. BLACK-WINGED SALTATOR

Saltator atripennis *

8.5". Top and sides of head and neck black (or with gray crown, 1). Long eyebrow and patch on ear coverts white. Back bright olive green; wings and tail black. Throat white, breast and belly light gray, under tail coverts cinnamon buff.

Upper tropical and subtropical zones. Andes

of COLOMBIA (w slope of E Andes, 1); w
ECUADOR, 1. Open woodland, pastures,
thickets.

3. GRAYISH SALTATOR

Saltator coerulescens *

8.5". Above light to dark gray, with slight
olive tinge in some races. Long eyebrow and
throat white to buffy white. Moustachial
streaks black. Underparts pale gray to buffy
gray, buff on center of abdomen, under tail
coverts cinnamon buff. Pattern very like 1
but back gray instead of green.

Tropical zone. Widespread e of Andes south
to e PERU, BOLIVIA, PARAGUAY, and n
ARGENTINA. W of Andes in Caribbean
COLOMBIA. Trinidad. [Mexico to Costa
Rica.] Scrub, gardens, edge of mangroves,
arid woodland, campos.

4. GREEN-WINGED SALTATOR

Saltator similis *

Chiefly distinguishable from 3 by bright
olive green edges to inner remiges, and olive
crown and mantle. Breast and belly pale
clay color instead of gray.

E and s BRAZIL from Goiás and Bahía s to
URUGUAY, ne ARGENTINA, PARA-
GUAY and ne BOLIVIA. Thickets, orchards, open woodland, capoeira, feeds on
ground or in treetops, cerradão.

5. ORINOCAN SALTATOR

Saltator orenocensis *

7". Sides of head and neck, back and wings
gray; tail black. Very broad eyebrow white.
Below white, flanks cinnamon rufous.
Under tail coverts cinnamon buff.

Tropical zone. VENEZUELA n of ríos
Orinoco and Apure; ne COLOMBIA.
Thickets, thorny arid scrub.

6. THICK-BILLED SALTATOR

Saltator maxillosus

8". Upperparts, wings and tail dusky gray.
Long eyebrow white, moustachial streaks
black. Throat ochraceous buff, rest of
underparts buffy gray, under tail coverts
clear buff. Much like 3 but bill much
thicker, more curved and shorter, black with
yellow blotch at base of mandible. ♀: Like ♂
but upperparts bright olive green.

E BRAZIL from Espírito Santo s to Rio

Grande do Sul; e PARAGUAY; w ARGEN-
TINA. Woodland undergrowth.

7. GOLDEN-BILLED SALTATOR

Saltator aurantiirostris *

8.5" (or 7.7", 1). Above gray; forehead,
sides of head and neck, and broad pectoral
band black (sometimes no band); long postocular streak white. Throat white to buffy
white; rest of underparts buff to cinnamon
buff, darkest on flanks and under tail
coverts; breast tinged gray. Tail black with
conspicuous white tips to two outer tail
feathers (or no white-tipped feathers, 1).
Bill orange yellow to red (or blackish above,
yellow to reddish below, ♀ or imm.).

Subtropical to temperate zone. PERU,
CHILE in Arica, BOLIVIA (except Tarija).
S BRAZIL, n and w ARGENTINA. BO-
LIVIA in Tarija, 1. Dry scrub, thickets.

8. BLACK-COWLED SALTATOR

Saltator nigriceps

9". Gray; head black, center of belly and
under tail coverts buff. Outer tail feathers
tipped white. Bill salmon red.

Subtropical zone. Sw ECUADOR from Loja
south to w Lambayeque, PERU. Arid scrub.

9. MASKED SALTATOR

Saltator cinctus

8.5". Above dark gray; mask, malar region
and upper throat black; lower throat and
upper breast white, pectoral band black.
Sides of body gray, belly and under tail
coverts white. Tail blackish, strongly graduated, three outer feathers broadly tipped
white.

Tropical zone. E ECUADOR (Cutucú).

10. BLACK-THROATED SALTATOR

Saltator atricollis

8.5". Above earthy brown with a suggestion
of streaking. Lores, cheeks and throat black;
ear coverts and sides of neck gray. Breast
and belly dull white, flanks and under tail
coverts buffy cinnamon. Tail dusky,
strongly graduated.

Campos of e and s BRAZIL from Maranhão
and Ceará south to n São Paulo and Mato
Grosso; PARAGUAY; ne BOLIVIA. Scrub,
capoeira, cerrado.

11. RUFOUS-BELLIED SALTATOR

Saltator rufiventris

9.5". Upperparts, throat and breast gray; lower breast and belly rufous. Broad eyebrow white. Wings and tail dusky, feathers edged gray.

Temperate zone of n and e BOLIVIA in La Paz, Cochabamba and Chuquisaca.

12. STREAKED SALTATOR

Saltator albicollis *

8". Above olive to grayish olive, grayer on rump; supraloral streak white. Tail gray. Below white, lightly to heavily streaked olive or gray (or unstreaked below, breast tinged yellow; eyebrow white, conspicuous, 1). Bill black with yellow tip.

Tropical, subtropical zones. N VENEZUELA from Barinas west to n and central COLOMBIA. From río Patía, COLOMBIA, south to w ECUADOR and w PERU to Ica, 1. PERU in upper Marañón Valley. [S Costa Rica; Panama.] Dry scrub, woodland borders.

13. YELLOW-GREEN GROSBEAK

Caryothraustes canadensis *

7". Mask and upper throat black. Back, wings and tail olive yellow; underparts bright yellow.

Tropical zone. GUIANAS; s VENEZUELA; se COLOMBIA; Amazonian BRAZIL from rios Negro and Madeira e to Amapá and Pará and from Maranhão to Ceará and s to Rio de Janeiro and e Minas Gerais. [E Panama.] Forest treetops, clearings.

Plate 19

14. YELLOW-SHOULDERED GROSBEAK

Caryothraustes humeralis

6.5". Crown and nape gray, broad stripe through eye black. Throat and malar region white, feathers edged black giving a scaled appearance. Back, wings and tail olive yellow; underparts gray. Wing coverts and under tail coverts bright yellow.

Tropical zone. E COLOMBIA (?). E ECUADOR. Sw Amazonian BRAZIL on upper rio Purús. Forest.

15. RED-AND-BLACK GROSBEAK

Periporphyrus erythromelas

8.5". Head black; back, wings and tail crimson; underparts rosy red. ♀: Head black; back, wings and tail olive; underparts dull yellow, olivaceous at sides of body.

Tropical zone. GUIANAS; se VENEZUELA. Ne BRAZIL s of the Amazon e of rio Tapajós. Forest.

Plate 19

16. SLATE-COLORED GROSBEAK

Pitylus grossus *

7.5". Dark blue gray above, wings and tail blackish. Lores, sides of neck and broad pectoral band black; center of throat white. Breast and belly gray, paler than back. Bill bright red. ♀: Paler than ♂, no black on neck and breast.

Tropical zone. GUIANAS; VENEZUELA s of the Orinoco; COLOMBIA; e and w ECUADOR; e PERU; nw BOLIVIA; Amazonian BRAZIL. [Nicaragua through Panama.] Forest undergrowth.

Plate 30

17. BLACK-THROATED GROSBEAK

Pitylus fuliginosus

8.5". Larger and darker than 16; no white on center of throat. Bill bright red. ♀: Differs from male by throat and breast dusky gray instead of deep black.

Se BRAZIL from Bahía to Rio Grande do Sul; e PARAGUAY; ne ARGENTINA in Misiones. Forest treetops.

18. YELLOW CARDINAL

Gubernatrix cristata

8". Crown and conspicuous crest black. Eyebrow and broad moustachial streaks bright yellow, throat black. Back olive, streaked black; breast and sides of body olive yellow, center of underparts bright yellow. Wings dusky brown, edged olive; lesser wing coverts bright yellow. Central four tail feathers dusky brown, rest mostly yellow. ♀: Differs from ♂ by white eyebrow and moustachial streaks, grayish ear coverts and upper breast.

Se BRAZIL in Rio Grande do Sul; e ARGENTINA s to Río Negro, acc. to Tucumán. Shrubbery.

Plate 19

19. RED-CRESTED CARDINAL

Paroaria coronata

7.5". Long crest, head, throat and center of upper breast scarlet. Above gray, below white. Tail black.

BRAZIL in Rio Grande do Sul and sw Mato Grosso; URUGUAY; PARAGUAY; se BOLIVIA; ARGENTINA s to Buenos Aires and La Pampa. Wet scrub, shrubbery.

20. RED-COWLED CARDINAL

Paroaria dominicana

7". Head, throat and center of upper breast scarlet. Upper back black, spotted with white; lower back gray, below white. Wings and tail black, remiges edged white.

E BRAZIL from s Maranhão to Ceará and south to n Minas Gerais.

21. RED-CAPPED CARDINAL

Paroaria gularis *

7". Head and upper throat crimson (with broad black stripe through eye, 1), lower throat black, black continued downward in a point to upper breast. Back, wings and tail glossy blue black; underparts white. Upper mandible black; lower, flesh color with black tip.

VENEZUELA in Orinoco Valley w to the llanos of e COLOMBIA, 1. From s Meta east across s VENEZUELA to GUIANAS; Amazonian BRAZIL; e ECUADOR; e PERU; n BOLIVIA. Trinidad. Wet scrub, plantations, mangroves, campos, lakes and river borders.
Plate 42

22. CRIMSON-FRONTED CARDINAL

Paroaria baeri *

Differs from 21 (1) by much deeper red forehead and throat, feathers of hindcrown only tipped red.

Central BRAZIL in Goiás, on the middle Araguaya and in ne Mato Grosso.

23. YELLOW-BILLED CARDINAL

Paroaria capitata *

Much like 21 but at once distinguishable by completely pale (brownish pink) bill and feet (brownish flesh color). Also by complete or virtually complete narrow white nuchal collar.

BRAZIL in w Mato Grosso; PARAGUAY; se BOLIVIA; n ARGENTINA. Shrubbery in humid areas.

24. VERMILION CARDINAL

Cardinalis phoeniceus

(Called *Pyrrhuloxia phoenicea* in *Sp. Bds. S. Amer.*)

8". Long crest, head and underparts rosy scarlet; back, wings and tail vermilion red. ♀: Crest rosy scarlet, front and sides of crown gray. Back sandy gray. Chin black, underparts ochraceous buff. Wings brown, tinged vermilion; tail dull vermilion.

Arid tropical zone. Littoral of VENEZUELA from Sucre w to Guajira Peninsula and the e base of the Santa Marta Mts., COLOMBIA. Margarita I. Thorny scrub, cacti, thickets.

25. YELLOW GROSBEAK

Pheucticus chrysopeplus *

8". Golden yellow; longer upper tail coverts black, tipped white. Wings black; bases of remiges, spots on inner remiges, and wing coverts white; tail black, outer feathers broadly tipped white. ♀: Differs from ♂ by dull yellow back profusely streaked blackish; wings brown, similarly marked; tail brown, outer feathers with small white tips.

Tropical to temperate zone. Coastal mts. of VENEZUELA from Sucre to Aragua, s Lara, and Perijá Mts.; COLOMBIA in Santa Marta Mts. and Nariño. Andes of ECUADOR s to Puno and Arequipa, PERU. [Highlands of w Mexico, Guatemala, Costa Rica, and w Panama.] Open woodland, river bottoms, forest borders, gardens.
Plate 42

26. BLACK-BACKED GROSBEAK

Pheucticus aureoventris *

8.5". Upperparts, throat and breast black (with yellow rump, 1; with rump, throat and center of breast yellow, 2). Lower breast and belly golden yellow, more or less spotted black, particularly at sides. Wings and back black, outer remiges basally white, lesser wing coverts yellow, median and greater wing coverts broadly tipped white. Tail black, outer feathers with broad white tips. ♀: Upperparts, wings and tail like respective males but browner, not as black; below yellow, somewhat spotted black.

Subtropical to temperate zone. Nw VENE-

ZUELA in Mérida; COLOMBIA in E and Central Andes, 1. From w Nariño s to Andes of ECUADOR, 2. E and central PERU south to n BOLIVIA; sw Mato Grosso, BRAZIL; PARAGUAY; n ARGENTINA. Forest tree-tops.

27. ROSE-BREASTED GROSBEAK

Pheucticus ludovicianus

7.5". Upperparts and throat black; rump white. Rosy red patch on breast continuing in narrow line over lower breast; sides of breast and rest of underparts white. Wings black, base of outer remiges and tips to greater wing coverts white, under wing coverts rosy red. Tail black, outer feathers broadly tipped white. ♀: Upperparts brown, streaked black; eyebrow and malar region white. Below buffy, streaked dusky; center of belly white. Wings brown, wing coverts and inner remiges with small white tips; tail uniform brown.

Winter resident (Oct.-Apr.). Tropical to temperate zone. N VENEZUELA and in Amazonas west to n COLOMBIA and e of Andes from Meta south to ne ECUADOR. Central PERU (Junín). Transient, Curaçao, Bonaire. [Breeds in N Amer. e of the Rockies; migrates through Mid. Amer.] Forest edge, cultivated lands.

28. BLUE-BLACK GROSBEAK

Cyanocompsa cyanoides *

6.7". Dark blue; forehead, eyebrow, spot at base of mandible and wing coverts brighter. Wings and tail black, feathers narrowly edged dark blue. ♀: Uniform reddish brown.

Tropical, lower subtropical zones. GUIANAS, VENEZUELA and COLOMBIA south to e PERU, n BOLIVIA and Amazonian BRAZIL. Trinidad. [Mid. Amer.] Forest, clearings, thickets, semiarid scrub.

Plate 42

29. ULTRAMARINE GROSBEAK

Cyanocompsa cyanea *

6"-6.7". Smaller (some races), but virtually indistinguishable in color from 28, but bill more curved, swollen and shorter. ♀: Much paler below than 28.

Tropical, lower subtropical zones. N VENE-ZUELA; w COLOMBIA in Dagua and Patía Valleys. N and e BOLIVIA; n and central ARGENTINA. E and s BRAZIL from Ceará

and Piauí s to Rio Grande do Sul and s Mato Grosso. Scrub, thickets near ground.

30. INDIGO GROSBEAK

Cyanoloxia glaucocaerulea

6". Above bright light blue with grayish cast; wing coverts light cobalt blue. Bill much smaller than 29. ♀: Very like 29 in color but bill much smaller, more curved.

S BRAZIL in w São Paulo, Paraná and Rio Grande do Sul; URUGUAY; e ARGEN-TINA to Buenos Aires. Dense thickets.

31. DICKCISSEL

Spiza americana

6.5". Like small meadowlark. Eyebrow and spot at base of mandible pale yellow, sides of head and neck gray. Chin and sides of throat white; center of lower throat and patch on breast black (no black in winter), remainder of breast pale yellow, belly white. Shoulders chestnut, bend of wing yellow. ♀: Sparrowlike. Above much like ♂, below whitish, lightly streaked black, moustachial streak black, shoulder dull chestnut.

Winter resident (Sept.-May). GUYANA and FRENCH GUIANA, n VENEZUELA, n COLOMBIA to Bolívar and the llanos del Meta. Acc. Aruba. Trinidad. [Breeds in N Amer. e of Rockies from Canada s to Texas. Winters in Mid. Amer.] Open country in flocks.

32. BLUE FINCH

Porphyrospiza caerulescens

5.5". Dark blue; bright cobalt blue on forehead, sides of head, throat, foreneck and rump; still brighter on lesser wing coverts. In very fresh plumage dorsal feathers broadly edged rufous. Bill yellow, conical, sharply pointed. ♀: Rusty brown above, feathers with dusky centers; below grayish white, lightly washed buff and narrowly streaked blackish.

Campos in interior BRAZIL from se Pará and Maranhão south to w Minas Gerais, s Mato Grosso and e BOLIVIA.

Plate 18

33. BLUE-BLACK GRASSQUIT

Volatinia jacarina *

4". Uniform glossy blue black. ♀: Brown above; below whitish, streaked brown.

Tropical zone. Widely distributed in shrubby areas, capoeira, cerrado and pastures south to n CHILE and ARGENTINA s to Buenos Aires and Mendoza. Margarita I., Trinidad, Tobago. [Mid. Amer.]

Plate 50

34. YELLOW-FACED GRASSQUIT

Tiaris olivacea*

4". Crown and sides of head blackish; eyebrow and upper throat yellow; lower throat and breast black; rest of plumage dull olive, paler below. ♀: Eyebrow and throat dull yellowish. Above and below dull olivaceous, belly pale grayish olive.

Tropical, subtropical zones. Nw VENEZUELA; COLOMBIA w of E Andes. [Mid. Amer., Greater Antilles, Cayman Is.] Cultivated lands, grassy borders at edge of woodland, grasslands.

Plate 19

35. BLACK-FACED GRASSQUIT

Tiaris bicolor*

4". Forecrown, sides of head, throat and breast black. Upperparts dull olivaceous, lower breast and belly gray. ♀: Above dull olivaceous gray; below light gray, whitish on center of abdomen.

Coastal VENEZUELA and in Mérida and w Lara. COLOMBIA in Guajira Peninsula, w Santander and upper Magdalena Valley. Aruba to Trinidad and Tobago. [The Bahamas, Antilles, Providencia and San Andrés.] Rice fields, open thorny scrub.

36. SOOTY GRASSQUIT

Tiaris fuliginosa*

4.5". Sooty black with slight olive wash; crown, sides of head, throat and breast black, becoming sooty gray on belly and sides. ♀: Differs from 35 by being darker and browner above, below darker.

Tropical, subtropical zones. GUYANA; coastal mts. of VENEZUELA, s of the Orinoco in se Bolívar. COLOMBIA in upper Magdalena and Patía valleys. E and s BRAZIL from Pernambuco s to São Paulo and Mato Grosso. Trinidad. Open country.

37. CINEREOUS FINCH

Piezorhina cinerea

6.5". Lores and malar region black. Pale

gray above, sides of rump white; whitish below, tinged pale gray on breast. Bill heavy, lemon yellow; legs dirty yellow.

Arid coastal n PERU s to Libertad.

Plate 14

38. WHITE-NAPED SEEDEATER

Dolospingus fringilloides

6". Head, upper throat, back, wings and tail black; back with slight bluish gloss. Patch on hindneck and larger one on rump white. Lesser wing coverts and small wing speculum white. Underparts white. Bill conical, thick, sharply pointed, horn color. ♀: Cinnamon brown; throat, center of lower breast and abdomen rufescent white.

Tropical zone from central Amazonas, VENEZUELA s to upper rios Negro and Xié, BRAZIL. Probably open country.

Sporophila

Sporophilas are small, somewhat gregarious finches with thick, grosbeaklike bills (except 50) found in grasslands, forest edge, thickets and marshes. The females of most species resemble each other closely and are very difficult to tell apart. Most are light olive brown to brown above, yellowish buff to buff below. They will not be described in the following text. Immature males resemble females but usually have a white wing speculum.

39. BUFFY-FRONTED SEEDEATER

Sporophila frontalis

5". Olivaceous brown above, short and narrow stripe behind eye white, forecrown white in old birds. Throat white, broad band across breast grayish brown, center of abdomen buffy white. Median and greater wing coverts tipped white. Bill thick, dull yellow. ♀: Wing coverts tipped buff, no stripe behind eye. The bill in this and the next two species differs from that of other species by having a very shallow upper mandible.

Se BRAZIL from Espírito Santo to São Paulo, Rio Grande do Sul; e PARAGUAY; ne ARGENTINA in Misiones. Shrubbery.

40. TEMMINCK'S SEEDEATER

Sporophila falcirostris

4.5". Light slaty gray, paler below; center of belly white, flanks and under tail coverts buffy brown. Wing speculum white, middle upper wing coverts tipped white. Bill yellow.

E BRAZIL from Bahía to São Paulo.

41. SLATE-COLORED SEEDEATER

Sporophila schistacea *

4.5". Slaty gray, darker than 40. Patch at sides of neck, center of breast and belly and under tail coverts white. Wing speculum white, wing coverts without white tips. Bill yellow, nails light colored.

Tropical zone. GUIANAS; s VENEZUELA and in n Mérida; n and w COLOMBIA; nw ECUADOR. Ne BRAZIL in Amapá and Pará. N BOLIVIA in Beni. [Costa Rica; Panama.] Forest, forest edge; usually in trees.

42. GRAY SEEDEATER

Sporophila intermedia *

Much like 41 but paler, blue gray rather than slaty gray (grayish black, 1). Upper mandible not noticeably shallow. Bill yellow, nails black.

Tropical, subtropical zones. GUYANA; n VENEZUELA. The llanos of COLOMBIA and w of Andes generally; in sw COLOMBIA, 1. Trinidad. Shrubbery, cultivated lands, pastures, llanos.

43. PLUMBEOUS SEEDEATER

Sporophila plumbea *

4.2". Blue gray above, paler below; upper throat and moustachial streaks pure white; neck, breast and sides of body pale gray; belly white. Tail black, remiges and wing coverts narrowly edged gray; wing speculum white. Bill black.

Tropical zone. GUIANAS; VENEZUELA in Bolívar, w Amazonas, Carabobo and w Zulia; ne COLOMBIA west to se Bolívar. E and s BRAZIL from Piauí to Paraná and Mato Grosso; PARAGUAY; n BOLIVIA from Beni to e Santa Cruz; ne ARGENTINA. Grassland, cerrado.

44. VARIABLE SEEDEATER

Sporophila americana *

4.5". Above glossy black with incomplete white nuchal collar and gray or white rump. Below white with narrow to very broad black pectoral band; upper throat sometimes black, sides of body pale gray in some races. Wings and tail black; inner remiges white basally; wing coverts tipped white, no white tips in more western races.

Tropical zone. GUIANAS; ne VENEZUELA. COLOMBIA e of Andes in Caquetá, w of them in Atrato Valley and Pacific lowlands; w ECUADOR; w PERU to Libertad and in Loreto. Amazonian BRAZIL from rio Solimões and Juruá eastward. Chacachacare I.; Tobago. [Mid. Amer.] Grassland, forest edge, gardens, fields.

45. RUSTY-COLLARED SEEDEATER

Sporophila collaris *

4.7". Top and sides of head black; spot at sides of forehead and below eye white. Mantle black; nuchal collar, incomplete in some races, buffy white to cinnamon; lower back grayish, rump buffy white to cinnamon. Throat white to buffy, pectoral band black, rest of underparts buff to bright cinnamon. Wings and tail black; two buffy to cinnamon wing bars, inner remiges broadly edged buffy gray to pale cinnamon; wing speculum white.

E BRAZIL from s Goiás to Rio Grande do Sul and Mato Grosso; URUGUAY; PARAGUAY; ARGENTINA s to La Rioja and Buenos Aires. Humid scrubland, weedpatches bordering lagoons.

46. LINED SEEDEATER

Sporophila lineola *

4.2". Glossy black above, rump white, sometimes center of crown white or with a few white spots. Throat black, broad moustachial streaks and underparts white. Wings and tail black, remiges basally white.

Tropical zone. GUIANAS; VENEZUELA; COLOMBIA e of Andes and in Magdalena Valley; e ECUADOR; e PERU south to Junín. BRAZIL south to s Amazonas, Mato Grosso and São Paulo; e BOLIVIA; PARAGUAY; ARGENTINA w of río Paraná s to Santa Fe and Tucumán. Grassland, shrubbery.

47. BLACK-AND-WHITE SEEDEATER

Sporophila luctuosa

4.5". Upperparts, throat, breast and sides of body glossy black; center of lower breast and belly white. Wings and tail black, outer remiges white basally.

Tropical, mostly subtropical zone. Nw VENEZUELA; COLOMBIA (except w Nariño); e and sw ECUADOR; w PERU in Ancash, and in the east s to Puno. N BOLIVIA Grassland.

48. YELLOW-BELLIED SEEDEATER

Sporophila nigricollis *

4.5". Crown, sides of head, throat and breast black; back, wings and tail olive; lower breast and belly pale yellow.

Tropical, subtropical zones. GUYANA, SURINAM, VENEZUELA and COLOMBIA south, e of Andes, to se PERU, ne BOLIVIA, BRAZIL to Mato Grosso and São Paulo and ne ARGENTINA. Trinidad, Tobago. [Sw Costa Rica southward. S Lesser Antilles.] Cultivated lands, shrubbery.

49. DUBOIS' SEEDEATER

Sporophila ardesiaca

Differs from 48 by gray instead of olive back, wings and tail; white instead of pale yellow lower breast and belly.

E BRAZIL in se Minas Gerais and Espírito Santo. Shrubbery.

50. DULL-COLORED SEEDEATER

Sporophila obscura *

4.2". Above dull, light reddish brown. Throat, breast and flanks brownish gray; whitish on abdomen (or below virtually uniform grayish brown, 1). Bill almost conical.

Tropical, subtropical zones. Nw VENEZUELA and COLOMBIA in Santa Marta Mts., 1. Sw COLOMBIA s through w ECUADOR to Arequipa, w PERU and from Libertad to Puno. BOLIVIA from La Paz to Tarija and nw ARGENTINA. Forest edge, grainfields.

51. DOUBLE-COLLARED SEEDEATER

Sporophila caerulescens *

4.6". Upperparts dull gray to brownish gray, browner on wings and tail. Upper throat and pectoral band black, lower throat white; moustachial streak, breast and belly white.

E and central BRAZIL from lower rio Tapajós e to Pará and s through Goiás and Bahía to URUGUAY, PARAGUAY, n BOLIVIA, se PERU and ARGENTINA to Buenos Aires and La Pampa. Shrubbery, cerrado.

52. WHITE-THROATED SEEDEATER

Sporophila albogularis

Differs from 51 mainly by entirely white throat; white bases of remiges; and black wings and tail, feathers edged gray.

E BRAZIL from Piauí and Pernambuco s to Bahía and Espírito Santo. Shrubbery at forest edge.

53. WHITE-BELLIED SEEDEATER

Sporophila leucoptera *

5". Upperparts, wings and tail gray (or glossy black, 1); underparts white. Base of remiges white. Bill clear, light brown.

E BRAZIL from mouth of the Amazon s to Rio de Janeiro and Mato Grosso; PARAGUAY; central n ARGENTINA. BOLIVIA in Santa Cruz and Beni, 1. Shrubbery at forest edge.

54. PARROT-BILLED SEEDEATER

Sporophila peruviana *

4.8". Above grayish brown, grayer on crown. Throat and breast black; patch at sides of neck, lower breast and belly white. Wings and tail dusky brown, edged grayish; wing speculum white. Bill very thick, very curved, dusky yellow.

Arid coastal zone from Manaví, sw ECUADOR, to Ica, PERU. Scrub, grainfields, arid scrub.

55. DRAB SEEDEATER

Sporophila simplex

4.3". Grayish brown above; breast pale grayish, throat and belly whitish. Double wing bars and wing speculum white. ♀: Differs from other species, except 39, by conspicuous buffy double wing bars.

Tropical, upper subtropical zones. PERU in upper Marañón Valley and Pacific slopes from Libertad to Ica.

56. BLACK-AND-TAWNY SEEDEATER

Sporophila nigrorufa

4.2". Cap, hindneck and mantle black; rest of plumage cinnamon rufous. Wings and tail black, wing speculum and margins of inner remiges white.

Tropical zone. E BOLIVIA (Chiquitos) and immediately adjacent Mato Grosso, BRAZIL. Campos.

57. CAPPED SEEDEATER

Sporophila bouvreuil *

4.2". Cap, wings and tail black; rest of plumage cinnamon rufous (or back pale grayish brown, feathers with dark centers; below cinnamon buff, 1). Wing speculum white.

SURINAM (Sipaliwini). E BRAZIL from mouth of the Amazon s through Goiás and Pernambuco to Rio de Janeiro and e São Paulo. In w and s São Paulo and Rio Grande do Sul, e PARAGUAY and ne ARGENTINA, 1. Shrubbery, cerradão.

58. TUMACO SEEDEATER

Sporophila insulata

4". Upperparts mouse gray, narrow band on rump and entire underparts rufous chestnut. Wings and tail black, both white basally.

Tumaco I. off coast of Nariño, COLOMBIA.

59. RUDDY-BREASTED SEEDEATER

Sporophila minuta *

4". Back, top and sides of head ashy gray (or with cheeks and auriculars tawny rufous, 1); rump and underparts orange rufous. Wings and tail dusky brown, feathers edged grayish brown; wing speculum white. ♀: Wing coverts dark brown conspicuously pale edged.

Tropical, subtropical zones. The GUIANAS, VENEZUELA, COLOMBIA, nw ECUADOR, ne BRAZIL. Se BRAZIL from s Goiás to Paraná and Mato Grosso, PARAGUAY, e BOLIVIA, n ARGENTINA from Formosa south to n Buenos Aires, 1 (*S. hypoxantha*, Tawny-bellied Seedeater, probably a distinct species). Los Frailes, Trinidad, Tobago. [Mid. Amer.] Tall grass, wasteland.

60. DARK-THROATED SEEDEATER

Sporophila ruficollis

4". Crown gray; cheeks, throat and sometimes upper breast black. Back gray, upper tail coverts rufescent. Underparts cinnamon buff. Wings and tail dark brown, remiges basally white (considered by Short probably a color phase of 59 [1]).

BRAZIL in Goiás, São Paulo and Mato Grosso; URUGUAY; PARAGUAY; BOLIVIA; n ARGENTINA s to Tucumán and Buenos Aires. Shrubby pastures.

61. MARSH SEEDEATER

Sporophila palustris

4". Crown, nape and mantle gray; cheeks, sides of neck, throat and upper breast white; rest of underparts and rump rufous chestnut. Wings and tail black, feathers edged gray; bend of wing, speculum, margins to greater wing coverts and inner remiges white.

S BRAZIL in w Rio Grande do Sul; PARAGUAY; URUGUAY; ARGENTINA in Entre Ríos. Marshes.

62. CHESTNUT-BELLIED SEEDEATER

Sporophila castaneiventris

4". Gray; throat, center of breast and belly, and the under tail coverts chestnut. Wings and tail black.

Tropical zone. GUIANAS; VENEZUELA in se Amazonas; se COLOMBIA; e ECUADOR; e PERU; n BOLIVIA; Amazonian BRAZIL e to rio Tapajós. Sandy wasteland, swampy fields, cultivated lands.

Plate 42

63. RUFOUS-RUMPED-SEEDEATER

Sporophila hypochroma

(*S. h. rothii* of Guyana is probably a hybrid between 59 and 62.)

4". Crown to below eye, nape, mantle and back gray; cheeks, ear coverts, sides of neck, rump and underparts chestnut. Wings and tail black, wing speculum white.

BOLIVIA in Santa Cruz and s Beni and Corrientes, ARGENTINA.

64. CHESTNUT SEEDEATER

Sporophila cinnamomea

4". Chestnut; cap gray. Wings and tail blackish, inner remiges basally white.

BRAZIL on upper rio Araguaia. E PARAGUAY (e of Villarica).

65. BLACK-BELLIED SEEDEATER

Sporophila melanogaster

4.2". Like 62 in pattern but gray parts of plumage much paler, and throat and central underparts black instead of chestnut. Inner remiges basally white.

Se BRAZIL in Minas Gerais, São Paulo and Rio Grande do Sul.

66. CHESTNUT-THROATED SEEDEATER

Sporophila telasco

4". Above gray, streaked dusky on crown and mantle. Upper throat chestnut, rest of underparts white. Wings and tail black. Inner remiges and tail basally white. ♀: Differs from all other *Sporophilas* by crown, back, breast and flanks streaked dusky. Above brown, below whitish.

Gorgona I. off coast of sw COLOMBIA. Coastal ECUADOR s through w PERU (also in upper Marañón Valley) to Arica, CHILE. Scrub.

67. LARGE-BILLED SEED-FINCH

Oryzoborus crassirostris

5.6"-5.8". All glossy black; wing speculum and under wing coverts white, rectrices sometimes basally white. Bill thick, bluish horn color, smooth and shiny. ♀: Earthy brown above, dull reddish brown below variable as to shade of color. Bill dusky.

Tropical zone. GUIANAS; VENEZUELA; n COLOMBIA s to Meta and w to Chocó. Ne PERU in n Loreto (Chayavetas, Xeberos, Chamicuros). BRAZIL n of the Amazon. Trinidad. Marshy open country, forest edge, clearings rice fields.

Plate 50

67bis. GREATER LARGE-BILLED SEED-FINCH

Oryzoborus maximiliani *

(Group considered conspecific with 67 in *Sp. Bds. of S. Amer.*)

5.8"-6.5". Differs from 67 only in size and proportions. Under wing coverts white (or black, 1). Bill much larger and thicker, pale horn color (or black, 2), bonelike in texture. Tail considerably longer. ♀: In color like 67 but bill much larger.

Tropical zone. GUYANA, FRENCH GUIANA, VENEZUELA in Orinoco Valley. Sw COLOMBIA in Nariño. Se COLOMBIA in Putumayo, 2. Ne PERU in n San Martín (Moyobamba), 1, 2. N BOLIVIA in Beni, 2. E and central BRAZIL from Goiás and

Bahía s to São Paulo and in Mato Grosso. Trinidad. [Nicaragua south to w Panama.] Hab. as in 67.

Plate 30

68. LESSER SEED-FINCH

Oryzoborus angolensis *

5.2". Glossy black (or lower breast and belly chestnut, 1). Wing speculum and under wing coverts white. Bill black. ♀: Earthy brown above, buffy brown (or sepia brown, 1) below. Under wing coverts white. Bill dark brown.

Tropical zone. Widespread e of Andes from the GUIANAS, VENEZUELA, and COLOMBIA south to e ECUADOR, ne PERU, BRAZIL to Rio Grande do Sul and Mato Grosso, n BOLIVIA, PARAGUAY and ne ARGENTINA, 1. W of Andes south to w ECUADOR. Caribbean COLOMBIA e to Santa Marta, where intermediates occur. [Mid. Amer.]. Woodland's edge, wasteland, shrubbery.

69. BLUE SEEDEATER

Amaurospiza concolor *

4.5". Dull indigo blue, slightly brighter on forehead and above eye; lores and ear coverts black. Under wing coverts white. ♀: Dark to rather light tawny brown, paler below.

Upper tropical zone. Sw COLOMBIA; w ECUADOR s to Loja. [Mexico; Honduras southward.] Forest, shady second growth.

70. BLACKISH-BLUE SEEDEATER

Amaurospiza moesta

5". Dark slaty blue gray; blackish on lores, chin, throat and breast. Wings and tail black, under wing coverts white. ♀: Above rather bright reddish brown, wings and tail dusky. Below light tawny brown.

E BRAZIL in Maranhão and from Río de Janeiro to Rio Grande do Sul. Ne ARGENTINA in Misiones. Shrubbery, bamboo thickets.

Plate 19

71. BAND-TAILED SEEDEATER

Catamenia analis *

5.5". Slaty gray, sometimes streaked dusky above; forehead and ocular region blackish (or gray, 1); under tail coverts chestnut.

Tail distinctive: black with inner webs of all but central pair of feathers having an oval white patch at the middle of the feather. Wings black, edged light gray; conspicuous wing speculum in some races. Bill yellow. ♀: Sparrowlike: above grayish brown (reddish brown, ♂ imm.), streaked dusky; below buffy white, streaked blackish. (See 97)

Temperate, páramo zones. COLOMBIA in Santa Marta Mts. and E and Central Andes, 1. ECUADOR, PERU, BOLIVIA, CHILE, ARGENTINA s to Mendoza and Buenos Aires. Shrubby or stony hillsides, irrigation ditches, weedpatches.

Plate 42

72. PLAIN-COLORED SEEDEATER

Catamenia inornata *

5.7" (or 5", 1). Light gray, back streaked black. Under tail coverts rufous chestnut. Tail dusky. Bill yellow. ♀: Differs from ♂ by brownish, black-streaked back.

Temperate, páramo zones. Nw VENE-ZUELA, Central Andes of COLOMBIA, ECUADOR and PERU s to Junín, 1. From Cuzco and Puno s through BOLIVIA to Mendoza and Córdoba, ARGENTINA. Shrubby hillsides.

73. PARAMO SEEDEATER

Catamenia homochroa *

5.3". Dark slaty gray; forehead and lores blackish; under tail coverts chestnut. Bill yellow. ♀: Dark olivaceous brown, streaked dusky above. Throat and breast grayish brown, becoming buffy on belly. Under tail coverts chestnut.

Subtropical to lower páramo zone. Nw VENEZUELA and in mts. of Bolívar and immediately adjacent BRAZIL; mts. of CO-LOMBIA s through ECUADOR and PERU to n BOLIVIA. (*C. oreophila* of *Sp. Bds. S. Amer.* is probably the S. Marta, Colombia, subspecies of *C. homochroa*. Ad. ♂ is unknown.)

74. SULPHUR-THROATED FINCH

Gnathospiza taczanowskii

5". Sparrowlike. Upperparts grayish brown, streaked brown on back. Ocular region white; eyebrow, malar region and upper throat bright yellow; underparts white, under tail coverts tinged yellow. Primaries edged pale yellow.

Arid tropical zone. Sw ECUADOR from Guayaquil s to Libertad, PERU. Grassy scrub.

Plate 18

75. STRIPE-TAILED YELLOW-FINCH

Sicalis citrina *

4.7". Above olive green, yellowish green on forecrown and rump, mantle streaked dusky. Below bright yellow, tinged olivaceous at sides of breast. Outer two tail feathers with large white stripe on inner web. ♀: Above brown, streaked dusky; rump olivaceous. Throat and breast dull yellow, streaked dusky; belly bright yellow. Tail as in ♂.

Tropical to temperate zone. GUYANA; VENEZUELA; COLOMBIA in Cundina-marca and Antioquia. Se PERU in Puno. Central and e BRAZIL in s Pará and Piauí s to Paraná and Mato Grosso. Nw ARGEN-TINA in Tucumán. Campos, open mountain slopes.

76. PUNA YELLOW-FINCH

Sicalis lutea

5.7". Above olive yellow; below bright yellow. Wings and tail dusky brown, feathers edged olive yellow. ♀: Above brown, feathers edged olive; crown, nape, rump, throat and center of breast olive yellow; sides of head grayish, belly and under tail coverts bright yellow. Inner remiges edged whitish.

Puna zone. S PERU in Arequipa, Cuzco and Puno. W BOLIVIA in Oruro and Potosí. Nw ARGENTINA in Jujuy and Salta. Shrubby pastures and grainfields, rocky slopes.

77. BRIGHT-RUMPED YELLOW-FINCH

Sicalis uropygialis *

5.5". Crown, nape, rump and upper tail coverts bright olive yellow. Lores and eye ring white; ear coverts, back and sides of body light gray, back narrowly streaked black. Throat and belly bright yellow, breast yellow clouded with olive. Wings and tail black, feathers edged grayish. Tail shorter than in other species. ♀: Differs from ♂ mainly by heavily streaked dusky crown, browner back.

Temperate, puna zones. PERU from Caja-marca s through w BOLIVIA to Potosí;

CHILE s to Antofagasta; nw ARGENTINA in Jujuy and Tucumán. Open slopes.

78. CITRON-HEADED YELLOW-FINCH

Sicalis luteocephala

6". Forecrown and sides of head olive yellow, hindcrown and nape gray, back brownish gray; throat, sides of head, band down center of underparts, and under tail coverts bright yellow; sides of body light gray, belly white. Wings and tail dusky brown, feathers edged bright yellow. ♀: Like ♂ but yellow of forecrown less extensive and back browner.

Temperate, puna zones. BOLIVIA in Cochabamba, Chuquisaca and Potosí.

79. GREATER YELLOW-FINCH

Sicalis auriventris

6.7". Head and underparts bright yellow; back greenish yellow. Wings dusky, coverts broadly edged light gray, remiges more narrowly so. Tail dusky, edged yellow basally, narrowly white distally. ♀: Differs from ♂ by browner back and throat; only center of underparts yellow; sides of body brownish gray, washed yellow.

Temperate zone. CHILE from Antofagasta to Talca and w ARGENTINA in Mendoza and Neuquén. Open slopes above 6000 ft.

80. GREENISH YELLOW-FINCH

Sicalis olivascens *

5.5". Above grayish brown, washed olive yellow; rump and upper tail coverts olive yellow. Underparts olive yellow, bright deep yellow on belly. ♀: Like ♂ but duller with sides of body light grayish brown.

Temperate zone. PERU in upper Marañón Valley, w slope of the w cordillera from Ancash southward; BOLIVIA in La Paz and Cochabamba s to Potosí; CHILE s to Coquimbo; w ARGENTINA from Jujuy to Mendoza. Open slopes.

81. PATAGONIAN YELLOW-FINCH

Sicalis lebruni

6". Feathers of upperparts, throat and breast olive yellow broadly edged light gray, producing splotched look. Center of both lower breast and belly bright yellow, sides pale gray, under tail coverts white. Upper wing coverts olive yellow, edged gray. Wings and tail dusky, primaries and rectrices edged whitish. ♀: Gray; belly tinged yellow.

S ARGENTINA from Río Negro, and CHILE from Magallanes, south to n Tierra del Fuego. Open plains.

82. ORANGE-FRONTED YELLOW-FINCH

Sicalis columbiana *

4.5". Crown silky orange red; back, wings and tail bright olive yellow; underparts bright golden yellow. ♀: Olive brown above, finely streaked darker; below whitish, lightly shaded brownish at sides of body. Wing and tail feathers edged olivaceous.

Tropical zone. VENEZUELA south to n Bolívar and n Amazonas. COLOMBIA in e Vichada. E PERU along the Ucayali; Amazonian BRAZIL from rios Negro and Purús e to Amapá and central Pará, and from Maranhão and Pernambuco s to São Paulo and Mato Grosso. Campos.

83. SAFFRON FINCH

Sicalis flaveola *

5.5" (or 5.2", 1). Crown bright orange; back olive yellow, streaked dusky (or forecrown dull brownish orange; back pale gray, tinged olive yellow, sharply streaked dusky, 1). Below bright golden yellow (or duller, breast clouded olive, flanks lightly streaked dusky, 1). Wings and tail dusky, edged olive. Young males have gray crown, streaked dusky; below white with broad yellow pectoral band and under tail coverts. ♀: Above brown, broadly streaked dusky; lower back strongly olivaceous (or no olivaceous on lower back, 1). Below white, sharply streaked dusky; breast and under tail coverts pale lemon yellow (or no yellow below, 1).

Tropical, casually subtropical zone. GUIANAS, VENEZUELA, n COLOMBIA w to lower Magdalena Valley and s to Meta. W ECUADOR, nw PERU s to Ancash. E BRAZIL from Maranhão and Pernambuco s to Paraná. BRAZIL from Santa Catarina s to Rio Grande do Sul and Mato Grosso, e and s BOLIVIA, PARAGUAY, URUGUAY and ARGENTINA s to Buenos Aires and Mendoza, 1. Trinidad. [Introduced into Panama and Jamaica.] Shrubbery, gardens, campos, palm groves.

Plate 42

84. GRASSLAND YELLOW-FINCH

Sicalis luteola *

4.5". Above olive, heavily streaked blackish; rump plain olive; lores, eye ring and underparts bright yellow (with grayish pectoral band in s part of range). ♀: Above like ♂ but browner; throat, breast and flanks light grayish brown, belly yellow.

Tropical to temperate zone. Widely distributed in unforested areas e of Andes s to Río Negro, ARGENTINA, and in Aysén, CHILE. [Mid. Amer. Introduced Lesser Antilles.] Grassland, alfalfa fields, borders of marshes, cliffs.

85. RAIMONDI'S YELLOW-FINCH

Sicalis raimondii

Very like 84 but back and sides of body grayish; back less heavily streaked; front and sides of crown and nape yellowish, center of crown and ear coverts gray. No eye ring or gray pectoral band.

Tropical, subtropical zones. W slope of Andes of PERU from Cajamarca to Arequipa. Rocky slopes.

86. WHITE-WINGED DIUCA-FINCH

Diuca speculifera *

7.2". Ashy gray; patch below eye, the throat, belly, under tail coverts, outer webs of primaries (conspicuous) and outer web of outer tail feather white. (See 95)

Puna zone from Ancash, PERU, s to Arica, CHILE, and La Paz and Cochabamba, BOLIVIA. Rocky slopes; sleeps in caves and glacial fissures.

Plate 19

87. COMMON DIUCA-FINCH

Diuca diuca *

7.2" (or 6.2", 1). Ashy gray, washed brownish on mantle; throat and band from lower breast to under tail coverts white; sides of vent chestnut. Tail dusky; four outer feathers with increasing amounts of white on inner web, outermost mostly white. ♀: Similar but browner. (See 94)

Se BRAZIL in w Rio Grande do Sul; URUGUAY; Argentina on lower slopes of Andes from Salta s to Santa Cruz; lowlands from Córdoba to Santa Cruz, 1. CHILE from Antofagasta to Aysén including Chiloé

l. Southern breeders migrate north to n Argentina and Brazil. Bushy hillsides, villages, gardens, sand dunes; arid gravelly hills, 1.

88. SHORT-TAILED FINCH

Idiopsar brachyurus

7.2". Leaden gray, paler below; wings and tail blackish. Bill long (.75"), slender; tail rather short.

Andean, puna zones. Se PERU in Puno (Huancarani, e slope of cordillera); BOLIVIA in La Paz and Cochabamba. Nw ARGENTINA from Salta to Catamarca. Steep mountain slopes with tussocks of grass and rocks.

Plate 19

89. PATAGONIAN SIERRA-FINCH

Phrygilus patagonicus

6". Head, wings and tail gray; back cinnamon; rump and underparts greenish yellow, bright yellow on center of abdomen. ♀: Differs from ♂ by dark olive back; lower parts paler, more strongly greenish.

Temperate wooded zone. ARGENTINA from w Neuquén and CHILE from Aconcagua s (including coastal islands) to Cape Horn. Bushy sides of ravines, especially those with dense vegetation and vines.

90. GRAY-HOODED SIERRA-FINCH

Phrygilus gayi *

7". Much like 89 but larger, head darker (or with black top and sides of head, 1); gray of throat bordered below by band of dusky green. Back cinnamon rufous (or olive, 1), rump ochraceous yellow, upper breast and sides of body ochraceous cinnamon, center of belly ochraceous yellow (or grayish white, 1). ♀: Like ♂ but underparts yellowish olive (or like ♂ but much duller with head gray instead of blackish, 1).

Upper subtropical to puna zone. PERU from Cajamarca s to Puno. Extreme se PERU and nw BOLIVIA in La Paz, 1. CHILE from Atacama to Colchagua, sea level in winter; w ARGENTINA from sw Salta s to Strait of Magellan. Open country, ravines, cliffs covered with creepers.

91. BLACK-HOODED SIERRA-FINCH

Phrygilus atriceps *

Very similar to 90 (1) but head, throat and

upper breast deep black with no green border below. Back olive, below ochraceous, center of belly white. ♀: Like ♂ but duller; head, throat and upper breast dusky gray.

Temperate, puna zones. Extreme sw PERU in Arequipa and Tacna; CHILE from Arica to Coquimbo; BOLIVIA from Cochabamba to Potosí; nw ARGENTINA from Jujuy to nw Catamarca. Pastures, shrubbery.

92. MOURNING SIERRA-FINCH

Phrygilus fructiceti*

6.5"-7.2". Above slate gray, streaked black (blacker in worn plumage); throat and breast black, sides gray, belly white. Double wing bar white. Bill orange yellow. Legs light brown. ♀: Above heavily streaked reddish brown and blackish; rump gray. Ear coverts reddish brown. Eyebrow white; moustachial streak black. Below dirty white, streaked dusky on throat and breast. Two prominent white wing bars.

Temperate, puna zones. PERU from Cajamarca s to Cochabamba and Potosí, BOLIVIA; CHILE s to Llanquihue and w ARGENTINA to Santa Cruz. Bushy and rocky slopes.

93. PLUMBEOUS SIERRA-FINCH

Phrygilus unicolor*

6". Leaden gray to pale gray, in some races lightly streaked blackish above. Wings and tail dusky. ♀: Above grayish brown (or reddish brown, 1), heavily streaked dusky; below dull white, heavily streaked dusky. Two whitish wing bars.

Upper temperate, páramo zones. Nw VENEZUELA, mts. of COLOMBIA (except W Andes) and ECUADOR, 1; thence s to Tierra del Fuego. Shrubby slopes.

Plate 50

94. RED-BACKED SIERRA-FINCH

Phrygilus dorsalis

7.2". Extraordinarily like 87 in color and pattern but back browner, lower breast and belly white instead of white only in center.

Puna zone. BOLIVIA in Potosí. CHILE in w Tarapacá; w ARGENTINA from Jujuy to Catamarca. Rocky open slopes.

95. WHITE-THROATED SIERRA-FINCH

Phrygilus erythronotus

7.4". Remarkably like 86. Differs by purer gray back, pinkish-tinged under tail coverts, but mainly by no conspicuous white wing marking. Bill smaller.

Puna zone. PERU in Arequipa and Tacna; BOLIVIA in Oruro and Potosí. Puna grassland.

96. ASH-BREASTED SIERRA-FINCH

Phrygilus plebejus*

5.4". Above grayish brown, streaked dusky; rump leaden gray. Below grayish white, tinged clay color on flanks. Young birds are much like ♀ of 97 but belly unstreaked, no white in tail, and legs dusky instead of yellow.

Temperate zone. ECUADOR s through Andes to Arica, CHILE, and Mendoza, ARGENTINA. Rocky and bushy slopes with sparse vegetation.

97. BAND-TAILED SIERRA-FINCH

Phrygilus alaudinus*

5.2" (or 6.8", 1). Head, throat and breast leaden gray; back brown (or gray, 1), heavily (or narrowly, 1) streaked black. Lower breast and belly (or belly only, 1) white. Tail black with large oval white patch on inner web. Bill and legs orange yellow. ♀: Brown above, streaked black; below white, streaked dusky on throat and breast. White patch in tail much smaller than in ♂. Legs yellow. (See 71)

Temperate zone. W ECUADOR and w PERU s to Arequipa, also sea level on arid coast, 1. PERU from Junín s through BOLIVIA to Córdoba, ARGENTINA, and CHILE to Valdivia. Terrestrial; rocky open country with scattered bushes.

98. CARBONATED SIERRA-FINCH

Phrygilus carbonarius

5.4". Above ashy gray, streaked black; feathers with brownish tips; rump brown. Forehead, lores, sides of head and underparts black; sides of body ashy gray, washed and streaked brown. Tail black. Bill and feet yellow. ♀: Brownish gray, streaked black above; below whitish narrowly streaked dusky on breast and sides. Bill and feet yellow.

ARGENTINA from s Buenos Aires and Córdoba s to Río Negro; in winter n to Tucumán and Santiago del Estero. Bushy ravines, pastures.

99. BLACK-THROATED FINCH

Melanodera melanodera *

5.7". Crown, nape and ear coverts gray; supraloral streak and eye ring white. Lores and throat black; throat bordered all around by white, broadly so at sides. Back olive gray, rump olive. Sides of breast gray, center of breast olive yellow; belly yellow, under tail coverts white. Wing coverts and edges of primaries bright canary yellow; outer tail feathers pale yellow, central ones olivaceous. ♀: Above brown, mottled with blackish; rump more reddish brown. Lores whitish; ear coverts and cheeks dark brown with dusky shaft streaks; throat white; underparts pale yellow, streaked gray; breast strongly tinged brown, sides of body whitish broadly streaked brown. Lesser wing coverts olive yellow, median and greater coverts tipped white, remiges edged olive yellow. Tail dark brown, outer feathers edged yellow, outermost mostly yellow.

S ARGENTINA from Santa Cruz and s CHILE from Magallanes, s to Tierra del Fuego. [Falkland Is.] Moist pastures, shrubbery.

Plates 19, 30

100. YELLOW-BRIDLED FINCH

Melanodera xanthogramma *

6.4". Much like 99 but supraloral streak and band around black of throat yellow instead of white. Above clear bluish gray, some feathers with olive yellow centers; outer tail feathers mostly yellow (or white, 1). A color phase exists in which upperparts and outer rectrices are largely greenish yellow. ♀: Above grayish brown, finely streaked on head and broadly on back with blackish; below dirty white, streaked dusky on sides of neck, breast and flanks.

ARGENTINA from Neuquén, and CHILE from Aconcagua, s to Strait of Magellan, 1. Tierra del Fuego and Cape Horn Archipelago. [Occasional in Falkland Is.] Rocky fields, shrubbery.

101. SLATY FINCH

Haplospiza rustica *

5". Uniform slaty gray. Bill rather long, slender, sharply pointed. ♀: Above sepia brown; below olive brown, obscurely streaked on throat and breast; center of belly whitish.

Upper tropical and subtropical zones. VENEZUELA in Dist. Federal, Perija Mts., and on Cerro Chimantá-tepui, se Bolívar. Andes of COLOMBIA, ECUADOR, PERU and nw BOLIVIA in La Paz and Cochabamba. [S Mexico to w Panama.] Forest edge, partly terrestrial.

Plate 50

102. UNIFORM FINCH

Haplospiza unicolor

Much like 101 but somewhat bluer and paler gray, under tail coverts with whitish edges. Bill shorter. ♀: Olive brown above. Below whitish, breast strongly shaded pale olivaceous and streaked dusky, sides olive brown.

Se BRAZIL from Minas Gerais to Rio Grande do Sul; e PARAGUAY; ne ARGENTINA in Misiones. Dense shrubbery, usually near water.

103. BLACK-CRESTED FINCH

Lophospingus pusillus

5.2". Long crest black. Top and sides of head dark brown, sides of crown black, long eyebrow white. Back grayish brown, paler than crown; rump gray. Throat black, sides of neck and center of belly white, breast and sides pale ashy gray. Median wing coverts tipped whitish, greater wing coverts pale ashy gray. Four central tail feathers blackish; rest broadly tipped white, increasing towards outermost. Lower mandible flesh color. ♀: Like ♂ but throat white (irregularly black, in old females?).

Tropical zone. E BOLIVIA in Santa Cruz and Tarija, PARAGUAY; w ARGENTINA s to San Luis. Open, shrubby plains.

Plate 19

104. GRAY-CRESTED FINCH

Lophospingus griseocristatus

5.8". Crested, longest crest feathers black. Pale gray above, below paler, center of abdomen and under tail coverts white. Tail as in 103. Lower mandible flesh color.

Subtropical zone. BOLIVIA from La Paz to Santa Cruz and Chuquisaca; nw ARGENTINA in Salta. Shrubbery.

105. COAL-CRESTED FINCH

Charitospiza eucosma

4.6". Crest, crown, preocular region, throat and center of upper breast black; cheeks and ear coverts white. Back pale gray, center of lower breast and belly chestnut, sides of breast and belly cinnamon buff. Lesser wing coverts gray, greater ones whitish; remiges black, inner ones edged gray; tail black, basal half of all but central feathers white.

Interior of BRAZIL from se Pará and s Maranhão s to Mato Grosso and nw São Paulo. Ne ARGENTINA in Misiones. Campos, cerrado.

Plate 18

106. RED-CRESTED FINCH

Coryphospingus cucullatus *

5.6". Prominent silky crest bright crimson, bordered black in front and at sides. Back dark wine red, rump crimson; underparts dark crimson; chin and preocular region whitish. Wings and tail blackish. ♀: Upperparts grayish brown, tinged vinous; rump dull crimson. Lores and throat white, rest of underparts rosy pink.

Tropical zone. GUIANAS; e BRAZIL from rio Tapajós e to Belém, and from w Minas Gerais and s Goiás south to Rio Grande do Sul; URUGUAY; PARAGUAY; BOLIVIA; e PERU to n Cajamarca (where possibly migrant). ARGENTINA s to Entre Ríos and La Rioja. Terrestrial; pastures, cleared land, gardens, scrub, cerrado.

Plate 19

107. PILEATED FINCH

Coryphospingus pileatus *

5". Prominent silky crest bright scarlet, bordered in front and at sides by black. Lores white. Back light gray. Throat, belly and under tail coverts white; breast and sides light gray. Tail black. ♀: Above pale sandy gray. Below like ♂ but breast streaked pale gray.

Arid tropical zone. N VENEZUELA and Margarita I. COLOMBIA n and s of Santa Marta Mts. and in dry parts of Magdalena Valley. Central-eastern BRAZIL from Maranhão and Ceará s to Rio de Janeiro. Dry scrub, thickets; terrestrial.

108. CRIMSON FINCH

Rhodospingus cruentus

4.2". Upperparts black, feathers edged grayish in fresh plumage. Center of crown scarlet. Underparts pinkish scarlet gradually fading to pinkish buff on lower belly and under tail coverts. Remiges with extensively white bases. Under wing coverts white. ♀: Above brown; below yellowish buff, brownish at sides of breast. Under wing coverts white.

Arid tropical zone. W ECUADOR from Esmeraldas to Piura, PERU. Dry scrub.

Plate 18

109. YELLOW-THROATED BRUSH-FINCH

Atlapetes gutturalis *

7". Sides of head and crown black with broad white coronal streak from between eyes to nape; back, wings and tail blackish gray, sometimes shaded olive. Throat bright yellow, rest of underparts white, flanks and under tail coverts brownish olive.

Subtropical zone of Andes of COLOMBIA. [Mid. Amer.] Thickets, woodland borders.

110. SANTA MARTA BRUSH-FINCH

Atlapetes melanocephalus

6.7". Head, including upper throat black; ear coverts silvery gray. Back, wings and tail dark gray; underparts bright yellow, olivaceous on flanks and under tail coverts.

Upper tropical and subtropical zones of Santa Marta Mts., COLOMBIA. Forest, scrub, open bushy places.

111. MOUSTACHED BRUSH-FINCH

Atlapetes albofrenatus *

7". Crown and nape chestnut; forehead, sides of head and neck black with white moustachial streak (with little black below moustachial streak, throat yellow, no black on forehead, 1). Back, wings and tail olive, center of throat white, rest of underparts bright yellow, sides and under tail coverts olive.

Subtropical zone. Andes of Mérida and

Táchira, VENEZUELA, 1; E Andes of CO-LOMBIA s to Cundinamarca. Forest.

112. PALE-NAPED BRUSH-FINCH

Atlapetes pallidinucha *

7". Forecrown cinnamon; center of hindcrown and nape, white; sides of crown and sides of head and neck black. Back, wings and tail dusky gray. Underparts olive yellow, throat bright yellow, flanks and under tail coverts olive.

Upper tropical to temperate zone. VENE-ZUELA in w Táchira; E and Central Andes, COLOMBIA; e and w ECUADOR. Forest, scrub.

113. RUFOUS-NAPED BRUSH-FINCH

Atlapetes rufinucha *

6.7". Crown and nape chestnut (or with forehead and upper throat black, 1; or forecrown chestnut, hindcrown cinnamon buff, 2). Back dusky grayish black (or pale gray, 1; or dark olive, 3; or glossy black, 4). Underparts yellow (with throat largely black, 4), flanks and under tail coverts olivaceous. Wings and tail like back (with prominent white wing speculum, 5).

Upper tropical and subtropical zones. VEN-EZUELA and COLOMBIA in Perijá Mts., 1. Andes of COLOMBIA, 5. E and w ECUA-DOR. W PERU in Piura, Cajamarca and Libertad, 2; in Amazonas, 5; in Cuzco and Puno to nw BOLIVIA, 4; in Santa Cruz, BOLIVIA, 3. Forest and scrub.

114. DUSKY-HEADED BRUSH-FINCH

Atlapetes fuscoolivaceus

6.5". Top and sides of head and ill-defined moustachial streak sooty black; back and sides dull olive, rest of underparts yellow. Wings and tail blackish, feathers edged olive. Tail very rounded.

Subtropical zone. Upper Magdalena Valley, COLOMBIA. Forest and scrub.

115. OLIVE-HEADED BRUSH-FINCH

Atlapetes flaviceps

6.5". Head and nape yellowish olive, feathers edged yellow; back olive. Lores, eye ring and underparts yellow; flanks and under tail coverts olivaceous. Wings and tail blackish, feathers edged olive. Tail very rounded.

Subtropical zone. E slope of Central Andes in Tolima, COLOMBIA. Forest.

116. TRICOLORED BRUSH-FINCH

Atlapetes tricolor

7.5". Crown and nape yellowish olive brown to old gold, back dusky olive to black (or crown and nape dull yellow, back dark olive brown, 1); sides of head black. Underparts yellow, light to dark olive at sides. Wings and tail like back.

Tropical, subtropical zones. Pacific COLOM-BIA south to w ECUADOR. Central PERU in Libertad and Junín, 1. Mossy forest.

117. OCHRE-BREASTED BRUSH-FINCH

Atlapetes semirufus *

6.5". Head, throat and breast orange rufous (with white center to throat, 1); back, wings and tail olive, center of belly yellow, flanks olive.

Upper tropical and temperate zones. VENE-ZUELA n of the Orinoco (in Táchira, 1); COLOMBIA on both slopes of E Andes s to Boyacá. Forest, scrub.

Plate 42

118. FULVOUS-HEADED BRUSH-FINCH

Atlapetes fulviceps

6.5". Top and sides of head and moustachial streak rufous chestnut; loral spot and underparts yellow; sides of body, back, wings and tail olive.

Subtropical zone. Andes of BOLIVIA and nw ARGENTINA in Jujuy. Dense forest undergrowth.

119. TEPUI BRUSH-FINCH

Atlapetes personatus *

6.7". Above black to sooty black. Throat (and in some races also breast) rufous to chestnut, rest of underparts yellow (or above dark gray, below yellow, sides of throat rufous, 1).

Subtropical zone. VENEZUELA on the isolated mountains in Bolívar and Amazonas, excepting Cerros Roraima, Ptari-tepui, Acopán-tepui and Aprada-tepui, on which, 1. Adjacent Amazonas, BRAZIL. Forest.

120. YELLOW-STRIPED BRUSH-FINCH

Atlapetes citrinellus

6.5". Upperparts, wings and tail brownish olive. Conspicuous eyebrow, throat and sides of neck bright yellow; conspicuous moustachial streak, ocular region and ear coverts black. Breast and sides of body yellow, center of lower breast and belly bright yellow.

Subtropical zone. Andes of nw ARGENTINA s to Tucumán and Catamarca. W PARAGUAY. Dense scrub.

121. RUFOUS-EARED BRUSH-FINCH

Atlapetes rufigenis *

7.5". Top and sides of head to nape bright rufous chestnut. Loral spot, throat and sides of neck white; moustachial streak black. Back, wings, tail and sides brownish gray; below white, clouded gray on breast (or grayer throughout, head chestnut, forecrown and ocular region black, 1).

Subtropical zone. Andes of central PERU and upper Marañón Valley from Cajamarca to Huánuco and Ancash; in temperate zone in Apurimac, 1.

122. WHITE-WINGED BRUSH-FINCH

Atlapetes leucopterus *

6". Crown cinnamon rufous becoming paler on nape; sides of head black, preocular spot white (or forehead white, forecrown and sides of crown black, rest of crown and nape cinnamon rufous, lores and ocular region white, ear coverts gray, 1). Back, wings and tail gray (or brownish gray, 1); conspicuous wing speculum white. Underparts white (or buffy white, 1); narrow moustachial streaks black.

Subtropical, temperate zones. W ECUADOR s to Chimbo Valley; sw ECUADOR from El Oro south in w PERU to Cajamarca, 1.

123. SLATY BRUSH-FINCH

Atlapetes schistaceus *

7.2". Crown and nape deep maroon chestnut to cinnamon chestnut, sides of crown black (with some black on forehead and a white spot above each nostril, 1; or forecrown black, with a white line above each nostril joining cinnamon rufous of rest of crown and nape, 2). Back blackish gray to dark gray. Sides of head and moustachial streak black (or no moustachial streak, 3). Throat white; rest of underparts gray, paler than back, whitish in center of belly. Wings and tail black (with a conspicuous white speculum, 1).

Subtropical, temperate zones. Andes of nw VENEZUELA and n part of E Andes of COLOMBIA. Andes in rest of COLOMBIA and e ECUADOR, 1. Central and e PERU in Huánuco and Junín, 2; in Cuzco, 3. Forest.

124. BAY-CROWNED BRUSH-FINCH

Atlapetes seebohmi *

7.2" (6.2", 1). Differs from 123 (1) chiefly by no white spot above nostril and no white wing speculum (or rather like 123 but considerably smaller, sides of neck white, much shorter black moustachial streak, ear coverts gray instead of black, back tinged brown; wings and tail brownish rather than black; outer web of outermost primary white; no white wing speculum, 1).

Subtropical zone. Sw ECUADOR in Loja. W PERU from Libertad to Ancash, 1.

125. RUSTY-BELLIED BRUSH-FINCH

Atlapetes nationi *

7". Crown and nape dusky brown, sometimes with scattered white feathers; forecrown and sides of head black (or crown dull reddish brown, forecrown and eyebrow grizzled with gray, eye ring whitish, subocular patch black, 1). Back, wings and tail grayish brown. Chin and short malar streak black; throat, upper breast and sides of neck white; breast pale ashy gray, rest of underparts cinnamon buff. Outer primary edged white.

Arid subtropical, temperate zones. West slope of w PERUVIAN Andes from Ancash to Lima and Ayacucho; in Arequipa, 1. Woods.

126. WHITE-HEADED BRUSH-FINCH

Atlapetes albiceps

6.7". Forecrown, sides of head and neck and the throat white; middle of hindcrown and nape blackish brown. Breast pale gray; rest of underparts light buffy brown, whitish on center of belly; under tail coverts pinkish buff. Back, wings and tail grayish brown. Base of remiges white, forming a large speculum.

Arid tropical, subtropical zones. Sw ECUADOR s to Cajamarca, w PERU.

127. PALE-HEADED BRUSH-FINCH

Atlapetes pallidiceps

6.7". Head dingy white with some brownish mottling on hindcrown; forehead very narrowly dark chestnut, stripe through eye pale brown. Back, wings and tail light brownish; conspicuous wing speculum white. Below white, grayish at sides; crissum washed buff.

Arid tropical, subtropical zones. Sw ECUADOR in Azuay. Scrub.

128. CHESTNUT-CAPPED BRUSH-FINCH

Atlapetes brunneinucha *

7.5". Forecrown black, with three short vertical white stripes; rest of crown chestnut, bordered laterally by cinnamon. Sides of head black; back and wings olive green. Throat, center of both breast and belly white, black band across chest (or no band, 1); sides of body mixed gray and olive. Tail blackish olive.

Upper tropical and subtropical zones. The three Andean ranges of COLOMBIA. W ECUADOR, 1. Forest, woodland borders.

129. STRIPE-HEADED BRUSH-FINCH

Atlapetes torquatus *

7.5". Coronal streak gray, sides of crown black, eyebrow gray (or white, 1). Back and wings olive, bend of wing yellow. Throat and center of underparts white, pectoral band black (or no pectoral band, 2); sides of body gray to olive or olive brown, sometimes the two colors mixed. Tail dusky (or olive, 3).

Upper tropical and subtropical zones. VENEZUELA from Sucre and Monagas to Carabobo, 1. From w Lara and Táchira w to Santa Marta Mts. and east slope of the W COLOMBIAN Andes. West slope of W COLOMBIAN Andes s through ECUADOR to central and w PERU, 2. Nw BOLIVIA e to Santa Cruz and s to Tarija and nw ARGENTINA, 1, 2, 3. Forest.

Fig. 19, p. 430

130. BLACK-HEADED BRUSH-FINCH

Atlapetes atricapillus *

8.5". Top and sides of head deep black. Back and wings bright olive. Below white, sides gray. Tail black.

Upper tropical zone. N COLOMBIA from w slope of E Andes in Santander westward.

[Costa Rica, Panama.] Forest borders, shady thickets.

131. WHITE-RIMMED BRUSH-FINCH

Atlapetes leucopis

7.5". Crown chestnut, narrow eyebrow, sides of head and neck black; eye ring and short streak behind eye white. Back, wings and tail black; lower back tinged olive brown. Throat dusky gray, rest of underparts dark olive green.

Subtropical zone. COLOMBIA from head of Magdalena Valley s along e slope of E Andes to e ECUADOR. Forest.

132. TANAGER-FINCH

Oreothraupis arremonops

8". Head black, broad coronal stripe and eyebrow pearl gray. Back and wings rufous chestnut. Lower throat, breast, sides of neck and body orange rufous, center belly pearl gray. Tail blackish.

Subtropical zone. Pacific COLOMBIA from Antioquia south to nw ECUADOR. Terrestrial, thick forest.

Plate 42

133. OLIVE FINCH

Lysurus castaneiceps

6". Crown and nape chestnut. Eyebrow, sides of head, throat and upper breast iron gray, rest of plumage olive, brighter and slightly yellower below. Tail black.

Upper tropical and subtropical zones. COLOMBIA on w slope of W Andes from Antioquia to Cauca, e slope of E Andes in Nariño; e and nw ECUADOR. Se PERU in Cuzco. Forest.

Plate 42

134. PECTORAL SPARROW

Arremon taciturnus *

6.5". Head black, coronal stripe gray, long eyebrow white. Back and wings bright olive (or remiges edged gray, 1); shoulders bright yellow (or olive, 2). Below white with black pectoral band (or with interrupted pectoral band, 2; or with black patch at sides of breast 1, 3). Tail dusky, edged olive (or gray, 1). Bill black (lower mandible yellow, 4). ♀: Differs from ♂ chiefly by buffy gray coronal stripe and buffy instead of white underparts. Pectoral band slightly indicated or absent. Bill as in ♂.

Tropical, lower subtropical zones. GUIANAS; VENEZUELA s of the Orinoco; e BRAZIL s to Rio de Janeiro and w to rios Negro and Madeira. From Rio de Janeiro to Rio Grande do Sul, 2, 3. W VENEZUELA from Portuguesa and Apure w to Arauca and Meta, COLOMBIA, 1, 3, 4. Se PERU in Cuzco and Puno and n BOLIVIA to Cochabamba and nw ARGENTINA, 3. Forest.

135. SAFFRON-BILLED SPARROW

Arremon flavirostris *

6.5". Very like 134, differing chiefly by gray upper mantle, gray-edged primaries and tail, shoulder with less yellow. Bill yellow with black ridge, instead of all black. ♀; Like ♂ but duller, sides of body pale brownish instead of gray; differs from ♀ of 134 by black pectoral band. Bill as in ♂.

Tropical, subtropical zones. Interior of e and s BRAZIL s to Paraná and s Mato Grosso; PARAGUAY; e BOLIVIA; n ARGENTINA south to n Catamarca and Corrientes. Dense forest undergrowth.

136. GOLDEN-WINGED SPARROW

Arremon schlegeli *

6.2". Immediately distinguishable from any other *Arremon* by uniform black top and sides of head without stripes. Otherwise very like 134 (1), but upper back gray (or back all gray only very slightly tinged olive on lower back, 1). Shoulders with little yellow. Below white, a black patch at each side of breast. Bill lemon yellow with black ridge. ♀: Differs from ♂ only in clay colored instead of gray flanks.

Tropical zone. N VENEZUELA from Dist. Federal w through Santa Marta and Guajira Peninsula s to n Bolívar, COLOMBIA; on w slope of E Andes in Santander, 1. Semiarid forest, thickets, near ground.

137. ORANGE-BILLED SPARROW

Arremon aurantiirostris *

6". Top and sides of head black, eyebrow white, broad coronal streak gray (or olive, 1). Back and sides olive, darker and duller than in foregoing species. Underparts white with narrow to very broad black pectoral band, sides of body gray to olive. Bend of

wing yellow to orange. Tail dusky brown. Bill orange. ♀: Much like ♂.

Tropical zone. COLOMBIA w of E Andes south to w ECUADOR. Se COLOMBIA south to e Huánuco, PERU, 1. [Mid. Amer.] Forest, woodland.

Plate 42

138. BLACK-CAPPED SPARROW

Arremon abeillei *

6". Top and sides of head black, long eyebrow white. Back gray (or bright olive, 1). Below white, narrow pectoral band black, sides of body gray. Wings and tail gray, no yellow at bend of wing, wing coverts tipped white (with lesser wing coverts olive; rest gray, narrowly edged whitish, 1). Bill black. ♀: Like ♂ but sides brownish gray.

Tropical zone. W ECUADOR s to Piura, w PERU; in upper Marañón Valley, 1. Arid scrub.

139. TOCUYO SPARROW

Arremonops tocuyensis

5". Stripe through eye and sides of crown black. Eyebrow whitish, coronal stripe pale gray. Back pale grayish brown. Underparts white, breast and sides tinged grayish brown. Wings and tail brownish, edged pale olivaceous. Bend of wing pale yellow. Much like brownish-backed specimens of 140 but considerably smaller.

Tropical zone. VENEZUELA in s Lara and from Falcón w to Guajira Peninsula, COLOMBIA. Arid scrub.

140. BLACK-STRIPED SPARROW

Arremonops conirostris *

6.5"-7.5". Stripe through eye and sides of crown black, eyebrow gray (or white), broad coronal stripe gray. Back dull grayish olive to brownish olive (or bright olive, 1). Below white, breast and sides of body shaded gray to brownish (or dark gray, throat and center belly white, 2). Wings and tail like back, bend of wing yellow.

Tropical zone. VENEZUELA n of the Orinoco, s of it in n Bolívar. BRAZIL in Roraima. COLOMBIA e of Andes from Norte de Santander to Meta and Vaupés, and across Caribbean lowlands to upper Sinú Valley. In middle and upper Magdalena Valley, 1. In humid region s of Lake

Maracaibo, VENEZUELA, and immediately adjacent COLOMBIA, 2. [Honduras through Panama.] Fields, plantations, woodland borders.

Plate 18

141. GRASSLAND SPARROW

Myospiza humeralis *

5″. Upperparts gray, streaked black; streaks edged rufous. Eyebrow yellow in front of eye, gray behind it; eye ring white. Below mostly whitish, chest and sides tinged buffy gray. Bend of wing yellow, inner remiges edged rufescent.

Tropical, subtropical zones. GUIANAS, VENEZUELA and COLOMBIA s through east and central BRAZIL to e BOLIVIA, URUGUAY and Río Negro, ARGENTINA. W of Andes in COLOMBIA to Cauca Valley. Grassland.

142. YELLOW-BROWED SPARROW

Myospiza aurifrons *

Much like 141; differs chiefly by yellow eye ring, eyebrow all yellow, yellow wash at base of lower mandible, olive-edged wing coverts and whiter underparts.

Tropical zone. W VENEZUELA; COLOMBIA e of Andes; e ECUADOR; e PERU; n and e BOLIVIA; Amazonian BRAZIL. Grassland.

Plate 50

143. GRASSHOPPER SPARROW

Ammodramus savannarum *

4.3″. Crown blackish, narrow median line buff; eyebrow buff, ochre yellow in front of eye; eye ring buffy, postocular streak black. Upper mantle gray, streaked chestnut; back feathers black, edged grayish and tipped chestnut. Throat, breast and under tail coverts pale buff; belly white. Bend of wing yellow. Tail feathers sharply pointed, dusky, edged sandy; outermost whitish buff.

Tropical zone, COLOMBIA in Cauca Valley. Temperate zone, w ECUADOR (Cayambe). Curaçao, Bonaire. [N and Mid. Amer. Northern migrants reach Guatemala, El Salvador and W Indies.] Grassland, xerophitic vegetation.

144. TUMBES SPARROW

Rhynchospiza stolzmanni

6″. Crown chestnut, coronal streak and eyebrow gray, postocular streak dusky. Back brown, streaked dusky; rump unstreaked. Below white, washed gray on breast, buffy on flanks and under tail coverts. Moustachial streak and short streak at gape black. Shoulder chestnut, margins of wing coverts pale chestnut, bend of wing yellow. Tail brown, edged buffy brown. Bill large and coarse (.5″).

Arid tropical zone. Sw ECUADOR; nw PERU south to n Libertad and Cajamarca. Scrub.

Plate 18

145. STRIPE-CAPPED SPARROW

Aimophila strigiceps *

6.5″. Center of crown gray, broad band at sides of crown and postocular streak hazel (or chestnut, 1); eyebrow white in front of eye, gray behind it, sides of head gray (with lores and subocular region, black, 1). Back light reddish brown, grayish on upper mantle, broadly streaked with blackish except on rump. Throat white, moustachial streak black; breast pale gray, rest of underparts white; under tail coverts buff. Tail rather long, dark brown; outermost feather edged white.

ARGENTINA in Chaco, Santiago del Estero, Entre Ríos, Santa Fe and Córdoba; in Jujuy, Salta and Tucumán, 1. Grassland.

Plate 18

146. GRAY-WINGED INCA-FINCH

Incaspiza ortizi

6.5″. Ad. ♂ unknown. ♀: Above brown, somewhat streaked; forehead, lores, ocular region and upper throat black; lower throat, breast and sides of neck and body gray; center of belly white. Inner remiges and greater wing coverts rufous on outer web. Tail black, outer two feathers largely white.

Subtropical zone. N PERU on e slope of the western cordillera in Cajamarca. Possibly also on w slope (imm. ♂, this species?).

47. GREAT INCA-FINCH

Incaspiza pulchra

6.5″. Upperparts dull reddish brown, lower back grayish. Lores, ocular region and throat black. Eyebrow, ear coverts, sides of head and neck, and breast gray; flanks buffy gray, belly buffy white. Lesser wing coverts gray, outer webs of greater wing coverts and inner remiges rufous. Tail black, two outermost feathers mostly white. Bill orange yellow, feet yellow.

Upper tropical and subtropical zones. Andes of PERU from Ancash to s Lima. Dry scrub, cactus, feeds on cactus fruits.

148. RUFOUS-BACKED INCA-FINCH

Incaspiza personata

6.5". Differs from 147 mainly by chestnut back, broader black frontal band, more restricted throat patch and no eyebrow. Facial pattern more as in 148. Bill and feet yellow.

Subtropical, temperate zones. Andes of PERU in Cajamarca, Libertad, Huánuco and Ancash.

149. BUFF-BRIDLED INCA-FINCH

Incaspiza laeta

5.7". Rather like 148 but crown and nape grayer, lower back much darker and almost blackish, but differs mainly by more extensive black throat patch, broadly bordered laterally by white. Outer two tail feathers virtually all white. Bill orange, feet yellow.

Arid subtropical, temperate zones. Andes of n PERU in Marañón drainage in Cajamarca, Libertad and n Huánuco.

Plate 16

150. LITTLE INCA-FINCH

Incaspiza watkinsi

5". Lores, chin and preocular region black. Crown and nape grayish brown, eyebrow and sides of head blue gray; upper throat white becoming gray on lower throat, sides of neck and breast; belly white. Back reddish brown, streaked black. Wing coverts and edges of remiges light gray. Bill and feet yellow.

Arid tropical zone in n PERU in Marañón drainage in Cajamarca.

151. RUFOUS-COLLARED SPARROW

Zonotrichia capensis *

5"-6.6". Head somewhat crested, gray with (or without, 1) two broad black lateral coronal stripes; postocular streak, line below

ear coverts and patch at sides of breast black. Nuchal collar extending to sides of breast rufous chestnut. Back reddish brown, streaked black; below white. Median and greater wing coverts tipped white. Tail dull brown. Imm. Above brown, streaked blackish. Below dirty white, finely streaked dusky. ♀: Like ♂ but no crest.

Tropical to temperate zone in cleared and open areas virtually throughout (but chiefly in the highlands in tropical latitudes) s to Río Negro, ARGENTINA, and immediately adjacent CHILE. ARGENTINA from Río Negro and CHILE from Aysén s to Tierra del Fuego, winters n to Jujuy, 1. Curaçao, Aruba. [S Mexico to central Panama. Hispaniola.] Open country, campos, cerrado, scattered brush, gardens, parks.

Plate 18

152. WEDGE-TAILED GRASS-FINCH

Emberizoides herbicola *

7"-8". Tail long, pointed, much graduated. Above sandy brown (or gray, 1) boldly streaked black; bend of wing yellow, wing coverts and edges to remiges yellowish olive. Lores and eye ring white. Below white, tinged clay color on breast and sides; flanks streaked in some races.

Tropical, lower subtropical zones. GUIANAS; VENEZUELA (in Barinas, Portuguesa, w Apure and immediately adjacent COLOMBIA, 1); COLOMBIA south to e and s BRAZIL, PARAGUAY, e BOLIVIA, ne ARGENTINA west to e Chaco. W of Andes in COLOMBIA. [Sw Costa Rica, Pacific Panama.] Grassland. For 152 bis, *E. ypiranganus* see p. 429.

Plate 42

153. BLACK-MASKED FINCH

Coryphaspiza melanotis

5.5". Top and sides of head black, long eyebrow white. Back olive brown broadly streaked black. Shoulder, bend of wing, under wing coverts and axillaries olive. Below white. Tail graduated, all but four central feathers with white patch at tip of inner web.

E BRAZIL on Marajó I. and in Minas Gerais, São Paulo and Mato Grosso; n BOLIVIA; PARAGUAY; ne ARGENTINA west to e Chaco and Santa Fe. Campos, coastal dunes.

Plate 30

154. SLENDER-BILLED FINCH

Xenospingus concolor

6.5". Upperparts, wings and tail blue gray; forehead, lores and point of chin black. Below pale bluish gray, whitish on center of belly. Slender bill and the feet yellow. ♀: Smaller and darker above than ♂.

Coast and w slope of Andes of PERU from Lima s to Tarapacá-Antofagasta border in CHILE. Thickets, marsh borders, campos, cultivated lands.

155. LONG-TAILED REED-FINCH

Donacospiza albifrons

6.5". Lores, eye ring and narrow eyebrow buffy white; preocular region blackish, ear coverts gray. Crown grayish brown shading to reddish brown on mantle, where streaked dusky; rufescent brown on rump. Underparts tawny buff, whitish on center of abdomen. Lesser and median wing coverts blue gray, greater coverts broadly edged tawny buff. Tail rather long; feathers graduated and pointed, dark brown, pale-edged. ♀: Differs from ♂ mainly by crown narrowly streaked, and back broadly streaked, blackish. Below paler.

E BRAZIL from Minas Gerais s to URUGUAY, PARAGUAY and e ARGENTINA s to Buenos Aires. Sawgrass near water.

156. BAY-CHESTED WARBLING-FINCH

Poospiza thoracica

5". Upperparts, wings and tail gray, tinged olivaceous; wing with conspicuous white speculum. Cheeks gray, line below eye white. Throat, center of breast and belly white; broad pectoral band and sides of body dark chestnut.

Se BRAZIL from Espírito Santo to Rio Grande do Sul.

157. BOLIVIAN WARBLING-FINCH

Poospiza boliviana

6.3". Above pale reddish brown; broad, long eyebrow white; ear coverts and sides of neck grayish brown. Below white, breast band and sides of body dark pinkish cinnamon. Wings and tail blackish, inner remiges edged cinnamon rufous; all but four central tail feathers tipped white, increasingly so to outermost.

Temperate zone. Andes of BOLIVIA in Cochabamba, Chuquisaca and Tarija.

158. PLAIN-TAILED WARBLING-FINCH

Poospiza alticola

6.3". Crown and ear coverts dark brown; broad, long eyebrow white; malar streak black. Back ashy brown; below dingy white, sides of upper breast orange rufous becoming pale cinnamon buff on sides of body. Wings and tail blackish, remiges and greater wing coverts edged ashy white. Tail like back, without white.

Temperate zone. N PERU in e Libertad and Ancash.

159. RUFOUS-SIDED WARBLING-FINCH

Poospiza hypochondria *

6.5". Above ashy brown; superciliary white, bordered black above; subocular patch white. Throat and sides of neck buffy white, narrow moustachial streak black. Pectoral band pale ashy gray, rest of underparts buffy white, flanks chestnut, under tail coverts buff. Wings and tail blackish, inner remiges broadly edged pale buffy brown; outer two tail feathers broadly tipped white, outermost mostly white.

Temperate zone. BOLIVIA from La Paz to Santa Cruz and s to Chuquisaca and Tarija; w ARGENTINA from Jujuy to Mendoza. Open scrub.

160. COLLARED WARBLING-FINCH

Poospiza hispaniolensis

5". Above gray, feathers of crown with black shaft streaks. Long eyebrow white, surmounted by a blackish line. Sides of head black, lower eyelid white. Below white, sides of breast and body gray, center of breast black, sides of vent chestnut. Wings black, wing coverts and inner remiges edged pinkish buff; tail black, inner webs of outer three feathers mostly white. ♀: Above brown, streaked dusky; rump gray; otherwise much like ♂. Tail grayish brown, outer two feathers with a little white on inner web near tip.

Arid tropical to temperate zone. Sw ECUADOR s to Ica, PERU. Arid scrub, cactus, farmland.

161. RINGED WARBLING-FINCH

Poospiza torquata *

Much like 160 but with much smaller bill, pectoral band all black, margins of greater wing coverts and wing speculum pure white; under tail coverts chestnut; tail black, the outermost white on outer web and on distal third of inner web, next white on inner web only (or similar but with broad black band above white superciliary, outer tail feather mostly white, next diagonally white for distal half of inner web, 1). ♀: Like ♂ but back and sides of body tinged brown.

Subtropical zone W BOLIVIA from La Paz to Chuquisaca. E BOLIVIA in Santa Cruz, w PARAGUAY and w ARGENTINA s to Mendoza and w Buenos Aires, 1. Low scrubby growth, thickets.

162. BLACK-CAPPED WARBLING-FINCH

Poospiza melanoleuca

5.2″. Top and sides of head black, back gray; below white. Wings black, feathers edged gray; tail blackish, three outer feathers tipped white, increasingly so to outermost.

Tropical, subtropical zones. BRAZIL in sw Mato Grosso; n and e BOLIVIA; PARAGUAY; w URUGUAY; ARGENTINA s to Córdoba and n Buenos Aires. Scattered bushes, sawgrass, on or near ground.

163. CINEREOUS WARBLING-FINCH

Poospiza cinerea

5.3″. Lores, subocular region and ear coverts black; top of head and back gray. Below white with yellowish wash on throat and chest. Wings blackish, the feathers edged gray; tail black, outer feather white, next with wedge-shaped black mark at end of inner web.

Campos of Minas Gerais, Goiás, n São Paulo and Mato Grosso, BRAZIL.

164. BLACK-AND-RUFOUS WARBLING-FINCH

Poospiza nigrorufa *

5.7″. Above dark grayish brown (or gray, feathers indistinctly edged olive brown, 1). Eyebrow white turning rufous behind eye; sides of head black, malar streak white. Chin white; throat, breast and sides of body orange rufous (or chestnut, 1). Wings like

back; tail brown, outer feathers tipped white (or tail black, distal half of outer, and distal third of next feathers white, 1).

Se BRAZIL in Rio Grande do Sul; URUGUAY; PARAGUAY; e ARGENTINA from Misiones to Río Negro. W ARGENTINA from Jujuy to w Córdoba, n and e BOLIVIA, 1. Bushes, woodland, gardens, marshes.

Plate 16

165. RUSTY-BROWED WARBLING-FINCH

Poospiza erythrophrys *

5.3″. Crown, nape, ear coverts and sides of neck gray; back olive gray. Eyebrow, lower eyelid, throat and breast deep rusty rufous; sides of belly and under tail coverts paler, center of belly white. Primaries and greater wing coverts edged white. Central tail feathers gray; rest black except white outermost, next with distal half white, next tipped white.

Subtropical, temperate zones. BOLIVIA in Cochabamba, Chuquisaca and Tarija; w ARGENTINA s to Catamarca. Woodland, shrubbery near or on ground.

166. RUFOUS-BREASTED WARBLING-FINCH

Poospiza rubecula

6.5″. Forecrown, eyebrow and entire underparts orange rufous; face, chin and very narrow frontal line black. Back gray suffused with olive; pure gray on rump and upper tail coverts. Wings and coverts blackish, edged gray; inner remiges edged olive brown. Tail black. (Cf. 171)

Temperate zone. PERU on both slopes of w cordillera from Libertad to Lima. Woodland, brush.

167. CINNAMON WARBLING-FINCH

Poospiza ornata

5.5″. Crown and upper tail coverts dark ashy gray; eyebrow light chestnut, bordered above by blackish; subocular spot white. Back dark chestnut brown. Cheeks, foreneck, breast and sides rich vinous chestnut; belly cinnamon rufous, under tail coverts pale cinnamon. Wings and tail dusky, lesser wing coverts ashy gray, middle coverts white forming bar; all but central tail feathers with white spot at tip of inner web. ♀: Much paler than ♂, cheeks and underparts pale cinnamon rufous.

ARGENTINA breeding from La Rioja to w La Pampa, sporadically to Buenos Aires; winters n to Salta. Pastures in bushes and low trees; feeds on ground.

168. RED-RUMPED WARBLING-FINCH

Poospiza lateralis*

5.5''. Above ashy gray, washed with olive on back (or upper back dull reddish brown, 1); rump and upper tail coverts chestnut (or rufous chestnut, 1). Supraloral streak white (or with long white eyebrow, 1). Throat and foreneck buff (or grayish white, tinged buff only on foreneck and upper breast, 1); center of breast and belly white, sides of body chestnut rufous. Wings and tail black, greater coverts and inner remiges edged white. Outer web and broad tip to outer tail feather white, next with small white tip. ♀: Differs from ♂ by no white outer web to outer tail feather.

Se BRAZIL from Minas Gerais and Espírito Santo to n São Paulo. From s São Paulo to ᵣURUGUAY, PARAGUAY and e ARGENTINA to n Buenos Aires, 1. Bushy woodland.

169. CHESTNUT-BREASTED MOUNTAIN-FINCH

Poospizopsis caesar

7.2''. Above slate gray; forecrown, lores and sides of head black; eyebrow, throat and center of belly white; sides gray; breast and under tail coverts chestnut. Tail black.

Temperate zone. PERU in Cuzco and Puno. Bushy slopes.

Plate 18

170. TUCUMAN MOUNTAIN-FINCH

Compsospiza baeri

7.3''. Forecrown, eyebrow, streak below eye, throat, extreme upper breast and under tail coverts orange rufous; rest of plumage gray, tinged olive on back and flanks; lower belly whitish.

Temperate zone. Nw ARGENTINA in Tucumán. Bushy pastures.

171. COCHABAMBA MOUNTAIN-FINCH

Compsospiza garleppi

7.3''. Differs from 170 by entire underparts

orange rufous, whitish on center of belly, back purer gray. Very like 166 but larger with different facial pattern.

Temperate zone. BOLIVIA in Cochabamba. *Polylepis* woodland interspersed with cultivated lands.

Plate 18

172. MANY-COLORED CHACO-FINCH

Saltatricula multicolor

6.5''. Above light sandy brown, rump gray. Forehead, lores, cheeks and sides of neck black; center of throat white; upper breast light gray, lower breast and sides of body pinkish cinnamon, center of underparts white. Tail rounded, blackish, outer three feathers broadly tipped white.

Se BOLIVIA in Tarija; PARAGUAY; URUGUAY; n and central ARGENTINA from Jujuy to Corrientes and s to La Rioja and Entre Ríos. Thickets bordering fields, bushes; feeds on ground.

Plate 18

173. BUFF-THROATED PAMPA-FINCH

Embernagra longicauda

8.7''. Above dull olive green, brighter and more yellowish on wings and tail. Lores blackish; supraloral streak, eyebrow, subocular spot and throat pale fawn; breast grayish with buff wash. Cheeks, ear coverts, sides of neck, and body grayish brown. Center of underparts white, tinged pinkish, becoming buff on flanks and under tail coverts. Tail much rounded.

Known only from Morro do Chapéu, 3600 ft., Bahía, BRAZIL.

174. GREAT PAMPA-FINCH

Embernagra platensis*

8.5''. Above olive green to grayish, tinged olive (more to less streaked black in imm. birds depending on age). Wing coverts and edges of primaries and rectrices bright yellowish olive. Below gray, whitish on center of abdomen, brownish on flanks and under tail coverts. Forepart of face dusky. Tail rounded.

E BRAZIL from Minas Gerais and Rio de Janeiro s to URUGUAY, e PARAGUAY, n and e BOLIVIA to Río Negro, ARGEN-

TINA. Marshy places, sawgrass, low bushes. Feeds on ground.

Plate 18

175. ANDEAN SISKIN

Spinus spinescens *

4". Cap black, back olive green, underparts olive yellow. Tip of greater wing coverts and basal part of remiges bright yellow; innermost remiges edged whitish terminally. Tail black, outer webs of feathers basally yellow, inner webs basally white. ♀: Differs from ♂ by no black cap, back duller; underparts grayish olive, center of belly white.

Temperate, páramo zones. Nw VENEZUELA, COLOMBIA in Andes and Santa Marta Mts. Open country, shrubbery.

176. YELLOW-FACED SISKIN

Spinus yarrellii

4". Cap black, back olive yellow; rump, upper tail coverts and entire underparts bright golden yellow. Wings black, tips of greater wing coverts and bases of remiges and rectrices golden yellow. ♀: Differs from ♂ chiefly by no black cap; crown olive yellow like back.

Tropical zone. N VENEZUELA in Carabobo. E BRAZIL from Ceará and Paraiba to n Bahía. Open country, shrubbery.

177. RED SISKIN

Spinus cucullatus

4". Head and throat black; nuchal collar, breast and sides of body and rump bright orange vermilion; back darker. Wings and tail black, bases of remiges and rectrices pale orange vermilion. ♀: Above dark gray, slightly tinged vermilion on lower back; rump and upper tail coverts vermilion. Lores whitish, throat and sides of head pearl gray; foreneck and breast orange vermilion; sides gray, rest of underparts white. Wings and tail as in ♂ but paler.

Tropical zone. N VENEZUELA in Monagas, Sucre, Dist. Federal and Mérida. Ne COLOMBIA in Norte de Santander. Trinidad, Monos and Gasparee I. Dry scrub, open country, shrubbery.

178. THICK-BILLED SISKIN

Spinus crassirostris *

5.5". Differs from other species by remark-ably thick bill. Head and throat black; underparts, incomplete nuchal band, and rump bright yellow; center of belly white; back olive, feather bases dark brown. Wings and tail brownish black, bases of remiges and rectrices yellow. ♀: Crown, throat and sides of head gray; breast pale olive, rest of underparts and incomplete nuchal collar whitish. Back grayish olive, rump olive yellow. Wings and tail as in ♂.

Temperate, puna zones. PERU in Puno, Tacna and Arequipa; w BOLIVIA in Potosí; w ARGENTINA from Jujuy to Mendoza; CHILE in Aconcagua, Santiago and Colchagua. Bushy slopes.

179. HOODED SISKIN

Spinus magellanicus *

5". Much like 178 in color but smaller. Bill normal; back brighter, olive yellow; below brighter and deeper yellow, no white center to belly; wings and tail blacker. ♀: Crown and back olive, rump bright yellow; throat and breast olive, belly dull yellow. Wings and tail as in ♂ (or much like 178 in color, but back slightly greener, head paler and more brownish gray, 1).

Tropical to temperate zone. GUYANA; s VENEZUELA in Bolívar and Apure; COLOMBIA on the Meta, in Central Andes and w Nariño. Sw ECUADOR; PERU (in Urubamba Valley, 1); BOLIVIA; PARAGUAY; URUGUAY; ARGENTINA s to Río Negro; n CHILE to Tarapacá; BRAZIL in Roraima, and in e and central portions from Piauí and Bahía to Rio Grande do Sul. Woodland savanna, palm groves, swampy lowlands, bushy pastures, parks, farmland.

Plate 50

180. SANTA CRUZ SISKIN

Spinus santaecrucis

4.7". Head and throat black, this color extending on foreneck to upper breast. Back olive green, spotted with black; rump and underparts bright yellow, center of belly white. Wings and tail much as in 179. ♀: Above dull olive, rump slightly brighter. Throat and breast dull olivaceous yellow, rest of underparts light yellow.

Tropical zone. Santa Cruz, BOLIVIA

181. SAFFRON SISKIN

Spinus siemiradzkii

4". Head and throat black; back bright olive yellow; underparts and nuchal collar bright saffron yellow. Wings and tail much as in 179. ♀: Much like 179 but considerably brighter and yellower.

Tropical zone. Guayaquil and Puná I., w ECUADOR. Arid scrub.

182. OLIVACEOUS SISKIN

Spinus olivaceus

4.3". Much like 180 but smaller. Back unspotted, and much yellower; narrow nuchal collar yellow; below darker yellow. ♀: Quite different from 180. Crown and back yellowish olive, rump slightly brighter; throat and breast bright olive yellow; center of abdomen and under tail coverts deep, bright yellow.

Subtropical zone. E ECUADOR; PERU from San Martín to Junín, Cuzco and Puno; n BOLIVIA in Santa Cruz and Cochabamba.

183. YELLOW-BELLIED SISKIN

Spinus xanthogaster *

4.6". Upper surface, throat and upper breast deep black, rest of underparts bright yellow. Wings and tail black, base of remiges and outer rectrices bright yellow. ♀: Head, throat and sides of head and neck dull grayish olive; underparts pale yellow, center of belly white. Back dark dull olive.

Subtropical, temperate zones. N VENE-ZUELA; COLOMBIA (except Santa Marta Mts. and Nariño). Sw ECUADOR. N BO-LIVIA in La Paz and Santa Cruz. [Costa Rica; w Panama.] Bushy slopes.

184. BLACK SISKIN

Spinus atratus

5". Black; center of belly and under tail coverts yellow. Base of remiges and all but central rectrices bright yellow. ♀: Brownish black, marked with yellow as in ♂.

Puna zone. PERU from Huánuco to Puno; w BOLIVIA from La Paz to Potosí; CHILE from Arica to Antofagasta and occasionally

Colchagua; w ARGENTINA from Jujuy to Mendoza. Rocky, bushy slopes, woodland, pastures.

185. YELLOW-RUMPED SISKIN

Spinus uropygialis *

Much like 183 but at once distinguishable by yellow rump; and narrow olive yellow margins on dorsal feathers, which disappear with wear. ♀: Like ♂ but not as deep black; yellow coloring paler.

Temperate zone. PERU from Lima and Huancavelica s to Arequipa and Puno; sw BOLIVIA in Potosí; CHILE from Atacama to Bío-Bío; w ARGENTINA from Jujuy to Mendoza. Bushy slopes and ravines.

186. BLACK-CHINNED SISKIN

Spinus barbatus

5.2". Crown, center of throat and foreneck black. Back olive yellow, feathers with dark centers; rump brighter and yellower. Line bordering hindcrown, the sides of neck and underparts bright yellow. Center of belly white, under tail coverts white with a central black streak. ♀: Crown and back olive, streaked dusky; forehead, long eyebrow pale yellow, underparts also pale yellow.

CHILE from Atacama, and ARGENTINA from Neuquén s to Cape Horn Archipelago. [Occasional in Falkland Is.] Bushes, weed-patches, woodland.

187. DARK-BACKED GOLDFINCH

Spinus psaltria *

4". Above glossy blue black; below golden yellow. Wings and tail black; wing speculum, edges to innermost remiges, and basal two thirds of outermost tail feather white. ♀: Olive brown above, dull yellow below. Wings brown, marked as in ♂; tail brown, no white.

Tropical, subtropical zones. VENEZUELA n of the Orinoco, s of it in nw Bolívar. COLOMBIA (except Vichada and the se); w ECUADOR; n PERU to w Cajamarca and Libertad. [Western US s through Mid. Amer.] Open country, shrubbery.

ADDENDA

The following two species have come to light too late for inclusion in the main part of this book.

27bis. LONG-TAILED CINCLODES *(Cinclodes pabsti)*

Cinclodes pabsti Sick, Beitr. Neotrop. Fauna, 1969, *6*, no. 2, p. 64 (between Tainhas and Tambezinho, 16 km. northeast of Tainhas on the road to Cambará, 1000 m., Rio Grande do Sul, Brazil).

Much like *Cinclodes fuscus* but considerably larger with a much longer tail, throat unspotted, and more white on outer three tail feathers.

Plateau region of southeastern BRAZIL in northern Rio Grande do Sul, 900-1200 m., and probably in southern Santa Catarina. (See p. 205 for position.)

152bis. LESSER GRASS-FINCH *(Emberizoides ypiranganus)*

Emberizoides herbicola ypiranganus von Ihering, Cat. Faúna Braz., 1907, *1*, p. 390 (Ypiranga, São Paulo, Brazil).

Differs from *E. herbicola* by smaller size, heavier black streaking above and by blackish instead of pale facial area.

BRAZIL in São Paulo, Santa Catarina and Rio Grande do Sul. ARGENTINA in Corrientes and Formosa. (See p. 422 for position.)

The distinctness of this overlooked species is based on collections made, but not reported, by Partridge in Argentina. Eisenmann and Short are reviewing the genus and have been kind enough to allow inclusion of the species in this book prior to the appearance of their paper.

The following is a list of corrections and additions to the text.

Page 98. BLUE AND YELLOW MACAW *(Ara ararauna)*. Recently recorded from nw Argentina (Salta).

Page 112, no. 9. SQUIRREL CUCKOO *(P. cayana)*. The orbital skin is red in the Orinoco basin, the Guianas and Amazonia.

Page 149, no. 141. BLACK-BREASTED HILLSTAR *(O. melanogaster)*. Add Cerro de Pasco and Huancavelica, Peru to range.

Page 158, no. 206. BEARDED MOUNTAINEER *(O. nobilis)*. The species inhabits arid regions with cacti and sisal plants.

Page 203. EARTHCREEPERS, CINCLODES and CANASTEROS (p. 214) carry their tails cocked up.

Page 217, no. 130. For *Spartanoica* read *Spartonoica*.

Page 343, no. 15. GLOSSY-BLACK THRUSH *(T. serranus)*. Recently recorded from Argentina (Jujuy, *fide* Olrog).

Page 403, no. 11. RUFOUS-BELLIED SALTATOR *(S. rufiventris)*. Recently recorded from Argentina (Jujuy, *fide* Olrog).

Page 405, no. 31. DICKCISSEL *(S. americana)*. Recently recorded from Brazil in Roraima (rio Mucajaí, March).

Since publication of *The Species of Birds of South America* the following new species have been discovered:

BRONZE-TAILED BARBTHROAT *(Threntes loehkeni),* p. 132, no. 9bis.
MARANHÃO HERMIT *(Phaethornis maranhaoensis),* p. 134, no. 25 bis.
COLORFUL PUFFLEG *(Eriocnemis mirabilis),* p. 155, no. 180.
LONG-TAILED CINCLODES *(Cinclodes pabsti),* p. 429, no. 27bis.
ELUSIVE ANTPITTA *(Grallaria eludens),* p. 255, no. 200.
OLROG'S TYRANNULET *(Tyranniscus australis),* p. 323, no. 293.
PALE-EYED BLACKBIRD *(Agelaius xanthophthalmus),* p. 358, no. 40.
Not listed was the LESSER GRASS-FINCH *(Emberizoides ypiranganus),* p. 429, no. 152bis, described many years ago, and only recently found to be a valid species.

In the last decade, 15 new species have been described from South America, 238 new species in this century which are currently regarded as valid. The greatest number of novelties have been found among the Formicariidae (45), Tyrannidae (37), and Furnariidae (31).

Fig. 19. STRIPE-HEADED BRUSH-FINCH
Atlaptes torquatus umbrinus
p. 419

APPENDIX

CASUAL, ACCIDENTAL, DOUBTFUL, AND INTRODUCED SPECIES

The following species have been recorded from South America but they represent birds occurring only casually or accidentally, or are birds known mostly from single specimens—in most cases probably hybrids or color variants (particularly among the hummingbirds) often from doubtful localities. Introduced species are also included.

SPHENISCIDAE

MACARONI PENGUIN *(Eudyptes chrysolophus)* Possibly acc. off Tierra del Fuego, Argentina.

PROCELLARIIDAE

BROAD-BILLED PRION *(Pachyptila forsteri)* Doubtfully recorded off Bahía, Brazil.
FLESH-FOOTED SHEARWATER *(Puffinus carneipes)* Occasionally reaches the coast of Chile.
BULWER'S PETREL *(Bulweria bulwerii*)* Recorded once off Trinidad.

ARDEIDAE

GRAY HERON *(Ardea cinerea*)* Acc. from Europe to Trinidad.
LITTLE EGRET *(Egretta garzetta*)* Acc. in Trinidad (once) from Europe.

THRESKIORNITHIDAE

GLOSSY IBIS *(Plegadis falcinellus*)* Acc. in Colombia.

ANATIDAE

MALLARD *(Anas platyrhynchos*)* Casual in Trinidad and Tobago.
GREEN-WINGED TEAL *(Anas crecca*)* Casual in Colombia and in Tobago.
RING-NECKED DUCK *(Aythya collaris)* Casual in Venezuela, Margarita I., Trinidad.

ACCIPITRIDAE

WHITE-COLLARED KITE *(Leptodon forbesi)* Known from a single specimen from Pernambuco, Brazil. Probably an aberrant example of *L. cayanensis*.
COOPER'S HAWK *(Accipiter cooperi)* Acc. in Colombia.

PHASIANIDAE

CALIFORNIA QUAIL *(Lophortyx californicus*)* Introduced and established in Chile and w Argentina.
COMMON PHEASANT *(Phasianus colchicus*)* Introduced into Chile, but unsuccessfully.

CHARADRIIDAE

PIPING PLOVER *(Charadrius melodus)* Taken once at Salinas, western Ecuador (Oct.).
RINGED PLOVER *(Charadrius hiaticula*)* Caught and released in Trinidad. Breeds in arctic. Winters to Africa.

SCOLOPACIDAE

CURLEW SANDPIPER *(Calidris ferruginea)* One old record from eastern Patagonia.
RUFF *(Philomachus pugnax)* Acc. in Colombia and Trinidad.

RECURVIROSTRIDAE

AMERICAN AVOCET *(Recurvirostra americana)* Acc. on Tobago.

PSITTACIDAE

WAGLER'S MACAW *(Ara caninde)* Status uncertain, possibly subspecies of *A. ararauna.*

COLUMBIDAE

ROCK DOVE *(Columba livia*)* This is the familiar domestic pigeon now widespread near towns mostly in southern South America. It is native to Eurasia.
MOURNING DOVE *(Zenaida macroura*)* Recorded once in nw Colombia (May).
DARK QUAIL-DOVE *(Geotrygon erythropareia)* E Ecuador; n Bolivia. Probably dark phase of *Geotrygon frenata.*

TROCHILIDAE

BEARDED COQUETTE *(Lophornis insignibarbis)* "Colombia." Known from one specimen.
DUSKY COQUETTE *(Lophornis melaenia)* "Colombia." Known from one specimen.
BERLEPSCH'S EMERALD *(Chlorostilbon inexpectatus)* "Bogotá," Colombia. Known from one specimen. Probably a variant of *C. poortmanni.*
CABANIS' EMERALD *(Chlorostilbon auratus)* "Peru." Probably a very coppery example of *Chlorostilbon poortmanni.*
NATTERER'S EMERALD *(Ptochoptera iolaema)* Ypanema, Brazil. Probably an artifact.
LERCH'S WOODNYMPH *(Thalurania lerchi)* "Bogotá," Colombia. Probably a hybrid, *Thalurania nigrofasciata* and *Chrysuronia oenone.*
BERLIOZ'S WOODNYMPH *(Augasma cyaneoberyllina)* "Bahía," Brazil. Status uncertain.
EMERALD WOODNYMPH *(Augasma smaragdinea)* Known from six old specimens from southeastern Brazil.
FLAME-RUMPED SAPHIRE *(Hylocharis pyropygia)* "Bahía," Brazil. Probably a hybrid, *Hylocharis cyanus* and *Chlorostilbon pucherani* but possibly a valid species. Known from five specimens.
BLUE-SPOTTED HUMMINGBIRD *(Amazilia cyaneotincta)* "Bogotá," Colombia. Known from two specimens.
LILAC-FRONTED STARFRONTLET *(Coeligena traviesi)* Known from several Bogotá skins. Possibly a hybrid, *Coeligena torquata* and *Coeligena* sp.
SÖDERSTRÖM'S PUFFLEG *(Eriocnemis soderstromi)* One specimen taken at Nono, w Ecuador. Possibly an aberration of *Eriocnemis godini.*

RAMPHASTIDAE

MAROON-BANDED ARAÇARI *(Pteroglossus olallae)* João Pessoa, rio Juruá, Brazil. The single known specimen is probably a hybrid, *Pteroglossus torquatus* and *Pteroglossus mariae.*

PICIDAE

RUSTY-NECKED PICULET *(Picumnus fuscus)* Known from one imm. specimen from w Mato Grosso, Brazil.
BLACKISH PICULET *(Picumnus asterias)* Known from type from "Brazil," possibly variant of *Picumnus pigmaeus.*

FURNARIIDAE

FORK-TAILED SPINETAIL *(Cranioleuca furcata)* Known from two specimens from Chirimoto, San Martín, Peru. Probably the young of *Cranioleuca curtata*.

COTINGIDAE

WHITE-TAILED TITYRA *(Tityra leucura)* Known from one specimen from upper rio Madeira, Brazil described in 1868.

PIPRIDAE

GOLDEN-CRESTED MANAKIN *(Heterocercus luteocephalus)* Known from one specimen from an unknown locality.

TYRANNIDAE

BERLIOZ'S TYRANT *(Knipolegus subflammulatus)* Known from four imm. examples from Bolivia. Probably immature examples of *Knipolegus cabanisi*.
HEINE'S KINGBIRD *(Tyrannus apolites)* Known from the type from "Rio de Janeiro," Brazil. Probably a hybrid.
BUFF-CHEEKED TODY-FLYCATCHER *(Todirostrum senex)* Known only from the type from the rio Madeira, Brazil.
BERLEPSCH'S TODY-TYRANT *(Todirostrum hypospodium)* "Bogotá," Colombia. Probably a variant of *Todirostrum sylvia.*
PELZELN'S TODY-TYRANT *(Idioptilon inornatum)* Known from the type from the rio Içaná, Brazil. Possibly a subspecies of *Idioptilon margaritaceiventer.*

MIMIDAE

CATBIRD *(Dumetella carolinensis)* Acc. in Colombia, recorded once from Ciénaga (March).
BROWN THRASHER *(Toxostoma rufum*)* Acc. on Curaçao, one record (Oct.).

TURDIDAE

WOOD THRUSH *(Hylocichla mustelina)* Acc. in Curaçao and Guyana.

VIREONIDAE

PHILADELPHIA VIREO *(Vireo philadelphicus)* Casual winter visitor to n and w Colombia (Oct.-Nov.).

PARULIDAE

BLUE-WINGED WARBLER *(Vermivora pinus)* Casual in Colombia, Santa Marta Mts. (March).
AMERICAN PARULA *(Parula americana*)* Casual in Curaçao and Los Roques, Venezuela.
MAGNOLIA WARBLER *(Dendroica magnolia*)* Casual in nw Colombia, Boyacá (Dec.).
MYRTLE WARBLER *(Dendroica caronata*)* Casual in n Colombia and Venezuela (Delta Amacuro). Curaçao.
BLACK-THROATED GREEN WARBLER *(Dendroica virens*)* Casual in ne Colombia and Venezuela (April).
YELLOW-THROATED WARBLER *(Dendroica dominica*)* A sight record from Barranquilla, Colombia (D.A. Easterla, Dec., 1969).
CAPE MAY WARBLER *(Dendroica tigrina)* Casual in Tobago.
CHESTNUT-SIDED WARBLER *(Dendroica pensylvanica)* Casual in n Venezuela and Colombia (April; Oct., Nov.).
BLACK-THROATED BLUE WARBLER *(Dendroica caerulescens*)* Casual in ne Colombia, Santa Marta Mts. (Dec.) and n Venezuela.
PALM WARBLER *(Dendroica palmarum*)* Casual in Aruba and Curaçao.
PRAIRIE WARBLER *(Dendroica discolor*)* Casual in Aruba.
COMMON YELLOWTHROAT *(Geothlypis trichas*)* Casual in Colombia, Chocó (June);

Santa Marta (April). Tobago. Possibly Venezuela.
HOODED WARBLER *(Wilsonia citrina)* Casual in n Venezuela, and Trinidad.

THRAUPIDAE

BLACK-THROATED EUPHONIA *(Euphonia vittata)* Known from a single "Rio" ♂. Probably a hybrid between *Euphonia pectoralis* and *Euphonia xanthogaster*.
ARNAULT'S TANAGER *(Tangara arnaulti)* Known from a single cage bird. Probably a hybrid between *Tanagra preciosa* and *Tanagra cayana.* Type examined.
CHERRY-THROATED TANAGER *(Nemosia rourei)* Known from a single specimen from Murariahié, Rio de Janeiro, Brazil, collected in 1870. Status uncertain.

FRINGILLIDAE

INDIGO BUNTING *(Passerina cayanea)* Casual winter visitor. Recorded from n Venezuela (Dec.), n Colombia (Jan., Feb., Mar.), Curaçao.
HOODED SEEDEATER *(Sporophila melanops)* Known from a specimen from Goiás, Brazil.
WHITE-THROATED SPARROW *(Zonotrichia albicollis)* Acc. in Aruba. Breeds in N. America; winters south to n Mexico.
EUROPEAN GOLDFINCH *(Carduelis carduelis*)* Introduced from w Europe to Uruguay and Buenos Aires (escaped cage birds?), Argentina.
EUROPEAN GREENFINCH *(Chloris chloris*)* Introduced from w Europe to Uruguay.

PLOCEIDAE

HOUSE SPARROW *(Passer domesticus*)* Introduced from Europe. Now widespread in settled parts of southern South America and western Peru.

ESTRILDIDAE

COMMON WAXBILL *(Estrilda astrild*)* A small brown bird with red bill and red stripe through eye. Established in southern and central Brazil in and near São Paulo, Rio de Janeiro, Bahía and Brasilia.

Fig. 20. SOUTHERN LAPWING
Vanellus chilensis cayennensis
p. 73

BIBLIOGRAPHY

The following currently available books will be found useful by students of South American ornithology. Most are illustrated with colored plates.

ARGENTINA

1959. Olrog, C. C. Las Aves Argentinas. Univ. Nac. Tucumán, Tucumán, Argentina.

BRAZIL

1964. Pinto, O. M. de O. Ornitologia Brasiliense, pt. 1. Rev. Mus. Paulista, São Paulo, Brazil.

Caribbean Islands

1955. Voous, J. K. De Vogels van de Nedelandse Antillen. Natuurvet. Werk. Ned. Ant., Curaçao.

1966. Bond, J. Birds of the West Indies. Collins, London.

Central America

1954-1969. Skutch, A. F. Life Histories of Central American Birds. Cooper Orn. Soc., Berkeley, California.

CHILE

1965-67. Johnson, A. W. The Birds of Chile, 2 vols. Buenos Aires, Argentina.

COLOMBIA

1964. Meyer de Schauensee, R. The Birds of Colombia. Livingston, Wynnewood, Pennsylvania.

GUYANA

1966. Snyder, D. The Birds of Guyana. Peabody Museum, Salem, Mass.

The Oceans

1936. Murphy, R. C. Oceanic Birds of South America. American Museum of Natural History, New York.

1954. Alexander, W. B. Birds of the Ocean. Putnam, New York.

Panama

1965-1968. Wetmore, A. The Birds of the Republic of Panama, 2 vols. Smithsonian Institution, Washington.

PERU

1970. Koepcke, M. The Birds of the Department of Lima, Peru. Livingston, Wynnewood, Pa.

435

Trinidad and Tobago

1961. Herklots, G. A. C. The Birds of Trinidad and Tobago. Collins, London.

South America

1966. Meyer de Schauensee, R. The Species of Birds of South America. Livingston, Wynnewood, Pa.

1968. Olrog, C. C. Las Aves Sudamericanas, vol. 1. Univ. Nac. Tucumán, Tucumán, Argentina.

North America

1966. Robbins, Bruun and Zim. Birds of North America. Golden Press, New York. (Colored figures of all North American migrants to South America.)

Fig. 21. RED-CAPPED MANAKIN
Pipra mentalis minor
p. 275.

INDEX

437

O

P